EMPIRE AND IDEOLOGY
GRAECO-ROMAN WO]

Benjamin Isaac is one of the most distinguished historians of the ancient world, with a number of landmark monographs to his name. This volume collects most of his published articles and book chapters of the last two decades, many of which are not easy to access, and republishes them for the first time along with some brand new chapters. The focus is on Roman concepts of state and empire and mechanisms of control and integration. Isaac also discusses ethnic and cultural relationships in the Roman Empire and the limits of tolerance and integration as well as attitudes to foreigners and minorities, including Jews. The book will appeal to scholars and students of ancient, imperial, and military history, as well as to those interested in the ancient history of problems which still resonate in today's societies.

BENJAMIN ISAAC is Lessing Professor of Ancient History Emeritus in the Department of Classics at Tel Aviv University. He is the author of *The Limits of Empire: The Roman Army in the East* (1990) and *The Origins of Racism in Classical Antiquity* (2004). He is a member of the Israel Academy of Sciences and Humanities and of the American Philosophical Society as well as being an Israel Prize Laureate.

EMPIRE AND IDEOLOGY IN THE GRAECO-ROMAN WORLD

Selected Papers

BENJAMIN ISAAC

Tel-Aviv University

CAMBRIDGE
UNIVERSITY PRESS

CAMBRIDGE
UNIVERSITY PRESS

University Printing House, Cambridge CB2 8BS, United Kingdom

One Liberty Plaza, 20th Floor, New York, NY 10006, USA

477 Williamstown Road, Port Melbourne, VIC 3207, Australia

314-321, 3rd Floor, Plot 3, Splendor Forum, Jasola District Centre, New Delhi - 110025, India

79 Anson Road, #06-04/06, Singapore 079906

Cambridge University Press is part of the University of Cambridge.

It furthers the University's mission by disseminating knowledge in the pursuit of education, learning and research at the highest international levels of excellence.

www.cambridge.org
Information on this title: www.cambridge.org/9781316501672
DOI: 10.1017/9781316476963

First published 2017
First paperback edition 2021

A catalogue record for this publication is available from the British Library

ISBN 978-1-107-13589-5 Hardback
ISBN 978-1-316-50167-2 Paperback

Cambridge University Press has no responsibility for the persistence or accuracy of URLs for external or third-party internet websites referred to in this publication, and does not guarantee that any content on such websites is, or will remain, accurate or appropriate.

Contents

Contents

Map of Judaea/Palaestina and Arabia

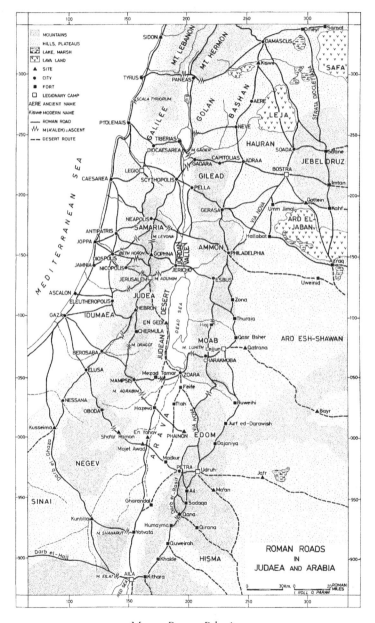

Map 1. Roman Palestine

Places of Original Publication

Roma Aeterna. *Historia* 2 (1998): 19–31 (in Hebrew).

Roman Victory Displayed: Symbols, Allegories, and Personifications? in Y. Eliav et al. (eds.), *The Sculptural Environment of the Near East: Reflections on Culture, Ideology and Power* (Leuven: Peeters, 2008), 575–604.

Army and Violence, originally published as 'Army and Power in the Roman World', in Angelos Chaniotis and Pierre Ducrey (eds.), *Army and Power in the Ancient World*. (Publications of the Seminar für alte Geschichte der Universität Heidelberg, Franz Steiner Verlag, 2002), 181–191.

Core-Periphery Notions, *Scripta Classica Israelica* 30 (2011): 63–82.

Attitudes towards Provincial Intellectuals in the Roman Empire. Originally published in Erich Gruen (ed.), *Cultural Identity and the Peoples of the Ancient Mediterranean* (Los Angeles: Getty Research Institute, 2011), 491–518.

Proto-Racism in Graeco-Roman Antiquity. *World Archaeology* 38.1 (2006): 32–47.

The Barbarian in Greek and Latin Literature. *Scripta Classica Israelica* 34 (2014): 117–37.

Romans and Nomads in the Fourth Century. This is a modified version of a paper originally published as: 'Ammianus on Foreigners' in Maijastina Kahlos (ed.), *The Faces of the Other: Religious and Ethnic Encounters in the Later Roman World* (Turnhout, Brepols, 2011), 237–58.

A Multicultural Mediterranean? Originally published as: B. Isaac 'A Multicultural Mediterranean? Erich S. Gruen, *Rethinking the Other in Antiquity*, Princeton 2010', Review article for *Scripta Classica Israelica* 23 (2013): 233–54.

Latin in Cities of the Roman Near East. Originally published in Hannah Cotton, R. G. Hoyland, J. J. Price, and D. J. Wasserstein (eds.), *From*

Hellenism to Islam: Cultural and Linguistic Change in the Roman Near East (Cambridge: Cambridge University Press, 2009), 43–72.

Ancient Antisemitism. Originally published as: 'The Ancient Mediterranean and the Pre-Christian Era', in Albert S. Lindeman and Richard S. Levy (eds.), *Antisemitism: A History* (Oxford: Oxford University Press, 2010), 34–64.

Roman Religious Policy and the Bar Kokhba War. Originally published in Peter Schäfer (ed.), *The Bar Kokhba War Reconsidered: New Perspectives on the Second Jewish Revolt Against Rome* (Tübingen: Mohr Siebeck, 2003), 37–54.

Jews, Christians, and Others in Palestine: The Evidence from Eusebius. Originally published in M. Goodman (ed.), *Jews in a Graeco-Roman World* (Oxford: Oxford University Press, 1998), 65–74.

Roman Organization in the Arabah in the Fourth Century AD. Originally published in Piotr Bienkowski and Katharina Galor (eds), *Crossing the Rift: Resources, Routes, Settlement Patterns and Interaction in the Wadi Arabah* (Oxford: Oxbow Books, 2006), 215–21.

'Hatra Against Rome and Persia: From Success to Destruction'. This is an expanded version of an article with the same title originally published in Lucinda Dirven (ed.), *Hatra: Politics, Culture and Religion between Parthia and Rome* (Stuttgart: Franz Steiner Verlag, 2013), 23–32.

Introduction

The papers collected in this book roughly deal with three topics concerning empire and ideology in the ancient world. The first six share in common the attempt to trace anachronisms in modern views of ancient empires, anachronisms which, as I suggest, lead to misinterpretations and distorted perspectives. The next nine deal with aspects of ethnic and cultural relationships, and Graeco-Roman views of others, foreigners, and minorities, and include two concerned with the Jews. These nine papers also contain examples of anachronistic views of the ancient world, but their aim is, first and foremost, to trace the limits of tolerance and integration in ancient empires; they also provide specific evidence for mixed or separate communities in Late Roman Palestine. The final two papers propose solutions to controversies over Roman control of desert routes, notably the priorities given to frontier defence or rather to security of communications.

Roma Aeterna

The concept of Eternal Rome is a familiar one. Nowadays we associate it with the city that once ruled an empire, became the world-capital of Roman Catholicism, continued to exist as one of the major cultural centres of the Western world, and is still there, a vibrant city for us to admire.

But what did *Roma aeterna* mean to the Romans as a concept? That is the topic of the first study in this book.

Scipio, as cited by the historian Polybius, expounded that nothing is eternal and therefore Rome would end like other cities before it. This explicitly denies the idea of an eternal Rome, whatever it represents. An insistence on eternity is first found in the work of Cicero: the army gave the Roman people its name and brought it eternal glory. Here eternity does not refer to the city as such, but to Rome as a people who are collectively eternal. We encounter something similar in the expression 'the eternal memory of your name'. The concept of 'the Roman name' has a

I

specific force and more will be said about this. In Cicero's *civitas*, in the sense of 'the state', empire and glory should be eternal. The idea of 'eternity' in most cases applies to these concepts, and only rarely to the city (once in a letter, *urbs*). We find the same pattern in the work of authors of the Augustan period. In Livy's work the city is described as eternal only twice. A similar tendency is found in the works of Tibullus and Ovid.

Many passages of various authors from the Augustan period which use the term 'eternal' mention Romulus, the founder of the city, the city's foundation, or crucial moments in Roman history. One of them, by Ovid in his *Fasti*, specifically mentions the eternity of the *numina Caesaris*. This is the only reference to the eternity of an emperor, rather than the city or the Empire, in the Julio-Claudian period, an indication that the idea was conceivable, but not regarded as appropriate at the time. Suetonius' criticism of Nero, who applied the concept to himself, is telling.

Velleius Paterculus and Valerius Maximus each refer to the eternity of the Roman Empire. Both the Elder and the Younger Pliny combine the ideas of the glory and eternity of the Empire.

The city as such is said on two further occasions to be eternal: in the work of Frontinus (on the city's aqueducts) and, much later, in that of Ammianus. In other words: to call the city eternal remained exceptional in Roman antiquity. We should note the existence of a cult to 'Roma Aeterna' (the state) in provinces, as testified by inscriptions.

The idea of an eternal Rome is thus sometimes associated with Rome as a city, but far more often with Rome as a state, a people, and, above all, an empire. This ambiguity has deeper roots. It is immediately connected with the fluidity of the concept of Rome itself. Rome began as a village that developed into a city-state and gradually expanded into an empire. The name 'Roma' could refer to the city, but also to the people, or rather, the collective citizenry. The Empire, of course, was called *Imperium Romanum*, but to translate that as 'the Roman Empire' is somewhat misleading, or a simplification, for the original meaning of the term was 'power', 'the power of the Roman Empire'. Even in the days of the Principate it was never a purely geographic concept. There was no simple term for 'the Roman state', for *civitas* was also a fluid term that could simply indicate a city, but also refer to its citizens. The expression that is most often used for the 'the Roman state' is *nomen Romanum*. Cicero is the first to use it frequently: 'For so great is the dignity of this empire, so great is the honour in which the Roman name is held among all nations.'[1] Here it

---

[1] Cicero, *Ver.* 2.5.150: *tanta enim huius imperi amplitudo, tanta nominis Romani dignitas est apud omnis nationes ut ista in nostros homines crudelitas nemini concessa esse videatur.*

can still be interpreted as merely a term for 'reputation'. That is no longer the case when Cicero says: 'Who has such a hatred, one might almost say for the Roman name, as to despise and reject the *Medea* of Ennius or the *Antiope* of Pacuvius, and give as his reason that though he enjoys the corresponding plays of Euripides he cannot endure books written in Latin?'[2] The expression *nomen Romanum* occurs frequently in Augustan literature, notably the work of Livy, again in phrases that may indicate 'the Roman reputation' or 'fame',[3] but also in the sense of 'people' or even 'power': 'Go, and with the help of the gods, restore the unconquerable Roman name!'[4] It is also used frequently as a term for 'the Roman people'.[5] In the fourth century the Isaurians are described as inhabiting a region 'in the middle of "the Roman name" '.[6] Here, of course, it refers to the Roman Empire. A proper understanding of the eternity which the Romans ascribed to Rome requires a lucid understanding of their various means of self-identification.

Roman Victory Displayed: Symbols, Allegories, and Personifications

The second essay in this book deals with a topic related to that of the first: the meaning and significance of what are usually regarded as symbols, allegories, and personifications that represent Roman superiority, conquest, and rule over other peoples. This is an attempt to clarify the ancient perspective as opposed to our modern approach, which is that personifications and allegories are 'abstract thinking made easy'. In our age ideas and concepts are given the shape of living persons, as in the case when justice is depicted as a blindfolded woman with scales and sword, or the USA appears as Uncle Sam. In the ancient world, on the other hand, similar images are used to express mythological entities, not abstract ones. Gaia, Uranus, Helios, Selene, Eros, etc. are at one and the same time physical phenomena as well as anthropomorphic gods, who fall in love, marry, have children, and, in the case of Uranus, get castrated.

Ancient ideas of collective or national identity are different from those of our times. Here we return to the subject of Chapter 1. For example, on its

---

[2] Cicero, *Fin.* 1.4.6: *quis enim tam inimicus paene nomini Romano est, qui Ennii Medeam aut Antiopam Pacuvii spernat aut reiciat?*

[3] Livy 4.33.5: *nominis Romani ac uirtutis patrum uestraeque memores.*

[4] Livy 7.10.4: *perge et nomen Romanum inuictum iuuantibus dis praesta.*

[5] For instance: Frontinus, *Str.* 1.2.2; Nepos, *Vit. Han.* 7.3; HA Severus Alexander 53: *nomen Romanum et imperium.*

[6] HA Tir. Tryg. 26: *in medio Romani nominis solo regio eorum.*

coins the city of Athens refers to itself as 'the Athenians', not as 'Athens'. As just noted, the Roman Empire was the *Imperium Romanum*, i.e. 'Roman power', and the city the *senatus populusque Romanus* or *Romanorum*, 'the senate and the people of Rome'. Rome, the state, is usually designated as *nomen Romanum*. In other words, the Roman Empire was not a single abstract entity, but the expression denoted Rome's military might, or a collective of the senate and the people of Rome. The alternative was a monarchy where the monarch *was* the state, Persia and Egypt being the classic examples. This is still the case in the work of Shakespeare: France, England, Lancaster, and York are persons – rulers and lords. The same was not true for the Roman emperor, who is never called *Roma* in the literature.

Symbols and Personifications

When considering Graeco-Roman images as symbols and personifications, we are attempting to understand pre-monotheistic concepts with conceptual models drawn from secular, post-Renaissance culture. It ought to be obvious, but is not generally regarded so, that we must be extremely cautious when interpreting material from the former period along lines familiar to us who live in a later period. Or, to put it differently, our modern approach is that personifications and allegories are abstract concepts, or impersonal or collective entities, depicted in the form of living individuals. Ideas are given the shape of human beings, as in the case just mentioned, when justice is depicted as a woman with scales. In the ancient world, on the other hand, similar images are used to show mythological figures, not abstract ones, as already noted in the case of Gaia, Uranus, Helios, Selene, and Eros. There is an essential difference: in Graeco-Roman antiquity it was thought that Gaia and Helios actually existed somewhere in reality. Nobody in modern times would imagine that Justice is alive in the shape of a woman. We should avoid confusing modern forms of abstraction with expressions of ancient religion and mythology.

Images of States and Peoples

Having established this line of reasoning we now return to ancient ideas of collective or national identity which are radically different from those of our times.

To start with the modern symbols of state: a modern flag has no meaning in itself, but is regarded as an object of value only because of what it symbolically represents, even if there may often be confusion and controversy, especially when nineteenth- and twentieth-century nationalism crossed the boundary between secular, collective self-identification and chauvinist mysticism.[7] Even so, a modern national flag is essentially a secular object that is respected, but not believed to have magical powers. Expressions of disrespect are just that – they are not believed to be actual sacrilege or harmful magic, although they may be prohibited by law. In antiquity it was the representation of the ruler himself that was regarded as sacred. The likeness of the emperor on coins or in the form of a statue was no mere symbol; it had magic significance in and of itself and any hostile or demeaning act aimed at the image was regarded as an act of sacrilege.[8] The distinction is not always kept in mind, which is the reason for Chapter 2.

Just as there is no ancient equivalent of a national flag, an impersonal object which represents the abstract concept of a modern nation-state, there is no ancient equivalent of an animal representing the state in modern times, such as a lion, dragon, or eagle. Such symbols have their roots in heraldry, the animals appearing on many medieval and later coats of arms, a custom developed in the High Middle Ages in order to identify individual combatants.[9] Ancient Athens is associated with the owl, the reason being that that animal was closely associated with the Athenian guardian divinity, Pallas Athena. Here again the distinction is one of abstract symbolism and genuine religion. Pallas Athena was a supernatural power and so was her owl. The American eagle is a secular abstraction, unlike the eagle now often associated with Rome. To the Romans the eagle was primarily associated with the legionary standard (*aquila*), an object of cultic significance, but, again, not a symbol of the state. The Roman eagle was an identifier of a military unit.

The patron-goddess of cities in Hellenistic and Roman times, Tyche, is not a personification but a guardian deity. The wolf was important in Roman myth, for it was a she-wolf who suckled Romulus and Remus. We

---

[7] The text of the Pledge of Allegiance of the United States, for instance, is confused and opaque and has been a subject of controversy, including a long list of court cases, especially since the addition of the words 'under God' in 1954. Cf. J. W. Baer, *The Pledge of Allegiance: A Revised History and Analysis, 1892–2007* (Annapolis, MD, 2007); J. J. Montgomery, 'Controversies over the Pledge of Allegiance in Public Schools: Case Studies Involving State Law, 9/11, and the Culture Wars' (Harvard PhD thesis, 2015, networked resource (DASH): http://nrs.harvard.edu/urn-3:HUL.InstRepos:16461048).

[8] This is to be distinguished again from the pre-modern idea of the divine right of kingship. The king may have believed he enjoyed his status as a result of divine will, but divinity did not extend to the king as a person or to his images, which had no magical or divine qualities.

[9] Army units of the Roman Empire were, of course, identified by the distinctive markings on their shields and by standards and eagles. These were not heraldic in the medieval sense, as they were associated with units, not with individuals or families.

cannot, therefore, claim that the wolf is some sort of national symbol for Rome. It was an important animal of mythological significance because of its role in the legendary origins of the city.

The first point of this chapter is thus that we must be far more cautious than is often the case in the modern literature in using terms like personification, allegory, and symbol when interpreting figures in art who somehow represent peoples and cities. On the one hand, these figures may often be deities; on the other hand, they may be meant as a typical, but not a collective, representation of a community.

The more specific question asked here is to what extent ancient art, when celebrating Roman victories over foreigners, introduced allegories and personifications.

In general it ought to be obvious that the term 'personification' is inappropriate when applied to Greek and Roman art. When an image of a woman in specific dress appears on a relief or coin with the inscription 'Gallia' underneath, it is often, without further ado, claimed that this is a personification. This implies that the province(s) or peoples of Gallia are conceived in Roman thought as an abstract entity, represented by a woman. This is modern thinking. 'Gallia' is a region, a number of Roman provinces, inhabited by numerous tribes. The woman depicted represents a typical specimen of one of its inhabitants. The view that it is a form of abstraction is influenced by eighteenth-century concepts.

A related topic is the interpretation of narrative art, images depicting a sequence or a series of events – as distinct from a single scene, or better, a historically significant moment. The latter may appear on coins or in sculpture. It is argued here that such single scenes allude to a significant moment in history, deemed familiar to the spectator. We should not, it is claimed here, interpret such scenes as allegories. When more space is available, as on the Columns of Trajan and Marcus Aurelius, we are faced with scenes from the entire war, from the beginning to the end. This is imperial art, concrete and explicit, but definitely not allegorical or symbolic by nature. The intention is to evoke the reality of war and Roman victory.

Victory Monuments in the Provinces, Trophies

A trophy is often depicted on Roman coins and monuments celebrating victories. The origin of the trophy is a sacrifice dedicated to the gods, taken from some of the spoils acquired in war. In due course these might be replaced by works of art made from or depicting them. It might seem obvious to call depictions of such trophies on coins and in sculpture symbols, but this misses the point. The trophies were a genuine form of sacrifice following victory and that is what they remained.

There is an extensive collection of victory monuments set up in the provinces to celebrate Roman victories. These may depict individuals from the provinces and are therefore regularly interpreted as 'personified peoples (*ethnē*]) and provinces whose common feature ... was that they were conquered, or deemed to have been conquered', by Rome. It is argued here that the images are not allegories, personifications, or symbols, they are a single image serving as illustration for each subjugated tribe. Clearly, the aim of such monuments was to convey the extent of the Empire, both its geographical spread and its ethnic variety.

The result of all this is that the conclusions of the two first chapters seem to reach opposite, or at least paradoxical, conclusions. The Rome that was eternal, according to Roman authors, was not the physical city as such, but the Roman people and the Empire. The terminology used to indicate the city, the state, and the Empire is not as straightforward as might be expected. In particular there is no obvious term for the state which usually is called *nomen Romanum*. Next follows the analysis of what are usually regarded as symbols, allegories, and personifications that represent Roman superiority, conquest, and rule over other peoples. Here it is argued that this represents anachronistic thinking. These depictions in art and on coins are not abstract symbols, allegories, and personifications, but images deriving from religion and myth or, alternatively, representations of concrete reality, such as conquered peoples, or enslaved cities.

These two chapters in fact deal with related topics: concepts of Roman self-identification and the manner in which Rome expressed the superiority of Roman imperial power. In both cases it is argued that anachronistic assumptions have prevented us from regarding these concepts from the ancient Roman perspective which is necessary for a proper understanding of Roman ideology.

The Roman Army and Violence

Political and military control, stability, and continuity are a precondition for imperial rule. The essential instrument to assure those aims as well as that of expansion, when desired, or defence, when necessary, was of course the army. In the case of the Roman army, unlike the armed organization of most modern states, the same military apparatus served to realize Rome's political aims directed outward – offence and defence – as well as the maintenance of internal control. In other words, there was no distinction between the imperial army, the organization which operated against foreigners and against foreign powers, and the police force which maintained internal control.

The exercise of violence is a basic feature of any army. In modern states it is usually assumed that the sort of armed aggression aimed at foreigners is not suitable for internal use. That is why there are different organizations for the realization of the aims of the regime – at least in well-ordered states. Since one and the same military organization fulfilled both aims in the Roman Empire, it is useful to pay attention to the efficacy of the Roman army as a police force.

This chapter therefore deals with the subject of the army and violence within the Empire, notably in major cities. Although this may not immediately be obvious, it is related to the subjects discussed in the first two chapters in this book, namely a conceptual difficulty in defining the essence of state, city, citizenship, and the instruments of physical control. When considering reasonably well-functioning states – and we might assume that the Roman Empire resembled such a state, given its longevity – we take a number of assumptions for granted. We regard it as likely that the state guarantees the physical and economic safety of its citizens at a minimum level. We assume that it does not abuse the citizens in a random fashion. A reasonable limit to the force exerted in order to maintain order and internal security is expected. There may be differences of opinion about what is permitted, what is necessary, and what is illegitimate, but these are part of a modern public discourse. The numerous states where these basic conditions do not apply are not regarded as essentially functional by our own standards.

In the Roman Empire the situation was clearly different from what we regard as desirable.

(1) Massive violence in cities. It appears from the sources that the use of combat troops for internal police duties resulted in a far more violent treatment of civilians than we would now consider reasonable or efficient for the purpose of maintaining control.

(2) Physical force in a judicial context. The lack of separation of judicial and police authority resulted in the exercise of physical force in judicial contexts. Non-citizens could be and were physically abused before legal proceedings or go without them altogether.

(3) Physical abuse of individuals by soldiers or civilians of superior social status. The social position of military men and the weaponry at their disposal allowed them to intimidate and abuse civilians without proper

checks. There is evidence of acts of random violence carried out by soldiers without any legal or judicial restraints. This was the result of the absence of a well-organized police force that could exert authority in the civilian sphere.

We are therefore faced with a paradox. One of the important features of modern states, the organization of justice, to some extent has its origins in Roman law. At the same time, however, the Roman Empire must be regarded a failure when we apply the norms of a modern constitutional state in which the exercise of governmental power is constrained by the law, and by rules defining what we regard as morally right.

Innovation and the Practice of Warfare in the Ancient World

A familiar pattern in recent centuries is the fact that warfare engenders spurts of technical development and innovation. The question here is not whether there existed science in the ancient world. It is a matter of fact that there was, even if it was different from science in the modern sense of the word. Instead we consider whether there was a demonstrable connection between science and war, and between war and innovation. It is argued here that there was no close connection and, more importantly, that it was not present even where one might have assumed it to have existed.

It is obvious that there existed technology and technological progress in antiquity, but this was not driven by scientific research, let alone research carried out in specific institutions set up for this purpose, which is the standard practice in our times. It reflected a process of learning by trial and error. Moreover, in matters of state and warfare, this was not an institutionalized process subject to rules and a reasoned method. We are facing conceptually simple technological innovation, not science contributing to change or war inspiring scientific progress.

First, war itself. There was no systematic work on a theory of warfare, no institutionalized effort to draw lessons from the past for future use. There are texts about specific aspects of warfare such as the collection of information, tactics, and stratagems. These do reflect the past, but it is clear that the Roman imperial army did not draw lessons systematically. Of the various branches of learning and technology that already existed in the past there are a few immediately relevant to warfare: geography, medicine, and engineering, notably the improvement of weaponry. The conclusion is drawn that all of these were applied to the needs of armies and fighting, but none were subject to systematic research for the sake of innovation and improvement in functionality. This is all the more remarkable since the Roman imperial army was the first professional force of its kind in history. Consequently, the medical services in the army were on a large scale and well organized, relatively speaking, but the innovation lies in the sphere of practical organization, of taking care of the well-being of soldiers, without a significant role being played by scientific inquiry for the advancement of medical science.

The conclusion is paradoxical: the science that existed was not employed for gain in warfare as one might have expected, and experience gained in war did not normally give the impetus to the kind of further scientific development that is taken for granted in modern times. The reasons are to be sought in the ancient social value-system and the consequent organization of the officer corps of the army. The Roman army was commanded by wealthy, aristocratic amateurs. No less essential is the absence, in antiquity, of a clear concept of progress. Where there is no such sense, there is no drive to make progress happen.

Chapter 4 emphasizes conceptual, intellectual, and practical differences between antiquity and our times where these have been underestimated, or even ignored, in the scholarly literature. It is claimed here that the apparent modernity of much in Greek and Roman culture tends to obscure the enormous differences.

Core–Periphery Notions

The next chapter, like the considerations of symbols and personifications in Chapter 2, again considers a case of popular but anachronistic views of the ancient world. It deals with a phenomenon that is related to, but different from, that discussed in the previous chapter on innovation, namely a fashionable model applied to the Roman Empire. It is argued here, first, that this model clashes with the manner in which the Romans themselves saw their empire and, second, that it distorts ancient reality, quite apart from how the ancients themselves saw their world. The modern theory is the Core–Periphery model developed by Immanuel Wallerstein. This is essentially an expansion of dependency theory, which is a body of social scientific theories predicated on the notion that resources flow from a 'periphery' of poor and underdeveloped states to a 'core' of wealthy states, enriching the latter at the expense of the former.

Before the validity of the modern theory is discussed, the ancient world-views are described. The Greeks, notably Herodotus, indeed regarded their country as situated in the centre of a circular world whose periphery was inhabited by distant peoples. The extreme regions of the earth were blessed by nature with the most remarkable productivity, while Greece (in the centre) enjoyed a more excellently tempered climate than any other country. This, of course, is far from a centre-and-periphery situation where the wealthy centre profits from the impoverished and dependent periphery. Aristotle combined this approach with an imperialist ideology: the Greeks, because of their ideal situation in between the cold lands of Europe and the gentle climate of Asia, live in the best part of the world and should therefore be capable of governing every other people – if only they could achieve political unity.

Roman authors offer three views, or images, of the world. The first sees three roughly concentric circles: Rome is in the middle, then the Mediterranean and Black Seas, with peoples around them, and finally there are peoples, regions, and natural features farther removed from the Mediterranean. The latter form the outer circle. Generally speaking, the farther away peoples are, the less they are worth incorporating into the Empire. The second idea is the claim that the city of Rome rules the entire world, a world that is circular or elliptic in shape. The third idea, related to the second, is that Rome, the city, and the entire world – round or elliptical – are one and the same. Obviously none of these ideas remotely resembles the modern concept of a core and a dependent periphery. As regards the Core–Periphery theory, developed by Wallerstein, my argument is that those who attempt to follow it in their discussion of ancient empires are using a model that is not suitable for their subject. They therefore rather freely adapt the theory to their needs, without analysing its proper application. The model, it is argued, is mostly inappropriate for the study of ancient empires. When applied, it leads to confusion rather than deeper understanding.

Next follows a brief consideration of another model, developed more recently by Peregrine Horden and Nicholas Purcell in their major influential work *The Corrupting Sea*, where the proposition is offered that the Roman Empire has to be viewed as consisting of interconnected 'micro-ecologies', or 'virtual islands'. I discuss one concrete example of the application of this model and suggest some possible modifications and additional considerations. The point of this discussion is to show that there are many instances where Roman administrative arrangements may give a sense of ancient geographical perspective that runs counter to that obtained by looking at modern maps. This is yet another of the numerous instances of anachronism encountered in modern research.

Names: Ethnic, Geographic, and Administrative

When considering names in the Roman Near East we are dealing with confusion. Many of the names are still in use in the present day and we therefore tend to think we know what they meant in antiquity as well. This is yet another instance of anachronistic thinking encountered frequently in these pages. However, the confusion is a real one. There is a good deal of inconsistency of various kinds that requires careful handling. An example of plain confusion or inconsistency is that Assyria, Syria, and Coele-Syria may all three be used in contemporary sources for the same geographical area. However, they can also mean different things: Coele-Syria can refer to the valley between the Lebanon and Anti-Lebanon (the Beqa and Jordan valleys); Assyria can refer to the original Assyrian heartland, centred on the Upper Tigris river in northern Mesopotamia. Syria is first and foremost a geographical concept, and then an administrative term, while neither is necessarily restricted to the region inhabited by ethnic Syrians. Ethnic Syrians may also be called Assyrians. Regarding ethnic indications it must be observed that these can, but need not, point very specifically to origin: the Greek poet Meleager of Gadara calls himself a Syrian, for instance, but he calls his city of origin 'Attic' because of its Hellenic culture. Ethnicity, language, dress, and culture often go together, but by no means always. The term Hellenic is used for and by communities that definitely did not claim to descend from Greeks in Greece or Asia Minor. They claimed to be Hellenic in culture and language. Professions such as farming and trading may also be regarded as ethnic features, e.g. by Strabo. Changes over time may be confusing: from the fifth century BC onwards 'Palestina/Palestine' is common in Greek as a geographical term for a part of Syria. It became an administrative appellation for a Roman province only in Hadrian's reign and had no ethnic connotations in antiquity until the period when the inhabitants of provinces came to be regarded as such (attested in the fourth century AD).

Another complex example is 'Judaea' in the ancient sources. At first it was the name of an Achaemenid satrapy. In the Hellenistic period and in the books of the Maccabees it could imply (a) the name of 'The Land of the Jews', in its narrow sense, and (b) an administrative district. Then, when the Jews gained political and military control over a broader area, Judaea naturally became successively the name of the Hasmonaean and Herodian kingdoms and, after the incorporation of Herod's kingdom, the name of that Roman province. Consequently it included various peoples and not just the Jews of Judaea in the original sense. Paradoxically the non-Jews are also included among the 'Ioudaioi' in several sources (Strabo, Plutarch).

Thus 'Ioudaioi' can be a term for all the inhabitants of the province, or of the region of Judaea only, besides being the name of the ethnic Jews. Thus the term has frequently lost both its religious and its ethnic content. After the Roman province was renamed Syria-Palaestina, the name of Judaea is still found, but, often, as in the case of Cassius Dio's writings, it refers again to the 'Land of the Jews' within the Province of Palaestina. The bottom line: Judaea can mean various things in different periods, depending on the context: geographical, administrative, ethnic, and social. In other words, when interpreting names we need to take into account that ideas concerning ethnicity in the Roman Near East were highly flexible and not necessarily what they might seem to us. The reason for this is not far to seek: in the ancient texts we are faced with what was in many respects a different approach to group identity from our contemporary concepts. Categories and definitions that seem clear to us often do not apply in antiquity. Conversely, recognizing the ancient perspective for what it was may contribute to a better understanding of social reality in the Roman Empire. As observed in this chapter, the very words *ethnos* and *natio* changed meaning in the Roman Empire over time: from an indication of ethnic identity these terms came to be used for the Latin *provincia*. In other words a social term became an administrative one – up to a point, for the collective designations 'Palaestini' and 'Ioudaioi' could have either administrative or ethnic meaning or could even, somehow, fulfil a combined function.

The separation of the concepts of descent, ethnic identity, language, and culture, and religion had consequences for Jewish history and, no less, for the growth of Christianity.

In Semitic languages in antiquity 'Arab' is a term for nomads, people with a specific way of life, rather than an ethnic or linguistic designation. By contrast, in Greek and Latin sources 'Arabs' or 'Arabians' is an ethnic (and geographic) designation, a people with a language of their own, to be distinguished from *scenitae* or nomads.

We are faced with a complex reality when we try to understand names in the Roman Near East. Their meanings shift, vary, and are not necessarily what they might seem to us because ideas concerning social identity in the Roman Near East were highly flexible.

Attitudes towards Provincial Intellectuals in the Roman Empire

Inhabitants of the provinces made a substantial contribution to intellectual and artistic life under Roman rule, as might be expected in an empire well-integrated in the sphere of administration, military control, law, taxation, economics, and, to some extent, culture. Less clear is the degree to which provincial intellectuals were integrated or felt themselves to be integrated in the upper class of the Empire as a whole and in the major cities of the Empire. Chapter 7 investigates the writings of a number of provincial intellectuals in order to try to answer this question. Various types of preserved works are considered: philosophy, poetry, literary prose, rhetoric, scientific writings, including medical treatises, in sum the works commonly known as the 'Second Sophistic'. The selection of authors shows various responses to the social situation in which they found themselves as citizens of the Roman Empire. A peculiarity of the High Empire is that many provincials in the Near East identified themselves not so much as 'Romans' or 'Syrians' or a similar ethnic group, but as 'Hellenes', thereby distinguishing themselves culturally and linguistically from their immediate surroundings. The tone and manner in which this is formulated varies, from one of denial to being defensive or assertive. Another point, as noted in Chapter 6, is the fact that the terms *ethnos* and *natio* were used for both 'people' and 'province'. A province seems gradually to have come to be seen as an ethnic unit.

With this topic we are far removed from the sphere of armed rebellion, small-scale resistance to the authorities, or internecine fighting. All authors were successful in their own circles and hence their works have at least in part been preserved. Even so it cannot be denied that this coexistence engendered complex social situations and tensions of various sorts which should not be ignored. These included tensions and manifestations of local jealousy or internal competition, a phenomenon that was as widespread as it was common. The cases discussed in this chapter cover the Roman Near East, Anatolia, North Africa, and Gaul. It cannot be denied that the Roman Empire was a successfully integrated system for centuries, but even so, the most successful provincials could still feel they were outsiders to some degree.

Proto-Racism in Graeco-Roman Antiquity

In spite of the usual assumption that racism is a form of prejudice which developed in recent history, it is argued here that prototypes of racism were prevalent in Greek and Roman thinking. Obviously, in classical antiquity racism did not exist in the modern form of a biological determinism, nor was there systematic persecution of any ethnic or presumed racial group by others, let alone the massive excesses to which state-imposed racist doctrine led in the twentieth century. Racism is taken here as representing a form of rationalizing and systematically justifying various forms of prejudice, a conceptual process which was part of Greek intellectual development in general. I have treated this subject at length in a book,[10] but it seems useful to offer the essence of the argument here in succinct form, since at least four of the following studies deal with related topics. It must be admitted that the evidence we have is of a restricted nature: we have to work with the available ancient texts and cannot trace more than that. We cannot know what people were saying in a pub in ancient Rome.

In antiquity, as in modern times, we constantly encounter the unquestioned assumption that it is possible and reasonable to relate to entire peoples as if they were a single or collective individual. This is the conceptual basis for all generalizations: a denial of individuality. One of the consequences of this attitude is that individuals belonging to a target group are thereby believed to have all the presumed characteristics of the group.

The manifestations of proto-racism – as I prefer to call it – were different from those encountered in the twentieth century and they did not lead to systematic persecution, but they had an impact at the time. They also deeply influenced later authors, in the age of the Enlightenment and afterwards, who accepted these ideas together with others which they found in Greek and Latin literature. The prevalent concepts in antiquity were different from what we now call racism. There was no biological determinism, but other models existed, based on ideas current in that period. These concepts are discussed here: environmental determinism, the heredity of acquired characters, a combination of these, and a belief in – and insistence on – pure lineage. Related issues involve ideas concerning the constitution and form of government of communities, autochthony, and pure lineage.

This discussion is followed by some thoughts regarding the connection between ancient views of slavery and concepts of empire in classical antiquity. If individual slavery was morally accepted, so was collective enslavement. The claim was that enslaved people were probably in that situation because they were inferior. Influential in this connection was also the sense that imperial expansion and migration inevitably lead to degeneration and collective deterioration through both the influence of debilitating climate and contamination with the flaws of inferior peoples.

Most, if not all, of these concepts and ideas were developed in ancient Greece and subsequently adopted in Rome. It is argued that the stereotyped views of foreign peoples described here may not have determined

[10] B. Isaac, *The Invention of Racism in Classical Antiquity* (Princeton, 2004).

imperial policy, but nevertheless had their impact on the political and military decisions that were made. In this respect this topic is of immediate relevance for my understanding of the mechanisms of ancient imperialism.

The Barbarian in Greek and Latin Literature

Various peoples have a term indicating all foreigners collectively, but few of those concepts have had such a long history as the ancient Greek *barbaros* which is still in use in many Western languages. An exception are the parallel terms in Chinese (*Yi* among others).[11] The meaning of *barbaros/barbarus* varied considerably over time. Chapter 9 argues that it is worth reconsidering carefully what the word says about Greek and Roman attitudes towards other peoples over time because it is immediately relevant to the essence of the subjects which the present collection of papers attempts to clarify: empire and ideology, ethnic and cultural relationships, and Graeco-Roman views of others, foreigners and minorities.

From the earliest attestations onwards language can be a factor determining the identity of a people as barbarians, but language was by no means the only one at any stage. The aim here is to gain a better understanding of what this term can teach us about Greek and Roman attitudes to non-Greeks and non-Romans. This is based on literary sources of all kinds, including poetry and tragedy from the eighth century BC right through to the fourth century AD. At various times and in various contexts the word can refer to language and culture, but origin, ethnicity, and citizenship are often viewed as central. Over time a wide array of stereotypes and prejudices are attested in connection with the use of this term. Personal names may be a characteristic of persons presumed to be 'barbarians', or irrationality, or, not surprisingly, peculiar dress or different weaponry. Effeminacy also comes up. Generally speaking there was a clear tendency in the course of the fifth century BC for the concept to bear an increasingly negative content. This may relate to a simple, odd external appearance, but can also apply, for instance, to a lack of sexual restraint. In the fourth century BC the term approached its use in modern English. An essential feature appeared in the later fifth century BC, namely a marked tendency toward the use of the term as part of an imperialist ideology. This ideological and political use is found in Euripides and Xenophon and gains force in the fourth century BC.

---

[11] Michèle Pirazzoli-t'Serstevens, 'Imperial Aura and the Image of the Other in Han Art', in F.-H. Mutschler and A. Mittag (eds.), *Conceiving the Empire: China and Rome Compared* (Oxford, 2008), 299–322, at 309–14.

At the same time we note another significant shift, namely the possibility of change: barbarians may become Greeks and Greeks can turn into barbarians, according to certain authors in some periods. Being Greek or barbarian is no longer a fixed, inherited form of identity.

Moving on to the Roman use of the term we see that it was employed differently in various ways from those found in Greek literature. As a consequence of conquest, empire, and the systematic grants of citizenship, there was never any doubt that it was possible for a barbarian to become a Roman. The overall impression is one of relative conceptual simplicity as compared with the Greeks. Of course its basic meaning of 'non-Greek' or 'non-Roman' is frequently implied, as might be expected, when enemies in war are mentioned, although not exclusively so. It will not come as a surprise either that it occurs with a dual meaning, both indicating non-Roman identity as well as including a negative qualification in the modern sense of the word. New, however, is the fact that it is frequently used in the modern, pejorative sense of 'barbarian' as a derogatory substantive or adjective, not immediately associated with foreignness. In other words, a Roman can be called a barbarian if his behaviour deviates from the norm, without any suggestion that he is actually a foreigner.

In Greek and Roman texts, we see that important differences and shades of meaning can be detected over time. Generalizations are common: foreigners are naturally wicked; with them loyalty depends upon success; they are treacherous, and impious. Both Greeks and Romans have in common their denial to the barbarian of the qualities which they themselves regard both as their own and as essential. In the case of the Romans, among the most important of those are: loyalty, honesty, piety, and discipline. However, the essence of what is seen as barbarism shifts in stages as a consequence of changes in self-perception, of ideology, and of imperial reality. An empire cannot be continuously successful if it relates to all others as though they were inferior and incapable of sharing in the Empire.

Romans and Nomads in the Fourth Century AD

The purpose of Chapter 10 is to fill a gap left in my book *The Invention of Racism in Classical Antiquity* (2004), namely aspects of Roman attitudes toward foreigners in fourth- and fifth-century AD literature. Fourth-century Latin, non-Christian literature, notably Ammianus' *History*, contains numerous value-judgements regarding foreigners and provincials. A great variety of negative descriptions, including many recurring stereotypes, can be found there. Clearly this reflects the increased intensity of warfare with foreign peoples as compared with previous centuries – wars which were not initiated by Rome as had usually been the case in the past. There is less agreement on the background and overall attitude reflected by those negative views.

It is argued here that these fourth-century attitudes are best seen through an analysis of statements about nomads who represent the bottom of the scale in the ancient hierarchy of reputations. Also, in this period the Roman Empire found itself in conflict with nomadic peoples more frequently than in the past. They were a source of concern in a way that they had not been before.

Ammianus describes the development over time of the collective of the Empire in terms of the existence of an individual rather than a group. He combines this with a certainty, familiar from Graeco-Roman culture, that the progress of time can only bring deterioration, not improvement. His excursuses on provincial peoples tend to be anachronistic: Gaul and parts of the Near East are described as if they had just been annexed. Subsequent developments over the centuries are ignored. His treatment of nomads, however, is different. The Saracens are described in terms that make them less than fully human, with comparisons to animals: they are half-naked, do not live in houses, are unproductive, and do not have regular marriages. The theme of drinking human blood comes up at least once. The Thracians, described in extremely anachronistic terms, practise human sacrifice and drink human blood out of skulls. The treatment of the Isaurians is replete with animal comparisons. A common accusation aimed at all nomads is that they do not fight honestly. Guerrilla tactics are seen not as a different manner of fighting, but as a despicable and cowardly form of soldiering. This fits the view, expressed by Ammianus, that all foreigners are lacking *fides* and *constantia*. They are not gentlemen. These descriptions are used with particular force, by Ammianus and later authors, in their treatment of the Huns in the fourth and fifth centuries. Their external appearance is not human, they are of unnatural descent, they have no fire, no homes, no morals, and no religion, and produce nothing. Indeed they are a sort of centaur, half horse and half human being.

We encounter here a consistent and coherent pattern which places nomads in a category apart. They are inferior in every respect and they are so by nature and pass on their inferiority from one generation to the next. The views of these authors display a gradual scale dividing groups of peoples into classes from superiority to inferiority, where those least regarded are associated with animals or classified as less than fully human. The repetition of specific themes is coherent and can legitimately be seen as an ideology based on an early form of racism. A further point arising from this chapter is the recognition of a shift over time. Nomads were always regarded as inferior and no effort was made to understand the social and economic reality of their lifestyle. However, when the military confrontation with nomadic peoples became fiercer and more threatening, the derogatory statements and descriptions increase markedly.

A Multicultural Mediterranean?

Chapter 11 was first published as a review article of Erich Gruen's important book, *Rethinking the Other in Antiquity* (Princeton, 2011), in which the author proposes an alternative interpretation of ancient views of others, or of 'the Other'. It deals with essential elements in our views of any society: group identity, tolerance or feelings of superiority, mutual appreciation or polarity between peoples. Gruen's book is learned and persuasive, but I disagree with many of the conclusions. As Gruen formulates it: 'This study offers an alternative vision to the widespread idea that framing the self requires postulating "the Other." The expression of collective character in antiquity ... owes less to insisting on distinctiveness from the alien than to postulating links with, adaptation to, and even incorporation of the alien.' Gruen goes so far as to declare the ancient Mediterranean 'a multicultural world'. The book thus argues that ancient society, as we know it, was different in kind from all that followed in terms of social acceptance. It does so in spite of our awareness that these were societies in which slavery, war, and conquest were an integral part of their system, morally accepted as a matter of course.

While expressing my great admiration for the scholarship, originality, elegance, and broad perspective to be found in Gruen's book, I point to what I regard as a number of methodological problems. My first question concerns the fact that an elementary distinction must be made between attitudes towards foreign, distant peoples and foreign minorities within Greece and Rome, especially in the large cities, and also between people in the present and those living in the distant past. It is only natural to assume that inhabitants of the city of Rome would regard Egyptians living in their midst in a different light from those living in their far-away homeland. Secondly, feelings about people in the present may be different from those about the same people in the recent, remote, or legendary past. Thus Romans of the first century AD would relate to Egyptian neighbours in their city in one way, but to the inhabitants of the Roman province of Egypt in another and to historical Egyptians, one of the oldest

civilized peoples known to them, in yet another. Third, attitudes towards
others usually change over time. That is true everywhere and at all times,
but would apply with specific force in a rapidly expanding empire. It is
my suggestion that Gruen underestimates the importance of these distinctions. Thus in my opinion it is undeniable that the sources show a change
in Greek attitudes towards the East, Persia in particular, in the course of
the fifth and fourth centuries BC, culminating in the Macedonian destruction of the Achaemenid Empire.

Similarly we must distinguish between Roman attitudes towards
its major enemy in the third century BC, Carthage, and that towards
Phoenicians who lived in Rome in the first century AD. The Gauls were a
formidable enemy in the fourth century BC. In the first century AD they
were fully incorporated into the Empire. Of course there was a shift in
Roman thinking about Gauls during these centuries.

A basic difference between Gruen's and my approaches is our interpretation of the limits of a sense of humour, especially in Tacitus, when he
discusses Germans or Jews. There is a point where hatred can masquerade
as if it were simple, good fun. The question is what emotional weight is
hidden behind a presumed sense of humour.

The second part of Gruen's book is particularly stimulating and original with chapters on 'Foundation Legends' (ch. 9), 'Fictitious Kinships'
(chs. 10 and 11), and 'Cultural Interlockings and Overlappings' (ch. 12).
Whether we agree or not, the issues raised are fascinating. They touch on
essential questions regarding the manner in which Greeks, Romans, and
Jews dealt with their own origins in various periods. The subject here is
the distant, mythical past and the manner in which contacts between and
relationships with other peoples in that mythical past were invented and
imagined. There is much to say about this, even if I disagree that it can
all be construed as evidence that the Greeks and Romans were tolerant
and that the ancient world was multicultural. The question is what these
fictions and legends meant to Greeks and Romans in the classical age.
I would say that this question remains to be answered. Gruen asserts: 'The
idea that nations had a common ancestor transcends conflict and warfare,
and challenges the concept of "otherness"' (257). I am not persuaded, but
I do agree that this is an important issue which demands careful thought.
To give just one example from another period: in the 1950s the Dutch had
no qualms about singing the (sixteenth-century) national anthem, containing the phrase: 'William of Orange I am of German blood ... the King
of Spain I have always honoured.' This does not mean there was uniform
approval in the Netherlands, immediately after the Second World War, of

Germans or the Spanish monarchy. It is important to understand what Greeks and Romans thought and meant when they dealt with their own legendary and mythical distant past. To mention just two central topics, what was the purpose of Athenian claims of autochthony, and what was the meaning of Roman manipulations of myths in order to prove their Trojan and Asiatic origins or, alternatively, Greek roots or a combination of the two? I would conclude that there is more work to be done, precisely because the questions are so interesting and important.[12]

I regard it as obvious that Greeks and Romans developed views of other peoples approaching what we now call racism in an ideological form, although this never led to systematic persecution on the basis of skin-colour or other forms of group identity (see Chapter 8). This leads to my conclusion that there is a tendency towards utopia in Gruen's book. Furthermore, essential points of method and approach need to be discussed. Gruen, I claim, ignores distinctions between categories of 'others' and differences over time, and also fails to deal with sources that contradict his thesis or interprets them in an anachronistic manner. That said, I emphasize the great contribution of this learned and elegant book towards the discussion of the subject as a whole. I would say that Rome in particular succeeded for so long in maintaining an integrated empire because it coped with the existence of these very real tensions, rather than as a result of an absence of such tensions.

Latin in Cities of the Roman Near East

In the Roman Near East, various languages were used for written and oral communication. The relative importance of these languages is a topic frequently studied and discussed. Two of the languages were imported by conquerors from the West. Of these, it is clear that Latin, unlike Greek, was never used widely, but it is also obvious that the first language of the Empire played a role in communications in its time. In Chapter 12 I consider the question of the extent to which Latin may have been more than the language of government and military organization in the cities of the Near East from Pompey to the third century AD. This is only one aspect

---

[12] See now D. J. Mattingly, *Imperialism, Power, and Identity: Experiencing the Roman Empire* (Princeton, 2011), esp. ch. 8: 'Identity and Discrepancy' and E. S. Gruen (ed.), *Cultural Identity in the Ancient Mediterranean* (Berkeley and Los Angeles, 2011). In both works many aspects are discussed that are not represented in this book, such as 'Power, Sex, and Empire'; 'Resources' (Mattingly); 'Myth and Identity'; Egyptian Culture and Roman Identity; 'Myths, Images, and the Typology of Identities in Early Greek Art' by T. Hölscher (Gruen); and more.

but an important one of the impact of Western, Roman influence on the cities of the Near East.

The question asked in this chapter is what we can learn from surviving texts, invariably inscriptions on stone, about the use of Latin in cities of the Roman East. The region considered for this purpose is limited to that of Syria, Judaea/Palaestina, and Arabia, excluding the numerous cities of Asia Minor. There are various reasons for this choice, the most important being that the process of Hellenization is so markedly different between the various regions. In the area under discussion the local languages were Semitic, while Greek arrived only with the establishment of Seleucid and Ptolemaic rule. The degree of Hellenization varied and is often difficult or impossible to trace. Whatever the relationship between the local Semitic languages and Greek, Greek was the second language introduced by imperial rulers in this region and Latin was the third. The ancient literature is not very informative on the use of Latin in non-Latin-speaking provinces. In this respect, the situation resembles a related and even larger and more complex topic, popularly called 'Romanization', referring to the political, economic, and cultural assimilation of subject peoples into Roman imperial society. For the present, far more modest subject, the material studied is the epigraphic record although it is in itself a question to what extent this is reliable evidence for social and cultural realities beyond that of epigraphic practices themselves.

In principle Latin may be expected to have been used by the following groups: Roman authorities and their representatives, the army, and settlers in Roman colonies. It is also conceivable that the last group to some extent exerted a Latinizing influence on people with Greek or a Semitic language who might have used Latin in order to interact with the speakers of that language who belonged to the local upper class. We must therefore try to see whether local civilians from these cities other than Roman settlers and their descendants set up inscriptions in Latin, and whether we can establish any kind of social context for those epigraphic Latin-speakers. There proves in fact to be little evidence for such a development, although there is some evidence of mixed nomenclature, the result, apparently, of mixed marriages or grants of citizenship, notably in Berytus. The case of Caesarea is more complex: it is argued here that this was not a Roman veteran colony, but a titular colony, where a strong Latin presence is attested because it was the provincial capital with an army unit stationed there.

My conclusion: the most obvious way of understanding the choice of language is as a reflection of political loyalty and of association with the imperial power. At Berytus there was a substantial Roman veteran colony where the Latin tradition was maintained for centuries after its foundation. The city produced members of the upper classes, and some of its citizens expressed themselves in Latin on public monuments and had proper Roman names. Elsewhere Latin does not simply represent one of the languages spoken locally, but had a particular social and political resonance, and the study of the epigraphic material opens up these resonances to historical analysis.

Ancient Antisemitism

Chapter 13 is a survey of hostile attitudes towards Jews in the Graeco-Roman world. It distinguishes between racist and non-racist forms of hostility according to reasonable, modern definitions. One of the purposes of the study is to decide which form of hostility we face in the ancient literature. Three different groups of sources should be considered separately: (a) Alexandrian authors; (b) Hellenistic, non-Egyptian authors; (c) Roman literature. Furthermore clear regional distinctions have to be made: Jews in Egypt, elsewhere in the Diaspora, and in Rome. Various types of hostility and criticism should be singled out. The discussion of Roman attitudes towards the Jews, which is more extensive than the treatment of Hellenistic attitudes, is divided into several sections: social criticism, criticism of the Jewish religion and its monotheism, as well as a number of specific topics: dietary restrictions, the Sabbath, and circumcision.

A set of questions is dealt with systematically:

(1) Was Greek and Roman hatred of the Jews essentially different from hatred toward other, non-Greek and non-Roman groups?
(2) Were Roman attitudes different from those encountered in the general Hellenistic and more specifically Alexandrian traditions?
(3) Can we feel an impact of the various wars and revolts on Roman attitudes towards Jews?
(4) What are the differences between common antisemitic stereotypes of later periods and those encountered in the literature of Graeco-Roman antiquity?

It is clear that Alexandrian traditions produced a form of hostility exceeding that of other groups of Greek and Latin authors. The Jews, it was asserted, had no sexual inhibitions, they practised human sacrifice and cannibalism. There are records of calls for the eradication of the Jewish people.

A Hellenistic, non-Alexandrian claim, familiar from modern antisemitism, is that the Jews made no contribution to human society.

More generally attested is the claim that Jews were not sociable. They are accused of cutting themselves off from the rest of humanity. This is found frequently in Roman texts: their god tolerated no others and they themselves refused to take part in meals with others. Related to this, and particularly significant, is the claim that proselytes were attracted to the Jewish religion and then became traitors to Rome. A further step is the assertion that 'the vanquished have given laws to their victors', that is to say, the Jews proselytized and in doing so became the religious and cultural masters of the Empire.

The most frequent expressions of disapproval concern the distinct and unusual Jewish lifestyle: monotheism, dietary restrictions, the Sabbath, and circumcision. All these engendered hostility, but no efforts were made to suppress them, for that was not how the Roman Empire functioned.

The paper ends with a number of conclusions:

(1) Ancient attitudes towards Jews are indeed quite different from those towards other foreigners. They should not be regarded as a form of ancient proto-racism.

(2) The Hellenized Egyptian and Alexandrian hatred of the Jews was different in scale.

(3) Roman attitudes were different from those encountered in the Hellenistic and Alexandrian tradition, partly because of the specific social situation in the major city of Alexandria, but also because of the policy of integration which made the Roman Empire as successful as it was.

(4) There are marked differences between ancient disapproval of the Jews and later forms of antisemitism. Absent in antiquity are the blood libel, which was a Christian invention, and the legend of the wandering Jew. Jews were definitely not depicted as typical Asiatics or Orientals, nor were they regarded as materialistic traders. Finally, they were never depicted as the rootless conspirators who aimed to gain world domination through secret plotting, in spite of the resentment caused by proselytism, whatever the scale on which it operated in antiquity. Causes for these differences are argued in the chapter.

It is essential to note how differently the Roman Empire, before it became Christian, responded to the Jews it subjected, a result of the politics of integration which made it a success.

Roman Religious Policy and the Bar Kokhba War

Following this discussion of ancient attitudes towards Jews, I consider a specific crisis between Romans and Jews. The cause or causes of the Bar Kokhba revolt are still reported in only two sources, for the documents discovered in recent years do not add any direct references to its origins. We have to choose between the information given by the Historia Augusta (*v. Had.* 14.2) and that given by Cassius Dio (69.12), or a combination of the two. If it could be shown that Jerusalem was refounded as Colonia Aelia Capitolina before the outbreak of the revolt that would reinforce the statement of Dio that this was the cause of the revolt. However, this in itself does not contradict or invalidate the explicit statement in the Historia Augusta that a general ban on circumcision was the cause. Generations of scholars have firmly expressed their preference for one cause or the other, or a combination of the two. Others have introduced additional theories which, however, are not attested in any source.

Chapter 14 considers the two alleged causes of the revolt in the light of what we know about Roman religious policy and Roman attitudes towards the Jews in general. The first important point to make is that both sources, and both alleged causes, mark the revolt as a religious war; this is an essential feature, for religious wars were rare in antiquity in general and in the Roman Empire in particular before the rise of Christianity. However the Maccabaean Revolt and the Jewish rebellions against Roman rule were clearly religious wars, connected with the exclusivity of monotheism. Apart from these instances, religious wars were initiated by the Roman imperial authorities only after the Empire had become Christian. This should be a significant factor in assessing the role of the Roman authorities before and after Constantine, both in general and in the specific case of the Second Jewish Revolt.

In this chapter I attempt to reinforce the arguments of those who conclude that there was never a general ban on circumcision for Jews. If there was no such ban, then it cannot have been a cause of the Revolt. On the other hand, there was a ban on circumcision for converts which is well attested in the sources. This, it is argued, was part of a long-term policy against conversion.

The absence of a general ban on circumcision makes sense in the light of what we know about Roman religious policy. However, the ban on the circumcision of converts to Judaism as part of a long-standing policy against proselytism also makes sense in Roman terms. Religion and ethnicity were closely associated. A people had a right to its religion, if it was well established and respectable (i.e. refrained from human sacrifice) and did not resist Roman rule. It could maintain its cults and customs, side by side with the religion of the Roman state and people. However, individuals had no right to change their religion, or their ethnicity, except by accepting Roman citizenship. Jews were explicitly allowed to practise their religion in spite of numerous objections against them and, above all, against their customs. More than anything else it was proselytism which engendered hostility and resistance on the part of individual Romans and of the authorities. The inhabitants of the Empire were not permitted to make an act of commitment to a new cult which would cut them off from their old ones. That, by the way, was also precisely what Christianity later meant to the authorities.

The bottom line is that there was nothing in the Roman pattern of behaviour which would have excluded the foundation of a Roman colony on the site of Jerusalem, which we know to have existed. A general ban on circumcision would not have been part of Roman policy. The former initiative of founding a *colonia*, however, was a common act, but in the case of Jerusalem it caused a major war.

Jews, Christians, and Others in Palestine: The Evidence from Eusebius

This chapter raises the question of the distribution of the various population groups – pagans, Jews, and Christian – in fourth-century AD Palestine. While it is now generally admitted that the cities had a mixed population, although not evenly spread, that was not the case for the countryside and its villages. Here it is frequently assumed as a matter of course that each community was dominated by a single group: Jews, Christians, or pagans. In this view the villages were monocultures inhabited by representatives of a single ethnic and religious group. Yet this is far from obvious. There is in fact little information about the process of Christianization of the countryside. If conversion took place on an individual more often than a group basis, many villages must inevitably have been inhabited by both unconverted pagans and converted Christians. In late antiquity we find many churches and synagogues in different small communities and, albeit rarely, both a church and a synagogue in the same community. Thus it is quite possible that Jews might have lived in a village with a church, or Christians or pagans in a village with a synagogue.

The present discussion focuses on the evidence from a unique source which merits closer scrutiny, namely the *Onomasticon of Biblical Place-Names* by Eusebius. This is a mine of information about Palestine in the

Roman and Byzantine periods, contemporary evidence of a kind that does not exist for any other part of the Roman Empire. It is unique because it is the only text which is concerned solely and consistently with regional matters. Of course the work has been studied intensively by scholars interested in the Holy Land, but it is not a text that has drawn much attention from historical geographers of the Roman Empire.

Among the large number of villages that Eusebius mentions there is a fairly small group which he qualifies in some manner. He refers to eleven 'villages of Jews'. Three villages are inhabited 'entirely by Christians' and two of these are also 'very big' villages. Eusebius further mentions four 'villages of Samaritans'. In the entire work he does not mention any specifically 'pagan' villages. These are very small numbers out of the hundreds of villages mentioned in the text. It is argued here that this is no coincidence and gives a faithful impression of the demographic situation at the time when the information was compiled.

On the basis of a survey of the information provided by Eusebius for the Palestinian countryside, the conclusion is that the overwhelming majority of villages had a mixed population: pagan, Jewish, Christian, and Samaritan. Eusebius would have considered that the norm and found it worth mentioning only if a settlement was purely Jewish, Christian, or Samaritan. Normally Jews, Christians, and gentiles lived side by side both in the cities and in the countryside. This does not necessarily mean they lived peacefully side by side – perhaps they did so at times or even usually. It can, however, be concluded that modern assumptions that they all lived separately in communities of their own are wrong. This could also be true for other parts of the Empire.

Roman Organization in the Arabah in the Fourth Century AD

The aim of the last two chapters in this volume is to help elucidate questions concerning the issue of frontier defence versus security of communications along the roads.[13]

The first focuses on Roman army organization in Palestine in the fourth century. Following the survey work carried out by Fritz Frank in the Negev, Albrecht Alt made an extensive attempt to trace a string of Diocletianic *castella* in the Wadi Arabah.[14] The assumption here was that there must have been a '*limes* system' in the Negev such as allegedly existed in Germany.

---

[13] This is the central topic in B. Isaac, *The Limits of Empire*, 2nd edn (Oxford, 1992).
[14] A. Alt, 'Aus der Araba II: Römische Kastelle und Strassen', *ZDPV* 58 (1935): 1–59.

The existence of such a system was firmly denied by Beno Rothenberg, who stated, based on his survey of the Arabah in the 1960s:

> The Diocletianic reform brought no essential military changes to the 'Arabah. Only three small fortlets were erected there, all sited at the extreme ends of the 'Arabah, and protecting essential water-sources on major west-east roads. There was never a line of fourth century castella in the 'Arabah, and no traces of any north-south road running all the way from the Dead Sea to the Red Sea have ever been found. A quantity of Byzantine sherds in the remains of an Iron Age watch-tower or a Nabataean khan do not make it a Roman fortress.[15]

Chapter 16 reconsiders the available sources in an attempt to assess the merits of these two contradictory opinions and any possible alternatives. It is argued that Rothenberg was right in challenging the view that there was a line of fourth-century *castella* in the Arabah, but wrong in denying the existence of a fourth-century north–south road through it. Furthermore, it is argued that the archaeological evidence attesting the existence of this road corresponds with the evidence from the literary sources as long as the dates of these sources are carefully interpreted. The literary sources are Eusebius' *Onomasticon* and the *Notitia Dignitatum*. Inscribed milestones in the Arabah and a Latin inscription found at Yotvetah provide decisive evidence. It is no longer possible to deny that a road was laid out through the Arabah in the fourth century, clearly coinciding with the transfer of a legion from Jerusalem to Aela (Elath). Aela was now linked with western Palestine just as it had previously been connected with Transjordan, and this fact was reflected in administrative terms by the transfer of the Negev to the province of Palaestina.

At the same time, however, it is clear that we once again have evidence of the Roman army's concern for safe communications rather than the organization of frontier defence.

Hatra Against Rome and Persia: From Success to Destruction

Hatra, located in northern Mesopotamia not far from the Tigris, was a crucially important centre in between the Roman and Persian Empires. Both powers attempted to gain control of it in the second and third centuries AD. Its location was clearly considered essential by those who wanted to gain control of Northern Mesopotamia. As is well known, the site has

---

[15] B. Rothenberg, 'The Arabah in Roman and Byzantine Times in the Light of New Research', in S. Applebaum (ed.), *Roman Frontier Studies* (Tel Aviv, 1967), 211–23, at 220.

been excavated and produced numerous inscriptions. Recently, in 2015, it became a major item in the news because of the destruction of its antiquities by religious fanatics.

Hatra was besieged three times: by Trajan during his Parthian campaign (AD 114–17), by Septimius Severus in AD 197/8, and by the Sassanian Ardashir in AD 239/40, who destroyed the city.

Hatra was clearly part of the region Trajan wanted to annex into the provincial system of the Empire. The fact that Septimius Severus spent time and effort taking the city during his march back again confirms the importance of the location. It is worth noting that, when he attacked Parthia, Severus marched south along the Euphrates but withdrew northwards along the Tigris and thus found Hatra on his route.

Why Septimius Severus felt the need to besiege Hatra is not explained in any text in our possession. However, Herodian reports that Barsemius, ruler of Hatra, sent Severus' enemy Niger a company of archers, which may have been considered a hostile act by Severus. The fact that Hatra sent troops to support a Roman pretender may also serve as evidence that it was a Roman client state, perhaps since the AD 160s as a result of the Roman campaigns in the region at that time. However, according to Dio, Severus' persistence was mainly a matter of honour.

Hatra was undoubtedly a Roman client state by AD 238–240 when a detachment of Roman troops was stationed there. That explains why Ardashir attacked the city.

As already noted, Hatra's location was considered essential by those who wanted to control Northern Mesopotamia – whether they were based in Babylonia or, if they controlled the North, wanted to engage militarily in the South. Hence the efforts made by Trajan, Septimius Severus, and Ardashir. Yet it was not a place that needed to function as a city, at least in the eyes of Ardashir, for he destroyed it. Its location remained essential for armies on the march, however, as is clear from the fact that Julian's army passed the site during its withdrawal in AD 363.

In contrast to the site's archaeological riches, the literary sources relating to the site are deficient and essential information is missing. This study assesses the role played by the city in war and peace and the reason why both powers attached such importance to it. A peculiar circumstance to be taken into account is that Persia preferred to destroy it altogether rather than leave it in Roman hands. The evidence concerning Hatra in peacetime is far less extensive and vivid than that from Palmyra, another site that has recently been vandalized. Yet there can be little doubt that it played a somewhat similar role. It was situated on a main road along the Tigris, parallel to the route along the Euphrates – which explains its importance in war as well. The importance in peacetime of cities controlling nodal points along the trade routes linking the two empires is clear from texts on other towns in various periods.

The extent of our ignorance concerning essential matters is shown by the fact that we do not have the slightest idea whether any other centre assumed the role Hatra must have played during the period of its prosperity, or how else its destruction affected trade along the Tigris route. It is clear, however, that sites which could play a key role in commercial traffic might also be strategically important. The cases of both Palmyra and Hatra show that ancient leaders, facing commercial prosperity combined with a strategic risk, did not hesitate in putting an end to both.

Conclusions

I conclude with a few words about the title of this collection 'Empire and Ideology in the Ancient World?' 'An empire is a multi-ethnic or multi-national state with political and/or military dominion over populations which are culturally and ethnically distinct from the imperial (ruling) ethnic group and its culture.'[16] This definition covers the reality of the Roman Empire. However, are there specific qualities that are not applicable to other ancient or later empires?

This volume essentially is devoted to three broad fields: (a) anachronisms in modern views of ancient empires; (b) problems in understanding the self-identification of ancient groups, views of others, and the role of religion in this sphere; (c) military matters. Most of these are – and will remain – matters of intense debate. For the present I will conclude with a few observations about possible directions for further thinking.

A consideration of the idea of 'Eternal Rome' suggests an obvious tension between the claim of an eternal empire and the overwhelming absence in antiquity of an idea of progress or, rather, a firm belief in the necessity of decline. Further, continued attention may be paid also to matters of nomenclature and terminology, notably the absence of an obvious name for the Roman state and its empire which may have had practical consequences. What I claim for the Near East is probably true for other parts of the Roman Empire not discussed here: terminology indicating social identity is far more fluid than may seem obvious. We have to determine

---

[16] *The Oxford English Reference Dictionary*, 2nd edn (Oxford, 2001), 461.

for each instance whether we are faced with geography, ethnicity, language, culture, administration, or a social group. The concept of the 'barbarian' – which often says more about those who use it than about their target – is one well-known and significant example of a term that changes meaning over time. The same may apply to the absence of abstractions, so familiar in our times, representing the state, justice, victory, etc. The images in ancient art so interpreted are clearly mythological figures and deities and must be regarded as such. They are not renderings of abstract concepts. Clarity is needed in all of these cases for a proper understanding of historical processes. This is true also for models attempting to portray the geographical, political, and economic relationship between parts of empires, such as the Core–Periphery theory. If they are to function, they need a more thorough and systematic analysis than is usually practised.

I have written elsewhere about the existence of racism in antiquity, involving approaches towards others: minorities and foreigners. It is my contention that too little distinction is made, even now, between attitudes towards minorities, which were actually present in ancient cities, and those towards distant peoples. The same goes for the distinction between contemporary peoples and those in the distant past. It bears further consideration what it meant for fifth-century Greeks when the city of Thebes claimed to have had a mythical Phoenician as founder. We have seen too that it is necessary to keep in mind that at the highest social level there still were status differences between provincials and Romans.

The Jews were strongly disliked by many Roman authors, but formal measures, initiated by the state, to suppress their freedom of religion are not reliably attested before the empire turned Christian. Freedom of religion, however, does not mean that conversion was allowed. In this connection it has been shown for the province of Syria Palaestina that the various population groups lived in mixed communities rather than separate ones. It will be useful to consider this question for other provinces of the Empire as well. It may be healthy, too, to pay more attention to the fundamental lack of an understanding of nomadism in Graeco-Roman antiquity, given the fact that large parts of the Roman Empire were eventually lost to nomads in central Europe and the Near East. Another question in need of further consideration and debate is whether we accept Erich Gruen's claim that the ancient Mediterranean could be called a multicultural world.

One of my subjects is military matters. In this connection topics that bear further thought are the absence anywhere in antiquity of a proper internal police force. The functions of an internal police force were fulfilled by the regular army without legal checks and balances. Material from the

Arabah once again confirms that the Roman army invested in communications and roads rather than frontier fortifications. This represents the well-known Roman expertise in organization and engineering. In this connection, elsewhere in this volume it is shown that Roman willingness to apply science and research to their accomplishments in the practice of warfare was seriously limited. Finally, I have indicated various uncertainties concerning Hatra and other sites in Mesopotamia, focusing again on its key role in controlling communications. Recent, disastrous developments are likely to exclude the possibility of such questions being investigated properly in the foreseeable future. That too is a matter for serious consideration.

It is a pleasure to thank Prof. Aron Shai, Rector of Tel Aviv University and Prof. Eyal Zisser, Dean of the Faculty of Humanities, for the generous financial support rendered in preparing this book for publication.

CHAPTER I

Roma Aeterna

The subject of this chapter has been discussed frequently in the modern literature.[1] The last of these discussions, however, seems to be forty years old and a somewhat different approach may prove to have some merit. I will be guided, in particular, by the feeling that earlier discussions tend to over-interpret single testimonies and ignore long-term trends.

We may start with a famous passage of Polybius where he described Scipio, the Roman commander who destroyed Carthage, at the time of the destruction which he witnessed:

> At the sight of the city utterly perishing amidst the flames Scipio burst into tears, and stood long reflecting on the inevitable change which awaits cit- ies, nations and dynasties, one and all, as it does every one of us men. This, he thought, had befallen Ilium, once a powerful city, and the once mighty empires of the Assyrians, Medes, Persians and that of Macedonia lately so splendid. And unintentionally or purposely he quoted, – the words perhaps escaping him unconsciously, –
> The day shall be when holy Troy shall fall
> And Priam, lord of spears, and Priam's folk.
> And on my asking him boldly (for I had been his tutor) what he meant by these words, he did not name Rome distinctly, but was evidently fearing for her, from this sight of the mutability of human affairs …
> Another still more remarkable saying of his I may record.
> … [When he had given the order for firing the town] he immediately turned round and grasped me by the hand and said: 'O Polybius, it is a

This is a revised version of a paper published originally in Hebrew in *Historia* 2 (1998): 19–31.

[1] F. G. Moore, 'On *Urbs Aeterna* and *Urbs Sacra*', *TAPA* 25 (1894): 34–60; F. Cumont, 'L'éternité des empereurs romains', *Revue d'histoire et de littérature religieuses* 1 (1896): 435–52; M. Charlesworth, '*Providentia* and *Aeternitas*', *HTR* 29 (1936): 107–32. For the early evidence esp.: H. V. Instinsky, 'Kaiser und Ewigkeit', *Hermes* 77 (1942): 313–55; J. Beaujeu, *La religion romaine à l'apogée de l'empire* (Paris, 1955), 141–52; R. Mellor, 'The Goddess Rome', *ANRW* 2.17.2 (1991), 950–1030, esp. 1018–25. See also: K. J. Pratt, 'Rome as Eternal', *Journal of the History of Ideas* 26 (1965): 25–44; C. Edwards, *Writing Rome: Textual Approaches to the City* (Cambridge, 1996), esp. 86–8, 141–52. Various further references will be found in works cited below.

grand thing, but, I know not how, I feel a terror and dread, lest someone
should one day give the same order about my own native city.'

(Polybius 38.21)

Here then the idea that Rome might be eternal is emphatically denied
by one of its major historians, citing one of the most famous and successful generals of the second century BC. It clearly was not seen always and by
everyone as obvious that Rome would be eternal.

Indeed, the concept appears first in the work of Cicero:

> This [sc.: military service] has gained the Roman people its name, has gained
> eternal glory for this city, and has compelled the world to obey this empire.[2]
>
> It is through the favour of the Senate and the Roman People that your
> honour is being enshrined in that temple and with that temple the eternal
> memory of your own name is being consecrated.[3]
>
> If you wish our state to be immortal, if you wish our empire to be eternal
> and our glory everlasting, it is our own greed that we must watch, we must
> watch men of violence, anxious for revolution, we must watch evil among
> ourselves, and conspiracies devised at home.[4]
>
> But private citizens often escape these punishments which even the most
> stupid can feel – poverty, exile, imprisonment and stripes – by taking refuge
> in swift death. But in the case of a state, death itself is a punishment, though
> it seems to individuals an escape from punishment; for a state ought to be
> so firmly grounded that it will live for ever. Hence death is not natural for
> a state as it is for a human being, for whom death is not only necessary, but
> frequently even desirable.[5]

A similar sentiment appears in a letter to Atticus, written in 49 BC, where
Cicero explains that he was in favour of avoiding civil war, 'for he, Caesar,
was mortal and might be removed in many ways, while we must preserve
our city and people, in so far as we can, for immortality'.[6] A related, but

---

[2] Cicero, *Mur.* 22.13: *Haec nomen populo Romano, haec huic urbi aeternam gloriam peperit, haec orbem terrarum parere huic imperio coegit.*

[3] Cicero, *Ver.* 2.4.69: *Tuus enim honos illo templo senatus populique Romani beneficio, tui nominis aeterna memoria simul cum templo illo consecratur ...*

[4] Cicero, *Pro Rabirio* (ed. Clark) 33.4: *Si immortalem hanc civitatem esse voltis, si aeternum hoc imperium, si gloriam sempiternam manere, nobis a nostris cupiditatibus, a turbulentis hominibus atque novarum rerum cupidis, ab intestinis malis, a domesticis consiliis est cavendum.*

[5] Cicero, *Rep.* 3.34 (fr.2): *Sed his poenis quas etiam stultissimi sentiunt, egestate, exilio, vinculis, verberibus, elabuntur saepe privati oblata mortis celeritate, civitatibus autem mors ipsa poena est, quae videtur a poena singulos vindicare; debet enim constituta sic esse civitas, ut aeterna sit. Itaque nullus interitus est rei publicae naturalis ut hominis, in quo mors non modo necessaria est, verum etiam optanda persaepe.* Trans. Keyes, Loeb.

[6] Cicero, *Ad Att.* 9.10.3: *hunc (Caesarem) primum mortalem esse, deinde etiam multis modis posse extingui cogitabam, urbem autem et populum nostrum servandum ad immortalitatem, quantum in nobis esset, putabat.*

modified sentiment is expressed in an oration held after Caesar's victory in the civil war: 'But is there a single person so ignorant … that he does not understand that his well-being depends on yours, and that the lives of all depend on Caesar? I myself … suffer at the idea that the state, which must be immortal, depends on the life of a single mortal being.'[7]

It may be observed that 'eternity', applied to the empire, to the state, glory and renown, is a recurrent theme in Cicero's work. It occurs repeatedly in his rhetorical work and is discussed extensively in his treatises. Since we have no contemporary body of Latin prose comparable to that of Cicero, it seems impossible to say whether this is a feature of his work or of a wider trend. It is, of course, conceivable that a period, which saw both civil war and unprecedented expansion of the empire, engendered a mixture of anxiety that the state could be destroyed from within and hope that it might be eternal and ever expanding. In any case, the notion that the state and the glory of the state and the memory of it must be eternal is frequent in Cicero's rhetorical work and it was clearly presumed common currency among his audience. It is also conceivable, but has to remain a speculation, that Cicero himself was, to some extent, responsible for the increased significance of the concept in the following period. Indeed, it occurs rather frequently in several authors in the reign of Augustus.

In prose we encounter the concept in the work of Livy:

> …The City founded for all eternity…[8]
>
> But (in 403 BC) they cried out, each (senator) for himself, from his elevated position (on the steps of the Senate House), to the multitude standing in the Comitium, and with words and gestures expressed the general happiness, declaring that the city was fortunate, invincible and eternal by this unity.[9]
>
> May Jupiter, the best and greatest not allow that our city, founded under proper auspices and with the consent of the gods for all eternity, exist but as long as this frail and mortal body.[10]

In poetry we encounter the concept in the work of Tibullus: 'Romulus had not yet built the walls of the eternal city'[11] and in the works of Ovid and Vergil.

---

[7] Cicero, *Pro Marcello* 22.

[8] Livy 4.4.4: *in aeternum urbe condita*. Cf. R. M. Ogilvie, *A Commentary on Livy, Books 1–5* (Oxford, 1965), 536.

[9] Livy 5.7.9.2: *sed pro se quisque ex superiore loco ad multitudinem in comitio stantem uoce manibusque significare publicam laetitiam, beatam urbem Romanam et inuictam et aeternam illa concordia dicere …*

[10] Livy 28.28.11 (Livy atrributes to Scipio a speech held in 206 BC): *Ne istuc Iuppiter optimus maximus sirit, urbem auspicato dis auctoribus in aeternum conditam huic fragili et mortali corpori aequalem esse.*

[11] Tibullus 2.5.23: *Romulus aeternae nondum formaverat urbis moenia.* Cf. P. Hardie, 'Augustan Poets and the Mutability of Rome', in A. Powell (ed.), *Roman Poetry and Propaganda in the Age of Augustus* (Bristol, 1991), 61.

'And now what had recently been woods and the retreats of cattle was a city, when the father of the eternal city spoke as follows: …'[12] However, the two passages most discussed in this connection are the following, by Ovid and Vergil, respectively:

> Over the eternal fire (of Vesta) presides the divinity of eternal Caesar. You see the pledges of empire combined.

This is an exceptional pronouncement for the Augustan period, because it combines the eternity of Vesta with that of Caesar.[13]

> For these I set neither bounds nor periods of empire; dominion without end have I bestowed.[14]

This is the best-known celebration of the boundlessness of Rome's empire.[15]

Most of these passages from the period of Augustus are connected with Romulus, the founder of the city, with its foundation, or with crucial moments in Roman history. Only one of them, Ovid in his *Fasti,* specifically mentions the eternity of the *numina Caesaris.* This is the only explicit reference to the eternity of the emperor, rather than the city or the empire in the Julio-Claudian period. The fact that the theme comes up several times in the literature of Augustus' reign inevitably has given rise to claims that it was an element of Augustan propaganda through the influence of Maecenas.[16] However, it is impossible to prove or to disprove that Maecenas told his clients to develop or, at least, insert this specific notion in their literary works. First, Tibullus who first uses the phrase, was not a client of Maecenas but of Messalla Corvinus.[17] Secondly, it is absent from the known elements of the Augustan propaganda programme, the essence

---

[12] Ovid, *Fasti* 3.72: *iam, modo quae fuerant silvae pecorumque recessus, urbs erat, aeternae cum pater urbis ait [sc. Romulus].*

[13] Ovid, *Fasti* 3.421: *ignis aeternis aeterni numina praesunt Caesaris: imperii pignora iuncta vides.* On this passage: G. Herbert-Brown, *Ovid and the Fasti: An Historical Study* (Oxford, 1994), 76–7.

[14] Vergil, *Aen.* 1.278: *his ego [sc. Iuppiter] nec metas rerum nec tempora pono: imperium sine fine dedi.* Trans. Fairclough, Loeb. Cf. R. G. Austin, *P. Vergili Maronis Aeneidos Liber Primus* (Oxford, 1971), comm. *ad loc.* on p. 106.

[15] Sometimes the phrase is misunderstood and *sine fine* interpreted in a spatial sense. That is clearly an error, as will be obvious, if not from the text itself, then from the comments in Servius, *In Vergilii Aeneidos Libros* (*Servii Grammatici Qui Feruntur in Vergilii Carmina Commentarii,* vols. 1–2, ed. G. Thilo, 1878–84) 1.278: *nec metas rervm nec tempora pono 'metas' ad terras rettulit, 'tempora' ad annos; Lavinio enim et Albae finem statuit, Romanis tribuit aeternitatem, {quia subiunxit 'imperium sine fine dedi'.}.* Clearly, *metas rerum* refers to the physical aspect, *tempora* and *sine fine* to the temporal element.

[16] Beaujeu, *La religion romaine,* 145 and references in n. 2.

[17] F. Cairns, *Tibullus: A Hellenistic Poet at Rome* (Cambridge, 1979), 133; R. Syme, *The Augustan Aristocracy* (Oxford, 1986), 200–26.

of which is so well represented in various art forms: prose, poetry, architecture, and sculpture.[18] Thus Augustan *pietas* found expression in religious building and Ovid's *Fasti*,[19] the campaign for family values in legislation, sculpture, and occasional poems.[20]

The entire complex of the new golden age for Rome and the recreation of a mythology around Rome's early history are well known.[21] While Rome's eternity is mentioned occasionally in the literature, we get the impression that the expression appears incidentally, rather than as a significant element in the programme. After all, the essence of public propaganda is that its message is conveyed with emphasis rather than a light and occasional touch. It is thus possible to consider that it was not an element of the Augustan programme, but a popular concept at the time. Certainly, the link with the emperor appears to be a secondary development. Confirmation of this may be found in the fact that Livy inserts the notion as no more than a rhetorical topos in several speeches that are not connected in any way with Romulus or with the new monarchy (in books 4, 5, and 28). No Maecenas was needed to persuade Augustus' contemporaries of the truth that the loss of the old republic had bought them an everlasting empire. To claim eternity for the emperor himself, however, was another matter at that stage. Among the literary men of Augustus' reign, only Ovid felt the need to cross that boundary although, as will be seen below, this may be found occasionally in first-century inscriptions and on coins.

In the first and early second centuries we encounter the concept of eternal Rome in several passages connected with emperors. First, in the reign of Tiberius, Velleius Paterculus describes the joy when Augustus made Tiberius his associate:

> The joy of that day, the congregation of the citizens, their pledges when they stretched their arms to heaven, and the hope which they gained for the perpetual security and the eternity of the Roman empire I will hardly be able to describe extensively in my full work of history, let alone that I should try to do so here.[22]

[18] P. Zanker, *The Power of Images in the Age of Augustus* (Ann Arbor, 1988).

[19] Zanker, *Power of Images*, 102–35.

[20] Zanker, *Power of Images*, 152–9.

[21] Mellor, 'The Goddess Rome'; Zanker, *Power of Images*, ch. 5.

[22] Velleius Paterculus 2.103.4: *Laetitiam illius diei concursumque ciuitatis et uota paene inserentium caelo manus spemque conceptam perpetuae securitatis aeternitatisque Romani imperii uix in illo iusto opere abunde persequi poterimus.*

Valerius Maximus, writing also in the reign of Tiberius, refers to Romulus, founder of the city, as the man who had given the Roman Empire its vitality for ever.[23]

Suetonius gives us an interesting perspective on the contemporary views of the eternal:

> At the games which he [sc. Nero] organized 'for the eternity of the empire' and which he wished to be called the 'Ludi Maximi', roles were played by several persons of both the orders (senatorial and equestrian) and of both sexes.[24]

In this connection we may mention Suetonius' critical comments on Nero: 'He had a craving for everlastingness and eternal fame, although it was ill-considered, and consequently he took away the old designations from many things and gave them new ones derived from his own name.'[25] Here then we have an interesting pronouncement describing Nero's acts as driven by a pathological craving for *aeternitas*. When Suetonius was writing many Romans still found it fitting to describe their city and empire as eternal, but not their rulers.

The elder Pliny may describe Vespasian as the greatest ruler of all times, but it still is Roman glory that is eternal, not the emperor himself:

> For mortal to aid mortal – this is god; and this is the road to eternal glory: by this road went our Roman leaders, by this road now proceeds with heavenward step, escorted by his children, the greatest ruler of all time, Vespasianus Augustus, coming to the aid of an exhausted world.[26]

The younger Pliny often refers to *gloria et laus et aeternitas*, but this is individual glory, praise, and eternity (e.g. *Ep.* 3.16.6; 3.21; 6.16; *Pan.*, frequently). Once he is relevant for our present subject:

---

[23] Valerius Maximus 5.3.1: *Vrbis nostrae parentem senatus in amplissimo dignitatis gradu ab eo conlocatus in curia lacerauit, nec duxit nefas ei uitam adimere, qui aeternum Romano imperio spiritum ingenerauerat.*

[24] Suetonius, *Nero* 11.2: *ludis, quos pro aeternitate imperii susceptos appellari 'maximos' uoluit, ex utroque ordine et sexu plerique ludicras partes sustinuerunt …*

[25] *erat illi aeternitatis perpetuaeque famae cupido, sed inconsulta. ideoque multis rebus ac locis uetere appellatione detracta nouam indixit ex suo nomine …* Cumont, 'L'éternité des empereurs romains', 437, assumes that the expression '*pro aeternitate imperii*' is ambiguous. It could refer to the *imperium* of the ruler and to the Roman Empire. See also Instinsky, 'Kaiser und Ewigkeit', 329–30, with further discussion and references regarding the *Neronia*.

[26] Pliny, *NH* 2.18.2: *deus est mortali iuvare mortalem, et haec ad aeternam gloriam via. hac proceres iere Romani, hac nunc caelesti passu cum liberis suis vadit maximus omnis aevi rector Vespasianus Augustus fessis rebus subveniens.* Incidentally, Pliny's work contains an interesting and unusual note, in this connection: the Jewish sect of the Essenes receives from the Elder Pliny the paradoxical accolade of 'being an eternal people in which no one is born'. *NH* 5.15.73: *ita per saeculorum milia – incredibile dictu – gens aeterna est, in qua nemo nascitur. tam fecunda illis aliorum vitae paenitentia est!*

We used to offer vows for the eternity of the empire and the well-being of the emperors, or, rather, for the well-being of the emperors and through them for the eternity of the empire …[27]

The subject of Pliny's oration is Trajan, but he carefully speaks only of the eternity of the empire and of the well-being of the emperors. Note, however, a Greek inscription cited below, which describes Trajan as eternal.

We have the first reference to the eternal city, as distinct from the eternal empire, or Rome in the broad sense of 'Roman Empire' in the work of Frontinus:

> The present queen and mistress of the world, second to or equalled by none, perceives from day to day this care displayed by the emperor Nerva, the most pious ruler and she will perceive it even more through the health of the eternal city as the number of the works, reservoirs, fountains and water-barriers increases.[28]

This then is the first occurrence of the phrase *aeterna urbs*. This will be no coincidence in a work about the water supply of the city.

One could hardly expect Tacitus to use the phrase in earnest, but he does apply it in speeches which he attributes to others, for instance one by Otho: 'the eternity of the state, the peace of the nations and my own well-being together with yours will be ascertained by the preservation of the Senate'.[29]

Tiberius, addressing the population after Germanicus' death, emphasizes that 'rulers are mortal, but the state is eternal'.[30] Tacitus here ascribes to Tiberius an explicit denial of the ruler-cult.

I will not trace 'Eternal Rome' in the subsequent literature. It will suffice to refer briefly to Ammianus Marcellinus.[31] He opens his fierce chapter on the sins of the Senate and the Roman people (*Senatus populique Romani vitia*) with the sentence: 'Meanwhile Orfitus was governing the eternal city with the authority of Prefect, behaving with a presumption beyond the measure of the

---

[27] Pliny, *Pan.* 67.3: *Nuncupare uota et pro aeternitate imperii et pro salute principum, immo pro salute principum ac propter illos pro aeternitate imperii solebamus.*

[28] Frontinus, *Aq.* 88.1: *sentit hanc curam imperatoris piissimi Nervae principis sui regina et domina orbis in dies, quae terrarum dea consistit, cui par nihil et nihil secundum, et magis sentiet salubritas eiusdem aeternae urbis aucto castellorum, operum, munerum et lacuum numero.* Some editors delete unnecessarily *aeternae urbis*.

[29] Tacitus, *Hist.* 1. 84: *aeternitas rerum et pax gentium et mea cum vestra salus incolumitate senatus firmatur.* Cf. R. Syme, *Tacitus* (Oxford, 1958), 208, n. 1; also: H. Heubner, *P. Cornelius Tacitus: Die Historien*, I (Heidelberg, 1963), 180–1.

[30] *Ann.* 3.6: … *principes mortalis, rem publicam aeternam esse.*

[31] J. F. Matthews, 'Ammianus and the Eternity of Rome', in C. Holdsworth and T. P. Wiseman (eds.), *The Inheritance of Historiography 350–900* (Exeter, 1986), 17–29.

position that had been entrusted to him.'[32] It is possible that the reference to the 'eternal city' here has an undertone of irony. Indeed, it recurs in another attack on the city:

> Among the Persians – as I told above – the perfidy of the King was provoking unanticipated commotion, and in the eastern regions there was a renewed upsurge of wars. At the same time, more than sixteen years after the death of Nepotianus, Bellona, raging through the Eternal City, set everything on fire …[33]

However, 'the eternal city' appears also in perfectly neutral references such as the one to Claudius as prefect of the city: 'when Claudius ruled the eternal city.'[34] It is therefore quite possible, or even likely, that Ammianus used the phrase, simply, as a familiar alternative to 'Rome'.[35] In Late Roman texts it is found more often in official documents.[36]

This survey would be incomplete without tracing the manner in which eternal Rome is attested on inscriptions and coins, in Rome, in Italy, and in the provinces. An inscription from Interamna, Umbria, from the reign of Tiberius, shows how different an attitude such documents may reflect, as compared with the literary works considered so far: 'providentiae Ti. Caesaris Augusti nati ad aeternitatem Romani Augusti' (*ILS* 157; *CIL* XI 4170). Here, in the reign of Tiberius, there is no compunction in describing the emperor himself as eternal. It is therefore, perhaps, surprising that some scholars found it remarkable that the Arval Brethren sacrificed a cow to the 'Aeternitati Imperii' in 66.[37] A *senatus consultum* from the reign of Claudius, twenty years earlier, describes the emperor as 'providing for … the eternity of all of Italy'.[38]

---

[32] Ammianus 14.6.1: *Inter haec Orfitus praefecti potestate regebat urbem aeternam, utra modum delatae dignitatis sese efferens insolenter.*

[33] 28.1.1: *Dum apud Persas (ut supra narravimus), perfidia regis motus agitat insperatos, et in eis tractibus bella rediviva consurgunt, anno sexto decimo et eo diutius post Nepotiani exitium, saeviens per urbem aeternam, urebat cuncta Bellona, ex primordiis minimis ad clades excita luctuosas …*

[34] 29.6.17: *Claudio regente urbem aeternam.*

[35] Moore, 'On *Urbs Aeterna* and *Urbs Sacra*', 37, with nineteenth-century dislike of the later Roman literature, considers it typical of Ammianus' bombastic style.

[36] As observed by Moore, 'On *Urbs Aeterna* and *Urbs Sacra*', 34–60, who gives examples from Symmachus and the *Codex Theodosianus*. For recent discussion: Mellor, 'The Goddess Rome', 1024–5, and, extensively: F. Paschoud, *Roma Aeterna* (Rome, 1967).

[37] *CIL* VI 2044 I c, lines 5–6. Cf. Instinsky, 'Kaiser und Ewigkeit', 329. Another inscription from the reign of Tiberius has tentatively been read: *pr(o) ae[ternitate] Caesarum* (*CIL* IX 42090. Instinsky, 'Kaiser und Ewigkeit', 323, n. 1, rejects this reading because it does not fit his views of the mentality of the Julio-Claudian period.

[38] *ILS* 6043 = *CIL* X 1401: *cum providentia optumi principis tectis quoque urbis nostrae et totius Italiae aeternitati prospexerit …*

A pair of interesting inscriptions was found in Como:[39] L. Caecilius Secundus is recorded as having started building a temple to the Aeternitas of both the goddess Roma and the Augusti, while his son dedicated the complex. This is a new expression of the imperial cult, although not for any specific living emperor. L. Caecilius Secundus was the younger Pliny's natural father, which dates the commencement of the temple shortly after 69, when Vespasian was emperor, and the dedication in 77/78.

While these are two testimonies from Italy outside Rome, 'Roma Aeterna' developed into a divinity in her own right in the provinces during the Principate, as is clear from a number of inscriptions that mention priests of this divinity.

(1) An undated inscription from Graz in Austria represents a dedication to Jupiter Optimus Maximus, dedicated by a 'priest of the Eternal City of Rome'.[40]

(2) *ILS* 6751 = *CIL* V 6991 *(Taurini):…Laur. Lavin [Sacerdot]i urbis Romae Aeternae*. Here another priest of the Eternal City of Rome is mentioned.

A number of inscriptions are dedicated to this divinity in combination with others:

(3) To Fortuna Redux (the Fortune of Return from duty in the provinces), Lar vialis (the guardian of roads and wayfarers) and Roma Aeterna.[41]

(4) To the Eternal City of Rome and the emperor.[42]

(5) To Jupiter Optimus Maximus, the immortal gods and goddesses and Eternal Rome.[43]

(6) To the gods [of] Eternal Rome and the genius (spirit) of the Province of Lower Moesia, dedicated by a provincial governor of Lower Moesia.[44]

(7) The *Feriale Duranum*, the official calendar of the military unit based at Dura Europos between 223 and 227, has a record of 'vows paid and

---

[39] *AE* 1983.443 a and b: *[Caeci]liae f(iliae) suae nomin[e] L(ucius) Ca[ceiliu]s C(ai) f(ilius) Ouf(entina tribu) Secundus praef(ectus) [fabr(um)] a co(n)s(ule) (quattuor) vir i(ure) d(icendo) pontif(ex) tem[plum] aeternitati Romae et Augu[stor(um)] [c]um porticibus et ornamentis incohavit [– Caeci]lius Secundus f(ilius) dedic(avit).*

[40] *ILS* 4852 = CIL *III* 5443: *I.O.M. Arubino L. Camp. Celer Sacerdos urbis Romae Aeternae et Iulia Honorata con. pro se et suis VSLM.*

[41] *ILS* 3636 = *CIL* III 1422 (Sarmizegetusa, Dacia): a dedication to *Fortunae reduci Lari viali Romae Aeternae, Q. Axius Aelianus VE proc. Aug[g]. Ioni.*

[42] *ILS* 3926 = *CIL* VIII 1427 (Thibursici, Africa): *Urbi Romae Aeternae Aug. resp. Municipi Severiani Antoniani Liberi Thibursicensium Bure.*

[43] ILS 3927 = CIL X 16 (Locri): *Iovi Optimo Maximo diis deabusque inmortalibus et Romae Aeternae Locrenses.*

[44] *AE* 1985.26 (date: 235–6): *divini[b]us Romae Aeternae genio provinciae Moes(iaea) inf(erioris).*

undertaken both for the welfare of our Lord Marcus Aurelius Severus Alexander and for the eternity of the empire of the Roman nation'.[45]

(8) From Africa we have a base of a statue of the goddess Roma Aeterna, set up in the joint reign of Valens, Gratianus, and Valentinianus (367–75).[46]

(9) Engaging is a dedication from Cirta of a statue of Venus 'with her Cupids' by a dignitary of the city of Cirta, mentioning also the eternal city of Rome.[47]

It will be clear that all these inscriptions, apart from no. 8, date to the period of the Principate. All of them refer to Rome, the city, and/or her Empire and none contain even an indirect or direct expression of the emperor cult. From Rome itself during the Late Empire came a pedestal dedicated to the 'invincible father Mars and the founders of his eternal city' (reign of Maxentius, 306–12)[48] and in the later period, we may mention a dedication to Iulius Festus Hymetius, *vicarius urbis Romae aeternae* in the reign of Valens, Gratianus and Valentinian.[49] There are also building inscriptions from the Later Roman Empire (Valens, Arcadius, after 365, and Honorius, 408) which refer to the *urbs aeterna*.[50]

Aeternitas personified appears on coins in a parallel development. It occurs first on a reverse type of 76 and is then found regularly on *aurei* of Vespasian and Titus.[51] Related reverse legends are found in the reign of Vespasian on issues from Illyricum and Gaul.[52] *Aeternitati Aug.* occurs on coins issued by Titus in his own name and in that of Divus Vespasianus (AD 80–1).[53] Here then the transition from 'Eternal Rome' to an 'Eternal

[45] R. O. Fink, *Roman Military Records on Papyrus* (Cleveland, OH, 1971), 423, no. 117, col. I, line 3: *[... ob aetern]ITATEM [imper]RI P[r...]*

[46] *AE* 1991.1644: *Temporum felicitate compellente ddd(ominorum) nnn(ostrorum) Valentis, Gratiani ac Valentiniani invictissimorum semper Augg(ustorum) aeternam Vrbem Romam Publicius Felix Hortensius fl(amen) p(er)p(etuus) cur(ator) r(ei) p(ublicae), cum ordine posui.*

[47] *ILS* 3181 = *CIL* VIII 6965: *Veneri Aug. L. Iulius L.f. Q. Martialis IIIvir et q. pot., simulacrum aureum Veneris cum aede sua et Cupidinibus ex liberalitate L. Iuli Martialis patris sui super aliam liberalitatem Romae aeternae, quam nomine Victoris fratris sui posuisset dedit dec. dec.*

[48] *CIL* VI 33856 = *ILS* 8935: *Marti invicto patri et aeternae urbis suae conditoribus …*

[49] *ILS* 1256: AD 367–75.

[50] *ILS* 769 = *CIL* VI 31402; *ILS* 797 = *CIL* VI 1189.

[51] H. Mattingly, *Coins of the Roman Empire in the British Museum* II (London, 1930), pp. xxxix–xxxx, 48, 49, 52, 53. It is not clear why Mattingly feels the issue should have been connected with any specific event, such as the death of Mucianus, as already observed by Beaujeu, *La religion romaine*, 148, n. 3. Mattingly even refers to the symbolism of *Aeternitas* as conceived by the later Stoics.

[52] Mattingly, *BMC Emp.* II, 86–8: 'Roma perpetua' is essentially the same as 'Aeternitas P(opuli) R(omani)' which occurs in AD 70 in Gaul: p. 194, at the same time as legends: 'Fortunae reduci' and others.

[53] Mattingly, *BMC Emp.* II, 265–6: AETERNIT AVG and AETERNIT AVGVST; Divus Augustus Vespasianus: 277.

Augustus' has been made. The same legend is found also on coins of Domitian.[54] *Aeternitas* as type continues under Trajan[55] and, more often under Hadrian.[56] The legend AETERNITAS is hardly found on Trajanic coins,[57] but in various forms on those of Hadrian, usually as variants of *aeternitas Augusti*.[58] Since these types and legends have become a regular feature by this time, it is hard to see why one would want to make them apply to specific elements in the propaganda of the moment.[59] As soon as we encounter the phrase *aeternitas Augusti* or *Augusta* this belongs to the sphere of the imperial cult rather than the celebration of the perpetuity of the city or Empire. Such elaborate interpretations of single items can never be more than speculations, unnecessary because the long-term pattern, from the mid-first century BC until the reign of Hadrian, is quite clear. Hadrian finally formalized the transformation of 'eternity' when he fully established a cult for *Aeternitas*, derived from Αἰών, in Rome and built his temple for Venus and Roma.

It will surprise no one that the notion of 'the eternal city' is found rarely in patristic literature.[60] Remarkably, however, the parallel expression is not encountered in Greek literature or epigraphy either.[61] This is true before and after the foundation of 'the New Rome'. By contrast, the emperors regularly are described as αἰώνιοι, sometimes individually (Trajan: *SEG* 12.94), more often in the standard phrase: ὑπὲρ τῆς τῶν Αὐτοκρατόρων νίκης καὶ αἰωνίου διαμονῆς (e.g. *IG* Bulg. III 1.904). The adjective came, in an inflationary development, to be extended to local officials, such as *gymnasiarchs* (*IG* V 1.305; 468) and *agoranomoi* (*IG* V 1.504). Conversely, the Latin expression *aeternus* is only applied to individual emperors from the fourth century onwards, in literature and inscriptions.[62] All this will

---

[54] Mattingly, *BMC Emp.* II, 362, 364, 374.

[55] *BMC Emp.* III (London, 1936), p. lxxix.

[56] *BMC Emp.* III, pp. cxlv, clxxxii–clxxxiii; see also cxxvii.

[57] *BMC Emp.* III, 81, 82–3, 87, 95.

[58] *BMC Emp.* III, 247, 251, 270, 419 (Divus Traianus), 465, 528. AETERNITAS without reference to Augustus: 378.

[59] See e.g. Mattingly, *BMC Emp.* II, p. lxxix: 'The type of Aeternitas represents the claim that the "optimus status rerum" under the "optimus princeps" has the power of indefinite continuance. Derived from the older thought of the Aeternitas of Rome, the "Aeternitas Augusta" is the sign that, though generations may pass, Rome under her Emperors continues.' With all due respect for a great scholar it must be admitted that Mattingly is reading in the coins what they cannot possibly tell anyone. Similarly I am not convinced by Instinsky's efforts (336–7) to explain away the explicit references to Trajan's *aeternitas* in Pliny's correspondence, *Ep.* 10.59; 83.

[60] Mellor, 'The Goddess Rome', 1024–5.

[61] As already observed by Moore, 'On *Urbs Aeterna* and *Urbs Sacra*', 42–3.

[62] *Pan. Lat.* 7.1 and passim, 8.13.3, cf. *imperium aeternum*: 7.12.6. Inscriptions: Diocletian: *ILS* 614; Diocletian and Maximian: *ILS* 644, 5900; Valentinian: *ILS* 8947.

have much to do with attitudes to Rome and, respectively, the emperor cult, in East and West.

To sum up: the notion of an eternal city and empire was not universally accepted in the days of the Republic. On the contrary, the Polybius passage cited shows that the inevitable decline and end of Rome were taken as a matter of course. This suits the ancient absence of an idea of progress. Decline, not progress, marks the course of history.

The idea of an eternal city is found first and frequently in the work of Cicero, while it is not clear whether this reflects a current trend, or Cicero's own thinking about the state. It is found occasionally in the literature of the Augustan period, but not with great emphasis and it did not represent an element in the Augustan propaganda programme. This pattern continues under Tiberius, although it has been observed that there is at least one inscription (*ILS* 157) which, in a rather roundabout way, describes the emperor himself as having been born for eternity. This, however, is an exception at that time. A few decades later, the emperor Nero craved for eternity, as we learn from his biographer, but contemporary documents do not ascribe to him this quality. For the time being, 'the eternal empire' continues to appear occasionally as topos in literature and 'Eternal Rome' is a goddess in her own right, as we learn from inscriptions, most of them undated. The first occurrence of *Aeternitas* on coins, however, is clearly dated in the reign of Vespasian and, shortly afterwards, in the reign of Titus, *Aeternitas August(i)* or *August(a)* makes an appearance, as opposed to simply *Aeternitas* without attribute. It is interesting to observe that the first formal and official association of eternity with the emperor, rather than the city or the state, is found under Titus rather than in the reign of Nero or Domitian. These developments culminated in the reign of Hadrian. That said, it must be admitted that the very idea of Rome as an eternal city as such is not typical of classical antiquity.

CHAPTER 2

Roman Victory Displayed
Symbols, Allegories, and Personifications?

The Problem of Interpreting Visual Images

Roman victory was communicated and proclaimed to the inhabitants of the Empire through various means, including visual images in the form of statuary and coinage. These images have been preserved for us to enjoy and interpret. The question is then how, or even whether, we can properly understand the messages which are represented and expressed by these images and which were meant for viewers two millennia in the past. Where possible modern scholars utilize all available material, i.e. the relevant written sources and various related images, but this does not usually produce an easy synthesis. When we see on coins an emperor, a palm tree, and a woman, or a trophy and seated prisoners, it is clear that this has something to do with a Roman victory in general. More specifically, however, it is not obvious what was meant by such representations, whether on coinage or in the form of statuary. There is no problem in describing them in terms of the public celebration of a Roman emperor, of his victory over a given people. However, it is usually assumed that we know more than that. We are led to believe that the women or prisoners depicted are personifications symbolizing abstract ideas. The modern literature often uses these terms and others, such as allegory and symbol, without offering a clear definition of their meaning and without explanation why in fact they are applicable.[1]

Indeed it is easy to imagine that we understand the underlying concepts and ideas. For example, when encountering political cartoons of Uncle

---

[1] In a recent article Amy C. Smith uses at least twenty such terms without properly defining or discussing them; see A. C. Smith, 'Eurymedon and the Evolution of Political Personifications in the Early Classical Period', *JHS* 119 (1999): 128–41. For an extensive and thoughtful discussion, see T. Hölscher, 'Images of War in Greece and Rome: Between Military Practice, Public Memory, and Cultural Symbolism', *JRS* 93 (2003): 1–17, and his earlier paper, T. Hölscher, 'Geschichtsauffassung in römischer Repräsentationskunst', *JdI* 97 (1980): 265–321; note esp. Hölscher's discussion of personifications, allegories, and symbols, 'Geschichtsauffassung', 273–9.

Sam, John Bull, and Marianne, many people immediately understand what is intended. In fact the cartoonists expect them to understand this and their work would have no impact if this were not true. It does not matter in this respect that only few of us would be able to explain the origins of the characters of John Bull and Uncle Sam[2] or of Marianne.[3] When considering the meaning of ancient images, modern interpreters often tend to assume that they can be equally confident in their understanding of the essential message of the ancient engraver or sculptor.[4] Yet, as observed by Alan Shapiro, 'the Greeks of the fifth century BC did not have a word for personification, and they most likely conceived of personified abstractions in terms very different from our own'.[5] While Uncle Sam and John Bull represent understandable cartoon figures with associations that are mostly clear to the general public, the Greeks and Romans – to point out a tremendous difference in perception between them and us – routinely transformed things and ideas into gods. The question is whether we are able to understand the ancient associations with works of art that have no obvious meaning for us and no accompanying text for clarification.

The Greeks and Romans, attempted to make abstract ideas understandable by thinking of them as magic and divine powers. The latter, as is evident in their many figural representations, looked like human beings with similar, but divine bodies. In our days we are used to thinking in terms of abstractions, although we amuse ourselves by illustrating such abstractions as if they were human beings. When we see *Justitia* on a public building in the shape of a woman with a blindfold, holding scales and a sword, we do not think of a goddess or supernatural power. We understand that this figure represents in visual form a number of principles: the state maintains justice with the aid of legitimate force (the sword) without prejudice (blindfolded) and according to objective and clearly apparent norms (the scales). These are merely the last conventional and frozen remnants of a much later and different culture, namely the European world of the

---

[2] This was the topic of an exhibition first put on in 1999 by the joint efforts of the British Library and the Library of Congress: 'John Bull and Uncle Sam'. Online: www.loc.gov/exhibits/british. For Uncle Sam: *Encyclopædia Britannica Online* www.britannica.com/EBchecked/topic/614065/Uncle-Sam, retrieved in May 2015; for John Bull: www.britannica.com/EBchecked/topic/304946/John-Bull.

[3] For Marianne see e.g. www.france.fr/en/institutions-and-values/marianne.html.

[4] Kenneth W. Harl remarks that the designs on coins were 'symbols of deeply felt beliefs'; see K. W. Harl, *Civic Coins and Civic Politics in the Roman East AD 180–275* (Berkeley, CA, 1987), 33–4. But the question remains, what is a symbol of a belief?

[5] H. A. Shapiro, *Personifications in Greek Art: The Representation of Abstract Concepts, 600–400 BC* (Zurich, 1993), 12.

sixteenth and seventeenth centuries in which such symbols and personifications were ubiquitous.[6] At the time these representations were part of the secularization of culture. At an earlier stage, we find an antecedent to *Justitia* in the archangel Michael, who uses the familiar scales to weigh souls at the Last Judgment.[7]

In other words, when considering Graeco-Roman images as symbols and personifications, we are attempting to understand pre-monotheistic concepts with conceptual models drawn from post-Renaissance culture. It ought to be obvious, but is not generally regarded so, that we must be extremely cautious when interpreting material from the former period along lines familiar to us who live in a later period. Or, to put it differently, our modern approach is that personifications and allegories are 'abstract thinking made easy'. Ideas are given the shape of living beings, as in the case just mentioned, when justice is depicted as a woman with scales. In the ancient world, on the other hand, similar images are used to express mythological concepts, not abstract ones. Gaia, Uranus, Helios, Selene, Eros, etc. are at one and the same time physical phenomena and anthropomorphic gods, who fall in love, marry, have children, and, in the case of Uranus, get castrated.

Images of States and Peoples

In the following analysis, one particular category of abstractions will be examined, namely that of state and people. Surely states and peoples were real, existing entities, but the concepts associated with these categories, current since the eighteenth century, did not exist in antiquity. Ancient ideas of collective or national identity are different from those of our times. For example, on its coins the city of Athens refers to itself as 'the Athenians', not as 'Athens'. The Roman Empire was the *Imperium Romanum*, i.e. 'Roman Power', and the city the *senatus populusque Romanus* or *Romanorum*, 'the senate and the people of Rome'. The expression that most often is used for the 'the Roman state' is *Nomen Romanum*. In other words, the Roman Empire was not a single abstract entity, but an expression of its military might, or a collective of the senate and the people of Rome. The alternative

---

[6] *Justitia* by Rafael (from 1511) appears with sword and scales, but not blindfolded, on the ceiling of the Stanza della Segnatura, in the Vatican Museum, Rome, and in a painting by Giuseppe Salviati (1542–59), now in the National Gallery in London.

[7] See e.g. the painting by the Dutch Renaissance artist Rogier van der Weyden (1399–1464), now in l'Hotel Dieu, Beaune, France.

was monarchy where the monarch *was* the state, Persia being the classic
example. This is still the case in the work of Shakespeare: France, England,
Lancaster, and York are persons – rulers and lords.[8] The same was not true
for the Roman emperor, who is never called 'Roma' in the literature. Roma
is a goddess of disputed status and about whom accordingly a good deal
has been written.[9] When a Roman provincial governor appeared on a coin
in the Republican period, it would not have occurred to any Roman or
provincial to call him 'Syria' or 'Gaul'.

What was meant or intended when an image of a person appears on a
coin with the name of a province added is a matter to be considered below.
Again, it is clear that the significance of the image on coins of an emperor
is quite different from that of a modern constitutional monarch. Under
the emperor Tiberius (14–37) it was prohibited to carry a ring or coin with
the image of the emperor into a privy or brothel.[10] Cassius Dio (late second
and early third century AD) relates that a young knight who had done precisely that was imprisoned to await execution.[11] Likewise his contemporary Philostratus relates that in Aspendus in Pamphylia a mutinous crowd
attacked the governor, intending to burn him alive,

> although he was clinging to the statues of the Emperor, which were more
> dreaded at that time and more inviolable than the Zeus in Olympia; for
> they were statues of Tiberius, in whose reign a master is said to have been
> held guilty of impiety, merely because he struck his own slave when he had
> on his person a silver drachma coined with the image of Tiberius.[12]

Not long ago politicians in the US suggested that the act of burning
the flag of the United States should be prohibited through an amendment to the Constitution. Here too it is obvious that there is an essential

---

[8] Most lucidly expressed in the phrase 'L'état c'est moi', whether Louis XIV actually said it or not;
cf. H. H. Rowen, ' "L'état c'est à moi", Louis XIV and the State', *French Historical Studies* 2 (1961),
83–98, emphasizing the element of property.

[9] For opposite viewpoints posited without discussion, see K. Lehmann, Review of P. G. Hamberg,
Studies in Roman Imperial Art, Art Bulletin 29 (1947): 136–9, in which Lehmann remarks that Roma is
as concrete a divinity as any other deity (138); see also M. Pfanner, *Der Titusbogen* (Mainz am Rhein,
1983), 67, who regards Roma as an independent goddess, equal to the emperor. For an alternative
view, see E. Keller, 'Studien zu den Cancellaria-Reliefs: Zur Ikonographie der Personifikationen und
Profectio – bzw. Adventus Darstellungen', *Klio* 49 (1967): 198–204, who, following Franz Richter's
discussion of Roma, identifies the goddess as 'merely a personification'; cf. F. Richter, 'Roma', in W.
H. Roscher (ed.), *Ausführliches Lexikon der griechischen und römischen Mythologie*, IV (Leipzig, 1915),
130, who argues that Roma could not have been a goddess in Roman eyes; rather, her identification
as a goddess was a distinctly Greek idea.

[10] Suetonius, *Tib.* 58.

[11] Cassius Dio, *Hist. Rom.* 78.16.5.

[12] Philostratus, *Vit. Apoll.* 1.15.

difference between the modern phenomenon, which is rooted in ideological and socio-political conceptions, and its ancient counterpart where they regarded the image with awe due to its divine powers. A modern flag has meaning in and by itself, but is regarded as an object of value only because of what it symbolically represents. In antiquity it was the representation itself of the ruler that was regarded as sacred. The likeness of the emperor on coins or in the form of a statue was no mere symbol; it had magic significance and power in itself and any hostile or demeaning act aimed at the image was regarded as sacrilege.

There is no ancient equivalent for a national flag, an impersonal object which represents the abstract concept of a nation-state. Similarly there is no ancient equivalent for an animal representing the state such as a lion, dragon, or eagle. All these symbols have their roots in heraldry, the animals appearing on many medieval and later coats of arms. Athens is associated with the owl, because that creature was closely associated with the Athenian guardian divinity, Pallas Athena.[13] This represents a long and genuine religious tradition and is thus conceptually entirely different from the medieval and later traditions linking cities with heraldic animals such as lions or bears. Coins show various eponymous nymphs as protectors of cities.[14] In the Hellenistic period, cities were represented by the Tyche or fortune of the place.[15] Tyche is a goddess, originating, perhaps, in the Near East and appearing often in art, notably on city coinage. It is important to note that Tyche is not the personification of a city, but its guardian divinity.[16] Her origins and continued significance as a deity should not

---

[13] The goddess is frequently attended by an owl, and in epic poetry her regular epithet is γλαυκῶπις, a composite of γλαύξ and ὤψ.

[14] F. W. Hamdorf, *Griechische Kulturpersonifikationen der vorhellenistischen Zeit* (Mainz am Rhein, 1964), 27–30, 90–3; although not a very lucid study, Hamdorf includes all gods with cults, such as Gaia, Eros, and Helios. It is not always certain whether there were cults for such guardian nymphs, but they are definitely honoured both with statues and on coinage.

[15] The earliest attestation is the statue made by Boupalos about 540 BC for the city of Smyrna, known exclusively through a literary source. It was the usual type: the goddess being represented with a *polos* (a cylindrical hat) on her head and the horn of Amaltheia in her hand; see Pausanias, *Descr.* 4.30.6. Cf. R. Hinks, *Myth and Allegory in Ancient Art* (London, 1939; repr. 1968), 76–83; Eva Christof expresses doubts concerning the accuracy of the information; see *Das Glück der Stadt: Die Tyche von Antiocheia und andere Stadttychen* (Frankfurt am Main, 2001), 51; for other early attestations see Christof, *Das Glück der Stadt*, 50–3. See also the discussion in W. Messerschmidt, *Prosop opoiia: Personifikationenpolitischen Charakters in spätklassischer und hellenistischer Kunst* (Cologne, 2003), 62–6.

[16] For an attempt to clarify the terminology, see Messerschmidt, *Prosopopoiia*, 69–74. There is no basis for the frequent assumption that such figures were allegorical; see e.g. J. M. C. Toynbee, *The Hadrianic School: A Chapter in the History of Greek Art* (Cambridge, 1934; repr. 1967), 7. Toynbee consistently denies the genuine religious content of the artworks she discusses, for instance when she describes Jupiter hurling his bolt at the Dacians as 'a fine personification of a thunderstorm

be doubted by anyone who considers the sources and iconography of her images.[17] For imperial Rome there was the Dea Roma, an object of a formal cult and in Greek texts definitely regarded as identical with the Tyche of the city of Rome.[18] The most famous statue of its kind is that of the Tyche of Antioch, made by Euthychides of Sikyon, a pupil of Lysippus, about 296 BC.[19] Her association with the city of Antioch on the Orontes is made clear by the rock on which she sits, illustrating the mountainous location and the small emerging river-god for the Orontes. Alexandria in Egypt actually had a Tyche sanctuary.[20] Influential also is the type of the Tyche of Caesarea Maritima which is modelled after the examples of an Amazon and the images of the Dea Roma in Rome.[21] This may well be politically and ideologically significant. The coinage of cities in Syria-Palaestina,

which seems to have assisted the invaders at this juncture'. Apparently she regards all Romans as unbelievers and the religious elements in Roman art as mere affectation. For a similar approach, see Messerschmidt, *Prosopopoiia*, 160, where he speaks of the 'Verfall des traditionellen Götterglaubens, der nach einer *communis opinio* in der Forschung die Entstehung der Personifikationen begünstigte'. Those who tend to assume traditional religion did not decline to such an extent may therefore hesitate to see personifications so frequently.

[17] Based on his analysis of the sources, Christof concludes that the Tyche of the city is not a divinity, but an abstract concept; see *Das Glück der Stadt*, 92. It is clear that it does occur as such, just like any other abstract concept which is also a divinity, like *themis*, but the material brought together in her book overwhelmingly shows that the Tyche of a town could be seen and was regarded as a genuine divinity, just like the Latin *genius* (for which, see *Das Glück der Stadt*, 97–9, 101–4) and *Fortuna* (for which, see 99–101). The Tyche of Caesarea Maritima is once addressed as *Genio Colonia[e]*; see R. Gersht, 'Representations of Deities and the Cults of Caesarea', in A. Raban and K. G. Holum (eds.), *Caesarea Maritima: A Retrospective After Two Millennia* (Leiden, 1996), 305–6, pl. 1.2. See also R. Gersht, 'The Tyche of Caesarea Maritima', *PEQ* 116 (1984): 110–14; R. Wenning, 'Die Stadtgöttin von Caesarea Maritima', *Boreas* 9 (1986): 113–29. Christof also observes that the Tyche of cities often was identified with their chief deity, as happened, for instance, in Gerasa, where there are coins with the legend ARTEMICTUXH GERASON (Artemis the Tyche of the people of Gerasa); see Christof, *Das Glück der Stadt*, 132. The female members of the imperial house could also be honoured as Tyche of cities. Julia Domna, for instance, the Syrian born second wife of the emperor Septimius Severus, is declared to be the *Tychē Mētropoleōs* on coins of Laodicea in Syria (Christof, *Das Glück der Stadt*, 154–5). Clearly, Julia Domna was not venerated as a personification or allegory of Laodicea but as guardian deity of the city.

[18] Christof, *Das Glück der Stadt*, 186–93. She appears on the *Gemma Augustea* (relief cameo gem cut from a double-layered Arabian onyx, now at the Kunsthistorisches Museum in Vienna), for which see below, and probably on the Great Trajanic Frieze; see A. M. L. Touati, *The Great Trajanic Frieze: The Study of a Monument and of the Mechanisms of Message Transmission in Roman Art* (Stockholm, 1987), 14–16. Touati refers to the Dea Roma and also to Victoria as personifications. For the Dea Roma as Tyche, see also the references in W. Roscher, *Lexikon der griechischen und römischen Mythologie*, s.v.'Roma', IV, 131, and 133–4.

[19] T. Dohrn, *Die Tyche von Antiochia* (Berlin, 1960); Christof, *Das Glück der Stadt*; Messerschmidt, *Prosopopoiia*, 91–119.

[20] Christof, *Das Glück der Stadt*, 183–6. The *Tychaion* apparently was built not long after the foundation of the city.

[21] Christof, *Das Glück der Stadt*; Gersht, 'Representations of Deities', 305–6; Gersht, 'The Tyche of Caesarea Maritima', 110–14; Wenning, 'Die Stadtgöttin', 113–29.

the Decapolis, and Provincia Arabia shows numerous types following that from Caesarea Maritima and these are very often placed in an architectural setting, evoking the placement of a statue in a sanctuary.[22] Whether or not these cities actually had Tyche statues, placed in shrines or temples, the images clearly suggest an actual deity, not a personified abstract concept. It is, in theory, still possible to assume that such a concept existed in antiquity and may be recognized on works of art, but the evidence does not point in this direction.

The wolf was important in Roman myth, for it was a she-wolf who suckled Romulus and Remus,[23] But we cannot claim that the wolf is some sort of national symbol for Rome. It was significant because of its role in the myths concerning the origins of the city. The eagle, now often associated with Rome, was to the Romans primarily the legionary standard (*aquila*), an object of cultic significance, but, again, not a symbol of the state.[24] The eagle with thunderbolt was also associated with monarchic power in general, first on Hellenistic coinage,[25] and later occasionally appearing as a companion on imperial statues.[26] It is a mistake to assume that it had the same meaning for Romans as the bald eagle of the Great Seal now has as the national bird of the United States. The American eagle was adopted in this capacity in spite of the resistance of Benjamin Franklin, who, in a personal letter to his daughter Sarah Bache (dated 26 January 1784), argued for the turkey because he regarded the bald eagle as 'a bird of bad moral character; like those among men who live by sharping and robbing, he is generally poor, and often very lousy'.[27] Clearly then, there was in the US at that time no idea that the eagle somehow represented more than a plain, secular symbol. When Jacob blesses his twelve sons in Genesis 49, some of them are compared with various wild animals. He describes Benjamin,

---

[22] Christof, *Das Glück der Stadt*, 175–7.

[23] Cf. B. Andreae, *L'art de l'ancienne Rome* (Paris, 1973), 37, who remarks: 'As the ubiquitous emblem of Rome, the she-wolf is so rife with symbolism, that it has no equal among cities past or present.' It is not clear to me what Andreae means with this statement.

[24] L. Keppie, *The Making of the Roman Army: From Republic to Empire* (London, 1984), 67. Originally there were five animal totems on legionary standards: the eagle, wolf, Minotaur, horse, and boar, but Marius, in 104 BC, gave pre-eminence to the eagle and abolished the others.

[25] C. M. Kraay and M. Hirmer, *Greek Coins* (London, 1966), no. 799 (Ptolemy I, 305–283 BC); see also no. 578 (Perseus of Macedon, 179–168 BC); nos. 806–7 (Ptolemy IV, 221–204 BC); without thunderbolt, see no. 751 (Alexander I Balas, 150–145 BC).

[26] H. G. Niemeyer, *Studien zur statuarischen Darstellung der römischen Kaiser* (Cologne, 1966), 61 and 125; for an imperial relief from the Sebasteion at Aphrodisias, see R. R. R. Smith, 'The Imperial Reliefs from the Sebasteion at Aphrodisias', *JRS* 77 (1987): 102, pl. 4.

[27] The turkey, of course, has other advantages over the bald eagle, whence it retained the privilege of being eaten on Thanksgiving.

his youngest, 'as a wolf that prowls, devouring his enemies in the morning and dividing up the spoils in the evening'.[28] This is, of course, no literary device, but ancient totemism, and as such to be taken seriously.

Again, a distinction must be made between modern, secular personifications, found mostly in cartoons, such as 'Uncle Sam', and the Greek 'eponymous heroes' or tribal heroes. The Athenian eponymous heroes were figures familiar from mainstream mythology such as Ajax and Erechtheus who, somehow, were associated with the ten tribes of Athens that were named after them. These cannot be called personifications by any reasonable definition, for they were famous heroes who somehow had taken part-time jobs, 'moonlighting' as patrons of Athenian districts.

I have argued thus far that we must be far more cautious than the modern literature often is in using terms like personification, allegory, and symbol when interpreting figures in art who somehow represent peoples and cities. On the one hand, these figures may often be deities; on the other hand, they may be meant as a typical, but not a collective, representation of a community.

Definitions

The *Oxford English Dictionary* offers the following definitions[29] for 'personification': (1) 'Attribution of personal form, nature, or characteristics; the representation of a thing or abstraction as a person: esp. as a rhetorical figure or species of metaphor. Also in art, the representation of a thing or abstraction by a human figure'; (2) 'An imaginary or ideal person conceived as representing a thing or abstraction.' Note that the implication is that the person is imaginary or ideal and does not exist in reality.[30]

---

[28] Gen 49:27; see also Thomas Mann, *Joseph, der Ernährer* (Stockholm, 1943), 522–642: '(Benjamin) war verdutzt es zu hören'.

[29] Messerschmidt, *Prosopopoiia*, 69–74, for a description of the manner in which the various terms have been used by different scholars. Messerschmidt does not attempt to give here any definitions of his own, but he does so once elsewhere: 'Der Begriff "Politische Personifikationen" umschreibt all jene abstract gedachten, in bildliche Darstellung personaler Art umgesetzten Konzeptionen der Griechen, von denen eine politisch-propagandistische Wirkung ausging' (160). He argues that the 'political personification' was not, in antiquity, a part of Nature filled with divine forces, but the embodiment of political abstract concepts and institutions. As such the concept anticipates modern secular thinking. It will be clear that this does not correspond to the approach advanced in this chapter. I cannot see that the widespread appearance of the Tyche of the *polis* in the Hellenistic period is best explained as a personification consciously developed to spread a political message. Referring to the beginning of this chapter, it can be said that on the conceptual level this approach converts Tyche into a phenomenon similar to Uncle Sam or the Russian bear.

[30] Similar definitions appear in *The Webster's Encyclopaedic Dictionary*. I cannot see in any of those definitions support for A. L. Kuttner's use of the term as 'corporate images or assemblages'; see A. L. Kuttner, *Dynasty and Empire in the Age of Augustus: The Case of the Boscoreale Cups* (Berkeley,

For 'allegory' the *Oxford English Dictionary* gives the following definitions: (1) 'Description of a subject under the guise of some other subject of aptly suggestive resemblance'; (2) 'An instance of such description; a figurative sentence, discourse, or narrative, in which properties and circumstances attributed to the apparent subject really refer to the subject they are meant to suggest; an extended or continued metaphor.'[31] The Greek term *allēgoria* does not appear before the Hellenistic age and is in that period a technical term of rhetoric and thus not relevant for the present discussion.[32]

Images of Victory

To what extent did ancient art, when celebrating Roman victories over foreigners, introduce allegories and personifications conforming to these definitions? Personification of abstract concepts is a complex and much disputed phenomenon in ancient religion. An early example which is apparently not disputed is the Indo-Iranian god Mithras, whose name means 'contract'. Greek religion in its earliest known forms included physical phenomena that were also anthropomorphic gods, such as Gaia, Uranus, Helios, and Selene. In the Homeric epic personified beings play a variety of roles, such as Themis, who dwells among the Olympians, but occurs also as a noun, meaning 'that which is laid down, established by custom, right'. In the next stage of development, such a figure receives an established cult, is given a genealogy, and obtains other characteristics of the known divinities.[33] It is in any case clear that for the Greeks in the archaic and classical periods 'Peace' as a goddess was not an abstract concept that somehow represented as an imaginary or ideal person. This is a process whereby important concepts were manifested as religious forces. In the fourth century BC this may have changed to some extent, when we see increasing numbers of statues, altars, and even temples erected for

CA, 1995), 73. As Kuttner observes, there is no sustained analysis of *groups* of personifications in Republican and Julio-Claudian art, nor any typological critique of the conceptual and formal contexts of ethnic personification iconography (69). Kuttner herself, however, does not provide any working definition of an 'ethnic personification'.

[31] For the development of the term in antiquity, see Hinks, *Myth and Allegory*, 4; Hamdorf, *Griechische Kultpersonifikationen*; H. A. Shapiro, 'The Origins of Allegory in Greek Art', *Boreas* 9 (1986): 4–23; Shapiro, *Personifications in Greek Art*, 16–18; Messerschmidt, *Prosopopoiia*.

[32] It is discussed by Cicero, *Or. Brut.* 94; *Att.* 2.20.3; Quintilian, *Instit. or.* 8.6.44, and later Greek authors. Cf. Hinks, *Myth and Allegory*, 4.

[33] Lehmann, Review of P. G. Hamberg, 138; T. B. L. Webster, 'Personification as a Mode of Greek Thought', *Journal of the Warburg and Courtauld Institutes* 17 (1954): 13–14.

figures such as Eirene and Homonoia, who constituted abstract forces. A related phenomenon is the absorption of abstract qualities by existing Olympic gods, such as Athena Hygieia, Athena Nike. These added names had the force of adjectives: Athena who grants health, Athena who delivers victory.[34]

The numismatic evidence is important. Both archaeologists and numismatists have recognized that many coin types were influenced by official reliefs, statues, and paintings.[35] As shown by Annalina Caló Levi, an origin from a sculpture or painting may be assumed whenever a representation is found on a coin for the first time. Later coins with the same representation copy the earlier coin type rather than the original sculpture or painting. Representations on coins directly inspired by sculpture include such figures as emperors, gods, prisoners, and inhabitants of the provinces. Particularly interesting among the coins of this kind are those which show figures of defeated foreigners – and there are many of those in the Near East. Naturally, adaptation was needed to fit the image onto the small surface of a coin. Multifigured scenes, for instance those where homage is paid to the emperor, are therefore rare on coins. Narrative scenes are unsuitable, for it is impossible to tell a story at length within the limitations of the flat and small reverse field.

Favourite subjects of coins are prisoners at the foot of a trophy, and the emperor or Victory with a prisoner at or under his/her feet. Such images are often called 'personifications', 'symbols',[36] or 'allegorical figures'.[37] It remains to be seen whether any of these is likely to be the correct term. Rivka Gersht uses the terms 'condensed' and 'indicative' in order to clarify that they really are snapshots, or rather, the essence in pictorial form, of what could be envisaged as a more elaborate display such as would have been produced if there were more space for it.[38] In other words, a coin depicting the emperor and a captive provincial conveys in different

---

[34] H. Usener, *Götternamen: Versuch einer Lehre von der religiösen Begriffsbildung* (Bonn, 1895; repr. Frankfurt/Main, 1948), 366–8. The relevance of this topic for the present volume may not be immediately obvious. Or rather, it is as relevant for any region of the empire as it is for the Near East. Many or most of the sculptures in the class here considered have been discovered in other regions. However, it is clear that such works of art were present in the Near East, and an attempt to advance the proper interpretation of them in general will be relevant for the Near East as well, as illustrated, it is hoped, by some of the examples discussed in this chapter.

[35] See A. C. Levi, *Barbarians on Roman Imperial Coins and Sculpture* (New York, 1952), 1.

[36] Levi, Barbarians, 25.

[37] Toynbee, *The Hadrianic School*, ch. 2; Hinks, *Myth and Allegory*, 74.

[38] R. Gersht, 'Roman Condensed Indicative Symbols and Emblems', in N. Kenaan-Kedar and A. Ovadiah (eds.), *The Metamorphosis of Marginal Images: From Antiquity to Present Time* (Tel Aviv, 2001), 49–58, at 52. Gersht distinguishes between two artistic formulas – the narrative and indicative.

form the same message as the lengthy sculptured spiral of Trajan's Column (which was, in itself, a novelty without tradition behind it). It is not immediately obvious that the differences imposed by the artistic media also entail drastic conceptual distinctions.

In general it should be obvious that the term 'personification' is inappropriate. When an image of a woman in specific dress appears on a relief or coin with the inscription 'Gallia' underneath, it is often, without further ado, claimed that this is a personification. This implies that the province(s) or peoples of Gallia are conceived as an abstract entity in Roman thought. It furthermore implies that such an abstract entity is represented as a female and, thirdly, that this female is supposed to look like a Gallic woman. In other words, we have a highly curious and roundabout argument. It starts with something concrete: Gauls are incorporated into a province of the empire. Then this province and its inhabitants are presumably elevated into something abstract (the idea of a province), believed to be represented in Roman art in personified, female form. This personified abstract province is finally given the concrete appearance of a typically concrete Gallic woman. This is a mental process which should not be taken as a matter of course. It is acceptable only if there is good evidence that this is how Romans thought. If there is not, other interpretations should be considered.

Narrative Art and Individual Scenes

What is the difference between narrative art – depicting a sequence or a series of events – as distinct from a single scene, or better, a historically significant moment? The earliest examples of stand-alone scenes on coins are Republican and quite specific: the reverse of a coin of 103 BC, for example, shows a Roman soldier fighting a non-Roman to protect a fallen comrade. Michael Crawford comments: 'The types doubtless allude to an act of martial heroism of one of the moneyer's ancestors – it is idle … to speculate which.'[39] In other words, here we have a concrete depiction of a concrete event in the past. The reverse of a coin of 55 BC shows a 'horseman r., holding reins in l. hand and with r. hand thrusting with spear at warrior below – warrior is about to drive sword through unarmed captive'. Crawford notes that this depicts 'an exploit of a member of the moneyer's family'.[40] This again appears to have been a specific event. We cannot therefore claim

[39] M. H. Crawford, *Roman Republican Coinage*, 2 vols. (London, 1974), I, 325, no. 319.
[40] Crawford, Roman Republican Coinage, I, no. 429.

that these images are in any way allegorical. They depict the climax of an historic event. There is nothing metaphorical about them.

The Greeks, unlike Egyptians, Assyrians, and Romans, tended to avoid the direct narrative representation of historical events. To put it in simple terms, there is no Greek antecedent for the Columns of Trajan and Marcus. Even so, however, it must be admitted that the Parthenon frieze shows the people of Athens in two processions that begin at the southwest corner and parade in opposite directions until they converge over the door of the *cella* at the east end of the Parthenon.[41] It is generally assumed that this represents the Panathenaic procession which was a central celebration in Athens during the classical period. It is not important for the present discussion whether this was an ideal or a specific Panathenaic procession. In either case this is a continuous representation of an event with actual citizens of Athens depicted as participating.

Jenifer Neils comments on the description of the frieze: 'Rather than one defining moment, the viewer is confronted with a series of excerpted events and is led physically from the city gates to the Acropolis and temporally from the preparations for the festival to its successful conclusion.'[42] It seems therefore that the frieze is essentially and conceptually similar to a column depicting events which took place in Trajan's Dacian war, moving the story along a spiral instead of a frieze. The Parthenon *metopes*, on the other hand, reflect a different conception, for they all show two figures fighting one another. On the east side are depicted scenes from the Gigantomachy, the giants in their battle with the gods. On the west are depicted fights between Greeks and Amazons, while on the north and south scenes are presented from the Trojan War and the story of the Centauromachy respectively. It is usually assumed that the common theme of all these mythological scenes is the struggle between Greeks and non-Greeks (or Greek gods and other divine beings), which would supposedly refer to the war between Greeks and Persians that was taking place at the time. This leaves unanswered the question why the artist thought the most effective way to evoke associations with the extraordinarily massive battles between Persia and Greece was through scenes of individual combat.[43] However that may be, they are all separate scenes, derived from the world

---

[41] The literature on the Parthenon frieze is vast; see lately J. Neils, *The Parthenon Frieze* (Cambridge, 2001); M. B. Cosmopoulos (ed.), *The Parthenon and its Sculptures* (New York, 2004); J. Neils (ed.), *The Parthenon: From Antiquity to the Present* (Cambridge, 2005).

[42] Neils, *The Parthenon Frieze*, 44. Curiously, in her discussion of the influence of the frieze on Roman sculpture (40–5), Trajan's and Marcus' Columns are not mentioned.

[43] On the significance in Greece of individual combat, see J. E. Lendon, *Soldiers and Ghosts: A History of Battle in Classical Antiquity* (New Haven, 2005).

of myth, showing a single Greek and a single non-Greek fighting one another.

While it may be possible that the Athenians looking at these sculptures would associate them with the Persian wars, it certainly cannot be maintained that they are to be interpreted along symbolic or allegorical lines, for the Greeks regarded their myths, the Trojan War included, as historical and not metaphorical. All that could be claimed as a hypothesis is that these familiar scenes of fighting between Greeks or Greek gods and non-Greeks would be understood as antecedents of what had happened in the recent past between Greeks and contemporary non-Greeks. In that case the sculptures were intended to evoke a sense of continuity and repetition rather than the uniqueness of the historical events to which they presumably allude. The latter was precisely the main topic of Herodotus' work, as observed in its first sentence: 'to preserve from decay the remembrance of what men have done, and of preventing the great and wonderful actions of the Greeks and the Barbarians from losing their due need of glory'.[44] In drama Aeschylus' *Persians* shows that Greek literature refers directly to specific, historical events even in a work that was not intended as historiography, but poetic drama.

Similar to the coin of 103 BC, which shows a Roman soldier fighting a non-Roman, the *metopes* on the Parthenon also depict anonymous combatants, here in known mythical or historical contexts. The coin refers to a known event with specific although nameless individuals participating.

Another example is a coin of 55 BC, issued by A. Plautius, *Aedilis Curulis*.[45] The reverse shows a camel facing right; before it a kneeling figure holds reins in his left hand and an olive-branch in his right hand. The legend reads BACCHIVS and IVDAE. Crawford comments on this scene: 'The reverse type presumably refers to the surrender of an Eastern ruler, doubtless in the course of Pompey's campaigns ... The interpretation of "Bacchius" is disputed.'[46] Whoever Bacchius was, he was a concrete ruler somehow connected with Judaea. He is not mentioned in any literary source.[47] He was no personification or allegory. The camel behind

[44] Herodotus, *Hist.* 1.1: Ἡροδότου Θουρίου ἱστορίης ἀπόδεξις ἥδε, ὡς μήτε τὰ γενόμενα ἐξ ἀνθρώπων τῷ χρόνῳ ἐξίτηλα γένηται, μήτε ἔργα μεγάλα τε καὶ θωμαστά, τὰ μὲν Ἕλλησι, τὰ δὲ βαρβάροισι ἀποδεχθέντα, ἀκλέα γένηται, τάτε ἄλλα καὶ δι᾽ ἣν αἰτίην ἐπολέμησαν ἀλλήλοισι.

[45] Crawford, *Roman Republican Coinage*, no. 431. R. M. Schneider, *Bunte Barbaren: Orientalenstatuen aus farbigem Marmor in der römischen Representationskunst* (Worms, 1986), 25.

[46] Crawford, *Roman Republican Coinage*, I, 454.

[47] See E. M. Smallwood, *The Jews under Roman Rule: From Pompey to Diocletian* (Leiden, 1981), 26, n. 16.

Bacchius therefore cannot be taken as a symbolic feature on the coin. This must be interpreted as a genuine depiction of the ruler and his animal. Even though the latter is certainly regarded as characteristic of the region, the scene cannot be described as allegorical in intent.

Similarly, from the reign of Augustus, a *denarius* of 18 BC from Rome shows a kneeling Parthian holding a Roman standard. The legend reads: *Caesar Augustus sign(is) rece(ptis)* (Caesar Augustus; standards retaken).[48] A similar image is found on the breastplate of the Augustus statue from Primaporta.[49] This celebrates the Parthian surrender of the spoils and military standards lost by Crassus and Antony.[50] It shows the essence of a historical event as seen by Augustan propaganda. Horace, one of the leading poets in the days of Augustus, describes Phraates as 'on his knees accepting the right and rule of Caesar' (*ius imperiumque Phraates Caesaris accepit genibus minor*).[51] There is even a glass paste ring showing *two* kneeling Parthians with standards held up before the Victory of Augustus on a globe.[52] Clearly neither the Parthian nor Augustus are personifications or allegories, for Augustus was himself ruler of the Roman Empire. The Parthian is shown in a specific action that excludes any allegorical interpretation according to the definitions cited.[53]

Another Late Republican instance of captive enemies dates from 37 BC. C. Sosius, *quaestor* of Antony and the governor of Syria and Cilicia, captured Jerusalem in that year. He struck a coin showing two captives seated at the foot of a trophy. The one on the left is female, with bowed head; she wears a long robe and has long, dishevelled hair. On the right is a man with his hands tied behind his back.[54] Such scenes are often explained as

---

[48] *BMCRE* Augustus, nos. 410, 412, 414–19, 421–3.

[49] H. Kähler, *Die Augustusstatue von Primaporta* (Cologne, 1959), 17–18, pl. 17.

[50] *Res gest. divi Aug.* 29.2; Velleius, 2.91.1; Cassius Dio, 54.8.1–2; Suetonius, *Aug.* 21.3; Suetonius, *Tib.* 9.1.

[51] Horace, *Epod.* 1.12.27.

[52] Paul Zanker, *The Power of Images in the Age of Augustus*, trans. A. Shapiro (Ann Arbor, 1988), 187 and fig. 147.

[53] Note also the *denarii* of 18 BC showing a kneeling Armenian, which celebrated the settlement of Armenia in 20 BC; see *BMCRR* 2:30108; Velleius, 2.94.4; Horace, *Ep.* 1.12.26-7. Levi points out that these representations derive from sculpture. She refers to triple arches erected at Pisidian Antioch (AD 212). From each of the two spandrels of the central archway come blocks with the relief figure of a barbarian kneeling and holding a Roman standard; see Levi, *Barbarians*, 7–8 (pl. 2.1–2).

[54] Toynbee, *The Hadrianic School*, 117–21, pl. 16. Toynbee unnecessarily suggests the possibility that this man may be the Hasmonaean prince Antigonus. The interpretation of such figures is quite random. Toynbee, 117–18, argues that a male and female couple of Jewish captives are intended to represent captives, or rather, the woman is assumed to represent a captive. However, a woman alone, unaccompanied by a male captive is assumed 'to portray *Iudaea* in a more abstract and "universal" manner, the figure personifying, not the conquered Jewish people, but the country as a whole'. There is no shred of evidence for this distinction.

personifications or allegories of 'native' peoples. As will be clear by now, it is the purpose of this chapter to raise doubts regarding precisely this certainty, shared by so many scholars. It is not clear to me that a captive Jewish man or woman on a coin or piece of sculpture fits any reasonable definition of personification or allegorical representation. The characters are truly defeated individuals realistically rendered.

When there is no such woman present on a monument another solution is found. Thus Toynbee acknowledges that there is no defeated Jew on the Arch of Titus: 'But in the narrow frieze above the archway on the side facing towards the Coliseum the recumbent figure of the river Jordan, acting as representative of his defeated people, is borne along in a litter in the Roman general's triumph-train.'[55] Why is the river god 'a representative of his people'? No reason is given and none could be given, for river gods do not represent peoples. They undoubtedly represent a geographic feature and, on a victory monument, they show how Roman power has subdued the elements in foreign lands. The most notorious instance of such a victory in a literary description is Caligula's subjugation of the Ocean.[56] An element of religiosity definitely must not be denied. Cities in Bithynia and Paphlagonia often struck coins with recumbent river gods. These rivers were important for the economy of their territories and their gods were the objects of local cults.[57] Obviously, the river god of the Jordan was not held in pious esteem by the Jews, but carried along during Titus' triumph he conveyed to the Roman public the message that not just the Jews and their land, but also the local divinities had been made captives.

The victory scenes described are not straightforward depictions of unique events which took place as shown. They are images that evoke glimpses of the culmination of success in warfare. As such they could be taken to represent a scene similar to those depicted on a single panel from Trajan's or Marcus Aurelius' Columns or the entire columns squeezed together into a single work of art. As already noted, it is often claimed that such motifs have no narrative intent and are therefore symbolic.[58] It is hard to see why a kneeling captive with his hands tied behind his back should be regarded

---

[55] Toynbee, *The Hadrianic School*, 118–19; for the Arch of Titus, see Pfanner, *Der Titusbogen*. There are definitely women on the sculptures from the Sebasteion at Aphrodisias. These are unusual images because they suggest that emperors, when conquering a province, actually kill the vanquished, see R. R. R. Smith, *The Marble Reliefs from the Julio-Claudian Sebasteion* (Darmstadt, 2013).

[56] Suetonius, *Cal.* 46.

[57] L. Robert, *A travers l'Asie Mineure: Poètes et prosateurs, monnaies grecques, voyageurs et géographie* (Paris, 1980), 165–201, with detailed discussion of the geography of the territories, the literary sources, and coinage.

[58] As claimed, e.g. by Levi, *Barbarians*, 4; Harl, *Civic Coins*, 33–4.

as a symbol of anything. It is a scene which vividly evokes the reality of
Roman victory and the suffering of the vanquished. If the artist had had a
triumphal arch or frieze at his disposal rather than a coin, the same image
would have been expanded and accompanied by other vivid depictions of
Roman triumph. To conclude: I doubt that the depiction of a single, significant moment in history in Roman art really requires the introduction
of concepts of an abstract or derivative nature.

'Symbolic' Objects?

A trophy is often depicted on Roman coins celebrating victories. This
stems from an old tradition. Victorious Greeks dedicated some of the
spoils taken from the enemy to gods as a form of sacrifice, either the
original spoils or works of art made from them. This could either be
done on the spot of the victory or in a sanctuary of the deity to whose
assistance the victory was ascribed. Delphi was full of such gifts.[59] In
the course of the fourth century BC trophies became permanent monuments on the site of the battle. The term is also applied to the images
of masses of arms on sculptured monuments, Hellenistic (for example
in Pergamum)[60] and Roman, such as the victory monuments at La
Turbie[61] and Adamklissi[62] and triumphal arches such as that at Orange.[63]
Likewise trophies are found on Roman coins. It might seem obvious
to call such trophies symbols, but this appellation misses the point.
The trophies were a genuine form of sacrifice following victory and
that is what they remained, for instance when Vespasian and his sons

---

[59] E.g. Pausanias, *Descr.* 10.13.9: the famous tripod on a bronze serpent dedicated from the spoils
taken at the battle of Platea; see also *Descr.* 10.15.6. G. C. Picard, *Les trophées romains: Contribution
à l'histoire de la religion et de l'art triomphal de Rome* (Paris, 1957); W. K. Pritchett, *The Greek State
at War*, III (Berkeley, CA, 1979), ch. 7. For most of the objects in Delphi we depend on Pausanias'
description. Here too it is my impression that there exists a tendency to interpret too easily in
terms of personification; e.g. Kuttner, *Dynasty and Empire*, 73. When Pausanias mentions 'an armed
woman, supposed to represent Aetolia', that is no proof of personification; see *Descr.* 10.18.7 (Jones,
Loeb trans.). The same is true for the following comment: 'The bronze horses and captive women
dedicated by the Tarentines were made from spoils taken from the Messapians'; see *Descr.* 10.10.6
(Jones). Such remarks do not necessarily imply personification. There can be no doubt, however,
that there existed Greek works of art in which women represented regions: e.g. *Descr.* 10.13.6, an
image of Aegina (ἄγαλμα Αἰγίνης); 10.15.6, an image of Cyrene and Libya. The question is then
whether these are personifications or deities and the objects of a formal cult.

[60] R. Bohn, *Das Heiligtum der Athena Polias Nikephoros* (Berlin, 1885). The temple has sculpted images
of Macedonian and Celtic weapons.

[61] J. Formigé, *Le trophée des Alpes (La Turbie)*, Gallia Suppl. 2 (Paris, 1949), two trophies with two
captives each.

[62] F. B. Florescu, *Monumentul de la Adamklissi: Tropaeum Traiani* (Bucharest, 1960).

[63] R. Amy et al., *L'Arc d'Orange*, 2 vols., Gallia Suppl. 15 (Paris, 1962).

consecrated trophies from Judaea to Isis and Sarapis, protectors of the *Fortuna Flavia* in Egypt, because of the role this province played at the time of Vespasian's proclamation.[64]

A substitute for the trophy was the palm tree. This is often, erroneously, associated only and exclusively with the Flavian suppression of the Jewish Revolt of 66–70. The palm tree, which appears on some of the Judaea Capta coins, is then believed to be representative of, or a symbol standing for, Judaea as a province. In fact the palm tree is associated with the Apollo cult on Delos already in the seventh century BC.[65] It was here that the tree began to be associated with victory.[66] It is quite clear that the palm tree was not especially associated with Judaea. Other defeated provincials are also depicted besides palm trees.[67] It is clear therefore that both images, trophies and palm trees, often seen on Roman monuments and coins in connection with victory, are to be regarded as belonging to the realm of the sacred rather than as items simply and vaguely evoking an idea of military dominance.

This may be clarified by comparison with a familiar religious symbol such as the cross in Christianity. In its bare form this may indeed be described as a symbol used by Christians to convey a concept concerned with man's relationship with the sacred or holy. However, when it appears on a painting of the crucifixion as described in the gospels it is no symbol, but the rendering of a historical instrument of execution and the painting as such vividly depicts a particularly significant moment in a religious narrative. When a cross is worn as an ornament by a private person it may serve as a charm; when it is worn by a church official it is part of the uniform indicating status within an organization.

---

[64] Picard, *Les trophées romains*, 342–7.

[65] W. Deonna, 'L'ex-voto de Cypsélos à Delphes: Le symbolisme du palmier et des grenouilles', *RHR* 139 (1951): 162–207; 140 (1951), 5–58; for the palm tree: 173–207, 5–16; Picard, *Les trophées romains*, 62–3. Note the bronze palm of Nicias at Delos (417 BC), mentioned in Plutarch, *Nic.* 3; Athenaeus, *Deipn.* 11.502b. Deonna points out that the palm plays a role in the art of the Near East and Egypt as well and argues that it may have been taken over as a sacred tree from these regions by Greeks in the archaic period. In Greece bronze palm trees were dedicated to Apollo in Delphi and Delos. They were planted also in the sanctuary of Artemis (in Aulis) and in other sanctuaries associated with Artemis in Tanagra, Ephesus, and Pygela. The palm tree was not only associated with Apollo and Artemis, but also with other gods, and not only with victory, but with phenomena such as fertility and endurance.

[66] Deonna, 'L'ex-voto de Cypsélos', 173–7.

[67] Florescu, *Adamklissi*, Gruppa i: Dacian prisoner in front of palm tree; Picard, *Les trophées romains*, 358: a German captive with palm tree on a cuirassed torso from Sabratha, probably from the Flavian period. Note also coins from Lugdunum of 15 BC with Tiberius and Drusus handing over their palms of victory to Augustus; see Zanker, *Power of Images*, 225 and fig. 179a.

Group Scenes and Monuments

The kneeling, vanquished captive and the seated, weeping female captive on both sides of a trophy depict the culmination of warfare and triumph for a Roman public and it is wrong to imagine that the modern observer can classify these images as symbols or any other such modern category. They are meant to evoke the reality of a war, fought by the emperor in person, such as the Romans would want it to be fought. Such an image is found on a panel from the Arch of Marcus Aurelius titled 'Clementia'.[68] It represents the emperor on horseback extending clemency to kneeling enemies. The composition is derived from the pictorial convention which shows an equestrian emperor trampling the enemy, similar to the way Trajan was depicted in a representation discussed below.[69] Here, however, Marcus Aurelius is represented both as victor and dispenser of clemency, a resolute and virtuous emperor before Germans who are humiliated and submit to Rome.

The most vivid rendering of such events is also found on the Column of Marcus Aurelius which shows women and children exclusively as defenceless victims of Roman soldiers. Their villages are set on fire, the men killed, the women and their children try to flee, but are caught and either killed, raped, or transported as captives. Rape is often suggested by showing women with bare breasts.[70] The Marcus Aurelius Column is the most expressive Roman monument in its depiction of such scenes, which, although less bloody, are still explicitly found in earlier works of art representing Roman triumph, such as the Gemma Augustea[71] and Trajan's

---

[68] I. S. Ryberg, *Panel Reliefs of Marcus Aurelius* (New York, 1967), 9–15, pls. 2 and 3; E. Angelicoussis, 'The Panel Reliefs of Marcus Aurelius', *MDAI* 91 (1984), 141–204, at 147–8, pl. 63.2; D. E. Kleiner, *Roman Sculpture* (New Haven, 1992), 292. The *Clementia* is now in the Museo del Palazzo dei Conservatori in Rome. Kneeling enemies appear already in fourth century BC Greek art. A vase by the Dareios painter now in Naples shows a kneeling Oriental; see Schneider, *Bunte Barbaren*, 23–5. In the reign of Augustus one finds a kneeling Parthian on the coins celebrating the return of the military standards in 20 BC, mentioned above; cf. Schneider, *Bunte Barbaren*, 29–30. A submission scene is found also on the second Boscoreale cup, depicting Augustus' visit to the northern frontier in 15 or 8 BC, where German chiefs wearing animal hides approach him on their knees. Augustus reaches out and mercifully accepts their submission; cf. Kuttner, *Dynasty and Empire*.

[69] The theme first appears on coins celebrating the victory in Judaea; see *BMCRE* 2: pl. 26.3.

[70] P. Zanker, 'Die Frauen und Kinder der Barbaren auf der Markussäule', in J. Scheid and V. Huet (eds.), *La colonne Aurélienne: Geste et image sur la colonne de Marc Aurèle à Rome* (Turnhout, 2000), 163–74, at 164–5. For a full collection of plates, see C. Caprino *et al.*, *La colonna di Marco Aurelio* (Rome, 1955).

[71] A. Rubeni, *Dissertatio de Gemma Augustea*, ed. H. Kähler (Berlin, 1968). The *gemma*, dated to approximately AD 10, shows a barbarian man with his hands bound on his back who sits next to a *tropaeum* that is being erected, probably referring to the victory over the Illyrians. Next to the barbarian, there is a mourning woman and another man surrendering on his knees, with his arms

Column.[72] Another artistic depiction on the so-called 'Great Trajanic Frieze', shows the emperor Trajan on horseback in personal triumph over the Dacian while he tramples one of the enemies beneath him.[73] Prisoners are presented dead and alive.[74]

The images which depict violence or just hint at it belong essentially to the same group of triumphal works of art which celebrate Roman superiority and the humiliation and dejection of the defeated enemy. That is the case with Caesar's coins already mentioned, and also in numerous other works of art in different form. For example, the Augustan so-called 'Grand Camée de France', now in the Bibliothèque Nationale in Paris, shows, in the lower register, subjected peoples: Germans and perhaps Syrians with their wives, one of them carrying a child. All appear depressed, looking downwards and sitting bowed.[75] In another example, the above-mentioned Augustan victory monument at La Turbie shows trophies and captives, kneeling and chained.[76] The two silver cups from Boscoreale which show groups of provincials provide further examples from the reigns of Augustus

positioned in supplication. Beside the supplicant, a woman is being pulled by her hair by a man (soldier?) towards the *tropaeum*. She may be trying to pull her dress together, an image possibly associated with rape; see Zanker, 'Die Frauen und Kinder', 165. See also J. Pollini, 'The Gemma Augustea: Ideology, Rhetorical Imagery, and the Creation of a Dynastic Narrative', in P. Holliday (ed.), *Narrative and Event in Ancient Art* (Cambridge, 1993), 258–98. For a particularly good photograph, see B. Andreae, *Römische Kunst* (Freiburg, 1973), pl. 57.

[72] For Trajan's Column, see S. Settis *et al.*, *La colonna Traiana* (Turin, 1988), fig. 32 (24-25.63-4): Dacians flee as their village is set on fire; fig. 36 (29-31.71-74): Dacian fighters are killed. In these scenes, the old men and children flee, animals are killed, the women and children are taken captive and transported in ships. Zanker believes that Trajan's Column is less bloody and cruel in its depiction of women and children because Trajan's war was one of conquest, while Marcus' war was necessary and defensive; see Zanker, 'Die Frauen und Kinder'. That interpretation is based on a set of anachronistic morals. Marcus' wars were a response to attack, but developed into an openly declared plan for expansion of the Empire; cf. B. Isaac, *The Limits of Empire: The Roman Army in the East*, 2nd edn (Oxford, 1992), 390–1.

[73] Cf. Touati, *The Great Trajanic Frieze*, 22–4 and pl. 3, 13.1; J. Elsner, *Imperial Rome and Christian Triumph* (Oxford, 1998), 82 and pl. 53.

[74] Touati, *The Great Trajanic Frieze*, pls. 4 and 14. There is considerable confusion regarding the identity of several figures on the frieze; see Touati, *The Great Trajanic Frieze*, 14–16. Whatever or whoever they are, the assumption is that they must be personifications, such as the person crowning the emperor, often thought to be Victoria. For similar confusion regarding figures on the Arch of Titus, see Pfanner, *Der Titusbogen*, 67; and on the Arch of Trajan in Benevento, see K. Fittchen, 'Das Bildprogramm des Trajansbogens zu Benevent', *AA* (1972): 742–88, at 754, 756–8. Cf. P. Veyne, 'Une hypothèse sur l'arc de Bénévent', *MEFR* 72 (1960), 191–219, at 192–4; T. Lorenz, *Leben und Regierung Trajans auf dem Bogen von Benevent* (Amsterdam, 1973). See also the reflections by T. Hölscher, 'Beobachtungen zu römischen historischen Denkmälern III', *AA* (1988): 523–41, at 523–7.

[75] For a description, see J. B. Giard, *Le Grand Camée de France* (Paris, 1998), 17–23. The identity of the various members of the imperial court is not of present concern. For a full bibliography, see W. R. Megow, *Kameen von Augustus bis Alexander Severus* (Berlin, 1987), 155–63.

[76] Formigé, *Le trophée*. Note also the arch at Glanum (southern France); see H. Rolland, *L'arc de Glanum*, Gallia Suppl. 31 (Paris, 1977), pls. 22–3.

and Tiberius. These are particularly significant because they represent Roman state reliefs which otherwise do not survive for this period.[77] Thus in this instance there is no allegory, but, as observed by Kuttner, 'a classic example of Roman documentary historical relief: an image that presents itself as the literal transcription of an actual and singular event as it would have been visible to a real observer'.[78] As Kuttner points out, it is different from most such scenes known today from Roman art, because the captives appear not to be brutalized.[79] They are subjected peoples, not vanquished foreigners.

Fascinating and puzzling are the Julio-Claudian imperial relief panels from the Sebasteion at Aphrodisias.[80] These include what is described as a series of 'personified peoples (*ethnē*]) and provinces whose common feature ... was that they were conquered, or deemed to have been conquered by Augustus'.[81] For the East these include Crete, Cyprus, Egypt, Judaea, and Arabia. The surviving reliefs show single, standing women, well differentiated in their costume, attributes, and posture. As pointed out by Smith, this is clearly a surviving, provincial monument, planned after the example of a number of such structures known from literary sources to have existed in Rome and Lyon.[82] Strabo's wording in his description of the latter is revealing: 'And it is a noteworthy altar, bearing an inscription of the names of the tribes, sixty in number; and also images from tribes, one from each tribe, and also another large altar.'[83] In other words, the images are not said to be allegories, personifications, or symbols; a single image serves as illustration for each subjugated tribe. Clearly, the aim of such monuments was to convey the extent of the Empire, both in its geographical spread and its ethnic variety.

The reliefs showing emperors and captives from the Sebasteion at Aphrodisias depict Augustus with Nike, a trophy, and, below it, a naked

---

[77] Kuttner, *Dynasty and Empire*, containing a systematic discussion of the imagery on the cups and their message as familiar elements of Augustan imperialism. See also A. Héron de Villefosse, *Le trésor de Boscoréale* (Paris, 1902).

[78] Kuttner, *Dynasty and Empire*, 95.

[79] Kuttner, *Dynasty and Empire*, 86–93, discusses a group of images from the reign of Augustus which she interprets as giving expression to a notion of a 'benevolent *imperium*', the primary examples being the *Ara Pacis Augustae* and the province group of the first Boscoreale cup. Kuttner recognizes, however, that it is a form of benevolence only from the Roman perspective.

[80] Smith, 'Imperial Reliefs', 88–138.

[81] Smith, 'Imperial Reliefs', 95–6.

[82] E.g. statues of fourteen *nationes* in Pompey's theatre in Rome – Pliny the Elder, *Nat.* 36.41; a cycle of statues in the Augustan structure known as Porticus ad Nationes – Servius, *In Vergil. carm. comm.* 8.721; Pliny the Elder, *Nat.* 36.39; inscriptions in the forum of Augustus – Velleius, 2.39.2; see also Smith, 'Imperial Reliefs', 95–6.

[83] Strabo, *Geogr.* 4.192: ἐπιγραφὴν ἔχων τῶν ἐθνῶν ἐξήκοντα τὸν ἀριθμὸν καὶ εἰκόνες τούτων ἑκάστου μία.

prisoner, seen from behind and arms bound at his back;[84] Germanicus with a captive, probably a German;[85] an unidentified commander with a trophy; a captive and the Roman people or Senate;[86] Claudius and Britannia;[87] Nero and Armenia;[88] and another unidentified (and unfinished) commander with a captive.[89] It is interesting to see that the captives here are in several cases smaller in stature than the Roman commanders and gods and they are always positioned below them.[90] This is a feature more common on coins dating from the end of the second century and later.[91] Several of the reliefs show another feature, common in later art, namely that the emperor or god seems rather unaware of the presence of the captive.[92] These clearly are devices to emphasize the abject position of the foreigners, a tendency fully developed by the reign of Trajan. The little enemy becomes an attribute.[93] It seems as if the provincial art from Aphrodisias in this respect anticipated mainstream triumphal art by a century or more.

Two reliefs from Aphrodisias are different in character. Claudius and Britannia are identified by inscriptions on the base, which read 'Tiberios Klaudios Kaisar' and 'Bretannia'. The emperor stands over a sprawling defeated woman. He pulls her head back by the hair to kill her. Nero and Armenia are also identified by inscriptions on the base: 'Armenia' and '[Nero] Klaudios Drousos Kaisar Sebastos Germanikos'.[94] Armenia, wearing oriental dress, collapses and is being supported by Nero with wide-striding legs. As pointed out by Smith, both reliefs are more directly inspired by classic Greek battle scenes than is typical in Roman art. Claudius and Britannia are reminiscent of, for instance, the Amazonomachies, and Nero and Armenia of Achilles and Penthesilea. In the case of Claudius and Britannia, this rather clashes with the normal spirit of imperial propaganda, which shows a triumphant Roman and a weeping, dejected provincial. In Aphrodisias, however, Claudius is clearly about to kill Britannia. This appears to be a

---

[84] Smith, 'Imperial Reliefs', 101–4, pl. 4.
[85] Smith, 'Imperial Reliefs', 110–12, pl. 10.
[86] Smith, 'Imperial Reliefs', 112–15, pl. 12.
[87] Smith, 'Imperial Reliefs', 115–17, pl. 14.
[88] Smith, 'Imperial Reliefs', 117–20, pl. 16.
[89] Smith, 'Imperial Reliefs', 120–3, pl. 18.
[90] Pls. 4, 10, 18.
[91] Levi, *Barbarians*, 25: 'Barbarians are increasingly small in size and appear as accessories to the larger figures of the emperor, Victory or other divinity.' This phenomenon is quite common in Egyptian and Near Eastern formal art, but that need not mean there was direct influence, which in any case is not my concern.
[92] Pls. 4, 10, 12, 18.
[93] Levi, *Barbarians*, 27.
[94] Smith, 'Imperial Reliefs', 117; Nero's name had been erased in antiquity.

local deviation from the norm.[95] There is perhaps little point in trying to decide how the contemporary visitors to the sanctuary envisaged Britannia and Armenia. We are faced here with imperial art, but modified by a strong Eastern, provincial, Hellenistic tradition. Yet, when Claudius is about to kill the woman identified as 'Britannia' it is hardly convincing to say that this is an allegory of what the empire did to a province. It is more likely that the message or intended association was that the Empire, under Claudius and Nero, defeated and subjugated the Britons and Armenians, and did so with much slaughter. The medium used to convey this message was art of the type which the Greeks traditionally employed to celebrate victories.

Other remains of imperial monuments show figures of unidentifiable women. Often it is assumed that these are personifications of provinces.[96] It has, however, also been suggested that these may represent measures of imperial policy. Alternatively, it has been proposed that not all such figures were meant to be identifiable and they may have formed a generic representation of the extent of imperial power.[97] Whatever the intention of the sculptor, it cannot be retraced with any certainty. No less serious a question is whether a Roman spectator would have been able to do so in the absence of inscriptions. Some monuments, after all, such as the reliefs from Aphrodisias, had such inscriptions. Greek vase paintings often have inscriptions naming heroes who ought to have been recognizable for anyone vaguely familiar with epic poetry. As noted above, we may not know enough of contemporary culture to gain a clear idea of how first-century spectators saw and interpreted these images.

Another dilemma concerns the proper analysis of non-Roman children depicted in group scenes on the first Boscoreale cup and the *Ara Pacis*. As pointed out by Kuttner, these are not babies and children such as one sees on submission scenes, but aristocratic hostages.[98] Some of them can even convincingly be identified.[99] These then are not personifications or allegorical figures. They are images of real individuals who find themselves in the company of members of the imperial court. Yet they appear on the same object as what has been described as 'an assemblage of numerous provincial/ethnic personifications representing the peoples of the empire'.[100] It

---

[95] Smith, 'Imperial Reliefs', 117: 'This puts it out of step with central ideology, and suggests a purely Aphrodisian design.'

[96] Hölscher, 'Beobachtungen', 523–41.

[97] Hölscher, 'Beobachtungen', 525, 527.

[98] Kuttner, *Dynasty and Empire*, 99–111.

[99] Kuttner, *Dynasty and Empire*, 102–4.

[100] Kuttner, *Dynasty and Empire*, 106.

should at least be asked whether the assumption of such a mixture is conceptually the best way to understand these scenes.

All that I have claimed thus far is not intended to negate the possibility that some abstraction did occur in artistic presentations. For example, in a well-known statue of the Emperor Hadrian from Hierapytna (Crete), now in Istanbul, the emperor places his foot on what almost certainly is a (minute) Jewish captive.[101] On coins from the days of the Emperor Domitian (81–96) onwards Roman authority often has his foot on the defeated enemy. In the fourth century AD, from the times of the Emperor Constantine onwards, coins often show a walking emperor or divinity dragging a small enemy by the hair. The emperor or god seems rather unaware of the presence of the barbarian even when he is represented doing this. It is often assumed without further discussion that such statuary groups offer, like the groups depicted on coins, a symbolical representation of the emperor's victory over his enemies.[102] Undoubtedly this sort of depiction of a victorious situation had become a topos, but that does not make it a symbolic representation. It has been suggested as well that oriental influence might be detected here. However, the precise image of a king placing his foot over the defeated enemy is not common in Eastern art.[103] A better assumption is that we have here a genuinely, concrete Roman conception of the emperor and his enemy.

In a similar vein, it has been suggested that the iconography of city Tychai immediately influenced the representation of Roman provinces in personified or allegorized form.[104] It is true that city Tychai, which are encountered in large numbers throughout the Empire, invariably give expression to the sense of pride and well-being of the citizens. The goddess is shown to be the source of prosperity of the city she protects. Foreign

---

[101] H. G. Niemeyer, *Studien zur statuarischen Darstellung der römischen Kaiser* (Berlin, 1968), no. 53, pl. 17.2. Cf. p. 49: 'Auf Statuen des Kaisers Hadrian und den griechisch sprechenden Teil des römischen Imperiums beschränkt ist ein symbolkräftiges Bildschema, in dem das Palladion von Rom mit der kapitolinischen Wölfin und zwei bekränzenden Victorien verbunden ist'; p. 52: 'Ein "Attribut" besonderer Art ist die Gestalt eines niedergeworfenen Barbaren, die seit Domitanischer Zeit mit kaiserlichen Panzerstatuen verbunden ist'. Cf. Levi, *Barbarians*, 17–18, on how such a statue was reproduced on coins. Compare a statue from Ramleh (Israel), now in the British Museum; see A. H. Smith, *A Catalogue of Sculptures by the Successors of Pheidias, in the British Museum*, III/1 of *A Catalogue of Sculpture in the Department of Greek and Roman Antiquities* (London, 1892), no. 1172; cf. P. v. Bieńkowski, 'Über eine Kaiserstatue in Pola', *Wiener Studien* 34 (1912): 272–81, who gives parallels from the second century AD. See also Picard, *Les trophées romains*, 421–2.

[102] Levi, *Barbarians*, 28.

[103] Sassanian reliefs show defeated enemies kneeling before the king, and old Egyptian reliefs show Pharaoh killing an enemy with a mace while holding him by the hair, but there does not seem to be any parallel for the Roman themes here discussed.

[104] Christof, *Das Glück der Stadt*, 218–26.

peoples or those inhabiting the Empire are the subject of imperial art only when they have been vanquished or are humble inhabitants of the provinces.[105] But at the same time, it may be safely said that any Roman citizen who saw a coin or large sculpture showing such a scene would be looking at very familiar imagery and, even if only three figures were depicted, he or she would imagine the rest. Modern spectators see an art form that may seem deceptively understandable, but living in a different culture, it may be salutary for us to maintain caution in interpreting these images with the intellectual tools familiar in our times, but not to Greeks and Romans.[106]

[105] Kuttner, *Dynasty and Empire*, 69–93; Kuttner points out that Rome is always dominant, but the relationship is variously depicted, ranging from the utter humiliation of the recently vanquished to the well-established association of ruler and ruled.

[106] For helpful advice I am obliged to Margalit Finkelberg and Rivka Gersht.

CHAPTER 3

Army and Violence in the Roman World

The following discussion focuses on a number of topics concerning the functioning of the Roman army within the Empire, namely the relationship between army and civilians in the Empire and the effect on the civilian population of large numbers of professional troops among them. I shall briefly survey three subjects:

(1) massive violence in cities;
(2) physical force in a judicial context;
(3) physical abuse of individuals by soldiers or civilians of social superior status.[1]

Before doing so, however, it should be elucidated that this discussion will necessarily focus on regions for which there is evidence in sufficient quantities and of sufficient quality. Notably the chapter will consider literary sources which, to some extent, give us a perspective of the civilian population living in close contact with military forces. Obviously, the resulting account will differ in essence from one based on a close study of, for instance, public inscriptions, which give the perspective of those belonging to the circle of military men and officials. The latter are meant to convey a message to be seen by those who are part of the provincial and imperial establishment, both in the military and judicial and the financial sphere. They express public loyalty to the emperor and the Roman state, satisfaction at whatever has been achieved, and cannot be regarded as statements of people's private views, let alone as being representative of the reality of daily life for the subjects of the Empire, living in the provinces. It is entirely legitimate to study government and army in the Roman provinces through the interpretation of public monuments, but it is necessary also to keep in

---

[1] These subjects are all treated in R. MacMullen, *Soldier and Civilian in the Later Roman Empire* (Cambridge, 1963), a seminal study. The present chapter mostly addresses the earlier period, not covered by MacMullen's book.

mind that the resulting impression is different from one which tries to see reality through the sources relating to the civilian population. If we want to understand why army and power in the Roman world were successful in achieving the aims of the authorities, proper answers can be reached only if we know something about the impact of the exercise of power at the lower end of the social scale. This is not to suggest that this chapter will result in an over-all view. Pierre Ducrey, for instance, pays much attention to the crucial question of political control over the military apparatus.[2] That is not a question raised in the present chapter, although some of the sources considered here suggest that the limits of control exercised by the authorities over the military were rather more flexible than one associates with proper government. It will be essential to keep in mind that an assessment of the quality of life in the Empire will always be influenced by the kind of sources we read. A dedication to a successful high officer gives a radically different view from a satirical description of brutal police action.

Massive Violence in Cities

Several extreme instances have been recorded of violence in major cities at the command of the emperor. In Alexandria, under Vespasian, 'so many of the Alexandrians were slaughtered by the soldiers stationed in the city that the swords grew heavy in the hands of those who used them'.[3] In 215 an imperial visit to Alexandria resulted in a massacre, the cause of which is not clearly explained in the sources.[4] Caracalla set troops on the city without warning. Severe repressive measures were taken after the massacre. Diocletian carried out a massacre after Eugenius' revolt in Antioch in AD 303.[5] Later there were fears of similar treatment at the hands of Theodosius to whom Libanius wrote:

> Rumour has it that you will unleash the military to pillage the property of us all, or to massacre the inhabitants of the city [sc. Antioch], or that you

[2] P. Ducrey, 'Armée et pouvoir dans la Grèce antique, d'Agamemnon à Alexandre', in A. Chaniotis and P. Ducrey (eds.), *Army and Power in the Ancient World* (Stuttgart, 2002), 51–60.
[3] Libanius, *Oratio* 20. 32, as trans. C. P. Jones, 'Egypt and Judaea under Vespasian', *Historia* 46 (1997): 249–53, at 251. In this article Jones discusses the testimonies of Dio Chrysostom, Josephus, Libanius, and the *Chronicle* of Eusebius about events in Alexandria under Vespasian. He convincingly brings them together as referring to an armed suppression of unrest in Alexandria in the last stage of the Jewish War.
[4] Dio 77.21–3; cf. Historia Augusta, *Antoninus Caracalla* 6; Herodian 4.9. F. Millar, *A Study of Cassius Dio* (Oxford, 1964), 156–8, for the evidence and discussion; C. R. Whittaker, *Herodian*, Loeb, I (Cambridge, 1969), 422, n. 1, for the reasons (local support for Geta?).
[5] Libanius, *Oratio* 20.17–20; 19.45; 2.11; 1.3.

will avenge this insult by a huge fine or by shedding the blood of the leading lights of the city council.[6]

On that occasion the matter ended without bloodshed and Libanius thanked the emperor in another oration in which he mentions again the various kinds of slaughter they had feared and expected.[7] Even Italian cities might suffer. Tiberius and Nero used Praetorian units to suppress unrest in Pollentia and Puteoli.[8] In emergencies, such as the great fires of AD 64 in Rome, the Praetorians took to looting, in which case, of course, they were not acting under orders.[9]

It appears from the sources that the use of combat troops for internal police duties resulted in a far more violent treatment of civilians than we would now consider reasonable or efficient for the purpose of maintaining control. Josephus provides extensive descriptions of the clashes between Roman troops under the command of the procurators and the Jewish civilian population in Judaea. The lack of effectiveness of regular troops in such circumstances is obvious throughout. Josephus himself ascribes the random and uncontrolled violence of those years primarily to the obstreperousness of the equestrian governors of Judaea. While it is clear that these were a particularly poor choice, it is none the less true that neither governors nor their forces were properly trained for the mission they had to perform. Occasionally the troops were used to suppress what would seem to have been real armed sedition,[10] but they were also used by Pilate to intimidate unarmed Jews, assembled in the stadium in Caesarea.[11] This is not the sort of activity to improve either the morale or the morals of any army, nor those of the civilian population which suffered from this sort of behaviour. Both Pilate and Florus used regular troops in Jerusalem with disastrous effect.[12] Pilate used troops, armed but disguised in civilian dress, to suppress unrest. According to Josephus, many civilians were killed

---

[6] Libanius, *Or.* 19 (To the Emperor Theodosius, About the Riots) 39: μὴ γὰρ δὴ τῶν θρυλουμένων μηδὲν εἰς ἔργον ἔλθοι. τίνα δὴ ταῦτ' ἔστιν; οἱ μὲν εἰς ἁρπαγὴν τῶν ὄντων ἑκάστοις χρημάτων φασὶν ἐπαφήσειν σε στρατιώτας οἱ δ' ἐπὶ σφαγὰς τῶν ἐχόντων τὴν πόλιν, οἱ δὲ διὰ μεγέθους καταδίκης ἀμυνεῖσθαι τὴν ὕβριν, οἱ δὲ ἵματι τῶν ἐν τῇ βουλῇ γνωριμωτέρων.

[7] Libanius, *Or.* 20; for the expectation of a massacre: 20. 5.

[8] Suetonius, *Tiberius* 37.3; Tacitus, *Ann.* 13.48 on which see also J. H. D'Arms, 'Tacitus, *Annals* 13.48 and a New Inscription from Puteoli', in B. Levick (ed.), *The Ancient Historian and his Materials: Essays in Honour of C. E. Stevens* (Farnborough, 1975), 155–66.

[9] Dio 62.17.1; Tacitus, *Ann.* 15.38.7; Josephus, *Ant.* 19 (160).

[10] *Ant.* 20.8.6 (167–72); *BJ* 2.13.5 (261–3).

[11] *BJ* 2.9.3 (172–4); *Ant.* 17.3.1 (57–9); cf. Philo, *Legatio*, 299–302.

[12] Pilate: *Ant.* 18.3.2 (60–2); *BJ* 2.9.4 (175–7). The latter source does not mention that the soldiers exceeded their orders.

because the troops inflicted much harder blows than the commander had ordered, hitting rioters and innocents indiscriminately. On two other occasions the misbehaviour of individual soldiers caused serious riots.[13] The first of these met with a response from the troops which, according to Josephus, resulted in massive and unnecessary loss of life. Incidents like these are often claimed to be unavoidable when large numbers of troops function as an occupying army among a much larger civilian population. However, experience shows that strict discipline and thorough training for such tasks go a long way in preventing excesses. Florus misused troops to provoke and intimidate the civilian population in Jerusalem.[14] He ordered the troops to sack the 'Upper Market' (τὴν ἄνω ἀγοράν). The soldiers not only plundered that quarter, but moved on to other quarters, plunged into every house and killed the inhabitants, causing a stampede and massacre. Josephus ascribes all this to the governor's active desire to cause a rebellion, said to be his only hope of covering up his crimes.[15] It is more likely that they represent the familiar pattern which occurs when a regular fighting force used to suppress a hostile city population does so with little competence and excessive bloodshed. We do not know much about the effect of the army presence on Judaea after Josephus ceased to record it, but it is significant, in this connection, that the number of soldiers serving in the province probably increased from around 3,000 to 18,000 by the reign of Hadrian.[16] It is clear, however, that such cases are to be distinguished from carefully planned large-scale massacres in major cities, such as that carried out by Caracalla in Alexandria. Furthermore it is, of course, quite likely that far more bloody clashes occurred in practice than our sources report. Literary sources would know about major conflicts in cities, but when the male population of a village in the Nile Delta was killed in an army action, we know about this only through the chance discovery of a papyrus, dealing with the problems in the collection of taxes that were the result.[17]

---

[13] A soldier exposed himself while standing guard on the Temple portico (*BJ* 2.12.1 (224); *Ant.* 20.5.3 (108)). Another soldier destroyed a copy of the Torah (*BJ* 2.9.2 (228–31); *Ant.* 20.5.4 (113–17)). While both incidents under Cumanus led to dangerous conflict, the first of them resulted in numerous civilian casualties, because the manner in which troops were called in caused panic in the city.

[14] *BJ* 2.14.6 (293–308); 15.5 (325–9).

[15] The misdeeds ascribed to Florus are sometimes puzzling. For instance, he is said to have scourged and nailed Jews of equestrian rank to the cross (Josephus, *BJ* 2.14.7 (308)). It is not clear how many such dignitaries there can have been in Judaea at that period.

[16] B. Isaac, *The Limits of Empire: the Roman Army in the East*, rev. edn (Oxford, 1992), 115–18.

[17] *P.Thmouis* 98, cited by R. Alston, *Soldier and Civilian in Roman Egypt: A Social History* (London, 1995), 83. Alston generally concludes that the soldiers in Egypt played a positive role (conclusions on p. 101), but his book does not contain a list of complaints about soldiers in papyri, a subject that

Physical Force in a Judicial Context

Ulpian sums up the duties of a proconsul as follows:

> He must, besides pursuing temple robbers, kidnappers and thieves, mete out to each of them the punishment he deserves and chastise people sheltering them; without them a robber cannot hide for very long.[18]

This legal text describes the duties of the proconsul in terms which leave no doubt that an active and forceful policy was considered to be the sign of a good governor. However, it does not make clear whether there were explicit rules defining and restricting the amount of force considered permissible. Since the proconsul had no police force at his disposal, it is also clear that the men used for these purposes came from the regular army, which, as far as we know, was trained for combat, not for police duties. It is obvious, but useful to remember that, as always in pre-modern times, judicial and police control was exercised by the same officials. This must, by definition, have resulted in a lack of sufficient checks and balances. It will be clear that, with this topic, we have moved on from massive clashes to individual conflict, whereby soldiers and officials were dealing with individuals in a formal capacity. The question is what measure of violence and physical force was considered acceptable according to contemporary norms and to what extent these norms were respected.

In our attempt to get an impression of reality in the life of the ordinary man, we may start with the famous description in the Book of Acts of Paul's arrest in Jerusalem. His presence in the Temple had resulted in a public riot. The local garrison, commanded by a tribune, interfered and Paul was arrested, bound, and brought to the barracks.[19] Eventually the tribune ordered his troops to interrogate Paul by scourging, which was only prevented by Paul's famous declaration that he was a Roman citizen,[20] whereupon the soldiers left him alone and he was untied. Paul's subsequent public appearance in Jerusalem caused further unrest, but he was protected by Roman soldiers, brought to the barracks, and, the following day, taken under escort to the governor in Caesarea.[21] All this is often cited as the classic proof of the protection Roman citizenship gave to an individual

---

presumably could be treated in this context, since the material exists. See my review in *American Historical Review* (1998): 1230–1.

[18] *Digest* 2.18.13, Praef.: *nam et sacrilegos latrones plagiarios fures conquirere debet et prout quisque deliquerit, in eum animaduertere, receptoresque eorum coercere, sine quibus latro diutius latere non potest.*

[19] Acts 21:30–4.

[20] Acts 22:24–9.

[21] Acts 23.

in this period. For our present purposes we should note the reverse impli-cation, namely that a provincial without citizenship would not enjoy this protection. The soldiers would have proceeded to bind and examine him by scourging without possibility of appeal. It is also less often emphasized that, according to the same source, the governor Felix, 'desiring to do the Jews a favour, left Paul bound' for two years.[22] It was only Felix's successor Festus who sent Paul to Rome when the latter appealed to Caesar.[23]

This was no exception. In the fourth century Libanius devotes an entire speech to the habit of governors of being quick to order detention, but very slow to come to a decision.[24] 'The prison is packed with bodies. No one comes out – or precious few, at least – though many go in.' In these cases governors apparently had the freedom to act against the accepted norms of the times, but there was little or no appeal – Libanius indeed was an important man, but we do not know what effect his speech had.

Juvenal's sixteenth satire shows that common civilians suffered the same disadvantages *vis-à-vis* soldiers inside Italy:

> Let us consider first then, the benefits common to all military men. Not least is the fact that no civilian would dare to give you a trashing – and if beaten up himself he'll keep quiet about it, he'd never dare show any magis-trate his knocked-out teeth, the blackened lumps and bruises all over his face, that surviving eye which the doctor offers no hope for. And if he seeks legal redress the case will come up before some hobnailed centurion and a benchful of brawny jurors, according to ancient military law: no soldier, it's stated, may sue or be tried except in camp, by court-martial. 'But still, a centurion's tribunal sticks to the rule-book. It's a soldier up on a charge, there'll be justice done. So if my complaint is legitimate I'm sure to get sat-isfaction.' But the whole regiment is against you, every company unites, as one man, to ensure that the 'redress' you get shall be something requiring a doctor, and worse than the first assault etc.[25]

---

[22] Acts 24, esp. θέλων τε χάριτα καταθέσθαι τοῖς Ἰουδαίοις ὁ Φῆλιξ κατέλιπε τὸν Παῦλον δεδεμένον:. Josephus describes the procurator Florus as having scourged and crucified even Jews of equestrian rank (Josephus, *BJ* 2.14.7 (308)); see above.

[23] He was dispatched to Rome only after Agrippa II had also heard him and concluded that Paul might have been released if he had not appealed to Caesar (26:32).

[24] Libanius, *Or.* 45.

[25] Juvenal, *Satire* 16 (trans. Peter Green, Penguin): *Commoda tractemus primum communia, quorum / haut minimum illud erit, ne te pulsare togatus / audeat, immo etsi pulsetur, dissimulet nec / audeat excussos / praetori ostendere dentes / et nigram in facie tumidis livoribus offam / atque oculum medico nil promittente relictum. / Bardaicus iudex datur haec punire volenti / calceus et grandes magna ad subsellia surae / legibus antiquis castrorum et more Camilli / servato, miles ne vallum litiget extra / et procul a signis. 'iustissima centurionum / cognitio est igitur de milite, nec mihi derit / ultio, si iustae defertur causa querellae.' / tota cohors tamen est inimica, omnesque manipli / consensu magno efficiunt curabilis ut sit / vindicta et gravior quam iniuria.* Cf. E. Courtney, *A Commentary on the Satires of Juvenal* (London, 1980), 613–22.

The following concrete information is to be derived from this satire:

(1) There is the common assumption that simple soldiers would beat up civilians. From the present passage it appears that this involved fairly extreme forms of physical force.

(2) In a matter of a conflict between a soldier and a civilian the judge would be a military man. The soldier had a great advantage over civilians. The civilian would suffer lengthy proceedings and constant adjournments. The soldier's case would be heard at a convenient moment and settled quickly (lines 42–50, not quoted here).

(3) The judge almost certainly would be a centurion.

(4) Any civilian who dared challenge a soldier who had beaten him up would suffer physical violence in the camp.

Libanius, discussing fourth-century Antioch, similarly describes the helplessness of simple citizens as victims of random violence and robbery by soldiers in town:

> A soldier provokes a market trader, mocking him and goading him, and then he lays hands on him, pulling him and dragging him about. Then he too perhaps is touched, but apparently the actions are not comparable: such men may not raise voice or hand against the soldier, and so this man, who is bound to suffer, is seized and finds himself at headquarters and buys exemption from being beaten to death.[26]

The similarities between Juvenal's satire and Libanius' ironic rhetoric are striking. The implication of Libanius' description is that any market trader was liable to be abused by soldiers and would find no protection of any kind through judicial channels at headquarters. We may assume that the situation in the Book of Acts and the imaginary scenes described by Juvenal and Libanius were typical of daily life. The point they were meant to convey would come across forcefully only if the reader or listener indeed recognized the reality around him in such descriptions.[27] Roman troops apparently used brute force both when they were acting under orders in a formal capacity (as with the riots in Jerusalem) and, without being provoked, in a non-military social context. The various sources cited here

---

[26] *Or.* 47.33; cf. ed. Reiske, II, 522, n. 37; J. H. G. W. Liebeschuetz, *Antioch: City and Imperial Administration in the Later Roman Empire* (Oxford, 1972), 115 with n. 4.

[27] Cf. J. B. Campbell, *The Emperor and the Roman Army* (Oxford, 1984), 235. Campbell notes that this picture of soldier and civilian in the Roman Empire is in stark contrast to the conventional encomion of Aelius Aristides and Dio of Prusa, 1.28. These had a different aim in their writings. One cannot expect social criticism in *encomia*.

explicitly convey the message that judicial channels did not lend support to civilians who had suffered unprovoked mistreatment from individual soldiers.

There may be some evidence that even the inhabitants of Italian cities were not safe from military men. For example, the following passage from Petronius' *Satyricon*:

(Eumolpus rushes into the street, repeatedly slapping his sword hilt):

> But then I drew the attention of a soldier – he may have been a trickster, or a mugger operating in the dark – who greeted me: 'Ho there comrade! What is your legion, who's your sergeant-major?' I wore a brave face as I lied about the officer and the detachment. 'So tell me,' he said, 'in your army do the troops go round in soft shoes?' Both my expression and my agitation showed I was lying. He ordered me to hand over my arms, and to keep out of harm's way. So not only was I robbed, but my plan for revenge was aborted.[28]

This passage should be interpreted with due caution, since it is satire rather than real life, but it illuminates another aspect, not mentioned by the author. Eumolpus is running around in an Italian city, armed and impersonating a soldier. A random soldier arrests him, checks his identity, and finds that he is not a soldier. He then confiscates his sword. The soldier has no formal authority to do this and he presumably keeps the sword for himself. This is the assumption attributed to Eumolpus, who says he was robbed. Yet the actions of the soldier were those we would expect of military police: to maintain discipline among those bearing arms on behalf of the state. Here, and in the story of Paul, we encounter a certain ambiguity, which we do not recognize in the simple abuse of military power recorded by Libanius.

Physical Abuse of Individuals by Soldiers or Civilians of Social Superior Status

To start from the top, any Roman emperor was constantly surrounded by armed soldiers, Praetorians and non-Roman guards. As Fergus Millar observes, this had an important influence on what it meant to appear

---

[28] Petronius, *Satyricon* 82 (trans. P. G. Walsh): *notavit me miles, sive ille planus fuit sive nocturnus grassator, et 'quid tu' inquit 'commilito, ex qua legione es aut cuius centuria?' cum constantissime et centurionem et legionem essem ementitus, 'age ergo' inquit ille 'in exercitu vestro phaecasiati milites ambulant?' cum deinde vultu atque ipsa trepidatione mendacium prodidissem, ponere iussit arma et malo cavere. despoliatus ergo, immo praecisa ultione retro ad deversorium tendo.*

before the emperor, and lent an increased immediacy and force to any sign of imperial displeasure.[29] The implication, clearly, is that physical force might be expected at any time, at least under certain emperors. There is no reason to assume that this presence of soldiers was only a symbolic one. It is also likely that this phenomenon was taken for granted by those living in the Empire. This was not the case when emperors indulged in brawling and debauchery at night in Rome,[30] like some vicious young noblemen.[31] Such behaviour was felt to be an outrage, even though there was nothing anyone could do about it.

Lower down the social scale, at the level of the individual, no ordinary inhabitant of the Empire would feel free to express anger at someone in a slightly higher position:

> It is like a man who stands up in the market place and defies the *bouleutes*. Those who heard him said to him: 'You utter fool, you defy the *bouleutes*?' What if he wanted to beat you or tear your clothes, or throw you in prison, what could you do to him? Or if he were a *qitron* (centurion), who is greater than him, how much more so! Or if he were a *hapatqas* (*hypatikos*, governor) who is greater than the two of them, how much more so![32]

This Talmudic source gives a nice impression of the relative social standing of the officials mentioned in the province of Palaestina. It is also quite obvious what means men of influence had at their disposal when they wanted to intimidate the ordinary citizens of a city. There was nothing to prevent them from using physical force or imprisoning citizens. There is no indication that it was important whether these officials were acting in a formal capacity, as agents of the state, or in a private quarrel and for personal reasons: ordinary people suffered violence if they dared to oppose men of superior status, who could be military men or civilian officials. All this is the implication of the Talmudic source, which invites comparison with other descriptions of urban life. Apuleius, in his *Metamorphoses*, describes how the aedile/*agoranomos* of a small Thessalian town abuses a little old fish merchant without good reason, emptying the man's basket onto the pavement and stamping on his fish. The official comments afterwards: 'It is sufficient for me … to have abused the old chap so thoroughly.'[33]

---

[29] F. Millar, *The Emperor in the Roman World: 31 BC–AD 337* (London, 1976), 61–6, 'Military Escorts and Bodygards'. Private guard of barbarians: 62–4.

[30] Nero: Tacitus, *Ann.* 13.25; cf. 47.2; Suetonius, *Nero* 26; Dio 61.8.1; Lucius Verus: SHA, *L. Verus* 4.7; Commodus: SHA, *Commodus* 3.7.

[31] Suetonius, *Otho* 2; Juvenal 3.278–30. Cf. W. Nippel, *Public Order in Ancient Rome* (Cambridge, 1995), 105.

[32] L. Finkelstein, *Siphre ad Deuteronomium* (1939, repr. New York, 1969), cccix, p. 348.

[33] Apuleius, *Met.*1.24–5. '*Sufficit mihi, o Luci,*' inquit 'seniculi tanta haec contumelia'.

Violent robbery under the guise of the exercise of legitimate authority recurs frequently in the literary and epigraphic sources. A well-known
example is provided again in Apuleius' satirical work: a soldier confiscates
an ass, falsely claiming that he needs it on official duty.[34] It is worth noting
what excuse the soldier produces in support of his claim:

> 'Well, I need his services,' said the other. 'He must carry our commanding
> officer's baggage from the nearby fort with all the other pack-animals.'[35]

This is very different from Pliny's and Trajan's insistence that such services
are only to be enjoyed by those travelling in the emperor's service and provided with up-to-date *diplomata*.[36] The soldier, incidentally, carries a *vitis*,
a staff, usually but not always the mark of the centurionate. In this inci-
dent, indeed, he uses it to thrash the civilian who did not want to give up
his ass.[37] The *vitis* was the symbol of the centurion's authority, but also an
actual instrument for inflicting punishment. The owner of the ass knocks
down the soldier and makes off. He is pursued and arrested, the soldier
takes the ass and loads him with his own baggage, carefully arranged with
the armour conspicuous so as 'to terrify poor travellers'.[38] After a while the
soldier and the ass come to a small town where they stay, not at an inn, but
in the house of a town-councillor. Once again, the soldier behaves as if he
is on official duty.[39] In the end the soldier sells the ass for his own profit,
when 'in dutiful obedience to an order from his tribune, he had to carry
a letter to the great emperor in Rome'.[40] In other words, when he sets out

---

[34] Apuleius, *Met.* 20.39–40; comments by F. Millar, 'The World of the Golden Ass', *JRS* 71 (1981):
67–8. In this article the resemblance is noted with Epictetus 4.1.79: 'If a requisition takes place and
a soldier takes (your mule), let it go, do not hold on to it, and do not complain. For if you do,
you will get a beating and lose your mule all the same.' (Trans. J. B. Campbell, *The Roman Army,
31 BC–AD 337: A Sourcebook*, London, 1994). Cf. R. G. Summers, 'Roman Justice and Apuleius'
Metamorphoses', *TAPA* 101 (1970): 511–31, on Apuleius' work as a subtle indictment of the administration of criminal justice in the Roman provinces.

[35] Apuleius, *Met.* 9.39: '*Sed mihi' inquit 'opera eius opus est; nam de proximo castello sarcinas praesidis
nostri cum ceteris iumentis debet aduehere'; et iniecta statim manu loro me, quo ducebar, arreptum
incipit trahere.*

[36] Pliny, *Ep.* 10. 45; 46; 120. For requisition of transport: Campbell, *The Emperor and the Roman Army*,
246–54.

[37] Cf. Tacitus, *Ann.* 1. 23.4, on the centurion Lucilius who was nicknamed *cedo alteram*, 'bring
another', because when he had broken one *vitis* on a man's back, he would call in a loud voice for
another and yet another. Also: Livy *Epitome* 57; Pliny, *NH* 14.19.

[38] Apuleius, *Met.* 10.1: *propter terrendos miseros viatores*

[39] Apuleius, *Met.* 10.1: *Confecta campestri nec adeo difficili uia ad quandam ciuitatulam peruenimus nec
in stabulo, sed in domo cuiusdam decurionis deuertimus.* On compulsory billeting, Isaac, *Limits of
Empire*, 297–304.

[40] Apuleius, *Met.* 10.13: *tribuni sui praecepto debitum sustinens obsequium, litteras ad magnum scriptas
principem Romam uersus perlaturus.*

on a genuine mission to the emperor in Rome, he sells the ass that he had stolen under false pretences. It is true that Apuleius is not historiography or a documentary source but a satirical work.[41] However, specific clauses in the *Digest* show that this sort of misbehaviour existed in real life: 'The governor must take care that nothing is done by individual soldiers exploiting their position and claiming unjust advantages for themselves, which does not pertain to the communal benefit of the army.'[42]

Generally speaking then, the assumption is that soldiers would be violent and rapacious, both when acting in their capacity as an internal police force, and when they were off duty. This resulted in endemic abuse and extortion as implied, for example, by the following passage in the Gospel according to Luke:

> Tax collectors also came to be baptized, and said to him, 'Teacher, what shall we do?' And he said to them, 'Collect no more than is appointed you.' Soldiers also asked him, 'And we, what shall we do?' And he said to them, 'Rob no one by violence or by false accusation, and be content with your wages.'[43]

In an edict published in 133–7 Mamertinus, the prefect of Egypt, declared that illegal and violent requisitions by troops had turned the local population against the Roman army: 'And so it has come about that private citizens are insulted and abused and the army is criticised for greed and injustice.'[44] It should be added that the army was especially powerful, for several papyri from Egypt show that centurions had judicial authority in rural areas (as, according to Juvenal's satire, they had also in Italy in disputes between soldiers and civilians). They are the recipients of complaints and requests for redress.[45] So, the troops not only acted as a police force, but also provided judges in the countryside. As in the case of the proconsul, discussed above, this means that there was no separation

---

[41] Satire makes fun of what exists in real life and provides relief from unbearable experiences by laughing at them. The passages quoted here clearly imply that more acceptable norms of behaviour were deemed possible.

[42] *Digest* 1.18.6, 5–7: *Ne quid sub nomine militum, quod ad utilitates eorum in commune non pertinet, a quibusdam propria sibi commoda inique indicantibus committatur, praeses prouinciae prouideat.*

[43] Luke 3:12–14.

[44] *Select Papyri* 2 (Cambridge, MA, 1932), no. 221 (AD 133/137): ἔπαρχος Αἰγύπτου λέγει· ἐπέγνων πολλοὺς τῶν στρατ[ι]ωτῶν ἄνευ διπλῆς διὰ τῆς χώρας πορευομένους πλοῖα καὶ κτήνη καὶ ἀνθρώπους αἰτεῖν παρὰ τὸ προσῆκον τὰ μὲν αὐτοὺς π[ρ]ὸς βίαν ἀποσπῶντας τὰ δὲ καὶ κατὰ χάριν η θεραπείαν {θαραπειαν} π[α]ρὰ τῶν στρατηγῶν λαμβάνοντας.

[45] P.Oxy. 2234 (AD 31); P.Ryl. 2.141 (AD 37); P.Mich. 175 (AD 193) cited by Campbell, *The Roman Army*, 172–3, nos. 286–8. Note also the instances listed by Alston, *Soldier and Civilian*, 88–90 (only part of the complaint listed there is relevant for the present discussion).

between police and judicial control. Even without evidence of what that would have meant in practice, it is clear that this must have led to abuse of authority and confused standards of behaviour.

In mid-fourth-century Egypt it had been common for army units to be engaged in collecting taxes, both *annona* and regular dues. While the *exactor* was responsible for the delivery, it was the soldiers who actually collected the taxes,[46] which frequently caused friction between the civilian and military authorities.[47] Soldiers are accused of looting and stealing cattle, of violent behaviour during the collection of taxes,[48] and of drunkenness combined with brutality.[49] We should remember that the same troops carried out policing duties in the region.[50] As so often, the evidence from Egypt is better than from other provinces, but it is by no means unique. Note, for instance, a well-known inscription from Africa referring to soldiers who arrested and tortured imperial tenants and beat up Roman citizens in an imperial domain.[51]

Conclusions

The Roman imperial army was for centuries successful in carrying out one of its main tasks: keeping the provincial population under control. This is the topic of the present chapter, for not considered here are the other roles of the army: to defend and expand the Empire in its conflicts with external armies or its task of protecting the regime against internal, armed enemies. The first point to make is that, over time, and as the Empire developed

---

[46] Isaac, *Limits of Empire*, ch. 6, 289–90, n. 129, referring to H. I. Bell *et al.*, *The Abinnaeus Archive* (Oxford, 1962), 55–8, no. 13. For the collection of *annona*: 73–5, no. 26; 78–9, no. 29.

[47] Cf. Isaac, *Limits of Empire*, 289–90. For the evidence from the Abinnaeus archives, see Bell *et al.*, *Abinnaeus Archive*, 55–60, nos. 13–15; nos. 26–9. Admittedly, these represent a brief period in a single district, but there is no lack of corroborating material from other periods and other areas, such as the well-known petition to the Emperors for redress from Philadelphia in Lydia: A. J. Abbott and A. C. Johnson, *Municipal Administration in the Roman Empire* (Princeton, 1926), 142. The document is translated by B. Levick in *The Government of the Roman Empire: A Sourcebook* (Beckenham, 1985), 222–3, no. 221. This contains the complaint of the villagers on an imperial estate protesting against the exactions of imperial officials and municipal magistrates. The immediate cause of complaint was the arrest of nine of the tenants by officers who claimed to be acting under the authority of the procurator.

[48] Bell *et al.*, *Abinnaeus Archive*, 75–6, no. 27; P.Oxy. 2, 184, no. 240; V. Ehrenberg and A. H. M. Jones, *Documents illustrating the Reigns of Augustus and Tiberius*, ed. D. L. Stockton (Oxford, 1976), 117 (Greek); trans. Levick, *Government*, 181, no. 168.

[49] Bell *et al.*, *Abinnaeus Archive*, 76–7, no. 28.

[50] Bell *et al.*, *Abinnaeus Archive*, 50–1, no. 9; 54–5, no. 12; 96–7, no. 42.

[51] *ILS* 6870; *CIL* VIII 10570, cf. 14464 (AD 180–3): ... *ut millis militib(us) in eiundem saltum Burunitanum alios nostrum adprehendi et vexari ali[os vinc]iri, nonnullos cives Romanos virgis et fusti-bus effligi iusse[rit]*.

into an integrated whole, the ethnic origin of the troops mattered less than their status and power among unarmed civilians. At the same time it is proper to observe that the successes of the troops in keeping the civilian population under control were achieved at a high cost and accompanied by serious imbalances. These are indicated in the present chapter. This is not to deny that there were substantial groups of people who profited from a military presence. Those who dedicated honorary inscriptions to officers of the local garrisons were not necessarily hypocrites. The point of the present chapter is that there were others who did not make such dedications, not only because they lacked the means to do so, but also because the relationship between army and civilians was often very tense.

First to be noted is a pattern of massacres carried out by regular troops in major cities, sometimes on instructions of the emperor, sometimes initiated by governors. A related phenomenon is cases of extreme violence in riot control. Urban unrest, of which there may have been far more than we know in the large cities of the Empire, was suppressed by troops not trained for the purpose and without maintaining adequate control mechanisms.

Second, the lack of separation of judicial and police authority resulted in the exercise of physical force in judicial contexts. Non-citizens could be and were physically abused before or entirely without legal proceedings. There is evidence of lengthy incarceration without legal justification.

Third, the social position of military men allowed them to intimidate and abuse civilians without proper checks. There is good evidence of acts of random violence carried out by soldiers without any legal or judicial restraints. Acts of robbery and illegal requisitions were common.

All this does not imply that the Roman Empire had a worse record than other ancient empires. This is not a comparative study, nor does it mean that ordinary men were worse off living under Roman rule than in smaller, more coherent states. The aim of this chapter is to indicate that the civilian population of the Empire paid a price for the long-term stability achieved with the aid of a permanent and widespread military presence.

CHAPTER 4

Innovation and the Practice of Warfare in the Ancient World

Was there science in antiquity? Undoubtedly there was, but not in the sense in which it is nowadays commonly understood. Was there war? Clearly, yes, there was. Was there a demonstrable connection between the two? That is the topic of this chapter. It will be argued that there was no close connection and, more important, it was not there even where one might have assumed it to have existed. I will then propose a tentative explanation of why this was so.

Science and Technology

Technology may be science-driven or not. We should distinguish between developing technology by trial and error and a development driven by science. Metallurgy, textile making, pottery, agriculture all developed long before the Greeks developed their recognized level of scientific enquiry. In these cases technological development was the result of a long and arduous process of learning by trial and error. The craftsmen experimented in a general, non-technical sense of the word. Their experiments were designed not to test a theory, but to improve the end-product of their work.

However important technological developments were for the evolution of civilization, they do not by themselves imply science, conscious theorizing, but reflect a developed ability to observe and to learn from experience. Learning from experience is in modern times a matter of routine for every bureaucracy, including military bureaucracies. This is not to say that this is true for antiquity in the same manner, for Greece and Rome did not have bureaucracies in a modern sense. However, to some extent this happened in war as well, whether concerning tactics, the production of weapons, or

This is the text of an unpublished lecture presented at a binational conference, 'Science and War; Science and Peace', organized by the Israel Academy of Sciences and Humanities and the Berlin-Brandenburg Academy of Sciences in December 2009.

the planning and execution of major campaigns. Evidence of the increasing complexity of warfare begins already in Herodotus: as in the case of the Persian expeditions to Greece – and, more especially as described by Thucydides, the development of the trireme. Yet this is conceptually simple technological innovation, not science contributing to change or war inspiring scientific progress.

What is Science?

It has been debated for decades how science is to be defined. As is well known, Latin *scientia,* and its derivatives in modern languages, is a term indicating systematic knowledge.[1] Let us consider a few definitions.

(1) The *New Oxford Dictionary* has: 'the intellectual and practical activity encompassing the systematic study of the structure and behaviour of the physical and natural world through observation and experiment'.

(2) Webster emphasizes the result rather than the activity: knowledge or a system of knowledge covering general truths or the operation of general laws especially as obtained and tested through scientific methods.

(3) A compromise may be proposed tentatively: 'Knowledge obtained by enquiry in accordance with an established method of investigation, which is tested through agreed methods of observation and experiment.'

Science is a modern, not an ancient category, not antedating the seventeenth century, if these definitions are accepted. It requires quantitative analysis, the use of hypotheses and postulates and experimental methods, following commonly accepted rules. However, there exist broader, relativist definitions that would allow for the existence of science in pre-modern cultures. These hold that

> the truth of a scientific theory is not settled by a direct correspondence to facts … but rather first by its internal consistency, and secondly by its ability to generate hypotheses that can yield predictions. The hypotheses *can* thus be evaluated, not that there is any suggestion that they are true of the world, only that they are adequate for the purposes of making and testing predictions.[2]

[1] English 'science' without further qualification is currently often taken to refer to the 'natural sciences' in particular.

[2] G. E. R. Lloyd, *Disciplines in the Making: Cross-Cultural Perspectives on Elites, Learning, and Innovation* (Oxford, 2009), 158. On 154–5, he observes that there is a contrast between a more restricted and a broader understanding of science.

The question is then: what was science in antiquity?

Marshall Clagett defines Greek science as: (a) the orderly and systematic comprehension, description, and/or explanation of natural phenomena; (b) the tools necessary for that undertaking, including, especially, logic and mathematics.[3]

Geoffrey Lloyd is more reserved:

> The Milesians did not have a fully articulated system of inquiry including a definite methodology and extending over the whole of what we call natural science. Their investigations were restricted to a very narrow range of topics. They had no conception of scientific method as such. Their innovations are a) the discovery of nature as a topic for rational and systematic inquiry (i.e. there is no room here for arguments derived from mythology or religion, but only from cause and effect). b) The practice of rational criticism and debate.[4]

Lloyd later suggested that 'on a broader view, science can be said to exist wherever there is a systematic understanding of a range of natural phenomena, whether or not that understanding is the result of the self-conscious application of a programme of research governed by an explicit "scientific method"'.

The history of differing conceptions of the aims and justifications of different modes of inquiry concerning nature is the main concern of historians of science. In antiquity science had clearly established branches:

Mathematics, which was hierarchically subdivided into arithmetic, geometry; then: optics, harmonics (music) and astronomy which included astrology.[5]

Physics

Biology and medicine

Geography

'Geometry' literally means the measurement of land. Herodotus 2.109 states that it originated in Egypt. Plato sees a contrast between abstract geometry, the measurement of lengths, breadths, and depths (*Laws* 817e), and the art of measurement that is appropriate for carpentry or architecture (*Philebus* 56e). There is a clear and hierarchical distinction between the training of the intellect, which is superior and the lower level of

---

[3] M. Clagett, *Greek Science in Antiquity* (London, 1957), 4.

[4] G. E. R. Lloyd, *Early Greek Science: Thales to Aristotle* (London, 1970), 8; see now Lloyd, *Disciplines in the Making*, ch. 8.

[5] Cf. Lloyd, *Disciplines in the Making*, 31.

applied, practical utility. We should keep in mind that astrology is, in fact, an applied sub-branch of astronomy. If accepted as valid, it is of practical utility (but was rejected by Cicero, *De divinatione* and regarded as speculative by the Epicureans). Astronomy was otherwise theoretical.

For present purposes it may be said that in the modern literature very often not enough attention is paid to the difference between technology and science. Technology there certainly was, in the sense of the improvement of existing material equipment for the sake of productivity and greater efficiency. Science is a different matter, if taken as systematic inquiry: questions asked, a method developed, hypothesis, testing of hypothesis, application in practice. Applied science was according to Greek norms almost a contradiction in terms, even though it did exist in some form and to a limited extent in the Hellenistic age (Alexandria). It was hardly taken up in Rome. Neither in Greece nor in Rome do we see the phenomenon familiar from recent times of science being developed for the sake of weapons development. The classic forms of applied science in modern times are the Manhattan Project and the German rocket programme.

Institutions

All branches of science were practised by individuals and their pupils, but not in any formal settings. Philo of Byzantium tells us that under the Ptolemies engineers were financed by them in their investigations. However, the circumstances of the Ptolemies' support for this kind of work were exceptional. The ancient world knew very few institutions set up to promote science and culture which were funded by rulers. First of these are, obviously, the Museum and Library in Alexandria.[6] Again, such institutions are an exception. In Athens Marcus Aurelius instituted a very limited number of posts for paid teachers of philosophy. There was a small number of public physicians in some Greek cities in the fifth century and in the Hellenistic period there were *archiatroi* who enjoyed certain privileges (tax exemption). In Greece the courts of 'tyrants' attracted poets, musicians, artists, and craftsmen, as well as philosophers. The entourages of Hellenistic kings and then of Roman emperors could provide supportive, if risky, environments for intellectuals (Vitruvius, Seneca, Galen).

In any case, science did not exist in Greece and Rome (and China) in the institutionalized sense of the past century. It was not organized in any

---

[6] P. Fraser, *Ptolemaic Alexandria*, 2 vols. (Oxford, 1972).

form such as we know it: in academic institutions, national academies, professional societies, or commercial bodies. Institutionalized support for science was not forthcoming. In particular the idea that science holds the key to material progress, and indeed the ideal of material progress itself, were largely lacking – more about this below.

What was the Possible Contribution of Science to Warfare in Antiquity?

What did the undertaking of systematic research owe to a perception of its possible practical applicability? In what areas was practical utility the chief stimulus to research? Conversely, how far did the actual technological advances made in early societies depend on input from the side of theorists?[7]

Aeneas Tacticus (fourth century BC) wrote the first military treatise extant in Greek. Aeneas stresses the importance of experience, of military intelligence; the use of spies, etc. These are all sensible lessons based on experience. He sheds light on the nature of life and the strategic and psychological preoccupations in a typical Greek city-state. We see what conditions were like. His recommendations derive from his own accumulated experience and from material he found in other writers, including Herodotus and Thucydides. There is no question of technology here at all. The same is true for the second-century authors Arrian and Polyaenus who discusses stratagems. None of them had any drawings or tables.[8] None of them present any coherent theory set forth in a systematic manner.

These authors draw lessons from the past. Although the evidence is poor, it is clear that the Roman imperial army did not draw such lessons systematically.[9] This is not to say that individual commanders failed to profit from their own experience – be it positive or negative. The point is that there was no organized system assisting commanders in profiting from knowledge acquired during wars in the past. Also, what we know of the reports by commanders on their exploits suggests that they aimed at conveying a rhetorical and political message more than providing factual and useful information.[10] It has been suggested that an innovation of

---

[7] For an earlier consideration of these questions see T. Bekker-Nielsen, 'Academic Science and Warfare in the Classical World', in T. Bekker-Nielsen and L. Hannestad (eds.), *War as a Cultural and Social Force: Essays on Warfare in Antiquity* (Copenhagen, 2001), 120–9.

[8] Bekker-Nielsen, 'Academic Science', 121–2, briefly considers, only to reject, the possibility that there was a connection between the science of geometry and tactics on the battlefield.

[9] B. Isaac, *The Limits of Empire: The Roman Army in the East* (Oxford, 1992), 401–6; S. P. Mattern, *Rome and the Enemy: Imperial Strategy in the Principate* (Berkeley, CA, 1999), ch. 2.

[10] Mattern, *Rome and the Enemy*, 33.

Greek and Roman warfare was rational analysis, unencumbered by religious, autocratic, or ideological distortion and control.[11] Whether true or not, this is not the topic of the present chapter. It is, in any event, clear that this has nothing to do with science in the sense accepted for present purposes.

When do we Find Science-Driven Technological Improvement in Warfare in the Pre-Modern World?

One main area where technological advances were made through the application of mechanical principles was in warfare,[12] especially the production and development of weapons, where we can supplement the written texts with the evidence from ancient weapons.

The engineers known to have contributed are Ctesibius (285–222 BC), Epimachus of Athens, who worked for Demetrius Poliorketes (305/4 BC)[13], Philo of Byzantium (3–2 BC), Asclepiodotus (first century BC), Bito (2 BC), Vitruvius, Hero of Alexandria (AD 1), Frontinus (AD 1), Polyaenus (AD 2), Vegetius (AD 4).[14]

Several of these produced texts that deal with weaponry (primarily artillery and siege craft). Philo, Vitruvius,[15] and Hero[16] wrote on the construction and improvement of various types of catapults – scorpions and ballistae – designed to hurl bolts or stones in both torsion and non-torsion varieties. The torsion principle exploited the power of skeins of twisted hair or sinew (catapults had an effective range of up to 365 m).

Ctesibius invented a new and accurate sort of catapult and a cannon, driven by compressed air.[17] Philo of Byzantium (3–2 BC) produced an

---

[11] V. D. Hanson and J. Heath, *Who Killed Homer: The Demise of Classical Education and the Recovery of Greek Wisdom* (New York, 1998), 72–5. Their hypothesis is unfortunately phrased in traditional chauvinist terms, opposing Western superiority to Oriental failure. Cf. B. Isaac, *The Invention of Racism in Classical Antiquity* (Princeton, 2004), 257–9 and *passim*.

[12] Y. Garlan, 'Hellenistic Science: Its Application in Peace and War', *Cambridge Ancient History*, VII.1, 2nd edn (Cambridge, 1984), 353–62.

[13] I. Pimouguet-Pédarros, 'Le siège de Rhodes par Démétrios et "l'apogée" de la poliorcétique grecque', *REA* 105 (2003): 371–92, esp. 377–9, argues that the merit and innovations of Demetrius and his men have been overrated.

[14] Onasander, *Strategikos* 42.8, has a chapter on the use of siege engines, but not on their construction, which was the responsibility of the workmen building them: 42.3: τῶν ἑπομένων ἀρχιτεκτόνων .. εἰς τὰς ὀργανικὰς κατασκευάς. It is the general's task to decide where and when to use them.

[15] Vitruvius 10.10 discusses ballistae, catapults and siege machines in a brief, but genuine technical description.

[16] H. A. Diels and E. Schramm, *Herons Belopoiika, Philons Belopoiika: Griechisch und Deutsch* (Berlin, 1918–19; repr. Leipzig, 1970).

[17] A. Reymond, *History of the Sciences in Greco-Roman Antiquity* (London, 1927), 78–9.

improved torsion catapult, based on systematic tests.[18] His work throws important light on the nature of those investigations: essential proved to be the diameter of the bore, that is, the circle that receives the twisted skeins. Experiments were therefore conducted to test the diameter till the optimal result was obtained.[19] This shows quite clearly that the ancients did, on occasion, appreciate the need to conduct systematic tests in order to isolate the relevant variables and determine the relationship between them. Philo also planned a repeater catapult, a sort of machine gun, which however, had serious problems that made it impossible to use.[20] Other siege instruments were developed or improved such as mines, tunnelling, incendiary projectiles, access ramps, wooden towers with swing bridges and shelters for groups of soldiers: 'porches' and 'tortoises'.

Best known are the inventions of Archimedes (284–ca. 212 BC), which perhaps reflects more Archimedes' stature as a scientist than the importance of these instruments for the material development of warfare. While Archimedes is recorded as having been active in the development of some weapons, it is obvious that he did so under the force of circumstances, not because this was in any way central to his activities as a scientist.[21] His city faced an existential threat. According to Plutarch, Archimedes did not consider the development of these weapons a serious endeavour, but his inventions were 'accessories of geometry practised for amusement at the request of King Hiero'.[22] It has been argued also that Archimedes did not in fact introduce major innovations. His only major innovation is said to have been crane arms mounted on the city walls to pick up enemy soldiers and ships.[23] This, however, was not conceptually new, but an increase in scale of equipment used previously.

---

[18] Philo of Byzantium (ca. 280–ca. 220 BC), also known as Philo Mechanicus. The military sections *Belopoeica* and *Poliorcetica* are extant in Greek, detailing missiles, the construction of fortresses, provisioning, attack, and defence, as are fragments of *Isagoge* and *Automatiopoeica* (ed. R. Schone, 1893, with German trans. in H. A. T. Köchly's *Griechische Kriegs-schriftsteller*, I, 1853; E. A. Rochas d'Aiglun, *Poliorcetique des Grecs*, 1872); Diels and Schramm, *Herons Belopoiika, Philons Belopoiika*; Y. Garlan, *Recherches de Poliorcétique grecque* (Paris, 1974), 279–404: 'Le Livre "V" de la *Syntaxe Mécanique* de Philon de Byzance, Texte, Traduction et Commentaire'. He discusses how one should organize a city so as to withstand a siege; how to build fortifications, granaries, and gives practical information, based on experience.

[19] *Belopoiika (On Artillery Construction)* 3.50.20–2, ed. Diels and Schramm, 8–9.

[20] Two flat-linked chains were connected to a windlass, which by winding back and forth would automatically fire the machine's arrows until its magazine was empty. Philo, however, notes that during fire it had to be kept absolutely steady, which in turn meant that the aim could not be adjusted. See Philo, *Belopoeica* 73.21–76.20. E. W. Marsden, *Greek and Roman Artillery: Technical Treatises* (Oxford, 1971), 146–8, 177–9. W. Soedel and V. Foley, 'Ancient Catapults', *Scientific American* 240.3 (March 1979): 124–5.

[21] Polybius 8.4–7; Plutarch, *Marcellus* 14–17.

[22] Plut., *Marc.* 14.4.

[23] Bekker-Nielsen, 'Academic Science and Warfare', 125.

While there can be little doubt that most improvements in weaponry were the hard-won outcome of experience on the field of battle, some on the Greek side appear to have come from deliberate experimental research into the principles at work. The improved catapult is an example of this.

It is important (says Lloyd) to realize that, in part of their theoretical explorations, some Greek authors went far beyond the limits of what was practicable: some of the devices in the technical literature were, in other words, merely plans that were never realized, because the inventions were not practicable.[24]

Victor Davis Hanson and John Heath claim that the Greeks introduced a series of innovations in Western warfare, partly driven by science.[25] They mention specifically advances in the technology of weapons and armour. The Greek, Macedonian, and Roman bronze and iron scale and plate protected better than anything their enemies had at their disposal. Their bronze and iron swords were more effective. While this is true, it confuses improvements in technology with science. Moreover, I cannot see that they are right in claiming that these innovations were made possible 'by their pragmatic society where religious coercion and state suppression played no role'. These are the usual old stereotypes. Persia was no democracy (nor were most Greek states or the Roman Empire), but there was no religious coercion or state suppression in Achaemenid, Parthian, and Sassanian Persia.

Geography

Eratosthenes secured his place in the history of scientific thought with his calculation of the circumference of the earth, based not on conjecture but on mathematics and astronomy. Eratosthenes was in fact the first geographer to draw parallel circles and meridians and develop them into a proper system. By means of known distances and the fixing of points within his system of co-ordinates, it was now possible for him to construct a new map of the *oikoumene* based on a compromise between the requirements of the system and the limited knowledge available.[26]

---

[24] For a revisionist article, see: A. Wilson, 'Machines, Power and the Ancient Economy', *JRS* 92 (2002): 1–32. This paper argues that the ancient technology was not as stagnant as claimed.

[25] Hanson and Heath, *Who Killed Homer*, 62–3.

[26] K. Geus, 'Measuring the Earth and the *Oikoumene*: Meridians, *sphragides* and Some Other Geographical Terms Used by Eratosthenes of Cyrene (276–194 BC)', in R. Talbert and K. Brodersen (eds.), *Space in the Roman World: Its Perception and Presentation* (Münster, 2004), 11–26. See also the earlier survey of ancient cartography by A. O. W. Dilke, 'The Culmination of Greek Cartography

Ptolemy of Alexandria (second century) was the first to present the locations of places in a uniform system of co-ordinates with details of the degrees. Calculation of latitude was relatively simple: (a) from the length of the shadow cast by a gnomon on the equinox or (b) from the length of the longest day. Longitude was harder: Hipparchus had the idea of using lunar eclipses for this purpose.[27]

The best-known, ancient map of the world as it was known at the time is the *Tabula Peutingeriana*.[28] The map is named after Konrad Peutinger, a German fifteenth–sixteenth-century humanist and antiquarian. It was discovered in a library in Worms by Conrad Celtes, who was unable to publish his find before his death and bequeathed the map in 1508 to Peutinger. It is conserved at the Österreichische Nationalbibliothek, Hofburg, Vienna. The existing copy of it, a medieval reproduction of a Late Roman scroll, was made by a monk in Colmar in the thirteenth century. It is a parchment scroll, 0.34 m high and 6.75 m long, assembled from eleven sections.

The inference is that such a large and ambitious work could only emerge from an established Roman cartographic tradition; it seems inconceivable for it to have been created as a ready-made product without precedent. Indeed there now exists evidence that more maps were produced in antiquity.[29] There is no need to go into this here. It is clear, in any event, that the Peutinger map, as it is, reflects a second-century stage as well as later additions. However, it has too many shortcomings to be of genuine

in Ptolemy', in J. B. Harley and D. Woodward (eds.), *History of Cartography*, I (Chicago, 1987), 177–200; and in the same volume: 'Maps in the Service of the State: Roman Cartography to the End of the Augustan Era', (201–11); 'Itineraries and Geographical Maps in the Early and Late Roman Empires' (234–57); 'Cartography in the Byzantine Empire' (258–75). Dilke argues that the value of maps to the Roman state and its generals was widely accepted. However, he also concludes (242) that the 'geographical manuscripts of Roman origin are of less cartographic interest than their Greek counterparts'. Note also the advice offered by the sixth-century Anonymous *Treatise on Strategy* 20, in G.B. Dennis, *Three Byzantine Military Treatises* (Washington, DC, 1985), 70, trans. 71: When troops march into hostile territory or are getting close to the enemy, it is 'a good plan … to make sketches of the more dangerous places, and more so of locations suitable for an ambush, so that if we have occasion to pass that way again, we may be on our guard'. Cf. Vegetius' advice to use *itineraria picta*. It is perfectly clear from this statement that the Byzantine commander is not expected to have any proper maps at his disposal. The *Treatise* merely offers sound advice, which is proof that there was no standing order to keep a good record of any kind of an expedition into enemy territory.

[27] A. Stückelberger, 'Ptolemy and the Problem of Scientific Perception of Space', in Talbert and Brodersen, *Space in the Roman World*, 27–40.

[28] K. Miller, *Die Peutingersche Tafel* (Stuttgart, 1916; repr. 1962); *Tabula Peutingeriana* (Graz, 1976); cf. R. Talbert, 'Cartography and Taste', in Talbert and Brodersen, *Space in the Roman World*, 133–41.

[29] One early Greek map that has survived is found on the famous Artemidorus papyrus for which, see C. Gallazzi, B. Kramer, and S. Settis (eds.), *Il papiro di Artemidoro (P. Artemid.)* (Milan, 2008). This represents a map of Spain, dating to the first century BC. It is an important discovery because it proves that such maps existed at the time. If one is now known to have existed, it is likely that there were more.

practical use. Travellers who tried to rely on it when making a journey would quickly encounter problems and frustrations. The users that the mapmaker had in mind must have been more detached. The mapmaker's main purpose is by some scholars thought to have been to boost Romans' pride in the range and greatness of Rome's rule.

For sea travel it must be observed that there was no tradition of navigational charts for plotting routes by sea or navigable rivers, such as the *portolanas* of the Middle Ages. Nothing comparable survives from Roman antiquity and it is doubtful that Roman sailors possessed such aids. Sailors followed the coast-line where possible, and were aided by verbal descriptions (*periploi*).[30] These represent a long, Greek tradition of geographic documents that list, in order, peoples, ports, and coastal landmarks, with approximate intervening distances, that sailors would find along a shore. Well-known texts that have survived are the *Periplus Ponti Euxini* ascribed to Skylax and dated to the fourth or third century BC;[31] the *Periplus Maris Erythraei*;[32] and the *Periplus Ponti Euxini*, written by Arrian in the mid-second century AD.[33] Like the later, Roman *itinera*, road descriptions over land, these are a typically linear way of looking at geography.

Scientific geography, in so far as it existed, was not used for practical purposes by historians or the authors of treatises on war and generalship (Onasandros, Frontinus, Polyaenus, Vegetius) and not in Polybius' work. Where Polybius comments on the qualities a general needs, he observes that it is best for him to be personally acquainted with the roads, the destination of his march, the nature of the terrain and the people he has to work with and rely upon. Next best it is to make a thorough inquiry and not to rely on accidental informants, but on reliable ones. In this connection he notes that one needs reliable guides,[34] but geography and cartography as fields of study are not mentioned. The general should have a theoretical knowledge of astronomy and geometry at a superficial level in order to establish the difference in length between day and night, necessary for the calculation of the distance traversed in a day's or a night's march.[35]

---

[30] B. Salway, 'Sea and River Travel in the Roman Itinerary Literature', in Talbert and Brodersen, *Space in the Roman World*, 43–96.

[31] P. Counillon, *Pseudo-Skylax: Le Périple du Pont-Euxin, Texte, traduction, commentaire philologique et historique* (Bordeaux, 2004); G. Shipley, *Pseudo-Skylax's Periplous: The Circumnavigation of the Inhabited World: Text, Translation and Commentary* (Exeter, 2011).

[32] L. Casson, *The Periplus Maris Erythraei: Text with Introduction, Translation, and Commentary* (Princeton, 1989).

[33] C. Muller, *Geographi Graeci Minores* 1.370–401 (repr. Hildesheim, 1990); A. Diller, *The Tradition of the Minor Greek Geographers* (Lancaster, 1952), 102–46.

[34] Polybius 9.14.1–5.

[35] Polybius 9.14.6; 9.15.

In general, Polybius says: 'These things are learnt by experience, by inquiry or by systematic investigation.'[36]

Influential geographic works were those of Pomponius Mela and the poem of Dionysius Periegetes. Both describe the shape of the land in words, following routes.[37] This again, fits the pattern already indicated: geography as texts rather than maps and illustrations, emphasizing a linear view, as experienced by the traveller along the road or coast.

Geographical knowledge was extremely limited for many regions. Although the idea that the earth was a globe goes back to the fifth century BC,[38] in the time of Plutarch, second-century-AD intellectuals were comfortably prepared to believe that the world looked like a dinner table. By the fifth century AD the cartographers of the Emperor Theodosius II believed that a map of the *totus orbis* would be more comprehensible if it could be made smaller.[39]

Castrametation

Castrametation is a practical application of geometry.[40] It is clear that surveying before the lay-out and construction of army camps and new towns and roads was common practice in the Roman Empire. It is not quite clear when the Roman technique of well-organized camp building developed. The earliest structures documented were found in Spain, near Numantia.[41] These go back to the middle of the second century BC. In roughly the same period Polybius gives an extensive description of the Roman camp and how troops would be accommodated in it.[42] This shows at least that the system had been developed by that time, but provides no more than a *terminus ante*. According to Frontinus the Romans learned how to design a camp by studying a camp of Pyrrhus in

---

[36] Polybius 9.14.1: Τῶν δὲ προειρημένων τὰ μὲν ἐκ τριβῆς, τὰ δ' ἐκ ἱστορίας, τὰ δὲ κατ' ἐμπειρίαν μεθοδικὴν θεωρεῖται.

[37] See K. Brodersen, *Studien zur römischen Raumerfassung* (Hildesheim, 1995), 78–81.

[38] It originated apparently in Pythagorean circles. The earliest reference is Plato, *Phaedo* 110b.

[39] Bekker-Nielsen, 'Academic Science and Warfare', 122–4, agrees that cartography did not make any great contribution to the military campaigns of the fourth to first centuries, but argues that these campaigns in themselves made a great contribution to the development of cartography. He provides no evidence for this claim, apart from the familiar existence of the work of Eratosthenes, Marinus, and Ptolemy and the map said to have been placed by Agrippa in the Porticus Vipsania.

[40] O. A. W. Dilke, *The Roman Land Surveyors: An Introduction to the Agrimensores* (Newton Abbot, 1971); Bekker-Nielsen, 'Academic Science and Warfare', 125–7.

[41] L. J. F. Keppie, *The Making of the Roman Army: From Republic to Empire* (London, 1984), 44–51 and references on 48.

[42] Polybius, 6.27–32; cf. Keppie, *Making of the Roman Army*, 36–51.

275 BC.[43] Plutarch, however, says that Pyrrhus looked at a Roman camp with admiration. These stories cannot both be right and even so it is not clear whether we have some sort of chronological indication here.[44] In any event, regular, orthogonal civilian towns were planned earlier than that, the best-known case being Miletus, planned by Hippodamus in the fifth century BC, and Roman Ostia (fourth century). Finally it must be admitted that geometric castrametation was an applied offshoot of academic geometry, but maybe it is going too far to see this as science contributing to warfare.

Medicine

As observed by G. E. R. Lloyd, both in China and, more especially, in Greece extensive efforts were made to systematize the key concepts in medical science, but also to accumulate medical experience.[45] Both in China and in Greece case histories of individual patients were regularly recorded. There was thus an essential difference in this respect between medicine and warfare, for, as has been observed above, the Roman imperial army did not draw lessons from past experience in war in any systematic manner.

Besides the compilation of past experience, a second avenue of increasing knowledge was dissection to investigate the bodies of humans and animals.[46] Aristotle was the first Greek to carry out animal dissection. Dissection and vivisection of humans started in Alexandria. It was controversial. Here too competition often was an important factor.

In the sphere of medicine Roman organization undoubtedly had a long-term impact and serious influence lasting till modern times.[47] The Roman forces were the first professional imperial army in history. The same is true for its medical service, both as an organization and in the technical sphere. In the Roman army medical services were established at a scale hitherto unknown. It was based on a fairly standardized empire-wide organization.

---

[43] Frontinus, *Stratagemata* 4.1.14. Livy 35.14.8, quotes Hannibal as saying Pyrrhus was the first to have his camps laid out by surveyors.

[44] Plutarch, *Pyrrhus* 16.4–5.

[45] Lloyd, *Disciplines in the Making*, ch. 4, 83. For Greek and Roman medicine: V. Nutton, *Ancient Medicine* (London, 2004).

[46] G. E. R. Lloyd, *The Revolutions of Wisdom* (Berkeley, CA, 1987), 160–7, points out that the study of anatomy originated in Greece with a distinctive programme.

[47] Ido Israelowich, *Patients and Healers in the High Roman Empire* (Baltimore, 2015), ch. 4. See also the older study: J. C. Wilmanns, *Der Sanitätsdienst im Römischen Reich: Eine sozialgeschichtliche Studie zum römischen Militärsanitätswesen nebst einer Prosopographie des Sanitätspersonals* (Hildesheim, 1995); C. F. Salazar, *The Treatment of War Wounds in Graeco-Roman Antiquity* (Leiden, 2000).

The supply of medicine was regulated between provinces; the military hospitals are a ubiquitous feature in Roman army installations, and treatment was based on commonly available handbooks, representing Hellenistic medical science. Greek army doctors are encountered in all parts of the Empire. However, as innovation this lies in the sphere of practical organization and practicalities, not scientific inquiry.

Science in War and Peace

We are faced with a paradox: the science that existed was not employed for gain in warfare as one might have expected and experience gained in war did not normally give the impetus to further scientific development that is taken for granted in modern times. There are at least two obvious reasons for this. First, there is the ancient value-system. Science and scholarship were highly regarded, up to a point, but, in spite of claims to the contrary, their practical application was not the work of gentlemen. Second, there is the absence of a clearly developed expectation of progress.

Values: Education of Upper Class

In his discussion of the qualities required for generalship Polybius advocates formal training for generals in tactics, astronomy, and geometry.[48] Astronomy makes it possible to calculate the length of the days and geometry the height of a town wall that one wants to scale. However, there is no indication that this advice was usually followed. Aratus' verse composition on astronomy, several times translated into Latin, was especially popular.[49] As regards the methods whereby a general acquires his skill Polybius lists (a) routine experience, (b) inquiry, and (c) experience systematically acquired.[50] Indeed, Roman education as described by Seneca the Elder or Quintilian was designed mainly to produce orators. Onasander has a chapter on the choice of a general.[51] He lists only character traits, not education,

---

[48] Polybius 9.12–20 and 11.8 with the comments by F. W. Walbank, *A Historical Commentary on Polybius*, 3 vols. (Oxford, 1957–79), II, 138–49. Cf. S. Mattern, *Rome and the Enemy: Imperial Strategy in the Principate* (Berkeley, CA, 1999), ch. 1, 15–16.

[49] Walbank, *Historical Commentary*, II, n. 51.

[50] Polybius 9.14.1; cf. 11.8 where he mentions (a) the study of history (ὑπομνήματα); (b) systematic instruction from experts, and (c) routine practice.

[51] Onasander, *Strategikos* 1.

training, or skills, apart from the need to be a good speaker. Emphasis was very much on literary and rhetoric skills.[52] Greek and Roman officers were amateurs, raised as gentlemen or, in Rome, as senators and members of the equestrian class. The most important subject taught was rhetoric, or the art of persuasion. Literature, mostly poetry, was a major topic.[53] Furthermore, much of the available geographical literature had a rhetorical and propagandistic character.[54] Geography was not a subject in its own right, but a part of geometry, itself regarded as unimportant, and so were arithmetic and astronomy. It is important also to observe that most professional subjects were taught through apprenticeship: that is how one became a lawyer or a medical doctor.

The pre-modern world did not have the senior commanding officers as familiar in modern armies, risen through the ranks. Professionally trained at a staff college, senior generals are appointed by the government. This, however, is a recent phenomenon. Only in the course of the nineteenth century did the view achieve recognition that would-be officers needed to be specially educated in military or semi-military institutions *before* obtaining a commission, whereas previously a haphazard system of apprenticeship *after* commissioning had been preferred.[55] Before the Napoleonic Wars armies and navies can scarcely be said to have been led by professionals as that term came to be understood in the nineteenth century. Officers were for the most part mercenaries or aristocrats: the former tended to view war as a business, the latter as a hobby. Not surprisingly, wealth, birth, and interest played a major part in determining advancement to high rank. Except in the artillery and engineers, the British army retained the system of purchasing commissions up to and including the rank of lieutenant

---

[52] The literature on ancient education is extensive, but clearly focuses consistently and systematically on literary, philosophical, rhetorical, and social topics. Mathematics and science is normally avoided. See the old work: P. Monroe, *Sourcebook for the History of Education for the Greek and Roman Period* (Basingstoke, 1901); H. Marrou, *History of Education in Antiquity* (Madison, WI, 1956); H. Marrou, *L'Histoire de l'éducation dans l'antiquité* (Paris, 1948); R. Barrow, *Greek and Roman Education* (London, 1976); Y. L. Too (ed.), *Education in Greek and Roman Antiquity* (Leiden, 2001); E. J. Watts, *City and School in Late Antique Athens and Alexandria* (Berkeley, CA, 2006); M. Joyal, I. McDougall, and J. C. Yardley, *Greek and Roman Education: A Sourcebook,* Routledge Sourcebooks for the Ancient World (London and New York, 2009): recent, but limited in scope; J. Yardley, *Greek and Roman Education: A Sourcebook* (Abingdon, 2009). Also: R. Cribiore, *Gymnastics of the Mind: Greek Education in Hellenistic and Roman Egypt* (Princeton, 2001); D. L. Clark, *Rhetoric in Greco-Roman Education* (Westport, CT, 1977; 1957).

[53] Brodersen, *Studien zur römischen Raumerfassung.*

[54] Mattern, *Rome and the Enemy,* ch. 2.

[55] B. Bond, *The Victorian Army and the Staff College 1854–1914* (London, 1972), 8.

colonel until 1871. In Rome there was no military academy; there was no staff college where senior officers learned the trade.[56] No ancient army underwent the process of professionalization that took place in all armies in the nineteenth century. Significantly, Clausewitz (1780–1831) nowhere mentions technology in his major work *On War*.

There existed among Roman historians a notion that a career pattern could be recognized among the Roman senatorial aristocracy showing that some of its members were singled out fairly early in their career as talented officers, suitable for the senior positions in the provincial army, which they subsequently obtained, following a series of particularly demanding military commands. However, this view has been criticized and is not now commonly accepted.[57] In Rome we can certainly observe an integration of military, intellectual, and political leadership, but this definitely did not include scientists and engineers – even if some leaders chose to write about technical subjects, such as Frontinus who wrote about aqueducts,[58] about military science (a treatise that has been lost), and about stratagems.[59] In this connection it is also important to note that there was no general staff, no military high command in the Roman Empire.[60] This too is a modern notion.

All this had an impact on the value-system of the preparation for war and its conduct. If wars are led by aristocratic amateurs that will influence the manner in which it is fought. The commanders did not receive an elementary education in the sciences, so they did not look to science for a solution for their problems. Conversely, the scientists had no impact on the planning and conduct of wars. They themselves were not usually much interested in applied science anyway. This state of affairs also had a serious impact on tactics and strategy.

---

[56] J. B. Campbell, 'Teach Yourself How to be a General', *Journal of Roman Studies* 77 (1987): 13–29. The title of this article itself recognizes that there was no institutionalized officer training in Rome. The author emphasizes the importance that military handbooks may have had, given the lack of institutionalized instruction.

[57] J. B. Campbell, 'Who were the "Viri Militares"', *Journal of Roman Studies* 65 (1975): 11–31 with reference to the scholars who advanced the idea of military specialization among Roman aristocrats, E. Birley, R. Syme, and G. Alföldy on p. 11, n. 1.

[58] Frontinus, *De aqueductu urbis Romae*, ed. with introduction and commentary by R. H. Rodgers (Cambridge, 2004).

[59] Frontinus, *Strategemata*, ed. R. I. Ireland (Leipzig, 1990).

[60] For the idea that it existed: G. Alföldy, 'Die Generalität des römischen Heeres', *Bonner Jahrbücher* 169 (1969): 233–46, reprinted in his *Römische Heeresgeschichte: Beitrage 1962–1985* (Amsterdam, 1987), 3–18.

The Idea of Progress

At another conceptual level it could be argued that the systematic pursuit of science can only be realized if, as in recent centuries, it is driven by a consistent and firm belief in the long-term progress of human society. If we define this as a consistent belief that humankind is evolving in a positive sense, in a long-term, linear process of improvement and advance, this hardly existed in antiquity. This has been shown in a classic study by E. R. Dodds against the theories advanced by Ludwig Edelstein.[61] Dodds agrees with Edelstein that the idea was not wholly foreign to antiquity, but argues that only during a limited period in the fifth century was it widely accepted by the educated public at large. Thereafter all the major philosophical schools were more or less hostile to the idea of linear progress. Where it was accepted, this is found in the works of scientists or works on science. The age of Augustus saw a short period of a state-sponsored belief in progress. Thus Vergil's Roman Empire had no boundaries and was to be eternal.[62] The very notion of a Golden Age, of course, excludes an idea of linear progress.[63] It is therefore no coincidence that Hesiod and later pessimistic authors hold the Golden Age to be ignorant of navigation. According to these views then, decline and dissolution are inevitable and communication between peoples reinforces these destructive processes.[64]

[61] The literature on progress in antiquity is extensive: L. Edelstein, *The Idea of Progress in Classical Antiquity* (Baltimore, 1967), argues that the idea of progress did exist throughout antiquity; this is denied by E. R. Dodds, *The Ancient Concept of Progress* (Oxford, 1973), ch. 1, 1–25. A different view, briefly stated and not really argued, is represented by E. Gabba, 'Literature', in M. Crawford (ed.), *Sources for Ancient History: Studies in the Uses of Historical Evidence* (Cambridge, 1983), 7. Gabba asserts that there was an assumption of linear progress in the past, leading up to the present, which forms the highest point in development. This is to be followed by decline and there is no prospect of a further growth in power or of a higher cultural level. It is hard to see what the basis is for the first of these assumptions other than, perhaps, the opening statements of Herodotus and Thucydides in their histories. W. Den Boer, 'Progress in the Greece of Thucydides', *Mededelingen der Koninklijke Nederlandse Akademie van Wetenschappen, Afd. Letterkunde*, NS 40.2 (1970), again discussed the topic. Den Boer, it seems, tries to make too much of his differences with Dodds. Dodds essentially says there was no idea of progress and is cautious in presenting his conclusions. Den Boer emphasizes Dodd's caution as if he really argues *for* an idea of progress in antiquity. See also the brief observations by P. Veyne, '*Humanitas:* Les Romains et les autres', in A. Giardina (ed.), *L'homme romain* (Paris, 1992), 421–59, esp. 423. See further references in W. Nippel, 'Progress, idea of', *Brill's New Pauly*. Antiquity volumes ed. H. Cancik and H. Schneider (Leiden, 2010: Brill Online).

[62] Vergil, *Aen.* 1.278: *ego nec metas rerum nec tempora pono: imperium sine fine dedi.*

[63] The Prometheus myth, as related by Hesiod, *Theogony* 510–616; *Works and Days* 42–89, also precludes progress or at least implies that the Gods do not wish men to possess arts and crafts. Aeschylus, *Prometheus Vinctus* has a different message, cf. Dodds, *Ancient Concept*, 5–7, 31–43.

[64] Cf. Isaac, *Invention of Racism*, 108, 243, 304, 310–11.

The belief in progress is usually considered the culmination of eighteenth-century thought, even if it is true that, at the same time, a notion of pessimism became a focus of attention for some Enlightenment authors.[65] The great doctrine of human progress was produced by Nicolas Condorcet (1733–94), who wrote his *Sketch for a Historical Picture of the Progress of the Human Spirit* while hiding from the French revolutionary authorities in 1793–4.[66] It contains precisely those elements relevant for the present study, for Condorcet argues that expanding achievements of the natural and social sciences necessarily lead to an ever more just world of individual freedom, material affluence, and moral compassion. No less relevant for us is that Condorcet's doctrine is not based on any classical set of ideas or theory. When published it was thoroughly original and modern.

The opposite is true for two other theories, fashionable in the Enlightenment and afterwards: the idea of decline and the idea of environmental determinism. Both have their roots firmly in Graeco-Roman thought. The former had an influential proponent in Bossuet (1627–1704), who examined the decline of the successor states formed from the empire of Alexander – a decline supposedly rooted, in the case of Syria, in softness and luxury.[67] The decadence of Rome he treats at greater length. Thanks to Bossuet the rise and fall of empires began to receive attention.[68]

Environmental determinism, combined with the notion of cycles in the existence of nations, their rise and decline, was widely accepted. It is encountered in the work of Bodin (1530–96), but more strongly emphasized by Saint-Evremond (1610–1703).[69] A series of thinkers preceding Montesquieu (1698–1755), but postdating Bodin (1530–96), were interested in climatic determinism, but Saint-Evremond was the first to emphasize it seriously. Also, Saint-Evremond accepted the ancient ideas regarding the rise and decline of nations. For present purposes it is essential that such ideas leave no room for a notion of progress, assured, and reinforced by the advance of science. To conclude this attempt at interpretation: whatever the contribution and role of Graeco-Roman science in antiquity and afterwards, the ideology, social attitudes, and basic outlook on life of that period all prevented science from playing the central role in life that is so obvious in our age.

[65] H. Vyverberg, *Historical Pessimism in the French Enlightenment* (Cambridge, 1958), 1.

[66] *Esquisse d'un tableau historique des progrès de l'esprit humain* (1795).

[67] See Isaac, *Invention of Racism*, 335–50, for precisely those ideas, advanced in Roman authors (and thus taken over by Bossuet).

[68] Vyverberg, *Historical Pessimism*, 20. Bossuet thus preceded Gibbon who conceived the idea to write his *Decline and Fall* in 1764. Note that Bossuet influenced Gibbon in various ways.

[69] For environmental determinism in antiquity and its influence on the authors of the Enlightenment, see Isaac, *Invention of Racism*, 9–13, 102–8. For Saint-Evremond, Vyverberg, *Historical Pessimism*, 32.

CHAPTER 5

Core–Periphery Notions

Introduction

The terms 'core and periphery' have become a household concept in recent years. It is therefore useful to keep in mind that we are dealing with a specific model that forms the basis and point of reference for the use of those terms. This is the work of Immanuel Wallerstein developed at extraordinary length in three books perhaps more often cited than actually studied.[1] An alarming lack of clarity has spread regarding the meaning of the terms and the modalities of the approach.

This chapter will briefly describe the constituent elements of the original model and the manner in which students of the Roman Empire have attempted to apply it. However, I will begin with a brief discussion of Greek and Roman images of the geography of the world and Roman views of the geography of their empire, to see to what extent this may have affected modern views of it, notably those dealing with 'core and periphery'. My argument is that those who claim to follow Wallerstein are using a model that is not suitable for the study of ancient empires and therefore freely adapt it to their needs without making this sufficiently clear. Next it will be argued that the model is mostly inappropriate for the study of ancient empires and, when applied, leads to confusion rather than deeper understanding. Then I will mention another model, developed more recently by Peregrine Horden and Nicholas Purcell in their major influential work *The Corrupting Sea*, where the proposition is offered that the Roman Empire has to be viewed as consisting of interconnected

---

A partial and modified version of this paper was read in February–March 2010 at a conference: 'Contact Zones of Empires in Europe and Japan', Fukuoda, Japan (ESF – Frontier Science Conference). It was then published in *Scripta Classica Israelica* 30 (2011): 63–82.

[1] Three of his works are particularly relevant: I. Wallerstein, *The Modern World-System: Capitalist Agriculture and the Origins of the European World-Economy in the Sixteenth Century* (New York and London, 1974); *The Capitalist World-Economy* (Cambridge and Paris, 1979); *Unthinking Social Science: The Limits of Nineteenth-Century Paradigms* (Cambridge, 1991).

'micro-ecologies', or 'virtual islands'.[2] Rather than dealing with all of the
eight hundred pages of the book, I will discuss one concrete example of
the application of this model and suggest some possible modifications and
additional considerations.

Ancient Greek Views

In the archaic period Ionic geography assumed that the world was circular in shape and surrounded by the legendary river Ocean.[3] This view
was criticized by Herodotus, who ridiculed the idea of a river surrounding a perfectly circular world.[4] Herodotus generally preferred an empirical
approach, trying to base himself on facts, taking account of what was actually known in his days about distant peoples. He accepted the concept of a
world population (οἰκουμένη) with Greeks in its centre and distant peoples
living in remote regions (ἐσχατιαί) encircling this world. There are clear
elements of environmental determinism in his approach:

> It seems as if the extreme regions of the earth were blessed by nature with
> the most excellent production, just in the same way that Greece (in the
> centre) enjoys a climate more excellently tempered than any other country.[5]

These remote regions, 'which surround the rest of the world and enclose
it within, seem to possess the things we consider most lovely and rarest'.[6]
Accordingly the centre and the periphery are the best parts. While the centre, of course, is populated by Greeks, the distant peoples living near the
borders of the *oikoumenē* are idealized and have mostly legendary traits.
Interestingly, Herodotus criticizes the Persians for their ethnocentric, chauvinist views, 'honouring most the peoples nearest to themselves … and
holding in the least honour those dwelling farthest'.[7] It has been pointed out

[2] P. Horden and N. Purcell, *The Corrupting Sea: A Study of Mediterranean History* (Oxford, 2000).
[3] J. S. Romm, *The Edges of the Earth in Ancient Thought: Geography, Exploration and Fiction* (Princeton, 1992), 9–31.
[4] Hdt. 2.23; 4.8; 4.36–45; cf. D. Asheri, A. Lloyd and A. Corcella, *A Commentary on Herodotus Books I–IV* (Oxford, 2007), 256, 608–9; Romm, *Edges of the Earth*, 33–41.
[5] Hdt. 3.106: Αἱ δ᾿ ἐσχατιαί κως τῆς οἰκεομένης τὰ κάλλιστα ἔλαχον, κατά περ ἡ Ἑλλὰς τὰς ὥρας πολλόν τι κάλλιστα κεκρημένας ἔλαχε. See also: 3.114–16. Cf. Asheri *et al.*, *Commentary on Herodotus*, 496–7, 500, 608–9; Romm, *Edges of the Earth*, 38–9. For Herodotus on the Ethiopians: Romm, *Edges of the Earth*, 54–60; for his description of the northern Hyperboraeans: 65–7.
[6] Hdt. 3.116: Αἱ δὲ ὦν ἐσχατιαί οἴκασι, περικληίουσαι τὴν ἄλλην χώρην καὶ ἐντὸς ἀπέργουσαι, τὰ κάλλιστα δοκέοντα ἡμῖν εἶναι καὶ σπανιώτατα ἔχειν αὐταί
[7] Hdt. 1.134; cf. Romm, *Edges of the Earth*, 54–5. Herodotus then continues to describe a hierarchical organization in the Median Empire which is imaginary: cf. Asheri *et al.*, *Commentary on Herodotus*, 169. If this is imaginary all of the chapter may not be reliable with its report about Persian chauvinism.

that two opposing approaches may be recognized in Greek literature: the first idealizing the centre and disparaging the periphery, the second doing the reverse. Herodotus appears to represent a third possibility: idealizing both the centre and the periphery.[8]

It will be obvious that there is no trace here of the modern model which sees a direct economic relationship between the centre and periphery.

A century later such ideas found expression in Aristotle's claim that the Greeks, because of their ideal situation in between the cold lands of Europe and the gentle climate of Asia, live in the best part of the world and should therefore be capable of governing every other people – if only they could achieve political unity.[9] We see here elements of environmental determinism in combination with geography and ethnography formulating an imperialist ideology which was later taken over by Roman authors. Whether Roman authors also speak in terms of a core and periphery is another matter.

Roman Views

Appian (*Praef.* 1.1) gives a broad and general description of the geography of the Roman Empire:

> Intending to write the history of the Romans, I have deemed it necessary to begin with the boundaries of the nations under their sway. They are as follows:[10] In the ocean, the major part of those who inhabit the British Isles. Then entering the Mediterranean by the Pillars of Hercules and circumnavigating the same we find under their rule all the islands and the mainland washed by that sea.

Then he describes, going around the Mediterranean counter clockwise, the peoples living on the coast and those farther inland, starting with the coast of North Africa:

> The nomad tribes whom the Romans call Numidians ... other Africans. Beyond Egypt there is Ethiopia. Beyond Syria-Palaestina is part of the Arab regions. Beyond Phoenician territory there is Coele-Syria, and the parts stretching from the sea as far inland as the river Euphrates, namely Palmyra and the sandy country round about ...

---

[8] Romm, *Edges of the Earth*, 38–9 and 46–7. For Herodotus on the Ethiopians: 54–60; for his description of the northern Hyperboraeans: 65–7.

[9] Aristotle, *Politics* 1327b. The idea was later taken over and applied to Italy by Roman authors: Vitruvius 6.2; Strabo 6.4.1 (ca. 286); Vergil, *Aeneid* 1.2; cf. B. Isaac, *The Invention of Racism in Classical Antiquity* (Princeton, 2004), 70–1, 82–7.

[10] Τὴν Ῥωμαϊκὴν ἱστορίαν ἀρχόμενος συγγράφειν ἀναγκαῖον ἡγησάμην προτάξαι τοὺς ὅρους, ὅσων ἐθνῶν ἄρχουσι Ῥωμαῖοι. εἰσὶ δὲ οἵδε·.

This should suffice for present purposes. The Empire is described as if it were an oval dinner table.

Does Appian, in his first sentence, mean boundaries, as the Loeb translation has it, or territories? From the text it is clear that he must mean 'territories' for he does not, in fact, indicate any boundaries or borders. He does not describe the boundaries of the Empire, but he lists its subject peoples and a few seas (note: Syria-Palaestina, a region, but 'Phoenicians', the people, and Coele-Syria, again a region). He mentions first the territories which encompass the Empire along the sea and then those further inland. That is to say: he first lists the peoples and the seas under Roman control: the Mediterranean, North Sea, and Black Sea. Then he lists the outer circle, the peoples and a few features that are not contiguous with any of those seas: these include the river Euphrates, the Caucasus, the rivers Rhine and Danube. By way of exception he mentions that some of the Celts across the Rhine and some of the Getae across the Danube, 'called Dacians', are subject to Roman rule. He does not mention any frontier of the Empire.

Essentially the empire is seen as roughly three concentric circles: Rome in the middle, then the Mediterranean and Black Sea, with peoples around it, and finally the peoples, regions, and natural features farther removed from the Mediterranean. These form the outer circle. Generally speaking, the farther away peoples are, the less they are worth incorporating into the Empire. For instance, Appian says: 'Crossing the Northern Ocean to Britain, which is an island greater than a large continent, they have taken possession of the better and larger part (i.e. the South), not caring for the remainder (i.e. the North). Indeed, the part they do hold is not very profitable to them' (*Praef.* 5). Another way of looking at this description is to note that the first part essentially represents a traditional *periplus*, a geographical document that lists, in order, the ports, peoples, and coastal landmarks, with approximate intervening distances, that the sailors would find along a shore.[11] Appian quite explicitly gives his description the form of a voyage along coasts. Parts of the empire that have no coastal sections or rivers as points of reference are located in relation to those that have.

---

[11] Well-known examples of texts that have survived are the *Periplus of the Black Sea* by Pseudo-Skylax (fourth–third century BC), the *Periplus Maris Erythraei* (mid-first century AD), and the *Periplus Ponti Euxini* by Arrian, second century AD. On this manner of describing the world, see: C. Nicolet, *Space, Geography, and Politics in the Early Roman Empire* (Ann Arbor, 1991), 58.

At the end of this description we recognize the well-known image: 'They surround the empire with great armies and they garrison the whole stretch of land and sea like a single stronghold.'[12]

There is, then, the vague notion of a cordon around the outer circle that functions like a wall around a city. This may have given some modern authors the misguided idea that a model of core and periphery is somehow recognized also in ancient texts. It is not. Many Roman texts differentiate between the various remote parts of the Empire. There are a number of authors, mostly Greek, who resisted imperial expansion in regions which, they thought, were not profitable and worth having. One encounters such statements in the work of Strabo, Appian, already mentioned, and Cassius Dio.[13] They were against wars engendered by 'a quarrel in a far-away country between people of whom we know nothing', as emphasized by a British prime minister in 1938, a politician who, of course, had been well trained in the Classics.[14] The point, then, is that some far-away countries are not worth conquering, but others are. There is no sense of a coherent outer zone. This is far from a view of the Empire as consisting of a core and periphery. Appian's description very much resembles the ideas of Aristides, who also speaks in terms of a circular structure, defended by the Roman army, as is discussed below. We have here undoubtedly the equivalent of the Latin *orbis*.[15]

The next idea, prevalent in Roman authors, that has to be considered here is related, but represents a shift in emphasis. It is the claim that the Roman Empire encompasses the entire inhabited world, the *oikoumenē*. According to Vogt it is Greek, not Roman, in origin. Of course, *oikoumenē* is a Greek term, in frequent use already in the work of Herodotus.[16] It is true also that traditionally there was a sense that the *oikoumenē*, seen as an island surrounded by the Ocean, was thought to be somehow circular in shape. Yet Vogt's precise statement is implausible. It is worthwhile briefly to trace the development of the concept. A genuinely Greek idea was

---

[12] Appian, *Praefatio* 28: τήν τε ἀρχὴν ἐν κύκλῳ περικάθηνται μεγάλοις στρατοπέδοις καὶ φυλάσσουσι τὴν τοσήνδε γῆν καὶ θάλασσαν ὥσπερ χωρίον.

[13] Cf. B. Isaac, *The Limits of Empire: The Roman Army in the East*, revised edn (Oxford, 1992), 26–8, 388–9.

[14] This is not to suggest that Neville Chamberlain, at Rugby School, read the texts of Strabo and Appian where these authors argue that Britain is a far-away place, worth subjecting only partly or not at all.

[15] Cf. J. Vogt, 'Orbis Romanus', in *Orbis: Ausgewählte Schriften zur Geschichte des Altertums* (Freiburg, 1960), 151–71 at 152–6 and 159. See on this: P. A. Brunt, 'Laus Imperii', in P. D. A. Garnsey and C. R. Whittaker (eds.), *Imperialism in the Ancient World* (Cambridge, 1978), 162–78.

[16] For *oikoumenē* in Herodotus' work: Romm, *Edges of the Earth*, 37.

indeed that of the world having an exact centre: the *omphalos*, the navel of the world, located in Delphi.[17] This was later taken over by Jews and Christians who transferred the centre and navel of the earth to Jerusalem.[18] *Oikoumenē* is the Greek equivalent of the Latin *orbis terrarum*. This then is relevant for the present chapter.

Polybius claimed that by 167 BC the whole, or virtually the whole *oikoumenē*, or its known parts, had come under Roman dominion. However, this does not mean that the idea as such was Greek, as Vogt seems to imply.[19] Polybius echoes a Roman view of the Empire.[20] Polybius, indeed, emphasizes that there had been empires in the past, but the Romans were the first 'to subjugate almost the whole inhabited world'.[21] Rome, says Polybius, demonstrated her superiority over Alexander and the Macedonians by her successes in the West over 'peoples who were not even known' to the Macedonians.[22] We may add that Polybius certainly knew better: he was aware that eastwards the Roman Empire definitely did not cover the entire inhabited world. He may have meant there was no serious rival to Rome, but it should be obvious that Polybius' insistence reflects a Roman political ideology rather than facts believed to be true. Thus, it may be repeated, we are dealing with a Roman, not a Greek idea.

This is particularly clear from what may be an early Latin instance. Livy attributes to Ti. Gracchus the remark that '(L. Cornelius Scipio Asiaticus) had spread the domination of the Roman people to the extreme confines of the earth'.[23] This may represent the language of Livy in the age of Augustus, rather than that of Ti. Gracchus in the early second century BC. It is a mere phrase when attributed to a speaker in the time of Scipio and was known

---

[17] C. Auffarth, 'Omphalos', in H. Cancik and H. Schneider (eds.), *Brill's New Pauly*, online edn (2010). See also K. Brodersen, *Studien zur römischen Raumerfassung* (Hildesheim, 1995), 110–33: Nichtkartographische Raumerfassung.

[18] P. S. Alexander, 'Jerusalem as the *Omphalos* of the World: On the History of a Geographic Concept', in L. I. Levine, *Jerusalem: Its Sanctity and Centrality to Judaism, Christianity, and Islam* (New York, 1999), 104–19.

[19] Admittedly, Hdt. 7.38 attributes to Xerxes boastful claims that, after conquering Greece, the Persians will bring all of humanity under their yoke. That, given the context, indeed represents no more than the Persian monarch's *hybris* as attributed to him by Herodotus.

[20] Romm, *Edges of the Earth*, 122, observes: 'In fact all three of the principal geographers of the early Empire – Strabo, who wrote in Greek but was nonetheless Roman in outlook, Pomponius Mela, and Pliny the Elder – seem bent on supporting this claim by showing that the *oikoumenē* (or in Roman terms the *orbis terrarum*) had at last been completely circumnavigated.' *Rhet. Her.* 4.13 (mid-first century BC) may be the earliest extant instance in Latin.

[21] Polybius 1.2.7: Ῥωμαῖοί γε μὴν οὐ τινὰ μέρη, σχεδὸν δὲ πᾶσαν πεποιημένοι τὴν οἰκουμένην ὑπήκοον αὐτοῖς, Cf. 1.1.5: ἐπὶ κρατηθέντα σχεδὸν ἅπαντα τὰ κατὰ τὴν οἰκουμένην.

[22] Polyb. 1.2.4-6. See also 3.1.4–5; 6.50.6; 15.9–5.

[23] Livy 38.60.5: *[L. Scipio] imperium populi Romani propagaverit in ultimos terrarum fines.*

to be a remarkable exaggeration, then and afterwards. After all, Scipio may have subjugated 'the wealthiest king in the world' (Antiochus III), but it was well known at the time that there were peoples farther to the East.

In the first century BC Cicero repeatedly contends that Pompey and Caesar had made the boundaries of the Empire coterminous with the *orbis terrarum*.[24] Pompey is said to have made the same boast for himself on a monument in honour of his deeds in Asia: he 'extended the frontiers of the Empire to the limits of the earth'.[25] Cicero regularly speaks casually as if Rome already ruled all peoples or the whole *orbis terrarum*.[26] This conception also appears in a rather bombastic preamble to a consular law of 58 BC: *imperio ampli]ficato [p]ace per orb[em terrarum confecta*.[27] In the time of the second triumvirate Cornelius Nepos could assert that Octavian and Antony both wanted to be the ruler, 'not only of the city of Rome, but of the whole world'.[28] In Virgil's *Aeneid* the walls of Rome figuratively enclose the Roman Empire.[29] Note further Ovid's claim: 'To other peoples was given land with fixed boundaries. The extent of the city of Rome is the same as that of the world.'[30] Writing about Tiberius, Velleius Paterculus says: 'By this decree the command of almost the entire world (*orbis*) was being entrusted to one man.'[31] Also in the first century AD the astrologer and poet Manilius writes: 'Italy belongs to the Balance, her rightful sign: beneath it Rome and her sovereignty of the world (*orbis*) were founded.'[32] A related theme is found in a Stoic tradition represented by Cicero who speaks of 'those who regard the entire world as one city'.[33]

---

[24] Cicero, *In Catilinam* 3.26; *Pro Sestio* 67; *De Provinciis Consularibus* 30, 33; *Pro Balbo* 64. Cf. Brunt, 'Laus Imperii', 162. Nicolet, *Space, Geography, and Politics*, 31 with n. 17, notes that *orbis* by itself, without *terrarum* dates from the Augustan period.

[25] Diodorus Siculus 40.4 (= *Const. Exc.* 40.4, 405–6): τὰ ὅρια τῆς ἡγεμονίας τοῖς ὅροις τῆς γῆς προσβιβάσας. The *oikoumenē* is not mentioned in the parallel text Pliny, *NH* 7.97–8; cf. Nicolet, *Space, Geography, and Politics*, 31–3.

[26] For instance: *De oratore* 1.14. Alternatively, Cicero speaks of Rome's power over all peoples, *In Verrem* II 4.81; *De Lege Agraria* 2.22; *De domo sua* 90; *Planc.* 11; *Phil.* 6.7.19. Cf. E. Bréguet, 'Urbi et Orbi', in J. Bibauw (ed.), *Hommages à Marcel Renard*, Collection Latomus 101 (Brussels, 1969), 140–52; Brunt, 'Laus Imperii', 168.

[27] *CIL* I² 2500.

[28] Nepos, *Att.* 20.5: ... *cum se uterque principem non solum urbis Romae sed orbis terrarum esse cuperet*. Also: 3.3: *in ea urbe in qua domicilium orbis terrarum esset imperii*.

[29] *Aen.* 8.714–15. See P. R. Hardie, *Virgil's Aeneid: Cosmos and Imperium* (Oxford, 1986), 364: 'The association of city and empire is basic to the whole conception of the Shield of Aeneas ...'

[30] Ovid, *Fasti* 2.683–4: *gentibus est aliis tellus data limite certo: Romanae spatium est urbis et orbis idem*. For other instances of this theme: F. Bömer's edition of the *Fasti* (*Die Fasten*, 2 vols., Heidelberg, 1957), II, 17 and 131–2. Other relevant passages in the *Fasti*: 1.284; 517; 529; 600; 616; 712; 717; 2.130; 136–7.

[31] Velleius Paterculus 2.31.2: *Quo scito paene totius terrarum orbis imperium uni viro deferebatur*.

[32] Manilius, *Astronomica* 773–5: *Libra ... qua condita Roma orbis et imperium retinet discrimina rerum*.

[33] Cic. *Paradoxa* 2.18.5: *qui omnem orbem terrarum unam urbem esse ducunt*.

Seneca has a related image: 'The very reason for our magnanimity in not shutting ourselves up within the walls of one city but in going forth into intercourse with the whole earth, and in claiming the world as our country, was that we might have a wider field for our virtue.'[34] Florus (writing at an uncertain date in the reigns of Hadrian to Marcus Aurelius) asserts: 'So widely have they extended their arms throughout the world (*orbis*), that those who read of their exploits are learning the history, not of a single people, but of the human race.'[35] The idea is still encountered in the fifth century in the work of Rutilius Namatianus: Rome 'has united all peoples into one nation and made all the world one city'.[36]

It is true, as noted by Brunt, that *orbis terrarum* was also used in a restricted sense of those parts of the world that formed the Roman political universe.[37] However, this is less frequently encountered than the use of the expression in a universal sense in general. Altogether more important is the fact that the numerous authors who make these claims of Roman universal rule knew it to be false. Nobody was unaware of the existence of an independent power, Parthia. The presence of numerous independent Germanic tribes beyond the Rhine, before the end of the first century BC and after AD 9 was familiar and so was the presence of numerous farther-away peoples. In the Augustan period Pompeius Trogus says the Romans and Parthians had divided the world between them.[38] An important aspect of this is that East–West distances are consistently underestimated by Greeks and Romans.[39] In Central Europe, for instance, it seems that only after the loss of Varus' army in AD 9 did the Romans begin to appreciate the size of the population they would have to keep under control if they wanted to hold Germany east of the Rhine.[40] This is clear, too, from Caesar's plans for an eastern campaign as described by

---

[34] Seneca, *De tranquillitate animi* 4.4: *Ideo magno animo nos non unius urbis moenibus clusimus, sed in totius orbis commercium emisimus patriamque nobis mundum professi sumus, ut liceret latiorem uirtuti campum dare.* Cf. Bréguet, 'Urbi et Orbi', 150.

[35] Flor. I. Praef.: *Deinceps ad Caesarem Augustum centum et quinquaginta anni, quibus totum orbem pacavit.* Note also: *ILS* 212: *gloria prolati imperi ultra Oceanum.*

[36] Rut. Namat. 65–6: *Dumque offers victis proprii consortia iuris / urbem fecisti quod prius orbis erat.* This refers to the grant of citizenship to the inhabitants of the provinces.

[37] Brunt, 'Laus Imperii', 323, n. 35: *SEG* 1.335; cf. Cic. *Att.* 4.1.7 (consular law of 57 *de annona*); Polyb. 1.1.5; 1.3.10; 3.1.4; 6.50.6; for his true meaning: 1.3.9; 15.9.5 with 2.14.7 and 4.2.2.

[38] Justinus, *Epitome* 41.1.1: *Parthi, penes quos uelut diuisione orbis cum Romanis facta nunc Orientis imperium est* ... Strabo advances a similar idea: 11.9.2 (515); 17.3.24 (840), but for a different view: 6.4.2 (288), where the Parthians are described as a dependent kingdom.

[39] This phenomenon goes far back in Greek geographical ideas as shown by M. Finkelberg, 'The Geography of *Prometheus Vinctus*', *RhM* 141 (1998): 119–42.

[40] C. M. Wells, *The German Policy of Augustus* (Oxford, 1972), 7–8.

Plutarch. Caesar is said to have intended to conquer Parthia, India, and subsequently Scythia and Germany.[41]

To sum up: two somewhat varying ideas are conveyed by these passages. One is the claim that the city of Rome rules the entire world, a world that is circular or elliptic in shape. This is found in the work of Cicero, in Pompey's victory inscription, in a legal source, and in the works of Nepos, Velleius, Manilius, and Florus. The second idea is that Rome, the city, and the entire world – round or elliptic – are one and the same. This is encountered in the work of Vergil, Ovid, Cicero, Seneca, and Rutilius Namatianus, cited above, and in that of Aristides, discussed below.

While these ideas are common in Latin authors, there are no parallels for such statements in Greek literature, apart from Greek authors strongly influenced by Roman concepts such as Polybius and Strabo. It is true that there are Greek precedents of seeing the world in the shape of a shield and having an *omphalos*, a navel, in the exact centre.[42] However, the Roman idea of the Empire, or the city as covering the entire circular world, the *orbis terrarum*, is a new concept. The world is circular in shape, but there is no centre and no periphery, for the two are in fact the same.

The idea of the identity of city and empire is prominent in Aristides' speech *Regarding Rome* which, of course, attempts to praise Rome in Roman terms: 'What a city is to its boundaries and its territories, so this city (of Rome) is to the whole inhabited world, as if it had been designated its common town'.[43]

The implication is that the Empire, and, with it, the entire inhabited world, is Rome's territory. Thus here again we see the conflation of city and empire. Note also the following passage in Aristides' work: 'Since the government is universal and like that of a single city ...'[44] This immediately

[41] Plutarch, *Caesar* 58.3; cf. Nicolaus of Damascus (Jacoby, *FGH* 90F 130.95). See on this: R. Syme, *The Provincial at Rome and Rome and the Balkans 80* BC–AD *14* (Exeter, 1999), 174–92, ch. 4: 'Caesar's Designs on Dacia and Parthia'. Syme discards the reports on a planned eastern campaign and argues that Caesar meant to go to Dacia. This does not concern us here. It suffices that Nicolaus and Plutarch, two well-informed authors, and, one may presume, their readers, found it credible that Caesar seriously contemplated such a campaign.

[42] Romm, *Edges of the Earth*, 14. The first Greek maps of the world portrayed the earth as a disk of land surrounded by Ocean: Agathemerus 1.1, in C. Müller *GGM* 2.471; Hdt. 4.36, and further references in Romm, 14, n. 14. In fact the similarity between these visual and verbal images was remarked as early as the second century AD by Crates of Mallos (reference in Romm, 14, n. 15) who called Achilles' shield a *kosmou mimēma* or 'image of the world'; the parallel thereafter became a commonplace among Stoic geographers and critics, for instance Strabo 1.1.7 (ca. 4): 'Again in the story of the making of the arms of Achilles, Homer places Oceanus in a circle round the outer edge of the shield of Achilles.'

[43] Aristides, *Or.* 61. Trans. C. A. Behr (Amsterdam, 1968).

[44] Aristid. *Or.* 65 (trans. Behr).

reminds the modern historian of the fact that Rome, to some extent, always remained a city whose magistrates also ruled the Empire.

In this light must be seen also Aristides' statement about the army:

> You (i.e. Rome) believed that it was base and inconsistent with your other conceptions to put walls about the city itself, as it were concealing it or fleeing your subjects, as if some master should show himself in fear of his own slaves. However, you did not neglect walls, but you put these about your empire, not your city. And you erected them as far off as possible … For beyond the outermost circle of the inhabited world, indeed like a second line of defence in the fortification of a city, you have drawn another circle, which is more flexible and more easily guarded, and here you have put up your defensive walls and have built border cities, filling each in a different place with inhabitants … Just as a trench encircles an army camp, all this can be called the circuit and perimeter of the walls, so that the circumference of this perimeter is not calculated at ten parasangs, nor twenty, nor a little more, nor as much as you would say right off, but by all that is enclosed by the inhabited portion of Ethiopia and the Phasis on the one side and the Euphrates inland, and to the west that final great island. These walls have not been built of bitumen or baked brick … This circuit, which is much greater and grander than those walls, is on every side in every way unbreakable and indissoluble … men who hold out their shields in protection of those walls, not believing in flight …[45]

Obviously all this is a metaphor inspired by imperial ideology, but it is also the perspective of an upper class representative living in Greece, who has no concrete conception of the remote provinces.[46] It is interesting as well to observe that Aristides, born in Asia Minor as he was, explicitly states that he does not speak of man-made and built barriers, but of an army located in a frontier zone. This does not refer to *limes*-works, rivers, or mountains. That, however, touches on the subject of frontiers, which is not our topic here. The point of interest for present purposes is that Aristides' images are in fact the opposite of a core–periphery model: the core and periphery are one and the same, part of a single structure. The army surrounds it all, but that has nothing to do with an idea of core and periphery. Also worth mentioning is Dionysius of Halicarnassus, who again refers to Rome as a city ruling an empire (1.3.3).

Connected with this idea is the rule that the *pomerium* (the formal boundary of the city of Rome) might be extended only by those who

---

[45] Aristid. *Or.* 80–4 (trans. Behr).
[46] Cf. T. J. Cornell, 'The End of Roman Imperial Expansion', in J. Rich and G. Shipley (eds.), *War and Society in the Roman World* (London, 1993), 139–70.

expanded the boundaries of the Empire.[47] There is thus a clear connection between city and the limits of empire. A concomitant idea was the universality of the Roman Empire: 'She is the first and only power ever to have made the risings and settings of the sun the boundaries of her power.'[48] This may have been inspired by a boastful phrase attributed by Herodotus to Xerxes: 'we shall extend the Persian land as far as Zeus's heaven stretches. The sun will then shine on no land beyond our territory.'[49] It is also an early predecessor of the claim that Charles V and Philip II ruled 'an empire on which the Sun never sets'.[50]

The concept of a universal empire is most famously encountered in Vergil's line: 'For these I set neither bounds nor periods of empire; dominion without end have I bestowed.'[51]

So far in this brief sketch of ancient authors, which aims to show how they envisaged the Roman Empire as part of the world in geographical terms, we have encountered two distinct levels or concepts. There are authors who see the Empire and the world in abstract, ideological terms. While they describe the world as circular, there is no clear distinction between a core and a periphery. Of course, this is ideology and not reality, as has been noted, but it reflects the manner in which the Empire was seen by some intellectuals. Rome rules the entire world; the city and all of the Empire are one and the same. The Roman Empire covers the entire inhabited world without any indication of a division between heartland and outlaying districts. This approach insists on the integration of city and empire in every respect: geographical, social, and military. Then there are authors with a genuine interest in geography and ethnography such as Strabo and Tacitus. Their descriptions certainly convey no sense of an empire consisting of a core and a periphery. For them the Empire, as well as the world, was complex and no centre and periphery can be recognized in those works.

If the idea that the Empire consists of a core and a periphery is not as such encountered in ancient literature, it can of course still be argued that

---

[47] Tacitus, *Ann.* 12.23: *Caesar, more prisco, quo iis qui protulere imperium etiam terminos urbis propagare datur.*

[48] Dionysius of Halicarnassus, *Ant. Rom.* 1.3.3.

[49] Hdt. 7.8.37: γῆν τὴν Περσίδα ἀποδέξομεν τῷ Διὸς αἰθέρι ὁμουρέουσαν· οὐ γὰρ δὴ χώρην γε οὐδεμίαν κατόψεται ἥλιος ὁμουρέουσαν τῇ ἡμετέρῃ,

[50] *El imperio en el que nunca se pone el sol.* The phrase became popular elsewhere too, notably in nineteenth-century Britain.

[51] Verg. *Aen.* 1.278 (trans. Fairclough, Loeb): *his ego nec metas rerum nec tempora pono: imperium sine fine dedi.* Bréguet, 'Urbi et Orbi', 151–2, briefly indicates the afterlife of the idea, in the Middle Ages and the Renaissance.

the core–periphery model is a productive way of analysing ancient realities for a modern historian. This possibility should now be discussed.

Core/Periphery in the Modern Literature

The idea that there existed a core and a periphery has been applied also to the Greek world. It is sometimes claimed, for instance, that Macedonia is peripheral to the Greek core. This is a misconception, for numerous Greek colonies were geographically farther from the Greek mainland than Macedonia: yet the cities in Southern Italy and Sicily, Libya, Egypt, and the Black Sea are not normally considered peripheral, even though they are much farther away than Macedonia. On the other hand, population groups closer to Athens could be regarded as non-Greeks by the ancient Greeks themselves, for instance the Dryopes who inhabited Euboea, the Cyclades, and the Peloponnese (Hdt. 8.46.4; Diod. Sic. 4.37.2) and the Aetolians in the later fifth and fourth centuries BC.[52]

We move on therefore to a brief consideration of the popular core–periphery model and various attempts to apply it to the Roman Empire. Wallerstein is a fairly late successor to Universalists like Spengler and Toynbee, but less of an historian and more of an abstract social scientist. Also, unlike these two historians, he is a consistent neo-Marxist.[53] Three of his works are relevant here.[54]

The core–periphery model is essentially an expansion of dependency theory, which is a body of social science theories predicated on the notion that resources flow from a 'periphery' of poor and underdeveloped states to a 'core' of wealthy states, enriching the latter at the expense of the former. It is a central contention of the dependency theory that poor states are impoverished and rich ones enriched by the way poor states are integrated into the 'world-system'.

---

[52] J. Hall, 'Contested Ethnicities: Perceptions of Macedonia within Evolving Definitions of Greek Identity', in I. Malkin (ed.), *Ancient Perceptions of Greek Ethnicity* (Cambridge, 2001), 159–86, at 166. For the Aetolians: C. Antonetti, *Les Etoliens: Image et religion* (Paris, 1990). The criticism cited here more or less echoes the observations of Horden and Purcell, *Corrupting Sea*, cited below, n. 89.

[53] Wallerstein, *Capitalist World-Economy*, 118: 'The next twenty-five years will probably determine the modalities and the speed of the ongoing transition to a socialist world government.' On pp. 109–11 he copies with approval an essay by Comrade Kim Il Sung, consisting of three full pages, published as 'an advertisement by the Office of the Permanent Observer of the Democratic People's Republic of Korea to the United Nations' in the *New York Times* (16 March 1975), 6–7.

[54] Wallerstein, *Modern World-System*; *Capitalist World-Economy*, part I; *Unthinking Social Science*, part VI: 'World-Systems Analysis as Unthinking', 227–72; esp. ch. 20: 'World-Systems Analysis: The Second Phase', 266–72.

The theory defines the difference between developed countries and developing countries, characterized e.g. by power or wealth. The core refers to developed countries, and the periphery is a synonym for the dependent developing countries. The main reason for the position of the developed countries is economic power.

Beginning in the fifteenth century, the Age of Discovery, Europeans took the capitalist system, which flourished at home, to distant lands, whose labour and productivity were then bound to the European core in an unequal colonial relationship. The result was the capitalist world-system, as Wallerstein terms it.[55] There was increasing economic and productive specialization among the world's regions, as a pattern of unequal exchange developed between the industrial commodities of the advanced European nations (at the world-system's core) and the raw materials from underdeveloped Asia, Africa, and the New World (at the world-system's periphery). By the eighteenth century a worldwide urban culture had come into existence. It took variant forms of economic, political, and urban organization in the colonizing core and in the colonized periphery.

Wallerstein's analysis of what he calls a 'world-system' makes an essential distinction between a 'world-economy' and a 'world-empire'. A world-system is, in his description, 'a unit with a single division of labour and multiple cultural systems' (i.e. countries, powers, political and military systems). If there is a common, that is, unified political system, then he speaks of a 'world-empire', if there is not, then it is a 'world-economy'. Wallerstein concludes:

> It turns out empirically that world-economies have historically been unstable structures leading either towards disintegration or conquest by one group and hence transformation into a world-empire. Examples of such world-empires emerging from world-economies are all the so-called great civilisations of pre-modern times, such as China, Egypt, Rome …

On the other hand, the so-called nineteenth-century empires, such as Great Britain or France, were not world-empires at all, according to Wallerstein, but nation-states with colonial appendages operating within the framework of a world-economy. If we want to analyse ancient empires such as Rome in Wallerstein's terms, we must then follow his qualifications of a 'world-empire'.[56]

---

[55] Wallerstein, *Modern World-System*.
[56] Wallerstein, *Capitalist World-Economy*, part I: 'The Inequalities of Core and Periphery', ch. 1: 'The Rise and Future Demise of the World Capitalist System: Concepts for Comparative Analysis', 5.

There have been three major mechanisms that have enabled world-systems to retain relative political stability, according to Wallerstein: 'One obviously is the concentration of military strength in the hands of the dominant forces ... A second mechanism is the pervasiveness of an ideological commitment to the system as a whole ... Three: the division of the majority into a larger lower stratum and a smaller middle stratum.'[57]

The normal condition of a world-system is a three layered structure. When this ceases, the world-system disintegrates. In a world-empire, the middle stratum is in fact accorded the role of maintaining the long-distance luxury trade, while the upper stratum concentrates its resources on controlling the military machine which can collect tribute, the crucial mode of redistributing surplus.[58] This is hardly an appropriate structural description of the Roman Empire.

However, the essential difference between the two types of world-systems is that a world-empire has a 'cultural' stratification (presumably meaning social and class distinctions), while a world-economy has: core, periphery, and semi-periphery states.[59]

The important conclusion for us is that core and periphery are concepts which Wallerstein uses, not in connection with a world-empire, which, in his terminology, includes the Roman Empire, but with a world-economy, and he uses them for a classification of states, not regions. The description of core, periphery, and semi-periphery refers to what he calls 'world-economic' systems, not to 'world-empires'.[60] This is relevant for the period of European domination from the fifteenth until the twentieth century, not to any ancient major empire that we try to understand here and now. He specifically and emphatically analyses the capitalist economy of those recent centuries and in fact says little about empires.[61] He insists: 'a "world-economy" is fundamentally different kind of social system from a "world-empire" ... both in formal structure and as a mode of production ... the mode of production is capitalist'.[62] Were China,

---

[57] Wallerstein, *Capitalist World-Economy*, 22.
[58] Wallerstein, *Capitalist World-Economy*, 23.
[59] There is extensive discussion throughout ch. 5 of 'Semiperipheral countries and the contemporary world crisis'. By 'semiperipheral countries' he means, for instance, those in Latin American regions.
[60] Wallerstein, *Capitalist World-Economy*, 20–1.
[61] Wallerstein, *Modern World-System*, 16. He defines an empire as a mechanism for collecting tribute, which 'means payments received for protection, but payments in excess of the cost of producing the protection'.
[62] Wallerstein, *Modern World-System*, 159. R. Blanton and G. Feinman, 'The Mesoamerican World-System', *American Anthropologist* 86 (1984): 673–82, try to apply Wallerstein to Mesoamerica, which they see as a pre-capitalist world-economy, not as an empire. In discussing a pre-capitalist economy

Egypt, and the Roman Empire capitalist?[63] Where in these empires was the 'semi-periphery'?[64]

Wallerstein explains:

> World-economies then are divided into core-states and peripheral areas. I do not say peripheral *states* because one characteristic of a peripheral area is that the indigenous state is weak, ranging from its nonexistence (that is, a colonial situation) to one with a low degree of autonomy (that is, a neo-colonial situation) … There are also semi-peripheral areas which are in between the core and the periphery on a series of dimensions … The semi-periphery is a necessary structural element in a world-economy.[65]

A further point: it is usually assumed that the location of the political centre becomes the capital where most of the political and administrative institutions of the state are located.[66] There seems to be confusion between political, administrative, and economic centres. It is obvious that these are not necessarily identical in modern history (Washington, DC, vs. New York; Amsterdam vs. The Hague; Ottawa vs. Toronto; Berlin/Bonn vs. Frankfurt; Jerusalem vs. Tel Aviv).

Rome was something different again: a city-state with an empire, not the capital or centre of a nation. In this connection it is interesting that it was transferable, as suggested by the passage intimating that Caesar considered moving it to Troy or Alexandria and realized in late antiquity.

The conclusion is clear: if we want to use terms like 'core', 'semi-periphery', and 'periphery' towards an understanding of ancient empires, we have to make it clear that we do not use them as concepts formulated

they already abandon Wallerstein's principles. However, they consider Wallerstein's model to provide a useful framework for macro-regional interaction. It is not clear what they mean when they use the terms core and periphery. They see pre-capitalist Mesoamerica as a world-economy with core state and peripheral cities, and further ignore Wallerstein's concept of a semi-periphery.

[63] J. Schneider, 'Was there a Pre-Capitalist World-System?', *Peasant Studies* 6 (1977): 20–9. Schneider proposes a hypothesis that there was a *pre-capitalist* world-system, in which core areas accumulated precious metals while exporting manufactures, whereas peripheral areas gave up these metals (and often slaves) against an inflow of finished goods. Whatever the merits of this hypothesis for an early modern study, it cannot apply to the Roman Empire.

[64] G. Woolf, 'World-Systems Analysis and the Roman Empire', *JRA* 3 (1990): 44–58, at 48: 'Nothing like a semi-periphery can be identified within the [Roman] empire: the inner provinces seem if anything to have been exploited more than the outer ones. The term semi-periphery must be used in a fairly precise sense.' Woolf then offers his own application of the idea of a semi-periphery to the Roman Empire which one may accept or not, but his proposition has no place in Wallerstein's concept of a semi-periphery.

[65] Wallerstein, *Modern World-System*, 349.

[66] J. Gottman, 'Confronting Centre and Periphery' in J. Gottman (ed.), *Centre and Periphery: Spatial Variation in Politics* (London 1980), 15; S. Rokka and D. Urwin, *The Politics of Territorial Identity* (London 1982), 5; M. Steed, 'Core–Periphery Dimension of British Politics', *Political Geography Quarterly* 5 (1986): 98.

by Wallerstein in part of his 'world-systems analysis', but in another sense. As observed by Woolf: 'Wallerstein's analysis of the extension of capitalism has been most often applied to pre-capitalist periods in a manner that runs directly contrary to his own conception of world history.'[67] In fact, I imagine that many of those studying the Roman Empire are strongly influenced in their choice of terminology and imagery by some of the views they encounter in ancient, Graeco-Roman texts. The difficulty is that they do not usually define their terminology. In fact, the term 'core' is often replaced by 'centre' without explanation. Most of them tend to apply Wallerstein's terminology not when writing about the type of economic relationship that is the subject of Wallerstein's work, but when discussing some of the usual subjects of interest to Roman historians: the exercise of Roman military and political power, and the degree of integration of peoples into the Empire. This is true for the work of Daphne Nash,[68] Colin Haselgrove,[69] Lotte Hedeager,[70] Barry Cunliffe,[71] Tom Bloemers,[72] Susan Alcock,[73] Richard Hingley,[74] and

---

[67] Woolf, 'World-Systems Analysis', 44.

[68] D. Nash, 'Imperial Expansion under the Roman Republic', in M. Rowlands et al. (eds.), Centre and Periphery in the Ancient World (Cambridge, 1987), 87–103. She distinguishes four zones: (1) Italy, (2) provinces, (3) allies, friends, and enemies, (4) a zone close to the empire, of economic importance, also described as 'a remote periphery which can be seen to have been recognizably involved in the economic maintenance of the Roman empire, but which lay outside the immediate political concerns of Rome'.

[69] C. Haselgrove, 'Culture Process on the Periphery: Belgic Gaul and Rome during the Late Republic and Early Empire', in Rowlands et al., Centre and Periphery, 104–24, discusses Gaul. He distinguishes between an 'outer' and an 'inner periphery'. On p. 112 he also speaks of the 'periphery' of the states of Central Gaul, which itself is apparently considered to be a core. I am not certain whether Nash's 'outer periphery' is the same thing as Haselgrove's 'remote periphery'.

[70] L. Hedeager, 'Empire, Frontier and the Barbarian Hinterland: Rome and Northern Europe from AD 1–400', in Rowlands et al., Centre and Periphery, 124–40. 'Free Germany' is the periphery to the Roman core.

[71] B. Cunliffe, Greeks, Romans and Barbarians: Spheres of Interaction (London, 1988), 2–9, 193–201; reviewed by G. Woolf, JRS 79 (1989): 236–9, esp. 237–8.

[72] J. H. F. Bloemers, 'Periphery in Pre- and Proto-History: Structure and Process in the Rhine-Meuse Basin between c. 600 BC and 500 AD', in R. F. J. Jones, J. H. F. Bloemers, S. L. Dyson, and M. Biddle (eds.), First Millennium Papers, BAR Series 401 (Oxford, 1988), 11–35 at 11–13. He equates 'periphery' with buffer zone. The periphery is part of the sphere of influence of the core. The elites in core and periphery collaborate.

[73] S. E. Alcock, 'Archaeology and Imperialism: Roman Expansion and the Greek City', Journal of Mediterranean Archaeology 2 (1989): 87–135. Alcock discusses the manner in which Greece was incorporated after the conquest and calls it periphery. Here then periphery is used for newly conquered and annexed territory, which is totally different from the views of those who study NW Europe, where the area beyond direct imperial political, judicial, and administrative control is meant.

[74] R. Hingley, 'Roman Britain: The Structure of Roman Imperialism and the Consequences of Imperialism on the Development of a Peripheral Province', in D. Miles (ed.), The Romano British Countryside: Studies in Rural Settlement and Economy, BAR (Oxford, 1981), 17–52. Hingley sets out to mix Wallerstein's concepts of a world-empire and a world-economy. He thus proposes to view the 'core' of the empire as having a relationship with 'peripheral provinces'. He ignores Wallerstein's

Michael Rowlands.[75] A collection of papers edited by Timothy Champion is concerned with the application of the theory to archaeology and less concerned with the Roman Empire.[76] A critical and systematic attempt to analyse the difficulties has been made by Greg Woolf. It is my impression that not much remains of the Wallerstein theory after Woolf has applied it to the Roman Empire.[77] Woolf analyses the Roman Empire in terms of Wallerstein's category of a 'world-empire', even though, according to Wallerstein's own definition, this is not applicable.[78] Woolf characterizes world-empires 'as centralised and extensive political units, comprising a number of tributary cells. The economy of a world-empire is subordinate to its political structure, as are its internal dynamics.'[79] Woolf acknowledges that the Roman Empire had no semi-periphery in Wallerstein's sense and observes that the frontiers of the Empire were major consumers of the tribute and taxation exacted from the rest of the Empire because of the presence of much of the imperial army there.[80] As already noted, the essential difference between Wallerstein's two types of world-systems is that a world-empire has a 'cultural' stratification, whatever this may mean, while a world-economy has: core, periphery, and semi-periphery states. This means that the entire notion of the Roman Empire consisting of a core and a periphery evaporates if Wallerstein's model is applied rigorously – which, admittedly, he does not do himself.[81]

emphasis on 'semi-periphery'. I am not at all sure that his description of the economic and social relationships in Roman Britain, however appropriate it may be, has anything to do with Wallerstein. For criticism of Hingley, see: M. Millett, 'Romanization: Historical Issues and Archaeological Interpretation', in T. Blagg and M. Millett (eds.), *The Early Roman Empire in the West* (Oxford, 1990), 35–41. Millett altogether rejects the attempts to apply Wallerstein's model to the reality of the Roman Empire.

[75] Rowlands *et al.*, *Centre and Periphery*. Rowlands in 'Part One: Theoretical Perspectives, Centre and Periphery: A Review of a Concept', 1–11, presents a theoretical and critical Marxist discussion in which he attempts to redefine Wallerstein's model so as to make it applicable to the ancient world. In doing so he does *not* refer to empires – he mentions Sumer, the Valley of Mexico, the Maya. However, he clearly uses 'periphery' in the sense of the remote areas of an empire.

[76] T. C. Champion (ed.), *Centre and Periphery: Comparative Studies in Archaeology* (London, 1989), Introduction by Champion. Chs. 7, 9, and 10 deal with specifically Roman topics.

[77] Woolf, 'World-Systems Analysis', 44–58.

[78] Woolf, 'World-Systems Analysis', 45.

[79] Woolf, 'World-Systems Analysis', 47.

[80] Woolf, 'World-Systems Analysis', 48. Note also the reservations expressed by H. Elton, *Frontiers of the Roman Empire: Spheres of Interaction* (Bloomington, 1996), 1. See also: T. C. Champion, *Centre and Periphery* (1995); M. T. Larsen (ed.), *Power and Propaganda: A Symposium on Ancient Empires* (Copenhagen, 1979).

[81] As noted, Wallerstein regards core–periphery as typical of a world-economy, not of a world-empire. Yet he himself uses the core–periphery idea in connection with empires: Wallerstein, *Modern World System*, I, 15.

The advantage of working with Wallerstein's model for Roman history, so it has been argued, is that it provides a tool 'for understanding the macro-scale structures and dynamics of the Roman Empire and its neighbours, and for facilitating comparisons between Rome and other early empires'.[82] However, if Wallerstein's ideas and his concepts are freely adapted without clear definitions of terminology and method, they cannot clarify or facilitate anything.[83] It has been claimed that the distinction between centre and periphery may be 'very useful and perhaps even indispensable'. But we must recognize that it is only a metaphor, and hence it has the weakness of all metaphors when we turn from generalizations to analyses of specific historical circumstances. 'We must be cognizant … of the dangers as well as the attractions of using models like the centre-periphery dichotomy.'[84] Indeed, the model has become a buzz word, or what *Fowler's Usage* calls a 'worsened word'.[85]

Regarding the views encountered in Greek and Roman authors, one point is clear: the *ancient* authors saw relationships in terms of politics, intellectuality, military and social culture and, from the fourth century onward, in terms of religion as well. They were not interested in economic dependency theories. This in itself, of course, does not invalidate attempts to develop such theories.

Furthermore, it is clear that the terms 'core' or 'centre', 'semi-periphery' and 'periphery' as such reflect modern, rather than ancient views of imperial geography, although some of those views may misleadingly suggest a core and periphery approach, if interpreted in a somewhat distorted manner. The world is shaped like a dinner table, an ellipsoid surface, surrounded by the Ocean with Greece or, respectively, Italy, forming the centre of a civilized Mediterranean world, encircled by barbarian lands which formed

[82] Woolf, 'World-Systems Analysis', 50: 'Above all the process of theoretical abstraction allows issues, structures and dynamics to be envisaged and debated with a clarity impossible in discussion at a more concrete level.' Woolf refers to Wallerstein's 'pre-capitalist world-economies'. Wallerstein, in fact, does not make it clear that he felt any such systems existed. The only world-economy he really discusses is the capitalist one. On pp. 51–2 Woolf goes on to refer to the 'frontier zone' and beyond as periphery *vis-à-vis* core. That is legitimate, but it is not the same as Wallerstein's concept of a periphery.

[83] Woolf, 'World-Systems Analysis', 45: Wallerstein's model has been 'customized for use in pre-capitalist contexts … But only a few of the many attempts to apply world-systems analysis to the pre-capitalist world face up to these challenges.'

[84] R. McC. Adams, 'Common Concerns But Different Standpoints: A Commentary', in Larsen, *Power and Propaganda*, 393–404 at 400–1.

[85] K. Clarke, *Between Geography and History: Hellenistic Constructions of the Roman World* (Oxford, 1999), has an item in the index: 'centre-periphery model' which, however, has nothing to do with all of the above.

the outer ring. This causes students of the Greek and Latin literature to find the concepts of 'centre and periphery' familiar and comfortable, whatever the exact content of the idea. It has to be admitted, too, that the geographic basis for the application of the terminology will remain simplistic as long as no extensive analysis has taken place, in the case of the Roman Empire, on what is regarded as core and what as periphery.

A final remark: a serious problem in working with the ideas of 'core' or 'centre' and 'periphery' is that many of those who try to do so keep us largely in the dark as to whether we are thinking in terms of geography, communications, power, military control, or social and economic relationships. It is somehow suggested that these spheres overlap. Of course they do not do so in fact. If a model is to generate clarity it requires minimal conceptual definition.[86]

The Micro Ecological Approach

This is the term introduced by Horden and Purcell in their major work, *The Corrupting Sea*. Their micro ecological approach seems the opposite of the core–periphery model.[87] They conceive that towns constitute the basic elements of the Empire less as separate and clearly definable entities and more as loci of contact or overlap between different ecologies.[88] The micro regions they consider have to be understood with reference to a wider setting and they therefore aim to show how micro regions can coalesce on a

---

[86] An interesting parallel showing the difficulties of working with a model of centre and periphery is found in the study of Jewish quarters in German towns in the late medieval period. See A. Haverkamp, 'The Jewish Quarters in German Towns during the Late Middle Ages', in R. Po-Chia Hsia and H. Lehmann, *In and Out of the Ghetto: Jewish–Gentile Relations in Late Medieval and Early Modern Germany* (Cambridge, 1995), 13–28 at 27: 'These findings also do not support the notion, widely found in research on Jewish quarters, that there was a negative social gradient from a town's center to its periphery ... The supposed gradients, particularly in such small urban settlements, were interrupted by the arrival of local highways that assigned a functionally central role to the outer areas. At least as important within the *regnum teutonicum*, with its diversified structure of lordship, were the conditions of constitutional topography, which, for example, could transform the geographical periphery by the existence of monasteries or other religious institutions, even in the suburbs, into centers of economic importance. Aspects of historical genesis, together with the constitutional topography, raise doubts about the applicability of modern social categories of 'central' versus "peripheral".'

[87] They refer to the core–periphery theory only once, on p. 133: 'The influential theories of Wallerstein about the nature of large scale social and economic systems will therefore apply to the Mediterranean, if at all, in a curious way: the core territories may be composed of far-flung coastlands whose functional proximity is the product of seaborne connectivity. Peripheral regions will be found in the interstices of this network as well as in geographically remote areas.'

[88] Horden and Purcell, *Corrupting Sea*, 100.

grand scale.[89] Part of their study considers 'four definite places': the Biqa (in Lebanon), South Etruria, Cyrenaica, and Melos.[90] It would be futile to attempt to discuss these complex matters as part of this chapter. However, it may be instructive to conclude by considering a recent work which attempts to apply the model of Horden and Purcell to yet another region.[91]

David Kennedy, in his interesting and stimulating book about Gerasa and its vicinity in modern Jordan, aims to consider this region as a 'virtual island', a micro region in terms of the approach proposed by Horden and Purcell. This is defined as a region 'isolated by the peculiar form of the geography and environment around it'. The question to be asked then should be: *was* this region indeed a 'virtual island' in the terms of Horden and Purcell's concept? I cannot avoid expressing serious doubts. While it is clear that the presence of the pre-desert and desert in the east and, perhaps, the lava lands of Trachonitis to the north demarcated it in those directions to some extent, no such isolating geographical feature existed to the south, west, and northwest.

There is, of course, a modern frontier now, separating two states, and it is conceivable that this conveys a sense of isolation to those archaeologists working in Jordan who are unfamiliar with the terrain west of the frontier, but that need have no implications for antiquity. It is not obvious that the Jordan valley as such ever was a significant barrier. Indeed there are indications that it was not. The province of Judaea extended east of the river and this included the cities of Gadara and Pella. This is still the reality in the late third–early fourth century, as shown by Eusebius' *Onomasticon*.[92] This is important, for Eusebius is very precise, as shown, for instance, by the entry on Arbela, a village in the territory of Pella, east of the Jordan. Eusebius says that this village marked the boundary of Judaea.[93] Through the centuries administrative units straddled both banks of the river. Scythopolis, west of the river, was one of the cities of the Decapolis. It has been a topic of discussion what exactly was the Decapolis, a term encountered in several

---

[89] The relationship between local and imperial is also the subject of a series of a recent series of papers edited by Tim Whitmarsh, *Local Knowledge and Microidentities in the Imperial Greek World* (Cambridge, 2010)

[90] Horden and Purcell, *Corrupting Sea*, part II, ch. 3: 'Four Definit Places', 53–88.

[91] D. Kennedy, *Gerasa and the Decapolis: A 'Virtual Island' in Northwest Jordan* (London, 2007); see my review in Ancient History Bulletin 22 (2008): 184–9.

[92] Iazer is described by Eusebius, *Onom.* 104.13 (Klostermann) as a city '10 miles west of Philadelphia, now in Peraea in Palestine beyond the Jordan'. Villages east of Pella, on the road to Gerasa are *not* described as belonging to Palestine. They are in Arabia Provincia.

[93] Euseb. *Onom.* 14.18 (Klostermann): Ἀρβηλά (Num 34, 11). Ὅριον ἀνατολικὸν τῆς Ἰουδαίας. ἔστι δὲ κώμη τις Ἀρβηλὰ πέραν τοῦ Ἰορδάνου ἐν ὁρίοις Πέλλης πόλεως Παλαιστίνης.

texts covering a varying number of cities, among them Gerasa.[94] The question of what is really represented by the term 'Decapolis' is central to the subject of Kennedy's book.

The Nabataean kingdom encompassed southern Jordan, the Negev to the west, and, to some extent, Sinai. In late antiquity the province of Palaestina III again included the Negev and the area which is now southern Jordan. As can be seen on pp. 88–95 of Kennedy's book, there were good Roman roads linking Judaea-Palaestina with Arabia.[95]

Map 1 (see p. vii), taken from p. 16 of Kennedy's book, illustrates the boundaries of the area discussed in his book with the aid of two circles with a 50 km radius. One circle has Gerasa for its centre. That is entirely appropriate if one writes about Gerasa and tries to see the world from the perspective of the Gerasenes. Scythopolis-Beth Shean, then, lies at the edge of the circle. However, it would be equally justified to draw a circle with Scythopolis at the centre. After all, Scythopolis was a large city, belonging to the Decapolis and, later, the capital of the province of Palaestina II, so it cannot be maintained that its natural location is at the edge of any circle. Modern Beth Shean is rather isolated, but that is a different matter, the result of modern political divisions. A circle of 50–60 km with Scythopolis at the centre, giving the perspective of, say, the governor of Palaestina II, would have Gerasa at the south-eastern edge. The circle would include Caesarea, port city and capital of Palaestina I on the Mediterranean, the Roman colony of Ptolemais-Acco in Syria-Phoenice to the northwest; Neapolis (Nablus, Shekhem) to the southwest and much of the Galilee, densely populated, including the cities of Tiberias and Diocaesarea-Sepphoris, to the northwest. To the north, just beyond the 60 km circle would be Gaulanitis, with numerous villages of mixed population. All of these locations could be reached via good Roman roads. If we focus on Damascus, which also belonged to the Decapolis according to the shorter of the two lists given by Pliny and Ptolemy, we move to an altogether different region.

---

[94] Pliny, *NH* 5.16.74 lists ten cities: Damascus, Philadelphia, Raphana, Scythopolis, Gadara, Hippos, Dion, Pella, Galasa (i.e. Gerasa), Canatha. Ptolemy 5.15.22–3 lists eighteen. He does not include Raphana, but mentions also nine others, including Heliopolis and Abila Lysaniae in the Lebanon. Cf. E. Schürer, *The History of the Jewish People in the Age of Jesus Christ (175 BC–AD 135)*, II, ed. G. Vermes, F. Millar, and M. Black (Edinburgh, 1979), 125–7.

[95] The most important of those was the road from Caesarea-on-the-Sea to Scythopolis-Beth Shean and thence to Pella and Gerasa: cf. B. Isaac and I. Roll, *Roman Roads in Judaea*, I, *The Legio-Scythopolis Road* (Oxford, 1982).

This is no mere speculation. As an approach it is reflected in Eusebius'
Onomasticon, where he says of Gadara that it is 'a city across the Jordan,
opposite Scythopolis and Tiberias, in the east, in the mountains'.[96] I do not
see therefore that the Decapolis was truly isolated or united in a geographical or environmental sense.

What then was the Decapolis? Undoubtedly it was a group of cities that
had something in common, for it is mentioned in the literary sources, even
if they disagree about the cities that belonged to it. In the first century, at
least, there was a Roman equestrian officer administering the Decapolis, an
indication that there was reason to keep the cities belonging to it together
in some form.[97] Since at least some of the cities were scattered physically
it seems best to assume that the Roman authorities recognized them as
united by another bond, and this was almost certainly Hellenic culture
and social organization, hence the claim by the citizens of Scythopolis
that their city was 'one of the Hellenic cities in Coele-Syria'.[98] The name
Decapolis may have lost its flavour when the cities came to belong to three
separate provinces in the second century. In the late third–early fourth
century Eusebius is rather vague: 'Decapolis: in the Gospels. It is in Peraea
in the neighbourhood of Hippos, Pella and Gadara.'[99] Yet the inhabitants still called themselves Greeks, as distinct from the Jews, Nabataeans,
Arabs, Ituraeans, Syrians, and other peoples in the region. In other words,
what united them and set them apart from the vicinity was not geography, environment, or presumed common descent, but social and cultural
identity. This implies that not descent, but their distinct language, social
organization, and culture were regarded as essential. These categories were
regarded as crucially important not only by those concerned, but also by
the Roman authorities.

Look at the situation before the Roman annexation. Petra was the capital of the Nabataean kingdom; Jerusalem, 'by far the most famous city of
the East and not of Judaea only'.[100] Rome transferred the capital of Arabia,

---

[96] Euseb. *Onom.* 74.10: Γάδαρα (Matt 8:28). πόλις πέραν τοῦ Ἰορδάνου, ἀντικρὺ Σκυθοπόλεως καὶ
Τιβεριάδος πρὸς ἀνατολαῖς ἐν τῷ ὄρει, …

[97] B. Isaac, 'The Decapolis in Syria, a Neglected Inscription', *ZPE* 44 (1981): 67–74; repr. in *The Near
East under Roman Rule: Selected Papers* (Leiden, 1998), 313–22.

[98] G. Foerster and Y. Tsafrir, 'Nysa-Scythopolis: A New Inscription of the City on its Coins', *Israel
Numismatic Journal* 9 (1986–7): 53–8. The inscription is dated 175/6 and describes the city as
'Hyera, asylos, of the Hellenic cities in Koile-Syria'.

[99] Euseb. *Onom.* 80.16 (Klostermann): Δεκάπολις (Matt 4:25). ἐν Εὐαγγελίοις. αὕτη ἐστὶν ἡ ἐπὶ τῇ
Περαίᾳ κειμένη ἀμφὶ τὴν Ἵππον καὶ Πέλλαν καὶ Γάδαραν.

[100] Pliny, *NH* 5.70 (M. Stern, *Greek and Latin Authors on Jews and Judaism*, I (Jerusalem, 1974), 468–
81, no. 204): (*Toparchia*) *Orine … in qua fuere Hierosolyma, longe clarissima urbium Orientis non*

after its annexation, to Bostra (not to Gerasa, which became the seat of the financial procurator). Jerusalem was destroyed while Caesarea-on-the-Sea was retained as provincial capital. Then, in the fourth century, Jerusalem again expanded rapidly. Both before 70 and after 235 the central position of the city, its prosperity, and large size were the consequence of its importance as a religious centre.

Horden and Purcell, in their major work, discuss several samples throughout the Empire, such as the Biqa in Lebanon. In the reign of Augustus this region was made part of the territory of the Roman colony of Berytus (Beirut) in spite of the fact that the Biqa was separated from Berytus by a mountain range.[101] This is only one of many instances where Roman administrative arrangements may give a sense of ancient geographical perspective that runs counter to that of one looking at modern maps. Another such region is Cyrenaica, which is also a sample in Horden and Purcell's work. It was some 300 km distance sailing from Crete with which it formed one Roman province.

To conclude: any consideration of the Roman Empire should not ignore the extent to which people are connected by culture, language, religion, and other factors that are not economic and geographic, but social and cultural. These too play a role in economic life. In the words of Owen Lattimore, it is one of the old rules of frontier history that 'the new frontiers were shaped less by geographical and material conditions than by the cultural momentum of those who created them'.[102]

Iudaeae modo. Cf. Joseph. *BJ* 7.4: Ἱεροσολύμοις … λαμπρᾷ τε πόλει καὶ παρὰ πᾶσιν ἀνθρώποις διαβοηθείσῃ.

[101] J.-P. Rey-Coquais, *Baalbek et Beqa: Inscriptions Grecques et Latines de la Syrie*, VI (Paris, 1967), 34, n. 9; 'Syrie romaine de Pompée à Dioclétien', *JRS* 68 (1978): 44–73, at 51–2; J. Lauffray, 'Beyrouth: Archéologie et histoire, époques gréco-romaines: I, Période hellénique et Haut Empire romain', *ANRW* 2.8 (1978): 135–63; F. Millar, 'The Roman *Coloniae* of the Near East', in H. Solin and M. Kajava (eds.), *Roman Eastern Policy and Other Studies in Roman History: Proceedings of a Colloquium at Tvärminne 2–3 October 1987* (Helsinki, 1990), 10–23, 31–4; Isaac, *Limits of Empire*, 318–21, 342–4; 'Latin in Cities of the Roman Near East', in H. M. Cotton *et al.* (eds.), *From Hellenism to Islam: Cultural and Linguistic Change in the Roman Near East* (Cambridge, 2009), 49–54.

[102] O. Lattimore, 'The Frontier in History', in *Studies in Frontier History: Collected Papers, 1928–1958* (Paris and The Hague, 1962), 470–91 at 489.

CHAPTER 6

Names
Ethnic, Geographic, and Administrative

Names are history, both at a personal and a collective level. Not so long ago one would find in an atlas names such as Bombay, Cambodia, Siam, Ceylon, Peking, Breslau, Danzig, and Leningrad. They have been replaced for political and ideological reasons. New York's Dutch past is still recognizable in names such as Brooklyn and the Bronx. Empires come and go and geographical and ethnic names either change with them or survive in spite of those changes.

In considering geographical, ethnic, and administrative names in the Roman Near East we are faced with problems at several levels. First, there is a measure of obscurity in the general terminology in ancient texts. This is true for all periods and regions of antiquity. Second, for the Near East specifically, there is confusion regarding the meaning and content of individual names. Third, there are developments over time that affect or compound the first two problems.[1]

Let me start with an example of the first problem: confusion in the use of names and terminology. Ethnicity is a popular topic, these days. We all know where the term comes from. We all know the meaning of the Greek word *ethnos*. Yet Cassius Dio uses it as a term for a Roman province and that is how we find it in an inscription mentioning a *beneficiarius* of the governor κατὰ ἔθνὸς Φοινίκῶν. The Phoenician people, if there was such an entity, had no governor, the Province of Syria-Phoenice had one.

Also, we know what a nation is, or rather, what Latin *natio* stands for. However, Tacitus uses it at least once as a term for a Roman province as

---

An early version of this chapter was read at the conference: 'The Future of Rome: Roman, Greek, Jewish and Christian Perspectives', 2–4 October 2013, Tel Aviv University.

[1] This chapter, therefore, focuses on various specific problems concerning nomenclature and terminology. It is no attempt to advance the subject of ethnicity, or deal with broad questions of identity and self-identification that are discussed in various works. A relevant work, recently published, is N. J. Andrade, *Syrian Identity in the Greco-Roman World* (Cambridge, 2013).

well and so does Jerome.[2] In some cases it is hard to decide whether a province or a people is meant, for instance when the Historia Augusta calls Camsisoleus, Gallienus' general, an Egyptian *natione*.[3]

Next, an example of the second problem: variations in the use of specific names in the Near East. The name Assyria is, in the narrower sense, understood as the heartland of the Assyrian Empire partly to the west and, more so, east of the Tigris (today approximately northern Iraq); in post-Assyrian times the term is often used in a wider sense. The Medes may have already taken over 'Assyria' as the name of the conquered non-Babylonian regions of the former Assyrian Empire.[4] However, in Pseudo-Skylax's *Periplous* of the fourth century BC the name 'Assyria' indicates a people in northern Asia Minor.[5] Josephus cites Alexander Polyhistor as stating that 'Assyria received its name from "Soures"'.[6] For Pausanias Assyrians can be Syrians in Ascalon. Meleager of Gadara describes the city where he was born as lying in Assyria. Lucian of Samosata on the Euphrates describes the local dress there as 'Assyrian style'. It is clear then that Greek-writing authors of the Hellenistic and Roman period, who knew the region very well, used both names, Syria and Assyria, interchangeably.[7]

Third, changes over time. The Roman province of Judaea was renamed Syria-Palaestina. As we know very well, that was a measure taken by Hadrian after the Bar Kokhba war. A name referring to an ethnic element, explicitely associated with Jews, was replaced by the purely geographic appellation Syria-Palaestina.[8] That the name Palaestina was originally associated with the Philistines is obvious. Less immediately obvious is the fact that in the second century 'Palaestina' had no ethnic association. However, two texts of the late fourth century mention 'Palaestini' as a clearly identified

[2] Jerome, *Vita Malchi* 42 (PL 23. 54), says of Malchus that he was *Syrus natione et lingua*, 'a Syrian by *natio* and language'. Malchus spoke Syriac rather than Greek which is not surprising. His belonging to the Syrian *natio* here indicates that he was a native of the province of Syria.

[3] SHA, *Tyr. Trig.* 26: *sed per Gallieni ducem Camsisoleum, natione Aegyptium ...*

[4] Wiley-Blackwell's *Encyclopedia of Ancient History*, *Brill's New Pauly*, s.v.

[5] G. Shipley, *Pseudo-Scylax's Periplous: The Circumnavigation of the Inhabited World, Text, Translation and Commentary* (Exeter, 2011), 89: μετὰ δὲ Χάλυβας Ἀσσυρία ἐστὶν ἔθνος; 90: μετὰ δ' Ἀσσυρίαν ἐστι Παφλαγονία ἔθνος. Comments, 159. For this text, see below.

[6] Josephus, *Ant.* 1.241: λέγει δὲ αὐτῶν καὶ τὰ ὀνόματα ὀνομάζων τρεῖς Ἀφέραν Σούρην Ἰάφραν. ἀπὸ Σούρου μὲν τὴν Ἀσσυρίαν κεκλῆσθαι ...

[7] See Andrade, *Syrian Identity*, *passim*. For a discussion of identity with emphasis on Britain and North Africa: D. J. Mattingly, *Imperialism, Power, and Identity: Experiencing the Roman Empire* (Princeton 2011), ch. 8.

[8] In this chapter I will use the English 'Jews' as the most appropriate translation of Greek *Ioudaioi* and Latin *Judaei*.

group. Thus following the regular pattern of this period, the inhabitants of a province became identified in ethnic terms.[9]

An apology is called for: it will not be possible to discuss these matters as systematically as is desirable, for many or most of the sources involved are relevant for more than one of the phenomena to be discussed, while repetition is best avoided. A further point to mention here is that we frequently encounter a lack of consistency or even internal logic in the ancient texts. We have to recognize this for what it is without trying to impose consistency where it is lacking in the sources. Now we shall move on to a consideration of these matters in detail.

Syria, Assyria, Coele-Syria

According to Herodotus, Scythians in 604 pillaged the temple of Celestial Aphrodite in Ascalon.

> ... they marched forward with the design of invading Egypt. When they had reached Palestine, however, Psammetichus the Egyptian king met them with gifts and prayers, and prevailed on them to advance no further. On their return, passing through Ascalon, a city of Syria, the greater part of them went their way without doing any damage; but some few who lagged behind pillaged the temple of Celestial Aphrodite. Having investigated the matter I conclude that the temple in Ascalon is the most ancient of all the temples to this deity; for the one in Cyprus, as the Cypriotes admit themselves, was built in imitation of it; and that in Cythera was established by the Phoenicians who belong to this part of Syria.[10]

Aphrodite Ourania is a Greek interpretation of the local form or variant of the 'dea Syria': Atargatis or Aštart. At Ascalon the goddess was Astarte in the shape of a fish with the head of a woman; fish and doves were sacred to her.[11]

---

[9] SHA, *Niger* 7.9: *idem Palaestinis rogantibus ut eorum censitio levaretur idcirco quod esset gravat respondit ... Severus* 14.6; 17.1: *Palaestinis poenam remisit quam ob causam Nigri meruerant. Not. Dig. Or.* 34.28: *Equites primi felices [sagittarii indigenae] Palaestini, Sabure sive Veterocariae.*

[10] Hdt. 1.105: Ἐνθεῦτεν δὲ ἤισαν ἐπ᾽ Αἴγυπτον. Καὶ ἐπείτε ἐγένοντο ἐν τῇ Παλαιστίνῃ Συρίῃ, Ψαμμήτιχός σφεας Αἰγύπτου βασιλεὺς ἀντιάσας δώροισί τε καὶ λιτῇσι ἀποτρέπει τὸ προσωτέρω μὴ πορεύεσθαι. Οἱ δὲ ἐπείτε ἀναχωρέοντες ὀπίσω ἐγίνοντο τῆς Συρίης ἐν Ἀσκάλωνι πόλι, τῶν πλεόνων Σκυθέων παρεξελθόντων ἀσινέων, ὀλίγοι τινὲς αὐτῶν ὑπολειφθέντες ἐσύλησαν τῆς Οὐρανίης Ἀφροδίτης τὸ ἱρόν. Ἔστι δὲ τοῦτο τὸ ἱρόν, ὡς ἐγὼ πυνθανόμενος εὑρίσκω, πάντων ἀρχαιότατον ἱρῶν, ὅσα ταύτης τῆς θεοῦ· καὶ γὰρ τὸ ἐν Κύπρῳ ἱρὸν ἐνθεῦτεν ἐγένετο, ὡς αὐτοὶ Κύπριοι λέγουσι, καὶ τὸ ἐν Κυθήροισι Φοίνικές εἰσι οἱ ἱδρυσάμενοι ἐκ ταύτης τῆς Συρίης ἐόντες.

[11] D. Asheri *et al.*, *A Commentary on Herodotus Books I–IV* (Oxford, 2007), 154–5, with further references. For the association of Atargatis with Ascalon: Athenaeus, *Deipnosophistae* 8.37. See also Diodorus 2.4.2–6 with comments and explanations. Philo, *De providentia* 2.64, tells that doves are sacred and forbidden food in Ascalon. For the cult of Atargatis-Derketo, see also M. Fischer with

Herodotus here refers to Palestine as a geographical entity. Ascalon is both in 'Palaestina Syria' and 'a city of Syria'.

Pausanias, writing in the second century AD, disagrees with Herodotus and claims that 'the first men to establish her cult [sc. of Heavenly Aphrodite] were the Assyrians, after the Assyrians, the Paphians of Cyprus and the Phoenicians who live at Ascalon in Palestine; the Phoenicians taught her worship to the people of Cythera'.[12] Are these Assyrians = Syrians? Undoubtedly they were, as will be clear again when we consider Meleager's description of Gadara in Assyria. Thus Pausanias distinguishes between Syrians and Phoenicians and is one of the authorities for the presence of Phoenicians in the Hellenistic/Roman period in coastal Palestine. If we leave aside the dispute about priority, what remains is the fact that Herodotus regards Celestial Aphrodite as originally established by Phoenicians in Ascalon, while Pausanias claims that Syrians were the first, followed by Phoenicians in Ascalon in Palestine which, again, is a geographical concept, like Syria, side by side with 'Syrians' as an ethnic notion. Another text mentioning Ascalon is relevant, namely an inscription from Egypt: 'Zeus Helios, Great Sarapis of Canopus, of the god of my fatherland, Heracles-Belus, invincible made by me, Marcus Aurelius Maximus, a Syrian from Ascalon …'[13] It is dated 12 April 228. Here then we see that a third-century citizen of Ascalon calls himself a Syrian on an inscription in Egypt, declaring that Heracles-Belus is the god of his fatherland.[14]

Matters are more complicated than that, however. An Ascalonian banker on Delos, Philostratos the son of Philostratos, dedicated an altar to the deity 'Astarte the Palestinian Aphrodite' in honour of his city, himself, his wife, and children.[15] Whatever the date of the inscription, it is worth

---

A. Krug and Z. Pearl, 'The Basilica of Ascalon', in J. H. Humphrey (ed.), *The Roman and Byzantine Near East* (Ann Arbor, 1995), 121–50, at 146. For the Syrian Goddesss, see now Andrade, *Syrian Identity*, part III, ch. 10.

[12] Pausanias 1.14.7.4 (trans. Jones and Ormerod, Loeb): πρώτοις δὲ ἀνθρώπων Ἀσσυρίοις κατέστη σέβεσθαι τὴν Οὐρανίαν, μετὰ δὲ Ἀσσυρίους Κυπρίων Παφίοις καὶ Φοινίκων τοῖς Ἀσκάλωνα ἔχουσιν ἐν τῇ Παλαιστίνῃ, παρὰ δὲ Φοινίκων Κυθήριοι μαθόντες σέβουσιν·

[13] A. Bernard, *Le Delta égyptien d'après les textes Grecs* (Cairo, 1970), I, 242–4, no. 14: Διὶ Ἡ[λίῳ] μεγά[λῳ] Σαράπιδι ἐν Κα[νώβῳ] θεὸν πάτρι[όν] μου Ἡρ[ακ]λῆ Βῆλον ἀνείκητον Μ(άρκος) Α(ὐρήλιος) Μάξιμο[ς Σύρος] Ἀ[σ]καλωνείτη[ς …

[14] See also A. Maiuri, *Nuova silloge epigrafica di Rodi e Cos* (Florence, 1925), no. 161: Ἀπολλωνίο(υ) Ἀσκαλωνίτου; no. 162: Εἰρηνας Ἀσκαλωνίτιδος; 175: Πλουσία Ἀσκαλωνῖτις, the wife of Ἀνταῖος Λαοδικεύς.

[15] P. Roussel and M. Launey, *Inscriptions de Délos* (Paris, 1937), 1719: Ἀστάρτηι Παλαιστινῆι Ἀφροδίτηι. The same man dedicated an inscription Ἀπόλλωνι καὶ Ἰταλικοῖς (1718) and Ποσειδῶνι Ἀσκαλ[ωνίτῃ] (1721–2). See also no. 2305. Cf. P. Bruneau, *Recherches sur les cultes de Délos à l'époque Hellénistique et à l'époque impériale* (Paris, 1970), 346–7, 474.

noting that the Ascalonian banker refers to Astarte, identifying her with Aphrodite, as a Palestinian, which can only be regarded here as an ethnic concept, the first such use of 'Palestine' in any ancient text, as far as I know. Would it be frivolous to suggest that Astarte was the first Palestinian?[16]

Another relatively early Greek source also mentions the town of Ascalon, namely Pseudo-Scylax's *Periplus* of the fourth century: 'There is after Kilikia the community of the Syroi (Syrians). And in Syria there live, in the seaward part, the Phoinikes (*Phoenicians*), a community, upon a narrow front less than up to 40 stades from the sea, and in some places not even up to 10 stades in width …'[17]

The text listing sites on the Palestinian coast is in bad shape and has been restored as follows: 'Doros (*Dor*) a city of Sidonioi, <Ioppe (*Jaffa*), a city;> they say it was here that Androm<eda> was < ex>posed <to the monster. Aska>lon, a city of Tyrioi and a royal seat. Her<e is the boundary of *Koile*> (*Hollow*) Syria.'[18]

There are several points to note here. First, Syrians are mentioned as a people and Syria as a geographic concept which is broader than the area inhabited by the Syrians, for it includes that inhabited by the Phoenicians, living in the coastal plain. In this connection we should note the identification of Dor as Sidonian and Ascalon as Tyrian.[19] Second, there is the specific statement that Ascalon was the southernmost coastal city of Koile-Syria thus, surprisingly, excluding Gaza. This is the first text that prefers to call this part of the Near East 'Coele-Syria' rather than Syria or Palestine (in Syria). The text gives the additional information that Coele-Syria extends from Thapsakos river (presumably the Orontes) as far as Ascalon.[20]

---

[16] It is not fanciful to assume that gods have an ethnic affiliation. Greek gods can even be called barbarians. Cf. Aristophanes, *Aves* 1573, where Poseidon addresses Triballus: 'Ugh! You cursed savage! You are by far the most barbarous of all the gods.' Οἴμωζε· πολὺ γὰρ δή σ' ἐγὼ ἑόρακα πάντων βαρβαρώτατον θεῶν.

[17] Shipley, *Pseudo-Scylax's Periplous*, 104.1: [Συρία καὶ Φοινίκη] ἔστι μετὰ Κιλικίαν ἔθνος Σύροι. ἐν δὲ τῇ Συρίᾳ οἰκοῦσι τὰ παρὰ θάλατταν Φοίνικες ἔθνος, ἐπὶ στενὸν ἔλαττον ἢ ἐπὶ τεσσαρακοντα σταδίους ἀπὸ θαλάττης, ἐνιαχῇ δὲ οὐδὲ ἐπὶ σταδίους ι' τὸ πλάτος. See also above, n. 5.

[18] Shipley, *Pseudo-Scylax's Periplous* 104.3: Δῶρος πόλις Σιδωνίων, κ[αὶ Ἰόππη πόλις· ἐκτε-]θῆναί φασιν ἐνταῦθα τὴν Ἀνδρομ[έδαν τῷ κήτει. Ἀσκά]λων πόλις Τυρίων καὶ βασίλεια. ἐνταῦ[θα ὅρος ἐστὶ τῆς Κοίλης] Συρίας also: M. Stern, *Greek and Latin Authors on Jews and Judaism*, 3 vols. (Jerusalem, 1974–84), III, no. 558; comments, 10–12.

[19] For Sidonians in Judaea, see B. Isaac, 'A Seleucid Inscription from Jamnia-on-the-Sea: Antiochus V and the Sidonians', *IEJ* 41 (1991), 132–44, reprinted with postscript in Isaac, *The Near East under Roman Rule* (Leiden, 1998), 3–20.

[20] 104.3: παράπλους Κοίλης Συρίας [ἀπὸ Θαψάκου ποταμοῦ μέχρι] Ἀσκάλωνος στάδια βψ'. Comments: Shipley, *Pseudo-Scylax's Periplous*, 179. For Coele-Syria, see E. Bikerman, 'La Coelé-Syrie: Notes de Géographie Historique', *Revue Biblique* 54 (1947), 256–68 and below: Rey-Coquais, Sartre, and Gatier. We may note that scholars disagree about the meaning and significance of the term. Some see 'Coele' as deriving from Greek κοῖλος, hollow, others as derived from the Aramaic

Coele-Syria thus is associated with the coastal region of Syria which some-how links it with the region of the Phoenicians who are said to live 'upon a narrow front less than up to 40 stades from the sea, and in some places not even up to 10 stades in width'. Finally it is worth noting that the source does not mention Jews.[21]

Moving on to the Hellenistic period, we see that the Ptolemaic king-dom included a satrapy of 'Syria and Phoenice'. This was conquered by the Seleucids around 200 BC and renamed 'Koile-Syria and Phoenice'.[22]

In the second century BC the poet Meleager describes himself as a native of Gadara (across the Jordan, southeast of the Sea of Galilee).[23]

> Island Tyre was my nurse, and Gadara, an Attic fatherland which lies in Assyria [sc. Syria] gave birth to me. From Eucrates I sprung, Meleager, who first by the help of the Muses ran abreast of the Graces of Menippus. What wonder if I am a Syrian? Stranger, we all inhabit one fatherland, one world. Once Chaos gave birth to all mortals …

The importance of this text and the following lies in the description of the author of himself, as will be noted in the next chapter: a Hellenized Syrian, referring to himself and his cultural environment. Meleager wrote in the second-first century BC.[24] The reason why these texts should be consid-ered again here is the ethnic and geographic nomenclature employed. As already noted above, Assyria is here obviously used as synonym for Syria, for that is the region in which Gadara lies. No local person would con-fuse the name Syria with what we now call Assyria, east of the Euphrates. While Assyria/Syria is here a geographical notion, 'Syrian' is here used as an ethnic adjective by Meleager himself. Gadara was an Attic fatherland because of its language and culture. There was no pretence here that the citizens were actually descendants of Athenians, as is shown immediately by the author's question whether it is a wonder that he is a Syrian. There

---

'kul' = all. For the latter: A. Schalit, 'Κοίλη Συρία from the Mid-Fourth Century to the Beginning of the Third Century BC', *Scripta Hierosolymitana* 1 (1954): 64–77.

[21] For the present discussion it may be worth observing that the name 'Ascalon' continued to be used for various unexpected purposes. It was the name of the lance used by St George to kill the dragon and, subsequently, of the British Second World War aeroplane used by Winston Churchill, named after the lance – an Avro York.

[22] Thus, for instance, in the *Aristeae Ep.*12, cited below.

[23] A. S. F. Gow and D. L. Page (eds.), *The Greek Anthology: Hellenistic Epigrams*, 2 vols. (Cambridge, 1965), I, 216, no. 2 (*Anthologia Palatina* 7.417): Νᾶσος ἐμὰ θρέπτειρα Τύρος· πάτρα δέ με τεκνοῖ / Ἀτθὶς ἐν Ἀσσυρίοις ναιομένα Γαδάρα· / Εὐκράτεω δ' ἔβλαστον ὁ σὺν Μούσαις Μελέαγρος / πρῶτα Μενιππείοις συντροχάσας Χάρισιν. / εἰ δὲ Σύρος, τί τὸ θαῦμα; μίαν, ξένε, πατρίδα κόσμον / ναίομεν, ἐν θνατοὺς πάντας ἔτικτε Χάος... /. For the reading Γαδάρα see Gow and Page, II, 607.

[24] Below, Chapter 7, p. 153.

are two points to be made here: (a) he is a Syrian by origin and (b), the question indicates that this is indeed an ambivalent status for someone who is so clearly a Hellenistic poet. So, to summarize: we have seen that Assyria, Syria, and Coele-Syria are all three used as geographic synonyms, while Syrian and Assyrian represent ethnic synonyms as well.[25] The second self-description of Meleager should be cited again for the same reasons:

> Tyre of the godlike boys and Gadara's holy earth made me a man; lovely Kos of the Meropes took care of me in my old age. So if you are a Syrian, Salaam! If you are a Phoenician, Naidios! If you are Greek, Chaire! And do you say the same [to me].[26]

'Syrian' and 'Phoenician' are here ethnic terms, but also associated with language as is emphasized by the last part of the poem, a call for what we now call 'multiculturalism' in a culture that did not cherish this phenomenon as an ideology. A variant combination occurs in an inscription from Italy, apparently of the second century AD: 'The tomb of Diodorus the son of Heliodorus from Gadara of the Syrian Decapolis.'[27] Given the find spot it is clear that 'Syrian' represents here geographic clarification.[28] About the Decapolis something more will be said.

Moving on, considering terminology in the Roman Near East we should first consider Strabo, late first century BC–early first century AD.

> We set down as parts of Syria, beginning at Cilicia and Mt. Amanus, both Commagene and the Seleucis of Syria, as the latter is called; and then Coele-Syria, and last, on the seaboard, Phoenicia, and, in the interior, Judaea. Some writers divide Syria as a whole into Coele-Syrians and Syrians and Phoenicians, and say that four other peoples are mixed up with these, namely, Jews, Idumaeans, Gazaeans and Azotians, and that they are partly farmers, as the Syrians and Coele-Syrians, and partly merchants as the Phoenicians.[29]

---

[25] For more sources referring to Coele-Syria in this period: M. Sartre, 'La Syrie Creuse n'existe pas', in P.-L. Gatier, B. Helly and J.-P. Rey-Coquais (eds.), *Géographie historique au Proche Orient: Syrie, Phénicie, Arabie, grecques, romaines, byzantines* (Paris, 1988), 15–40 at 22–5.

[26] Gow and Page, *The Greek Anthology*, I, 217, no. 4 (*Anthologia Palatina* 7.419): ...ὃν θεόπαις ἤνδρωσε Τύρος Γαδάρων θ'ἱερὰ χθών, / Κῶς δ'ἐρατὴ Μερόπων πρέσβυν ἐγηροτρόφει. / ἀλλ'εἰμὲν Σύρος ἐσσί, σαλάμ· εἰδ' οὖν σύ γε Φοῖνιξ, / ναίδιος· εἰ δ'Ἕλλην, χαῖρε· τὸ δ'αὐτὸ φράσον.

[27] P.-L. Gatier, 'Décapole et Coelé-Syrie: Deux inscriptions nouvelles', *Syria* 67 (1990): 204–6 at 204: Διοδώρου Ἡλιοδώρου ἀπὸ Συριακῆς Δεκαπόλεως Γαδάρων ταφεών.

[28] Gatier, 'Décapole et Coelé-Syrie', 205, refers for comparison to Josephus, *Vita* 341: τὰς ἐν τῇ Συρίᾳ δέκα πόλεις; to *Vita* 410: οἱ πρῶτοι τῶν τῆς Συρίας δέκα πόλεων and to *IGRR* III, 1057 from the Thracian Chersonnesus: Δεκαπόλεως τῆς ἐν Συρίᾳ, for which see B. Isaac, *The Near East under Roman Rule* (Leiden, 1998), 313–21.

[29] Strabo 16.2.2 (749): Μέρη δ' αὐτῆς τίθεμεν ἀπὸ τῆς Κιλικίας ἀρξάμενοι καὶ τοῦ Ἀμανοῦ τήν τε Κομμαγηνὴν καὶ τὴν Σελευκίδα καλουμένην τῆς Συρίας, ἔπειτα τὴν κοίλην Συρίαν, τελευταίαν

This gives variant descriptions: the first is exclusively geographical: it divides Syria into three parts: Coele-Syria, Phoenicia, and Judaea; the second refers to ethnic groups: 'Coele-Syrians', which is distinguished from Syrians, Phoenicians, and the others mentioned here – Jews, Idumaeans and the inhabitants of two cities (including ethnic stereotypes). This shows that, for Strabo, the reference by name to a region or to a people may have no more force than a variation in terminology. Many or most regions are not named in terms of geography, but of inhabitants, such as the 'Coele-Syrians', except in cases where the intention is quite obvious, as in the following instance. To be noted is that here 'Coele Syria' for the first time is unambiguously given as a subdivision of Syria.

To continue reviewing Strabo's information: 'Here are two mountains, Libanus and Antilibanus, which form Coele-Syria, as it is called, and are approximately parallel to each other. They both begin slightly above the sea – Libanus above the sea near Tripolis and nearest to Theuprosopon and Antilibanus above the sea near Sidon'.[30]

Coele-Syria, here designated again as a region of Syria, means the Orontes, Beqa, and Jordan valleys down to the Dead Sea region.

> Now the whole of the country above the territory of Seleucis, extending approximately to Egypt and Arabia, is called Coele-Syria, but the country marked off by the Libanus and the Antilibanus is called by that name in a special sense. Of the remainder the seaboard from Orthosia to Pelusium is called Phoenicia, which is a narrow country and lies flat along the sea, whereas the interior above Phoenicia, as far as the Arabs, between Gaza and Antilibanus, is called Judaea.[31]

Strabo is clear enough. He is aware of Coele-Syria in the narrow sense of the valley between Libanus and Antilibanus, but also uses the term for all of the Near East from Seleucis to Arabia and Egypt. He calls the entire coastal strip Phoenice. Judaea is for him the strip of land between Phoenice

---

δ' ἐν μὲν τῇ παραλίᾳ τὴν Φοινίκην, ἐν δὲ τῇ μεσογαίᾳ τὴν Ἰουδαίαν. ἔνιοι δὲ τὴν Συρίαν ὅλην εἴς τε Κοιλοσύρους [καὶ Σύρους] καὶ Φοίνικας διελόντες τούτοις ἀναμεμῖχθαί φασι τέτταρα ἔθνη, Ἰουδαίους Ἰδουμαίους Γαζαίους Ἀζωτίους, γεωργικοὺς μέν, ὡς τοὺς Σύρους καὶ Κοιλοσύρους, ἐμπορικοὺς δέ, ὡς τοὺς Φοίνικας.

[30] Strabo 16.2.16 (755): Δύο δὲ ταῦτ' ἐστὶν ὄρη τὰ ποιοῦντα τὴν κοίλην καλουμένην Συρίαν ὡς ἂν παράλληλα, ὅ τε Λίβανος καὶ ὁ Ἀντιλίβανος μικρὸν ὕπερθεν τῆς θαλάττης ἀρχόμενα ἄμφω, ὁ μὲν Λίβανος τῆς κατὰ Τρίπολιν, κατὰ τὸ τοῦ Θεοῦ μάλιστα πρόσωπον, ὁ δ' Ἀντιλίβανος τῆς κατὰ Σιδῶνα·

[31] Strabo 16.2.21 (756): Ἅπασα μὲν οὖν ἡ ὑπὲρ τῆς Σελευκίδος ὡς ἐπὶ τὴν Αἴγυπτον καὶ τὴν Ἀραβίαν ἀνίσχουσα χώρα κοίλη Συρία καλεῖται, ἰδίως δ' ἡ τῷ Λιβάνῳ καὶ τῷ Ἀντιλιβάνῳ ἀφωρισμένη. τῆς δὲ λοιπῆς ἡ μὲν ἀπὸ Ὀρθωσίας μέχρι Πηλουσίου παραλία Φοινίκη καλεῖται, στενή τις καὶ ἁλιτενής· ἡ δ' ὑπὲρ ταύτης μεσόγαια μέχρι τῶν Ἀράβων ἡ μεταξὺ Γάζης καὶ Ἀντιλιβάνου Ἰουδαία λέγεται..

(the coastal strip) and Coele-Syria (i.e. the Jordan valley). Coele-Syria in the broader sense is for him Syria east of the coastal strip. All this is geographic, not ethnic, apart from 'the Arabs'.[32]

Later in the first century one poem deserves brief mention. Statius apparently addresses the grandfather of Septimius Severus – or one of his older relatives.

> Did Leptis that loses itself in the distant Syrtes beget you? ... Who would not think that my sweet Septimius had crawled an infant on all the hills of Rome? ... Neither your speech nor your dress is Punic, yours is no stranger's mind: Italian are you, Italian! Yet in our city and among the knights of Rome Libya has sons who would adorn her.[33]

The poem, while flattering Septimius Severus, clearly states that one would expect a man from Leptis Magna, a Poenus, to speak, dress, and think like a foreigner. Language, dress, and mental qualities are the essential features mentioned here. Leptis Magna was indeed an old Punic city, but by the time of the Flavians it had the status of a *municipium* and Trajan gave it colonial status. The Septimii Severi were therefore members of the colonial upper class.

In the late first–early second century Plutarch uses 'Syrians' once in a context indubitably associated with language, as well as 'Hebraioi'. Cleopatra spoke in their own languages to various peoples, including *Hebraioi*, Arabs, and Syrians.[34]

From the second century the first to be mentioned is Appian.

> In this way the Romans, without fighting, came into possession of Cilicia, inland Syria and Coele-Syria, Phoenicia, Palestine and all the other countries bearing the Syrian name from the Euphrates to Egypt and the sea. The Jewish nation alone still resisted and Pompey conquered them ...[35]

Appian sees Syria in the broadest geographical sense as subdivided into the parts he mentions. Palestine is clearly more than the Jews and the region

---

[32] For 'the Arabs' and 'Scenitae', see 16.2.11 (753). For Arabs/Arabians see below. For the terms ἡ ἄνω Συρία and 'Seleucis', see Sartre, 'La Syrie Creuse n'existe pas', 19–20.

[33] Statius, *Silvae* 4.5.29–48 (trans. J. H. Mozley, Loeb): ... *non sermo Poenus, non habitus tibi, externa non mens: Italus, Italus. / sunt Vrbe Romanisque turmis / qui Libyam deceant alumni*. For this poem, see also below, Chapter 7, Provincial Intellectuals.

[34] Plutarch, *Ant.* 27.4: τοῖς δὲ πλείστοις αὐτὴ δι' αὑτῆς ἀπεδίδου τὰς ἀποκρίσεις, οἷον Αἰθίοψι Τρωγλοδύταις Ἑβραίοις Ἄραψι Σύροις Μήδοις Παρθυαίοις; cited also below.

[35] Appian, *Syr.* 251–2: οὕτω μὲν δὴ Κιλικίας τε καὶ Συρίας τῆς τε μεσογαίου καὶ Κοίλης καὶ Φοινίκης καὶ Παλαιστίνης, καὶ ὅσα ἄλλα Συρίας ἀπὸ Εὐφράτου μέχρις Αἰγύπτου καὶ μέχρι. θαλάσσης ὀνόματα, ἀμαχεὶ Ῥωμαῖοι κατέσχον. ἐν δὲ γένος ἔτι, τὸ Ἰουδαίων, ἐνιστάμενον ὁ Πομπήιος ἐξεῖλε κατὰ κράτος...

they control. It is the entire province of that name in Appian's days. Inland Syria presumably means here the eastern part; Coele-Syria is here used in an unspecified narrow sense. The terminology here is geographic, apart from 'the Jewish nation' (ἐν δὲ γένος ἔτι, τὸ Ἰουδαίων).[36]

The term Coele-Syria is still encountered on an inscription inscribed on an altar dedicated to an emperor who is probably Marcus Aurelius (161–80) by the people of Scythopolis (Beth Shean) one of τῶν κατὰ Κοίλην Συρίαν Ἑλληνίδων πόλεων. Thus the city of Nysa-Scythopolis is here referred to as 'one of the Hellenic cities in Coele-Syria'.[37]

'Coele-Syria' here cannot possibly mean the Beqa and Jordan valley, even though Scythopolis lies in the Jordan valley, for the authors of the text would not want to exclude a large number of important Hellenic cities in the region, such as Damascus, Gerasa, and Philadelphia. Thus the city of Nysa-Scythopolis is referred to as 'one of the Hellenic cities in Coele-Syria'. Scythopolis belonged to the province of Syria-Palaestina, but that is not an entity mentioned on the inscription, for the Hellenic cities referred to were in three separate provinces by this time. Clearly Coele-Syria is here used in a broader (intermediate) sense, which approaches that of 'The Decapolis', the cities of which, originally, all were assigned to the province of Syria.[38] 'Hellenic' is used as Meleager does in the case of Gadara: it refers to culture and language, not to origin. There is an important conclusion here to be drawn concerning Roman policy: when the region was incorporated into the Empire in 63 BC, it was regarded as desirable to include Hellenic cities into the Roman province of Syria, under the authority of a Roman governor and not to leave them under the rule of client kings. This is true for all of the cities of the Decapolis, but also for some Palestinian cities, such as Gaza and Ascalon. With the incorporation of Judaea and, afterward, Arabia into the Empire as provinces, there was no reason to

---

[36] Cf. Appian, *Mithr.* 16.106 (498): ἐπολέμησε δὲ καὶ Ἄραψι τοῖς Ναβαταίοις, Ἀρέτα βασιλεύοντος αὐτῶν, καὶ Ἰουδαίοις, Ἀριστοβούλου τοῦ βασιλέως ἀποστάντος, ἕως εἷλεν Ἱεροσόλυμα, τὴν ἁγιωτάτην αὐτοῖς πόλιν. καὶ Κιλικίας δέ, ὅσα οὔπω Ῥωμαίοις ὑπήκουε, καὶ τὴν ἄλλην Συρίαν, ὅση τε περὶ Εὐφράτην ἐστὶ καὶ Κοίλη καὶ Φοινίκη καὶ Παλαιστίνη λέγεται, καὶ τὴν Ἰδουμαίων καὶ Ἰτουραίων καὶ ὅσα ἄλλα ὀνόματα Συρίας, ἐπιὼν ἀμαχεὶ Ῥωμαίοις καθίστατο.

[37] G. Foerster and Y. Tsafrir, 'Nysa-Scythopolis: A New Inscription and the Titles of the City on its Coins', *Israel Numismatic Journal* 9 (1986–7): 53–8. Cf. Gatier, 'Décapole et Coelé-Syrie'. Gatier points out that the meaning of the phrase is not entirely clear, signifying either 'the Hellenic cities of Coele-Syria' or 'those cities of Coele-Syria that are Hellenic'. For the meaning of Coele-Syria, see Gatier, 'Décapole et Coelé-Syrie' and his earlier reference in 'Philadelphie et Gerasa du Royaume Nabatéen a la Province d'Arabie', *Géographie historique au Proche Orient* (Paris, 1988), 159–70, at 164. For a different view: J.-P. Rey-Coquais, 'Philadelphie de Coelesyrie', *ADAJ* 25 (1981): 25–31; Sartre, 'La Syrie Creuse n'existe pas': the latter see the term as an administrative one, associated with the imperial cult. See also above, n. 20, Bikerman, 'La Coelé-Syrie'.

[38] Gatier, 'Philadelphie et Gerasa', 162–3. See also Chapter 5.

leave those cities part of Syria. The essence of Roman policy was that the cities should be part of the responsibility of Roman governors, not that they should belong to one and the same province. The inscription from Scythopolis shows that cities like Scythopolis still considered themselves as belonging to a specific group, separate from the non-Hellenic environment, irrespective of the Roman province to which they belonged.

Οἱ ἐν Δαναβοις Ἕλληνες Μηνοφίλῳ εὐνοίας ἕνεκεν.

The Hellenes in Danaba ...[39]

Just as 'Hellenic' in the previous inscription, 'Hellenes' is used here as a cultural marker. It must refer to language, as in the case of Meleager, but also to intellectual life and cult practices.

Another Greek author from the Roman Near East of interest is Lucian of Samosata (125–80). He is discussed below in his capacity as a provincial intellectual.[40] Here he merits attention already for his use of ethnic terminology. In *The Fisherman* we read: 'I am a Syrian, Philosophy, from the banks of the Euphrates. But what of that? I know that some of my opponents here are just as barbarian as I.'[41] 'Syrian' is used here as an ethnic term, further qualified by geography and associated with a lack of culture.

A passage in *The Double Indictment* seems to contain elements of an autobiographic dialogue or at least of a scene taken from real life. The speaker here is Rhetoric accusing her husband, a Syrian, before a court of justice: 'When this man was a mere boy, gentlemen of the jury, still speaking with a foreign accent and I might almost say wearing a caftan in the Assyrian [sc. Syrian] style.'[42] Accented Greek and foreign dress are typical of an ethnic Syrian.

Damascus is given at least once as a form of origin, a subdivision of Syrians: 'We Syrians are Damascus men by birth.'[43] However, there is also 'A Syrian from Palestine'.[44]

The second-century texts cited here appear to be rather free in their usage of ethnic and geographic terminology, while various cultural aspects

---

[39] M. Sartre, in A. Calbi *et al.* (eds.), *L'epigrafia del villaggio: Actes du VIIe colloque international Borghesi à l'occasion du cinquantenaire d'Epigraphica (Forlì, 27–30 septembre 1990)* (Faenza, 1993), 133–5; *Année Épigraphique* 1993: 1636.

[40] Cf. below, p. 164.

[41] *Reviviscentes sive Piscator* 19.6 (*The Fisherman*): Σύρος, ὦ Φιλοσοφία, τῶν Ἐπευφρατιδίων. ἀλλὰ τί τοῦτο; καὶ γὰρ τούτων τινὰς οἶδα τῶν ἀντιδίκων μου οὐχ ἧττον ἐμοῦ βαρβάρους τὸ γένος

[42] *Bis Accusatus* 27 (*The Double Indictment*): Ἐγὼ γάρ, ὦ ἄνδρες δικασταί, τουτονὶ κομιδῇ μειράκιον ὄντα, βάρβαρον ἔτι τὴν φωνὴν καὶ μονονουχὶ κάνδυν ἐνδεδυκότα εἰς τὸν Ἀσσύριον τρόπον,

[43] *Podagra* 265: Σύροι μέν ἐσμεν, ἐκ Δαμασκοῦ τῷ γένει,

[44] *Philopseudes* 16.4-5: τὸν Σύρον τὸν ἐκ τῆς Παλαιστίνης

are associated with those terms without obvious consistency: language, accent, culture, clothing, all appear as frequent and important elements.

Syrians are still recognized – or stigmatized – as a separate ethnic group in the fourth century, as is clear from a passage in the Historia Augusta on Severus Alexander:

> He [sc. the Emperor Severus Alexander] wished it to be thought that he derived his descent from the Roman people, for he was ashamed at being called a Syrian, particularly because, on a certain festival, the people of Antioch and of Egypt and Alexandria had angered him with jibes, as they are wont to do, calling him both a Syrian *archisynagogus* and a high priest.[45]

In this case the author does not mean Syrians in the sense of inhabitants of the province of Syria, for the people of Antioch are described as jeering the emperor, clearly because he was regarded as an ethnic and cultural Syrian as opposed to the Hellenized urban population of Antioch. The source somehow brings Judaism also in the equation.

To sum up: Syria is, first, a geographic concept, then an administrative term, while neither is necessarily restricted to the region inhabited by ethnic Syrians. It is sometimes, confusingly, called Assyria and Coele-Syria, just as Syrians may also be called Assyrians. This is not a matter of ignorance, for Meleager of Gadara and Lucian of Samosata also refer to Assyria and Assyrians. The Phoenicians are described as a people inhabiting the coastal plain from the Orontes to Ascalon in the south, including a number of Palestinian cities. When considering subdivisions the picture may be even more confusing. Coele-Syria can be used in a broad sense as almost the equivalent of Syria, and in a narrow sense, for the Beqa and Jordan valleys, or in an intermediate sense as covering the coastal region of Syria from the mouth of the Orontes to Ascalon, roughly the equivalent of some instances in the use of 'Phoenice'.

Regarding the ethnic indications it remains to be observed that these can, but need not point very specifically to origin: the Greek poet Meleager of Gadara calls himself a Syrian, for instance, but his city of origin is Attic because of its culture. Often, however, ethnicity, language, dress and culture go together. The term Hellenic is used for and by communities that definitely did not claim to descend from Greeks in Greece or Asia Minor. Professions such as farming and trading may also be regarded as ethnic features, e.g. by Strabo.[46]

---

[45] SHA, *Severus Alexander* 28.7: *volebat videri originem de Romanorum gente trahere, quia eum pudebat Syrum dici, maxime quod quodam tempore festo, ut solent, Antiochenses, Agyptii, Alexandrini lacessiverant conviciolis, et Syrum archisynagogum eum vocantes et archiereum.*

[46] Below it is noted that 'Arab' in Semitic languages indicates a nomad, while in Greek or Latin it usually is an ethnic indication.

Palestine

In Greek and Latin texts the name Palestine (Συρίη ἡ Παλαιστίνη or Παλαιστίνη Συρίη) occurs first in the fifth century BC in several passages in the work of Herodotus.[47] One of these, in book I, has already been cited above. In Herodotus' work it is a geographic concept referring to the coastal plain from Phoenicia to Gaza. It is an open question how the name Palaestina got associated with all of the coastal area up to Phoenicia in the north, or how the name reached a Greek author in the fifth century, for the Philistines had disappeared as a people centuries earlier. Herodotus does not use Ioudaia/Judaea as a term. Of the existence of Jews he is unaware, although he may possibly be referring to them when he mentions 'The Phoenicians and Syrians of Palestine' who acknowledged having learnt the custom of circumcision from the Egyptians.[48] It would be interesting to know whether Herodotus indeed knew of the Jews without giving them a name of their own, but referring to an ethnic group in a specific geographical area. 'Palaistine' is a Greek transliteration of the Hebrew Plšth, 'the land of the Philistines'. The Philistines lived in the southern part of the coastal plain. Note that, clearly, the name Palestine is not quite familiar, for Herodotus speaks of 'the land called Syria-Palestine' or, when referring to the inhabitants, of 'the so-called Syrians of Palestine'.[49] It is for Herodotus purely a geographic term: there is a part of Syria that is called Palestine or, rather, Palestinian Syria. There is no ethnic term 'Palestinians' in Herodotus, for there is no such ethnic group known to him. The inhabitants of the region are 'Syrians of Palestine' as already noted, or Syrians in Palestine.[50] In the fourth century BC Aristotle also uses the name, but only on one occasion, clearly as a geographic concept, which here includes the Dead Sea as well.[51]

In the Hellenistic period, the Ptolemaic satrapy of 'Syria and Phoenice' was conquered by the Seleucids around 200 BC and renamed 'Koile-Syria and Phoenice'. It included all of what is known to us as Palestine or Judaea in the broader sense. It is significant that, side by side with this administrative nomenclature, 'Palestinian Syria' continued to be used as a

---

[47] Hdt. 1.104–5, cited above; 2.106: ἐν δὲ τῇ Παλαιστίνῃ Συρίῃ; 3.91 Φοινίκη τε πᾶσα καὶ Συρίη ἡ Παλαιστίνη καλεομένη; for which cf. Asheri, *Commentary*, 484–5; Hdt. 4.39, 7.89.

[48] Hdt. 2.104.3: Φοίνικες δὲ καὶ Σύριοι οἱ ἐν τῇ Παλαιστίνῃ καὶ αὐτοὶ ὁμολογέουσι παρ' Αἰγυπτίων μεμαθηκέναι.

[49] Hdt. 3.5.3: Συρίων τῶν Παλαιστίνων καλεομένων.

[50] Hdt. 7.89.3: Συρίοισι τοῖσι ἐν τῇ Παλαιστίνῃ.

[51] Aristotle, *Meteorologica* 359a.16: εἰ δ' ἔστιν ὥσπερ μυθολογοῦσί τινες ἐν Παλαιστίνῃ τοιαύτη λίμνη …

geographical term without ethnic (or administrative) implications within the satrapy of (Koile) Syria and Phoenice. Ioudaia/Judaea still was used in its narrow sense, for 'the Land of the Jews' at this stage. The Jewish author Philo, discussing the biblical period, equates 'Syria Palaestina' or, rather 'Palestinian Syria', with biblical Canaan as a geographical and ethnical term. He uses contemporary geographical terms: 'Phoenicia, Coele-Syria and Palestine which then was called Canaan.'[52] Judaea became the name of a political entity only under the Hasmonaeans. Under Roman rule Judaea was the name first of Herod's kingdom and, after annexation, of a province attached to the larger province of Syria. Thus Strabo uses the name Judaea,[53] except when he cites an earlier source.[54] Some authors, such as Pomponius Mela[55] and Pliny,[56] are not quite clear regarding the relationship between Syria, Palestine, and Judaea as geographical terms. However this may be, Judaea was the name of the province from its annexation until the reign of Hadrian. It is the usual name in e.g. Josephus,[57] Philo,[58] Tacitus,[59] and in inscriptions.[60]

Following the suppression of the Bar Kokhba revolt, the province was renamed Syria-Palaestina. The change of the name is neatly illustrated by inscriptions mentioning Julius Severus as governor of Judaea on *ILS*

---

[52] Philo, *De Abrahamo* 133: ἡ Σοδομιτῶν χώρα μοῖρα τῆς Χανανίτιδος γῆς, ἣν ὕστερον ὠνόμασαν Συρίαν Παλαιστίνην; *de vita Mosis* 1.163: τὴν ἀποικίαν ἔστελλεν εἰς Φοινίκην καὶ Συρίαν τὴν κοίλην καὶ Παλαιστίνην, ἣ τότε. προσηγορεύετο Χαναναίων, ἧς οἱ ὅροι τριῶν ἡμερῶν ὁδὸν διειστήκεσαν ἀπ᾽ Αἰγύπτου. For Canaanites as an ethnic designation: *De virtutibus* 221.1 Θάμαρ ἦν τῶν ἀπὸ τῆς Παλαιστίνης Συρίας γύναιον, 'Tamar was a woman from Palestinian Syria'.

[53] E.g. Strabo 16.1.1; 16.2.2 (cited above); 16.2.21: ἡ δ᾽ ὑπὲρ ταύτης μεσόγαια μέχρι τῶν Ἀράβων ἡ μεταξὺ Γάζης καὶ Ἀντιλιβάνου Ἰουδαία λέγεται.

[54] Strabo 16.4.18.

[55] Pomponius Mela 1.11.62–3: *Syria late litora tenet, terrasque etiam latius introrsus, aliis aliisque nuncupata nominibus: nam et Coele dicitur et Mesopotamia et Damascene et Adiabene et Babylonia et Iudaea et Commagene et Sophene. Hic Palaestine est qua tangit Arabas, tum Phoenice ...*

[56] Pliny, *NH* 5.66: *Iuxta Syria litus occupat, quondam terrarum maxuma et plurimis distincta nominibus. Namque Palaestinae vocabatur qua contingit Arabas, et Iudaea et Coele, den Phoenice et qua recedit intus Damascena ...* Stern, *Greek and Latin Authors*, I, 472, suggests that Pliny may have followed Mela which seems likely. *NH* 5.68: *Ostracine Arabia finitur, a Pelusio LXV p. mox Idumaea incipit et Palaestina ab emersu Sirbonis lacus, quem quidam CL circuitu tradidere.* 5.70: *Supra Idumaeam et Samari<a>m Iudaea longe lateque funditur. Pars eius Syriae iuncta Galilaea vocatur, Arabiae vero et Aegypto proxima Peraea, asperis dispersa montibus et a ceteris Iudaeis Iordane amne discreta.* For a different interpretation: Sartre, 'La Syrie Creuse n'existe pas', 20–1.

[57] Josephus, *Ant.* 20.105: Στάσεως δ᾽ ἐμπεσούσης τῇ τῶν Ἱεροσολυμιτῶν πόλει Κουμανοῦ τὰ κατὰ τὴν Ἰουδαίαν πράγματα διοικοῦντος ἐφθάρησαν ὑπὸ ταύτης πολλοὶ τῶν Ἰουδαίων. Note that Josephus does not usually see a need to clarify whether he means the Kingdom/Province of Judaea or Judaea in the narrow sense, for which e.g. *BJ* 3.51–6.

[58] Philo, *Legatio* 299: Πιλᾶτος ἦν τῶν ὑπάρχων ἐπίτροπος ἀποδεδειγμένος τῆς Ἰουδαίας·.

[59] Tacitus, *Ann.* 12.23.

[60] *Année Épigraphique* 1999: 1681; L. Boffo, *Iscrizioni greche e latine per lo studio della bibbia* (Brescia, 1994), 219, 303, 317; *CIL* XVI 33, a military diploma of AD 86.

1056,[61] but of Syria-Palaestina on an inscription of AD 134.[62] In non-Christian texts the old name, Judaea, is still used occasionally although rarely. However, still in the second century, Ptolemy uses both names without distinction.[63]

Thus Rome removed from the nomenclature the name Judaea derived from the Jewish people, replacing it with the traditional, geographic Graeco-Latin 'Syria-Palaestina', familiar since the fifth century, obviously one of the steps taken to punish the Jewish rebels. The name 'Judaea' was, at the time, clearly associated with the Jewish people. It was not a purely geographic concept. In the case of Palestine, however, the emphasis must be laid on 'geographic'. In the second century there was no ethnic group that called itself 'Palestinians'. A few texts of the late fourth century mention 'Palaestini', which, according to the regular pattern of this period, identifies the inhabitants of a province in ethnic terms.[64] As already noted, the Greek term for a province can be *ethnos* (ἔθνος) and a Latin variant is sometimes *natio*.[65]

The Islamic conquest in the 630s marks the end of this survey – but not, of course, of the use of the name Palestine which, soon after the Islamic conquest, was organized by the Moslems as 'Jund Filastin', 'the military district of Palestine'.

Again, it must be stressed that, throughout the period considered here, the name 'Palestine' was used in a geographic sense or as an administrative term. It does not refer to an ethnic group, apart from the instances in the fourth century AD.

An unusual reference occurs in Stephanus Byzantius where Hyrcania is described as 'a village of Palaestine, near Judaea', where the latter, perhaps,

---

[61] *ILS* 1056: ... *leg. pr. pr. [pr]ovinciae Iudeae, [l]eg. pr. pr. [provi]nciae Suriae. Huic [senatus a]uctore [imp. Tra]iano Hadrian[o Au]g. ornamenta triu[mp]halia decrevit ob res in [Iu]dea prospere ge[st]as. [D.] d ...*

[62] *Année Épigraphique* 1904: 9 (AD 134): *Cn(aeo) Iul(io) S[evero] / co(n)s(uli) le[g(ato) Aug(usti)] / pr(o) pr(aetore) pr[ovinciae] / Syriae Pa[laestinae] / triunf[alib(us)! ornamen]/tis [honorato —*

[63] Ptolemy, *Geographia* 5.C.16.1: Παλαιστίνης Ἰουδαίας; 5.15.8.14: παρὰ δὲ τὴν Ἰουδαίαν; 5.16.1.2: Ἡ Παλαιστίνη (Συρία), ἥτις καὶ Ἰουδαία καλεῖται; 5.17.1.3: τῇ τε Παλαιστίνη Ἰουδαίᾳ.

[64] SHA, *Niger* 7.9: *idem Palaestinis rogantibus ut eorum censitio levaretur idcirco quod esset gravat respondit ... Severus* 14.6: *Palaestinis poenam remisit quam ob causam Nigri meruerant.* 17.1: *In itinere Palaestinis plurima iura fundavit. Not. Dig. Or.* 34.28: *Equites primi felices [sagittarii indigenae] Palaestini, Sabure sive Veterocariae*

[65] See F. Mitthof, 'Zur Neustiftung von Identität unter imperialer Herrschaft: Die Provinzen des Römischen Reiches als ethnische Identitäten', in W. Pohl, C. Gantner, and R. E. Payne (eds.), *Visions of Community in the Post-Roman World: The West, Byzantium and the Islamic World, 300–1100* (Farnham, 2012), 61–72. Mitthof cites a text mention τὸ τῆς Ἀσίας ἔθνος (MAMA 8.508). He lists examples of the indication of *natio* on tombstones of soldiers from Misenum and Praetorian soldiers from the Danube and Balkan areas, where *natio* clearly represents a province.

is used in its narrower, pre-Hasmonaean sense.[66] Stephanus sometimes refers to Palaestine as the name of a province[67] and sometimes to Judaea.[68]

To sum up: from the fifth century BC onwards 'Palestina/Palestine' is common in Greek as a geographical term for a part of Syria. It became an administrative appellation only under Hadrian and had no ethnic connotations in antiquity until the period when the inhabitants of provinces came to be regarded as such.

Judaea

The name of Ioudaia/Judaea was the Greek rendering of the Persian satrapy of Yahud (538–332 BC) which, in turn, somehow indicated the formal tribal area of Judah of biblical times.[69]

The earliest appearance of the name in Greek occurs in Hecataeus of Abdera (300 BC), 'the land now called Judaea'.[70] It is clear that he means Judaea in the original, narrower sense: the land of the Jews.[71] In other words: the land is named after the people rather than the reverse. In the same period Clearchus of Soli states the opposite: the people are named after the land they inhabit, but he also claims that they, the Jews, are descendants from Indian philosophers,[72] an interpretation based upon theory only, derived from information transmitted through other authors.

In the third century BC Manetho twice mentions 'what is now called Judaea'.[73] Lysimachus of Alexandria (undated, perhaps second or first century BC) gives the Egyptian version of the exodus story as found later in Tacitus and says that the Jews 'came to the country now called Judaea'.[74] In the first

---

[66] Stephanus Byz. s.v. Ὑρκανία, … ἔστι καὶ Ὑρκανία κώμη τῆς Παλαιστίνης πλησίον τῆς Ἰουδαίας, ἀπὸ Ὑρκανοῦ τοῦ ἐξάρχου τῶν Ἰουδαίων.

[67] Stephanus Byz. 48.13: Αἰλία, πόλις Παλαιστίνης, ἡ πάλαι Ἱεροσόλυμα,

[68] For instance: Τιβεριάς, πόλις τῆς Ἰουδαίας

[69] J. W. Betlyon, 'The Provincial Government of Persian Period Judea and the Yehud Coins', *Journal of Biblical Literature* 106 (1986): 633–42.

[70] Hecataeus of Abdera, fr. 3a, 264, F.6* (Stern, *Greek and Latin Authors*, I, no. 11): ὁ δὲ πολὺς λεὼς ἐξέπεσεν εἰς τὴν νῦν καλουμένην Ἰουδαίαν, οὐ πόρρω μὲν κειμένην τῆς Αἰγύπτου, παντελῶς δὲ ἔρημον οὖσαν κατ᾽ ἐκείνους τοὺς χρόνους. Cf. Josephus, *Contra Apionem* 1.195–9.

[71] Hecataeus, fr. 3a, 264, F.21.43 (Stern, *Greek and Latin Authors*, I, no. 12): ἡ γὰρ Ἰουδαία τοσαύτη πλῆθός ἐστιν

[72] Clearchus, ap. Stern, *Greek and Latin Authors*, I, no. 15 (Josephus, *Contra Apionem* 1.179): κἀκεῖνος τοίνυν τὸ μὲν γένος ἦν Ἰουδαῖος ἐκ τῆς Κοίλης Συρίας, οὗτοι δ᾽ εἰσὶν ἀπόγονοι τῶν ἐν Ἰνδοῖς φιλοσόφων. καλοῦνται δέ, ὥς φασιν, οἱ φιλόσοφοι παρὰ μὲν Ἰνδοῖς Καλανοί, παρὰ δὲ Σύροις Ἰουδαῖοι, τοὔνομα λαβόντες ἀπὸ τοῦ τόπου. προσαγορεύεται γὰρ ὃν κατοικοῦσι τόπον Ἰουδαία.

[73] Manetho, *FHG* 2 42.90: ἐν τῇ νῦν Ἰουδαίᾳ καλουμένῃ; this refers to the foundation of Jerusalem; 54.8; *FHG* 609 F 10a (Josephus, *Contra Apionem* 1.228).

[74] Ap. Josephus, *Contra Apionem* 1.310 (Stern, *Greek and Latin Authors*, I, no. 158): ἐλθεῖν εἰς τὴν νῦν Ἰουδαίαν προσαγορευομένην,

half of the first century Apion, as cited by Josephus, uses the same expression.[75] Hellenistic authors apparently use Judaea as a contemporary name while lacking information concerning an older name for the country.

Another early reference occurs in the Letter of Aristeas (third-second century BC), which is a Jewish text and therefore represents a different perspective from the others which derive from non-Jewish authors discussing Jewish history. It uses the name in the sense of 'the country of the Jews',[76] as in the phrase: 'When we arrived in the land we saw the city situated in the middle of the whole of Judea on the top of a mountain of considerable altitude.'[77] The name is here used in the narrow sense, excluding Samaritis and Idumaea.[78] Elsewhere the Letter speaks of 'those who had been transported (to Egypt) from Judaea' or 'from the country of the Jews'.[79] Thus 'Judaea' and 'the country of the Jews' are synonyms.

In the books of the Maccabees 'Judaea' is, naturally, used in the narrow sense – there was no extended Judaea at the time.[80] Note also the opening sentence of 2 Macc 1:1: 'To their brothers, the Jews in Egypt, [greetings,] their brothers in Jerusalem and those in the land of Judaea a perfect peace.'[81] Judaea is here mentioned as the territory (*chora*) of Jerusalem, a fact which, incidentally, should be taken into account when considering whether Jerusalem was a *polis*.[82]

In the later Hellenistic period the Hasmonaeans became Kings of Judaea. Under Roman rule Judaea became the name, first of Herod's kingdom and, after annexation, of the province which was attached to the larger province of Syria. It is clear that 'Judaea' as an administrative and political name originated in the period when it was a Roman client kingdom. As

---

[75] Ap. Josephus, *Contra Apionem* 2.21 (Stern, *Greek and Latin Authors*, I, no. 165): εἰς τὴν χώραν τὴν νῦν Ἰουδαίαν λεγομένην.

[76] *Aristeae Epistula* 4.3: περὶ τῶν μετοικισθέντων εἰς Αἴγυπτον ἐκ τῆς Ἰουδαίας ὑπὸ τοῦ πατρὸς τοῦ βασιλέως,; 11.4:χαρακτῆρσι γὰρ ἰδίοις κατὰ τὴν Ἰουδαίαν χρῶνται,; 184.3: οἱ παραγινόμενοι πρὸς αὐτὸν ἀπὸ τῆς Ἰουδαίας; also: 12.4; 318.2.

[77] *Aristeae Epistula* 83–4: ἐθεωροῦμεν τὴν πόλιν μέσην κειμένην τῆς ὅλης Ἰουδαίας ἐπ᾽ ὄρους ὑψηλὴν ἔχοντος τὴν ἀνάτασιν.

[78] Samaritis: *Aristeae Epistula* 107 (Σαμαρεῖτιν); Idumaia: *Aristeae Epistula* 107.4 (τῇ τῶν Ἰδουμαίων χώρᾳ).

[79] *Aristeae Epistula* 12: τῶν μετηγμένων ἐκ τῆς Ἰουδαίας and: ἐκ τῆς τῶν Ἰουδαίων χώρας εἰς Αἴγυπτον.

[80] 1 Macc 5:23: it excludes the Galilee; 9:50: Bacchides builds fortresses in Judaea in sites, all of them in Judaea proper; 10:38 and 11:334: three districts transferred from Samaritis to Judaea: Apheraima, Lydda, and Ramathaim.

[81] 2 Macc 1:1: οἱ ἐν Ἱεροσολύμοις Ἰουδαῖοι καὶ οἱ ἐν τῇ χώρᾳ τῆς Ἰουδαίας εἰρήνην ἀγαθήν·

[82] V. Tcherikover, 'Was Jerusalem a Polis?', *IEJ* 14 (1964): 61–78, argued that it did not have the characteristics and institutions required. However, if it had a territory, that would be enough, in principle, make it a *polis* in ancient terms. Tcherikover's argument seems to be redundant.

such it covered a much wider area than the original Judaea in the narrow, ethnic sense, and included numerous non-Jewish inhabitants. Thus Strabo uses the name Judaea for this region, except when he cites an earlier source. He does so also when referring, e.g. to the activities of Pompey in 63 BC.[83] As already noted, some authors, such as Pomponius Mela and Pliny, are not quite clear regarding the relationship between Syria, Palestine, and Judaea as geographical terms. However this may be, Judaea was the name of the province from its annexation until the reign of Hadrian.

Strabo notes that the western parts of Judaea 'towards Casius' and by the lake are occupied by the Idumaeans. He states that the north of Judaea

> is inhabited in general, as is each place in particular, by mixed groups of people from Aegyptian and Arabian and Phoenician tribes; for such are those who occupy Galilee and Hiericus and Philadelphia and Samaria, which last Herod surnamed Sebaste. But though the inhabitants are mixed up thus, the most prevalent of the accredited reports in regard to the temple at Jerusalem represent the ancestors of the present Jews, as they are called, as Aegyptians.[84]

Strabo also refers to Judaea as (the country of) the *Ioudaioi* which there, clearly, does not mean 'Jews', but 'the people of Judaea', all of them, Jews and others. This is clear, for instance, when he writes: 'The first people who occupy Arabia Felix, after the Syrians and *Ioudaioi*, are farmers.'[85] Here then *Ioudaioi* are not just Jews, but 'all of those living in Judaea'.[86]

---

[83] Strabo, fr. 2a, 91, F.14.8 (Stern, *Greek and Latin Authors*, I, no. 103; Josephus, *Ant.* 14.35): μέμνηται δὲ τοῦ δώρου καὶ Στράβων ὁ Καππάδοξ λέγων οὕτως· "ἦλθεν δὲ καὶ ἐξ Αἰγύπτου πρεσβεία καὶ στέφανος ἀπὸ χρυσῶν τετρακισχιλίων, καὶ ἐκ τῆς Ἰουδαίας εἴτε ἄμπελος εἴτε κῆπος· τερπωλὴν ὠνόμαζον τὸ δημιούργημα.

[84] Strabo 16.2.34 (761): ταῦτα μὲν προσάρκτια· τὰ πολλὰ δ᾽ ὡς ἕκαστα ἐστιν ὑπὸ φύλων οἰκούμενα μικτῶν ἔκ τε Αἰγυπτίων ἐθνῶν καὶ Ἀραβίων καὶ Φοινίκων· τοιοῦτοι γὰρ οἱ τὴν Γαλιλαίαν ἔχοντες καὶ τὸν Ἱερικοῦντα καὶ τὴν Φιλαδέλφειαν καὶ Σαμάρειαν, ἣν Ἡρώδης Σεβαστὴν ἐπωνόμασεν. οὕτω δ᾽ ὄντων μιγάδων ἡ κρατοῦσα μάλιστα φήμη τῶν περὶ τὸ ἱερὸν τὸ ἐν τοῖς Ἱεροσολύμοις πιστευομένων Αἰγυπτίους ἀποφαίνει τοὺς προγόνους τῶν νῦν Ἰουδαίων λεγομένων. Cf. Stern's comments, *Greek and Latin Authors*, I, 304–5.

[85] Strabo 16.4.2 (767): ἔχουσι δ᾽ αὐτὴν οἱ μὲν πρῶτοι μετὰ τοὺς Σύρους καὶ τοὺς Ἰουδαίους ἄνθρωποι γεωργοί·

[86] This is no idiosyncracy of Strabo. Below we see the same in the case of Plutarch. This is one of various reasons why I do not accept the claim that Jews in antiquity ought to be called 'Judaeans' rather than 'Jews'. Cf. S. Mason, 'Jews, Judaeans, Judaizing, Judaism: Problems of Categorization in Ancient History', *Journal for the Study of Judaism* 38 (2007): 457–512; the original idea has been discussed extensively by S. J. D. Cohen, *The Beginnings of Jewishness* (Berkeley, CA, 1999), ch. 3, and by D. R. Schwartz, '"Judaean" or "Jew"? How Should We Translate *Ioudaios* in Josephus?', in J. Frey *et al.* (eds.), *Jewish Identity in the Graeco-Roman World* (Leiden, 2007), 3–28. From Pompey to Hadrian Judaeans were all the peoples inhabiting the kingdom, later the province, of Judaea. Note also the fact that Dio 37.16–17, discussed below, explicitly contradicts the theory that 'Judaeans' would be a more suitable appellation than 'Jews'. One could argue that Strabo's and Plutarch's

To be observed also is Strabo's frequent use of 'those called now ...' (τῶν νῦν Ἰουδαίων λεγομένων..). That is a term reserved for a precise, contemporary ethnic appellation.

It is clear that Strabo always refers to Judaea as a geographic term in the broad sense. He describes its inhabitants as mixed. The 'present-day Jews' are identified with the Temple in Jerusalem and were originally descendants of the Egyptians in his work. This is the hostile version, represented also by Celsus, Diodorus,[87] and Chaeremon,[88] but not found in Hecataeus and Clearchus. Strabo omits the claim that the Jews were lepers expelled from Egypt, a tradition that is found in an early (and nuanced) version in Hecataeus.[89] However, a little further on Strabo refers to Judaea as 'being ruled by tyrants', so here it is indicated as a political entity.[90] There are also clear instances in Strabo's work of the use of the name Judaea in a purely geographical sense, e.g. where it is described as a country suitable for the growing of palms.[91]

Plutarch mentions Judaea in the time of Pompey as a kingdom.[92] In enumerating the triumph of Pompey he mentions 'Mesopotamia and the region of Phoenice, Palestine, Judaea, Arabia'.[93] For rhetorical effect both Palestine and Judaea are mentioned, but that should not be taken as meaning there was a difference between the two. Plutarch several times speaks of *Ioudaioi* when, clearly, he means (all of) Judaea in a political or geographical sense, for instance when he calls Aristoboulos 'King of the Jews'.[94] He was in fact king of Judaea, i.e. all peoples living in Judaea, Jews and non-Jews. In 37–36 BC Antony gave Cleopatra the following addition to her dominions, as Plutarch formulates it: 'Phoenicia, Coele Syria, Cyprus and

---

Ioudaioi ought to be translated as 'Judaeans' because they include all inhabitants of Judaea, including those who were not Jews in a religious or ethnic sense.

[87] Diodorus 34/35.1, one of the most negative passages regarding Jews, where it is reported that a majority of the advisors of Antiochus Sidetes favoured completely wiping out the Jewish people. Chaeremon is cited by Josephus, *Contra Apionem* 1.288; see Stern, I, no. 178, with comments on p. 420 and a discussion of the related papyrus *PSI* no.982 = *CPJ* no. 520.

[88] See the comments by Stern, *Greek and Latin Authors*, I, 305.

[89] Ap. Diodorus 40.3; Stern, *Greek and Latin Authors*, I, no. 11.

[90] Strabo 16.2.40: Ἤδη δ' οὖν φανερῶς τυραννουμένης τῆς Ἰουδαίας πρῶτος ἀνθ' ἱερέως ἀνέδειξεν ἑαυτὸν βασιλέα Ἀλέξανδρος·

[91] Strabo 17.51.6 (818): θαυμάζειν οὖν ἄξιον πῶς ταὐτὸ κλίμα οἰκοῦντες τῇ Ἰουδαίᾳ καὶ ὅμοροι οἱ περὶ τὸ Δέλτα καὶ τὴν Ἀλεξάνδρειαν τοσοῦτον διαλλάττουσιν, ἐκείνης πρὸς ἄλλῳ φοίνικι καὶ τὸν καρυωτὸν γεννώσης, οὐ πολὺ κρείττονα τοῦ Βαβυλωνίου.

[92] Plutarch, *Pompey* 39.2: τὴν δὲ Ἰουδαίαν κατεστρέψατο, καὶ συνέλαβεν Ἀριστόβουλον τὸν βασιλέα.

[93] Plutarch, *Pompey* 45.2: ἦν δὲ τάδε· Πόντος, Ἀρμενία, Καππαδοκία, Παφλαγονία, Μηδία, Κολχίς, Ἴβηρες, Ἀλβανοί, Συρία, Κιλικία, Μεσοποταμία, τὰ περὶ Φοινίκην καὶ Παλαιστίνην, Ἰουδαία, Ἀραβία, τὸ πειρατικὸν ἅπαν ἐν γῇ καὶ θαλάσσῃ καταπεπολεμημένον.

[94] Plutarch, *Pompey* 45.4.5: βασιλεὺς Ἰουδαίων Ἀριστόβουλος.

a large part of Cilicia; and still further, the balsam-producing part of the *Ioudaioi*, and all that part of Arabia of the Nabataeans which slopes toward the outer sea.'[95] It is not quite certain what Coele Syria here means, but, obviously the balsam-producing part of the *Ioudaioi* here is a geographical idea. It is hard not to say that *Ioudaioi*, normally indicating a people, here = *Ioudaia* in a geographical sense, a region. As regards 'Arabia of the Nabataeans', it is clear that this assumes the Nabataeans occupied part of a larger region, Arabia.

'While in my time [i.e. Appian's time, ca. 95–ca. 165] when the Roman Emperor Trajan was exterminating the Jewish people in Egypt (τὸ ἐν Αἰγύπτῳ Ἰουδαίων γένος) …'[96] Here, therefore we have 'The Jewish people; those of Jewish origin (*genos*) in Egypt'. There is a very clear distinction between *ethnos* and *genos*. As already noted, *ethnos* can be the Greek term for Latin *provincia*.[97] *Genos* here explicitly refers to those of Jewish origin, living in Egypt.

As already observed, in this period the name 'Iudaea' is well-attested in texts, on inscriptions and coins, while 'Palestine' is hardly encountered.

A variant may be found in Tacitus,[98] where, instead of Ituraea and Judaea he writes 'the Ituraeans and Jews' who were 'added to [the province of Syria]'. This refers to the people rather than the region and suits the common phenomenon whereby peoples rather than territories are indicated as subject of authority,[99] but at the same time reinforces the point made here, that ethnic and geographic appellations often are used interchangeably because the distinction is not seen as essential.

Occasionally we find an eponymous ancestor for the Jews in Hellenistic authors, notably Alexander Polyhistor,[100] who refers to the 'children of Semiramis, Juda and Idumaea', and Plutarch who reports

---

[95] Plutarch, *Ant.* 36.3: Φοινίκην, Κοίλην Συρίαν, Κύπρον, Κιλικίας πολλήν· ἔτι δὲ τῆς τ᾽ Ἰουδαίων τὴν τὸ βάλσαμον φέρουσαν καὶ τῆς Ναβαταίων Ἀραβίας ὅση πρὸς τὴν ἐκτὸς ἀποκλίνει θάλασσαν. For the chronology, see Stern, *Greek and Latin Authors*, I, 569–72.

[96] Appian, *BC* 13.90: ὅπερ ἐπ᾽ ἐμοῦ κατὰ Ῥωμαίων αὐτοκράτορα Τραϊανόν, ἐξολλύντα τὸ ἐν Αἰγύπτῳ Ἰουδαίων γένος, ὑπὸ τῶν Ἰουδαίων ἐς τὰς τοῦ πολέμου χρείας κατηρείφθη..

[97] Cf. the complex use of ethnic terminology in Herodotus as analysed by C. P. Jones, 'ἔθνος and γένος in Herodotus', *CQ* 46 (1996): 315–20.

[98] Tacitus, *Ann.* 12.23: *Ituraeique et Iudaei defunctis regibus Sohaema atque Agrippa provinciae Suriae additi*. For the usual terminology in Tacitus, e.g. *Hist.* 5.1: *Eiusdem anni principio Caesar Titus, perdomandae Iudaeae delectus a pater* … For the extent of the province of Judaea: *Hist.* 5.5: *Terra finesque qua ad Orientem vergunt Arabia terminantur, a meridie Aegyptus obiacet, ab occasu Phoenices et mare, septentrionem e latere Syriae longe prospectant*.

[99] Cf. B. Isaac, *The Limits of Empire: The Roman Army in the East* (Oxford, 1992), 394–97.

[100] Stephanus Byz. s.v.: Ἰουδαία. Ἀλέξανδρος ὁ πολυίστωρ, ἀπὸ τῶν παίδων Σεμιράμιδος Ἰούδα καὶ Ἰδουμαία,

with disapproval a tradition that Typhon was the father of Hierosolymus and Judaeus.[101]

An important passage of Cassius Dio deserves full consideration:

> This happened at that time [68 BC] in Palestine; for this has long been the name of the whole province (*ethnos*) extending from Phoenicia to Egypt along the inner sea. They (plural) have also another name that they have acquired: for the land (*chora*) has been named Judaea, and the people themselves Jews (*Ioudaioi*). I do not know how they acquired this appellation, but it applies also to all the other people who follow their customs even if they are of other origin (*alloethneis*; Cary, Loeb: of alien race). This group exists also among the Romans, and though often repressed has increased very much and has gained a right of freedom in its observances.[102]

Dio uses the regular name of the province in his days, Palaestina – he says it has long been the name, presumably aware of its appearance as a geographic concept from Herodotus onward – and then the term *ethnos* is given here as the equivalent of the Latin *provincia*, as already noted twice above. Dio refers to it as an administrative unit within a specific territory. He then moves on smoothly to consider the Jews as a people, as is clear from his use of the plural '*they* also have another name'. He says that 'their land was called "Judaea"'[103] and they themselves 'Ioudaioi', but the origin of the name is unknown to him. Like other Greek and Latin authors he is unaware of the original tribal association with the name Juda. However, and this is essential, he recognizes them as a people and observes what was an anomaly in his days: those who are of different descent, but adopt their customs are also called Jews. Dio thus recognizes an exception to the rule that people could not change their ethnicity, except in so far as they received the Roman citizenship – which undoubtedly formed a conceptual basis for the idea. Anyone could become a Jew who accepted Jewish customs, as he formulates it.[104] The fact that this phenomenon could be a

---

[101] Plutarch, *De Iside et Osiride* 31 (Stern, *Greek and Latin Authors*, I, no. 259).

[102] Dio 37.16–17: ταῦτα μὲν τότε ἐν τῇ Παλαιστίνῃ ἐγένετο· οὕτω γὰρ τὸ σύμπαν ἔθνος, ὅσον ἀπὸ τῆς Φοινίκης μέχρι τῆς Αἰγύπτου παρὰ τὴν θάλασσαν τὴν ἔσω παρήκει, ἀπὸ παλαιοῦ κέκληται. ἔχουσι δὲ καὶ ἕτερον ὄνομα ἐπίκτητον· ἥ τε γὰρ χώρα Ἰουδαία καὶ αὐτοὶ Ἰουδαῖοι ὠνομάδαται. ἡ δὲ ἐπίκλησις αὕτη ἐκείνοις μὲν οὐκ οἶδ' ὅθεν ἤρξατο γενέσθαι, φέρει δὲ καὶ ἐπὶ τοὺς ἄλλους ἀνθρώπους ὅσοι τὰ νόμιμα αὐτῶν, καίπερ ἀλλοεθνεῖς ὄντες, ζηλοῦσι. καὶ ἔστι καὶ παρὰ τοῖς Ῥωμαίοις τὸ γένος τοῦτο, κολουσθὲν <μὲν> πολλάκις, αὐξηθὲν δὲ ἐπὶ πλεῖστον, ὥστε καὶ ἐς παρρησίαν τῆς νομίσεως ἐκνικῆσαι.

[103] For the use of χώρα in this connection, see also 2 Macc 1:1, cited above: Judaea was the *chora* of Jerusalem.

[104] I disagree with the interpretation of Mason, 'Jews, Judaeans, Judaizing, Judaism', 457–512, at 509–10. This is not a proper occasion to discuss Jewish proselytism and what Tacitus has to say about proselytes in *Hist.* 5.5.

social reality was seen much earlier by Strabo in connection with the con-version of the Idumaeans.[105] The separation of the concepts of descent, eth-nic identity, and religion had tremendous consequences for Jewish history and, no less, for the growth of Christianity.

To sum up our considerations of the use of 'Judaea' in ancient sources: to begin with it was the name of an Achaemenid satrapy. In the Hellenistic period it could imply (a) the name of 'The Land of the Jews', in its narrow sense and (b) an administrative district. In the Books of the Maccabees it is also used in its former sense. Then, when the Jews gained political and military control, it naturally became successively the name of the Hasmonaean and Herodian kingdoms and thereafter of the Roman province. The Hasmonaeans and Herod expanded their control over neighbouring peoples and cities. As a result of these conquests and gains it became a term indicating a wider region than the original Jewish area in the narrow sense. Consequently it included various peoples and not just the Jews of Judaea in the original, narrow sense. Paradoxically the non-Jews are also included among the *Ioudaioi* in several sources (Strabo, Plutarch). Thus, *Ioudaioi* can be a term for all the inhabitants of the prov-ince, or of the region of Judaea only. We may take this argument one step further: Plutarch, at least, also writes *Ioudaioi* when he actually means *Ioudaia* in a geographical sense. When used thus the term has lost both its religious and its ethnic content. After the province was renamed Syria-Palaestina, the name of Judaea is still found, but, often, as in the case of Cassius Dio, it refers again to the 'Land of the Jews' within the Province of Palaestina. The bottom line: Judaea can mean various things in dif-ferent periods, depending on the context: geographical, administrative, ethnic, and social. In other words, in any interpretation we need to take into account that ideas concerning ethnicity in the Roman Near East were highly flexible.

Hebraioi

This appellation was in common use for Jews in the Septuagint.[106] Thus we find it also in the books of the Maccabees.[107] The first non-Jewish author to use it is Alexander Polyhistor (second-first century BC).[108]

---

[105] Strabo cited by Josephus, *Ant.* 13.319.
[106] Gen 39:17: ὁ παῖς ὁ Εβραῖος; Exod 1:22; Reg 1.4.9.2: τοῖς Εβραίοις,
[107] 2 Macc 7:31; 11:13; 15:37.
[108] Stern, *Greek and Latin Authors*, I, 29, no. 51a.

It is used by Plutarch in a context of language: Cleopatra 'made her replies to most of (the barbarians) herself and unassisted, whether they were Ethiopians, Troglodytes, Hebrews, Arabs, Syrians, Medes or Parthians'.[109]

We then find it in the work of Statius,[110] Antonius Diogenes,[111] Tacitus,[112] Charax of Pergamum (second century),[113] Appian,[114] and others.[115] Could it be that this name became more widespread after the Jewish revolts?

Arabs/Arabians

In Semitic languages in antiquity 'Arab' is a term for nomads rather than an ethnic or linguistic designation.[116] The question here is therefore whether an ethnic appellation or a social one (nomads) is meant in the Greek and Latin sources.

We may start with Strabo: 'whereas the interior above Phoenicia, as far as the Arabs, between Gaza and Antilibanus, is called Judaea'.[117] All this is geographic, not ethnic, apart, perhaps, from 'the Arabs' which here indicates territory inhabited by a named group.[118]

The next passage is decisive:

> Bordering on the country of the Apameians on the east is the Parapotamia, as it is called of the Arabian chieftains, as also Chalcidice, which extends down from Massyas, and all the country to the south of the Apameians, which belongs for the most part to Scenitae. These Scenitae are similar to

---

[109] Plutarch, *Ant.* 27.4: τοῖς δὲ πλείστοις αὐτὴ δι᾽ αὑτῆς ἀπεδίδου τὰς ἀποκρίσεις, οἷον Αἰθίοψι Τρωγλοδύταις Ἑβραίοις Ἄραψι Σύροις Μήδοις Παρθυαίοις.

[110] Statius, *Silvae* 5.1.213: *Palaestini simul Hebraeique liquores* (first occurence in Latin literature, second half of the first century AD).

[111] Porphyrius, *V. Pythagorae* 11 (Stern, *Greek and Latin Authors*, I, no. 250).

[112] Tacitus, *Hist.* 5.2.3: *Hebraeae terrae.*

[113] Stephanus Byz. 259.6: Ἑβραῖοι. οὕτως Ἰουδαῖοι ἀπὸ Ἀβράμωνος, ὥς φησι Χάραξ. Cf. Stern's comments, *Greek and Latin Authors*, II, 161, no. 335.

[114] Appian, *BC* 2.10.71.294: καὶ Κιλικία καὶ Συρία καὶ Φοινίκη καὶ τὸ Ἑβραίων γένος καὶ Ἄραβες οἱ τούτων ἐχόμενοι Κύπριοί τε καὶ Ῥόδιοι καὶ Κρῆτες σφενδονῆται καὶ ὅσοι ἄλλοι νησιῶται. Appian here refers to the Jews as *Hebraioi* in the present.

[115] See Stern, *Greek and Latin Authors*, II, 161, for references.

[116] For the meaning of the term 'Arab' indicating 'nomadic' or 'of nomadic origin' in the sense of a way of life, see R. Zadok, *On West Semites in Babylonia during the Chaldaean and Achaemenian Periods: An Onomastic Study* (Jerusalem, 1977), 192; I. Eph'al, '"Ishmael" and "Arabs": A Transformation of Ethnological Terms', *Journal of Near Eastern Studies* 35 (1976): 225–35; *The Ancient Arabs: Nomads on the Borders of the Fertile Crescent 9th–5th Centuries bc* (Leiden, 1982). B. Aggoula, *Inventaire des inscriptions Hatréennes* (Paris, 1991), translates 'ARABY' as 'Bédouins', e.g. nos. 336, 343. This is anachronistic.

[117] Strabo 16.2.21 (756): Ἅπασα μὲν οὖν ἡ ὑπὲρ τῆς Σελευκίδος ὡς ἐπὶ τὴν Αἴγυπτον καὶ τὴν Ἀραβίαν ἀνίσχουσα χώρα κοίλη Συρία καλεῖται, ... ἡ δ᾽ ὑπὲρ ταύτης μεσόγαια μέχρι τῶν Ἀράβων ἡ μεταξὺ Γάζης καὶ Ἀντιλιβάνου Ἰουδαία λέγεται.

[118] For 'the Arabs' and 'Scenitae', see 16.2.11 (753), cited in the next note and also: Herodian 3.1.3.

the nomads in Mesopotamia. And it is always the case that the peoples are more civilized in proportion to their proximity to the Syrians, and that the Arabs and Scenitae are less so, the former having governments that are better organized.[119]

Clearly, 'Scenitae' is a social term, roughly the same as 'nomads', as Strabo says.[120] They are here mentioned as distinct from 'the Arabs'. The only possible interpretation of the distinction between 'Scenitae' and 'Arabs' is that the latter is an ethnic term, representing a named people with a slightly better reputation than the anonymous 'tent-dwellers'. Only slightly, as is clear from the next passage:

'Now all the mountainous parts are held by Ituraeans and Arabs, all of whom are robbers, but the people in the plains are farmers; and when the latter are harassed by the robbers at different times they require different kinds of help. These robbers use strongholds as bases of operation.'[121]

A famous inscription records the Roman subjugation of an Ituraean fortress in the Lebanon Mountains.[122] In due course of time Ituraeans came to serve the Empire in their own capacity, as archers in the Roman army.[123]

Again it is clear that 'Arabs' here is an ethnic term, like 'Ituraeans' but one that is, for Strabo, immediately associated with an irregular lifestyle. Here the emphasis is not on nomadism, but on the contrast between productive farming and unproductive, rapacious and destructive mountain-dwelling.[124] This is an intermediate category in the valuation of the time: at the top of the scale is an urbanized society; next come farmers; then, at a far lower level are mountaineers, such as Arabs and Ituraeans. Sometimes Jews are included in this category. At the lowest level we find the nomads,

---

[119] Strabo 16.2.11 (753): Ὅμορος δ' ἐστὶ τῇ Ἀπαμέων πρὸς ἕω μὲν ἡ τῶν φυλάρχων Ἀράβων καλουμένη Παραποταμία καὶ ἡ Χαλκιδικὴ ἀπὸ τοῦ Μασσύου καθήκουσα καὶ πᾶσα ἡ πρὸς νότον τοῖς Ἀπαμεῦσιν, ἀνδρῶν σκηνιτῶν τὸ πλέον· παραπλήσιοι δ' εἰσὶ τοῖς ἐν τῇ Μεσοποταμίᾳ νομάσιν· ἀεὶ δ' οἱ πλησιαίτεροι τοῖς Σύροις ἡμερώτεροι καὶ ἧττον Ἄραβες καὶ σκηνῖται, ἡγεμονίας ἔχοντες συντεταγμένας μᾶλλον,

[120] Besides the nomads in Syria, Strabo also mentions them ('Scenitae') in Mesopotamia: 16.3.1 (765).

[121] Strabo 16.2.18 (755): τὰ μὲν οὖν ὀρεινὰ ἔχουσι πάντα Ἰτουραῖοί τε καὶ Ἄραβες, κακοῦργοι πάντες, οἱ δ' ἐν τοῖς πεδίοις γεωργοί· κακούμενοι δ' ὑπ' ἐκείνων ἄλλοτε ἄλλης βοηθείας δέονται. ὁρμητηρίοις δ' ἐρυμνοῖς χρῶνται,

[122] *CIL* III 6687; *ILS* 2683; Boffo, *Iscrizioni greche e latine*, no. 23: Q. *Aemilius Secundus … missu Quirini adversus Ituraeos in Libano monte castellum eorum cepi.*

[123] Caesar, *BA* 20: *sagittariisque ex omnibus navibus Ityraeis Syris et cuiusque generis ductis in castra compluribus frequentabat suas copias.* Diploma of AD 110: *CIL* XV 57: *cohors I Augusta Ituraeorum sagittaria.* Arrian includes Ἰτυραῖοι among his mounted archers: Arrian, *Acies contra Alanos* 1.9; 18.3. See also Cicero, *Phil.* 2.8.19; 2.44.112: to Cicero's fury Antony brought intimidating Ituraean archers to a session of the Senate in Rome: *homines omnium gentium maxime barbaros.* Also: 13.8.18; Lucan, *BC* 7.230; 7.514.

[124] Cf. B. Isaac, *Invention of Racism* (Princeton, 2004), ch. 10, esp. 407–9. For the image of nomads in the literature of late antiquity, see Chapter 10 below.

who, in the Near East, only in a fairly late period, receive an ethnic appellation of their own, 'Saracens', a name of obscure origin. The help needed by the farmers is to be supplied by the omnipresent source of law and order, the Roman Empire, which is one of Strabo's favourite themes.

Strabo, referring to Eratosthenes (third century BC), states that Arabia consists of two parts: the northern which is the Syrian Desert, inhabited by nomads, and the southern, Arabia Felix, which is settled. The northern part is bordered by 'the Coele-Syrians (Κοιλοσύρων = Syrians), the *Ioudaioi* (τῶν Ἰουδαίων)'. 'The first people who occupy Arabia Felix, after the Syrians and *Ioudaioi* are farmers.'[125] Above we saw that, according to Strabo, Judaea is inhabited by various peoples, so here *Ioudaioi* are not only Jews, but all the 'people of Judaea'. He uses the ethnic appellations, rather than the names of the regions, perhaps because the difference is considered relevant as an indication of lifestyle and culture since the subject here is the difference between settled people, farmers, and nomads.

Plutarch once uses the term Arabs in a context clearly associated with language.[126] Elsewhere he mentions 'Arabia of the Nabataeans',[127] which shows that the *Nabataioi* owned at least part of Arabia (here Arabia Petraea is meant). Ptolemy of Alexandria, in the middle of the second century has three chapters on regions called Arabia.[128]

Noteworthy is the importance of the cavalry and archers, said to be Arabs, for instance in connection with the city of Hatra.[129] Cassius Dio refers to the Arabs of Hatra in an ethnic sense, as is clear from a statement that Septimius Severus expected 'the Arabs to come to terms'.[130] Dio obviously means the Hatrene ruler and his people, the citizens of the city of Hatra. They were not nomads, but urban and settled. In local inscriptions the rulers of Hatra are

---

[125] Strabo 16.4.2 (767): ἔχουσι δ᾽ αὐτὴν οἱ μὲν πρῶτοι μετὰ τοὺς Σύρους καὶ τοὺς Ἰουδαίους ἄνθρωποι γεωργοί·

[126] Plutarch, *Ant.* 27.4, cited above, in connection with *Hebraioi*.

[127] Plut. *Ant.*, 36.3: τῆς Ναβαταίων Ἀραβίας, cited above.

[128] 5.17 (Ἡ Πετραία Ἀραβία); 19 (ἡ Ἔρημος Ἀραβία); 6.7 (Ἡ Εὐδαίμων Ἀραβία). Cf. G. W. Bowersock, 'The Three Arabias in Ptolemy's Geography', in P.-L. Gatier, B. Helly, and J.-P. Rey-Coquais (eds.), *Géographie historique au Proche Orient: Syrie, Phénicie, Arabie, grecques, romaines, byzantines* (Paris, 1988), 47–53.

[129] Dio 75.11.2: συχνοὶ μὲν γὰρ καὶ ἐν ταῖς προ νομαῖς ἐφθείροντο, τῆς βαρβαρικῆς ἵππου (φημὶ δὴ τῆς τῶν Ἀραβίων) πανταχοῦ ὀξέως τε καὶ σφοδρῶς ἐπιπιπτούσης αὐτοῖς· For the relationship between Hatra and the nomads in the region, see K. Dijkstra, 'State and Steppe: The Socio-Political Implications of Hatra Inscription 79', *Journal of Semitic Studies* 35 (1990): 81–98 with references to earlier discussion, 90–3, nn. 26–31. For Hatra see now L. Dirven (ed.), *Hatra: Politics, Culture and Religion between Partia and Rome* (Stuttgart, 2013) and below, Chapter 17.

[130] Dio 75.12: καὶ προσεδόκησεν ἐθελοντὶ τοὺς Ἀραβίους, ἵνα μὴ βίᾳ ἁλόντες ἀνδραποδισθῶσιν, ὁμολογήσειν.

described as sovereigns of Hatra and of Arabs.[131] Arabs were therefore understood to be non-urban *Hatreni*, or rather, nomads, as usual in the languages of the region. The importance of Ituraeans as archers has already been mentioned.

The name of the province of Arabia, *Arabia Provincia*, established in Trajan's reign, also indicates that the Romans understood this to be an ethnic designation, for they were well aware that the Nabataeans in Petra and Bostra were no nomads. There is no obvious reason why they refrained from calling the new province 'Nabataea'. It is not unlikely that the name 'Arabia' had broader associations than 'Nabataea'. The Province of Arabia had a grandiose name, like the two provinces of Germania which somehow conveyed the message that Rome controlled all of Germania. Note that Strabo, for instance, calls Nabataea 'Nabataea of the Arabs'.[132] So, if the province annexed was *de facto* 'Nabataea of the Arabs' it is no giant step to call the province simply 'Arabia'.[133]

As noted, in Semitic languages in antiquity 'Arab' is a term for nomads rather than an ethnic or linguistic designation. It is now clear that this is not the case in the Greek and Latin literature. 'Arabs' or 'Arabians' is an ethnic (and geographic) designation, a people with a language of their own, to be distinguished from nomads, who were called 'Scenitae' or 'nomads'. This does not mean the Arabs were highly regarded. They were not, but they were more respectable than the unnamed nomads and could be integrated into the Roman army. The rule, as formulated by Strabo, is that peoples are more civilized in proportion to their proximity to the Roman provinces, and that the Arabs and Scenitae are less so, although the former are better organized.

Conclusions

We have seen that there can exist several names for the same entity without obvious reason: Syria, Assyria, and Coele-Syria may mean the same thing. That is not necessarily always true, for Coele-Syria may also indicate one of two specific regions within the larger area of Syria.

---

[131] The king, Sanatruq, and his son are called "mlk' d'arab", king of Arabia, e.g. in Hatra inscriptions nos. 79, 195–9, 373, 378.

[132] Strabo 17.21 (803): καὶ ἐκ τῆς Ἀραβίας δὲ τῆς Ναβαταίων.

[133] For a different explanation, see Bowersock, 'Three Arabias', 51–2, where it is argued that the omission of the Nabataeans in the name must be due to the unofficial *damnatio* accorded to a defunct dynasty, to rulers who have been overthrown. For a recent paper with yet another approach: J. Retsö, 'The Nabataeans: Problems of Defining Ethnicity in the Ancient World', in W. Pohl, C. Gantner, and R. E. Payne (eds.), *Visions of Community in the Post-Roman World* (Farnham, 2012), 73–9.

There are also changes over time: Herodotus speaks of Ascalon in a geographic region 'Palaistine Syria' while he also calls it simply 'a city in Syria'. In the second century AD the name of the Roman province of Judaea became Syria-Palaestina. Syria is, first, a geographic concept, then an administrative term, while neither is necessarily restricted to the region inhabited by speakers of Syriac. Syria covered a very broad area, including many peoples and cities. Thus it included Phoenicia until the reign of Septimius Severus. Judaea was, obviously, 'the Land of the Jews', but it was also an administrative district in the Achaemenid Empire, a Hellenistic kingdom and, subsequently a Roman province until Hadrian's reign. As such it included non-Jews (who might yet be called *Ioudaioi* in Greek sources). Jews, however, are sometimes called *Hebraioi*. Cassius Dio says that the name 'Jews' applies not only to those who are so by origin, but also to all the other people who follow their customs even if they are of other origin. After the province was no longer called Judaea, we still encounter the name as indicating the 'Land of the Jews' within the Province of Palaestina. The bottom line: Judaea can mean various things in different periods depending also on the context: geographical, administrative, ethnic, and social.

There is another related varying factor, insufficiently recognized in some modern studies: names can have different content that is not always specified: geography, ethnic, cultural, linguistic, administrative, and even economic. Palestine was, originally, a geographic concept (although in a distant past it derived from an ethnic name, the Philistines). In the second century AD it became an administrative unit without ethnic associations. However, there are instances, in the case of Palestine as in other cases, where a Roman administrative term became an ethnic name (*Palaestini*). A related phenomenon is that there appears to be little consistency in the use of ethnic names or territorial ones: 'The Syrians' can refer to 'Syria' and the reverse. One reason for this is that the ancient texts are more interested in peoples than in territories.[134] Another reason may be that the Greeks and Romans were far less focused on maps and the graphic representation of geography than we are. The Greek-writing author Meleager calls himself an Assyrian, meaning he is of Syrian origin and his city is in Syria – yet his city, like he himself, is Attic (in language and culture). The term Hellenic is used for and by communities that definitely did not claim to descend from Greeks in Greece or Asia Minor. Professions such as farming and trading may also be regarded as ethnic features, e.g. by Strabo. Here too there are

---

[134] Isaac, *Limits of Empire*, 394–401.

complications. In ancient Semitic languages 'Arab' is term for nomads; in Greek and Latin texts it is an ethnic appellation for the non-nomadic Arabs and not used for nomadic groups, as nomads are indicated by other terms. Only later do we encounter the ethnic 'Saracens' as a name for ethnic nomads.

The case of the Jews was even more complicated than that of other peoples because it was recognized at least by some authors, in some periods, that they attracted foreigners in a manner that was not usual or generally acceptable at the time.

Rome itself was not as obvious a concept as it might seem. In Caesar's time there were rumours among the population of Rome that Julius Caesar 'planned to move to Alexandria or Ilium, take the wealth of the empire with him, exhaust Italy by levies and leave the care of the city to his friends'.[135] Thus, before Antony established himself in Alexandria with Cleopatra, Alexandria could be the subject of such rumours, while the presumed choice of Ilium shows that, long before the transformation of Byzantium into Constantinople, this was seen as an area from where the Empire could conceivably be ruled.[136] One might speculate that there was an ideological basis for this idea rather than a practical one. The view that Rome was in fact a reconstituted Troy, propagated by Augustan ideology, may have been around before Vergil started composing the *Aeneid*. Constantine actually moved Rome to Constantinople (rather than Ilium) and yet Rome remained Rome and the Roman Empire remained Roman.

When we try to understand questions of ethnicity in the Roman Near East we are faced with the reality that things are not necessarily what they might seem to us. We need to take into account that ideas concerning ethnicity in the Roman Near East were highly flexible and complex. The reason for this is clear: in the ancient texts we are faced with what was in many respects a different approach to group identity from our contemporary concepts. Categories and definitions that seem clear to us often do not apply in antiquity. Conversely, recognizing the ancient perspective for what it was, may contribute to a better understanding of social reality in the Roman Empire.

---

[135] Suetonius, *Divus Iulius* 79.3: *Quin etiam varia fama percrebruit migraturum Alexandream vel Ilium, translatis simul opibus imperii exhaustaque Italia dilectibus et procuratione urbis amicis permissa.*

[136] Suetonius clearly suggests that this was associated with a putative take-over of the Empire by the eastern part of it, for he mentions both Ilium and Alexandria as possible imperial capitals.

CHAPTER 7

Attitudes towards Provincial Intellectuals in the Roman Empire

Inhabitants of the provinces made a substantial contribution to the intellectual and artistic life under Roman rule, as might be expected in an Empire well-integrated in the sphere of administration, military control, law, taxation and economics and, to some extent, culturally. The degree to which provincial intellectuals were integrated or felt themselves to be integrated in the upper class of the Empire as a whole and at the centre is less clear.

Syme, in his posthumously published *The Provincial at Rome*,[1] devotes a brief chapter to 'Prejudice against Provincials', focusing on resistance against admission to the Senate of Roman citizens from the provinces. He concludes that 'for most purposes the senators from Spain and Narbonensis were hardly to be distinguished from the new men from municipal Italy, of the Transpadana in particular. They are marked by the same excellent qualities.' That may be true, but even so he himself cites Cicero as evidence that there was deprecation even of respectable men from the towns in Italy. Antony, says Cicero, expressed scorn for Octavian's ancestry. His mother came from Aricia (one of the oldest towns of Latium). 'You might think,' says Cicero, 'he [Antony] was speaking of a woman from Tralles or Ephesus! Note how all of us who come from the *municipia* are despised – that is absolutely all of us – for how few of us do not come from the *municipia*?'[2] In the time of Cicero then, it was still possible to quibble

A first version of this paper was delivered as a lecture in 2006 in the Shu'ubiyya Colloquium at the Institute for Advanced Study, Princeton, organized by the late Patricia Crone. I have profited from comments made on various occasions by Stanley Burstein, Deborah Gera, Jonathan Hall, Ron Mellor, and Josephine Quinn. It was published originally in E. Gruen (ed.), *Cultural Identity and the Peoples of the Ancient Mediterranean* (Los Angeles, 2011), 491–518. It was written before the publication of N. J. Andrade, *Syrian Identity in the Greco-Roman World* (Cambridge, 2013) and therefore less account could be taken of this work than it deserves.

[1] R. Syme, *The Provincial at Rome and Rome and the Balkans 80 BC–AD 14*, ed. A. Birley (Exeter, 1999).
[2] Cicero, *Philippic* 3.6.15: 'Aricina mater'. *Trallianam aut Ephesiam putes dicere. Videte quam despicia-mur omnes qui sumus e municipiis id est, omnes plane: quotus enim quisque nostrum non est?* Caligula

about the aristocratic merit of Romans from an ancient town some 25 km from Rome. Something else also needs to be said, however: there clearly was full agreement that anyone with a mother from Ephesus or Tralles, two ancient Greek cities in Asia Minor, would be despicable, or at least it was unthinkable that he would belong to the genuine Roman aristocracy. What Cicero would say of an enemy from Spain may be seen in the case of L. Decidius Saxa, a tribune of the plebs who espoused the cause of Antony. He is described as a wild Celtiberian, *ex ultima Celtiberia*,[3] although he probably was a respectable Roman from a colony in Spain.[4] It is the aim of the present chapter to see what we know about the level and integration during the Principate of people from other, non-Latin parts of the Empire and originating in less exalted circles than those considered by Cicero.

It may be instructive to investigate the writings of provincial intellectuals in order to see to what extent they saw themselves as accepted by and integrated into cosmopolitan society in Rome and other major cities of the Empire. It is not unlikely that any results of such an investigation will tell us something about social relationships between the urban elites in central cities such as Rome, Athens, and Alexandria and those in the provinces. Generally speaking, provincial intellectuals came from the locally distinguished families, notable and wealthy in their cities, all over the Greek East.[5] To be considered for this purpose are all types of works preserved: philosophy, poetry, literary prose, rhetoric, scientific writings, including medical treatises, notably the works commonly known as 'the second sophistic'.

First, we should note that the number of distinguished authors from the provinces, particularly those in the eastern part of the Empire, was quite substantial, even if the works of relatively few of them have been preserved. Obviously there were major authors from Syria, some of them to be discussed below, from cities such as Apamea (Posidonius), Damascus (Nicolaus), Emesa, and Samosata (Lucian). It will not surprise either that cities such as Tyre[6] and Berytus, with its famous law

asserted that his great-grandmother Livia was of low birth, for her maternal grandfather had been a magistrate at Fundi, another town in Latium: Suetonius, *Caligula* 23.2. Suetonius adds that, on the contrary, he held high offices at Rome.

[3] Cicero, *Philippic* 11.12: *Accedit Saxa nescio quis, quem nobis Caesar ex ultima Celtiberia tribunum plebis dedit, castrorum antea metator, nunc, ut sperat, urbis: …*

[4] Syme, *Provincial at Rome*, 24.

[5] G. W. Bowersock, *Greek Sophists and the Roman Empire* (Oxford, 1969), 21–5.

[6] Tyre: the Platonist Maximus. Heraclitus, fellow-student of Antiochus of Ascalon who settled in Alexandria: J. Glucker, *Antiochus and the Late Academy* (Göttingen, 1978). Paul of Tyre, orator in the reign of Hadrian: Suda *P* 809, cf. *RE* 18.4.2373; A. Birley, *Hadrian: The Restless Emperor* (London, 1995), 227–8; F. Millar, *The Roman Near East* (Cambridge, 1999), 289. Hadrian of Tyre, teacher of

schools,[7] and Naucratis[8] produced significant authors. This is less obvious for several Palestinian cities, such as Ascalon,[9] Gaza,[10] Acco,[11] Scythopolis,[12] Neapolis,[13] Caesarea on the Sea[14] which Apollonius of Tyana, or another author using his name, praises for its 'Greek manners'

Proclus of Naucratis, friend of Flavius Boethus and acquaintance of Galen. He held the chair of rhetoric in Athens and died *ab epistulis Graecis* of Commodus: Philostratus, *VS* 2.585; cf. J. Geiger, 'Notes on the Second Sophistic in Palestine', *Illinois Classical Studies* 9 (1994): 221–30. See now in general: J. Geiger, *Hellenism in the East: Studies on Greek Intellectuals in Palestine* (Stuttgart, 2014). Tyre or Berytus: Calvisius or Calvenus Taurus, private tutor, active in Athens, taught Platonic philosophy (second century AD): Glucker, *Antiochus and the Late Academy*, 142–3. There is also the little-known Euphrates of Tyre: see the entry in R. Sorabji (ed.), 'Aristotle and After', *Bulletin of the Institute of Classical Studies*, suppl. 68 (1997): 1–11. The major philosopher to have been born there was Porphyry (third century).

[7] L.J. Hall, *Roman Berytus: Beirut in Late Antiquity* (London, 2004). Note also Hermippus of Berytus: Suda *E* 3045: Ἕρμιππος Βηρύτιος ἀπὸ κώμης μεσογαίου; 'from an inland village, a disciple of Philo of Byblos ... in the time of the Emperor Hadrian, a freedman, quite erudite. He wrote extensively, among other things a work "Concerning Dreams"'; cf. *RE* 8.853–4 s.v. The hapless authors of the entry in the *Neue Pauly*, V, col. 440 write: 'einem Dorf im inneren Phöniziens, nicht der Stadt am Mittelmeer'. Of course the Suda means that he came from a village off the coast in the territory of Berytus.

[8] Athenaeus, author of the *Deipnosophists* (second–third century), and Proclus of Naucratis, pupil of Hadrian of Tyre and teacher of Philostratus: see A. Wasserstein, 'Rabban Gamaliel and Proclus the Philosopher (Mishna Aboda Zara 3.4)', *Zion* 45 (1980): 257–67 (Hebrew).

[9] Philosophers of the Late Academy: Antiochus and his brother Aristus, an acquaintance of Brutus, cf. Glucker, *Antiochus and the Late Academy*, 25–6. Euenus, a poet of the first century BC: J. Geiger, 'Euenus of Ascalon', *Scripta Classica Israelica* 11 (1991–2): 114–22; Julian of Ascalon, a fifth-century architect who wrote on metrology: Geiger, 'Julian of Ascalon', *Journal of Hellenic Studies* 112 (1992): 31–43; for the Byzantine period note also Ulpian the Sophist, Zosimus, and Eutocius, the mathematician. Cf. Geiger, 'Greek Intellectuals from Ascalon', *Cathedra* 60 (1991): 5–16 (Hebrew) and see now Geiger, *Hellenism in the East*, and the entry on Ascalon in the *Corpus Inscriptionum Iudaeae/Palaestinae*, III (2014).

[10] Gaza flowered as a centre for rhetorical and literary studies towards the end of the fifth century, with Procopius and his pupil Choricius as central figures, see C. Glucker, *The City of Gaza in the Roman and Byzantine Periods* (Oxford, 1987), 51–3; G. A. Kennedy, *Greek Rhetoric under Christian Emperors* (Princeton, 1983), 169–77. See now the relevant entry in the *Corpus*, III (previous note).

[11] Acco produced at least one distinguished person: the consular Flavius Boethus, governor of Palestine, 162–6, known from the works of Galen as a scholar and philosopher with an interest in medicine, cf. M. E. Smallwood, *The Jews under Roman Rule*, 2nd edn (Leiden, 1981), 552; *PIR*² F229; W. Eck, D. Isac, and I. Piso, 'Militärdiplom aus der Provinz Dacia Porolissensis', *ZPE* 100 (1994), 582–5; C. M. Lehmann and K. G. Holum, *The Greek and Latin Inscriptions of Caesarea Maritima* (Boston, 2000), 60, no. 30 = *CIIP* II, no. 1229; I. Israelowich, *Patients and Healers in the High Roman Empire* (Baltimore, 2014), 63, 74. He was a friend of Hadrian of Tyre: above, n. 6.

[12] A city 'rather out of the way' according to Ammianus 19.12.8. However, the Stoic philosopher Basilides, teacher of Marcus Aurelius, was a native from Scythopolis: Geiger, 'Notes on the Second Sophistic', 222.

[13] Two orators: Andromachus, son of Zonas or Sabinus who taught in Nicomedia in the reign of Diocletian: Suda *A* 2185; and Siricius, a pupil of his: Suda *G* 475; cf. Geiger, 'Notes on the Second Sophistic', 227; M. Heath, 'Theon and the History of the Progymnasmata', *Greek, Roman, and Byzantine Studies* 43 (2002–3): 129–60, at 132.

[14] Two fourth-century orators: Acacius, a rival of Libanius, and Thespesius. Then there are the fifth-century grammarian Priscio and the orator Orion and, most famous, the historian Procopius. See Geiger, 'Notes on the Second Sophistic', 228–9.

and for showing them by setting up 'public inscriptions'.[15] The province of Arabia also had its fair share of well-known figures.[16] Gerasa was a significant centre.[17] Over a considerable period a remarkable number came from Gadara, a city of Judaea – Palaestina, immediately east of the Jordan.[18] Some of these will be discussed more extensively below.[19]

It is important here to note that the inhabitants of these cities themselves attached great importance to being 'Hellenic', as is clear, for instance, from an inscription from Scythopolis (Beth Shean) on an altar dedicated to an emperor who is probably Marcus Aurelius (161–80). The city is there described as 'one of the Hellenic cities in Coele-Syria'.[20] There is even an inscription from Dhunaybeh (Danaba) in Trachonitis in Southern Syria which mentions: 'The Hellenes in Danaba'.[21] This indicates the existence of a social group in a rural community there that sees itself as Hellenic and separate from the non-Hellenic environment. The discovery of such a text at precisely this location is no coincidence, for it is one of the sites where Herod planted military colonies to secure the region between the Galilee and the poorly controlled region of Trachonitis. A question less easy to answer is the sense in which these people regarded themselves as Hellenic. Did they claim to descend from Greek immigrants? Or did they

---

[15] Apollonius of Tyana, *Ep.* 11, which may not be genuine. For the inscriptions, see now the *Corpus Inscriptionum Iudaeae/Palaestinae*, II, *Caesarea and the Middle Coast* (2011).

[16] Geiger, 'Notes on the Second Sophistic', 225–6: Heliodorus of Arabia, a well-known sophist in the time of Septimius Severus; Genethlius of Petra, active in Athens in the third century, rival of Callinicus of Petra (Suda *K* 231); Epiphanius, son of Ulpian, of Petra (?), sophist and orator who taught in Petra and in Athens in the fourth century (Suda *E* 2741); Gessius from Petra, 'iatrosophist', in the fifth century, pupil of the Jew Domnus; the orator Gaudentius 'from Nabataea'.

[17] Nicomachus, the Neopythagorean philosopher and mathematician (second century): A. H. Criddle, 'The Chronology of Nicomachus of Gerasa', *Classical Quarterly* 42 (1998): 324–6; Ariston the orator, Kerykos the sophist, and a jurist Plato: see Stephanus of Byzantium, s.v. Gerasa.

[18] J. Geiger, 'Athens in Syria: Greek Intellectuals in Gadara', *Cathedra* 35 (1985): 3–16 (Hebrew); 'Notes on the Second Sophistic', 223.

[19] Strabo 16.2.30 (759) mentions Philodemus, the Epicurean, Meleager, and Menippus, the satirist, and Theodorus the rhetorician. Theodorus, a truly eminent rhetorician, was teacher of Tiberius: G. Kennedy, *The Art of Rhetoric in the Roman World 300* BC–AD *300* (Princeton, 1972), 340–2; *A New History of Classical Rhetoric* (Princeton, 1994), 160. His son was a senator: Bowersock, *Greek Sophists*, 28, n. 6. Apsines 'the Phoenician' (*VS* 2.628) is possibly, but not certainly identical with the Athenian orator of that name (third century): Kennedy, *New History*, 226; M. Heath, 'Apsines and Pseudo-Apsines', *AJP* 119 (1998): 89–111. For the cynic critic of religion Oenomaus (second century): J. Hammerstaedt, *Die Orakelkritik des Kynikers Oenomaus* (Frankfurt, 1988). For the mathematician Philo: T. L. Heath, *A History of Greek Mathematics* (Oxford, 1922), I, 226; Geiger, 'Notes on the Second Sophistic', 224.

[20] G. Foerster and Y. Tsafrir, 'Nysa-Scythopolis: A New Inscription and the Titles of the City on its Coins', *Israel Numismatic Journal* 9 (1986–7): 53–8: τῶν κατὰ Κοίλην Συρίαν Ἑλληνίδων πόλεων.

[21] M. Sartre, in A. Calbi *et al.* (eds.), *L'epigrafia del villaggio* (Faenza, 1993), 133–5; IGLS XV 228; AE 1993: 1636: Οἱ ἐν Δαναβοις Ἕλληνες Μηνοφίλῳ εὐνοίας ἕνεκεν. See also above, p. 132, and below, p. 283.

see Hellenism as an expression of cultural and linguistic identity? It is possible that the meaning varies from place to place and over time. In the
well-known Augustan edicts from Cyrene being Greek means (a) not having the Roman citizenship, (b) being a citizen of a Greek city, speaking the
language and being Greek in culture. This excluded the non-urban tribes
in the province and immigrants without rights in the cities such as Jews.[22]

The authors considered in the present chapter came also from a wide
variety of provincial cities in various parts of the Empire: besides those
already mentioned in the Near East, there are representatives from the
western Mediterranean such as Madaurus in Africa Proconsularis, Arelate
in Gaul, Tarsus in Cilicia, Cirta in Numidia.[23] We shall see whether their
provincial origin plays a role anywhere in the extant works of these authors
and, if so, whether any common trait can be found in the manner in which
they view themselves, their place in wider Roman society, and in their
attitudes towards other provincials. I shall not discuss texts in languages
other than Greek and Latin. Furthermore I shall exclude from systematic discussion two authors who might seem obvious candidates: Philo of
Alexandria and Flavius Josephus. They are writing explicitly as Jews and
do not fully identify with the intellectual environment of the integrated
Roman Empire. Neither author calls himself a Hellene.[24]

Another important sector not dealt with here are the Christian authors
who consciously and systematically developed arguments which placed
themselves in a category apart.[25]

We may start with Posidonius who came from the Syrian city of Apamea
on the Orontes (ca. 135–ca. 51 BC). His work has not survived, but a fairly
large number of direct quotations by later authors are available for consideration. Interesting for our inquiry is a passage in which he tells of the
cities in Syria and how luxurious they were, writing as follows:

> The people in the cities, at any rate, because of the great plenty which their
> land afforded, [were relieved] of any distress regarding the necessaries of life;
> hence they held many gatherings at which they feasted continually, using

---

[22] V. Ehrenberg and A. H. M. Jones, *Documents illustrating the Reigns of Augustus and Tiberius*, ed. D.
L. Stockton (Oxford, 1976), no. 311. The Roman citizens were designated as οἱ Ῥωμαῖοι ἐν τῆι περὶ
Κυρήνην ἐπαρχήαι while the Greeks are simply οἱ Ἕλληνες.

[23] Cf. E. Champlin, *Fronto and Antonine Rome* (Cambridge, 1980), 16–20.

[24] For Josephus, see T. Rajak, 'Ethnic Identities in Josephus', in *The Jewish Dialogue with Greece and
Rome: Studies in Cultural and Social Interaction* (Leiden, 2002), 137–46. For Greek as a cultural
entity in Josephus: 142–4.

[25] D. K. Buell, *Why This New Race: Ethnic Reasoning in Early Christianity* (New York, 2005) and her
article 'Early Christian Universalism and Modern Forms of Racism', in M. Eliav-Feldon, B. Isaac,
and J. Ziegler (eds.), *The Origins of Racism in the West* (Cambridge, 2009), 109–31.

the gymnasia as if they were baths, anointing themselves with expensive oil and perfumes, and living in the 'bonds' – for so they called the commons where the diners met – as though they were their private houses, and putting in the greater part of the day there in filling their bellies – there, in the midst of wines and foods so abundant that they even carried a great deal home with them besides – and in delighting their ears with sounds from a loud-twanging tortoise-shell (i.e. a lyre), so that their towns rang from end to end with such noises.[26]

As mentioned, Posidonius himself was born in the Syrian city of Apamea, but he was trained in Athens and settled in Rhodes. The text above is quoted by Athenaeus of Naucratis in Egypt (ca. AD 200), following a passage about Lucullus who, after his victories in the East, was the first to live extravagantly. The beginning of decadence is a familiar theme in Roman historiography.[27] Baths as a symptom of luxurious decadence are a common topic in Roman literature. Elsewhere Posidonius notes the sturdy simplicity of the early inhabitants of Italy, also a popular theme: 'Even those who were very well off for a livelihood, trained their sons in drinking water, mostly, and in eating whatever they happened to have. And often, he tells us, a father or mother would ask a son whether he preferred to make his dinner of pears or walnuts, and after eating some of these he was satisfied and went to bed …'[28] Besides being an economic reality, it obviously was a popular commonplace. Scipio Africanus, criticized in his own times for extravagant living,[29] was centuries afterwards praised for his sobriety.[30]

---

[26] Athenaeus 12.527E–F (F62a, Kidd): Ποσειδώνιος δ᾽ ἑκκαιδεκάτη Ἱστοριῶν περὶ τῶν κατὰ τὴν ΣΥΡΙΑΝ πόλεων λέγων ὡς ἐτρύφων γράφει καὶ ταῦτα· "τῶν γοῦν ἐν ταῖς πόλεσιν ἀνθρώπων διὰ τὴν εὐβοσίαν τῆς χώρας ἀπὸ τῆς περὶ τὰ ἀναγκαῖα κακοπαθείας συνόδους νεμόντων πλείονας, ἐν αἷς εὐωχοῦντο συνεχῶς, τοῖς μὲν γυμνασίοις ὡς βαλανείοις χρώμενοι, ἀλειφόμενοι [δ᾽] ἐλαίῳ πολυτελεῖ καὶ μύροις· τοῖς δὲ γραμματείοις – οὕτως γὰρ ἐκάλουν τὰ κοινὰ τῶν συνδείπνων – ὡς οἰκητηρίοις ἐνδιαιτώμενοι, [καὶ] τὸ πλεῖον τῆς ἡμέρας γαστριζόμενοι ἐν αὐτοῖς οἴνοις καὶ βρώμασιν, ὥστε καὶ προσαποφέρειν πολλὰ καὶ καταυλουμένους πρὸς χελωνίδος πολυκρότου ψόφον, ὥστε τὰς πόλεις ὅλας τοιούτοις κελάδοις συνηχεῖσθαι." See also Athenaeus 5.210E–F (F62b, Kidd).

[27] See B. Isaac, *The Invention of Racism in Classical Antiquity* (Princeton, 2004), ch. 5. For Sallust it began with Sulla's eastern campaigns. The Elder Pliny, living more than a century afterwards, went further back in the past and saw the conquest of Asia Minor in 189 BC as the start of Roman decline and decadence.

[28] Athenaeus 6.109 (F267, Kidd): πρότερον δὲ οὕτως ὀλιγοδεεῖς ἦσαν οἱ τὴν Ἰταλίαν κατοικοῦντες ὥστε καὶ καθ᾽ ἡμᾶς ἔτι, φησὶν ὁ Ποσειδώνιος, οἱ σφόδρα εὐκαιρούμενοι τοῖς βίοις ἦγον τοὺς υἱοὺς ὕδωρ μὲν ὡς τὸ πολὺ πίνοντας, ἐσθίοντας δ᾽ ὅ τι ἂν τύχῃ. καὶ πολλάκις, φησίν, πατὴρ ἢ μήτηρ υἱὸν ἠρώτα πότερον ἀπίους ἢ κάρυα βούλεται δειπνῆσαι, καὶ τούτων τι φαγὼν ἠρκεῖτο καὶ ἐκοιμᾶτο.

[29] Plutarch, *Cato Maior* 3.5–7.

[30] Athenaeus 6.105; Seneca, *Ep.* 86.4ff.

Posidonius does not identify himself as a Syrian. His negative view of Syrians and Syria echoes the usual stereotypes of weak, decadent easterners found in Greece and Rome, just as his positive views of Italians echo their own chauvinist views of their own ancestors. Apparently he fully identifies with the familiar prejudices of the imperial elite and prefers not to insist on his own origins in Syria.

Posidonius does not mention himself at all in this passage. By contrast, the next author to be mentioned here places himself at the centre. Meleager of Gadara, living in roughly the same age, second–first century BC, came from a city already mentioned for its remarkable contribution to Greek culture over the centuries. Among his extant works is a short Greek autobiographical poem in the form of an epitaph:

> Island Tyre was my nurse, and Gadara, an Attic fatherland which lies among Assyrians [sc. Syrians] gave birth to me. From Eucrates I sprung, Meleager, who first by the help of the Muses ran abreast of the Graces of Menippus. What wonder if I am a Syrian? Stranger, we all inhabit one fatherland, one world. Once Chaos gave birth to all mortals ...[31]

Meleager emphasizes the point by saying 'an Attic fatherland among Syrians – Gadara' rather than 'an Attic fatherland in Syrian Gadara'. He also makes it clear that he competed with the elegant work of his fellow Gadarene, Menippus. Meleager is called 'the cynic' by Athenaeus[32] and the claim that all men are equal and compatriots fits this description. The idea goes far back, as far perhaps as Antiphon in the late fifth century BC.[33] However, it is undeniable that there is an apologetic and defensive element in the poem. He emphasizes that his fatherland is 'Attic' but apparently that is only part of his identity. Gadara is Attic among the Syrians. He is

---

[31] A. S. F. Gow and D. L. Page (eds.), *The Greek Anthology: Hellenistic Epigrams* (Cambridge, 1965), I, 216, no. 2 (*Anthologia Palatina* 7.417): Νᾶσος ἐμὰ θρέπτειρα Τύρος· πάτρα δέ με τεκνοῖ / Ἀτθὶς ἐν Ἀσσυρίοις ναιομένα Γαδάρα· / Εὐκράτεω δ' ἔβλαστον ὁ σὺν Μούσαις Μελέαγρος / πρῶτα Μενιππείοις συντροχάσας Χάρισιν. / εἰ δὲ Σύρος, τί τὸ θαῦμα; μίαν, ξένε, πατρίδα κόσμον / ναίομεν, ἐν θνατοὺς πάντας ἔτικτε Χάος... /. For the reading Γαδάρα see Gow and Page, *The Greek Anthology*, II, 607. Cf. Andrade, *Syrian Identity* (2013), 109–10. For 'Syrians' in Josephus, see Rajak, 'Ethnic Identities in Josephus', in *The Jewish Dialogue with Greece and Rome* (2002), 140–1.

[32] 11.107.12 and the passage cited also below: 4.45.33.

[33] Antiphon, *De veritate*: M. Ostwald, '*Nomos* and *Phusis* in Antiphon's περὶ ἀληθείας', in M. Griffith and D. J. Mastonarde (eds.), *Cabinet of the Muses: Essays on Classics and Comparative Literature in Honor of Thomas G. Rosenmeyer* (Atlanta, GA, 1990), 293–306; Isaac, *Invention of Racism*, 173–5. It is found again in the letters ascribed to Apollonius of Tyana: 44.2: 'It is an honourable thing to regard the whole earth as one's ancestral city (πᾶσάν τε γῆν πατρίδα νομίζειν) and all humans as his brothers and friends ...' However, there are reservations: 'No, kinship cannot be argued away, and everything that is akin responds to its own kind' (trans. C. P. Jones, Loeb).

therefore a Syrian (by origin), he says, but that should not affect his credentials, for all men have one common *patris*, namely the *kosmos*.

There is a second, similar and related poem: 'Tyre of the godlike boys and Gadara's holy earth made me a man; lovely Kos of the Meropes took care of me in my old age. So if you are a Syrian, Salaam! If you are a Phoenician, Naidios! If you are Greek, Chaire! And do you say the same [to me].'[34]

Here again Meleager is defiantly cosmopolitan: again he identifies himself as being from Gadara which is called 'holy', but its Attic identity is not mentioned. I am not sure why the earth there is called holy; perhaps simply because it was his fatherland?[35] It certainly is unconventional to introduce Aramaic and Phoenician words in a Greek poem.

A final engaging point is transmitted also by Athenaeus,[36] where Meleager is cited indirectly as claiming that Homer was a Syrian by birth and therefore depicted the Achaeans as abstaining from fish as customary in Syria, even though the Hellespont was full of fish.[37] Meleager's tone is quite different from Posidonius: he clearly identifies his background and claims that it does not prevent him from being genuinely Hellenic, a claim reinforced by the assertion that Homer himself was Syrian.

At this point a brief discussion of terminology is unavoidable, because it is historically and socially relevant. Meleager calls himself a Syrian, but also mentions a Phoenician, speaking his own language. The reference to a Phoenician is interesting for both Apsines and Menippus of Gadara, Meleager's city, are at least once called 'Phoenician'.[38] It is not clear to me why this ethnic indication would be applied to the citizens of a city east of the river Jordan, well beyond the region usually associated with Phoenicia. Although there is a record of Phoenician settlements in some towns in Palestine, we do not know that there was such an establishment at Gadara. Also, the settlements in Palestine are called 'Sidonian', not Phoenician.[39]

---

[34] *The Greek Anthology*, I, 217, no. 4 (*Anthologia Palatina* 7.419): ... ὃν θεόπαις ἤνδρωσε Τύρος / Γαδάρων θ' ἱερὰ χθών, / Κῶς δ' ἐρατὴ Μερόπων πρέσβυν ἐγηροτρόφει. / ἀλλ' εἰ μὲν Σύρος ἐσσί, / σαλάμ· εἰ δ' οὖν σύ γε Φοῖνιξ, / ναίδιος· εἰ δ' Ἕλλην, χαῖρε· τὸ δ' αὐτὸ φράσον.

[35] Cf. J. Geiger, 'Language, Culture and Identity in Ancient Palestine', in E. N. Ostenfeld (ed.), *Greek Romans and Roman Greeks: Studies in Cultural Interaction* (Aarhus, 2002), 233–46, at 233–4.

[36] Athenaeus, *Deipnosophistae* 4.45.38, citing Parmeniscus, the grammarian, *The Cynics' Symposium*.

[37] τὸν Ὅμηρον Σύρον ὄντα τὸ γένος κατὰ τὰ πάτρια ἰχθύων ἀπεχομένους τοὺς Ἀχαιούς. Also: 2.50.19; Plutarch, *Quaestiones convivales* 730C (where the point that Homer would have been Syrian himself is missing, not surprisingly).

[38] Philostratus, *VS* 2.628: Ἀψίνης ὁ Φοῖνιξ; Diogenes Laertius 6.98: Menippus was Φοίνικα τὸ γένος.

[39] B. Isaac, 'A Seleucid Inscription from Jamnia-on-the-Sea', in Isaac, *The Near East under Roman Rule* (Leiden, 1997), 3–20: Sidonians are found in Jamnia-on-the-Sea, Shekhem (Nablus), and Marissa (Maresha).

There can be no connection with the name of the Roman province of Syria-Phoenice, for that is an innovation of the end of the second century AD.

For several of the texts here discussed it will be interesting that, both in Latin and, more particularly, in Greek, no distinction in terminology is made between a 'people' and a 'province'. This is clear from the use of the Greek term *ethnos*. Thus an undated grave inscription mentions a *beneficiarius* of the governor κατὰ ἐθνὸς Φοινίκων.[40] The context shows unambiguously that this refers to the 'province of Syria-Phoenice', not to 'the people of the Phoenicians'. Tacitus refers to 'an official who was Roman governor of Egypt which was his own *natio*'.[41] The point of this piece of information for us is that a Roman province could be called a *natio*. It might indicate that Tacitus still considered the Egyptians a people under Roman rule, but it is more likely that the term is used here as an alternative to *provincia*, just as the term *ethnos Phoinikon* was seen to indicate the province of Syria-Phoenice. Yet it cannot be denied that an element of heredity and origin here seems to be implied. In this connection we may note that Jerome says of Malchus that he was *Syrus natione et lingua*, 'a Syrian by *natio* and language'.[42] Malchus spoke Syriac rather than Greek; that is not surprising, but in what sense was Syria his *natio*? Since there was a Syriac language, this in itself might have made the Syrians a nation or a people, but it is more likely that the term indicates that Syria was his province of origin. Or were the Syrians a people after all and does *natio* refer to heredity? Again it may be noted that the Historia Augusta speaks of 'Pal<a>estini' when referring in general to the inhabitants of the province of Syria Palaestina.[43] Finally we should consider a third–fourth century reference to Iamblichus, author of the *Babyloniaca*:[44]

> This Iamblichus was a Syrian by origin on both his father's and his mother's side, a Syrian not in the sense of the Greeks who have settled in Syria, but of the native ones (*autochthones*), familiar with the Syrian language and living by their customs.

---

[40] P. Le Bas and H. Waddington, *Inscriptions grecques et latines recueillies en Grèce et en Asie Mineure* (Paris, 1970), III, 2432, from Nedjan in the southern part of Trachonitis.

[41] Tacitus, *Hist.* 1.11: *regebat tum Tiberius Alexander, eiusdem nationis*. The phrase indicates that Alexander himself came from Egypt where he was governor.

[42] Jerome, *Vita Malchi* 42 (*PL* 23. 54).

[43] SHA *Niger* 7, 9. The passage contains a spurious statement, but that is not important here. Also: SHA *Severus*14.6 and 17.1; cf. the comments in M. Stern, *Greek and Latin Authors on Jews and Judaism* (Jerusalem, 1980), II, 623–5.

[44] Photius, *Bibliotheca* (marginal note): Οὗτος ὁ Ἰάμβλιχος Σύρος ἦν γένος πατρόθεν καὶ μητρόθεν, Σύρος δὲ οὐχὶ τῶν ἐπῳκότων τὴν Συρίαν Ἑλλήνων, ἀλλὰ τῶν αὐτοχθόνων, γλῶσσαν δὲ σύραν εἰδώς. R. Henry (ed. and trans.), *Photius, Bibliothèque* (Paris, 1960), II, 40, n. 1, for the Greek text of the note. Cf. F. Millar, *The Roman Near East: 31 BC–AD 337* (Cambridge, 1993), 491.

This text then refers to two categories of Syrians: Greek(-speaking) descendants of immigrant settlers and locals who know Syriac and have Syrian customs. Iamblichus is a Syrian, but not a Greek Syrian by birth, and his Greek was acquired later as a foreign language. The distinction made is both cultural-linguistic and a matter of origin or heredity. Even though he himself is, culturally, a successfully Hellenized Syrian the text still regards being Hellenic and being Syrian in language and culture as historically and inextricably linked with origin. A Syrian by origin will always remain a Syrian, whether he acquires Hellenic culture or not. It is a matter of heredity that cannot be changed. To return to Meleager's self-description as a Syrian from an Attic fatherland: this is clearly a complex notion, which may have been less obviously right to part of his readers than he would have wished.

Proceeding in roughly chronological order we come to Dio Chrysostom (ca. AD 40/50–after 110). We change to another literary genre, it should be noted. While Posidonius wrote scholarly prose and Meleager poetry, we are now dealing with public oratory with a partly philosophical, partly sophistic interest.[45] Dio, a native of Prusa, addresses the citizens of Tarsus and asks what would be the impression of a person hearing the sound of their voices from a distance: 'And would anyone call you [sc. the citizens of Tarsus] colonists from Argos, as you claim to be, or more likely colonists of those abominable Aradians? Would he call you Greeks, or the most licentious of Phoenicians?'[46] Dio's remarks about Tarsus in Cilicia have to be seen in perspective. The city was not a Phoenician foundation, but by the time Dio visited it, it was definitely venerable and had been Hellenic in culture for centuries. Strabo, writing not very long before Dio, claims that the people of Tarsus 'have surpassed Athens, Alexandria, or any other place that can be named' in their devotion to philosophy.[47] By contrast Prusa in Cilicia was established (in place of the older settlement named Kios) by Prusias I in 202 BC, so this is a cheeky accusation of Dio, to say the least.[48] This, however, may be regarded as no more than traditional rivalry between Hellenized Anatolian cities. It is the comparison of Tarsus with the equally Hellenized

[45] C. P. Jones, *The Roman World of Dio Chrysostom* (Cambridge, 1978); S. Swain, *Hellenism and Empire: Language, Classicism and Power in the Greek World* AD 50–250 (Oxford, 1996), 187–241.
[46] *Or.* 33: καὶ πότερον ὑμᾶς Ἀργείων ἀποίκους, ὡς λέγετε, φήσει τις ἢ μᾶλλον ἐκείνων Ἀραδίων; καὶ πότερον Ἕλληνας ἢ Φοινίκων τοὺς ἀσελγεστάτους; Cf. Jones, *Roman World of Dio Chrysostom*, 71–82.
[47] Strabo 14.13–15 (673–5).
[48] Note a related objection against the descendants of the Ionians who have become Romanized, according to a letter ascribed to Apollonius of Tyana, see below, p. 166.

Arados, described as licentiously Phoenician, that is striking.[49] Apparently, the worst that a person from Prusa could say to the inhabitants of Tarsus is that they were 'Phoenician colonists'. The point that interests us is to what extent the attitude of a provincial great man towards a provincial community not his own could be condescending and hostile.

A similar phenomenon may be found a century later in the work of Ptolemy of Alexandria (ca. 146–ca. 170) in his *Tetrabiblos*, the work in which he attempted to adapt horoscopic astrology to the Aristotelian natural philosophy of his day.[50] Here we are faced with yet another type of text: scientific prose. It is fascinating to see how this work repeats the usual stereotypes concerning various peoples of the Roman Empire, basing them very firmly on astrological analysis. Thus northern peoples, especially those of Western Europe are

> independent, liberty-loving, fond of arms, industrious, very warlike, with qualities of leadership, cleanly and magnanimous ... but without passion for women and they look down upon the pleasures of love, but are better satisfied with ... men.[51] Gaul, Britain, Germany and Bastrania are ... fierce, more headstrong and bestial.[52]

However, men from the western Mediterranean are clearly superior and destined to rule: 'Italy, Apulia, Cisalpine Gaul and Sicily ... are more masterful, benevolent and co-operative.' The same is true for Greece and its neighbours:

> [The peoples in] the parts of this quarter which are situated about the centre of the inhabited world, Thrace, Macedonia, Illyria, Hellas, Archaia, Crete, and likewise the Cyclades, and the coastal regions of Asia Minor and Cyprus ... have qualities of leadership and are noble and independent, because of Mars; they are liberty-loving and self-governing, democratic and framers of law, through Jupiter ...[53]

When he comes to the peoples of the Near East, neighbours or in the vicinity of his own province of Egypt, the tone changes drastically:

---

[49] Strabo describes Aradus as a prosperous city, acting with prudence and industry in maritime affairs: Strabo 16.2.14 (754). For the city see: H. Seyrig, 'Arados et Baetocaece', *Syria* 29 (1951): 191–220; J.-P. Rey-Coquais, *Arados et sa Pérée aux époques grecque, romaine et byzantine* (Paris, 1974); for legends on its origins: 250–1.

[50] Cf. K. E. Müller, *Geschichte der antiken Ethnographie* (Wiesbaden, 1980), II, 172–3; Isaac, *Invention of Racism*, 99–101.

[51] Ptolemy, *Tetrabiblos*, 2.3.13.4–8.

[52] 2.3.14.1–3.

[53] 2.3.17.1–20.1.

Idumaea, Coele Syria, Judaea, Phoenicia, Chaldaea, Orchinia and Arabia Felix ... more gifted in trade and exchange; they are more unscrupulous, despicable cowards, treacherous, servile, and in general fickle ... Of these, again, the inhabitants of Coele Syria, Idumaea, and Judaea are ... in general bold, godless and scheming.[54]

All this repeats in general terms the usual stereotypes for those peoples. The only true exception is the description of Ptolemy's native Egypt: 'Lower Egypt: thoughtful and intelligent and facile in all things, especially in the search for wisdom and religion; they are magicians and performers of secret mysteries and in general skilled in mathematics.'[55] This is entirely different from the familiar complex of negative stereotypes found about Egypt throughout antiquity: the Egyptians are fraudulent, promiscuous, greedy, fickle, rebellious, etc. etc.[56] It is in itself interesting to see the flexibility of astrology as applied to ethnography, but that is not the issue of the present chapter. The point to be considered here is the obvious indication of ill-will and hostility that could exist between neighbouring peoples and provinces of what undoubtedly was a reasonably well-integrated empire at the height of its power. Ptolemy is chauvinistic regarding his own provincial background, but aggressively negative about neighbouring peoples and provinces and those farther away. We must realize that these assessments are voiced by one of the most prominent scientists and authors of his time. Whether similar sentiments would be uttered in pubs and the markets we cannot know. However, here we are investigating the attitudes of provincial intellectuals and there is no doubt that Ptolemy the Geographer, like Dio Chrysostom, belonged to this category.

For an interesting contrast we may look at the attitude of Philo of Byblos, who lived earlier than Ptolemy – his dates are uncertain but certainly first–second century. Philo was a scholar, the author of grammatical, lexical, and historical works. Substantial fragments of his *Phoenician History* in Greek are cited by Eusebius of Caesarea.[57] Enough survives to conclude with confidence that Philo consistently reflects the perspective of a chauvinist Phoenician. He regularly asserts that everything important

[54] 2.3.31–2.
[55] 2.3.49.1–50.1.
[56] Isaac, *Invention of Racism*, 352–70.
[57] A. I. Baumgarten, *The Phoenician History of Philo of Byblos: A Commentary* (Leiden, 1981); H. W. Attridge and R. A. Oden, *Philo of Byblos: The Phoenician History, Introduction, Critical Text, Translation, Notes*, CBQMS 9 (Washington, DC, 1981); J. Ebach, *Weltentstehung und Kulturentwicklung bei Philo von Byblos: Ein Beitrag zur Uberlieferung der biblischen Urgeschichte im Rahmen des altorientalischen und antiken Schopfungsglaubens* (Stuttgart, 1979).

was first discovered by Phoenicians whose great god Taautos, the inventor of writing, was their model in this respect.[58] The account of the wars of Kronos and Ouranos in Hesiod and other Greek authors presumably derives from a Phoenician story.[59] It was 'the most ancient of the barbarians, and especially Phoenicians and Egyptians, from whom the rest of mankind received their traditions'.[60] Pherekydes of Syros (sixth century BC) was an autodidact who learned all from the Phoenicians: 'He trained himself, having acquired the secret books of the Phoenicians.'[61] Philo insists that he gives genuine Phoenician sources which he contrasts with the derivative and distorted versions found in Greek literature:

> These discoveries were made by us, who have earnestly desired to understand Phoenician culture and who have investigated much material apart from that in Greek authors, for this is inconsistent and composed by some people more for the sake of disputation than for truth ... It came to us to be convinced [of this] ... when we saw the inconsistency in Greek authors ...[62]

The Greeks are not originators but imitators, and bad imitators at that.[63] The Egyptians and the Phoenicians were two of the most ancient peoples who worshipped their gods similarly.[64] The Egyptians, unlike the Greeks, are not a nation that copied and borrowed the treasures of others, but are among the originators.[65] However, Phoenicia takes precedence: Phoenicia was the first land settled by mortal men.[66] Byblos was the first city founded.[67] Civilization began in Phoenicia before Kronos assigned Egypt to Thoth and gave the kingdom of Attica to his daughter Athena.[68] The insistence on precedence and antiquity are familiar from Josephus' *Contra*

---

[58] The name Taautos presumably derives from the Egyptian Thoth, but was perceived as that of a Phoenician god: Attridge and Oden, *Philo of Byblos*, fr. 1 Preface, 24; cf. Baumgarten, *The Phoenician History of Philo of Byblos*, 68–74. Baumgarten emphasizes the chauvinist character of Philo's attitude. Attridge and Oden, 3, also comment on this, while it is entirely ignored in Ebach's earlier, extensive study, although he has detailed chapters on 'Die Entstehung von Kultur und Zivilisation nach den Philo-Fragmenten' and on 'Die Errungenschaften in den Philo-Fragmenten'.

[59] Baumgarten 813: 11–22 and pp. 235–42; Attridge and Oden, fr. 2B, 8. In order to avoid confusion I follow the references as given by Baumgarten and by Attridge and Oden without attempt at compilation.

[60] Attridge and Oden, fr. 1, 29.

[61] Baumgarten 815: 22–5; Attridge and Oden, fr. 4F, 50 and n. 159 and Suidas, s.v. Phi 214.

[62] Attridge and Oden, fr. 1 Preface, 27–8.

[63] Attridge and Oden, fr. 2D, 40–1.

[64] Baumgarten, pp. 256–7.

[65] Baumgarten 805: 26–7.

[66] Baumgarten 807: 22; pp. 148–9.

[67] Attridge and Oden, fr. 2C, 20.

[68] Baumgarten 812: 27–9; Attridge and Oden, fr. 2B, 5; 10; C15; 20; D32; 38.

Apionem.[69] The farther back a people could trace its origins and merit, the higher its status among the peoples of the ancient Mediterranean.

An interesting passage for comparison is found in Pausanias, a younger contemporary of Philo.[70] The author tells he visited a shrine of Asklepios near Eileithyia in Achaia. There he met a confrontational Sidonian:

> In this sanctuary of Asklepios a man of Sidon entered upon an argument with me. He declared that the Phoenicians had better notions about the gods than the Greeks, giving as an instance that to Asklepios they assign Apollo as father, but no mortal woman as his mother. Asklepios, he went on, is air, bringing health to mankind and to all animals likewise; Apollo is the sun, and most rightly is he named father of Asklepios, because the sun, by adapting his course to the seasons, imparts to the air its healthfulness.

When referring to 'Asklepios' Pausanias' Sidonian must have meant Eshmun, whose father was a god associated with the sun, as noted by Baumgarten.

We have seen, therefore a quite fierce tendency towards provincial, or national, chauvinism on the part of Egyptians (Ptolemy) and Phoenicians (Philo of Byblos; Pausanias' Sidonian). Ptolemy combines his local pride with respect for Graeco-Roman culture and a good deal of disparagement of all the other regional peoples, while Philo is competitive with respect to both Egyptians and Greeks, the former being more respectable in many respects than the latter. In this connection we should mention Josephus' *Contra Apionem*, a polemic essay aimed at mostly Graeco-Egyptian authors who disparage the Jewish people, often through arguments demonstrating the antiquity of Jewish history and traditions. A remarkable literary elaboration of this theme may be found in the work of Philostratus. Apollonius of Tyana finds approval in the eyes of the Indians because they are quoted by Philostratus as saying that the visitors

> who come here from Egypt ... malign the people of the Hellenes, and while declaring that they themselves are holy men and wise, and the true law-givers who fixed all the sacrifices and rites of initiation which are in vogue among the Greeks, they deny to the latter any and every sort of good quality, declaring them to be ruffians, and a mixed herd addicted to every sort of anarchy, and lovers of legend and miracle mongers, and though indeed poor, yet making their poverty not a title of dignity, but a mere excuse for stealing.[71]

---

[69] Josephus, *Contra Apionem* 11–14: Hebrew history is much more ancient and better preserved than Greek history.

[70] Pausanias 7.23.7–8. Cf. Baumgarten, pp. 230–1.

[71] Philostratus, *Life of Apollonius of Tyana* 3.32 (trans. Conybeare, Loeb).

This is not the place to attempt to analyse the process which led to disparagement of Greeks on the part of Indians in a work of fiction written in the third century by a Greek author who inhabited the Roman Empire. What is remarkable, again, is the use of historical stereotypes to demonstrate the superiority of one people over another, while both were part of the Roman Empire. In any case, there can be no doubt that there was a good deal of competitive tension between some of the peoples under Roman rule.

We now return to Syria, to an author roughly contemporary with Ptolemy the Geographer, namely Lucian of Samosata, born ca. 120, a prolific author of Greek prose who came from Samosata on the Euphrates, the old capital of Commagene, one of the kingdoms annexed to the province of Syria. His Greek was impeccable and he was quite intolerant of others whose Greek he found lacking.[72] Lucian frequently refers to Syrians among Greeks and to Greeks in Rome and allows us a glimpse of the tensions engendered by the presence of persons of different ethnic and geographic origin in Greece and Rome. It is often difficult to interpret satirical literature properly because we may not be sufficiently familiar with the social context and common ground among the intended readers.[73] There are, however, passages in the work of Lucian that strongly suggest specific attitudes of interest for the present chapter.

Lucian is being accused of abusing philosophy by all great philosophers of the past while Philosophy acts as judge. Lucian addresses them:

> I am a Syrian, Philosophy, from the banks of the Euphrates. But what of that? I know that some of my opponents here are just as barbarian as I: but in their manners and culture they are not like men of Soli or Cyprus or Babylon or Stagira. Yet as far as you are concerned it would make no difference even if a man's speech were foreign, if only his way of thinking were manifestly right and just.[74]

---

[72] As pointed out by Swain, *Hellenism and Empire*, 46.

[73] The literature is very extensive: N. Rudd, *Themes in Roman Satire* (London, 1986), ch. 1; W. S. Anderson, *Essays on Roman Satire* (Princeton, 1982), p. viii; J. Henderson, *Writing down Rome: Satire, Comedy, and Other Offences in Latin Poetry* (Oxford, 1999); K. Freudenburg, *The Cambridge Companion to Roman Satire* (Cambridge, 2005); D.M. Hooley, *Roman Satire* (Oxford, 2007). For Lucian: J. Hall, *Lucian's Satire* (New York, 1981); C. P. Jones, *Culture and Society in Lucian* (Cambridge, 1986); G. Anderson, *The Second Sophistic: A Cultural Phenomenon in the Roman Empire* (London, 1993); Swain, *Hellenism and Empire*, 298–329 and esp. 298–308. See now Andrade, *Syrian Identity* (2013), ch. 10 on the work ascribed to Lucian 'On the Syrian Goddess'.

[74] *Reviviscentes sive Piscator* 19.6 (*The Fisherman*) [344]: Σύρος, ὦ Φιλοσοφία, τῶν Ἐπευφρατιδίων. ἀλλὰ τί τοῦτο; καὶ γὰρ τούτων τινὰς οἶδα τῶν ἀντιδίκων μου οὐχ ἧττον ἐμοῦ βαρβάρους τὸ γένος· ὁ τρόπος δὲ καὶ ἡ παιδεία οὐ κατὰ Σολέας ἢ Κυπρίους ἢ Βαβυλωνίους ἢ Σταγειρίτας. καίτοι πρός γε σὲ οὐδὲν ἂν ἔλαττον γένοιτο οὐδ' εἰ τὴν φωνὴν βάρβαρος εἴη τις, εἴπερ ἡ γνώμη ὀρθὴ καὶ δικαία φαίνοιτο οὖσα.

The argument made in this passage is a familiar cosmopolitan, cynic point, asserting the essential equality of human beings throughout the inhabited world.[75] More specifically, for present purposes, Lucian's tone is apologetic: even though he is a Syrian barbarian and speaks Greek with a foreign accent, his judgement can be right and his morals correct.

Next we will consider a passage from 'The Double Indictment' which has a different emphasis on a related theme: a Syrian, who moves to a Greek environment, gives up his non-Greek lifestyle and acquires Hellenic culture. This text seems to contain elements of an autobiographic dialogue or at least of a scene taken from real life. The speaker here is Oratory, accusing her husband who might well be Lucian himself, a Syrian, before a court of justice. The present passage describes the state in which Oratory first found Lucian.

> When this man was a mere boy, gentlemen of the jury, still speaking with a foreign φωνή [accent; or: speaking a foreign language] and I might almost say wearing a caftan in the Assyrian [sc. Syrian] style, I found him still wandering about in Ionia, not knowing what to do with himself; so I took him in hand and gave him an education. As it seemed to me that he was an apt pupil and paid strict attention to me – for he was subservient to me in those days and paid court to me and admired none but me – I turned my back upon all the others who were suing for my hand, although they were rich and good-looking and of splendid ancestry, and plighted myself to this ingratiate, who was poor and insignificant and young, bringing him a considerable dowry consisting in many marvellous speeches. Then, after we were married, I got him irregularly registered among my own clansmen and made him a citizen, so that those who had failed to secure my hand in marriage choked with envy.[76]

Barbarian φωνή could mean either Aramaic or provincial, accented Greek.[77] I think it means the latter because Lucian usually uses *glossa* for 'language'. The tone of the accusation is here that clothing, culture, and accent go together as well as poverty. They can all be changed, unlike character, as

---

[75] The choice of Soli, Cyprus, Babylon, and Stagira is incomprehensible to me.

[76] *Bis Accusatus* 27 (*The Double Indictment*): Ἐγὼ γάρ, ὦ ἄνδρες δικασταί, τουτονὶ κομιδῇ μειράκιον ὄντα, βάρβαρον ἔτι τὴν φωνὴν καὶ μονονουχὶ κάνδυν ἐνδεδυκότα εἰς τὸν Ἀσσύριον τρόπον, περὶ τὴν Ἰωνίαν εὑροῦσα πλαζόμενον ἔτι καὶ ὅ τι χρήσαιτο ἑαυτῷ οὐκ εἰδότα παραλαβοῦσα ἐπαίδευσα. καὶ ἐπειδὴ ἐδόκει μοι εὐμαθὴς εἶναι καὶ ἀτενὲς ὁρᾶν εἰς ἐμέ – ὑπέπτησσε γὰρ τότε καὶ ἐθεράπευεν καὶ μόνην ἐθαύμαζεν – ἀπολιποῦσα τοὺς ἄλλους ὁπόσοι ἐμνήστευόν με πλούσιοι καὶ καλοὶ καὶ λαμπροὶ τὰ προγονικά, τῷ ἀχαρίστῳ τούτῳ ἐμαυτὴν ἐνεγγύησα πένητι καὶ ἀφανεῖ καὶ νέῳ προῖκα οὐ μικρὰν ἐπενεγκαμένη πολλοὺς καὶ θαυμασίους λόγους. εἶτα ἀγαγοῦσα αὐτὸν εἰς τοὺς φυλέτας τοὺς ἐμοὺς παρενέγραψα καὶ ἀστὸν ἀπέφηνα, ὥστε τοὺς διαμαρτόντας τῆς ἐγγύης ἀποπνίγεσθαι.

[77] See J. L. Lightfoot, *Lucian on the Syrian Goddess* (Oxford, 2003), 205 with n. 554 for references.

is clear from the subsequent developments. Once the Syrian has acquired Hellenic culture and is accepted as a member of respectable society, his true character shows itself: he is an ungrateful profiteer. In other words: culture can be acquired, but character is basic, inherited, and a Syrian has a bad character by birth. A barbarian character will show, whatever the Hellenic veneer. Obviously this is not necessarily Lucian's own opinion of Syrians in Greek society. This accusation is actually ascribed to 'Oratory'. However, this passage may plausibly be interpreted as a satirical rendering of the stereotypes current among Greek rhetoricians against the easterners among them.

The third and last passage associated with well-to-do Syrians in Greek society is taken from 'The Ignorant Book-Collector'.[78] Lucian asks why this unlettered rich man collects books.[79] Perhaps it is only to display his wealth. 'Come now, as far as I know – and I too am a Syrian – if you had not smuggled yourself into that old man's will with all speed, you would be starving to death by now, and would be putting up your books at auction!' The implication of the words 'I too am a Syrian' is that the other man behaves like a typical Syrian or, rather, like a stereotypical Syrian. He was an ignorant pauper who got rich thanks to dishonest machinations and used his money to build up a façade of intellectuality. Again, this is satire and can plausibly be interpreted as representing a humorous imitation of Greek prejudice concerning Syrians. The three passages from Lucian cited here are concerned with varying situations. What they have in common is the view that Syrians cannot be genuine Greek, intellectual gentlemen. They have to defend themselves against prejudice because of their foreign accents or are seen as profiteers or frauds.

Several elements represented in these passages are clearly echoed by the following letter, ascribed to Apollonius of Tyana and addressed to the stoic philosopher Euphrates of Tyre (second century AD):

> You have travelled the provinces as far as Italy starting from Syria, showing yourself off in so-called 'king's robes'. Once you had a cheap cloak, a long white beard, and nothing more. So how is it that you now return by sea with a boatload of silver, gold, vessels of every kind, embroidered clothing, all kinds of furniture, clothing of various colours, every other sort of

---

[78] *Adversus Indoctum* 19.20–20.1 (*The Ignorant Book-Collector*) [342]: καὶ μὴν ὅσα γε κἀμὲ Σύρον ὄντα εἰδέναι, εἰ μὴ σαυτὸν φέρων ταῖς τοῦ γέροντος ἐκείνου διαθήκαις παρενέγραψας, ἀπωλώλεις ἂν ὑπὸ λιμοῦ ἤδη καὶ ἀγορὰν προὐτίθεις τῶν βιβλίων.

[79] The Loeb edn, I, by A. M. Harmon, 1953, adds by way of clarification: 'he may or may not have been of Semitic stock'.

adornment, conceit, effrontery, disgrace? What kind of cargo or trafficking does this novel trade involve? Zeno was a merchant in dried fruits.[80]

The suggestion here, clearly resembling some of those of Lucian, is that a philosopher from Syria lacked integrity and used his trade successfully for opportunistic, material gain.[81]

In the works of Lucian there are other Syrian immigrants, who do not move in circles of wealth and intellectuality. They are poor immigrants who make a living as quacks, thus in *Podagra*:

> We Syrians are, Damascus men by birth,
> But forced by hunger and by poverty,
> We wander far afield o'er land and sea,
> We have an ointment here, our fathers' gift
> With which we comfort woes of sufferers.[82]

A somewhat related figure appears in the *Philopseudes* 16.4–5: He is a Syrian from Palestine, not a specific person, but a familiar type, apparently, someone who exorcizes spirits for a large fee, and it is clearly suggested that men like this one are quacks who charge huge sums for their services.

> Everyone knows about the Syrian from Palestine, the adept in [exorcising spirits], how many he takes in hand who fall down in the light of the moon and roll their eyes and fill their mouths with foam; nevertheless, he restores them to health and sends them away normal in mind, delivering them from their straits for a large fee.[83]

The essence again is that it is typical of him as a Syrian from Palestine, that he is a quack, exploiting superstition and credulity for gain. These

---

[80] Philostratus, *Apollonius of Tyana, Letters of Apollonius*, ed. and trans. C. P. Jones (Cambridge, 2006), *Ep.* 3: Ἐπῆλθες ἔθνη τὰ μεταξὺ τῆς Ἰταλίας ἀπὸ Συρίας ἀρξάμενος, ἐπιδεικνὺς σεαυτὸν ἐν ταῖς τῶν βασιλέων λεγομέναις διπλαῖς. τρίβων δέ σοι πότε καὶ πώγων λευκὸς καὶ μέγας, πλέον δὲ οὐδέν, εἶτα πῶς διὰ θαλάττης νῦν ὑποστρέφεις ἄγων φορτίδα μεστὴν ἀργυρίου, χρυσίου σκευῶν παντοδαπῶν, ἐσθῆτος ποικίλων, κόσμου τοῦ λοιποῦ, τύφου καὶ ἀλαζονείας καὶ κακοδαιμονίας· τίς ὁ φόρτος καὶ ὁ τρόπος τῆς καινῆς ἐμπορίας; Ζήνων τραγημάτων ἦν ἔμπορος. I cite these letters several times, but have not treated them as the work of a single, datable author, since there is no reason to assume that that is what they are.

[81] Similarly, *Ep.* 5; 8.2.

[82] *Podagra* 265 [345]: Σύροι μέν ἐσμεν, ἐκ Δαμασκοῦ τῷ γένει, / λιμῷ δὲ πολλῷ καὶ πενίᾳ κρατούμενοι / γῆν καὶ θάλασσαν ἐφέπομεν πλανώμενοι· / ἔχομεν δὲ χρῖσμα πατροδώρητον τόδε, / ἐν ᾧ παρηγοροῦμεν ἀλγούντων πόνους..

[83] ἀλλὰ πάντες ἴσασι τὸν Σύρον τὸν ἐκ τῆς Παλαιστίνης, τὸν ἐπὶ τούτῳ σοφιστήν, ὅσους παραλαβὼν καταπίπτοντας πρὸς τὴν σελήνην καὶ τὼ ὀφθαλμὼ διαστρέφοντας καὶ ἀφροῦ πιμπλαμένους τὸ στόμα ὅμως ἀνίστησι καὶ ἀποπέμπει ἀρτίους τὴν γνώμην, ἐπὶ μισθῷ μεγάλῳ ἀπαλλάξας τῶν δεινῶν. There is a good deal of discussion regarding the identity of this man as to whether he is Jewish, non-Jewish, or Christian: Stern, *Greek and Latin Authors on Jews and Judaism*, II, 221, no. 372; Isaac, *Invention of Racism*, 347 and n. 101.

passages in Lucian's work related to Syrians all show subtle differences, but what they have in common is a suggestion that the dominant stereotype for them is that of dishonesty and it does not seem farfetched to detect an apologetic tone in these passages. We should remember here, that being 'Syrian' is not a straightforward issue, as we saw above. It can denote origin from the province of Syria, but is unavoidably part of a more complex package. There is little doubt that Lucian's audience was a general, Greek-reading intellectual part of the population, while he focused in these cases on the position of Syrians who had moved to other provinces.[84]

There is, however, another relationship which also must have played a significant role in his life, namely that of the position of Greeks in the city of Rome. In the following passage in *On Hirelings*, Lucian, Greek in culture, from Samosata in Syria, satirizes the local, Roman response to the presence of Greeks in the society of contemporary Rome:

> That was still left for us in addition to our other afflictions, to play second fiddle to men who have just come into the household, and it is only these Greeks who have the freedom of the city of Rome. And yet, why is it that they are preferred to us? Is it not true that they think they confer a tremendous benefit by turning phrases?[85]

The speaker here is a fictional character, a local Roman who feels he is being pushed aside in Roman society by Greeks with their smooth talk. In another passage of the same work, 40, there is a suggestion that there was an automatic presumption that every Greek is less reliable than any local Roman.[86] In the passages discussed here Lucian thus covers two groups of people who were the target of negative stereotypes: Hellenized Syrians who had moved to other provinces and Italy and Greeks in Rome.

If we compare the attitudes which Lucian attributes to his fictional characters, as they appear in these passages, then it will be clear that they do

---

[84] *Alexander* 48.19: Speaking of Marcus' war with the Marcomanni and Quadi, Lucian refers to the enemy as οἱ βάρβαροι, to the Roman troops as 'ours' (αὐτίκα δὲ τὸ μέγιστον τραῦμα τοῖς ἡμετέροις ἐγένετο). Some scholars regard this as significant. It certainly is not. Lucian had every reason to use the third person in this case. Cf. *Hist. conscr.* 29.5: 'Nobody would dare attack us – we have beaten everybody already.'

[85] *De mercede conductis* 17 (*On Hirelings*): Τοῦτο ἡμῖν πρὸς τοῖς ἄλλοις δεινοῖς ἐλείπετο, καὶ τῶν ἄρτι εἰσεληλυθότων εἰς τὴν οἰκίαν δευτέρους εἶναι, καὶ μόνοις τοῖς Ἕλλησι τούτοις ἀνέῳκται ἡ Ῥωμαίων πόλις· καίτοι τί ἐστιν ἐφ' ὅτῳ προτιμῶνται ἡμῶν· οὐ ῥημάτια δύστηνα λέγοντες οἴονταί τι παμμέγεθες ὠφελεῖν.

[86] I have not included any passages from *De Dea Syria* attributed to Lucian. While this is an extremely interesting text the difficulties involved in understanding it are such that they preclude useful discussion here. See Lightfoot, *Lucian On the Syrian Goddess*; cf. Andrade, *Syrian Identity* (2013), ch. 10. Personally I do not believe the work is by Lucian. In Lucian's satire there are always at least two parties involved.

not resemble the position taken by Posidonius in his scholarly work, where he does not identify himself as a Syrian and took his distance. Meleager's on the other hand clearly identifies his background, but claims that it does not prevent him from being genuinely Hellenic while, at the same time defending the view that all men are born equal and should be judged on the basis of intrinsic merit, not origin or ancestry. Lucian, writing satire, seems to imply that there always remained a social barrier that could not be overcome.

It is, unfortunately, not profitable to discuss Arrian, historian, senator, and high official (ca. 95–175), originally from Nicomedia in Bithynia in Asia Minor. In his *Bithynica* he proudly declared himself to have been born, raised, and educated in Nicomedia.[87] The most interesting reference to his fatherland (πατρίς) and 'his own land'[88] is a matter of lively and unresolved dispute, namely whether Arrian means thereby Nicomedia or Rome, perhaps even Athens or a combination of these cities.[89] Whatever he means, he declares his name, *patris*, family, and career to be well known, while he claims to be the proper man to write Alexander's history precisely because he is prominent as a Greek writer as Alexander was in arms. Here, then, we have a second-century author from Asia Minor who is thoroughly at ease in the Empire as a prominent intellectual. Even if we do not know whether he presented himself first and foremost as a Roman citizen or as a native of Nicomedia, his remarkable self-assurance is worthy of note.

Another rough contemporary of these men was Fronto, who belonged to quite a different social class (ca. 95–166). Fronto descended from a respectable Italian family in Cirta, the old capital of Numidia.[90] It became a city of colonial rank in the reign of Augustus.[91] His reputation as a Latin orator is second only to that of Cicero. In a letter, written in Greek in 143 to Domitia Lucilla, the Emperor Antoninus' mother, Fronto apologizes for any possible infelicities in his Attic and adds that Anacharsis is also said to have been imperfect in Greek, 'but he was praised for his meaning and his thoughts. I will compare myself, then, with Anacharsis, not, by heaven, in

---

[87] Arrian, *Bithynicorum fragmenta* 1, 1.7 (Roos 197): Νικομήδειον γάρ [τι] τὸ γένος αὑτοῦ ἐν ταύτῃ τῇ συγγραφῇ διορίζει, ἐν αὑτῇ τε γεννηθῆναι καὶ τραφῆναι καὶ παιδευθῆναι,.

[88] Arrian, *History of Alexander* 1.12.5.

[89] B. A. Bosworth, *A Historical Commentary on Arrian's History of Alexander* (Oxford, 1980), 106: Nicomedia; P. A. Stadter, *Arrian of Nicomedia* (Chapel Hill, NC, 1980), 65, n. 19; 181: 'my own land' is Rome; P. A. Brunt (ed. and trans.), *Arrian: Anabasis Alexandri and Indica*, 2 vols. (Cambridge, 1976–83), II, 538–9: Rome is both his fatherland and his own land; Swain, *Hellenism and Empire*, 244–6: both refer to Nicomedia. Further references to modern literature in Swain.

[90] Champlin, *Fronto*, ch. 1, 5–19.

[91] Champlin, *Fronto*, 6.

wisdom, but as being like him a barbarian. For he was a Scythian of the nomad Scythians … and … I am a Libyan of the Libyan nomads.'[92] In a letter to Marcus Aurelius Fronto refers to his writing as 'by the hand of this foreigner, in speech little short of a barbarian, but as regards judgment, as I think, not wholly wanting in sagacity'.[93]

Fronto identifies himself as a rustic provincial even though he is clearly a very superior one and he certainly does not mean he really has anything to do with nomads.[94] That is an affectation, a little pre-emptive strike. We may note that Lucian also compares himself with Anacharsis.[95] Here too the comparison is immediately qualified by what seems to be false modesty.[96] A further point of interest is that Fronto here is apologizing for his Greek. As mentioned, as a Latin author he was second to none in his time and he would never have apologized for that, but he does not mention his Latin. He is writing here as someone who appears to feel that Greek is the language that really distinguishes between a true gentleman and a barbarian.

Another provincial intellectual from North Africa to be mentioned briefly is Apuleius, best-known through his *Golden Ass* (*Metamorphoses*). He came from Madaurus,[97] a Roman colony in the province of Africa Proconsularis where his father was a *duumvir*. Apuleius was wealthy, studied in Carthage, Athens, and Rome.[98] His *Apologia* is a speech defending himself against an accusation that he indulged in magic practices.

> Concerning my fatherland, as you have shown on the basis of my own writings, it lies on the very border of Numidia and Gaetulia. I have in fact

---

[92] *Epist. Graecae* 1.10 (Naber 239–42; trans. C. R. Haines, Loeb): εἴ τι τῶν ὀνομάτων ἐν ταῖς ἐπιστολαῖς ταύταις εἴη ἄκυρον ἢ βάρβαρον ἢ ἄλλως ἀδόκιμον ἢ μὴ πάνυ Ἀττικόν, ἀλλὰ … τοῦ ὀνόματος σ᾽ ἀξιῶ τήν γε διάνοιαν σκοπεῖν αὐτὴν καθ᾽ αὑτήν· οἶσθα γὰρ ὅτι ἐν αὐτοῖς ὀνόμασιν καὶ αὐτῇ διαλέκτῳ διατρίβω. καὶ γὰρ τὸν Σκύθην ἐκεῖνον τὸν Ἀνάχαρσιν οὐ πάνυ τι ἀττικίσαι φασίν, ἐπαινεθῆναι δ᾽ ἐκ τῆς διανοίας καὶ τῶν ἐνθυμημάτων. παραβαλῶ δὴ ἐμαυτὸν Ἀναχάρσιδι οὐ μὰ Δία κατὰ τὴν σοφίαν ἀλλὰ κατὰ τὸ βάρβαρος ὁμοίως εἶναι. ἦν γὰρ ὁ μὲν Σκύθης τῶν νομάδων Σκυθῶν.

[93] *Epist. Graecae* 8 (Naber, 255; trans. Haines): τὸ δὲ δὴ τρίτον διὰ τοῦδε τοῦ ξένου ἀνδρός, τὴν μὲν φωνὴν ὀλίγου δεῖν βαρβάρου, τὴν δὲ γνώμην, ὡς ἐγῷμαι, οὐ πάνυ ἀξυνέτου.

[94] See, however, Champlin, *Fronto*, 7–8.

[95] In various fictional letters attributed to him Anacharsis appears as a spokesman for a Cynic theme – the importance of judging people by inner worth and not by external trappings. See C D. N. Costa, *Greek Fictional Letters: A Selection with Introduction, Translation and Commentary* (Oxford, 2001), 69, where the emphasis is placed on the unimportance of accent and idiomatic purity of spoken Greek.

[96] Lucian, *Scytha* 9.6ff.

[97] M'daurouch in modern Algeria.

[98] For information about Apuleius' background and biography: S. J. Harrison, *Apuleius: A Latin Sophist* (Oxford, 2000), 1–10.

declared in my public declarations made in the presence of the honourable
Lollianus Avitus that I am half Numidian and half Gaetulian. However, I do
not see what there is in this for me to be ashamed of, any more than there
was for the Elder Cyrus, being of mixed origin, half Mede and half Persian.
After all it is not where a man was born but his way of life that should be
considered, nor in what region, but how he lives his life ... Have we not seen
that in all periods and among all peoples different characters occur, while
some appear more remarkable for their stupidity or their cleverness? The
wise Anacharsis was born among the extremely foolish Scythians, among
the intelligent Athenians, the silly Meletides. And yet I have not spoken out
of shame for my country, even if we were still the town of Syphax [i.e. still
belonged to the kingdom of the late King Syphax]. After the latter's defeat
we found ourselves under the authority of king Masinissa by the grant of
the Roman people. Later our city was re-founded by the establishment of
veteran soldiers and we are now a most splendid colony. In this colony my
father reached the rank of *duumvir* after passing through all the ranks of the
municipal administration. His status in the city, ever since I was a member
of the council, I maintain without demeaning it, with equal honour and
respect, I hope.

Here too we encounter presumptuous comparisons: this time with Cyrus,
but also, for the third time, with Anacharsis. He returns to the argument
encountered in Meleager, going back to Antiphon, that it does not really
matter where you are born. It is important how you live, what culture you
have, how you behave. Yet he does not deny the truth of stereotypes. He
merely asserts that there are exceptions everywhere. He also seems to feel a
mixed origin is problematic, a common attitude in antiquity,[99] but here too
he asserts that there are exceptions: clever individuals among stupid people
and the reverse. A third point at issue is the character of his native city of
Madaurus. It is, apparently, felt necessary to point out the difference between
a notable from a Roman citizen colony, and a provincial native from among
the rural subject peoples.[100] While much of the *Apologia* is very aggressive
where he is on the attack, here he speaks as one who is on the defence. Yet,
as pointed out by Harrison, 'He belongs not to an African subculture, but to
the mainstream of Latin culture and literature, with his much-vaunted flu-
ency in Greek acquired as it would be by a well-educated Roman.'[101]

---

[99] Isaac, *Invention of Racism*, 90, 118–21, 126, 136, 144.
[100] He had only partial success. The online Wikipedia without hesitation calls Apuleius 'a thoroughly Romanized Berber' (later revised: 'He was a Numidian Berber and lived under the Roman
Empire'), referring to the entry 'Berbers' in the *Encyclopedia Americana* (2004), III, 569: where it
solemnly says: 'The best known of them were the Roman author Apuleius, the Roman emperor
Septimius Severus, and St. Augustine.'
[101] Harrison, *Apuleius*, 4.

We remain in North Africa, to consider the background of the Emperor Septimius Severus.[102] In the reign of Domitian, Statius addresses a Septimius Severus who was perhaps the grandfather and certainly an older relative of the future emperor:

> Did Leptis that loses itself in the distant Syrtes beget you? ... Who would not think that my sweet Septimius had crawled an infant on all the hills of Rome? ... Neither your speech nor your dress is Punic, yours is no stranger's mind: Italian are you, Italian! Indeed in our city and among the knights of Rome, Libya has sons who would adorn her.[103]

Ostensibly this pays Septimius Severus a compliment by declaring him indistinguishable from a genuine Roman. At the same time, however, it shows the condescension towards a man who was a provincial and yet was regarded as respectable by Romans in Rome. Obviously, most foreigners were less successfully adapted to Roman society. Statius' words may imply that a man from Leptis in North Africa, staying in Rome, might be remarkable there for his Punic speech and dress. It is the absence of those features that is regarded as remarkable. Moreover, not all representatives of the Roman elite were as tolerant (and as proud of it) as Statius. When all is said and done, Septimius still does not really belong.

According to the Historia Augusta the Emperor Septimius Severus was ashamed of his sister from Leptis because she could scarcely speak Latin. The emperor himself, however, was drilled in the Latin and Greek literatures as a child, according to the same source.[104]

The point regarding the sister will have been pure invention – as one may expect from this particular source;[105] the one regarding the emperor's schooling was undoubtedly true. The essence for us here is that the Historia Augusta still represents and writes for an audience among the imperial upper class that maintained the old attitudes towards provincial elites. It may be noted that the non-Roman background associated with the three North Africans cited here differs: Fronto from the Roman colony of Cirta in Numidia declares himself to be a 'Libyan nomad'; Apuleius from the

---

[102] T. D. Barnes, 'The Family and Career of Septimius Severus', *Historia* 16 (1967): 87–107.

[103] Statius, *Silvae* 4.5.29–48: *tene in remotis Syrtibus avia / Leptis creavit? ... / quis non in omni vertice Romuli / reptasse dulcem Septimium putet? ... non sermo Poenus, non habitus tibi, externa non mens: Italus, Italus. / sunt Vrbe Romanisque turmis / qui Libyam deceant alumni.* For this poem, see also above, Chapter 6, 'Names: Ethnic, Geographic, and Administrative.'

[104] SHA, *Severus* 17.7; 1.4.

[105] Similarly, Apuleius, *Apologia* 98 claims that his stepson and adversary, Sicinius Pudens, 'speaks never anything but Punic, or perhaps one or two words of Greek which come from his mother [Apuleius' wife]. Speaking Latin is beyond his wish and his grasp', trans. V. Hunink, in S. J. Harrison (ed.), *Apuleius Rhetorical Works* (Oxford, 2001), 116. Cf. Barnes, 'Family and Career', 96.

Roman colony of Madaurus in Numidia claims to be half a Numidian and half a Gaetulian (Berber) nomad. It was quite a common view in antiquity that nomads represented a far lower level of civilization than regular non-Greek and non-Roman urban society, for it was assumed that nomads in fact represented a totally unstructured form of society in social, political, and economic respects. This is the subject of Chapter 10.

The Septimii Severi, from Leptis (in Tripolitania, modern Libya) are, by contrast, associated with a Punic background. The city was indeed an old Punic city, but by the time of the Flavians it had the status of a *municipium* and Trajan gave it colonial status. It is remarkable to see that the colonial identity of the home-towns of Fronto, Apuleius, and Septimius Severus did not in those times convey a sense of Latin respectability which it should have if their colonial rank had genuinely preserved its old flavour as a mark of genuine Roman identity, as asserted in a well-known passage by Aulus Gellius (AD 123–70). Here it is stated that the rank of a *colonia* 'is thought preferable and superior because of the greatness and majesty of the Roman people, of which those colonies seem to be miniatures, as it were, and in a way copies'.[106] The opposite approach, however, goes far back. L. Calpurnius Piso, Caesar's father-in-law and an enemy of Cicero, had a grandfather from Placentia which was founded in 218 BC as a Latin colony in Cisalpine Gaul. Cicero suggests that the grandfather was really an Insubrian Gaul, or even a barbarian from Gaul beyond the Alps.[107] In the reign of Claudius there were those who resisted the emperor's decision to admit to the Senate men from Gallia Comata. According to Tacitus they asked whether it was not enough that 'Veneti and Insubres have already burst into the Senate-house … ?'[108] The senators from northern Italy were no tribal Veneti and Insubres; they belonged to highly respectable families from the colonies and *municipia* in Transpadane Italy.

The Historia Augusta also has something to say about the Emperor Severus Alexander, who came from Arca Caesarea in Syria: 'He wished it to be thought that he derived his descent from the Roman people, for he was ashamed at being called a Syrian, particularly because, on a certain festival,

---

[106] Aulus Gellius, *Noctes Atticae* 16.13.9: *Quae tamen condicio, cum sit magis obnoxia et minus libera, potior tamen et praestabilior existimatur propter amplitudinem maiestatemque populi Romani, cuius istae coloniae quasi effigies parvae simulacraque esse quaedam videntur …*

[107] Asconius, *Pis.* 4.3.fr10: *Hic cum a domo <profectus> Placentiae forte consedisset, pauci<s post annis> in eam civitatem-nam tum erat … … -ascendit. Prius enim Gallus, dein Gallica<nus>, extremo Placentinus haberi <coeptus> est.* Asconius, *Pis.* 5.3.fr11a: *Insuber quidam fuit, idem mercator et praeco … Cf.* Syme, *Provincial at Rome*, 41.

[108] Tacitus, *Ann.* 11.23.4: *an parum quod Veneti et Insubres curiam inruperint, nisi coetus alienigenarum velut captivitas inferatur?*

the people of Antioch and of Egypt and Alexandria had angered him with jibes, as they are wont to do, calling him both a Syrian *archisynagogus* and a high priest.'[109]

Whatever the meaning of a Syrian *archisynagogus* and a high priest could supposedly be, it was not intended or interpreted as a compliment.[110] The emphasis here is on the Syrian, non-Roman background of the emperor. Since this particular biography is one of the most fanciful of the series, all we should learn from it is that the author and his intended readers would find the idea natural – and even funny – for a Syrian emperor to be ashamed of his origins, vaguely associated with Judaism, and, perhaps, various unspecified Eastern cults.

So far we have encountered intellectuals from the Near East, notably Syria, but also Phoenicia, Asia Minor, and Egypt. There were several from North Africa too, but Gauls have only been mentioned in passing. There is at least one prominent figure from Gallia across the Alps to discuss here. Favorinus was a pupil of Dio Chrysostom and friend of many of the important men in the reigns of Hadrian and Antoninus, including Fronto, mentioned above. In spite of the judgement of Ronald Syme, who observed that his nullity is convincingly attested,[111] he was regarded in his own days as a prominent sophist and philosopher.[112] He came from Latin-speaking Arelate (Arles) in Gaul, was educated perhaps in Massilia, and made his name as a Greek orator and thinker.[113] According to Philostratus, 'he used to say in the ambiguous style of an oracle, that there were in the story of his life these three paradoxes: Though he was a Gaul he led the life of a Hellene; a eunuch he had been tried for adultery; he had quarrelled with an Emperor and was still alive ...'[114]

In the Corinthian oration attributed to him Favorinus says as follows:

> Indeed it seems that he [sc. Favorinus] has been equipped by the gods for this express purpose – for the Greeks, so that the natives of that land may have an

---

[109] SHA, *Severus Alexander* 28.7: *volebat videri originem de Romanorum gente trahere, quia eum pudebat Syrum dici, maxime quod quodam tempore festo, ut solent, Antiochenses, Agyptii, Alexandrini lacessiverant conviciolis, et Syrum archisynagogum eum vocantes et archiereum.* See also 44.3 and 64.3.

[110] See the comments in Stern, *Greek and Latin Authors*, II, 630, no. 521.

[111] R. Syme, *Tacitus* (Oxford, 1958), 505.

[112] A. Barigazzi, *Favorino di Arelate: Opere* (Florence, 1966); E. Amato (ed.) and Y. Julien (trans.), *Favorinos d'Arles, Œuvres*, I, *Introduction général – Témoignages – Discours aux Corinthiens – Sur la Fortune* (Paris, 2005).

[113] See Amato, *Favorinos d'Arles*, Introduction, 1–37, for full references regarding his life and chronology.

[114] Philostratus, *VS* I.8 (489): ὅθεν ὡς παράδοξα ἐπεχρησμῴδει τῷ ἑαυτοῦ βίῳ τρία ταῦτα· Γαλάτης ὢν ἑλληνίζειν, εὐνοῦχος ὢν μοιχείας κρίνεσθαι, βασιλεῖ διαφέρεσθαι καὶ ζῆν.

example before them to show that culture is no whit inferior to birth with respect to renown; for Romans, so that not even those who are wrapped up in their own self-esteem may disregard culture with respect to real esteem; for Celts, so that no one even of the barbarians may despair of attaining the culture of Greece when he looks upon this man.[115]

Being a native of Arelate in Gallia Narbonensis, a significant city and a Roman veteran colony, Favorinus ought not to have felt inferior in any way, but for a man from Gaul to be accepted as an equal in Greek circles was a difficult feat. In the lines quoted from what are, apparently, his own words, it is clear that he feels a need to impress on his audience that culture knows no boundaries and is more essential than birth, an assertion directed both at Greeks from Greece who should not feel that they have a monopoly on Greek culture and at Romans who tend to regard themselves as superior. In his oration Favorinus describes himself as a Roman of equestrian rank, as he was.

The idea that birth was more important than culture is familiar and an issue particularly in this period, as will be discussed below. It is surprising, however, to see that Favorinus also implies that he somehow belongs to the Celts and barbarians. It would not occur to any modern visitor to Arles to think of the ancient remains still standing in the city as representing those of a Celtic town. Arelate had been firmly Roman for more than two centuries when Favorinus spoke and was established as a genuine veteran colony by Julius Caesar.[116] Again, we see that colonial status does not prevent an author from identifying with the original non-Roman inhabitants of the region. This echoes the apparently disingenuous references to North African nomads in the writings of Fronto and Apuleius, cited above. In the case of Favorinus there is at least a hint that this was not an affectation, for Philostratus himself says that 'he came from the Gauls of the West'[117] and cites Favorinus as asserting that 'he, Favorinus, was a Gaul leading the life of a Hellene'.[118] Here again we should remember that the term 'Gaul' could

---

[115] *Corinthian Oration* 37.27: ἐπ' αὐτὸ γὰρ τοῦτο καὶ ἐδόκει ὑπὸ τῶν θεῶν οἷον ἐξεπίτηδες κατεσκευάσθαι, Ἕλλησι μέν, ἵνα ἔχωσιν οἱ ἐπιχώριοι τῆς Ἑλλάδος παράδειγμα ὡς οὐδὲν τὸ παιδευθῆναι τοῦ φῦναι πρὸς τὸ δοκεῖν διαφέρει· Ῥωμαίοις δέ, ἵνα μηδ' οἱ τὸ ἴδιον ἀξίωμα περιβεβλημένοι τὸ παιδεύεσθαι πρὸς τὸ ἀξίωμα παρορῶσι· Κελτοῖς δέ, ἵνα μηδὲ τῶν βαρβάρων μηδεὶς ἀπογιγνώσκῃ τῆς Ἑλληνικῆς παιδείας, βλέπων εἰς τοῦτον … with comments by Amato, 448–9.

[116] Note also the later, fourth-century description of Arelate as a large and prosperous city with an admirable population in the *Expositio Totius Mundi et Gentium* 58 (ed. Rougé).

[117] Philostratus, *VS* 1.8 (489): ἦν μὲν γὰρ τῶν ἑσπερίων Γαλατῶν οὗτος, This need not mean more than that Philostratus himself shared such prejudices. See Amato, *Favorinos d'Arles*, 10, n. 27, for extensive discussion whether Favorinus' mother tongue had been Celtic. That seems unnecessary.

[118] Γαλάτης ὢν ἑλληνίζειν. E. Amato, 'Luciano e l'anonimo filosofo Celta di *Hercules* 4: Proposta di identificazione', *Symbolae Osloenses* 79 (2004): 128–49 and A. Hofeneder, 'Favorinus von Arleate

and did indicate a person from the province of Gallia, but also an ethnic Gaul, a Celt, and that, even in the second century, raised associations with a lower cultural and social level.

A fierce enemy of Favorinus was the pompous, influential orator and practitioner of physiognomics, Polemon of Laodicea (88–145). An invective in his work almost certainly aimed at Favorinus refers to him as 'the Celt'.[119] Ilaria Romeo has pointed out that the hostility between Favorinus and Polemon was not only a personal conflict, but also a fiercely ideological one, as Polemon recognized only Greeks of pure lineage as genuine. For him Greek identity was a matter of descent, not of culture.[120] Romeo has shown also that Polemon was by no means alone in this view. The Panhellenic League, established in the reign of Hadrian in 131/2, selected its members clearly on the basis of a definition of the concept of *genos* in terms of blood ties, and ancestral Greekness was essential to qualify for admission.[121] Clearly then in this period there existed a powerful ideology which would insist on the priority of lineage over that of culture, an ideology supported, apparently by the emperor himself.

We may mention, in this connection, the assertion of Josephus that his enemy Apion merely claimed to be an Alexandrian, while he was in reality born in the Great Oasis in Upper Egypt and therefore 'more Egyptian than them all'. Given this false claim, says Josephus, he thus 'admitted the ignominy of his people'.[122] The situation is not fully comparable, but this is at least yet another instance where native, provincial origin is applied

---

und die keltische Religion', *Keltische Forschungen* 1 (2006): 29–58, have argued that Favorinus is identical with an anonymous 'Celtic philosopher' who explained an image of the God Ogmios in Lucianus, *Hercules* 4.2. Personally I doubt whether Lucian would describe Favorinus as 'a Celt, not uneducated in our culture as was clear because he spoke good Greek, a philosopher, I believe, in the local affairs' (Κελτὸς δέ τις παρεστὼς οὐκ ἀπαίδευτος τὰ ἡμέτερα, ὡς ἔδειξεν ἀκριβῶς Ἑλλάδα φωνὴν ἀφιείς, φιλόσοφος, οἶμαι, τὰ ἐπιχώρια,). Amato and Hofeneder may well be right in arguing that the Celt was not a Druid, but that does not mean we must assume that Favorinus would be described by Lucian in this fashion.

[119] Polemon, *De Physiognomonia* 1.160–1; Anonymi, *De Physiognomonia* 40 (André); cf. Isaac, *Invention of Racism*, 156–7.

[120] I. Romeo, 'The Panhellenion and Ethnic Identity in Hadrianic Greece', *Classical Philology* 97 (2002): 21–40, at 32–5. Note especially paragraph 35 (of the Arabic version as translated into Latin) of Polemon's *Physiognomica*, in R. Förster (ed.), *Scriptores Physiognomonici Graeci et Latini* (Leipzig, 1894), 240–2: *De Graecis et eorum genere puro*.

[121] Romeo, 'The Panhellenion', 26–31. Romeo (p. 35) suggests that Polemon, who was close to Hadrian in the 120s may have influenced the Emperor in formulating the ideology of the Panhellenic league.

[122] Josephus, *Contra Apionem* 2.29: αὐτὸς γὰρ περὶ αὑτοῦ τοὐναντίον ἐψεύδετο καὶ γεγενημένος ἐν Ὀάσει τῆς Αἰγύπτου πάντων Αἰγυπτίων πρῶτος ὤν, ὡς ἄν εἴποι τις, τὴν μὲν ἀληθῆ πατρίδα καὶ τὸ γένος ἐξωμόσατο, Ἀλεξανδρεὺς δὲ εἶναι καταψευδόμενος ὁμολογεῖ τὴν μοχθηρίαν τοῦ γένους.

to someone of indubitably Greek or Roman culture and interpreted in a negative sense.[123]

I am aware of only one Greek text that expresses strong disapproval of what is perceived as being a process of Romanization of true Greeks. This is to be found in one of the letters ascribed to Apollonius of Tyana and addressed to the Ionians: 'Most of you, however, do not even keep your names, and your recent prosperity has made you lose the marks of your ancestors ... Your names used once to be those of heroes, admirals and lawgivers, but now are those of a Lucullus, a Fabricius, a Lucanius, the lucky people! For me "Mimnermus" would be a preferable name.'[124] Whether authentic or not, the letter clearly expresses the opinion of someone who dislikes the adoption of Roman names by Greeks who received the Roman citizenship.[125] The attitude might be described as the Greek counterpart of the Roman distinction made between the admirable Greeks of the classic age and the inferior contemporary Greek subjects of the Roman Empire.[126]

Later, in the fourth century, Ammianus goes to great lengths in describing the arrogant and boorish attitude of Roman grandees towards foreigners.[127] They despise men of culture and prefer coarse plebeians at their extravagant banquets.

To sum up: the modest selection of authors cited in this paper shows various responses to the social situation in which provincial authors found themselves as citizens of the Roman Empire. We are far removed here from the sphere of armed rebellion, small-scale resistance to the authorities, or internecine fighting. All authors were successful in their own sphere and, hence their works have been preserved at least in part. Even so it cannot be denied that the coexistence that existed engendered complex social situations and tensions of various sorts that should not be ignored.

---

[123] Aulus Gellius, *Noctes Atticae* 19.9 describes an altercation between Greeks and a Latin rhetorician from Spain. There is no point in discussing this here because the real subject of dispute is the merit of Latin as compared with Greek poetry. Even so the Greeks accuse the man from Spain of being *tamquam prorsus barbarum et agrestem, qui ortus terra Hispania foret.*

[124] Apollonius, *Ep.* 71 (ed. and trans. C. P. Jones): ἀλλ᾽ ὑμῶν γε οὐδὲ τὰ ὀνόματα μένει τοῖς πολλοῖς, ἀλλ᾽ ὑπὸ τῆς νέας ταύτης εὐδαιμονίας ἀπολωλέκατε τὰ τῶν προγόνων σύμβολα ... εἴ γε πρότερον ἡρώων ἦν ὀνόματα καὶ ναυμάχων καὶ νομοθετῶν, νυνὶ δὲ Λουκούλλων τε καὶ Φαβρικίων καὶ Λευκανίων τῶν μακαρίων, ἐμοὶ μὲν εἴη μᾶλλον ὄνομα Μίμνερμος.

[125] Compare the far cruder claim by Dio Chrysostom that the citizens of Tarsus have lost their Hellenic quality to become orientalized, above, p. 159f.

[126] See Isaac, *Invention of Racism*, ch. 9: Roman views of Greeks.

[127] Ammianus 14.6.12–19.

CHAPTER 8

Proto-Racism in Graeco-Roman Antiquity

Preliminary Remarks

There appears to be a consensus that racism as such originates in modern times. Since it is thought not to be attested earlier, conventional wisdom usually denies that there was any race hatred in the ancient world.[1] The prejudices that existed, so it is believed, were ethnic or cultural, not racial. In this chapter I shall discuss three topics. First, I shall argue that proto-types of racism were common in the Graeco-Roman world. My second point will be to describe the close links between those forms of prejudice and ancient ideas about slavery. Finally I shall have something to say about the connection between these concepts and ancient imperialism. The ideas proposed in this chapter are fully discussed in two recent books.[2]

Obviously, in classical antiquity racism did not exist in the modern form of a biological determinism. Clearly too there was no systematic persecution of any ethnic or presumed racial group by another, let alone the massive excesses to which state-imposed racist doctrine led in the twentieth century. However, I shall argue that it is justified to speak of early forms of racism, or 'proto-racism' as a widespread phenomenon in antiquity. I do not claim that prejudice and bigotry are invented in the West; I claim that the specific form of rationalizing these prejudices and attempting to base them in systematic, abstract thought was developed in antiquity and taken over in early modern Europe. Nobody will deny that racism as an ideology developed in Europe, not in China, Japan, or India. It is generally accepted that Greek civilization was the first to raise the level of abstract, systematic abstract thought to a level that we

---

[1] G. M. Fredrickson, *Racism: A Short History* (Princeton, 2002), 17; unsatisfactory: I. Hannaford, *Race: The History of an Idea in the West* (Baltimore, 1996), chs. 2 and 3. For a different view: C. Delacampagne, *L'invention du racisme: Antiquité et Moyen Age* (Paris, 1983).

[2] B. Isaac, *The Invention of Racism in Classical Antiquity* (Princeton, 2004); M. Eliav-Feldon, B. Isaac, and J. Ziegler, *The Origins of Racism in the West* (Cambridge, 2010).

now recognize as approaching our own. I assert that the Greeks not only contributed the first attempt to think systematically about, e.g. political systems, but also the first effort to find a rational and systematic basis for their own sense of superiority and their claim that others were inferior. The subject of my study is precisely the conceptual mechanisms which they developed towards this purpose and which were taken over with alacrity by later thinkers.

Hostility towards foreigners occurs in every society, but in widely differing degrees, social settings, and moral environments. An essential component of such hostility is always the tendency to generalize and simplify, so that whole nations are viewed as if they were a single individual with a single personality. I should emphasize at the outset that one of the difficulties in studying group prejudices in antiquity is the lack of any term in Greek and Latin for 'racism', for 'prejudice', or 'discrimination'. Anticipating the conclusions of this chapter I would like to suggest that the lack of such terminology stems from the fact that there existed no intellectual, moral, or emotional objections against such generalizations. We must therefore trace the development of ideas and attitudes for which there existed no terminology in the culture under consideration. It will be clear from this description that this chapter is concerned exclusively with the history of specific ideas, not with the social history of antiquity or with the practice of discrimination and persecution in Greece and Rome. While I do not underestimate the importance of these topics as such, the justification for this approach is that the ancient ideas are found in Greek and Latin literature. This literature was widely read for centuries in the West and the ideas found there had a profound influence on later generations. This leads me to a second point that requires explanation. This chapter focuses on literary sources, that is, on the writings of the male elites in Greece and Rome. Quite clearly we cannot assume that the ideas expressed by members of those circles are identical with those of the representatives of other classes in Greece and Rome. Simple traders, farmers, and professional soldiers did not leave us their ideas, so we cannot study them, nor can we interview common people on the streets of ancient cities. Since there is, however, a substantial body of ancient literature, there is work to do and it is worth doing it, particularly because, as already noted, these authors continued to be read till the present time.

Modern definitions of race are numerous, definitions of racism a little less so, and it is the latter that are needed here, for I am studying attitudes of mind and their development. It will be clear that the nature of the definition always reflects the focus and outlook of the definer. My definition of racism is as follows:

> an attitude towards individuals and groups of peoples which posits a direct and linear connection between physical and mental qualities. It therefore attributes to those individuals and groups of peoples collective traits, physical, mental and moral, which are constant and unalterable by human will, because they are caused by hereditary factors or external influences, such as climate or geography.

This is long, but it covers the subject. The essence of racism is then that it regards individuals as superior or inferior because they are believed to share imagined physical, mental, and moral attributes with the group to which they are deemed to belong, and it is assumed that they cannot change these traits individually. This is held to be impossible, because these traits are determined by their physical make-up. This is a relatively broad, yet precise definition, broader than the ones usually employed. I am not the first to search for a flexible yet precise definition. Another author who did so was Albert Memmi in his lucid and influential book on the subject.[3] He rightly observes that too narrow a definition will not allow us forms of racism which fail to correspond with the forms of it which dominated in the 1920s, 1930s, and 1940s. Miles and Brown also emphasize the fluidity of racism as an ideology which is applied in different periods and different societies to various groups while still maintaining definable characteristics.[4]

A somewhat wider definition makes it possible recognize forms of racism that are not steered exclusively by biological determinism. Indeed, few historians now would deny that many authors of the Enlightenment, in the seventeenth and eighteenth centuries, adhered to a form of racism which was common before Darwin's revolution. It was his scientific breakthrough which made it possible to develop a pseudo-scientific form of racism, based on current biological theory. The advantage for the racist of the latter concept was that it seemed to give a justification for prejudice, based on influences entirely from within. Genetics were used to build a theory of constant and unchangeable characteristics for entire groups of people. These characteristics, it was then claimed, were passed on from

---

[3] A. Memmi, *Racism* (Minneapolis, 2000).

[4] R. Miles and M. Brown, *Racism*, 2nd edn (London, 2000), 103–13. The literature is massive. For a recent overview: C. Loring Brace, *'Race' is a Four-Letter Word: The Genesis of the Concept* (Oxford, 2005) (unsatisfactory for the pre-modern periods); for antiquity: D. E. McCoskey, *Race: Antiquity and its Legacy* (Oxford, 2012); M. Kahlos (ed.), *The Faces of the Other: Religious Rivalry and Ethnic Encounters in the Later Roman World* (Turnhout, 2011). Additional works come out all the time.

one generation to the next. The essence can best be illustrated with an example: in nineteenth-century Germany and Austria Jews who converted to Christianity became thereby in principle eligible for certain official positions. This represents an attitude of religious and social intolerance. Under the Nazi regime it made no difference whether a Jew was converted or not: their descent was all that mattered.

However, before Darwin there existed other forms of racism, based on the idea that external influences, such as climate and geography, determined the basic characteristics of entire peoples. These may be found in the works of French authors such as Jean Bodin (1530–96), John Arbuthnot (1667–1735), and, most influential, Montesquieu (1689–1755). In Germany Herder and Christoph Meiners represent this school of thought.[5] It is well known that these authors read their classical literature thoroughly and it is therefore only natural to look for precursors of these particular ideas in the ancient authors which they read. 'The authority of Greek and Roman texts should not be underestimated in providing ruling-class men (of the eighteenth century), in particular, with the distinction between themselves and barbarians ...'[6]

I will now briefly consider five concepts which, together, were in antiquity commonly held to determine the collective nature of groups, or the character of peoples. These are: environmental determinism, the heredity of acquired characters, a combination of these two ideas, the constitution and form of government, autochthony, and pure lineage. This will be followed by some thoughts about the connection between those ideas and the ideology of ancient imperialism.

Environmental Determinism

In both Greek and Latin literature from the middle of the fifth century BC onwards we encounter an almost generally accepted form of environmental determinism. This is first explicitly and extensively presented in the medical treatise *Airs, Waters, Places*, written at an uncertain date in the second half of the fifth century BC. The particular form of environmental determinism first found in this work became the generally accepted model in Greece and, afterwards, with variations, in Rome. According to this view, collective characteristics of groups of people are permanently determined

---

[5] Isaac, *Invention of Racism*, 56–7, 102–8.
[6] R. Wheeler, *The Complexion of Race: Categories of Difference in Eighteenth-Century British Culture* (Philadelphia, 2000), 15.

by climate and geography. The implication is that the essential features of body and mind come from the outside and are not the result of either genetic evolution, social environment, or conscious choice. Individuality and individual change are thereby ignored and even excluded. This is definitely related to racist attitudes as here defined. Entire nations are believed to have common characteristics determined wholly by factors outside themselves and which are, by implication, stable and unchangeable. These presumed characteristics are then subject to value judgements, in which foreigners are usually rejected as being inferior to the observer, or approved of as being untainted and superior in some respects. Such descriptions are, of course, not based on objective observations of reality. They are expressions of ethnic stereotypes and proto-racism.

The essence of the concept of environmental determinism is found again in the work of Aristotle, with some interesting variations. It is worth citing the text at some length:

> The peoples of cold countries generally, and particularly those of Europe, are full of spirit, but deficient in skill and intelligence; and this is why they continue to remain comparatively free, but attain no political development and show no capacity for governing others. The peoples of Asia are endowed with skill and intelligence, but are deficient in spirit; and this is why they continue to be peoples of subjects and slaves. The Greeks, intermediate in geographical position, unite the qualities of both sets of peoples. They possess both spirit and intelligence: the one quality makes them continue free; the other enables them to attain the heights of political development and to show a capacity for governing every other people – if only they could once achieve political unity.[7]

Strabo 6.4.1 (286) claims the same for Italy.

Aristotle, as is well known, was tutor to Alexander of Macedonia. The claims cited here made environmental determinism a useful ideological tool for ambitious imperialists, because it justified the conclusion that the Greeks were ideally capable of ruling others. Clearly, Aristotle was not the first person ever to justify imperial expansion. It is characteristic, one may presume of many or all expanding states that they claim to have good reasons for their expansion. Aristotle, however, is definitely the first to base such claims on a rationalization of the superiority of his people, as distinct from a God-given or self-evident superiority. Roman authors took over these ideas, duly substituting themselves as the ideal rulers, and with

---

[7] Aristotle, *Politics* 1327b (trans. E. Barker). On ethnocentrism: J. S. Romm, *The Edges of the Earth in Ancient Thought: Geography, Exploration and Fiction* (Princeton, 1992), 46–8, 54–5.

some variations. Instead of the contrast between Europe and Asia, which the Greeks found essential, the geographical poles for most Roman authors are North and East. As clear examples of this pattern I shall later describe ancient views of the Germans and Syrians.

It is appropriate here to indicate also how environmental determinism related to more distant foreigners, notably the Ethiopians, as blacks were usually called by the Greeks.[8] Ethiopians are mentioned fairly frequently already in some earlier sources, but usually as representatives of peoples living near the edge of the world. In Homer they are 'the furthest of men'. They are 'blameless' and their country is so prosperous as to furnish the ample sacrificial feasts which the gods relish.[9] In Herodotus 1.134, they occur as the ideal example of the far-away good barbarians.[10] In later periods blacks did not form much of an actual presence in the Greek and Roman worlds. They were regarded as remarkable, but relatively few of them lived among the Greeks and Romans and no country inhabited by a majority of blacks was ever part of the Greek and Roman Empires. They were present in fifth-century Athens, but as a rare and expensive type of slave, the possession of which enhanced the status of the owner.[11] Questions about the cause of their appearance appear in the literature from the fourth century onwards. An undated Pseudo Aristotelian chapter in *Problemata* asks: 'Why are those who live in climates of extreme cold or heat brutish in manners and appearance?'[12] This text further elaborates on the favourable effect on body and mind of the 'best mixture' of qualities and the harmful effects of the extreme climates. As examples of the physical effect of extreme heat, for instance, the text gives the bandy legs and curly hair of the Ethiopians and Egyptians. This is explained by analogy: just as planks are warped when they dry, so are the bodies of living beings.[13] The text adds that those who live in the south have dark eyes while northern peoples have grey eyes and this is explained by the influence of the temperature on the balance of moisture in the body.[14] The text also goes a step further: a person who is thought to fit the physical stereotype of a certain nation is

[8] F. M. Snowden, 'Greeks and Ethiopians', in J. E. Coleman and C. A. Walz (eds.), *Greeks and Barbarians: Essays on the Interactions between Greeks and Non-Greeks in Antiquity and the Consequences for Eurocentrism* (Bethesda, MD, 1997), 103–26, esp. 111–13.

[9] Romm, *Edges of the Earth*, 49–55.

[10] Cf. Romm, *Edges of the Earth*, 55–60.

[11] M. C. Miller, *Athens and Persia in the Fifth Century bc: A Study in Cultural Receptivity* (Cambridge, 1997), 212–17.

[12] Ps. Aristotle, *Problemata* 909a.

[13] Ps. Aristotle, *Problemata* 909a.27–32.

[14] Ps. Aristotle, *Problemata* 910a.12.

assumed to have the (mostly negative) mental and moral characteristics attributed to that nation, even if he does not belong to the nation. Thus not only are all Egyptians believed to be cunning, fickle, etc., but also all people who have curly hair like the Egyptians. A fourth-century treatise on physiognomy gives an example: Egyptians and Ethiopians, being dark, are cowards (however, women, who have light skins, are also cowards).[15] F. M. Snowden concludes that generally there were no such prejudices in antiquity. These views were not accepted by Thompson.[16] The least that can be said is that ancient views of the Ethiopians were not uniform. Herodotus certainly gives a different perspective.[17] In Athens there also was a fashion for vases in the form of heads of blacks.[18] It is hard to say what feelings such images would convey to the public for which they were produced, for the emotional responses to physical differences vary a good deal over time and between cultures.

As remarked above, the environmental theories of antiquity were widely accepted by the European authors of the Enlightenment and thus contributed to the later development of racism. Yet, if the environmental theories of antiquity had been the only form of collective prejudice to be found in the literature, it might still be possible to claim that this is not enough to conclude that this was an ancient form of proto-racism. However, it is just one concept encountered besides, and in combination with other ideas that will now be discussed.

The Heredity of Acquired Characters

A second conceptual mechanism which was generally accepted in Graeco-Roman antiquity is a belief in the heredity of acquired characters. In modern times this has been popular and was identified mainly with the theories of Lamarck, but it is now no longer accepted. In antiquity, however, it was accepted as a matter of course by many authors. It is explicitly propounded in some works, for instance in the treatise mentioned earlier, *Airs, Waters, Places*, in the work of Aristotle, and elsewhere, mostly in technical

---

[15] Ps. Aristotle, *Physiognomonica* 812a.

[16] F. M. Snowden Jr., *Before Color Prejudice* (Cambridge, 1983); L. A. Thompson, *Romans and Blacks* (Norman, OK, 1989).

[17] R. Bichler, *Herodots Welt: Der Aufbau der Historie am Bild der fremden Länder und Völker, ihrer Zivilisation und ihrer Geschichte* (Berlin, 2000), 31.

[18] F. M. Snowden Jr., *Blacks in Antiquity* (Cambridge, 1970), 24–5; 'Iconographical Evidence on the Black Populations in Greco-Roman Antiquity', in J. Vercoutter *et al.* (eds.), *L'image du Noir dans L'art occidental*, I (Fribourg, 1976), 133–245.

treatises. This was illustrated by reputed cases, where children inherited scars from wounds of their parents, or even tattoos. Indeed, it is clear from many implicit references that the principle was taken for granted throughout antiquity. The best known example, found in the treatise *Airs, Waters, Places*, ch. 14, is the case of the people who artificially elongated the skulls of their children, a feature which reputedly became hereditary after a couple of generations. The theory recurs, for instance, in the work of the geographer Strabo who wrote in the reigns of Augustus and Tiberius. Strabo discusses the cause of the colour of the skin of Ethiopians and the texture of their hair, which he attributes to scorching by the sun. He then observes that the Indians 'do not have woolly hair and that their skin is not so mercilessly burnt'. Strabo continues: 'And already in the womb children, by seminal communication, become like their parents; for congenital illnesses and other similarities are also thus explained.'[19] Later in the first century, the elder Pliny wrote in his *Naturalis Historia* that the Ethiopians are 'scorched by the heat of the sun which is nearby and are born with a singed appearance, with curled beard and hair'.[20] Pliny has interesting observations about the transmission of characters in book 7 of his work. 'It is also well known that ... deformed parents ... may have children with ... the same deformity, that some marks and moles and even scars reappear in the offspring, in some cases a birthmark on the arm reappearing in the fourth generation.'[21] As I said, these are random examples; it is easy to add more. It has, in fact, been recognized by others that this theory goes back to classical authors:

> What Lamarck really did was to accept the hypothesis that acquired characters were heritable, a notion which had been held almost universally for well over two thousand years and which his contemporaries accepted as a matter of course, and to assume that the results of such inheritance were cumulative from generation to generation, thus producing, in time, new species.[22]

A Combination of These Factors

Many authors combine environmental determinism with a belief in the heredity of acquired characters. When applied to human groups,

---

[19] Strabo 15.1.24 (696).
[20] Pliny, *NH* 2.80.189.
[21] Pliny, *NH* 7.50. Cf. the earlier claims by Aristotle, *De generatione animalium* 721b, 724a.
[22] C. Zirkle, 'The Early History of the Idea of the Inheritance of Acquired Characters and of Pangenesis', *Transactions of the American Philosophical Society*, NS 35 (1946): 91.

this leads somewhat paradoxically to an assumption that characteristics acquired through outside influences then somehow are passed on to the next generation and become uniform and constant. One example must suffice, taken from Livy's account of a speech made by the commander Cn. Manlius before his troops in 189 BC. The troops were about to give battle to mixed forces of a people descended from Celts who had moved from Europe to Asia Minor. The commander tells his troops (Livy 38.17.9–10): 'These (Celtic units) are now degenerate, of mixed stock and really Gallogrecians, as they are called; just as in the case of crops and animals, the seeds are not as good in preserving their natural quality as the character of the soil and the climate in which they grow have the power to change it.'[23] Climate and geography have definite effects on all people being born in a given region. These effects then become permanent traits because they become hereditary in one or two generations. The result of this combination is a powerful incentive to discriminatory attitudes. It is this combination which definitely justifies describing ancient ethnic-prejudice as a form of proto-racism, for it turns what could just be an external influence which can be variable (environmental influence) into something that is fixed and permanent (such as skin colour).

If there were any doubt as to the validity of this conclusion, it should be enough to indicate that modern racism has seen a similar combination of ideas. This is encountered already in the work of the influential German scholar Friedrich Ratzel.[24] He was followed by Semple, who, well-read in the classics, explicitly sees herself as writing in the tradition of Montesquieu.[25] She works with the same categories as the Greek treatise *Airs*, mentioned above: the effect of mountains, isolation, climate (heat, cold, moisture, aridity). 'The influence of climate upon race temperament, both as a direct and indirect effect, cannot be doubted.'[26] These ideas themselves were influenced by contemporary theories regarding the evolution of species through the influence of climate.[27] Matthew was 'thoroughly convinced that the whole of evolutionary progress may be interpreted as a response to external stimuli'.[28] The most elaborate defence of environmental theories

---

[23] Cf. Florus' later paraphrase: *mixta et adulterata*, mixed and impure, bastards (Florus 1.27.3–4).

[24] F. Ratzel, *The History of Mankind*, trans. from the 2nd German edn, 3 vols. (London and New York, 1896), 23.

[25] E. C. Semple, *Influences of Geographic Environment* (New York, 1911), 18.

[26] Semple, *Influences*, 620.

[27] W. D. Matthew, 'Climate and Evolution', *Annals of the New York Academy of Sciences* 24 (1915): 171–318; *Climate and Evolution*, 2nd edn with additions (New York, 1939; repr. 1974).

[28] Matthew, *Climate and Evolution*, 33.

may be found in the work of Griffith Taylor.[29] This work represents a major attempt to combine racist theory typical of this period with environmental determinism. The racist treatment rests heavily on German theories of the time, notably those of Eickstedt, but is combined with speculations from current endocrinal theories which held that climate affects the functioning of glands and thus influences human evolution.[30] Taylor offers a, relatively speaking, mild form of racism: he regards most races as roughly equal in quality, apart from the blacks, whose 'poor achievements in world-history are probably due to their non-stimulating environment. To this also is due their small advance from a primitive stage of racial evolution.'[31] 'As regards the future, it seems clear that *environment* will be the most potent factor in moulding every race and nation.'[32] The classic work of 1954 against prejudice by Allport still firmly believes in the existence of human races and postulates a direct connection between climate and the differences between the 'Mongol physique … the Negroid … and the Caucasoid'.[33] It is obvious that there is a lack of consistency in the combination of such ideas, but when we discuss racism, ancient or modern, it should be obvious that we cannot expect consistency and lucid logic. As recently as 1948 Sir Arthur Keith stated without hesitation that 'the nation of to-day is the lineal representative of the local group of Palaeolithic times; nations are now the race-making units of Europe'.[34] Racism is by definition a fallacy and we should not be surprised if it consists of elements that do not fit together as they should. It is then not the analysis which is to be blamed, but the intellectual inconsistency of the ideas analysed.

The Constitution and Form of Government

In the view of many of the relevant authors there is yet another important factor. A good form of government is an essential ingredient in shaping a people. Under a bad ruler or government no people can function well. The most obvious example from the fourth century BC is Isocrates' firm belief that Persia must be a weak nation, because it is ruled by too powerful a king. This, clearly, is not a racist or proto-racist concept, if only because it

---

[29] T. G. Taylor, *Environment, Race and Migration*, 2nd enlarged edn (Chicago, 1945), an expansion of Taylor, *Environment and Race: A Study of the Evolution, Migration, Settlement and Status of the Races of Man* (London, 1927).

[30] Taylor, *Environment, Race and Migration*, 276.

[31] Taylor, *Environment, Race and Migration*, 476.

[32] Taylor, *Environment, Race and Migration*, 477.

[33] G. W. Allport, *The Nature of Prejudice* (Reading, 1954; repr. 1979), 111.

[34] A. Keith, *A New Theory of Human Evolution* (London, 1948), 338.

is liable to change. It is a social condition. The last chapter of Xenophon's *The Education of Cyrus*, the *Cyropaedia*, claims that Persia was strong when it had a good king, and deteriorated when the kings did. This is essentially a socio-political view. We should understand that our authors are considering different levels here. The environment determines basic qualities: a good constitution is essential, but can exist only when basic human qualities exist. This may be compared with a statement which most of us would accept now: a proper education will determine the level at which an individual functions, but the precondition for the success of a good education is an appropriate level of intelligence.

Autochthony and Pure Lineage

The fifth and last concept to be mentioned here is that of autochthony and pure lineage.[35] The Athenians attached enormous importance to the dual myth that they had lived in their own land from the beginnings of time without ever abandoning it, and that they were a people of unmixed lineage. They saw themselves as originally having sprung from the soil itself, the earth serving as their collective mother. This myth served various purposes: (a) It was used as argument that they and only they held legitimate possession of their soil. (b) They regarded themselves as a people uncontaminated by an admixture of foreign elements, and were therefore superior. The uniqueness of their origins is deemed obvious by many fifth-century authors. Indeed a law promulgated by Pericles in 451/0 awarded citizenship only to the children of two citizens, the intention being to preserve the purity of lineage of the Athenians.[36] All the fourth-century authors who mention these subjects, mostly orators, are convinced of the value of pure descent. They are agreed that the Athenians are uniquely pure in their origins and superior to all other peoples of the world. Other Greek states have produced comparable myths, but only Athens insisted on this to such a great extent. Their insistence was still accepted in Roman literature.

The idea as such had a broad appeal, mostly in a negative sense, among other Greeks and, later, among Roman authors: intermarriage and mixed

---

[35] V. J. Rosivach, 'Autochthony and the Athenians', *Classical Quarterly* 37 (1987): 294–306; H. A. Shapiro, 'Autochthony and the Visual Arts in Fifth-Century Athens', in D. Boedeker and K. Raaflaub, *Democracy, Empire and the Arts* (Cambridge, 1998), 127–51; Isaac, *Invention of Racism*, 109–24.

[36] C. Patterson, *Pericles' Citizenship Law of 451–50 bc* (New York, 1981).

blood are considered bad and conducive to degeneration. The Celts already mentioned, who had migrated to Asia Minor, deteriorated for two reasons: first, because of their move to another environment, and, second, because they were a mixed people and thus of lesser quality: 'degenerate and mixed', *degeneres sunt, mixti ...*,[37] or, in Florus' later paraphrase: *mixta et adulterata*, mixed and impure, bastards.[38] This is the negative equivalent of the view held by the Athenians that they were superior because their ancestors were not mixed with migrants. The belief that marriage with outsiders produces offspring of lesser quality appears firmly entrenched in Greece as well as in Rome. In this form the concept of pure lineage emerges in the works of many Roman authors, even though the Romans in practice liberally granted citizenship to subject peoples. Best known are Tacitus' comments on the Germans, whom he described in terms in which the Athenians describe themselves: they were 'indigenous, and not mixed at all with other peoples through immigration or intercourse'.[39] As we know, the idea was taken up enthusiastically by the Germans in recent history. To be fair I must note here that some ancient authors are critical of such ideas, for instance Lucian and Apuleius. It may be no coincidence that these two originated in the Roman provinces, respectively Syria and North Africa, although they were of Greek and Latin culture.

Clearly, of all the concepts briefly described so far, this is the one which most closely approaches modern racism, for it establishes a hierarchy of peoples, based on the fiction that some are of pure lineage, while others are of mixed descent. It could even be said that the Athenians regarded themselves as a 'race' in modern terms. Furthermore, it is clear that these ideas were influential later as well, for they appear in authors who have been read widely ever since the Renaissance.

Ancient Imperialism

The ideas here described were a significant element in ancient concepts of imperialism. As with so many other relevant topics the essence of this is first encountered in the treatise *Airs, Waters, Places*, which insists that the inhabitants of Asia are soft because of their good climate and resources.[40] They are less belligerent and gentler in character than the Europeans,

---

[37] Livy 38.17.9–10.
[38] Florus 1.27.3–4.
[39] Tacitus, *Germania* 1, 4.
[40] *Airs, Waters, Places* 16, 23.

who are more courageous and belligerent. Aristotle then claimed that the Greeks, combining the best qualities of both groups were therefore capable of ruling all mankind – an early, if not the first text to suggest that Greeks should achieve universal rule.[41]

No less important: these ideas were taken over, suitably adapted, by the Romans. We find them, for instance, in Vitruvius 6.1; the Elder Pliny, *Naturalis Historia* 2.80.190; Vegetius 1.2. For them, Italy was ideally situated in the middle, but now the middle was between North and East, rather than between Europe and Asia.

One further significant concept should be emphasized, again in connection with Greek and Roman imperialist ideas, namely that of decline and degeneration. Just as there are believed to be environments which are good or even ideal for the creation of an imperial power, so there are those that are unfavourable. A related idea, that also is part of the complex of environmental theories, is that of decline as a result of migration. It is first attested in the work of Herodotus, where Cyrus says that the Persians, if they move from rugged Persia to a better country, should not expect to continue as rulers, 'but to prepare for being ruled by others – soft countries give birth to soft men. There is no land which produces the most remarkable fruit, and at the same time men good at warfare.'[42] This idea was fully accepted in Rome, for instance in the case of the Celts who established themselves in Asia Minor and, in the opinion of the Romans, subsequently degenerated. I cite Livy again: 'The Macedonians who rule Alexandria in Egypt, who rule Seleucia and Babylon and other colonies spread all over the world, have degenerated into Syrians, Parthians and Egyptians; … whatever grows in its own soil, prospers better; transplanted to alien soil, it changes and it degenerates to conform to the soil which feeds it.'[43] It is essential to recognize that no account is taken anywhere of the possibility of improvement: strong people become feeble in a soft environment, but the reverse never occurs. This idea is still echoed by recent environmentalists who worried about the effect of a tropical climate on white colonists. 'Our study of the historical movements of peoples in the northern hemisphere revealed a steady influx from colder into tropical and sub-tropical lands, followed always by enervation and loss of national efficiency, due partly to the debilitating heat of the new habitat, partly to its easier conditions of living.'[44]

---

[41] Aristotle, *Politics* 1327b. Curiously, Herodotus 5.3 says something similar about the Thracians. See below, Chapter.10, p. 241.
[42] Hdt. 9.122.
[43] Livy 38.17.12.
[44] Semple, *Influences*, 627.

Individual and Collective Slavery

In considering Greek and Roman society we must be aware that slavery hardly represented a moral dilemma as it has done in modern history. The existence of slavery as such was not a relevant topic of discussion in antiquity, but there were arguments about specifics, notably there was a controversy about the difference in nature between free men and slaves, an issue important for the justification of slavery. If an essential difference, mentally and physically, between free men and slaves could be demonstrated, it was easier to claim that their difference in status was justified and reasonable. If there was no essential difference, slavery was harder to justify, for it would depend only on brute force. Was slavery contrary to justice and also contrary to nature? Aristotle responds to arguments along these lines by contending that slavery was both natural and just, because some human beings were so shaped by nature that they lacked some of the essential qualities of fully fledged men.[45] They were therefore fit only to serve as instruments for those who had all those qualities. Here we move from the sphere of the individual into that of the collective and the group.

Relevant for our subject are ideas which assign not just to individuals, but to specific groups of people an inferior place in society on the grounds that they are deficient in various ways and need therefore to be subordinated to their intellectual and moral superiors in a master/slave relationship. That is to say, specific, non-Greek peoples are described as collectively having the qualities which slaves of the Greeks should have. Being less than human, or even subhuman, they live best in a symbiotic relationship with fully human masters. The arguments applied by Aristotle to individual slaves and masters are frequently and easily applied by other authors to entire groups and peoples. This is clear from the terminology employed: δούλωσις and δουλεία i.e. 'enslavement' and related forms are commonly used by Thucydides and by other authors to express the subjection of one state to another.[46] Slavery, δουλεία and similar terms are frequently used to denote political subjection generally.[47] It should be observed that the contrast between free man and slave, ἐλεύθερος-δοῦλος, originated in the domestic sphere and was first broadened out into the realm of politics in the early fifth century. The justification of individual slavery becomes then applicable also to collective

---

[45] Aristotle's discussion of slavery in his *Politics*; P. Garnsey, *Ideas of Slavery from Aristotle to Augustine* (Cambridge, 1996). For a recent study, see Y. Rotman, *Byzantine Slavery and the Mediterranean World* (Cambridge, MA, 2009).

[46] Thucydides 1.98.4; 1.141.1; 2.63.1 on possible domination of Athens by Sparta.

[47] A. W. Gomme, *A Historical Commentary on Thucydides*, III (Oxford, 1956), 646.

subjugation and thus becomes part of imperialist ideology which we should now discuss briefly. These views are again best expressed by Aristotle, whose words are now cited:

> From this it follows that even warfare is by nature a form of acquisition – for the art of hunting is part of it – which is applied against wild animals and against those men who are not prepared to be ruled, even though they are born for subjection, in so far as this war is just by nature.[48]

War then is a form of acquisition, just like hunting, and the object of this process is the procurement of slaves among those peoples who are slaves by nature, but resist Greek demands that they submit to their proper fate in the world.[49]

The Athenians assimilated the relation between imperial states and their subjects to that between master and slave. At least, they do so in a speech which Thucydides attributes to them:

> Of the gods we believe, and of men we know, that by a necessary law of their nature they rule wherever they can. And it is not as if we were the first to make this law, or to act upon it when made: we found it existing before us, and shall leave it to exist for ever after us; all we do is to make use of it, knowing that you and everybody else, having the same power as we have, would do the same as we do.[50]

The Athenians do not claim that this is just and right, nor do they claim that both sides profit from the unequal relationship, as does Aristotle in his theory of natural slavery. The Athenians merely claim it is inevitable.[51] Callicles, speaking in Plato's *Gorgias*, goes a step further towards Aristotle in claiming that this is not merely inevitable, but indeed just and right:

> But I believe that nature itself reveals that it is a just thing for the better man and the more capable man to have a greater share than the worse man and the less capable man. Nature shows that this is so in many places ...[52] both among the other animals and in whole cities and nations of men, it shows that this is what justice has been decided to be: that the superior rule the inferior and have a greater share than they ...[53]

---

[48] Aristotle, *Politics* 1256b 23–6.

[49] R. Schlaifer, 'Greek Theories of Slavery from Homer to Aristotle', *Harvard Studies in Classical Philology* 47 (1936): 165–204, repr. in M. I. Finley (ed.), *Slavery in Classical Antiquity* (Cambridge, 1968), 93–132.

[50] Thucydides 5.105.2 (trans. R. Crawley); 1.76.2; 4.61.5. A. W. Gomme *et al.*, *A Historical Commentary on Thucydides*, IV (Oxford, 1970), 162–4.

[51] J. de Romilly, *Thucydides and Athenian Imperialism* (Oxford, 1963), 56.

[52] E. R. Dodds, *Plato, Gorgias: A Revised Text with Introduction and Commentary* (Oxford, 1959), 267.

[53] Plato, *Gorgias* 483c–e.

To turn now to Roman literature, Cicero is far more explicit in describing the benefits of empire to the ruled than Aristotle ever is.[54] He claims that the existence of the Empire is justified because of genuine advantages to the provincials. The attitude of Cicero and other Romans comes closer to the modern concept of the 'White Man's Burden'.

In the age of Augustus, Dionysius of Halicarnassus is writing for Greeks in Greek to persuade them that Rome deserves her empire

> that they, the Greeks, may neither feel indignation at their present subjection, which is grounded on reason (for by a universal law of nature, which time cannot destroy, it is ordained that superiors shall ever govern their inferiors), nor rail at Fortune for having wantonly bestowed upon an undeserving city a supremacy so great and already of so long continuance ...[55]

So far this brief demonstration of the connection between classical ideas of slavery and imperialism. It is now proper to point to yet another influential complex of ideas in this sphere. Besides the common ancient assumption that those who have been enslaved deserve to be in that position, there is another common belief which holds that people, once enslaved, degenerate irrevocably into servile characters. Homer, later cited by Plato, says: 'If you make a man a slave, that very day / Far-sounding Zeus takes half his wits away.'[56] For a similar sentiment in a major Roman author we may turn to Cicero. Servitude is a central motive in his thinking about contemporary Greeks. Cicero advises his brother, proconsul of Africa, to be cautious in his dealings with the Greeks in his province, 'In your province there are a great many who are deceitful and unstable, and trained by a long course of servitude to show an excess of sycophancy.'[57] Cicero was certain that a state of subjugation distorts and degenerates character. Indeed, many Roman authors assume as a matter of course that the conquest of a people and their subjection to another inevitably set in motion a process whereby they increasingly lose their belligerency, their sense of freedom and their virility, the longer they are subjects. Cicero, Josephus, and Tacitus agree that it is an irreversible process.[58] In fact, only those who are born in freedom have a chance of regaining it after they have been subjected. It is a sentiment echoed, for instance, by the third-century historian

---

[54] Cicero, *De officiis* 22; cf. Augustine, *De civitate dei* 14.23.
[55] Dionysius of Halicarnassus 1.5.2.
[56] Homer, *Odyssea* 17.322–3; cited by Plato, *Laws* 776e–777a. Cf. Garnsey, *Ideas of Slavery*, 89 with discussion on pp. 93–4.
[57] Cicero, *Ad Quintum fratrem* 1.1.16.
[58] Josephus, *Bellum Judaicum* 2.15.4 (356–8); Tacitus, *Agricola* 21; *Hist.* 4.17; 4.64.3.

Cassius Dio in the pre-battle speech which he attributes to the British rebel queen Boudicca: '– let us, I say, do our duty while we still remember what freedom is, that we may leave to our children not only its appellation but also its reality. For, if we utterly forget the happy state in which we were born and bred, what, pray, will they do, reared in bondage?'[59]

There is at least one other reason why it is important to study an imperial power's attitudes to foreign peoples. The current stereotypes and commonplaces in an imperial capital may not decide imperial policy, but it is definitely true that it is an important factor in its formation. Both France under Napoleon and Germany under Hitler invaded Russia. For both these nations these campaigns ended in the loss, not just of a battle or campaign, but of their entire wars of expansion, wars that had been successful before they attacked Russia. They embarked upon these expeditions only because they were convinced that they would succeed. This means that there was an extraordinary discrepancy between their image of Russia as a country and reality. It is therefore useful to consider the image, for instance, of Persia in fourth-century Greece and of the Germans and Parthians/Persians in imperial Rome, for it is at least likely that the current views of these peoples helped in shaping imperial policy.

The last part of this chapter will be devoted to two unambiguous examples of what I would call proto-racist attitudes of Roman authors to other peoples, whereby it is clear that these attitudes also played a substantial role in the way the Romans conceived the relationship of these peoples with the Empire. The various topics of this article come together if we briefly look at Roman ideas about two peoples: the Syrians and Germans. First, the Syrians.[60] They were *born* for slavery according to the familiar formula.[61] The presumed qualities of the Syrians and other Asiatic peoples which earn them the description of having been born for slavery are: servility, effeminacy, perversity. Homosexuality, self-castration, perverted cults are all associated with this presumed lack of masculinity. They were no fighters, it was thought. Connected with this is the accusation of luxurious living. The Syrians are good at feasting, they tend to go to the baths rather than exercise, and they over-eat. This means that they represent the opposite of what Romans think real men ought to be. Roman ideas about Syrians constitute a complex of stereotypes with what I would call proto-racist characteristics. Their presumed qualities were also regarded as infectious. When effeminate

---

[59] Dio 62.4.3 (trans. E. Cary, Loeb).
[60] Isaac, *Invention of Racism*, ch. 6, 335–50.
[61] Cicero, *De provinciis consularibus* 2.5.10; Livy 35.49.8; 36.17.4–5.

Syrians and Romans are brought together the Romans become soft and the Syrians remain as they are. The reverse would never apply: Syrians do not become sturdy fighters under the influence of Roman conquerors.

The Germans, ever since Varus' defeat in AD 9, were to the Romans a constant reminder of failure and by many authors they were regarded as a major threat. Roman authors saw them as the ultimate northern people.[62] Accordingly, a full assortment of environmental stereotypes was applied to them. Tacitus, however, as already mentioned, attributes their specific characteristics rather to their pure lineage, a significant idea, even if we ignore its influence in later history. The Germans were of pure blood because they lived far to the north and apart from others and therefore were not corrupted into civilized degeneracy of any kind, except those living closest to other peoples. The Germans were tall, brave, and firm, prone to anger. They cannot stand hard work nor can they stand heat or thirst, but they are inured to cold and hunger. They love fighting, sleeping, and feasting; they hate peace and serious work and so forth. With all their weaknesses, however, the Germans represented the ultimate form of virility. Many of their virtues were the opposite of Roman decadence, especially in Tacitus' *Germania*. The Roman imperial view of itself and others saw here an unavoidable logic: subject people eventually lose their independence of mind. Conversely the Germans, if they are *not* subjected, remain dangerous. Combine this with the essential pessimism and belief in inevitable decline of the ancient world, and the German presence is indeed a serious long-term threat. Being uncorrupted and powerful, they were the most dangerous people that had not been conquered.

For our purposes it is important to note that, in the case of the Germans we encounter a strong combination of forms of proto-racism: environmental stereotypes are reinforced by the belief in pure lineage and sociocultural integrity. These notions in turn played a significant role in the ideas about the relationship between the Empire and the Germanic peoples. Thus Roman views – and especially those of Tacitus – on the Germans are probably the best example to be found anywhere in ancient literature of a full integration of proto-racist stereotypes and imperialist ideology. To conquer and rule them was not only the ultimate test of a warrior-empire, it was also a necessity for its long-term survival. It so happens that these ideas were absorbed by a nation particularly susceptible to them in the early modern and modern periods.

To sum up: in antiquity, as in modern times, we constantly encounter the unquestioned assumption that it is possible and reasonable to relate

---

[62] Isaac, *Invention of Racism*, ch. 12, 427–39.

to entire peoples as if they were a single or collective individual. The conceptual means employed to this end were not the same in antiquity as in modern history, although they are still quite familiar. They were the environmental theory and the belief in the heredity of acquired characters, concepts broadly accepted in Greece and Rome. These hold that collective characteristics of groups of people are permanently determined by climate and geography. The implication is that the essential features of body and mind come from the outside and are stable. They do not occur through genetic evolution, or conscious choice. Social interaction plays a secondary role. Individuality and individual change are thereby ignored. When applied to human groups these ideas lead to a belief that their characteristics are uniform and constant, once acquired, unless people migrate. The latter would lead to decline and degeneration through displacement and contamination. The presumed characteristics that resulted were subject to value judgements, in which the foreigners were usually rejected as being inferior to the observer, or, in rare instances, approved of as being untainted and superior. Greeks in the fourth century developed the environmental theory further, adding two elements which made it an essential tool for imperialists. They claimed that Greece occupies the very best environment between Europe and Asia and produces therefore people ideally capable of ruling others. More specifically this was directed at the Persian Empire and the inhabitants of Asia, who were said to be servile by nature, or natural slaves, and therefore suited to be subjects of the Greeks. These and similar ideas are found in many Roman authors in a popularized form, adapted to the specific needs and circumstances of the times. The Romans duly substitute themselves as the ideal rulers. A related idea, accepted by many Roman authors, held that long-term imperial rule reduces a people to a state almost identical to that of natural slavery. As a result masters and slaves, rulers and subject peoples, live in a symbiosis beneficial to both parties. Other relevant concepts are autochthony and pure lineage. The Athenians, in their period of imperial expansion, developed an emotional attachment to these interrelated ideas. Rome made no claim of being autochthonous or of pure blood, but applied those ideas to other peoples. Particularly important is the strong disapproval of mixed blood. There is a firm conviction, encountered in numerous texts, that mixing leads to degeneration. The idea is not so much that purity of lineage will lead to improvement, the reverse is true: any form of mixture will result in something worse. This, as has been shown, is connected with the absence of a belief in progress in antiquity.

CHAPTER 9

The Barbarian in Greek and Latin Literature

Various peoples have a term indicating all foreigners collectively,[1] but few of those concepts have had such a long history as the ancient Greek *barbaros* which is still in use in many Western languages. Its meaning varied over time. It is the argument of the present chapter that it is worth reconsidering carefully what the word says about Greek and Roman attitudes towards other peoples over time. This is not an attempt to make an essential contribution to questions of ethnicity – Greek and non-Greek, or Greek self-definition through the recorded views of others.[2] The aim is to understand somewhat better what this intriguing term can teach us about Greek and Roman attitudes to non-Greeks and non-Romans. This will be based on literary sources of all kinds, including poetry and tragedy from the eighth century BC until the fourth century AD. This is justified because the aim is not to trace objective practicalities, such as e.g. the manner in which foreigners were treated, but ideas and concepts that may be expressed in different literary forms. The first source discussed is a good example of this.

Greek

The term occurs first, once only, in Homer in the *Iliad* (2.867) where the Carians are called *barbarophonoi*, that is, 'of foreign speech'.[3] This may or

[1] See E. Hall, *Inventing the Barbarian: Greek Self-Definition through Tragedy* (Oxford, 1989), 4, n. 1, for the terms for foreigners used in various languages. For a Chinese perspective, see: H. Yang, 'Perceptions of the Barbarian in Ancient Greece and China', *Center for Hellenic Studies Research Bulletin* 2 (2013); Yang, 'Invention of Barbarian and Emergence of Orientalism: Classical Greece', *Journal of Chinese Philosophy* 37 (2010): 556–66. For the terminology see also K. C. Wu, *The Chinese Heritage* (New York, 1982), 106–8.

[2] Hall, *Inventing the Barbarian*; J. Hall, *Ethnic Identity in Greek Antiquity* (Cambridge, 1997); J. Hall, *Hellenicity: Between Ethnicity and Culture* (Chicago, 2002); I. Malkin, *Ancient Perceptions of Greek Identity* (Cambridge, 2001); M. Finkelberg, *Greeks and Pre-Greeks* (Cambridge, 2005); D. Konstan, 'Defining Ancient Greek Ethnicity', *Diaspora* 6 (1997): 97–110; K. Vlassopoulos, *Greeks and Barbarians* (Cambridge, 2013).

[3] See A. D. Kelly, in M. Finkelberg (ed.), *The Homer Encyclopedia* (Oxford, 2011), I, 123; see also J. McInerney, at I, 265–7. Cf. Hall, *Inventing the Barbarian*, 9.

may not be derogatory. In either case, it has often been misinterpreted as indicating an original linguistic basis for the term *barbaros* itself. This, however, is by no means obvious; for in the *Iliad* the term may mean no more than that the people mentioned spoke a foreign (barbarian) language. Generally speaking, all *barbaroi* are undoubtedly *barbarophonoi*, but that does not mean that the essence of being a *barbaros* is the difference in language. It may be just one of the characteristics of *barbaroi*. Another passage, in the *Odyssey*, may be related: When Hephaistos had been expelled from Olympus he landed on Lemnos where he received succour from the 'wild-speaking' Sintians.[4]

Thereafter, in the seventh century BC the term occurs in a fragment of the Spartan poet Alcman.

Alcman Fr. 10a 38–45:[5] γ]ὰρ εἰ διὰ [τ]ὴν σοφία[ν πολίτην ἐπ[ο]ιήσαντο
ἐστιν ἑα[υ]τοῦ κατη[γορεῖν ·η τοῖς ἄ[ισ]μασι τὸν ['Αλκμᾶνα καὶ λέγειν ὅτι
βά[ρβαρος ἦν καὶ Λυδὸς ὑπερλ[π]ατρίδος καὶ γε[·]ου καιτο[·]·[

Alcman's origin was a matter of dispute even in antiquity. He is frequently assumed to have been born in Sardis, capital of ancient Lydia, but the Suda states that Alcman was a Laconian.[6] The present fragment is not conclusive and even contradictory,[7] but it is in any case a fact that reference is made here to his being a barbarian and a Lydian. This then, obviously, does not refer to language or culture, but to origin and citizenship. There certainly is no reason to assume that Alcman would refer to himself as a foreigner with the irony and sarcasm encountered in the work of Lucian of Samosata or Apuleius, for that is not the sort of literature he produced.[8] If Alcman calls himself a barbarian, this refers to his presumed origin in Lydia, not his deficient Greek. In other words, the term designates geographic origin, not language.

The sixth century provides us with more instances. It appears in a fragment ascribed to Anacreon (570–488?) which is too far gone to tell us much, but it seems to refer to barbarian speech.[9]

---

[4] *Od.* 8.293–4: ἀλλά που ἤδη οἴχεται ἐς Λῆμνον μετὰ Σίντιας ἀγριοφώνους (i.e. non-Greek; see also *Il.* 1.593–4).

[5] D. L. Page, *Poetae Melici Graeci* (Oxford, 1962), 30 with comments; M. Davies, *Poetarum melicorum Graecorum fragmenta* (Oxford, 1991), 6–10; cf. C. Calame, *Alcman: Introduction, texte critique, témoignages, traduction et commentaire* (Rome, 1983), T5, 4–6; T6; T8.

[6] Suda, s.v. Ἀλκμάν. Calame, *Alcman*, pp. xiv–xvi; Cf. D. A. Campbell, *Greek Lyric* (Cambridge, 1938), II, 402–6. For his date, see also G. O. Hutchinson, *Greek Lyric Poetry: A Commentary on Selected Larger Poems* (Oxford, 2001), 71.

[7] See the comments by Page, above. Cf. Campbell, *Greek Lyric*, 13c and d on 404–5; 16 on 408.

[8] For these authors about their origin, see above, Chapter 7.

[9] D. L. Page, *Supplementum Lyricis Graecis* (Oxford, 1974), S 313: ὁ γὰρ Ἀνακρέων φησί· (a) κοίμισον δέ, Ζεῦ, σόλοικον φθόγγον (b) μή πως βάρβαρα βάξῃς. Page explains in his comments that he cannot make sense of the Greek as it stands.

The term *barbarian* occurs in at least one fragment from the work of Hecataeus of Miletus (ca. 550–ca. 476): 'Hecataeus of Miletus says that barbarians lived in the Peloponnese before the Hellenes. In fact, almost all of Hellas was inhabited by barbarians in ancient times, as we can infer from the traditional tales themselves.'[10] As observed in the commentary to this fragment, it is unclear whether the whole of this passage in Strabo 7.7.1, cited there, should be attributed to Hecataeus, or just the first sentence. According to Hecataeus, pre-Greek peoples (i.e. Pelasgians) occupied the Peloponnese before the Hellenes.[11] If not just the first sentence, but all of the passage in Strabo may be attributed to Hecataeus that is of interest for historical reasons, but it does not affect the meaning of 'barbarian' as used here. To remove any doubt of this the sequel may be cited here:

> Pelops led his people from Phrygia to the Peloponnese, which is named after him, and Danaos brought his people from Egypt. There are Dryopes, Kaukones, Pelasgians and Leleges and other such peoples who occupied the regions on the Peloponnesian side of the Isthmos, and the other side too. The Thracians who came with Eumolpos took possession of Attica, while Tereus occupied Daulis in Phokis, and the Phoenicians who came with Kadmos the Kadmeia, and the Aones, Temmikes and Hyantes (as Pindar says [F 83 Maehler]: 'There was a time when they called the Boiotian people "syas" [swine]'). And their barbarian origin is indicated by their names, such as Kekrops, Kodros, Aiklos, Kothos, Drymas and Krinakos. The Thracians, Illyrians and Epeirotes even to this day are on the flanks [i.e. of Greece], even more so formerly than now, since the barbarians possess a large portion of the territory that is at present indisputably part of Greece. The Thracians hold Macedonia and a large part of Thessaly, while the Thesprotians, Kassopaians, Amphilocheans, Molossians and Athamanes, Epeirote peoples, occupy the upper parts of Akarnania and Aitolia.[12]

---

[10] *Brill's New Jacoby* 1 F 119: Ἑκαταῖος μὲν οὖν ὁ Μιλήσιος περὶ τῆς Πελοποννήσου φησίν, διότι πρὸ τῶν Ἑλλήνων ᾤκησαν αὐτὴν βάρβαροι. σχεδὸν δέ τι καὶ ἡ σύμπασα Ἑλλὰς κατοικία βαρβάρων ὑπῆρξε τὸ παλαιόν, ἀπ' αὐτῶν λογιζομένοις τῶν μνημονευομένων·

[11] See R. L. Fowler, 'Pelasgians', in E. Csapo and M. C. Miller (eds.), *Poetry, Theory, Praxis: The Social Life of Myth, Word and Image in Ancient Greece* (Oxford, 2003), 2–18, at 9–10, and C. Sourvinou-Inwood, 'Herodotus (and others) on Pelasgians: Some Perceptions of Ethnicity', in P. Derow and R. Parker (eds.), *Herodotus and his World* (Oxford, 2003), 103–44; for a discussion of Hdt. 1.56–8: 122–31; for the traditions concerning the descent of these heroes, see Finkelberg, *Greeks and Pre-Greeks* (2005), chs. 2 and 4. See also below, on Herodotus.

[12] Πέλοπος μὲν ἐκ τῆς Φρυγίας ἐπαγομένου λαὸν εἰς τὴν ἀπ' αὐτοῦ κληθεῖσαν Πελοπόννησον, Δαναοῦ δὲ ἐξ Αἰγύπτου, Δρυόπων τε καὶ Καυκώνων καὶ Πελασγῶν καὶ Λελέγων καὶ ἄλλων τοιούτων κατανειμαμένων τὰ ἐντὸς Ἰσθμοῦ καὶ τὰ ἐκτὸς δέ· τὴν μὲν γὰρ Ἀττικὴν οἱ μετὰ Εὐμόλπου Θρᾷκες ἔσχον, τῆς δὲ Φωκίδος τὴν Δαυλίδα Τηρεύς, τὴν δὲ Καδμείαν οἱ μετὰ Κάδμου Φοίνικες, αὐτὴν δὲ τὴν Βοιωτίαν Ἄονες καὶ Τέμμικες καὶ Ὕαντες (ὡς δὲ Πίνδαρός φησιν «ἦν ὅτε σύας Βοιώτιον ἔθνος ἔνεπον»). καὶ ἀπὸ τῶν ὀνομάτων δὲ ἐνίων τὸ βάρβαρον ἐμφαίνεται· Κέκροψ καὶ Κόδρος καὶ Αἶκλος καὶ Κόθος καὶ Δρύμας καὶ Κρίνακος. οἱ δὲ Θρᾷκες καὶ Ἰλλυριοὶ καὶ Ἠπειρῶται καὶ μέχρι νῦν ἐν πλευραῖς εἰσιν· ἔτι μέντοι μᾶλλον πρότερον ἢ νῦν, ὅπου γε καὶ

We see here that Hecataeus mentions *barbaroi* purely in an ethnic sense, as representing non-Greeks, descendants from non-Greeks, inhabiting parts of the mainland of Greece. If the sequel may be attributed to him, rather than to Strabo – which is not at all clear – he also identifies non-Greeks by their non-Greek personal names.

At least one fragment of Heraclitus (535–475) may suggest that in his opinion there existed a typically non-Greek mentality:[13]

> Poor witnesses for people are eyes and ears if they possess barbarian souls.[14]

Marcovich says that 'if they have' is only conditional, not causal. The fragment, he comments, stresses the need of personal intelligence or insight for the apprehension of the Logos (which, we may add, barbarians lack by definition). Sextus Empiricus, who quotes this passage, adds: 'It is as if he had said: "It is characteristic of barbarian souls to trust in irrational senses."'[15] Emphasis here is thus on rationality versus irrationality, while Sextus Empiricus adds more bluntly that barbarians are irrational, and Greeks rational.[16]

> (Thales) used to say that he was grateful to fate for three reasons: first because he was born a man and not an animal, second, a man and not a woman, third a Greek and not a barbarian.[17]

Whatever the date of this pronouncement, here we have, for the first time, a remarkably derogatory statement: someone is quoted as saying he is grateful for three things: being a man and not an animal, a man and not a woman and, thirdly, a Greek and not a barbarian. A related phrase still forms part of the traditional Jewish morning prayer, except that

---

τῆς ἐν τῶι παρόντι Ἑλλάδος ἀναντιλέκτως οὔσης [τὴν] πολλὴν οἱ βάρβαροι ἔχουσι Μακεδονίαν μὲν Θρᾶικες καί τινα μέρη τῆς Θετταλίας, Ἀκαρνανίας δε καὶ Αἰτωλίας <τὰ> ἄνω Θεσπρωτοὶ καὶ <Κ>ασσωπαῖοι καὶ Ἀμφίλοχοι καὶ Μολοττοὶ καὶ Ἀθαμᾶνες, Ἠπειρωτικὰ ἔθνη.

13 Fr. 107: κακοὶ μάρτυρες ἀνθρώποισιν ὀφθαλμοὶ καὶ ὦτα βαρβάρους ψυχὰς ἐχόντων. See M. Marcovich, *Heraclitus: Greek Text with a Short Commentary*, Editio Maior (Merida, 1967), Fr. 13 (107, Diels Kranz), comm. on 47–8; M. Conché, *Héraclite, Fragments* (Paris, 1986), 266–8.

14 My trans. See also the trans. by Conché, *Héraclite, Fragments*, 266: 'Mauvais témoins pour les homes, les yeux qui on des âmes barbares.' Marcovich translates: 'Evil witnesses are eyes and ears for men, if they have souls that do not understand their language.'

15 Sextus Empiricus, *Against the Mathematicians* 7.126–34 (31, Mutschmann): 'κακοὶ ... ἐχόντων' [B 107], ὅπερ ἴσον ἦν τῶι 'βαρβάρων ἐστὶ ψυχῶν ταῖς ἀλόγοις αἰσθήσεσι πιστεύειν'.

16 Conché, *Héraclite, Fragments*, lays heavy emphasis on language, as being comprehensible or not. Those who have barbarian souls are incapable of speaking or understanding rationally, but the text as it is does not justify this and Conché's approach may be based on conventional assumptions.

17 F. W. A. Mullach, *Fragmenta philosophorum Graecorum* (Paris, 1860; repr. Aalen, 1968), I, 227 (Diogenes Laertius 1.33): *Apophthegmata* 5.9.1: Ἔφασκε τριῶν τούτων ἕνεκα χάριν ἔχειν τῇ τύχῃ, πρῶτον μὲν ὅτι ἄνθρωπος ἐγένετο καὶ οὐ θηρίον, εἶτα ὅτι ἀνὴρ καὶ οὐ γυνή, τρίτον ὅτι Ἕλλην καὶ οὐ βάρβαρος.

here the undesirable forms of existence are: non-Jew, slave and woman, in that order.

The term occurs more frequently in the surviving plays of Aeschylus (ca. 525/524–ca. 456/455 BC).[18] In the *Supplices* the King of Argos addresses the suppliants as follows: 'Whence come these barbarians? What shall we call you? So outlandishly arrayed in the barbaric luxury of robes and crowns, and not in Argive fashion, nor in Greek?' Thus it refers here to dress which, if un-Hellenic, is therefore by definition barbaric. The suppliants are recognized as foreigners by their clothes.[19]

In the *Seven against Thebes* the scout describes Eteocles' mares: before the attack they have muzzle-gear which, 'filled with the breath of their proud nostrils, pipes in barbaric style'. Here barbaric refers to an unusual noise, produced by horses.[20] This may not mean more than 'unusual' or 'strange' or, even, fiercer: grating on the ear. It probably expresses dislike, but it would be farfetched to claim it is a comparison with non-Greek speech.

In the *Agamemnon* Agamemnon says to Clytemnestra: 'For the rest, pamper me not after woman's wise, nor, like some barbarian, grovel to me with wide-mouthed acclaim …'[21] This is behaviour, treating Agamemnon as if he were a woman or a barbarian. As paraphrased by Fraenkel: 'do not pamper me like a woman': 'do not prostrate yourself in homage before me, as if I were a barbarian'.[22] Agamemnon, being Greek, does not want the sort of grovelling (προσκύνησις) expected by barbarians. Unspoken, but indubitably implied, is the stereotype assuming that oriental barbarians are effeminate.[23] As used in this passage, the term has the full negative force of alien manners and style.

Again, in the *Agamemnon*, Clytemnestra turns to the Chorus and says about Cassandra: 'Well, if her speech be not strange and outlandish,

[18] See in general: Hall, *Inventing the Barbarian*.

[19] Aesch. *Supp.* 234–6: ποδαπὸν ὅμιλον τόνδ᾽ ἀνελληνόστολον πέπλοισι βαρβάροισι κἀμπυκώμασι χλίοντα προσφωνοῦμεν; this and the other translations from Aeschylus are H. R. Smyth, Loeb. Cf. the comments by H. F. Johansen and E. W. Whittle, *Aeschylus the Suppliants*, 3 vols. (Copenhagen, 1980), II, comm. *ad loc.*: ἀνελληνόστολον, a hapax. 'Strangers' clothing regularly excites attention as an indication of their race', with parallels. For barbaric, i.e. pompous dress, see also Eur., *Iphigenia Aulidensis* 74: βαρβάρωι χλιδήματι,.

[20] *Septem.* 463: φιμοὶ δὲ συρίζουσι βάρβαρον βρόμον, βρόμον is here an emendation for τρόπον MSS.

[21] *Agamemnon* 918–20: καὶ τἄλλα μὴ γυναικὸς ἐν τρόποις ἐμὲ ἅβρυνε, μηδὲ βαρβάρου φωτὸς δίκην χαμαιπετὲς βόαμα προσχάνῃς ἐμοί,

[22] E. Fraenkel, *Agamemnon Edited with a Commentary*, 3 vols. (Oxford, 1950), II, and comm. *ad loc.* D. Raeburn and O. Thomas, *The Agamemnon of Aeschylus* (Oxford, 2011), unlike Fraenkel, take the subject of βαρβάρου φωτὸς δίκην as being Clytemnestra.

[23] For the effeminacy attributed to oriental peoples, see B. Isaac, *The Invention of Racism in Classical Antiquity* (Princeton, 2004), index s.v.

even as a swallow's, I must speak within the compass of her wits and move her to comply.' Here the term refers to language, non-Greek speech being compared with the sounds produced by swallows.[24] Not surprisingly, in Aeschylus' work the term occurs most often in the *Persae*, namely ten times.

In Atossa's dream she saw one woman living in the Land of Hellas, the other in a barbarian land.[25] It refers therefore to land: any land not Hellas is barbarian, even when a Persian queen is speaking. When the messenger reports to Atossa about the destruction of the king's army, their own forces, he regularly refers to the barbarian forces[26] and so do Atossa[27] and the Chorus.[28] The implication is clear: if Persians are speaking and represented as speaking in Greek, they refer to themselves simply as Persians or barbarians and a Greek audience did not assume that the latter is an incongruous term, to be used by foreigners referring to themselves. In other words, it is here a neutral term for 'alien' or non-Greek.

In one instance the term is applied to speech when the Chorus addresses a prayer to the dead and the divine spirit of Darius: 'Doth then our sainted and godlike king hear me as I utter, in obscure barbaric speech, these my dismal and dolorous cries of varied sort?'[29]

Next, Pindar (522–443 BC):

> Countless continuous roads have been cut extending without a break or continuously for your fine deeds, both beyond the springs of the Nile and through the land of the Hyperboreans [i.e. beyond the ends of the world].[30] There is no city so barbarous or so strange in its speech [25][31] that it does not

---

[24] *Agamemnon* 1050–3 (Clytemnestra to the chorus about Cassandra): ἀλλ' εἴπερ ἐστὶ μὴ χελιδόνος δίκην ἀγνῶτα φωνὴν βάρβαρον κεκτημένη, ἔσω φρενῶν λέγουσα πείθω νιν λόγῳ. Cf. Fraenkel, *Agamemnon Edited with a Commentary*, II, 476–7; Raeburn and Thomas, *The Agamemnon of Aeschylus*, 183: 'The twittering swallow was a common simile in Greek for foreign speech.' Similarly: Sophocles, *Ant.* 1002: βεβαρβαρωμένῳ·; Hdt. 2.57: αἱ γυναῖκες, διότι βάρβαροι ἦσαν, ἐδόκεον δέ σφι ὁμοίως ὄρνισι φθέγγεσθαι.

[25] Aeschylus, *Persae* 186–7: πάτραν δ' ἔναιον ἡ μὲν Ἑλλάδα κλήρῳ λαχοῦσα γαῖαν, ἡ δὲ βάρβαρον.

[26] *Persae* 255: στρατὸς γὰρ πᾶς ὄλωλε βαρβάρων. Similarly: 337; 391; 423.

[27] *Persae* 433–4: αἰαῖ, κακῶν δὴ πέλαγος ἔρρωγεν μέγα Πέρσαις τε καὶ πρόπαντι βαρβάρων γένει. Also: 475 (the fallen at Marathon).

[28] *Persae* 798: πῶς εἶπας; οὐ γὰρ πᾶν στράτευμα βαρβάρων περᾷ τὸν Ἕλλης πορθμὸν Εὐρώπης ἄπο; also: 844.

[29] *Persae* 633–6: ἦ ῥ' ἀίει μου μακαρίτας ἰσοδαίμων βασιλεὺς βάρβαρα σαφηνῆ ἱέντος τὰ παναίολ' αἰανῆ δύσθροα βάγματα.

[30] U. v. Wilamowitz-Moellendorff, *Pindaros*, 2nd edn (Berlin, 1966), 182, n. 2: 'Im Munde eines Griechen, der eine ordentlich gehaltene Landstraße überhaupt nicht kannte, ist die Vorstellung höchst merkwürdig.'

[31] L. R. Farnell, *The Works of Pindar; Translated with Literary and Critical Commentaries* (London, 1932; repr. Amsterdam, 1965), 359–61; for παλίγγλωσσος, see 248 and 360: 'speech contrary to the natural = perverse'.

know the fame of the hero Peleus, the fortunate in-law of gods, or of Aias and his father Telamon.[32]

The passage refers to the fame of Greek heroes beyond the ends of the world. It might be argued that 'barbarous' here is almost a synonym of παλίγγλωσσος, but that is not necessary. It can be naturally taken as referring to basic culture, information, and knowledge. Here it does *not* refer to language but to knowledge of the Greek heroes.

In the fifth century Herodotus uses the term 'barbarians', but not in any disparaging manner.[33] In his history of the wars between the Greeks and the Persians he describes the enemy respectfully as a formidable political and military power. The Persians were courageous (7.238), he writes, and fought valiantly (8.86; 9.71). They were also wont to honour those who did so. The Lydians too were brave and warlike (1.79). He pays much and varied attention to Egypt in a substantial part of his work, not marked by xenophobia.

Herodotus observes that the predecessors of the Greeks in their land were the Pelasgi (1.57), who spoke a barbarian language.[34] 'If so ... the Attic people, who were certainly Pelasgi, must have changed their language at the same time that they passed into the Hellenic community ...' In this view language and ethnic identity are inseparably connected. Consequently, the Athenians were once upon a time barbarians, speaking a barbarian language, but subsequently became Greek-speaking Hellenes. This is an explicitly formulated view of the essence of ethnicity – and therefore much discussed. Being Hellene or barbarian were categories that could change over time together with language, as opposed to the very common view that gives priority to descent. This is not to deny that Herodotus held the Greeks to be superior: more intelligent than other peoples, for instance (1.60.3). Yet his attitude was criticized in antiquity, notably in Plutarch's essay *The Malice of Herodotus,* which attacks the author's sympathy for barbarians, but that was written in the Roman period. In 8.144 Herodotus represents the Athenians as explaining why they could not have supported the Persians: first because of the destruction of Athenian sanctuaries, second because of 'the Hellenic ties, that is, our relationship, common

[32] *Isthmia* 6.22–7: μυρίαι δ᾽ ἔργων καλῶν τέτ᾽μανθ᾽ ἑκατόμπεδοι ἐν σχερῷ κέλευθοι καὶ πέραν Νείλοιο παγᾶν καὶ δι᾽ Ὑπερβορέους· καὶ πέραν Νείλοιο παγᾶν καὶ δι᾽ Ὑπερβορέους· οὐδ᾽ ἔστιν οὕτω βάρβαρος οὔτε παλίγγλωσσος πόλις, ἅτις οὐ Πηλέος ἀίει κλέος ἥρωος, εὐδαίμονος γαμβροῦ θεῶν, οὐδ᾽ ἅτις Αἴαντος Τελαμωνιάδα καὶ πατρός·

[33] See also the earlier discussion in Isaac, *Invention of Racism*, ch. 4.

[34] See above, on Hekataios. Cf. D. Asheri *et al., A Commentary on Herodotus Books I–IV* (Oxford, 2007), 117–119; for Pelasgi see also above, n. 11; cf. Finkelberg, *Greeks and Pre-Greeks*, ch. 2.

language, the joint altars and sacrifices and the common customs, which it would not be well for the Athenians to betray'. It has to be considered in context: the essence of the passage, usually overlooked, is that the issue itself needed to be clarified. If it had been obvious there would have been no need to say it (or for Herodotus: to write it). It remains true that the Athenians here are represented as emphasizing kinship, language, cult, and customs as essential features, determining collective relationships.

To be noted is also the admiration expressed in some sources for various remote barbarians, such as the Scythians with their sage Anacharsis, and the Ethiopians.[35] All this shows that the notion of 'barbarian' in Athens in the first half of the fifth century did not necessarily and immediately have all of the heavy negative load that the term carries in modern English, even if Greeks thought of themselves as being superior.

In the work of Thucydides (460–395 BC) the term frequently occurs as a simple indication of foreigners or foreign troops, often the Persians, as distinct from Greeks and their forces.[36] Thucydides has an interesting historical observation which represents, as far as I know, an approach totally novel at the time: '[Homer] does not even use the term barbarian, probably because the Hellenes had not yet been marked off from the rest of the world by one distinctive appellation.' Homer does not use Hellas and Hellenes to indicate all of the Greeks and he does not use the term *barbaroi* because there is no single name yet to indicate all of the Greeks collectively.

Thucydides points out the development of cultural differences between Greeks and barbarians over time, notably in dress. 'And there are many other points in which a likeness might be shown between the life of the Hellenic world of old and the barbarian of to-day.'[37] The implication here is that the Greeks evolved, while the non-Greeks remained stuck in an early stage of development. This is an interesting affirmation of a belief in progress – although in the past. Progress is a concept that otherwise is hardly found in antiquity.[38] Besides dress, language is of course emphasized as the essence of Hellenicity: Argos in Amphilochia was a Greek colony. At some stage, in need of reinforcement, 'they called in the Ambraciots, their neighbours on the Amphilochian border, to join their colony; and it was

---

[35] Cf. Romm, Edges of the Earth, 45–7; 74–6: Scythians and Anacharsis; 54–60: Ethiopians.

[36] Thuc. 1.1; 1.5; 1.6; 1.14.3 (Persians); 1.23.2; 1.118; Thucydides also uses the singular for a collective, thus 1.18.2: ὁ βάρβαρος, 'The Barbarian' for 'The Persians'; 1.73: φαμὲν γὰρ Μαραθῶνί τε μόνοι προκινδυνεῦσαι τῷ βαρβάρῳ. Note also 1.24.2: Ταυλάντιοι βάρβαροι, Ἰλλυρικὸν ἔθνος;

[37] Thuc. 1.6.6: πολλὰ δ' ἂν καὶ ἄλλα τις ἀποδείξειε τὸ παλαιὸν Ἑλληνικὸν ὁμοιότροπα τῷ νῦν βαρβαρικῷ διαιτώμενον.

[38] Cf. Isaac, Invention of Racism, 243, with references in n. 68; 310–11.

by this union with Argos that the Ambraciots learnt their present Hellenic speech, the rest of the Amphilochians being barbarians'.[39] The Ambraciots who joined Argos as citizens and began to speak Greek thus were no longer barbarians. Here again we see that Greek identity can be acquired and does not depend solely on descent. Another, related aspect of this is that there are degrees of barbarianism, or barbarity. When *barbaros* simply means 'non-Greek' it is an absolute characteristic. There are no variations. When it approaches the modern meaning of the term, this changes matters. Thus we find the word in the superlative in Thucydides' work:

> Upon this revolution taking place, the party of Pisander and Alexicles, and the chiefs of the oligarchs immediately withdrew to Decelea, with the single exception of Aristarchus, one of the generals, who hastily took some of the most barbarian of the archers and marched to Oenoe.[40]

It is the argument of this chapter that there is a marked change in attitudes toward foreigners, especially the Persians, in the course of the fifth century or, rather, in the second half of that century. Thus, we find one of the clearest expressions of a derogatory judgement of barbarians in Thucydides' remark on the Thracians: 'the Thracian race, like the bloodiest of the barbarians, being even more so when it has nothing to fear'.[41] This is interesting, given the personal ties of the author with Thrace and the Thracians. The occasion of the remark is the bloody conquest of Mycalessus by Thracians. Here, then, the term has a decidedly moral content: the Thracians are fearful murderers like the worst barbarians.

Towards the end of the fifth century attitudes hardened. Unlike the plays of Sophocles,[42] those of Euripides are rich in relevant statements, whereby it should be obvious that these do not represent opinions expressed on his own behalf, but phrases attributed by the author to his dramatic personae. Yet, these frequently represent concepts and ideas that are not encountered before, in earlier authors. Thus in 412 Euripides attributes to Helen,

---

[39] Thuc. 2.68: ὕστερον πιεζόμενοι Ἀμπρακιώτας ὁμόρους ὄντας τῇ Ἀμφιλοχικῇ ξυνοίκους ἐπηγάγοντο, καὶ ἡλληνίσθησαν τὴν νῦν γλῶσσαν τότε πρῶτον ἀπὸ τῶν Ἀμπρακιωτῶν ξυνοικησάντων· οἱ δὲ ἄλλοι Ἀμφίλοχοι βάρβαροί εἰσιν. For problems of interpretation, see A. W. Gomme, *A Historical Commentary on Thucydides* (Oxford, 1956), II, 201–2; S. Hornblower, *A Commentary on Thucydides*, 3 vols. (Oxford, 1991–2008), I, 352–3.

[40] Thuc. 8.98 (trans. J. M. Dent): Ἐν δὲ τῇ μεταβολῇ ταύτῃ εὐθὺς οἱ μὲν περὶ τὸν Πείσανδρον καὶ Ἀλεξικλέα καὶ ὅσοι ἦσαν τῆς ὀλιγαρχίας μάλιστα ὑπεξέρχονται ἐς τὴν Δεκέλειαν· Ἀρίσταρχος δὲ αὐτῶν μόνος (ἔτυχε γὰρ καὶ στρατηγῶν) λαβὼν κατὰ τάχος τοξότας τινὰς τοὺς βαρβαρωτάτους ἐχώρει πρὸς τὴν Οἰνόην.

[41] Thuc. 7.29: τὸ γὰρ γένος τὸ τῶν Θρᾳκῶν ὁμοῖα τοῖς μάλιστα τοῦ βαρβαρικοῦ, ἐν ᾧ ἂν θαρσήσῃ, φονικώτατόν ἐστιν.

[42] See above, n. 24; Sophocles, *Tr.* 236 and *El.* 95: land; *Aj.* 1263: language; 1289 and 1292: descent.

exiled in Egypt, the words:[43] 'A slave am I, the daughter of free parents, for among the barbarians all are slaves except one.'[44] This passage is particularly significant, for it is an explicit confirmation of the close relationship between barbarians and slavery in Greek eyes by this time. The same point is expressed again in *Iphigenia in Aulis*: 'And it is right, mother, that Hellenes should rule barbarians, but not barbarians Hellenes, those being slaves, while these are free.'[45] This is the clearest statement of an imperial ideology to be found in the Greek literature of the time. Moreover, it is no coincidence that we find it towards the end of the fifth century and not earlier.

The term also occurs in connection with land.[46] Furthermore, as we saw above, dress is one of the marks of Greek or non-Greek identity, in other texts as well.[47] 'Hellenic dress and fashion in his robes doth he no doubt adopts, but deeds like these betray the barbarian. Thou, sirrah, tell me straight the country whence thou camest thither.'[48] In Euripides' phrase, attributed to Demophon, dress may be adopted, but behaviour will reveal true identity. Barbarian armour is strange. Antigone says of Tydeus, the Aetolian: 'What a foreign look his armour has! A half-barbarian he!'[49] A remarkable instance of the complex use of the term may be found in the *Troades:* 'O barbarous ills devised by Greeks.'[50]

Barbarians do not know sexual restraint, according to several texts.

> Such is all the race of barbarians; father and daughter, mother and son, sister and brother mate together; the nearest and dearest stain their path with each other's blood [i.e. commit incest], and no law restrains such horrors. Bring not these crimes amongst us, for here we count it shame that one man should have the control of two wives, and men are content to turn to one lawful love, that is, all who care to live an honourable life.[51]

---

[43] Only a few representative examples are cited here.

[44] *Helen* 275–6: τὰ βαρβάρων γὰρ δοῦλα πάντα πλὴν ἑνός; cf. *Orestes* 1115: οὐδὲν τὸ δοῦλον πρὸς τὸ μὴ δοῦλον γένος.

[45] *Iph. Aul.* 1400: βαρβάρων δ᾽ Ἕλληνας ἄρχειν εἰκός, ἀλλ᾽ οὐ βαρβάρους μῆτερ, Ἑλλήνων· τὸ μὲν γὰρ δοῦλον, οἱ δ᾽ ἐλεύθεροι

[46] Eur. *Medea* 256: ἐκ γῆς βαρβάρου; 536: Ἑλλάδ᾽ ἀντὶ βαρβάρου χθονὸς γαῖαν κατοικεῖς; 1330.

[47] Aesch. *Supp.* 234–6; Thuc. 1.6.6, both cited above.

[48] Eur. *Heracleidae* 131(trans. Coleridge): καὶ μὴν στολήν γ᾽ Ἕλληνα καὶ ῥυθμὸν πέπλων ἔχει, τὰ δ᾽ ἔργα βαρβάρου χερὸς τάδε. It is to be noted that the subject of these comments is Copreus from Argos. See also *Heracleidae* 423–4 οὐ γὰρ τυραννίδ᾽ ὥστε βαρβάρων ἔχω· ἀλλ᾽, ἣν δίκαια δρῶ, δίκαια πείσομαι.

[49] Eur. *Phoenissae* 138: ὡς ἀλλόχρως ὅπλοισι, μειξοβάρβαρος. See below, n. 67.

[50] Eur. *Troades* 763: ὦ βάρβαρ᾽ ἐξευρόντες Ἕλληνες κακά, This is cited by Plutarch, *Ages.* 15.2.

[51] Eur. *Andromache* 173–80: τοιοῦτον πᾶν τὸ βάρβαρον γένος· πατήρ τε θυγατρὶ παῖς τε μητρὶ μείγνυται κόρη τ᾽ ἀδελφῷ, διὰ φόνου δ᾽ οἱ φίλτατοι χωροῦσι, καὶ τῶνδ᾽ οὐδὲν ἐξείργει νόμος. ἃ μὴ παρ᾽ ἡμᾶς ἔσφερ᾽· οὐδὲ γὰρ καλὸν δυοῖν γυναικοῖν ἄνδρ᾽ ἕν᾽ ἡνίας ἔχειν, ἀλλ᾽ ἐς μίαν βλέποντες εὐναίαν Κύπριν στέργουσιν, ὅστις μὴ κακῶς οἰκεῖν θέλῃ.

'Barbarians' laws are no standard for a Greek city.'[52] True friendship is impossible between the two groups, Greeks and barbarians.[53] Their music is strange,[54] their rites are foolish.[55] Acculturation is possible, but, it seems, almost exclusively as a form of deterioration. One can become a barbarian, but barbarians becoming Greek are exceptional: '[Tyndareus to Menelaus]: You have been so long among barbarians that you have become one of them.'[56]

In the work of Xenophon (430–354 BC) the term occurs very frequently. In his major works, the *Anabasis* and the *Hellenica,* it occurs most often in the sense of non-Greeks (Persians) as distinct from Greeks.[57] In the *Anabasis* it almost always refers to Cyrus' non-Greek forces.[58] Xenophon attributes the use of it also to Cyrus himself when addressing Greeks,[59] even telling the Greeks that they are braver and stronger than many barbarians.[60] We do not know, of course, what Cyrus told his non-Greek men. It can be used for languages: Pategyas, a member of Cyrus' staff is described as shouting 'in the barbarian language and in Greek'.[61] This does not mean that language is the essence of barbarian identity. It can also apply to dress,[62] to weaponry,[63] and to valuable Persian cups and carpets.[64] It is used as an adjective in the superlative: the Mossynoccians, friendly to the Greek forces, were 'the most barbaric' (βαρβαρωτάτους) people Xenophon's forces met and the farthest removed from Greek customs.[65] The reason Xenophon gives for his judgement may be worth noting: they wanted to

---

[52] Eur. *Andromache* 243: οὐ βαρβάρων νόμοισιν οἰκοῦμεν πόλιν..

[53] Eur. *Hecuba* 1199–1201: ἀλλ', ὦ κάκιστε, πρῶτον οὔποτ' ἂν φίλον τὸ βάρβαρον γένοιτ' ἂν Ἕλλησιν γένος οὐδ' ἂν δύναιτο.

[54] Eur. *Iph. in Taur.* 179–81: ἀντιψάλμους ᾠδὰς ὕμνων τ' Ἀσιητᾶν σοι βάρβαρον ἀχάν, δέσποιν', ἐξαυδάσω; *Iphig. Aul.* 576: βάρβαρα συρίζων,

[55] *Bacchae* 482–3: {Δι.} πᾶς ἀναχορεύει βαρβάρων τάδ' ὄργια. {Πε.} φρονοῦσι γὰρ κάκιον Ἑλλήνων πολύ. As observed by E. R. Dodds, *Euripides Bacchae*, 2nd edn (Oxford, 1969), 138: 'Everyone of the foreigners' is more emphatic than πάντες βάρβαροι.

[56] *Orestes* 485: βεβαρβάρωσαι, χρόνιος ὢν ἐν βαρβάροις.

[57] E.g. *Hell.* 1.6.8; 1.6.11; 3.1.19; 3.2.12.

[58] E.g. *An.* 1.1.5: καὶ τῶν παρ' ἑαυτῷ δὲ βαρβάρων ἐπεμελεῖτο ὡς πολεμεῖν τε ἱκανοὶ εἶησαν; *An.* 1.2.8: καὶ ἀθροίζει ὡς ἐπὶ τούτους τό τε βαρβαρικὸν καὶ τὸ Ἑλληνικόν; *An.* 1.2.14: βουλόμενος οὖν ἐπὶ δεῖξαι ἐξέτασιν ποιεῖται ἐν τῷ πεδίῳ τῶν Ἑλλήνων καὶ τῶν βαρβάρων.

[59] *An.* 1.5.16: κακῶς γὰρ τῶν ἡμετέρων ἐχόντων πάντες οὗτοι οὓς ὁρᾶτε βάρβαροι πολεμιώτεροι ἡμῖν ἔσονται τῶν παρὰ βασιλεῖ ὄντων.

[60] *An.* 1.7.3: Ὦ ἄνδρες Ἕλληνες, οὐκ ἀνθρώπων ἀπορῶν βαρβάρων συμμάχους ὑμᾶς ἄγω, ἀλλὰ νομίζων ἀμείνονας καὶ κρείττους πολλῶν βαρβάρων ὑμᾶς εἶναι,

[61] *An.* 1.8.1: ἐβόα καὶ βαρβαρικῶς καὶ ἑλληνικῶς.

[62] *An.* 4.5.33: Ἀρμενίους παῖδας σὺν ταῖς βαρβαρικαῖς στολαῖς·.

[63] *An.*4.8.7: ἐντεῦθεν διδόασιν οἱ Μάκρωνες βαρβαρικὴν λόγχην τοῖς Ἕλλησιν, οἱ δὲ Ἕλληνες ἐκείνοις Ἑλληνικήν·.

[64] *An.* 7.3.18: ἐκπώματα καὶ τάπιδας βαρβαρικάς,

[65] *An.* 5.4.34: τούτους ἔλεγον οἱ στρατευσάμενοι βαρβαρωτάτους διελθεῖν καὶ πλεῖστον τῶν Ἑλληνικῶν νόμων κεχωρισμένους.

have intercourse openly with the women who accompanied the Greeks, for that was their custom. They continuously did publicly what other peoples would do only in private, etc. etc. This is a rare case where we see that Xenophon does not merely relate to *barbaroi* as non-Greeks. Hellenicity is a standard. As for non-Greeks, the farther they are removed from Greek values, the more barbaric they are. As already noted on Thucydides' similar use of the term, when there are degrees of barbarism it no longer is an almost neutral term for 'foreigner', but has become an issue of judgement. In other words, the term here approaches its meaning in modern European languages. Aristophanes uses it similarly. That of course is in comedy, but it is there, when Poseidon addresses Triballus: 'Ugh! You cursed savage! You are by far the most barbarous of all the gods.'[66]

In his *Hellenica* Xenophon uses a rare word: the term μιξοβάρβαροι, 'mixed barbarians'. This might have indicated a mixture of barbarians, but, in fact, refers to the inhabitants of a city who are partly Hellenes, partly non-Greek.[67]

In his minor works there are notable occurrences of the term: 'Very well, in the first place, it is clear as day that both Greeks and barbarians believe that the gods know everything both present and to come …'[68] Both Greeks and non-Greeks here represent all of humanity.

In his *Ways and Means* Xenophon proposes measures regarding the metics (Greek resident aliens). They could, among other things, serve in the army and he remarks: 'The state would gain if the citizens served in the ranks together, and no longer found themselves in the same company with Lydians, Phrygians, Syrians and barbarians of all sorts, of whom a large part of our alien population consists.'[69]

---

[66] Aristophanes, *Av.* 1573 (trans. O'Neill): Οἴμωζε· πολὺ γὰρ δή σ' ἐγὼ ἑόρακα πάντων βαρβαρώτατον θεῶν.

[67] *Hell.* 2.1.15.: καὶ προσβαλὼν πόλει τῶν Ἀθηναίων συμμάχῳ ὄνομα Κεδρείαις τῇ ὑστεραίᾳ προσβολῇ κατὰ κράτος αἱρεῖ καὶ ἐξηνδραπόδισεν. ἦσαν δὲ μιξοβάρβαροι οἱ ἐνοικοῦντες. Cf. Euripides, *Phoenissae* 138: μειξοβάρβαρος. See above, n. 49. Plato, *Menex.* 245d4: οὐ γὰρ Πέλοπες οὐδὲ Κάδμοι οὐδὲ Αἴγυπτοί τε καὶ Δαναοὶ οὐδὲ ἄλλοι πολλοὶ φύσει μὲν βάρβαροι ὄντες, νόμῳ δὲ Ἕλληνες, συνοικοῦσιν ἡμῖν, ἀλλ' αὐτοὶ Ἕλληνες, οὐ μειξοβάρβαροι οἰκοῦμεν, The Athenians are pure Hellenes and not half foreigners. Cf. Finkelberg, *Greeks and Pre-Greeks*, 37. For a variant terminology, cf. Thucydides 4.109: οἰκοῦνται ξυμμείκτοις ἔθνεσι βαρβάρων διγλώσσων,. This refers to foreigners who spoke their own language and Greek as well; cf. Gomme, *A Historical Commentary on Thucydides*, III, 588–9. Usually ξύμμεικτος is used by Thucydides for an unspecified mixture, e.g. 2.98; 3.61; 4.106; 6.4; 6.17.

[68] *Symp* 4.47.1 Οὐκοῦν ὡς μὲν καὶ Ἕλληνες καὶ βάρβαροι τοὺς θεοὺς ἡγοῦνται πάντα εἰδέναι τά τε ὄντα καὶ τὰ μέλλοντα εὔδηλον.

[69] *Vect* 2.3–4: ἀλλὰ μὴν καὶ ἡ πόλις γ' ἂν ὠφεληθείη, εἰ οἱ πολῖται μετ' ἀλλήλων στρατεύοιντο μᾶλλον ἢ εἰ συντάττοιντο αὐτοῖς, ὥσπερ νῦν, Λυδοὶ καὶ Φρύγες καὶ Σύροι καὶ ἄλλοι παντοδαποὶ βάρβαροι· πολλοὶ γὰρ τοιοῦτοι τῶν μετοίκων.

An interesting episode is related by Xenophon in his *Life of Agesilaus* (king of Sparta, 400–360 BC).

> Moreover, believing that contempt for the enemy would kindle the fighting spirit, he gave instructions to his heralds that the barbarians captured in the raids should be exposed for sale naked. So when his soldiers saw them white because they never stripped, and fat and lazy through constant riding in carriages, they believed that the war would be exactly like fighting with women.[70]

This represents the fourth-century attitude towards Persians which is not normally encountered in the fifth century, marked by elements of contempt, intended humiliation, and the claim that they were effeminate. *The Life of Agesilaus* is an early text that regularly, and as a matter of course, emphasizes the need not merely to save Greece, but to subdue Asia.[71]

Xenophon's *On Hunting* opens with a lengthy praise of hunting which was taught by Cheiron to many heroes of myth, including Achilles. This section concludes with an ideological statement:

> These, whom the good love even to this day and the evil envy, were made so perfect through the care they learned of Cheiron that, when trouble fell upon any state or any king in Greece, it was solved through their influence; or if all Greece was at strife or at war with all the Barbarian powers, these brought victory to the Greeks so that they made Greece invincible.[72]

One may question the logic of this statement of Xenophon, but that is irrelevant here. Xenophon claims that hunting has to be learned by the young so that they may become good in war and 'in all things out of which must come excellence in thought and word and deed'.[73] Given that this is his persuasion it is to be noted that Xenophon here raises the possibility that 'all of Greece' would be at war with 'all the Barbarians'. It is a programme for which there was no precedent in Greece.[74] Indeed, it may be

---

[70] *Ages.* 1.28 (trans. Marchant, Loeb): ἡγούμενος δὲ καὶ τὸ καταφρονεῖν τῶν πολεμίων ῥώμην τινὰ ἐμβαλεῖν πρὸς τὸ μάχεσθαι, προεῖπε τοῖς κήρυξι τοὺς ὑπὸ τῶν λῃστῶν ἁλισκομένους βαρβάρους γυμνοὺς πωλεῖν. ὁρῶντες οὖν οἱ στρατιῶται λευκοὺς μὲν διὰ τὸ μηδέποτε ἐκδύεσθαι, πίονας δὲ καὶ ἀπόνους διὰ τὸ ἀεὶ ἐπ' ὀχημάτων εἶναι, ἐνόμισαν μηδὲν διοίσειν τὸν πόλεμον ἢ εἰ γυναιξὶ δέοι μάχεσθαι. The same story is told by Plutarch, *Ages.* 9.5.5.

[71] Xenophon, *Ages.* 1.8: κάλλιστον δὲ πάντων ἐκρίνετο <τὸ> μὴ περὶ τῆς Ἑλλάδος ἀλλὰ περὶ τῆς Ἀσίας τὸν ἀγῶνα καθιστάναι.

[72] *Cyn.* 17: οὗτοι δὲ τοιοῦτοι ἐγένοντο ἐκ τῆς ἐπιμελείας τῆς παρὰ Χείρωνος, ἧς οἱ μὲν ἀγαθοὶ ἔτι καὶ νῦν ἐρῶσιν, οἱ δὲ κακοὶ φθονοῦσιν, ὥστ' ἐν μὲν τῇ Ἑλλάδι εἴ τῳ συμφοραὶ ἐγίγνοντο ἢ πόλει ἢ βασιλεῖ, ἐλύοντο <δι'> αὐτούς· εἰ δὲ πρὸς τοὺς βαρβάρους πάντας πάσῃ τῇ Ἑλλάδι νεῖκος ἢ πόλεμος ἦν, διὰ τούτους οἱ Ἕλληνες ἐκράτουν, ὥστε ἀνίκητον τὴν Ἑλλάδα παρέχεσθαι.

[73] *Cyn.* 1.18: ἐκ τούτων γὰρ γίγνονται τὰ εἰς τὸν πόλεμον ἀγαθοὶ καὶ [εἰς] τὰ ἄλλα ἐξ ὧν ἀνάγκη καλῶς νοεῖν καὶ λέγειν καὶ πράττειν.

[74] Note however, arguments for earlier roots of a Pan Hellenic ideology: M. A. Flower, 'From Simonides to Isocrates: The Fifth Century Origins of Fourth-Century Pan Hellenism', *CA* 19 (2000): 65–101.

a remarkably early description of what in modern times came to be called
'Total War'. This is usually associated with nineteenth- and twentieth-
century wars, although a claim has been made that the Napoleonic Wars
could already be described in those terms.[75] The involvement of civilians
in warfare, typical of what is nowadays called 'total war', was, of course, a
feature of much pre-modern warfare which entailed sieges and the destruction of crops.

We have seen a selection of passages in which the term 'barbarian' is
used from the beginning until the fourth century. Is there a conclusion
to be drawn? Obviously it is used frequently as a plain term distinguishing Greeks from non-Greeks. As such it appears most often in the works
of the historians: Hekataios of Miletus, Herodotus, Thucydides, and
Xenophon, but also in the work of Aeschylus. Descent is found early on
(Alcman, Hekataios, Herodotus). Descent and geography are combined by
Hekataios of Miletos. It is frequently associated with language throughout
the period, in the works of Homer, Aeschylus, Herodotus, Thucydides, and
Xenophon. Herodotus at least once directly links language, religion, and
customs with ethnicity. Pindar links it with culture (familiarity with Greek
heroes). Dress and weapons can have barbarian characteristics according
to Aeschylus, Thucydides, and Euripides. One fragment of Heraclitus
associates it directly with mentality. Closely related is the association with
behaviour: slavish and effeminate (Aeschylus, Euripides, and Xenophon).
Morals and laws are considered essential in the works of Thucydides and
Euripides. The latter also includes sexuality and sexual customs among
aspects of barbarism. Religion and religious customs are brought out by
Herodotus and Euripides.

An essential feature appears in the later fifth century, namely a marked
tendency towards the use of the term in an imperialist ideology. As such it
is found in Euripides and Xenophon and will gain force in the fourth century in works postdating the chronological limits of this chapter.[76]

Two further points are significant: there are degrees of barbarism in
the works of Thucydides and Xenophon (and Aristophanes). Second,
Herodotus and Thucydides both see the possibility of change: barbarians
may become Greeks and the reverse may also occur, not easily, but the
former is attested in historical sources, and the latter at least mentioned as

[75] D. A. Bell, *The First Total War: Napoleon's Europe and the Birth of Warfare as We Know it* (Boston, MA 2007). Whatever happened in practice, the term *Der totale Krieg* seems first to have been used by Ludendorff.
[76] Isocrates, Plato, Aristotle are discussed in this sense in Isaac, *Invention of Racism*, 70–3, 175–81, 283–8, 299–301.

a possibility. This removes the quality of being barbarian out of the realm of descent and into the cultural and social sphere. Of course it is possible to associate a belief in descent and bloodline with mental and physical characteristics. However, when *barbaroi* can become Greeks or the reverse that no longer applies.

Can we draw clear-cut conclusions from this list? The term *barbaros* always refers to foreigners, except in a few cases of comparison, and is clearly associated with a variety of characteristics, depending on the perspective of the source. It is sometimes seen as a matter of pure bloodline, of descent. Whether or not this is the case, the accompanying qualities are many. It cannot be maintained that language is *the* central element, but neither are collective merit, behaviour, or outward appearance.[77] One feature stands out: in the course of the fifth century there are indications of increased polarization and moral disapproval. The earlier authors who celebrated the successful defence of the Greeks against the Persian invaders spoke of barbarians in terms that are different from those used by later ones. These prepared the moral and intellectual ground for the Greek counter-invasion.

Latin (Roman) Authors

Moving on to the Roman use of the term we shall see that it was used in various ways different from those found in Greek literature. The overall impression is one of relative conceptual simplicity as compared with the use of the word in Greek. It is employed, first, as indicating non-Greek, when Roman authors let Greek characters talk about foreigners. Second, in a majority of cases it indicates non-Romans, mostly referring to the enemy in conflict, in battle situations and, less frequently, to the enemy in war in a broader sense as well as in hostile diplomacy. Clearly, we find *barbari* in other contexts, but those are a minority of the sources in which the term occurs. Third, it is used frequently in the modern, negative sense of 'barbarian' as a derogatory substantive or adjective, not immediately associated with foreignness. Finally the term 'barbarian' occurs with a dual meaning, indicating both non-Roman identity as well as including a derogatory qualification in the modern sense of the word.

---

[77] Cf. the complex use of ethnic terminology in Herodotus is analysed by C. P. Jones, 'ἔθνος and γένος in Herodotus', *CQ* 46 (1996): 315–20.

Non-Greek

In specific contexts *Barbarus* can indicate non-Greeks in Roman literature. A special case is the passage in Plautus' *Captivi* where a Greek calls barbarian (sc. Italian) cities 'unpleasant'. Another early, much discussed text is given by Pliny where he cites the elder Cato:

> They [sc. Greek medical practitioners] have conspired among themselves to murder all barbarians with their medicine; a profession which they exercise for lucre, in order that they may win our confidence, and dispatch us all the more easily. They are in the common habit, too, of calling us barbarians, and stigmatize us beyond all other nations, by giving us the abominable appellation of Opici [i.e. an ancient Italic people]. I forbid you to have anything to do with physicians.[78]

Cato's letter to his son has been frequently discussed and variously interpreted.[79] It will not concern us here what it says about Roman prejudices against Greek medical practitioners. The point is that Cato twice mentions the word *barbari*, where he cites Greeks as referring to Romans. The first instance is probably meant to be ironic or cynical. When he uses the word for the second time, he is explicitly and fiercely critical of the application of the term by Greeks towards Romans

Cicero considers the division of mankind.[80] His categories are: sex, nation, country, family, age. As regards nation, the question is whether a stranger is Greek or a barbarian.

Roman authors, when dealing with Greek history or geography, use the term for non-Greeks as a matter of course.[81] Greek authors writing under Roman rule may refer to non-Greeks in a context where they deal with Greeks and others. When discussing they use the term in connection with non-Romans. Diodorus, for instance, does both, depending on the context.[82] Josephus mentions 'Hellenes and barbarians', but also calls the Sarmatians barbarians when discussing Roman frontier

---

[78] Pliny, *NH* 29.14.8 (citing Cato, writing to his son): *quandoque ista gens suas litteras dabit, omnia corrumpet, tum etiam magis, si medicos suos hoc mittet. iurarunt inter se barbaros necare omnes medicina, sed hoc ipsum mercede faciunt, ut fides iis sit et facile disperdant. nos quoque dictitant barbaros et spurcius nos quam alios Ὀπικῶν appellatione foedant. interdixi tibi de medicis.*

[79] Cf. Isaac, *Invention of Racism*, 226–8.

[80] Cicero, *Inv.* 1.35.7: *mortalium autem pars in hominum, pars in bestiarum genere numerantur. atque hominum genus et in sexu consideratur, virile an muliebre sit, et in natione, patria, cognatione, aetate. natione, Graius an barbarus; patria, Atheniensis an Lacedaemonius; cognatione, quibus maioribus, quibus consanguineis;*

[81] For instance Nepos, *Themistocles* 4.5; *Agesilaus* 3.1; Pliny, *NH* 127.3 (3).

[82] Diodorus Siculus 4.82.6: παρὰ τοῖς βαρβάροις, ἀλλὰ καὶ παρὰ τοῖς Ἕλλησι.; 38/39.21 ὁ Σπάρτακος ὁ βάρβαρος.

problems.[83] The same is true for the work of Cassius Dio.[84] In poetry, Ovid uses the term at least once for someone non-Greek, when he attributes a letter written by Briseis to Achilles which she herself is said to have described as 'written hardly in Greek with a barbarian hand'.[85]

Finally, Juvenal divides mankind into three categories: Greeks, Romans, and barbarians.[86]

Non-Roman

(a) *The Enemy in Battle*

The most frequent, regular occurrence of the term is in connection with battles where the barbarians are the non-Roman enemy. There is no need to cite examples in full. Livy probably has more instances than any other author.[87] However, it is common throughout.[88]

(b) *The Enemy in War in a Broader Sense*

This is fairly common and the term may apply to any enemy, Persians, Thracians, Spanish, and Illyrians. As in the previous category, and unlike the first, discussed above, it is not intended to be disparaging. It simply refers to a non-Roman enemy in war, or to non-Romans in the Roman army.[89]

A few examples will suffice. Cicero refers to Thracian raiders in Macedonia as *barbari*.[90] Livy calls the Illyrian king a barbarian.[91] Again, the fact that in such cases the term need not imply a value judgement is clear from Tacitus who describes a man who had commanded the royal fleet of Pontus as a barbarian slave.[92] Fronto calls the Parthian king a *barbarus*. 'A few days before Lucius of his own accord had sent a letter to Vologaesus to

---

[83] Josephus, *Ant.* 4.12: οὔτε παρ' Ἕλλησιν οὔτε παρὰ βαρβάροις; *BJ* 7.94 (Sarmatians).

[84] Dio 7.25: συμπεσόντες δὲ τοῖς βαρβάροις; 36.1b.2.1 καὶ αὐτὸν οἱ βάρβαροι τῇ τε τοξείᾳ καὶ τῇ νάφθα κατὰ τῶν μηχανῶν χεομένῃ δεινῶς ἐκάκωσαν. 38.34.6 ὁ βάρβαρος = Ariovistus.

[85] Ovid, *Heroides* 3.3.4: *Quam legis, a rapta Briseide littera venit, vix bene barbarica Graeca notata manu.*

[86] Juvenal 10.138: *Romanus Graiusque ac barbarus induperator.*

[87] E.g. Livy 23.18.2: *ubi ad moenia accessere, quia silentium erat, solitudo uisa; metuque concessum barbarus ratus moliri portas et claustra refringere parat.*

[88] *Bellum Africum* 93.1.5; *Bellum Alexandrinum* 43.2.4; Tacitus, *Ann.* 12.17; 12.29; 12.35; Ammianus 19.11.10; 19.11.13–14.

[89] Sallust, *Catilina* 19: Spanish cavalry; *Bellum Africum* 51.6.3, where *equites barbari* are non-Roman cavalry in the Roman army; also: SHA, *Max.* 7.4: *tribuni barbari.*

[90] Cicero, *De prov. cons.* 2.3.5; 2.4.

[91] Livy 43.20.4: Perseus of Macedon seeks Gentius as an ally, but his envoys *remittuntur sine mentione pecuniae, qua una barbarus inops inpelli ad bellum [non] poterat.*

[92] Tacitus, *Hist.* 3.47: [Anicetus, a freedman of Polemon of Pontus] *subita per Pontum arma barbarum mancipium, regiae quondam classis praefectus, moverat.*

put an end to the war by agreement, if he would; but the barbarian, while he spurned the offer of peace, paid dearly for it.'[93] In the fourth century the Historia Augusta states in a much discussed passage: 'In this period and frequently on other occasions in numerous regions where the barbarians are kept out not by rivers but by *limites*, Hadrian kept them apart by high stakes dug deep into the ground … so as to form a palisade.'[94]

(c)   Foreigners in a Civilian, Non-Military Context

Of course there are references to non-Romans in a context other than battle or warfare. They are not very numerous however, and relatively late. Tacitus says of Vonones, the new Parthian king: 'The barbarians [i.e. the Parthians], too, welcomed him with rejoicing, as is usual with new rulers'.[95] In Tacitus' facetious description of the Frisian envoys to Rome in AD 58 they are called *barbari*.[96] There is no hostility in these passages. In this connection we may note the use of *barbaricum* and *barbaria* for non-Roman territory.[97]

A special case that may be mentioned is that of the Isauri who are described in the Historia Augusta as having reverted to the status of barbarians because they were (no longer) Romans. They were barbarians again because they successfully excluded themselves from Roman authority.[98] A special case of poetic fancy is when Ovid calls himself a barbarian because, at Tomi, nobody understands him: 'the barbarians … they speak their own language and I have to express myself with gestures. I am the barbarian here, for nobody understands me.'[99]

---

[93] Fronto, *Princ.* 2.14.12: *Paucis ante diebus L<uciu>s ad Vologaesum litteras ultro dederat, bellum, si vellet, condicionibus poneret; dum oblatam pacem spernit barbarus, male mulcatus est.* Cf. *Princ.* 2.14.14: 2.16, 'the barbarians' had a high regard for Lucius Verus' justice and clemency.

[94] SHA, *Hadrian* 12.6: *per ea tempora et alias frequenter in p<l>urimis locis, in quibus barbari non fluminibus sed limitibus dividuntur, stipitibus magnis i<n> modum muralis saepis funditus iactis atque conexis barbaros separavit.*

[95] Tac. *Ann.* 2.2: *barbari laetantes, ut ferme ad nova imperia.*

[96] *Ann.* 13.54.13: *profectique Romam dum aliis curis intentum Neronem opperiuntur, inter ea quae barbaris ostentantur intravere Pompei theatrum,* See also various instances in the Historia Augusta: SHA, *Pius* 5.4.3; *Marcus Antoninus* 14.1; *Avidius Cassius* 4.9.2; *Severus Alexander* 45.2–3; 48.3; *Max.* 12.1; 62.2; 5; *Gord.* 14.1; *Gall.* 4.6; 13.7.

[97] E.g. Ovid, *Tr.* 3.1.18; 3.3.46: *barbara terra*; 3.11.7; 4.4.86; 5.2.31: *barbara tellus*; Ovid, *Pont.* 3.1.5: *barbaria*; SHA, *Severus Alexander* 47.1; *Max.* 10.2; 12.1: *barbaricum*; *Tyr. Trig.* 5.4: *in solo barbarico*; *Severus Alexander* 58.5: *barbaria.*

[98] SHA, *Tir. Tryg.* 26: *denique post Trebellianum pro barbaris habentur; et<eni>m in medio Romani nominis solo regio eorum novo genere custodiarum quasi limes includitur, locis defensa, non <h>om<i>nibus.* Note, however, the different phrasing in *Probus* 16.5, where mention is made of 'the barbarians who live among the Isauri'.

[99] Ovid, *Pont.* 10.27–38: … *exercent illi sociae commercia linguae: / per gestum res est significanda mihi. barbarus hic ego sum, qui non intellegor ulli.*

Barbarian in the Negative Sense of the Word –
Close to Modern English Usage

It is found several times already in the work of Plautus (ca. 254–184 BC), not in any clear-cut single meaning, but invariably negative.[100] It can indicate ignorance: 'O Lydus, why, what a barbarian you are, you, whom I had deemed to be far wiser than Thales himself. Go to, you are more foolish than Potitius, the barbarian, who, at an age so advanced, knew not the names of the Divinities.'[101] It may be used in the sphere of the old stereotype of decadent Orientals, eating too much.[102] Barbarian cities are disagreeable.[103]

While this chapter does not aim to give a full survey of the occurrence of the word, let alone provide reliable statistics, it is immediately clear that one of the most prolific suppliers of 'barbarian' in a multitude of negative passages is Cicero – particularly, but not exclusively, in his judicial rhetoric. It will suffice here to give a number of examples.

> [Unnecessarily cruel:] What bandit was ever so wicked, what pirate was ever so barbarous, as to prefer stripping off his spoils from his victim stained with his blood, which he might possess his plunder unstained, without blood?[104]
>
> [Ignorant:] But there is a word written in those documents, which that barbarian and profligate man never noticed, and would not have understood if he had.[105]
>
> [Impious:] There is a temple of Minerva in the island, of which I have already spoken, which Marcellus did not touch, which he left full of its treasures and ornaments, but which was so stripped and plundered by Verres, that it seems to have been in the hands, not of any enemy, – for enemies, even in war, respect the rites of religion, and the customs of the country, – but of some barbarian pirates.[106]

---

[100] *Captivi* 3.1 (32): *barbarica lege*, the meaning is disputed.

[101] Plautus, *Bacchides* 1, 2, 15 (trans. Riley): *An non putasti esse umquam? o Lyde, es barbarus; quem ego sapere nimio censui plus quam Thalem, is stultior es barbaro poticio, qui tantus natu deorum nescis nomina.*

[102] *Casina* 3.1 (32) (trans. Riley): *nil moror barbarico ritu esse* 'I want to have a charming meal. I really don't care, now, to be eating in the style of your sumptuous foreigners.'

[103] *Captivi* 4.2 (104): *barbaricas urbes* said to be *asperae* (unpleasant). As noted above, this is a rare case where a Greek is cited as referring to Rome or Italy in those terms.

[104] *S. Rosc.* 146.8 (trans. C. D. Yonge): *Quis umquam praedo fuit tam nefarius, quis pirata tam barbarus ut, cum integram praedam sine sanguine habere posset, cruenta spolia detrahere mallet?* Also: *Dom.* 140.8; *Flac.* 24.9; *Cat.* 3.25.11.

[105] *Verr.* 2.5.148.7 (trans. Yonge): *Sed scriptum exstat in isdem litteris quod iste homo barbarus ac dissolutus neque attendere umquam neque intellegere potuit.* Also: *Phil.* 3.15.1.

[106] *Verr.* 2.4.122 (trans. Yonge): *Aedis Minervae est in Insula, de qua ante dixi; quam Marcellus non attigit, quam plenam atque ornatam reliquit; quae ab isto sic spoliata atque direpta est non ut ab hoste*

Cicero also uses it to indicate a combination of undesirable characteristics:

> Him [sc. Apronius] did Verres employ as his chief agent in all his adulter-
> ies, in all his plundering of temples, in all his debauched banquets; and the
> similarity of their manners caused such a friendship and unanimity between
> them, that Apronius, whom everyone else thought a boor and a barbarian,
> appeared to him alone an agreeable and an accomplished man;[107]

Ovid, having struck his beloved, Corinna, exclaims: 'Who will not say
"madman, barbarian!" to me?'[108] However, on another occasion she, herself
is a *barbara*.[109]

Another author who easily provides examples of foreigners described in
negative terms is Tacitus. Thus he attributes a speech to Severus Caecina in
the Senate against the presence of spouses of Roman officials on duty in the
provinces: 'A train of women involves delays through luxury in peace and
through panic in war, and converts a Roman army on the march into the
likeness of a barbarian progress.'[110] The assumption is that foreign, or more
precisely, Eastern rulers always are accompanied by a train of women and serv-
ants. Whatever Caecina may have said, the stereotype of Eastern luxury and
lack of moderation is familiar, like that of immoderate banqueting by decadent Orientals, used by Plautus above. In a much later passage Tacitus praises
Seleucia on the Tigris which, in spite of the fact that it was under Parthian rule,
remained 'a powerful and fortified city which had not lapsed into barbarism,
but had clung loyally to its founder Seleucus'.[111] Tacitus implies that oriental
rule corrupts and causes degeneration – aspects, he feels, of barbarism.

Barbarian in a Combined Sense: Both Non-Roman
and Derogatory as in Modern Usage

As might be expected, Cicero provides a good number of instances. Callanus,
the Indian philosopher whom Alexander met was 'an untutored barbarian,
born at the foot of the Hindu Kush'.[112] Gauls who attacked Fonteius were 'a

---

aliquo, qui tamen in bello religionem et consuetudinis iura retineret, sed ut a barbaris praedonibus
vexata esse videatur.

[107] Verr. 2.3.23.10: tantamque habet morum similitudo coniunctionem atque concordiam ut Apronius, qui
aliis inhumanus ac barbarus, isti uni commodus ac disertus videretur;

[108] Ovid, Amores 1.7.19: Quis mihi non 'demens!' quis non mihi 'barbare!' dixit?

[109] Amores 3.1.48: quid, cum me munus natali mittis, at illa rumpit et adposita barbara mersat aqua?

[110] Tac. Ann. 3.33 (trans. M. Hadas): inesse mulierum mulierum comitatui quae pacem luxu, bellum
formidine morentur et Romanum agmen ad simillitudinem barbari incessus convertant.

[111] Ann. 6.42: [Seleucia] civitas potens saepta muris neque in barbarum corrupta, sed conditoris Seleuci
retinens

[112] Tusc. 2.22.52: Callanus Indus, indoctus ac barbarus, in radicibus Caucasi natus.

savage and intolerable band of barbarians'.[113] Especially telling is the following passage which deserves being quoted in full:

> Did you [Verres] dare to take away out of Enna the statue of Ceres? Did you attempt at Enna to wrench Victory out of the hand of Ceres? To tear one goddess from the other? – nothing of which those men dared to violate, or even to touch, whose qualities were all more akin to wickedness than to religion. For while Publius Popillius and Publius Rupilius were consuls, slaves, runaway slaves, and barbarians, and enemies, were in possession of that place; but yet the slaves were not so much slaves to their own masters, as you are to your passions; nor did the runaways flee from their masters as far as you flee from all laws and from all right; nor were the barbarians as barbarous in language and in descent as you were in your nature and your habits; nor were the enemies as much enemies to men as you are to the immortal gods. How, then, can a man beg for any mercy who has surpassed slaves in baseness, runaway slaves in rashness, barbarians in wickedness, and enemies in cruelty?[114]

To sum up: in this text barbarians are barbarous in language and by descent, they are wicked and cruel.

Livy is another author well represented. In 205 Scipio seeks to gain Syphax, a Carthaginian ally, as ally for Rome. 'At that time the king had a treaty with the Carthaginians; and Scipio, thinking it would have for Syphax no more weight and sanctity than is usual for barbarians, with whom loyalty depends upon success, sent Gaius Laelius as an envoy to him with gifts.' He was successful, of course.[115] According to Frontinus: 'When Ventidius was waging war against the Parthian king Pacorus ... he turned the treachery of the barbarian to his own advantage...'[116] Next: Tacitus. During the Revolt of Boudicca, the rebels stormed Camulodunum and: 'In their rage and their triumph they spared no variety of a barbarian's cruelty.'[117] In the *Germania* the Sennones are described as having publicly

---

[113] Cic. *Font.* 20.44: *Video, iudices; sed multis et firmis praesidiis vobis adiutoribus isti immani atque intolerandae barbariae resistemus.*

[114] *Verr.* 2.4.112.6 (trans. Yonge): *Tenuerunt enim P. Popilio P. Rupilio consulibus illum locum servi, fugitivi, barbari, hostes; sed neque tam servi illi dominorum quam tu libidinum, neque tam fugitivi illi ab dominis quam tu ab iure et ab legibus, neque tam barbari lingua et natione illi quam tu natura et moribus, neque tam illi hostes hominibus quam tu dis immortalibus. Quae deprecatio est igitur ei reliqua qui indignitate servos, temeritate fugitivos, scelere barbaros, crudelitate hostes vicerit?*

[115] Livy 28.17: *foedus ea tempestate regi cum Carthaginiensibus erat, quod haud grauius ei sanctiusque quam uolgo barbaris, quibus ex fortuna pendet fides.* See also 27.17.9; 28.18.6.

[116] Frontinus, *Stratagemata* 1.1.6: *Ventidius Parthico bello adversus Pacorum regem ... perfidiam barbari ad utilitates suas convertit.* Tacitus too claims that perfidy and treacherousness are characteristic of barbarians: Tac. *Hist.* 3.48.5.

[117] Tac. *Agr.* 16: *expugnatis praesidiis ipsam coloniam invasere ut sedem servitutis, nec ullum in barbaris [ingeniis] saevitiae genus omisit ira et victoria.*

slaughtered a human victim, as they celebrate the horrible beginning of their barbarous rite.[118] Barbarians lack interest and curiosity in natural phenomena[119] and are ignorant of military engines and the skilful management of sieges, contrary to the Romans.[120] In fact, in their view any kind of action and courage is better than sound planning and caution: 'With barbarians, indecision is a slave's weakness, prompt action king-like', he comments, when telling of Tiberius' diplomacy and the Parthians.[121] In the Historia Augusta Maximinus Thrax is a fine target for comments on barbarians. He was a 'half barbarian and scarcely yet master of the Latin tongue, speaking almost pure Thracian'.[122] Severus saw him 'rioting in his barbarian way among the crowd'.[123]

Particularly prolific in this sphere is Ovid, already mentioned, who uses the term 'Barbarus' and derivatives at least seventy-three times, more than half of them concerning his banishment to the Black Sea, to Tomi which he describes as more of a Thracian environment than a Greek one. 'Who would believe there are Greek cities among the place-names of the inhuman barbarians'?[124] Tomi is inhabited by a 'barbarian crowd, mixed with Greeks (which) frightens us, for they live with us without separation, the barbarians'.[125] He lives a life of barbarian shackles,[126] 'in *Barbaria*',[127] where they speak a barbarian language.[128]

Conclusions

The essence of what is seen as barbarism shifts over time as a consequence of changes in self-perception.

The term 'barbarian' originated in Greek and, in modern English, it has, almost three thousand years after it is first attested, a fairly straightforward meaning: it indicates a rude, wild, uncivilized person; an uncultured

---

[118] Tac. *Germ.* 39.2: *caesoque publice homine celebrant barbari ritus horrenda primordia.*

[119] *Germ.* 45.5.

[120] *Ann.* 12.45: *nihil tam ignarum barbaris quam machinamenta et astus oppugnationum: at nobis ea pars militiae maxime gnara est.*

[121] Tac. *Ann.* 6.32: *et barbaris cunctatio servilis, statim exequi regium videtur;* see also for similar pronouncements: 1.57, 1.68.

[122] SHA, *Maximini* 2.5: *semibarbarus et vix adhuc Latinae linguae, prope Thraecica.*

[123] SHA, *Maximini* 3.2: *in turba exultantem more barbarico.* See also 12.3; 12.8–9.

[124] *Tr.* 3.9.2: *Hic quoque sunt igitur Graiae -quis crederet?- urbes inter inhumanae nomina barbariae.*

[125] *Tr.* 5.10.27: *... et tamen intus mixta facit Graecis barbara turba metum. quippe simul nobis habitat discrimine nullo barbarus ...* See also above, p. 214.

[126] *Tr.* 2.1.206: *barbara vincla.*

[127] *Tr.* 3.10.4: *me sciat in media vivere barbaria.*

[128] *Tr.* 5.2.67.

person; as an adjective it refers to someone who is uncivilized, rude, savage, barbarous, the opposite of being British. This is therefore usually, but not necessarily, applied to foreigners. It is quite common to call a compatriot 'barbarian', suggesting that she or he behaves like a foreigner.

In Greek and Roman texts, we have seen there are important differences and shades of meaning to be detected over time. In Greek literature the word almost always refers to foreigners, hardly ever to Greeks, except for the sake of comparison. In ancient Greek texts the determining factors of being Greek are complex and, as a consequence, the same is true for being barbarian: language is one of them, but by no means the only one or the most important one, as claimed very often. Significant in this respect is the fact that it was recognized that one can change one's language. However, no less important are: geographic origin, descent, religion and citizenship. Here too the possibility of change was acknowledged, in the case of religion and citizenship, but others are fixed and cannot be changed. The accompanying characteristics are many and are closely connected with varying and developing attitudes towards group identity: the essence may be a combination of factors: customs, morals, behaviour (effeminacy), basic culture, and external appearance (dress). Towards the end of the fifth century there is a clear and strong shift towards negative judgement and moral disapproval. Then, in the course of the fourth century ideology becomes a dominant force: foreigners are regarded as slaves by nature, cruel, murderous, and sexually uninhibited. This is part of a pattern that developed in tandem with the surge of Greek imperialism.

By contrast, in Latin literature it is easier to distinguish clear-cut patterns. The determining characteristics, complex in Greece, are straightforward for Romans. Since there was no argument about what it was to be a Roman, it was obvious who was not a Roman, i.e. a barbarian. The term may refer to non-Greeks in texts dealing with Greeks, or citing Greeks, or to non-Romans, but also, as in modern English, in a derogatory sense, to Romans themselves. In Roman texts there is no doubt or question as to what makes someone a Greek or non-Greek, a Roman or non-Roman. As a consequence of conquest, empire and the systematic grants of citizenship, there never was any doubt that it was possible for a barbarian to become a Roman.[129] *Barbari* is the usual term for non-Romans in passages associated

---

[129] So far nobody has written a book *Becoming Greek*, while there is a well-known monograph by Greg Woolf, *Becoming Roman: The Origins of Provincial Civilization in Gaul* (Cambridge, 1998). See now Woolf's recent discussion 'Saving the Barbarian', in Gruen, *Cultural Identity in the Ancient Mediterranean* (Los Angeles, 2011), 255–71, with special emphasis on Ammianus' ethnography of the Gauls.

with battle or warfare. In such a context it may be used without any negative or derogatory associations. However, negative qualities are predominant in non-military contexts where the word often indicates untutored
savages, people barbarous in language and by descent. Generalizations are
common: foreigners are naturally wicked; loyalty for them depends upon
success; they are treacherous, and impious. Their rites are immoral and
bloody; they are ignorant and lack intellectual curiosity, discipline, and
inhibition. They are unnecessarily cruel. The shift from Greece to Rome
is obvious: both cultures deny the barbarian the qualities which they
themselves regard as essential. In the case of the Romans among the most
important of those are: loyalty, honesty, piety, and discipline. Finally: the
negative characteristics are also, not infrequently, applied to Romans, as
in modern English, where a barbarian could be a compatriot regarded as
resembling an uncivilized foreigner.

CHAPTER 10

Romans and Nomads in the Fourth Century

The fourth-century Latin, non-Christian literature contains numerous value-judgements regarding foreigners and provincials. A great variety of negative descriptions, many of them recurring stereotypes, is found there. That much is obvious to everybody who reads the texts. Clear also is that this reflects an increased intensity of warfare with foreign peoples as compared with previous centuries. There may be less agreement on the background of – and overall attitude reflected by – those views. The argument of the present chapter is that the various forms of stereotypes and patterns of prejudice which can be found in the Greek and Roman literature of this period form a coherent ideology, dividing groups of people into fixed categories of superior and inferior levels. I shall argue that we can detect here a systematic approach that is best described as an early form of racism.[1] The following topics will be discussed:

(1) Attitudes towards provincials. These are to be divided into (a) urbanized and settled peoples and (b) nomads.
(2) Attitudes towards foreigners living outside the Roman Empire, again including settled peoples and nomads.

The focus here will be on the non-urbanized provincials and on outsiders, notably nomads.[2] To be considered in particular are the common stereotypes encountered towards all these peoples – an attempt is made to

---

[1] This is a continuation of the discussion in B. Isaac, *The Invention of Racism in Classical Antiquity* (Princeton, 2004) where neither the fourth-century sources nor attitudes towards nomads are taken into account in any systematic manner. It is a modified and expanded version of the following article: 'Ammianus on Foreigners', in M. Kahlos (ed.), *The Faces of the Other: Religious and Ethnic Encounters in the Later Roman World* (Turnhout, 2011), 237–58.

[2] To be excluded here is the origins of the Parthians as nomadic horsemen for which see Isaac, *Invention of Racism*, 371–80; S. R. Hauser, 'Die ewigen Nomaden? Bemerkungen zu Herkunft, Militär, Staatsaufbau und nomadischen Traditionen der Arsakiden', in B. Meissner, O. Schmitt, and M. Sommer (eds.), *Krieg – Gesellschaft – Institutionen: Beiträge zu einer vergleichenden Kriegsgeschichte* (Berlin, 2005), 163–203. By the time the Romans faced the Arsacids they were not seen as nomads.

determine whether these should be regarded as simple ethnic stereotypes, as a set of vague forms of prejudice, or rather as part of an ideology, that is, as expressions of early, pre-modern racist attitudes.[3]

The author supplying most of our evidence is Ammianus Marcellinus.[4] Other contemporary works such as the *Expositio Totius Mundi* will be occasionally mentioned.[5] It must be emphasized that the collection of sources discussed here is by no means complete. I have selected passages that I considered relevant and make no claim to have done more than that.

The Roman Empire

We may begin with some thoughts of Ammianus (14.6.3) comparing the stages of the existence of Rome with those of an individual:

(1) From the cradle to the end of childhood are Rome's first three hundred years; wars were fought in the vicinity of the city.
(2) During the second stage, youth and manhood, triumphs were celebrated all over the world.
(3) The third stage is adult life: during the Late Republic Rome crossed the Alps and the sea.
(4) The fourth stage, in which Ammianus himself lived, is old age, victories were celebrated in name alone; Rome enjoyed a quiet existence.

---

[3] Note the broad view, from a different perspective, published by P. Heather, 'The Barbarian in Late Antiquity: Image, Reality and Transformation', in R. Miles (ed.), *Constructing Identities in Late Antiquity* (London, 1999), 235–58. Heather here shows the importance of texts in the development of a dominant ideology concerning *Romanitas* and foreigners in the fourth and fifth centuries. Two essential studies on the subject have been published by B. D. Shaw, ' "Eaters of Flesh, Drinkers of Milk": The Ancient Mediterranean Ideology of the Pastoral Nomad', *Ancient Society* 13/14 (1982–3): 3–52, reprinted in Shaw, *Environment and Society in Roman North Africa: Studies in History and Archaeology* (Aldershot, 1995); and: 'Fear and Loathing: the Nomad Menace and Roman Africa', in C. M. Wells (ed.), *Roman Africa /L'Afrique romaine: The 1980 Governor-General Vaniers Lectures, Revue de l'Université d'Ottawa* 52 (Ottawa, 1982), 25–46, reprinted in Shaw, *Rulers, Nomads, and Christians in Roman North Africa* (Aldershot, 1995). Note also the lucid remarks by P. Trousset, 'Signification d'une frontière: Nomades et sedentaires dans la zone du limes d'Afrique', in W. S. Hanson and L. J. F. Keppie (eds.), *Roman Frontier Studies 1979: Papers Presented to the 12th International Congress of Roman Frontier Studies* (Oxford, 1980), III, 931–43. The broadest treatment of these issues in historical perspective is the monumental work by P. Horden and N. Purcess, *The Corrupting Sea: A Study of Mediterranean History* (Oxford, 2000). See the review article by G. Algazi, *Mediterranean Historical Review* 20 (2005), 227–45. For nomads in Mesopotamia in an earlier period: J. S. Castillo (ed.), *Nomads and Sedentary Peoples* (Mexico, 1981).

[4] See J. Matthews, *The Roman Empire of Ammianus* (Baltimore and London, 1989), ch. 14: Barbarians and Bandits.

[5] The Historia Augusta is discussed rather extensively in the work cited in n. 1 and it would be repetitive to return to this text here.

The equation of a state with an individual is a common pattern of thought, as is the opposite: the assumption that an individual necessarily has all the collective characteristics of the group to which he belongs. Both ideas confuse the individual and the group, deny the individual his individuality and the group its diversity. There is a second aspect to Ammianus' approach worth observing here, namely the certainty that the progress of time can only bring deterioration, not improvement.[6] Thus he cites Cato the Censor as a model of virtue (14.6.8) and idealizes the Republic with its simple soldiers as opposed to the decadent present. These are common patterns of thought in antiquity and part of a complex of ideas which must be kept in mind if we want to understand ancient attitudes towards other peoples and foreigners.

Romans and Greeks

Next we shall do well to see how, in the fourth century, one of the old and complex issues of relationships within the Empire is expressed, namely the status of Greeks among the Latin-speaking Romans.[7] From the second century BC onwards this was ambivalent or negative, even if there was admiration for the Greeks in their classical period. Ammianus gives us a glimpse of the sort of friction that existed in the fourth century. The Emperor Julian emphatically saw himself as Greek, or rather, as Thracian by origin and Greek by culture.[8] When, as Caesar, he was campaigning in Gaul, generally with success, there came a point where his soldiers went hungry. The mutinous troops then called him 'an Asiatic, a Greekling, a deceiver, and a fool with a show of wisdom'.[9] The level of Julian's Gallic soldiers is depicted as remarkably low. At one point they are described as 'wild animals in cages'.[10] However, Julian was disparaged in similar terms not only at that level. At court he was called 'a nanny-goat and no man, insufferable with his victories, hairy, a chattering mole and an ape in purple, and a Greekish pedant'.[11] Clearly, then, a Greek-speaking

---

[6] More on this above, Chapter 4.

[7] See Isaac, *Invention of Racism*, ch. 9 for the attitudes from the second century BC onwards.

[8] Julian, *Misopogon* 40. Cf. Isaac, *Invention of Racism*, 402.

[9] 17.9.3: *Iulianum, Asianum, Graeculum, fallacem specie sapientiae, stolidam.* Cf. P. de Jonge, *Philological and Historical Commentary on Ammianus Marcellinus XVII* (Groningen, 1976), 237. The expression 'Asianus' usually refers to a style of rhetoric, but here clearly is meant to describe Julian's entire personality and style.

[10] 19.6.3–4: *utque dentatae in caveis bestiae.*

[11] 17.11.1: *In odium venit cum victoriis suis capella, non homo, ut hirsutum Iulianum carpentes, appellantesque 'loquacem talpam' et 'purpuratam simiam' et 'litterionem Graecum' et his congruentia plurima.*

emperor, even one whose Latin was good,[12] but one who identified with Greek culture and society, could evoke a traditional mixture of negative associations: dishonesty, intellectual pretence, pedantry, and lack of masculinity.[13]

Ammianus himself had a positive attitude towards Greek language and culture, for instance, speaking of the historian Timagenes, he calls him 'a true Greek in accuracy as well as language'.[14] He also greatly admired Julian and, even if he saw him as Greek in culture, he paradoxically regarded him also as a model of the traditional, old-fashioned Roman virtue, which Ammianus cherished. Thus, in 16.1, he compares him with the best emperors: Titus, Trajan, Antoninus Pius, and Marcus Aurelius. He explains in a lengthy eulogy (16.5) that Julian practised the old Republican virtues of frugality and sobriety. He was a philosopher and intellectual, passed his days in brilliant and witty conversation, had mastered rhetoric, knew Latin well enough, thoroughly prepared for battle, and instituted reforms in civil administration. The implication of all this is that in Ammianus' eyes Julian combined the best qualities of both the ancient Romans and the Greeks. This is not an ideal encountered in earlier centuries, but quite understandable if we find it in the works of a Latin-writing historian from the eastern part of the Empire. One of the few characters who forms the subject of even more paradoxical praise is Eutherius, the chief chamberlain, a eunuch, but – here is the paradox – a model of loyalty and virtue, who criticized even Julian as 'having been raised in the manners of Asia',[15] embodying a quite negative complex of characteristics which is in general regarded as typical precisely of eunuchs.

The examples of attitudes towards various groups of provincials and foreigners found in Ammianus and other contemporary Latin authors are consistent. There is tension between East and West, Greek and Latin, expressed sometimes in very strong language, but this is cultural and social hostility, significant, but not racist.

Cf. de Jonge, *Commentary ... XVII*, 266–7. *Capella*, a kid or young goat, and *hirsutus* refer to Julian's philosopher's beard.

[12] Ammianus 16.5.8: *Super his aderat Latine quoque disserendi sufficiens sermo*; Libanius, *Or.* 12.92. Cf. de Jonge, *Philological and Historical Commentary on Ammianus Marcellinus XVI* (Groningen, 1972), 34–5.

[13] In the sixth century Justinian's soldiers are accused of being 'Greeks' to the dissatisfaction of Procopius, *Anecdota* 24.7.

[14] 15.9.1: *et diligentia Graecus et lingua*. Cf. P. de Jonge, *Philological and Historical Commentary on Ammianus Marcellinus XV, 6–13* (Groningen, 1953), 49.

[15] 16.6: *Asiaticis coalitum moribus*. Cf. de Jonge, *Commentary ... XVI*, 67.

The Provinces: Gauls

The next topic: Ammianus describes a number of provincial peoples in anachronistic terms, as if there had been no change at all from the moment of their final absorption into the Empire. There is no obvious explanation for this, except to say that those peoples were seen as having lost their identity and place in history once they became Roman provincials.

The first to be mentioned here are the Gauls as described in an excursus (15.9.1–8; 12). It opens with a reference to his sources, Timagenes being the most recent, a Greek author of the first century BC. The entire treatment has been made to look as if it was written about the time of Caesar's conquest and annexation of Transalpine Gaul. The social reality is depicted in terms of the stereotypes of that period: thus the Belgae had the reputation of being the most valiant, because they were far removed from civilized life and not been made effeminate by imported luxuries, an observation obviously copied from Caesar himself.[16] The Aquitanians in the south, on the contrary, had their characters weakened to effeminacy because of their proximity to Rome, the deteriorating effect of which was also asserted by Caesar himself. Thus they easily came under the sway of Rome (15.11.4–5).

Then there is the next chapter, 15.12, on the manners and customs of the Gauls which is difficult to see as anything other than satire:

> Almost all the Gauls are of tall stature, fair and ruddy, terrible for the fierceness of their eyes, fond of quarrelling, and of overbearing insolence. In fact, a whole band of foreigners will be unable to cope with one of them in a fight, if he call in his wife, stronger than he by far and with flashing eyes; least of all when she swells her neck and gnashes her teeth, and posing her huge white arms, proceeds to rain punches mingled with kicks, like shots, discharged by the twisted cords of a catapult.[17]

This might have come straight from an Asterix album. It is, in fact, an embellishment of a similar statement in an earlier text, predating Caesar's conquest: 'The women of the Gauls are not only like the men in their great stature, but they are a match for them in courage as well.'[18] This reflects

---

[16] For my views on Caesar's opinions expressed in *BG* 1.1; 2.4; 2.15.4: Isaac, *Invention of Racism*, 415.

[17] 15.12.1: *Celsioris staturae et candidi paene Galli sunt omnes et rutili luminum que toruitate terribiles, auidi iurgiorum et sublatius insolentes. | nec enim eorum quemquam adhibita uxore rixantem multo se fortiore et glauca peregrinorum ferre poterit globus tum maxime, cum illa inflata ceruice suffrendens ponderans que niueas ulnas et uastas | admixtis calcibus emittere coeperit pugnos ut catapultas tortilibus neruis excussas.*

[18] Diodorus 5.32.2: αἱ δὲ γυναῖκες τῶν Γαλατῶν οὐ μόνον τοῖς μεγέθεσι παραπλήσιοι τοῖς ἀνδράσιν εἰσίν, ἀλλὰ καὶ ταῖς ἀλκαῖς ἐνάμιλλοι.

common attitudes towards what the Romans called barbarians: as so often in Greek and Latin literature, the male and female roles are reversed – such as in Egypt – which is characteristic of their perversity.

There is no objective reason for such anachronisms.[19] The *Expositio Totius Mundi*, written in what was roughly Ammianus' age, gives a brief but fully up-to-date description of Gaul.[20]

Arabia

The treatment of the Eastern Provinces of the Empire (14.8) again does not refer to anything that happened after the end of the first century AD, except the section about Arabia which mentions the annexation by Trajan (14.8.3). On the whole, one gets the impression that Ammianus places himself normally at the time of the annexation in such excurses, as if development and history stop at that point. A people loses its independent history once it is part of the Empire. All of the subsequent developments, which we call Romanization, acculturation, urbanization, and so on, and which we regard as serious topics for investigation, are in fact ignored. In other words, whatever happened to the Gauls and some of the peoples of the Near East between the mid-first century BC and the mid-fourth century AD has not affected the stereotypes attached to them. These seem to be frozen at the moment of incorporation into the Empire.

Persians

Turning now to Rome's neighbours, the first to be mentioned here are the Persians, the only major empire neighbouring Rome. During the early Empire the Parthians appear in the sources as redoubtable but distant enemies. We encounter stereotypes, but not those typically attached to other Eastern peoples. There is no obvious pattern of ethnic prejudice, let alone racism.[21] This changed drastically over the centuries. In the literature of the

---

[19] T. Mommsen, 'Ammians Geographica', *Hermes* 16 (1881): 602–36 = *Ges. Schr.* 7.393–425 at 395–7, already notes the schematic character of Ammianus' provincial excurses. See now Greg Woolf's recent discussion 'Saving the Barbarian', in Gruen, *Cultural Identity in the Ancient Mediterranean* (Los Angeles, 2011), 255–71, with special emphasis on Ammianus' ethnography of the Gauls. Woolf's paper became accessible to me only after I wrote the present chapter.

[20] *Expositio totius mundi et gentium* 58 (ed. Rougé). It mentions the imperial residence at Trier, a large city, and Arles. 'The entire region has valiant and noble men, which is why they say that the army of the Gauls is in time of war very numerous and brave. It is in every respect an admirable province.'

[21] For the Persians in Greek and Roman sources, see Isaac, *Invention of Racism*, ch. 8. Ammianus has an extensive description of the Persian kingdom: 23.6.

Byzantine period we encounter attitudes of far greater hostility towards Persia than was apparent in earlier centuries.[22] This is true especially for sixth-century authors such as Agathias in his excursus on Persian religion and Procopius: the Persians were considered perverted. They did not bury their dead properly, they exposed the sick instead of allowing them to recover. They practised consanguineous marriage and incest. They were incapable of understanding or producing genuine philosophy.[23] From the fourth century we have at least one text worth mentioning here, because it might indicate a transition from the earlier to the later attitudes. This is the *Expositio*, which describes the Persians briefly, combining stereotypes in a manner somewhat unusual as compared with earlier sources. The text asserts that they are remarkable in everything that is bad, but courageous in war. Then they say that the Persians commit great impieties: they ignore the dignity of nature and, like dumb animals, sleep with their mothers and sisters. They act in a manner without piety towards the god who made them. On the other hand, it is said that they have everything in abundance; since they allow commercial relations with the peoples who are their neighbours.[24]

The text admits that the Persians are courageous in war and prosperous in peace because of sensible trade policies. There is no precedent for this in earlier texts concerning the Parthians. Thereafter, however, follows the common fare, which was missing in earlier sources on the Parthians, but forms the staple of hostile prejudice against foreigners in general: the denial of regular morals, sexual and religious: like other foreigners they are like animals.

Nomads

First and for the record, there is a well-known fact to be noted. The Greeks and Romans thoroughly misunderstood the essence of pastoral nomadism. Pastoral nomads, who depend on domesticated livestock, migrate in an established territory to find pasturage for their animals. Most groups

---

[22] See B. Isaac, *The Near East under Roman Rule: Selected Papers* (Leiden, 1998), 439–41; A. Chauvot, *Opinions romaines face aux barbares au iv* siècle ap. J.-C. (Paris, 1998), 32–4, 45, 109–10.

[23] For Agathias: A. Cameron, 'Agathias on the Sassanians', *Dumbarton Oaks Papers* 23–4 (1969–70), 67–183, at 78–80 with comments on 90–1.

[24] *Expositio* 19–20 (Rougé): *Post hos sunt Persae, Romanis propinquantes, qui historiantur valde in malis omnibus … et <in> bellis esse fortes. Et impietates ab eis magnas agi dicunt: non cognoscentes naturae dignitatem, sicuti multa animalia, matribus et sororibus condormiunt. Et impie faciunt in illum qui fecit eos deum. Alias autem abundare dicuntur in omnibus; data enim <potestate negotii gentibus adpropinquantiubs suae regionis, ad eos omnia> abundare videntur.*

have fixed sites that they occupy for considerable periods of the year. Some pastoralists depend entirely on their herds; others also hunt or gather, practise some agriculture, or trade with agricultural peoples for grain and other goods. The Greek and Roman literature gives a different view of such societies. This is the next topic to be considered here.

The sense of timelessness encountered above is not found in the excurses on less settled peoples who were pastoral nomads in the past, and still lived in this manner when Ammianus wrote. This is true for the Saracens, 'whom we never found desirable either as friends or as enemies, ranging up and down the country, and who in a brief space of time laid waste whatever they could find, like rapacious kites which, whenever they have caught sight of any prey from on high, seize it with swift swoop, and directly they have seized it make off'.[25] They are nomads, i.e. homeless wanderers. Note the animal comparison which we encountered also in the case of Julian's Gallic soldiers. Ammianus describes the Saracens as an egalitarian society of warriors, 'half-nude, clad in dyed cloaks as far as the loins'.[26] Nudity is a sign of inferior culture; half nudity represents an intermediate level. Nomadism means to Ammianus, as it does to other Roman authors, a life without agriculture or cultivation, people 'roving continually over wide and extensive tracts without a home, without fixed abodes or laws'.[27] Homeless wandering has a long history of stigmatization, best known from the legends concerning the Wandering Jew[28] and the Flying Dutchman. The gypsies have been focus of discrimination and racism for centuries.[29] Their marriages are a temporary, commercial transaction.[30] Nomadic existence is the ultimate form of unstructured, unproductive, and immoral life, the opposite of *polis* and Empire. Elsewhere Ammianus gives a remarkable example of the sort of image the Saracens

---

[25] 14.4.1: *Saraceni, tamen nec amici nobis umquam nec hostes optandi, ultro citroque discursantes, quicquid inveniri poterat momento temporis parvi pastabant, milvorum rapacium similes, qui si praedam dispexerint celsius, volatu rapiunt celeri, ac si imptraverint, non immorantur.* Cf. Matthews, *Roman Empire of Ammianus*, 342–5.

[26] 14.4.3: *omnes pari sorte sunt bellatores, seminudi coloratis sagulis pube tenus amicti …*

[27] 7.4.6 (311): *sed errant semper per spatia longe lateque distenta, sine lare sine sedibus fixis aut legibus …*

[28] Cf. for the Wandering Jew: E. Isaac-Edersheim, 'Messias, Golem, Ahasver: Drei mythische Gestalten des Judentums' (The Messiah, Golem and Ahasuerus: Three Mythical Figures of the Jews), *Internationale Zeitschrift für Psychoanalyse und Imago* 26.1 (1941): 50–80, 26.2: 177–213, and 26.3–4: 287–315.

[29] For the gypsies see: M. Eliav-Feldon, 'Vagrants or Vermin? Attitudes towards Gypsies in Early Modern Europe', in M. Eliav-Feldon, B. Isaac, and J. Ziegler, *The Origins of Racism in the West* (Cambridge, 2009), 276–91.

[30] Ammianus 14.4.4. Cf. Pomponius Mela 2.21, where it is reported that Thracians auction their daughters, giving them in marriage to the highest bidder.

had at the time. At the battle of Hadrianople (AD 378), one of them, 'with long hair and naked except for a loin-cloth, uttering hoarse and dismal cries, with drawn dagger rushed into the thick of the Gothic army, and after killing a man applied his lips to his throat and sucked the blood that poured out'.[31] This thoroughly demoralized the Goths. It may not quite be cannibalism, but is somehow related. It is the sort of story, reminiscent of later vampire-superstition, which will be told about a group indulging in unnatural behaviour and therefore regarded as less than human. The drinking of blood is a recurring theme.

Ammianus says nothing about the Saracen diet, but for this we may turn instead to Jerome, *Life of Malchus* 4: 'half raw meat and camel's milk'.[32] This may have been true or not, but in any case this fits the overall impression of Saracens as crude savages, living to some extent like animals. In general it is thought to be characteristic of nomads that they live off their herds, and on milk and cheese.[33] They do not produce, do not store food, and do not engage in trade.

Two of the characteristics attributed to the Saracens recur in the treatment of Thrace. 'A description of Thrace would be easy, if the pens of the earlier writers agreed; but since their obscurity and their differences lend no aid to a work whose aim is truth, it will suffice to set forth what I myself remember to have seen.'[34] Ammianus would have preferred to rely on Greek authors of the later Republic or early Empire as he did for Gaul. However, the sources are unreliable, he says, because they disagree among themselves. In other words: he would have sought the material to rely upon for a description of Thrace in the earlier authors, if they had not been contradictory.[35] He then proceeds to say something about the Scordisci, Celts who clashed regularly with Roman troops in the second and first centuries BC, but who were fully subjected towards the end of the first century BC and then resided in Pannonia Inferior, Moesia Superior, and

---

[31] 31.16.6: *nudus omnia praeter pubem, subraucum et lugubre strepens, educto pugione, agmini se medio Gothorum inseruit, et interfecti hostis iugulo labra admovit, effusumque cruorem exsuxit.*

[32] Cf. Matthews, *Roman Empire of Ammianus*, 337–8; S. Weingarten, *The Saint's Saints* (Leiden, 2005), 180–1. Weingarten points out that there is a term in the Babylonian Talmud (b. Pesahim 41a) for half-raw, half-roasted meat, which, she argues, implies that this is a real, local food, not just a literary stereotype. The former, however, does not exclude the latter. For the ideologically significant connection between nomadism and diet in ancient texts, see Shaw, '"Eaters of Flesh, Drinkers of Milk"'.

[33] E.g. Strabo 7.3.7 (300) and in general Shaw's article cited in the previous note.

[34] 27.4.2: *Erat Thraciarum descriptio facilis, si veteres concinerent stili, quorum obscura varietas, quoniam opus veritatem professum non iuvat, sufficiet ea quae vidisse meminimus expedire.*

[35] 27.4.9–13 gives a condensed account of the Roman conquest of the region.

Dalmatia.[36] Ammianus, while observing that they no longer live in Thrace, says that they 'used to offer prisoners to Bellona and Mars and drink their blood out of human skulls'.[37] So, here we have a combination of two forms of ultimate barbarism: human sacrifice and drinking of human blood. It is a familiar combination, for Herodotus already reported of the Scythians that they sacrificed one out of every hundred of their captive enemies and drank their blood (each Scythian the blood of his first victim).[38] The use of the skulls of killed enemies is similarly attributed first by Herodotus to the Scythians.[39] Ammianus quite frequently echoes Herodotus, applying his extreme stories to any nomads, while Herodotus writes about the Scythians only – real people living far away, but who could also be seen in Athens in Herodotus' days. Ammianus transfers these stories to the nomads of his own days, some of them hardly known within the Empire and whom most Romans had never met. In this connection it is undoubtedly significant that many authors of the fourth and fifth centuries designated the contemporary Goths as 'Scythians'. It is remarkable not that Ammianus and others copy descriptions of foreign peoples from the distant past, but that it was also regarded as self-evident that those characterizations were applicable to other foreigners in the present. Thus the timelessness observed in the descriptions of Gauls and other provincials is present in another manner in the treatment of foreigners regarded as barbarians. They never change, an assumption that is one of the essential ingredients of racism.

The Thracian Odrysae are singled out for their uniquely savage cruelty, but this is represented as belonging to the past.[40] We may note that the roughly contemporary *Expositio* again has a brief and up-to-date

---

[36] Note also: Florus 1.39.12: *saevissimi omnium Thracum Scordisci fuere, sed calliditas quoque ad robur accesserat.* J. J. Wilkes, *Dalmatia* (London, 1969), 171–2; Jan Burian, *Der Neue Pauly* online edn., s.v. 'Scordisci' with references.

[37] 27.4.4: *hostiis captivorum Bellonae litantes et Marti, humanumque sanguinem in ossibus capitum cavis bibentes avidius …*

[38] Hdt. 4.62; 64. Strabo 7.3.7 (300) asserts that the Scythians practised human sacrifice and were cannibals, but also mentions reports different in tone: 7.3.8 (301) and 7.3.9 (302), citing Ephorus.

[39] Hdt. 4.65; cf. D. Asheri *et al.*, *A Commentary on Herodotus Books I–IV* (Oxford, 2007), comments by A. Corcella, 629. Subsequently: Plato, *Euth.* 299e; Strabo 7.3.7 (300); Pomponius Mela 2.13 and cf. A. Silberman (ed.), *Pomponius Mela, Chorographie* (Paris, 1988), 171–2, n. 3. Note also the Essedonians who ate the corpses of their parents and then prepared their skulls to serve as drinking cups, according to Hdt. 4.26, followed by Mela 2.9. Herodotus attributes the latter custom also to the Scythians, as already noted. See also, for a comparative approach: H. Yang, 'Perceiving the Nomadic Other: A Note on Herodotus' Scythians and Sima Qian's Xiongnu', in A. Heil, M. and J. Sauer (eds.), *Noctes Sinenses: Festschrift für Fritz-Heiner Mutschler zum 65. Geburtstag* (Heidelberg, 2011), 196-20.

[40] 27.4.9: *e quibus praeter alios ut immaniter efferati memorantur Odrysae.* I am not sure what source Ammianus could have had for this. In the classical Greek historians this is not a common view.

paragraph on Thrace.[41] It is wealthy, has good fighters, and therefore supplies the Roman army frequently with troops. It has two splendid cities: Constantinople and Heraclea.

The Isaurians, mountain dwellers in southern Asia Minor, were known for their fairly frequent unruliness and attacks on the surrounding cities and countryside.[42] In connection with such events in 353–4 Ammianus cites Cicero, *Pro Cluentio* 15.67: ' "as even wild animals, when warned by hunger, generally return to the place where they were once fed," so they all, swooping like a whirlwind down from their steep and rugged mountains, made for the districts near the sea'.[43]

In his description of renewed rebellion in 359, Ammianus says that the Isaurians 'gradually coming to life again just as snakes are wont to dart forth from their holes in the spring time, sallying forth from their rocky and inaccessible mountain fastnesses, and massed together in dense bands, were harrying their neighbours with thefts and brigandage, eluding the frontier-defences of our soldiers by their skill as mountaineers'.[44] It is not the aim of the present chapter to analyse Ammianus' narrative. Relevant here are the repeated animal comparisons which we found also in connection with Julian's Gallic soldiers, with descriptions of the Saracens, and which will be encountered again in the case of the Huns and others, for instance the Alemanni.[45] As I have argued elsewhere, animal comparisons are a significant phenomenon in ancient literature.[46] The implication is clear: in comparing barbarous peoples with animals it is implied that they, somehow, should be classified as not quite human – they are not actually animals, but do resemble them to some extent. Some remote foreigners indeed were thought to turn temporarily into animals, as Herodotus first records in an early version of werewolf superstition.[47]

---

[41] *Expositio* 50: *Dives in fructibus et maximos habens viros et fortes in bello; propter quod et frequenter inde milites tolluntur. Habet autem civitates splendidas Constantinopolim et Heracleam.* See also the *Expositio* on Gaul, above, p. 226.

[42] Matthews, *Roman Empire of Ammianus*, 355–67.

[43] 14.2.2: *Atque, (ut Tullius ait) ut etiam bestiae fame monitae plerumque ad eum locum ubi aliquando pastae sunt revertuntur, ita omnes instar turbinis degressi montibus impeditis et arduis loca petevere mari confinia.*

[44] 19.13.1: *His temporibus Isauri diu quieti … paulatim reviviscentes, ut solent verno tempore foveis exsilire serpentes, saltibus degressi scrupulosis et inviis, confertique in cuneos densos per furta et latrocinia finitimos afflictabant …*

[45] Ammianus 16.6.17: *utque bestiae custodum neglegentia raptu vivere solitae … armenta vel greges incursant, ita etiam illi cunctis, quae diripuere, consumptis fame urgente agebant aliquotiens praedas …*

[46] Isaac, *Invention of Racism*, 194–207.

[47] The Neuri: Hdt. 4.65 and 105, followed by Pomponius Mela 2.14 with a somewhat different version. Pomponius Mela is echoed by Solinus 15.2. See references in A. Corcella's commentary, *Libro IV: La Scizia e la Libia/Erodoto* (Rome, 1993), 316–17.

An essential ingredient in the list of objections against these enemies is their manner of fighting. Instead of launching proper heavy infantry against superior Roman legions they engage in guerrilla tactics, raids, light-armed attacks and the like, unlike gentlemen fighters. That is why the Saracens are like kites and the Isaurians like wild animals. The idea is expressed again in a speech of Constantius in 358, following a defeat of the Sarmatians.

> Our enemies ... were laying waste our farthest frontiers, crossing the rivers now in dug-out canoes and sometimes on foot; they did not trust to engagements nor to arms and strength, but, as is their custom, to lurking brigandage, with the craft and various methods of deceit dreaded also by our forefathers from our very first knowledge of this people.[48]

The emperor, of course, objected to the enemy's laying waste of the frontier regions, but that is not the essential point of this passage. Roman troops did the same thing to enemy frontier zones. This is what happened in war all around. The emperor's moral indignation is inspired by the reliance on speed and surprise, rather than brute force – tactics seen as 'craft', 'brigandage', and 'deceit'. Zosimus, apparently following Eunapius, has a peculiar view of the reasons for these tactics: the Huns were incapable of fighting a regular infantry battle, because they could not stand with their legs on the ground, being accustomed to spending all day on their horses, even sleeping on them.[49] These are deeply felt objections against unconventional forms of warfare, characteristic of nomad operations and their manner of fighting. They do not apply to all enemies.

There are, however, in Ammianus' view, also negative characteristics applying to all foreigners, not just nomads. Thus '[all] barbarians are of unstable loyalty' and: 'Chondomas, like all barbarians, was as submissive in disaster as he was the opposite in successes'.[50] Non-Romans, it appears, have no character. When victorious they are over-confident; in defeat they become spineless. They have no self-control. They are all inherently

---

[48] 17.13.27: *Persultabat Illyricum furor hostilis ... variisque discursibus vastabat extima limitum, nunc cavatis roboribus, aliquotiens peragrans pedibus flumina, non congressibus nec armis fretus aut viribus, sed latrociniis assuetus occultis, astu et ludificandi varietate, iam inde ab instuta gente nostris quoque maioribus formidatus.*

[49] Zosimus 4.20.4; cf. F. Paschoud (ed.), *Zosime, Histoire Nouvelle* (Paris, 1979), II/2, 372, n. 142. Ammianus, who describes the Alani as resembling the Huns but less savage, says that their 'young men who are used to riding from their earliest boyhood, regard it as below their dignity to go on foot; and all are trained in various manners to be skilled warriors' (Ammianus 31.2.20).

[50] 18.2.18: *ut sunt fluxioris fidei barbari*; 16.12.61: *Utque nativo more sunt barbari humiles in adversis, disparesque in secundis ...*

disloyal and inconstant. *Fides* and *constantia* are qualities reserved for Romans, which is not to say that all Romans have them, but that all non-Romans lack them.[51] Another quality which foreigners are regarded as lacking is rationality. As Themistius (fourth century) asserts: 'There is in each of us a barbarian tribe, extremely overbearing and intractable – I mean the temper and the insatiate desires, which stand opposed to the rational elements as the Scythians [i.e. the Goths] and Germans do to the Romans.'[52]

However, more alien and horrifying than any of the peoples mentioned so far were the Huns who are also the subject of an excursus by Ammianus.[53] This is not a text about a people subjected long ago and has therefore none of the anachronisms encountered in the treatment of Gaul and Arabia. However, his description of the Huns follows in part stereotypical impressions of nomads in earlier sources.[54]

> They ... are so monstrously ugly and misshapen, that one might take them for two-legged beasts or for the stumps, rough-hewn into images that are used in putting sides to bridges. But although they have the form of men, however ugly, they are so hardy in their mode of life that they have no need of fire nor of savoury food, but eat the roots of wild plants and the half-raw flesh of any kind of animal whatever, which they put between their thighs and the backs of their horses, and thus warm it a little.[55]

This is a variant of a familiar stereotype already noted. Pomponius Mela (fl. AD 40) asserted that the Germans ate raw meat.[56] It is interesting to see that

---

[51] Such accusations were aimed at many peoples. See Isaac, *Invention of Racism*, 412–14, 417: Gauls; 331, 393: Greeks; 331: Phoenicians; 349: Syrians and Africans; 365: Egyptians.

[52] Themistius, *Or.* 10.199/131, trans. P. Heather and J. Matthews, *The Goths in the Fourth Century* (Liverpool, 1991), 38–9.

[53] Ammianus 31.2. J. O. Maenchen-Helfen, *The World of the Huns: Studies in their History and Culture*, ed. M. Knight (Berkeley, CA, 1973), 9–15; W. Richter, 'Die Darstellung der Hunnen bei Ammianus Marcellinus', *Historia* 23 (1974): 343–72, who rejects the reliability of Ammianus altogether: 'der ganze Exkurs ist eine ethnographische Fiktion' (374). On the Huns in general there are also the antiquated works of E. A. Thompson, *A History of Attila and the Huns* (Oxford, 1948; 2nd revised edn 1996) and F. Altheim, *Attila und die Hunnen* (Baden Baden, 1951), both superseded by Maenchen-Helfen. For the archaeological material there is I. Bóna, *Das Hunnenreich* (Stuttgart, 1991); for the impact of the Hunnic presence on the Goths: P. J. Heather, *The Goths* (Oxford, 1996), ch. 4. Most recently: T. Stickler, *Die Hunnen* (Munich, 2007). See also Matthews, *Roman Empire of Ammianus*, 332–42. This paper discusses only a selection of the sources referring to the Huns and ignores many relevant texts, such as, for instance, Jerome, *Epp.* 60.16; 78.8.

[54] See Maenchen-Helfen, *World of the Huns*, 14–15.

[55] 31.2.1: *In hominum autem figura, licet insuavi, ita victu sunt asperi, ut neque igni neque saporatis indigeant cibis, sed radicibus herbarum agrestium, et semicruda cuiusvis pecoris carne vescantur, quam inter femora sua equorumque terga subsertam, fotu calefaciunt brevi.*

[56] Pomponius Mela 3.3.2. Ammianus' claim concerning the Huns was taken over by Jerome, *Adv. Iovinian* 2.7, *PL* 23. 295.

the features of the Huns evoked such strong feelings.[57] They are, in fact, the only people encountered in Ammianus' work whose external appearance alone elicited such extreme language, although Ammianus implies that they are after all not real animals, but human beings. That said, Ammianus explains that their way of life also is hardly human. They did not know fire and therefore ate only raw food, including their meat.[58] The notion that they warmed their meat a little by putting it between their thighs and the backs of their horses combines the stereotypical view of the way of life of nomads with the idea that such people lacked the habits of basic civilization, including fire.[59] Thus they represent a pre-Promethean phase of development. These features are in addition to their repulsive external appearance.

Ammianus' brief treatment of the Huns should be compared with the later treatment in Jordanes, *Getica*, which is based on Cassiodorus (ca. 485–ca. 585).[60]

> But after a short space of time … the people of the Huns, fiercer than ferocity itself, flamed forth against the Goths. We learn from old traditions that their origin was as follows: Filimers, king of the Goths … found among his people certain witches … Suspecting these women, he expelled them from the midst of his people and compelled them to wander in solitary exile afar from his army. There the unclean spirits, who beheld them as they wandered through the wilderness, gave themselves to the women's embraces in sexual intercourse and produced this savage people, which dwelt at first in the swamps – a stunted, hideous and puny tribe, scarcely human, unrecognizable by any language save something which bore only slight resemblance to human speech. Such was the descent of the Huns who came to the country of the Goths.[61]

---

[57] Cf. Maenchen-Helfen, *World of the Huns*, 360–4, for the physical appearance of the Huns in ancient sources.

[58] Shaw, ' "Eaters of Flesh, Drinkers of Milk" '.

[59] Maenchen-Helfen, *World of the Huns*, 14–15, points out that Ammianus' description is a mixture of good observation and a traditional topos. That they ate the roots of wild plants is quite credible; that they warmed raw meat while on horseback might be true, for the custom is attested for a later period. However, they did know the use of fire, of course.

[60] For Jordanes' *Getica* see P. J. Heather, *Goths and Romans 332–489* (Oxford, 1991), chs. 1 and 2; for the date (mid-sixth century): B. Croke, 'Cassiodorus and the Getica of Jordanes', *Classical Philology* 82 (1987): 117–34.

[61] Jordanes, *Getae* 121–2: *Post autem non longi temporis intervallum, ut refert Orosius, Hunnorum gens omni ferocitate atrocior exarsit in Gothos. Nam hos, ut refert antiquitas, ita exstitisse comperimus: Filimer, rex Gothorum … repperit in populo suo quasdam magas mulieres … easque habens suspectas, de medio sui proturbat longeque ab exercitu suo fugatas in solitudinem coegit errare. Quas spiritus immundi per heremum vagantes quum vidissent et earum se complexibus in coitu miscuissent, genus hoc ferocissimum ediderunt, quae fuit primum inter paludes, minutum, taetrum atque exile quasi hominum genus, nec alia voce notum nisi quod humani sermonis imaginem assignabat. Tali igitur Hunni stirpe*

For by the terror of their features they inspired great fear in those whom perhaps they did not really surpass in war. They made their foes flee in horror because their swarthy aspect was fearful, and they had, if I may call it so, a sort of hideous lump, not a head, with pinholes rather than eyes. Their audacity is evident in their threatening appearance, and they are beings who are cruel to their children on the very day they are born ... They are short in stature, quick in bodily movement; alert horsemen, broad shouldered, ready in the use of bow and arrow, and have firm-set necks which are ever erect in pride. Though they have human shape, they live with the savagery of beasts.[62]

The Huns then were descendants of Gothic witches who were expelled from the community of Goths and of unclean spirits, living in the wilderness. Such an effort to denigrate ancestry reminds us to some extent of the distorted version of the Exodus story in Hellenistic sources and Tacitus which claims that the Jews in Judaea were the descendants of impious lepers, expelled from Egypt to the desert.[63] In this insistence on poor lineage the Huns were claimed to be a truly separate, savage race in every modern sense of the term. They dwelt at first in swamps – 'a stunted, hideous and puny tribe, scarcely human, unrecognizable by any language, save something which bore only slight resemblance to human speech'. The horror of their external appearance echoes that of Ammianus. Their language too is regarded as scarcely human. Their victory is due more to the enemy's fear of their appearance than to actual military merit.[64] Then, hardly consistent, the text claims that their outward shape may be human, but their savagery is animal. So far Jordanes, relying on an earlier source.

Back to Ammianus – he displays the hazy impression of a nomadic way of life usually found in ancient sources, concluding that they are treacherous: 'Like unreasoning beasts, they are utterly ignorant of the difference between right and wrong; they are deceitful and ambiguous in speech,

---

creati, Gothorum finibus advenerunt. See Maenchen-Helfen, *World of the Huns,* 244–51, for a suggestion regarding the background of the tale. See also A. S. Christensen, *Cassiodorus, Jordanes and the History of the Goths* (Copenhagen, 2002), 241–2; W. Goffart, *The Narrators of Barbarian History* (AD 550–800): *Jordanes, Gregory of Tours, Bede, and Paul the Deacon* (Princeton, 1988), 84.

[62] 127–8: *Nam et quos bello forsitan minime superabant, vultus sui terrore nimium pavorem ingerentes, terribilitate fugabant, eo quod erat eis species pavenda nigredinis et velut quaedam, si dici fas est, informis offa, non facies, habensque magis puncta quam lumina. Quorum animi fiduciam torvus prodit aspectus, qui etiam in pignora sua primo die nata desaeviunt ... Exigui quidem forma, sed argutis motibus expediti et ad equitandum promptissimi, scapulis latis, et ad arcus sagittasque parati, firmis cervicibus et superbia semper erectis. Hi vero sub hominum figura vivunt beluina saevitia.*

[63] P. Schäfer, *Judaeophobia* (Cambridge, 1997), 15–33.

[64] This is not to deny that the Huns really caused terror on the battlefield, see, for instance, Procopius, *BV* 3.13–19.

never bound by any reverence for religion or for other religious beliefs.'[65] They have no morals. Claudian compares them with centaurs, themselves half-animals, half-human beings. They literally have a double nature.[66]

The Huns are said to be unproductive and have no homes. Ammianus claims that 'no one in their country ever ploughs a field or touches a plough-handle'.[67] This derives from a description of the Scythians by Pompeius Trogus: 'The people have no landmarks, for they neither cultivate the soil, nor have they any house, dwelling, or settled place of abode, but are always engaged in feeding herds and flocks, and wandering through uncultivated deserts. They carry their wives and children with them in wagons, which, as they are covered with hides against the rain and cold, they use instead of houses.'[68] Ammianus similarly describes the constant roaming of the Alans:

> They have no cottages, and never use the plough, but live solely on meat and plenty of milk, mounted on their wagons, which they cover with a curved awning made of the bark of trees, and then drive them through their boundless deserts. And when they come to any pasture-land, they pitch their wagons in a circle, and live like a herd of beasts, eating up all the forage – carrying, as it were, their cities with them in their wagons.[69]

This description combines a series of familiar themes: the nomads have no homes, do not work on the fields and are not productive, but live off their animals, consuming meat and milk. They are therefore like animals.

Maenchen-Helfen has shown that, in spite of the denial of ancient and also modern literature, the Huns did in fact practise agriculture, spun wool and made linen. Yet it was commonly assumed in ancient sources that nomads produce nothing and only consume. As Aristotle asserts in his discussion of the various modes of production and consumption of humanity,

---

[65] Ammianus 32.2.10: *Per indutias infidi et inconstantes, ad omnem auram incidentis spei novae perquam mobiles, totum furori incitatissimo tribuentes. Inconsultorum animalium ritu, quid honestum inhonestumve sit, penitus ignorantes, flexiloqui et obscuri, nullius religionis vel superstitionis reverentia aliquando districti ...* (cf. Matthews, *Roman Empire of Ammianus*, 340).

[66] Claudian, *In Rufinum* 1.329–30: *nec plus nubigenas duplex natura biformes / cognatis aptavit equis.*

[67] Ammianus 30.2.10: *Nemo apud eos arat nec stivam aliquando contingit.* Cf. Claudian, *In Ruf.* 1.327. Maenchen-Helfen, *World of the Huns*, 174–8.

[68] Justin, *Epit.* 2.2.3–4: *Hominibus inter se nulli fines. Neque enim agrum exercent, nec domus illis ulla aut tectum aut sedes est, armenta et pecora semper pascentibus et per incultas solitudines errare solitis. Uxores liberosque secum in plaustris uehunt, quibus coriis imbrium hiemisque causa tectis pro domibus utuntur.*

[69] 31.2.18: *Bipertiti per utramque mundi plagam Halani – quorum gentes varias nunc recensere non refert – licet dirempti spatiis longis, per pagos ut Nomades vagantur inmensos, aevi tamen progressu ad unum concessere vocabulum et summatim omnes Halani cognominantur ob mores et modum efferatum vivendi eandemque armaturam. nec enim ulla sunt illisce tuguria aut versandi vomeris cura, sed carne et copia victitant lactis, plaustris supersidentes, quae operimentis curvatis corticum per solitudines conferunt sine fine distentas.*

'The idlest men are nomads (for to procure food from domesticated animals involves not toil or industry, but as it is necessary for the herds to move from place to place because of the pastures, the people themselves are forced to follow along with them, as though they were farming a live farm).'[70] The idea that the nomads are idle is the distant predecessor of the accusation aimed at other peoples in conflict situations, such as the Jews, that they are unproductive, living as parasites on the backs of other people.

We observe a constantly repeated ambivalence about the humanity of the Huns: their physical shape, origin, and language are dubious, but also their morals: they are fickle, savage, and have no true religion. Like other nomads, they lack any social organization, regular economy, and, like animals, eat their food raw. This fully fits the concept of a proto-racist attitude towards foreigners, for a reasoned, consistent, and emphatic denial of other people's humanity is what distinguishes racism from hostile ethnic stereotype. It transforms vague hostility into a well-defined ideology.

In Ammianus' work this approach recurs in remarks about peoples who lived beyond the Alans, 'the Vidini and the Geloni, exceedingly savage races, who strip the skins from their slain enemies to make clothing for themselves and coverings for their horses in war'.[71] This is a curious variant of an accusation of cannibalism, creating a fantasy world of nomadic cruelty. The employment of human skins for garments or other practical use is like the association of nomadism with the drinking of human blood, found also in earlier sources, and ultimately goes back again to Herodotus' excursus on the Scythians.[72]

'And when they come to a place rich in grass, they place their carts in a circle and feed like wild beasts.'[73] It is not quite clear how we are supposed to imagine the feeding habits of the Vidini and Geloni. Were they eating grass? In any case their customs definitely placed them well beyond the bounds of humanity. However, an extraordinarily repulsive form of bestiality, in the classical tradition, is cannibalism (Aristotle, *Nicomachean Ethics* 1148b). Ammianus also mentions having heard of nomadic cannibals (*Anthropophagi*) living beyond the Alans, in the huge realm between them

---

[70] Aristotle, *Pol.* 1256a. See the analysis by Shaw, ' "Eaters of Flesh, Drinkers of Milk" ', 17–20.

[71] 32.2.17: *Post quos Vidini sunt et Geloni, perquam feri, qui detractis peremptorum hostium cutibus, indumenta sibi equisque tegmina conficiunt bellatoria.* Cf. Pomponius Mela 2.1.14.

[72] Hdt. 4.64; cf. comments by Corcella, *Erodoto*, 285–6. It recurs in Pliny, *NH* 7.12, a separate chapter on cannibalism, and in Pomponius Mela, 2.14, who, like Ammianus, associates it with the Geloni. Cf. Silberman (ed.), *Pomponius Mela*, 171–2, n. 3. Strabo reports having heard that the inhabitants of Ireland were cannibals and regarded it as honourable to devour their fathers after they died (4.5.4 (201)), an assertion found first in Hdt. 4.26 concerning the Essedonians (above, n. 39).

[73] 32.2.18: *Cumque ad graminea venerint in orbiculatam figuram locatis sarracis ferino ritu vescuntur ...*

and the Chinese.[74] The expression 'as I have heard' (*accepimus*) suggests contemporary, personal information, but in fact the report again echoes Herodotus.[75] Ammianus adds a note saying that all their former neighbours have moved away from them because of their repulsive feeding habits. This is a statement not found in Herodotus in this form.[76] The latter describes them as 'a people separate and by no means Scythian. Beyond them there is only true desolation, where no group of men lives, as far as we know.' For Herodotus then they were the most remote of men displaying a commensurate lack of civilization. For Ammianus their cannibalism drove away their less brutish neighbours and led to complete isolation. In other words: Herodotus sees their remoteness as the cause of their lack of culture, while Ammianus regards this lack as the cause of their isolation.[77]

Even if much in these reports is based on earlier texts, the treatment of hostile peoples at the edge of the Empire or beyond it definitely is formulated as if it depicts Ammianus' own times. The author in fact claims to describe only what he has seen himself, even where only a small part of a description may be based on autopsy.[78] As I emphasize again and again, stereotypes are far from meaningless: they reflect what is commonly accepted as true and are a symptom of the failure to employ critical, independent thought and basic rules of objective observation. The foreign peoples dealt with in this manner, especially the nomads, are consistently described in terms that question or almost deny their humanity in various respects: physical, moral, social, religious, and cultural. Thus these attitudes should be termed an ideology rather than a random collection of prejudices or stereotypes. As such they should be regarded as a form of racism.

If we recognize here a pattern of ancient racism as encountered in earlier centuries as well, do we also encounter the early scientific theories which formed the intellectual basis for the rationalization of prejudice and collective hostility? Two examples will at least indicate that the theories were

---

[74] Ammianus 31.2.15: *Post hos Melanchlaenas et Anthropophagos palari accepimus per diversa, humanis corporibus victitantes, quibus ob haec alimenta nefanda desertis, finitimi omnes longa petiere terrarum.*

[75] Hdt. 4.106: 'The *androphagoi* are the most savage of all men; they do not respect justice and respect no lawful customs. They are nomads and … are the only ones recorded as eating men', according to Herodotus. The earliest representation of cannibalism in Greek literature is the story of the cyclops: Homer, *Od.* 9.106; cf. the analysis by Shaw, ' "Eaters of Flesh, Drinkers of Milk" ', 21–4.

[76] Hdt. 4.18: μετὰ δὲ τὴν ἔρημον Ἀνδροφάγοι οἰκέουσι, ἔθνος ἐὸν ἴδιον καὶ οὐδαμῶς Σκυθικόν. τὸ δὲ τούτων κατύπερθε ἔρημος ἤδη ἀληθέως καὶ ἔθνος ἀνθρώπων οὐδέν, ὅσον ἡμεῖς ἴδμεν.

[77] Another distinction is that for Herodotus these people lived at the edge of the world, while Ammianus was aware of the Seres (Chinese), living far to the East.

[78] Ammianus 27.4.2: *Sufficiet ea meminisse quae vidisse meminimus expedire.* Yet in the subsequent chapter he cites Homer and refers to the past more than to the present.

still around and to some extent influential. Vegetius is the last author in antiquity known to me as having given, in adapted form, the standard formulation of environmental determinism. As in earlier texts, it occurs in a technical treatise, the *Epitome of Military Science* (late fourth–early fifth century):

> They tell us that all peoples that are near the sun, being parched by great heat, are more intelligent but have less blood, and therefore lack steadiness and confidence to fight at close quarters, because those who are conscious of having less blood are afraid of wounds. On the other hand the peoples of the north, remote from the sun's heat are less intelligent, but having a super-abundance of blood are readiest for wars. Recruits should therefore be raised from the more temperate climes. The plenteousness of their blood gives them contempt for wounds and death, and intelligence cannot be lacking either which preserves discipline in camp and is of no little assistance with counsel in battle.[79]

This is environmental determinism in its classic form. The differences between northern and southern climates have consequences for the physical qualities of the population as well as for their mental and moral characteristics. Those living in the middle, in a temperate climate, display the best of both, an idea first enunciated by Aristotle. The immediate occasion for Vegietus to raise the topic is to show where the best soldiers may be recruited.

It recurs at least once in the extant work of Ammianus:

> Now it is well known, as constant reports have spread abroad, that almost all the country folk who dwell in the high mountains throughout the lands just described surpass us in health and strength, and in the prerogative (so to speak) of prolonging life; and it is thought that this is due to abstinence from a conglomeration of diet and from hot baths,[80] and a lasting freshness knits their bodies through cold sprinklings with dew; and they enjoy the sweetness of a purer air; further they are first of all to feel the rays of the sun …[81]

---

[79] Vegetius 1.2 (trans. N. P. Milner): *Omnes nationes, quae uicinae sunt soli, nimio calore siccatas, amplius quidem sapere, sed minus habere sanguinis dicunt ac propterea constantiam ac fiduciam comminus non habere pugnandi, quia metuunt uulnera qui exiguum sanguinem se habere nouerunt. Contra septentrionales populi, remoti a solis ardoribus, inconsultiores quidem, sed tamen largo sanguine redundantes, sunt ad bella promptissimi. Tirones igitur de temperatioribus legendi sunt plagis, quibus et copia sanguinis suppetat ad uulnerum mortis que contemptum et non possit deesse prudentia, quae et modestiam seruat in castris et non parum prodest in dimicatione consiliis.* Cf. Isaac, *Invention of Racism*, 87.

[80] Or: hot food. There is a textual problem here, cf. M.-A. Marié (ed.), *Ammien Marcellin, Histoire*, V (Paris, 1984), 248, n. 214.

[81] Ammianus 27.4.14: *Constat autem … omnes paene agrestes, qui per regiones praedictas montium circumcolunt altitudines, salubriate virium et praerogativa quadam vitae longius propagandae, nos anteire, idque inde congigere arbitrantur, quod colluvione ciborum abstinent calidisque, et perenni viriditate*

This is environmental determinism, focusing on the opposition between mountain-dwellers and plainsmen, a variant encountered already in the fifth century BC.[82] The beneficial influence of the mountain climate is combined with a healthy way of life resulting in superior physical qualities for the local population. The harmfulness of hot baths is a familiar theme in the ancient literature from Posidonius onwards,[83] but that is a matter of lifestyle, not of the environment. The collective influence of the quality of air and quantity of moisture on the physical and mental characteristics of peoples is a long-standing concept. Yet, it is possible that environmental determinism lost some of its force in this period, for it seems to be less prevalent in the texts than in earlier centuries. Another concept that makes itself felt less regularly than in the past is the theory of natural slavery in its later development.[84] The influence of Greek medical and philosophical writing on ethnographic thinking may have weakened in the course of the third and fourth centuries, but this requires further study.

To conclude: I hope to have shown the presence of a clear pattern in the views of the Roman Empire and of various foreign peoples in the fourth century. Ammianus describes the development over time of the collective of the Empire in terms of the existence of an individual rather than a group. He combines this with the certainty, familiar from Graeco-Roman culture, that the progress of time can only bring deterioration, not improvement. His excurses on provincial peoples tend to be anachronistic: Gaul and parts of the Near East are described as if they had just been annexed. Subsequent developments over the centuries are ignored. Much of this chapter, however, is devoted to fourth-century views, not of the Empire, but of nomadic peoples and pastoralists. The Saracens are described in terms that make them less than fully human: there are animal comparisons, they are half-naked, do not live in houses, are unproductive, and do not have regular marriages. The theme of drinking human blood comes up at least once. The Thracians, described in extremely anachronistic terms, practise human sacrifice and drink human blood out of skulls. This is far removed from the admiration which Herodotus expressed in

---

roris asperginibus gelidis corpora constringente, aurae purioris dulcedine potiuntur, radiosque solis ...
primi omnium sentiunt ...

[82] Hdt. 9.122; *Airs, Waters, Places* 24.2–3 with special reference to air and moisture. Cf. Isaac, *Invention of Racism*, ch. 10.

[83] Posidonius F61a, b, Kidd (Athenaeus, *Deipnosophistae* 12.540B–C; 5.210C–D); F62a, b (Athenaeus, 12.527E–F; 5.210E–F).

[84] See Isaac, *Invention of Racism*, 170–94.

the fifth century.[85] The treatment of the Isaurians is replete with animal comparisons. A common accusation aimed at all nomads is that they do not fight honestly. Guerrilla tactics are seen not as a different manner of fighting, but as a despicable and cowardly form of soldiering. This fits the view, expressed by Ammianus, that all foreigners are lacking *fides* and *constantia*. All these features are applied with particular force to the treatment of the Huns in the fourth and fifth centuries. Their external appearance is not human. They are of unnatural descent. They have no fire, no homes, no morals, no religion, and they produce nothing. Indeed they are a sort of centaurs, half horses and half human beings.

All this leads me to conclude that we encounter here a consistent and coherent pattern which places the nomads in a category apart. They are inferior in every respect and they are so by nature and pass on their inferiority from one generation to the next. These views display a gradual scale from superiority to inferiority, dividing groups of peoples into classes where those least regarded are associated with animals or classified as less than fully human. The repetition of specific themes is coherent and can legitimately be seen as an ideology based on an early form of racism.

---

[85] Hdt. 5.3: The Thracians are the most powerful people in the world except, of course, the Indians; and if they had one head, or were agreed among themselves, it is my belief that their match could not be found anywhere, and that they would very far surpass all other nations. Curiously, this approaches Aristotle's assertion concerning the Greeks themselves. See above, Chapter 8, p. 182.

A Multicultural Mediterranean?

This erudite, lucid, and absorbingly written book [Erich S. Gruen, *Rethinking the Other in Antiquity*, Princeton: Princeton University Press, 2011] has a highly ambitious aim: in it the author proposes an alternative impression of ancient views of others, or of the 'Other'. It deals with essential elements in our views of any society: group identity, tolerance or feelings of superiority, mutual appreciation or polarity between peoples, and it does so with passion, profound scholarship, and elegance. How does one review such an important work if, in the end, the reviewer is himself persuaded only partially? The sum of the work is far more than a remarkable collection of interpretations of authors writing throughout antiquity and representing societies from Gaul in the Northwest to Egypt and Persia. It argues that ancient society, as we know it, was different in kind from all that followed in terms of social acceptance. It does so in spite of our awareness that these were societies in which slavery, war, and conquest were an integral part of their system, morally accepted as a matter of course. The question before us is not just whether negative stereotypes and generalizations were balanced by a positive acceptance of others, but whether the latter was an essential feature of ancient worldviews. As Erich Gruen states: 'This study offers an alternative vision to the widespread idea that framing the self requires postulating the "Other". The expression of collective character in antiquity ... owes less to insisting on distinctiveness from the alien than to postulating links with, adaptation to, and even incorporation of the alien'. In other words, the book not only claims to rethink the 'Other', as the title indicates, but also to rethink the 'Self' (352). The author goes so far as to declare the ancient Mediterranean 'a multicultural world' (253, 287–99, 306, 264–5).

This chapter was originally published as: 'A Multicultural Mediterranean? Erich S. Gruen, Rethinking the Other in Antiquity, Princeton 2010', review article for *Scripta Classica Israelica* 23 (2013): 233–54.

The present reviewer is himself on record as having argued at length that Greeks and Romans developed views of other peoples that approach what we now call racism, which certainly does not deny the fact that many important ancient authors had quite different attitudes.[1] The aim of my study was to demonstrate the existence of various forms of stereotypes, prejudice, and xenophobia in Greek and Roman societies. This review recognizes that the work under discussion adds numerous fascinating insights to the subject. There are many topics and specific points which I accept with admiration. Nevertheless, I shall also argue that, to put it succinctly, there is a good deal of utopia in the book.

At this point it may as well be noted that to some extent the study follows a string of publications that question or defend the contribution of Greece and Rome to later societies and cultures. In the 1980s and 1990s there was a widespread reaction to traditional views about the centrality of the West taken up by classicists who denied or defended the uniqueness of Greece which gave, or did not, give the world democracy, free enquiry, freedom, and other major features of modern society.[2] That, however, is not our subject. We are concerned with Gruen's book and its contribution to our understanding of ancient society and its views of foreigners.

My first question regards method and concerns whether an elementary distinction can be made between attitudes towards foreign, distant peoples and foreign minorities within Greece and Rome. I would regard it highly likely that in antiquity, as in our own days, distinct mechanisms are to be observed when one focuses on attitudes towards different categories of others: one category is neighbours in a city, who belong to other religions, ethnic groups, or social classes – these possibly include immigrants and indeed often do so; another category is neighbouring countries, whether friendly or not; a third group is distant peoples who are hardly known.

A further complication is that feelings about people in the present may be different from those about the same people in the recent, remote, or legendary past. Thus Romans of the first century AD would relate to Egyptian neighbours in their city in one way, but to the inhabitants of

---

[1] B. Isaac, *The Invention of Racism in Classical Antiquity* (Princeton, 2004); M. Eliav-Feldon, B. Isaac, and J. Ziegler (eds.), *The Origins of Racism in the West* (Cambridge, 2009).

[2] The publication of M. Bernal's *Black Athena* (New Brunswick, NJ, 1987) and the polemics that followed essentially focused on the question of whether Greek culture was original or a derivative of an older, African culture. Quite apart from this, a fierce discussion about Greek legacy developed, especially in the US. For an extreme example of such polemics on the part of classicists: V. D. Hanson and J. Heath, *Who Killed Homer? The Demise of Classical Education and the Recovery of Greek Wisdom* (New York, 1998); for a judicious review: J. Connolly, in *BMCR* 98.5.13.

the Roman province of Egypt in another and to historical Egyptians, one of the oldest civilized peoples known to them, in yet another. Those same Romans knew Greeks as a conquered people, and lived with a Greek presence in their town, but their attitude to those Greeks was by no means the same as the opinions they held with regard to Periclean Athens or the Homeric heroes of the Trojan War. Finally there is yet another complication: attitudes change over time. In our days this is obvious: Germans in Goethe's days related to German Jews in a manner different from that of many Germans in the 1930s or in the 1990s. Similar variations should be postulated for antiquity. In this connection it is also essential to take into account the social fabric that formed the basis of 'self-perception'. The citizens of a Greek *polis* in the fifth century BC belonged to a cohesive society. Romans were citizens of a town that gradually incorporated an empire.

Gruen's work does not sufficiently take these distinctions into account. Egypt was to the Greeks an old and venerable country with a brilliant history, but odd customs. For the Romans it was, first, a Hellenistic power, and then a province incorporated into the Empire. Many of Rome's inhabitants lived as a minority in their own city. Herodotus, remarkable for his even-handed willingness to concede barbarian achievements on the same terms as those of Greeks, visited Egypt extensively in the fifth century BC. His treatment has for generations been recognized as a classic source of information and intellectual history. Gruen rightly analyses him in detail.

Plutarch, one of the major Greek authors of the Roman period, despised Herodotus, notably his sympathy for non-Greeks. He calls Herodotus *philobarbaros*.[3] Plutarch accuses Herodotus of acquitting the legendary king Busiris of alleged human sacrifice and guest-murder. He objects to his claim that the Egyptians have a strong sense of religion and justice.[4] He criticizes Herodotus' version of myth (Helen and Menelaus).[5] Here it is clear that Plutarch objects to any ethical or moral appreciation of Egyptians. He goes on to attack Herodotus for his respectful treatment of Egyptian religion (*De malign.* 13, *Mor.* 857 C–D). Gruen dismisses Plutarch in two brief notes for his 'naïve and superficial judgment'.[6] However, what should interest us is not Plutarch's profundity or the reverse, but the fact that he, writing late in the first and early in the second century, expressed this

---

[3] Plut. *De malign.* 12 (*Mor.* 857A): φιλοβάρβαρος. For this treatise see: A. Bowen, *Plutarch, The Malice of Herodotus (De Malignitate Herodoti)* (Warminster, 1992); J. Marincola, 'Plutarch's Refutation of Herodotus', *AncW* 20 (1994): 191–203.

[4] Plut. *De malign.* 12, on Hdt. 2.45; 2.37.1 and 65.1.

[5] On Hdt. 2.119.

[6] E. S. Gruen, *Rethinking the Other in Antiquity* (Princeton, 2011), 30 with n. 115, 81 with n. 32.

sort of opinion at all. Gruen, with his usual eloquence, writes: 'It is easy enough to cite authors from Cicero to Juvenal, and beyond, to accumulate ostensibly hostile comments about Egypt, and to pile up numbers that seem impressive at first glance.[7] Do they show that Rome seethed with anti-Egyptian prejudice?' Indeed, it is easy to cite hostile comments, because they exist, but nobody claims that Rome was seething. What has been argued is that there was a measure of hostility. Juvenal, who disliked Egyptians very much, was no historian discussing pharaonic Egypt: his target was contemporary Egyptians living in Rome. Juvenal was a satirist, which means that he may be assumed to have reflected the opinions of many of those who read his poems – citizens of Rome who disliked foreigners. Herodotus, on the other hand, visited the Egyptians in Egypt. He did not meet them in Athens.

Herodotus wrote about Persia as the major power that had failed in an attempt to subjugate the Greeks not long before he produced his work. It was a major achievement for the Greeks and a spectacular failure for the Persians. I agree with Gruen's assessment of Herodotus' attitude and of that represented by Aeschylus' *Persae*.[8] Where we disagree is on the subsequent development of Greek views of Persia, marked by an increasingly aggressive attitude. The treatise *Airs, Water, Places* by (Pseudo-)Hippocrates, written probably not long after Herodotus' work, is tucked away by Gruen in a footnote.[9] Gruen is formally right in claiming that in this work 'nothing asserts a polarization of Greeks and Persians'. However, the treatise absolutely emphasizes polarization between Europe and Asia, stressing numerous essentialist characteristics.[10] It is true that the Persians are not mentioned in the treatise, but neither are the Greeks, who are nevertheless a dominant factor in the treatise even if they are not named.

---

[7] Gruen, Rethinking the Other, 107, n. 173: seven modern works are cited. Cf. 111: 'The sum of all this is decidedly smaller than its parts. Romans had no fixation on Egypt and were not preoccupied with deploring the nation. They retailed stereotypes …' I am not aware of any scholar who believes that the Romans had a fixation or were preoccupied, but the stereotypes are easy to find and need to be taken seriously as an expression of friction.

[8] Gruen, *Rethinking the Other*, 9–21 on Aeschylus; 21–39 on Herodotus. Note, however, the different view of J. S. Romm, *The Edges of the Earth in Ancient Thought* (Princeton, 1992), 54–60: 'Herodotus employs the Persians … throughout the *Histories* to represent a traditional type of ethnocentrism, which sees a central position in the world as the bases of cultural superiority' (60). In 1.134 Herodotus declares that the Persians honour most the peoples nearest to themselves, next the people next to those, etc. Romm notes that Herodotus disapproves of this attitude. It is *hybris* that brings disaster on itself. On visual representations, 40–53, there is some agreement with the essay, unknown to Gruen at the time, by H. A. Shapiro, 'The Invention of Persia in Classical Athens', in Eliav-Feldon *et al.* (eds.), *Origins of Racism*, 57–87.

[9] Gruen, *Rethinking the Other*, 39, n. 168.

[10] As argued and, I claim, demonstrated by Isaac, in Eliav-Feldon *et al.* (eds.), *Origins of Racism*, 60–9.

The background should be clear: Herodotus and Aeschylus wrote in the immediate aftermath of the war between Persia and Greece. Unlike those two, the author of the treatise was not an historian or a tragedian. He sought to interpret common stereotypes about the collective influence of climate and geography on human beings. He did so in the spirit of these stereotypes which, obviously, included Persians.

Gruen is one of numerous scholars who have tried to make sense of the problematic last chapter of Xenophon's *Cyropaedia* 8.8, describing Persia's decline after books full of praise of the elder Cyrus.[11] Gruen proposes the following solution: it is sardonic, farcical, exaggerated. Xenophon does not believe what he writes. On the contrary, he claims, it is a caricature of contemporary stereotypes. To me this would be altogether uncharacteristic of Xenophon, but, more important: this interpretation recognizes the existence and reality of contemporary stereotypes about Persians found in Greek literature: Ctesias, Plato, and Isocrates. Yet Gruen regards the last of these three as 'hardly … representative of widespread Hellenic opinion'. I prefer the assessment of Peter Brunt: 'Isocrates' *Panegyricus* … certainly reflects ideas already current in the fifth century.'[12] A further point: if we look at the key events in history we see that, in the early fifth century BC, Persia attempted but failed to conquer mainland Greece. A century and a half afterwards Greeks successfully conquered Persia. It is not a far-fetched idea that a gradual development in Greek ideology can be traced to reflect the sense of victory following the failed Persian invasions, leading to war initiated by Greeks to conquer Persia.

On Phoenicians and Carthaginians there is partial agreement. Gruen argues that 'The construct of *Punica fides* as antithesis of all that Rome stood for could provide a valuable vehicle for projecting that desirable image, and would bring a reassurance of moral superiority … Yet the picture may be too simple and too monochromatic' (115–16). This somewhat overstates the case that he is arguing against. Modern discussions of Roman attitudes towards Carthage have been varied and sometimes subtle.[14] Gruen declares that (the Phoenicians) 'were not the most obvious candidates to serve as foils for the Romans or to represent the "Other"' (116). I am not aware of anyone who claims that this is how they were presented. More important, one should distinguish between the image of Phoenicians and that of

---

[11] Gruen, *Rethinking the Other*, 58–65, and Isaac, *Invention of Racism*, 290–6. I have nothing to add to what I wrote at the time.

[12] P. A. Brunt, 'Laus Imperii', in P. A. Brunt, *Roman Imperial Themes* (Oxford, 1990), 161. Ample references are found in Gruen's footnotes.

Carthage, taking into account developments over time. Carthage was the major power Rome faced throughout the third century BC. It was a dangerous enemy during two large-scale wars and finally destroyed by Rome in the second century BC, when Carthage was no longer dangerous. The Phoenicians were never a threat. From Homer onwards, their image was a decidedly mixed one, as craftsmen and traders. Incorporated as part of the province of Syria by Pompey, they were known to urban Romans mostly as a minority in their city which inspired negative views, as stated in quite a number of sources from Lucilius onward (second century BC). That said, I would note Gruen's very interesting observations about bilingualism in Rome (128–30). He is also undoubtedly correct that there is no noticeable ethnic hatred before or after the destruction of Carthage (130–2). However, as I have argued, xenophobia and ethnic hatred are often aimed at minorities at home, and do not always play a significant role in the moral and political climate before and immediately after a major war.

At this point I ought to mention that Gruen, far more than I would regard as convincing, accepts the possibility of reconstructing Persian, Egyptian, and Punic perspectives on the basis of Greek and Latin sources.[13] Even if Greek and Roman authors were somehow acquainted with texts in Persian, Egyptian, and Phoenician, we cannot know where they found access to them and how they interpreted them.[14]

The Gauls were, for centuries, until their final incorporation into the Empire by Caesar, a formidable and nearby presence. Gruen, in a fine chapter (ch. 5) which focuses on Caesar in particular, concedes the existence of a string of stereotypes in several authors: Polybius, Diodorus, Cicero,[15] and Caesar. The latter, who fought the Gauls for almost a decade, repeats several of the usual stereotypes, observed by Gruen. I agree with Gruen that this is less important than the unconventional elements in Caesar's description indicating respect for them. For instance he speaks with admiration of Vercingetorix (*BG* 7.89.1–2) and emphasizes that the Gauls fought for their freedom (*BG* 3.8.4). These features indeed do go beyond the usual trick of exaggerating a defeated enemy's strength in order to enhance one's own victory.

Regarding the Germans, Gruen extensively considers one source, Tacitus' *Germania*, one of the most discussed works to have come to us

---

[13] Egyptian: 80–1, 90, 265–7, 266–72; Persian: 256–7, 260; Punic: 272–6.

[14] Sall. *Jug.* 17.7 claims to have consulted 'Punic books' by King Hiempsal II, translated for him.

[15] Gruen is clearly right in describing Cicero's *Pro Fonteio* as judicial rhetoric. That is no reason to dismiss it as evidence of popular views, however, for a good Roman lawyer will always employ rhetorical and judicial artifices that work among his audience.

from antiquity (ch. 6). The aim and message of the monograph have been considered in numerous ways and Gruen has added his own, original view on the work in a chapter full of subtle insights.[16] 'Germans, it is often presumed, were in Roman eyes the quintessential "barbarians". If so, Tacitus certainly does not perpetuate the stereotype' (161). Whatever Tacitus thought about the Germans, it was certainly not his aim to convey such a simple message and I am not sure that any modern authors would claim it was. Gruen is right in insisting on the complexity of Tacitus' views. 'The *Germania* remains an ambivalent and slippery text', as G. observes toward the end of his chapter (178).

When all is said and done, however, one has a feeling that it did not actually have a clear-cut aim or message, as Gruen interprets it. 'The historian serves up innuendos and imputations with balanced roguery. He aims not to underscore the "Otherness" of the Germans but to dissect and deconstruct it, to complicate and confuse it. For Tacitus, irony regularly trumps ideology' (178). Every reader may decide whether to accept this or not. It is my view that for Tacitus irony and rhetoric are instruments in conveying ideology and this ideology is not likely to have been the deconstruction of the 'Otherness' of the Germans.

In this connection there are two points to raise. First, there is Tacitus' insistence on the fact that the Germans are of pure lineage, 'not mixed at all with other peoples through immigration or intercourse'.[17] Tacitus (*Germ.* 4) repeats that he is of the opinion that 'the peoples of Germany have never contaminated themselves by intermarriage with foreign nations and that they appear as distinct, of pure blood, like none but themselves'. This, repeated twice at the beginning of the work, makes it hard to deny that Tacitus sees them as 'Others'. Second, there is Tacitus's insistence on the *libertas* of the Germani (discussed by Gruen on 169–72). I interpret this in not quite the same sense as Gruen. We need to clarify what kind of *libertas* is meant: collective or individual. I would say that it refers to the collective, the group: to collective freedom as the opposite of collective slavery/foreign rule, not to personal and individual liberty. Tacitus does not deny the internal social hierarchy which existed among the Germans, but here discusses freedom from foreign rule and absence of internal tyranny or domination by one man. There is ideology in this: the Germans did not live under foreign domination or tyranny, while the Romans did,

---

[16] E.g. the observations about *virtus*, 173–4 and the *interpretatio Romana*, 174–7.

[17] *Germ.* 1, discussed in Isaac, *Invention of Racism*, 137–40. Tacitus' claims of German pure blood are mentioned only in passing by Gruen, 162.

since the Principate had robbed them of their *libertas*. On Germans Gruen considers only Tacitus. It is not difficult to cite respectable authors who were far less subtle about Germans, such as Galen, who was no more in favour of them than of 'wolves and bears or other wild animals'.[18]

Next, Gruen relates to Tacitus' excursus on the Jews (ch. 7), another text that has been considered by generations of scholars. It attests to Gruen's originality that he manages to interpret such a well-known text in a novel manner. Whether we accept his view is another matter.

Gruen recognizes that Tacitus does not like Jews. However, the excursus is not a simple condemnation but a teasing, cunning, cynical text, full of paradoxes. Gruen frequently attempts to moderate hostile criticism by claiming that it is irony that needs to be taken *cum grano salis*. We see the same in the case of Xenophon, *Cyropaedia* 8.8, which he explains as a caricature (64–5), and of Juvenal's mockery of the Egyptians (110–11) and of people of colour (207). Gruen also uses it to moderate Juvenal's hostility towards the Jews: 'it is hazardous to place too serious an interpretation on Juvenal's sardonic wit' (182–3). This is a dangerous argument that could be applied to virtually every form of antisemitic and racist propaganda. Gruen further makes the point that Tacitus' many derogatory remarks about Jewish customs must be seen in perspective. He also skewers other groups he does not like, such as the Caesars and imperial freedmen. This is highly interesting and indubitably true, but does that reduce his animosity towards the Jews?

It is possible to read too much even into an author as complex and ambiguous as Tacitus. In *Historiae* 5.13, he at length criticizes the Jews for their misinterpretation and mishandling of threatening portents in AD 70, during the siege of Jerusalem by Titus. Gruen (194–5) argues that this is not a rebuke of Jewish belief, practice, and trust in the divine: 'one might well ask just how much faith Tacitus himself put in prodigies'. I see no reason to ask this question. Tacitus was quite capable of taking omens seriously. At the beginning of the revolt of Boudicca, 'without any evident cause, the statue of Victory at Camulodunum fell prostrate and turned its back to the enemy, as though it fled before them … and in the estuary of the Tamesa had been seen the appearance of an overthrown town; even the ocean had worn the aspect of blood' (*Ann.* 14.32). Tacitus tended to respect religion in such circumstances.[19] As Gruen agrees (195), Tacitus does not

---

[18] Gal. *San. tu.* 6.6.5: ἀλλ' ἡμεῖς γε νῦν οὔτε Γερμανοῖς οὔτε ἄλλοις τισὶν ἀγρίοις ἢ βαρβάροις ἀνθρώποις ταῦτα γράφομεν, οὐ μᾶλλον ἢ ἄρκτοις ἢ λέουσιν ἢ κάπροις ἢ τισι τῶν ἄλλων θηρίων, ἀλλ' Ἕλλησι καὶ ὅσοι τῷ γένει μὲν ἔφυσαν βάρβαροι, ζηλοῦσι δὲ τὰ τῶν Ἑλλήνων ἐπιτηδεύματα.

[19] R. Syme, *Tacitus* (Oxford, 1958), 523–7.

like the Jews, but unlike Gruen, I would argue that even for him there is a limit to paradox, cunning, and cynicism.

In my opinion there are three points to consider in Tacitus' attitude toward the Jews that Gruen appears not to regard as relevant. First, Tacitus wrote his excursus as introduction to his lost account of the siege of Jerusalem, but his acquaintance with Jews clearly goes back to their presence as a minority in Rome. His excursus is therefore part ethnography and history of a distant people and partly a reflection of his views on the minority in the city. Second, many Romans disapproved of Jews because of what they *did*, not because of what they *were*, because of their peculiar ways and manner of living, not because of any presumed inborn qualities. Third, Jewish monotheism as such was not so much an issue: the Jews were free to restrict their own pantheon as much as they wanted, but it was unacceptable that they rejected other people's gods. The rest followed from this. The bottom-line, as I see it, while Gruen does not, is that rejection, even if it is not racist, is still moral and social condemnation.

Chapter 8 deals with the People of Colour.[20] Here again it is essential to distinguish between attitudes towards the people of colour actually living among Greeks and Romans, and legendary Ethiopians who already appear in the work of Homer.[21] The Ethiopians are said to be autochthonous, a dubious compliment applied mostly to remote peoples such as the Britons, Germans, Indians, but also to some Greeks by those Greeks themselves: Athenians and Thebans. I call it dubious because the idea that pure lineage produces peoples of better quality than mixed stock has a pernicious later history, as has the notion of a connection between 'blood and soil'. Gruen rightly observes that the Ethiopians, once they appear as real people rather than legend, frequently come off well (201–4). However, in some texts there are also negative qualifications that, in my opinion, need to be recognized for what they are.

The Pseudo-Aristotelian *Physiognomica* asserts that blacks and curly-haired, namely Ethiopians and Egyptians, are cowardly.[22] Gruen (105) says this is an exception. I cannot agree. Physiognomics was a highly popular (pseudo-)science in antiquity and is represented by several treatises. A fourth-century AD essay, based on a lost one by Polemon, combines

---

[20] Gruen does not mention the work of D. Goldenberg, *The Curse of Ham: Race and Slavery in Early Judaism, Christianity, and Islam* (Princeton, 2003).

[21] For the legendary Ethiopians, see Romm, *Edges of the Earth*, 49–60.

[22] Ps. Arist. *Phgn.* 6.812a–b; cf. Gruen, *Rethinking the Other*, 205. For physiognomy and opinions on other peoples in antiquity, cf. Isaac, *Invention of Racism*, 149–62. For physiognomy and proto-racism between 1200 and 1500, see J. Ziegler, in Eliav-Feldon *et al.* (eds.), *Origins of Racism*, 181–99.

ethnic stereotypes with physiognomics: Egyptians and Ethiopians, because of their dark skins, are said to be 'frivolous, peaceful, cowardly and shrewd. Peoples with light skins, living in northern regions, are said to be courageous and bold and so forth'.[23] This is a popular form of stereotyping based on environmental determinism. It is part of an often repeated idea about the effect of northern and southern climates not only on the physical, but also on the mental qualities of groups.

Here we are concerned with distant peoples. However, there were dark-skinned people living among Greeks and Romans. Petronius, and especially Martial and Juvenal, refer to them in clearly unflattering terms. Gruen (207–9) again suggests that 'Satirists must have their due … One need not conclude that their parodist ethnic jabs represent widespread public prejudice'. I certainly agree with Gruen that there is no need to conclude that this is evidence of 'seething Roman hostility against blacks' – I am not aware of anyone claiming that this is the case, but neither am I convinced by Gruen's generous interpretation in a sphere of innocent and harmless fun.

In the second part of the book Gruen offers what may well be the most stimulating and original part: on 'Foundation Legends' (ch. 9), 'Fictitious Kinships' (chs. 10 and 11), and 'Cultural Interlockings and Overlappings' (ch. 12). Even if not all of us may agree with the conclusions, it is immediately clear that here we have a series of topics that are important and relevant for the discussion, besides being fascinating in their own right. They touch on essential questions regarding the manner in which Greeks, Romans, and Jews dealt with their own origins in various periods. These chapters undoubtedly will engender much exchange and further work.

The subject here is the distant, mythical past and the manner in which contacts and relationships with other peoples in that mythical past were invented and imagined. The legendary past was manipulated in surprising ways. This is a highly interesting topic, but it is a pity that so much material is analysed with so much care, exclusively in order to prove that the Greeks and Romans were tolerant and that the ancient world was multicultural. It is quite possible that there is more to it than that.

The essence of all this is that it concerns the mythical past. It remains to be seen and understood what this meant to Greeks and Romans in their

---

[23] Anonymi, *De physiognomonia* (ed. J. André, *Anonyme Latin Traité de Physiognomonie*, Paris, 1981), 79: *Color niger levem, imbellem, timidum, versutum indicat: refertur ad eos qui in meridiana plaga habitant, ut sunt Aethiopes, Aegyptii et qui his iuncti sunt. Color albus subrubeus fortes et animosos indicat: refertur ad eos qui in septentrione commorantur.*

classical age. Gruen asserts: 'The idea that nations had a common ancestor transcends conflict and warfare, and challenges the concept of "otherness"' (257). I am not persuaded, but I do agree with Gruen that this is an important issue which demands careful thinking.[24]

Gruen is not the first to devote extensive discussion to the issue of Athenian claims of autochthony and their descent from the original native population, the mythical Pelasgians (236–43). Many scholars have analysed the sources. It will suffice here to say that Gruen's arguments have not persuaded me to revise my published views.[25] I do not see that it is legitimate to discard Plato's *Menexenus* as mockery, Herodotus' relevant paragraphs (1.56–8) as muddle, and Isocrates' speeches *Helen* and *Panathenaicus* as rhetoric. Gruen does not mention Pericles' citizenship law of 451/0 BC which reserved the status of full citizenship for those who could prove that both parents were Athenian citizens.[26] Others have found this relevant. 'Pelasgians versus Hellenes' is a subject that demands more reflection than the question whether authors of the fifth century BC wrote in a spirit of kindness about their imagined predecessors. Gruen observes that 'Pelasgians are commonly conceived as "barbarians". Yet the designation nowhere carries a pejorative connotation' (242). It needs to be repeated: the Pelasgians are an imaginary people in the past and not a reality to fifth-century BC Greeks.

Furthermore, concerning the Greeks a distinction must be made between Hellenic chauvinism and chauvinism at the local or regional level. The Athenians saw themselves as autochthonous, but the Spartans or Corinthians made no such claim. Many Greeks had no serious thoughts about pure lineage, but it definitely exists as a theme in Greek thinking about origins. It is the great merit of Gruen's analysis that it shows that most Greeks did not mind having mixed ancestors in the distant past. This does not change the fact that they regarded contemporary non-Greeks as inferior.

'The ancient Mediterranean was a multicultural world' is the first sentence of chapter 10 (253). The *OED* defines 'multicultural' as follows: 'Of or relating to a society consisting of a number of cultural groups, esp.

---

[24] Note, in this connection, the observations by T. Hölscher, 'Myths, Images, and the Typology of Identities in Early Greek Art', in Gruen (ed.), *Cultural Identity in the Ancient Mediterranean* (Los Angeles, 2011), 47–65, at 48–50, 57–60.

[25] Isaac, *Invention of Racism*, 114–24 and *passim*.

[26] C. Patterson, *Pericles' Citizenship Law of 451–50 bc* (New York, 1981), 97–104, 133; D. Ogden, *Greek Bastardy in the Classical and Hellenistic Periods* (Oxford, 1996), 169–70, for the connection between autochthony and the citizenship law.

in which the distinctive cultural identity of each group is maintained'. This means that Gruen declares the ancient Mediterranean to be a single, coherent society adhering to an ideology that respected internal diversity in which the cultural identity of each group was maintained. It is a challenging statement that invites discussion. This review cannot do more than suggest that the subject should be debated.

Quite apart from the question how the Greeks and Romans related to other Mediterranean peoples, the statement above implies that the other Mediterranean peoples, such as the Egyptians, Phoenicians, Persians, and Jews, had a similar outlook and agreed with the Greeks and Romans on such matters. The Jews are the subject of separate treatment in Chapter 11. In Chapter 10 various episodes are discussed which, according to Gruen, provide evidence of a multicultural outlook on the part of the Egyptians and Persians. Herodotus (2.91) reports on Egyptians at Chemnis, who celebrate games in Greek style, 'because it was the home town of Danaus and of Lynceus, ancestor of Perseus'. Here we have a serious question of method. What can we really deduce about Egyptian attitudes in the fifth century BC from what Herodotus says about Egyptian customs involving Greek mythological characters? Gruen accepts that Herodotus' report contains precise and genuine information about Egyptian customs and their significance for Egyptian attitudes towards Greeks. The Egyptians respected kinship ties in this period, he says: 'The Chemnitans took the initiative here, adapting Hellenic modes of paying tribute to a Greek hero whom they claimed as their own by virtue of his Egyptian lineage' (85–6, 259). Alternative interpretations exist: 'To Herodotus the Greek character of the festival of Perseus was so striking in the light of Egyptian distaste for foreign customs that it became a θῶμα.'[27] 'At Chemnis (Perseus) had evidently been identified with a local deity who must be either Horus or Min-Hor … We can only assume that, when Perseus was identified with the local god, Greeks resident in the area introduced games of a Hellenic type which were celebrated in association with the cult of the Egyptian god.'[28]

The next topic is a Mesopotamian affiliation for Perseus, as reported by Herodotus 6.54: 'According to the Persian story, Perseus was an Assyrian who became a Greek; his ancestors, therefore, according to them, were not Greeks.' Herodotus was not a direct source for Persia, as he was, somehow, for Egypt, because he had visited it. Yet Gruen concludes: 'But it appears

---

[27] D. Asheri et al., *A Commentary on Herodotus, Books I–IV* (Oxford, 2007), *ad loc.*, 302–3, with references to 2.79.1 and to pp. 234–7.

[28] Gruen regards this as 'an unnecessary hypothesis' (259). He insists that Egyptians, not local Greeks, were the agents.

that Persian fictions, drawing on the reshaping of Hellenic legend, connected their own history in diverse ways with Assyrians, Greeks and even Egyptians, a genuinely multicultural mix' (260). What we have, however, is just one Greek author who did not even read Persian.[29]

Perseus, as Gruen interprets it, also has a Jewish connection (260–1). The basis for this claim is the identification of Joppe/Jaffa with the site of Perseus' rescue of Andromeda from the sea monster. G. calls this 'Jewish appropriation of the classical myth'. This identification is first attested in Pseudo-Scylax's *Periplous* of the fourth century.[30] The text, in bad shape, also describes the city as one 'of the Sidonians', i.e. controlled by Phoenicians. There is good evidence that these were Hellenized Phoenicians. The Jews obtained control over Jaffa and its port only in the Hasmonaean period, after the middle of the second century BC, under the leadership of Simon the Maccabee.[31] The transfer of Perseus' and Andromeda's adventure to Jaffa was therefore the initiative of Hellenized Sidonians, long before the Jews took control over the city.

Gruen concludes (264): 'Perseus is the quintessential Hellenic hero, ancestor of Doric kings. He had a mother with Egyptian roots. Egyptians appropriated him for their own. Persians happily accepted Perseus as a forebear, but they tampered with his ancestry. Phoenicians and Jews attached themselves to the multicultural blend.' The material is fascinating, but, in my opinion, requires further investigation. The Jewish connection here is quite uncertain.

Then there are the origins of Rome. Virgil's *Aeneid* is familiar: Aeneas, Aphrodite's son and a Trojan, migrated to Italy and became the ancestor of the founders of Rome. Thus the destruction of Troy by the ancestors of the Greeks would have resulted in the foundation of Rome as a new Troy. Gruen analyses the various versions and alternatives of the legends surrounding the prehistory of Rome's foundation (243–9). Rome was a city that acquired an empire, unlike any Greek city before Alexander including Athens which, after all, only dominated other Greek cities for some time, but not foreign peoples. As Gruen rightly observes, 'The most celebrated

---

[29] Hdt. 7.150 cites envoys of Xerxes who accepted the regular Greek view. Let us just say that they were diplomats.

[30] G. Shipley, *Pseudo-Scylax's Periplous: The Circumnavigation of the Inhabited World, Text, Translation and Commentary* (Bristol, 2011), 104.3: Δῶρος πόλις Σιδωνίων, κ[αὶ Ἰόππη πόλις· ἐκτε]θῆναί φασιν ἐνταῦθα τὴν Ἀνδρομ[έδαν τῷ κήτει. Ἀσκά]λων πόλις Τυρίων καὶ βασίλεια. ἐνταῦ[θα ὄρος ἐστὶ τῆς Κοίλης] Συρίας. Cf. Gruen, pp. 260–4.

[31] See on Jaffa in the *Corpus Inscriptionum Judaeae/Palaestinae* (Berlin, 2014), III, with the historical introduction.

and familiar case of fictitious foreign kinships must surely be that of Troy and Rome. Readers of Vergil from antiquity to the present have the tale of Rome's linkage to the survivors of the Trojan War as a fixture in their consciousness' (243). The fact that Rome as a city claimed that it had roots in Asia Minor is important and should be evaluated. Undoubtedly Gruen is right in concluding that the idea of autochthony or indigenous origins never made much headway in Rome – at least for the Romans themselves. Gruen discusses a complex web of associations and relationships in the mythical past: Rome's association with Troy, Greece's legendary enemy through Aeneas, is one such tie. Another is the assertion that Evander the Arcadian (son of Hermes) planted a colony, Pallantion, on the Palatine. Yet another is the claim of an association of Aeneas with Arcadia.[32] Thus Rome had Greek roots as well. As Gruen says rightly, this is complex. There is no simple, linear story.

Further thought may be given to the contemporary significance, attached in imperial Rome to foreign descent in the legendary past. Romans did not claim to be autochthonous. Perhaps it was therefore seen as desirable to have an association with Phoenicians and Egyptians, Greeks and other Asiatics in the past, when they were at the pinnacle of greatness. I am not certain that such ideas are a testimony of Roman tolerance. Perhaps an indication of this may be found in Cato's work: the Spartans were among the ancestors of the Sabines. According to Cato that was where Roman toughness originated.[33] In other words: Spartan toughness in the distant past was the progenitor of Roman toughness in the present. It is one thing to identify with past glory, another to respect your foreign contemporaries.

All of Chapter 11 is devoted to 'Fictitious Kinships, Jews and Others'. I am not competent to assess Gruen's discussion of the Bible. Two points to be made, however, are the following: if the people of Israel had a joint ancestor with the Ishmaelites, that did not reduce the enmity felt through the ages and, in fact, the enmity there was appears to have had its origin in the treatment of Ishmael by his father and Sarah. Second, there is a long list of mixed marriages in the biblical tradition, as Gruen points out. This undoubtedly says something about biblical attitudes towards such

---

[32] Cf. Tania S. Scheer, 'Ways of Becoming Arcadian: Arcadian Foundation Myths', in E. Gruen, *Cultural Identity*, 11–25.

[33] Cato F 2.22 (Beck and Walter), cited by Gruen, *Rethinking the Other*, 248, n. 148. Cato was not so anti-Greek as is usually claimed, argues Gruen (245–6) with a reference to A. Henrichs, 'Graecia Capta: Roman Views of Greek Culture', *HSCP* 97 (1995): 243–61, at 244–50. All I can find in this study is evidence that Cato knew Greek well.

marriages, but I cannot begin to evaluate the significance of this phenomenon for the social attitudes it represents.[34]

We owe Gruen an enormous debt for his beautifully written, provocative study. It gives due weight to a topic central to our evaluation of ancient social relationships. It will stimulate intensive exchange about the moral standards of Greeks, Romans, and Jews in their attitude towards foreigners.

Rather than summarize and describe the contents and architecture of the book, let me give the basics of its contents:

Part I: Impressions of the 'Other'
Chapter 1: 'Persian in the Greek Perception: Aeschylus and Herodotus'
Chapter 2: 'Persia in the Greek Perception: Xenophon and Alexander'
Chapter 3: 'Egypt in the Classical Imagination'
Chapter 4: '*Punica Fides*'
Chapter 5: 'Caesar on the Gauls'
Chapter 6: 'Tacitus on the Germans'
Chapter 7: 'Tacitus and the Defamation of the Jews'
Chapter 8: 'People of Color'
Part II: Connections with the 'Other'
Chapter 9: 'Foundation Legends'
Chapter 10: 'Fictitious Kinships: Greeks and Others'
Chapter 11: 'Fictitious Kinships: Jews and Others'
Chapter 12: 'Cultural Interlockings and Overlappings'
Conclusion

---

[34] Gruen, *Rethinking the Other*, 250–2: The Jews also claimed to have numerous foreign ancestors in the Hellenistic and Roman traditions. I shall leave it to others to consider these remarkable assertions. They belong to biblical as much as to Hellenistic culture and I am here out of my depth.

Latin in Cities of the Roman Near East

Four languages are appropriately used in the world. And these are: Greek for song. Latin for war. Syriac (Aramaic) for mourning. Hebrew for speaking.[1]

Rabbi Jonathan of Eleutheropolis (third century) is the author of this famous statement regarding the respective qualities of the four languages: Greek, Latin, Syriac, and Hebrew. According to his view, Greek is most suitable for 'zemer', which in this instance means song in the broader sense of the word – poetry.[2] The other qualifications do not require comment.

In the Roman Near East, various languages were used for written and oral communication. The relative importance of these languages is a topic frequently studied and discussed. Two of the languages were imported by conquerors from the West. Of these, it is clear that Latin, unlike Greek, was never used widely, but it is also obvious that the first language of the Empire played a role in communications. In the present chapter I shall attempt to consider the question of the extent to which Latin may have been more than the language of government and military organization in the cities of the Near East from Pompey to the third century. This is only one aspect – but an important one – of the impact of Western, Roman influence on the cities of the Near East.[3]

The region to be considered for present purposes is more narrowly that of Syria, Judaea/Palaestina, and Arabia, excluding the numerous cities of

---

An early version of this paper was delivered at a conference 'Epigraphy and Beyond', Institute for Advanced Studies, Jerusalem, 30 June–2 July 2003. An expanded version was originally intended for a volume in honour of Fergus Millar, the publication of which was cancelled. The chapter as published owes much to the diligent and careful editorial work of Richard Alston. It was then published in H. M. Cotton *et al.* (eds.), *From Hellenism to Islam: Cultural and Linguistic Change in the Roman Near East* (Cambridge, 2009), 43–72. Here it has been revised slightly to take account of recent publications.

[1] Y. Megilla I 71b, col. 748.

[2] S. Lieberman, *Greek in Jewish Palestine* (New York and Jerusalem, 1994), 21.

[3] Clearly, there are other aspects, not to be discussed here, such as the presence of amphitheatres in eastern cities. These are found not just in Roman colonies like Caesarea, but in regular *poleis* such as Scythopolis, Neapolis, Eleutheropolis, and Gerasa.

Asia Minor. This is appropriate because the cultural and linguistic differences between these regions are such that a comparison might well result
in misleading conclusions. Any attempt to lump them together would
ignore essential aspects of linguistic culture and I therefore follow the precedent of major recent works of synthesis which exclude Anatolia in their
treatment of the Roman Near East.[4] For the present study, this is appropriate all the more because the process of Hellenization is so markedly different between the various regions. Ephesus on the coast of the Aegean was
an important Greek *polis* from the archaic period onwards. Its language
always was Greek and the introduction of Latin as the language of government under the Principate was due to its status as a *conventus* centre, seat of
the governor and chief centre for the Roman ruler cult. Perge in Pamphylia
may have had its origins as a Hittite city, but its claims to Hellenic status
go back centuries before the arrival of Roman rule. The latter is true also
for a city like Side. Greek was the norm in those cities. Latin could never
achieve predominance, except in communities of Latin-speaking settlers
such those in southern Asia Minor.[5] The situation in the area of the Eastern
Levant, here to be considered, was different. The city populations and those
of the surrounding territories were always linguistically mixed. The local
languages were Semitic, and Greek arrived only with the establishment of
Seleucid and Ptolemaic rule. While some cities, such as Apamea, Gadara,
and Ascalon, produced highly respectable Greek intellectuals at some stage
and while others certainly wished to be regarded in the Greek heartland as
genuinely Greek, there is good evidence to show that this was a vain hope.[6]
The degree of Hellenization varied and is today often difficult to trace.
Whatever the relationship between the local Semitic languages and Greek,
Greek was the second language introduced by imperial rulers in this region
and Latin was the third. It seems therefore questionable whether the use of
Latin can be profitably compared in these two different regions and I will
restrict myself to Syria, Judaea-Palaestina, and Arabia.[7]

---

[4] F. Millar, *The Roman Near East: 31 BC–AD 337* (Cambridge, 1993); W. Ball, *Rome in the East: The Transformation of an Empire* (London, 2000); M. Sartre, *D'Alexandre à Zénobie, Histoire du Levant antique iv* siècle avant J.-C. iii* siècle après J.-C.* (Paris, 2003). It will be obvious that the present chapter focuses on a relatively small part of the Empire. Much can be said – and has been said – about
other regions, such as, for instance, North Africa. See e.g. F. Millar, 'Local Cultures in the Roman
Empire: Libyan, Punic and Latin in Roman Africa', *JRS* 58 (1968): 126–34; M. Benabou, *La résistance
africaine à la Romanisation* (Paris, 1976) with C. R. Whittaker's review in *JRS* 68 (1978): 190–2.
[5] B. Levick, *Roman Colonies in Southern Asia Minor* (Oxford, 1967).
[6] See the conclusions to this chapter and above, Chapter 7: 'Attitudes towards Provincial Intellectuals
in the Roman Empire'.
[7] It will be clear that these assumptions are not shared by my colleague Werner Eck, whose paper
in the volume in which the present article was originally published discusses Anatolian cities for

The ancient literature is not very informative on the use of Latin in non-Latin-speaking provinces. In this respect, the situation resembles a related and even larger topic, which is popularly called 'Romanization', an only apparently transparent term for political, economic, and cultural accultur-ation or the assimilation of subject peoples to Roman imperial society. For the present, far more modest subject, the obvious material to study is the epigraphic record and this immediately raises the question of the extent to which this is reliable evidence for social and cultural issues beyond that of epigraphic practices themselves. Can we take language use in epigraphic contexts as representative of issues of non-epigraphic language use or cul-tural identity, for instance?

Language use is determined by many factors, as will be obvious if we think of more recent parallels. In India, Hindi was declared the official language after independence alongside some eighteen officially recognized languages. English, however, in many ways a remnant of British colonial rule, continued to be a widely used *lingua franca*, especially by educated Indians in business, government, and academic life, and even more than half a century after independence, the English press remains influential. At another level, English serves as the means of communication between central government and the non-Hindi-speaking states. Yet it remains the first language of only a small percentage of the population. By compari-son, in Indonesia, formerly a Dutch colony, Bahasa Indonesia, originally a Malay dialect, was declared the official language and functions as such, though a multitude of other languages are in common use; Dutch has dis-appeared altogether, apart from a few loanwords. Again, in Laos, Vietnam, and Cambodia, formerly French Indochina, the French language did not penetrate deeply. In countries under German occupation during the Second World War, German was the language of communication between the occupying powers and the local authorities, but the language did not otherwise penetrate the society of the occupied. It is clear that these dif-ferences have been caused by combinations of factors, to be sought in the policies and practices of the rulers, in the social and linguistic situation of the ruled, in the length of time during which the foreign language was officially dominant, and, not least, in the circumstances surrounding the ousting of the occupying power. Whatever the reasons, their complexity

similar purposes: W. Eck, 'The Language of Power: Latin in the Roman Near East', in Cotton *et al.* (eds.), *From Hellenism to Islam*, 15–42. It is clear also that we disagree about the nature of society in Caesarea-on-the-Sea from the Flavian period onwards, and I hope that the contrasting arguments produced in these two papers will eventually contribute to scholarly clarity – if not agreement – in these complex matters.

and the variety of post-occupation linguistic reactions show how cautious we must be in drawing conclusions regarding language use in societies for which the extant evidence is scarce, or in drawing, consciously or unconsciously, on modern parallels in considering the ancient situation.[8]

In assessing the impact of Latin in the Roman Near East, we must keep in mind that there are several mechanisms at work.[9] First, there are the Roman authorities who used Latin for themselves and sometimes, but not always, Greek in their communications with the locals. Second, there is the Roman army, which functioned mostly in Latin and continued doing so for centuries even when recruitment was overwhelmingly local. Third, there was the settlement of speakers of Latin in a few parts of the region. Such settlers were in part drawn from retired soldiers. Finally, it is conceivable that in centres with a substantial Latin-speaking population this language was adopted to some extent by people with Greek or a Semitic language in order to interact with the speakers of Latin. This leads us to another large and related topic, that of bilingualism. In the Near East and

---

[8] There are several extensive older publications on the use of Latin and Greek in the Roman Empire: L. Hahn, *Rom und Romanismus im griechisch-römischen Osten mit besonderer Berücksichtigung der Sprache* (Leipzig, 1906), 110–18, 208–23; 'Zum Sprachenkampf im römischen Reich bis auf die Zeit Justinians', *Philologus*, suppl. 10 (1907), 675–718; A. Buturas, *Ein Kapitel der historischen Grammatik der griechischen Sprache: Über die gegenseitigen Beziehungen der griechischen und der fremden Sprachen, besonders über die fremden Einflüsse auf das Griechische seit der nachklassischen Periode bis zur Gegenwart* (Leipzig, 1910), 55–8. For the Eastern Roman Empire, see H. Zilliacus, *Zum Kampf der Weltsprachen im oströmischen Reich* (Helsingfors, 1935; repr. Amsterdam, 1965). Note the more recent paper by M. Dubuisson, 'Y a-t-il une politique linguistique romaine?', *Ktema* 7 (1982): 187–210, where it is argued that there was no Roman policy attempting to stimulate, let alone impose, the use of Latin in the provinces.

[9] B. Rochette, *Le Latin dans le monde grec: Recherches sur la diffusion de la langue et des lettres latines dans les provinces hellénophones de l'Empire Romain* (Brussels, 1997); W. Eck, 'Latein als Sprache politischer Kommunikation in Städten der östlichen Provinzen', *Chiron* 3 (2000): 641–60, discusses several inscriptions from Perge; W. Eck, 'Ein Spiegel der Macht: Lateinische Inschriften römischer Zeit in Iudaea/Syria Palaestina', *ZPalV* 117 (2001): 47–63; Eck, 'The Language of Power: Latin in the Inscriptions of Iudaea/Syria Palaestina', in L. H. Schiffman (ed.), *Semitic Papyrology in Context* (Leiden, 2003), 123–44; R. Schmitt, 'Die Sprachverhältnisse in den östlichen Provinzen des Römischen Reiches', *ANRW* 2.29.2 (1983): 554–86, esp. 561–3. S. Schwartz, 'Language, Power and Identity in Ancient Palestine', *P&P* 148 (1995): 3–47, is, in spite of its title, concerned only with the use of Hebrew and Aramaic by Jews. For local languages in the Roman Empire see R. MacMullen, 'Provincial Languages in the Roman Empire', *AJA* 87 (1966): 1–17, with discussion of the use of Syriac, Coptic, Punic, and Celtic in the Empire. For the (local) languages in Palestine, from 200 BC till AD 200 see J. C. Greenfield, 'The Languages of Palestine, 200 BCE–200 CE', in H. H. Paper (ed.), *Jewish Languages: Theme and Variations* (Cambridge, 1978), 143–54, with responses by H. C. Youtie, 'Response to Greenfield', 155–7, and F. E. Peters, 'Response to Greenfield', 159–64. H. B. Rosén, 'Die Sprachsituation im römischen Palästina', in G. Neumann and J. Untermann (eds.), *Die Sprachen im römischen Reich der Kaiserzeit: Kolloquium vom 8. bis 10. April 1974* (Cologne and Bonn, 1980), 215–39, at 219, claims that Latin had only administrative significance in Roman Palestine. R. Schmitt, 'Die Sprachverhältnisse in den östlichen Provinzen des Römischen Reiches', *ANRW* 2.29.2 (1983): 554–86, states that in Syria Latin was used only in the army and in Berytus.

in many or most of the provinces of the Roman Empire, bilingualism was a widespread phenomenon. Adams' recent study of the role of Latin and bilingualism in Egypt has demonstrated the need to reassess the available source material for all provinces.[10] In this chapter I am concerned with the role of Latin in cities, notably the Roman citizen colonies.[11] However, my discussion here is heavily dependent on our understanding of the role of Latin in the army and among the authorities. Concerning language use in the army, Adams concludes:

> A persistent misconception is that Latin was the 'official' language of the army ... While it is true that service in the army gave recruits, if they were not Latin speakers, the opportunity to acquire the language and although there might have been pressure on them to do so, in that training in the skills of Latin literacy seems to have been provided, some excessively sweeping generalisations have been made about the role of Latin as the official language of the army.[12]

Adams cites military documents from Egypt with the aim of showing that Greek was acceptable for official purposes.[13] Latin, however, was, as formulated by Adams, 'a sort of supreme or super-high language in the army, which was bound to be used in certain circumstances, e.g. correspondence with the Emperor'.[14] Or, as formulated by Valerius Maximus in a frequently cited passage:

> How carefully the magistrates of old regulated their conduct to keep intact the majesty of the Roman people and their own can be seen from the fact

---

[10] J. N. Adams, M. Janse, and S. Swain (eds.), *Bilingualism in Ancient Society: Language Contact and the Written Text* (Oxford, 2002); J. N. Adams, *Bilingualism and the Latin Language* (Cambridge, 2003).

[11] Rochette, *Le Latin dans le monde grec*, does not seriously discuss the subject at hand.

[12] Adams, *Bilingualism*, 599.

[13] J. N. Adams, 'Language Use in the Army in Egypt', in Adams *et al.*, *Bilingualism*, 599–623: 'There was no rigid adherence to a policy of using Latin for public documents in the army; on the contrary, there were occasions when a decision was taken to use Greek instead' (602). 'Greek was acceptable for record keeping even if there was a scribe to hand who could have used Latin' (607). '... matters of an official kind were regularly handled in Greek, both in dealings with outsiders to the unit and in internal record keeping' (608).

[14] Adams, 'Language Use in the Army in Egypt', 608–17. The *dux Aegypti* did not respond in Latin when he received a petition in Greek. Latin would be used when a superior wished to assert his power over a subordinate, or when a subordinate wished to make a potent appeal to a higher authority. It was used for the transmission of orders, receipts and promissory notes, *diplomata*, dedications to emperors. The incidents often cited in this respect may be more significant as exceptions than as a true reflection of the rule of behaviour. These are described by Suetonius, *Tiberius* 71: describing Tiberius' reluctance to use Greek loanwords in the Senate, he also relates that the Emperor prohibited a soldier from giving testimony in Greek. Suetonius, *Claudius* 16.2, reports that Claudius removed a Greek dignitary from the list of jurors and also took away his Roman citizenship because he did not know Latin. Dio 60.17.4 says he was a Lycian.

that among other indications of their duty to preserve dignity they stead-
fastly kept to the rule never to make replies to Greeks except in Latin.
Indeed they obliged the Greeks themselves to discard the volubility, which
is their greatest asset, and speak through an interpreter, not only in Rome
but in Greece and Asia also, intending no doubt that the dignity of Latin
speech be the more widely venerated throughout all nations ... (Thinking)
it unmeet that the weight and authority of empire be sacrificed to the seduc-
tive charm of letters.[15]

All this may have been true for the 'old magistrates' but it follows that it
was no longer the reality of the first century AD when Valerius Maximus
wrote these lines.[16] The same is true for a rather similar pronouncement by
John the Lydian.[17]

Since the cities of the East have not produced the abundance of papyri
available for Egypt, we must have recourse to the inscriptions on stone of
which many have been found.[18] Clearly, however, the usual type of public
inscriptions encountered in the inscriptions of the Roman East do not
require any serious knowledge of the language and are not evidence of
the language commonly spoken or written by those who set them up.
Nevertheless, the languages used for public declarations of political, cultural, and social identity in the various cities of the Roman East are important in themselves.

In the present chapter, therefore, I shall consider the various categories
of inscriptions in Latin that are found in a number of cities of the Roman
East and attempt to formulate conclusions about the use of this language
in documents meant to be read by or displayed to the public. The analysis
depends very much on the availability of published material. Preservation
and publication are very uneven for the various cities of the region, and
this, of course, raises methodological issues when considering the relative

---

[15] Valerius Maximus 2.2.2 (trans. Shackleton-Bailey): *Magistratus uero prisci quantopere suam populique
Romani maiestatem retinentes se gesserint hinc cognosci potest, quod inter cetera obtinendae grauitatis
indicia illud quoque magna cum perseuerantia custodiebant, ne Graecis umquam nisi latine responsa
darent. quin etiam ipsos linguae uolubilitate, qua plurimum ualent, excussa per interpretem loqui coge-
bant non in urbe tantum nostra, sed etiam in Graecia et Asia, quo scilicet Latinae uocis honos per omnes
gentes uenerabilior diffunderetur. nec illis deerant studia doctrinae, sed nulla non in re pallium togae
subici debere arbitrabantur, indignum esse existimantes inlecebris et suauitati litterarum imperii pondus
et auctoritatem donari.*

[16] As observed by Dubuisson, 'Y a-t-il une politique linguistique romaine?', 195.

[17] Joannes Laurentius Lydus, *De magistratibus populi Romani*, 2.12 and 3.42; cf. Dubuisson, 'Y a-t-il
une politique linguistique romaine?', 196; M. Maas, *John Lydus and the Roman Past* (London and
New York, 1992), 25, 32, 87.

[18] Adams, *Bilingualism and the Latin Language*, 617: 'An epitaph might be seen as the ultimate definition of a person's identity.'

incidence of Latin inscriptions at the various sites. In spite of the paucity of evidence, one category excluded from the analysis is inscribed milestones. Since these were formal texts set up by the army on instructions from the provincial authorities, they were obviously in Latin. By the end of the second century, in the reign of Severus, we find the first milestones which use Greek, in particular for distances.[19] The reason for this is that the responsibility for the maintenance of the road-system and, with it, the erection of milestones, fell increasingly upon the local authorities and has more to do with the development of provincial administration than with the topic at hand. In the remaining categories of Latin inscriptions from the Eastern cities and their territories, my analysis attempts to determine whether their erection and the choice of language in the inscriptions were the responsibility of the Roman authorities, such as the governor and procurator and their staffs; the Roman army, either active-duty soldiers or officers; veterans, either of local origin or settled after service in the area; local civilian speakers of Latin who may have been descendants of veterans settled in Roman citizen colonies or local citizens who served in the army and their relatives; or other civilians.

The use of Latin is more expected if army personnel and provincial authorities are involved, and it is thus of particular interest to attempt to assess the use of the language outside those circles. We know that Latin was used to some extent in Eastern cities with colonial status, as is clear from their coin inscriptions as well as from the fairly numerous inscriptions on stone so far published. The point of interest is whether and why local civilians from these cities set up inscriptions in Latin, and whether we can establish any kind of social context for those epigraphic Latinists.

The Roman colonies in the East were, like those in the West, either genuine veteran colonies such as Berytus (which presumably at first included Heliopolis and vicinity), Acco-Ptolemais, and Aelia Capitolina, or titular colonies, the most important of which for our purposes are Caesarea-on-the-Sea, Bostra, and Gerasa. Veteran colonies were reorganized at the time of the foundation, and veterans from the Roman legions were settled there and received land. They formed a local elite imposed upon the existing communities. By contrast, the titular colonies were established through political reorganization and a change in status, unaccompanied by the settlement of veterans or other foreigners. There is therefore an essential

---

[19] Cf. B. Isaac, 'Milestones in Judaea', in B. Isaac, *The Near East under Roman Rule: Selected Papers* (Leiden, 1998), 48–75, at 62–5. Tetrarchic milestones and those of Constantine and his colleagues are usually in Latin.

difference: the establishment of a veteran colony represented a serious disruption of social and economic life in a community and the imposition of a foreign upper class.[20]

Heliopolis-Baalbek

The fullest, most accessible, and therefore instructive collection is that of Heliopolis-Baalbek. The legal status of Heliopolis in the first and second centuries AD should not concern us here. It was either founded as a separate colony by Augustus or was part of the territory of Berytus, founded by Augustus no later than 14 BC. In the reign of Severus, it is on record as a separate colony.[21] Whatever the case, the city was occupied by veterans of the legions *V Macedonica* and *VIII Augusta* in the time of Augustus. In spite of this early occupation by veterans, the earliest imperial texts from the region are relatively late: two rock-cut inscriptions along the Heliopolis–Damascus road which mention Nero.[22] In the town the earliest dated inscription mentions Vespasian on a dedication.[23]

There are 306 inscriptions in Greek and Latin from the town, the sanctuary, and the vicinity, of which 131 are in Latin.[24] The exceptional nature of the Latin epigraphic record becomes obvious if we compare this corpus of inscriptions with that from the major city of Emesa, which has not produced a single Latin inscription, apart from milestones and boundary stones.[25] Yet one might have expected Emesa to produce some Latin texts

---

[20] It will suffice to refer to the establishment of the veteran colony at Camulodunum (Colchester). Tacitus, *Ann.* 12.32, states that a strong body of veterans was installed on expropriated land and describes vividly the procedure: the veterans ejected Britons from their homes, confiscated their land, and treated them as slaves. The town was 'the seat of servitude' in the eyes of the Britons and we are told of their fierce hatred of the veterans. Elsewhere, in a speech which Tacitus puts in the mouth of Arminius, the leader of the Germanic revolt, the essence of Roman provincial rule is expressed by the phrase *dominos et colonias novas: Ann.*1.59.8. Appian, *BC* 5.12–14, describes problems caused by the settlement of veterans in Italy. The walls of Colonia Agrippinensis (Cologne) are referred to as *munimenta servitii* (Tacitus, *Hist.* 4.64).

[21] References and discussion by J.-P. Rey-Coquais, *Inscriptions Grecques et Latines de la Syrie (IGLS)*, VI, *Baalbek et Beqa* (Paris, 1967), 34, n. 9 (for references to earlier discussion) and Rey-Coquais, 'Syrie romaine de Pompée à Dioclétien', *JRS* 68 (1978): 51–73; F. Millar, 'The Roman *Coloniae* of the Near East: A Study of Cultural Relations', in H. Solin and F. M. Kajave (eds.), *Roman Policy in the East and Other Studies in Roman History, Proceedings of a Colloquium at Tvärmine, 1987* (Helsinki, 1990), 7–57, at 10–23, 31–4; B. Isaac, *The Limits of Empire: The Roman Army in the East*, revised edn (Oxford, 1992), 318–21, 342–4; Millar, *Roman Near East*.

[22] *IGLS* VI, 2968.

[23] *IGLS* VI, 2762.

[24] All numbers derive from the collection in *IGLS* VI.

[25] *IGLS* 5 (Émésène). Latin boundary stones: nos. 2549, 2552. Milestones: 2672, 2674–6; see also 2704, 2708. Cf. Millar, *Roman Near East*, 300–9.

since its citizens served in units named after the city and at least one of those was a *cohors milliaria c(ivium) R(omanorum)*.[26] The first group of inscriptions from Heliopolis to be mentioned is dedications to Iupiter Optimus Maximus Heliopolitanus. There are nineteen of those, two of them erected by military men[27] and two by freedmen.[28] Then there are fourteen inscriptions on statue bases for emperors; on four of these the donors are private individuals. Two inscriptions record dedications to kings: Sohaemus of Emesa and Agrippa (either I or II), who apparently had a close relationship with the colony.[29] There are also five inscriptions in honour of provincial governors. For three of these it is not clear who dedicated them. Of the inscriptions with known dedicators, one was set up by the governor's *equites singulares*, the other (2779) by a centurion of the *legio VII Gemina*. Such dedications could have come from any urban centre which the governor regularly visited. Finally, there are forty-five inscriptions in Latin which mention people of local origin (as distinct from military personnel or officials who were not citizens of the colony, but present temporarily on duty). Two of these were members of senatorial families.[30] One remarkable equestrian career is recorded on a statue base, 2796, for C. Velius Rufus, clearly from Heliopolis, who was active in the second half of the first century. Several of his descendants were senators. There are two other equestrian careers: 2781 recording the career of L. Antonius Naso, who became a tribune of the Praetorian Guard and procurator.[31] The second is recorded

---

[26] J. Fitz, *Les Syriens à Intercisa* (Brussels, 1972).

[27] *IGLS* VI, 2711, dated AD 212–17, by Aurelius Antonius Longinus, a *speculator* of the *legio III Gal.*, stationed at Raphanaeae. The name is characteristic for a recent grant of citizenship and it is therefore not clear what connection the dedicant had with Heliopolis. There is no such doubt in the case of L. Antonius Silo (no. 2714, AD 128–38), *eques* of the *III Aug.*, *Heliopolitanus*, by his heirs, all four of the *tribus Fabia*, and therefore also Heliopolitans.

[28] *IGLS* VI, 2713, origin not certain, and 2719.

[29] *IGLS* VI, 2760 for Sohaemus, '*Patronus Coloniae* ... set up by L Vitellius L f Fab Sossianus'. *IGLS* VI, 2759 for Agrippa, *patronus coloniae*.

[30] *IGLS* VI, 2795: T. Statilius Maximus, for whose senatorial career see comments *ad loc*. A relative of his, Titus Statilius Maximus Bromiacus, is attested at Berytus (see below). *IGLS* VI, 2797: a senatorial descendant of the equestrian officer C. Velius Rufus, honoured in *IGLS* VI, 2796. *IGLS* VI, 2795 refers to a member of a senatorial family which produced three consuls in the second century and is also mentioned at Berytus (2796, 2798). Cf. G. W. Bowersock, 'Roman Senators from the Near East: Syria, Judaea, Arabia, Mesopotamia', in *Atti del colloquio internazionale AIEQL su epigrafia e ordine senatorio, Roma 1981* (Rome, 1982), II, 651–68, esp. 665–6, nos. 16–18. Note also *IGLS* VI 2785 honouring Sex. Attius Suburanus, twice consul under Trajan. The inscription dates to the end of the first century, while he was still an *eques*. There is no evidence of a personal connection with Heliopolis apart from this dedication by the brothers of his *cornicularius*.

[31] Cf. *IGLS* VI, no. 2761, where it is suggested that Antonius Taurus, mentioned on the base of a statue of Vespasian, is the tribune of the praetorians mentioned by Tacitus, *Hist.* 1.20, together with Antonius Naso. In that case, we would have another Heliopolitan *eques*.

on two statue bases (2793, 2794): P. Statilius Justus Sentianus, who was *praefectus fabrum* and tribune of the legion *II Traiana* as well as *decurio coloniae*. Nine inscriptions refer to military careers of local men below the equestrian level.[32] Five other Latin inscriptions mention locally significant men with Roman names who did not, apparently, have imperial careers outside the city.[33] Twenty-one fragmentary Latin inscriptions are too far gone to be instructive for the present topic.

No less significant is the number of Latin inscriptions from the vicinity of Heliopolis, which shows that there were Latin speakers, clearly descendants of the original colonists and locals, who were integrated with their families in the territory of the colony. I count twenty-three private individuals, twelve of them identified by their *tria nomina*.[34] Remarkable is a dedication on an altar for 'Iupiter Optimus Beelseddes' by three men, named Viveius Cand(idus?), Septimius Sator(ninus), and Adrus (2925). We may note also a boundary stone of a village from the territory.[35] Eleven additional Latin inscriptions are too fragmentary for profitable interpretation.

Of special interest is the material from Niha, in the Beqa valley, where a series of inscriptions in Latin records the existence of a sanctuary of the Syrian Goddess of Niha', Hadaranes, or Atargatis.[36] One of those mentions the *Pagus Augustus*, presumably an association of Latin-speaking Roman citizens which will have been settled there at the time of the foundation of the Roman colony. At this sanctuary some evidence of social integration

---

[32] *IGLS* VI, 2782: a *primus pilus*; I2783: a centurion; 2786 and 2787: L. Gerellanus who became *primus pilus* of the legion X Fretensis and *praefectus castrorum* of the legion XII Fulminata fulfilled functions in the colony. The statues were set up by respectively a centurion of legion X Fretensis and M. Antonius Sosipatrus, a friend. 2789: a statue of a *hastatus* of the XIII Gemina set up by his son, a centurion of the I Adiutrix. Their connection with Heliopolis is not clear. 2798: a fragmentary inscription on a statue base for a *primus pilus* who was honoured by the city, perhaps because he was of local origin. *IGLS* VI, 2844 is the epitaph of a *protector*, by his brother, also a *protector* (late third century). It is not unlikely that they were local citizens. 2788 is too fragmentary to tell us anything, apart from the rank of the honorand.

[33] *IGLS* VI, 2780, 2784, 2790–2.

[34] *IGLS* VI, 2898: M. Rufus Valens Honoratus; 2904: C. Antonius Abimmes. For this Aramaic name, see the comments on *IGLS* VI, 2898. pp. 181–2; *IGLS* VI, 2911: M. Cl. Cornelianus; 2921: M. Sentius Valens and his son; 2922: L. Licinius Felix; 2923: Q. Baebius Rufus; 2949: L. Sevius Rufinus; 2953: C. Iulius Magnus, son of Rufus (dated by the consuls of AD 96); 2955: epitaph of Cn. Iulius Rufus, *primus pilus*, probably father of the previous; 2956: L. Iulius Li(g)us; 2966: C. Aetrius Cresces Mundus and his family; 2976: M. Longinus Falcidianus.

[35] *IGLS* VI, 2894: *Oblig(atum)* or *Oblig(ata) Caphargmi*.

[36] *IGLS* VI, 2936. The inscriptions from Niha are *IGLS* VI, 2928–45. For *pagi*, country districts or communities attached to cities and *vici*, rural settlements, *RE* 18.2318–39. For *pagi* at Ptolemais see below.

has been detected.[37] The sanctuary preserved its indigenous character, and the gods did not receive Graeco-Roman names. In contrast to the sanctuary at Heliopolis itself, the priests and prophetesses were *peregrini,* but the inscriptions also mention at least six Roman citizens and their relatives.[38] A sanctuary nearby is identified by a dedication in Latin to the god Mifsenus.[39]

Finally we ought to notice a number of relevant inscriptions from other regions of the Empire.[40] They record citizens from Heliopolis as serving soldiers and officers in various regions.[41]

The figures are not in themselves statistically significant but they do show that some Roman citizens of local origin in Heliopolis used Latin on public monuments. These Romans belong to various social classes, from senatorial and equestrian families to families who use a mixture of Semitic, Greek, and Roman personal names, but all preferred to use Latin for their public declarations. We encounter some military careers at lower and middle levels, again of people of proven local origin, both in Heliopolis and its vicinity, and in other parts of the Empire. Particularly in the surrounding territory, we also encounter some evidence of integration and mixed culture. All this is what one would expect of an Eastern citizen colony where a substantial group of veterans settled in close proximity with Greek- and Semitic-speaking others. The situation resulted in a tendency in individuals to use of Latin on private monuments even if they were not of the original group of veteran settlers or their direct descendants.

---

[37] Cf. J.-P. Rey-Coquais, 'Des montagnes au désert: Baetocécé, le *Pagus Augustus* de Niha, la Ghouta à l'Est de Damas', in E. Frézouls (ed.), *Sociétés urbaines, sociétés rurales dans l'Asie Mineure et la Syrie hellénistiques et romaines, Actes du colloque organisé à Strasbourg (novembre 1985)* (Strasbourg, 1987), 191–216, esp. 198–207, pls. II–IV, 1.

[38] *IGLS* VI, 2928; 2929 (bilingual), set up by a veteran, Sex. Allius Iullus. Note also *IGLS* VI, 2933: L. Iulius Apollinaris; also 2937 (fragmentary); 2938(?); 2940 (Greek), mentioning the sons of C. Clodius Marcellus (who have Semitic names); 2942: Q. Vesius Petilianus, *flamen aug(ustalis)* and *decurio Berytensis, quaestor col.*; 2943: Q. Vesius M[agnus]; 2944: L. Vesius Verecundus.

[39] 2946, cf. Rey-Coquais, 'Des montagnes au désert', 203. In charge are five persons with Aramaic names and four with Roman names (*praenomina* only).

[40] Cited in *IGLS* VI, p. 40.

[41] Trebonius Sossianus appears in Rome as *centurio frumentarius* of the *legio III Fl(aviae) Gordianae* (*ILS* 4287) and later as *primus pilus* in Philippopolis (*ILS* 9005). *CIL* VIII 18084, ll. 75, 92: M. Domitius Valens and M. Atilius Saturninus are soldiers of the *Legio III Augusta* in Lambaesis. Since these date to the early second century and are described as 'Heliop(olitanus)' it has been suggested that this might be evidence of the existence of the city as a separate colony by that time (*IGLS* VI, p. 35). G. Ch. Picard, *Castellum Dimmidi* (Paris, 1945), 198, 22B, left column, l. 11: *[S]aturnin[us] in c(olonia) Helub (Heliupoli)*, as read by H.-G. Pflaum. *CIL* VI 2385.5, l. 14: *[Hel]iopo[li]* on a list of praetorians in Rome. Interesting is also *CIL* X 1579; *ILS* 4291 indicating the existence of a *corpus Heliopolitanorum* at Puteoli.

Berytus

> A city most charming that has law schools which assure the stability of all of the Roman legal system. Thence learned men come who assist judges all over the world and protect the provinces with their knowledge of the laws …[42]

Although there is far less published material from Berytus than from Heliopolis, the pattern of what there is resembles that of Heliopolis. Gregorius Thaumaturgus describes Berytus as being a 'city rather Roman in character and credited with being a school for legal studies'.[43] The planned corpus of inscriptions from the city is not yet available. Veterans were settled at Berytus at the same time as at Heliopolis, in 14 BC by Agrippa.[44] The existence of a distinguished school, or schools, of Roman law at Berytus has always been seen as an indication of the Latin character of this town from the third century until the end of the fourth century.[45] A famous inscription, originally set up at Berytus, honours an equestrian officer who, in the course of his career, was dispatched by the governor of Syria at the beginning of the first century to destroy a fortress of the Ituraeans in the mountains of the Lebanon.[46] The inscription is relevant for our topic because the officer later became *quaestor, aedilis, duumvir,* and *pontifex* of the colony.

There is evidence of at least two senators from Berytus, which shows that it produced members of the imperial upper class.[47] Four (or possibly

---

[42] *Expositio Totius Mundi et Gentium* (ed. Jean Rougé) 25: <*Post istam*> *Berytus, civitas valde deliciosa et auditoria legum habens per quam omnia iudicia Romanorum* <*stare videntur*>. *Inde enim viri docti in omnem orbem terrarum adsident iudicibus et scientes leges custodiunt provincias …*

[43] Gregorius Thaumaturgus, *Orat. Panegyr. ad Origenem* 5. *PG* 10. 1066: πόλις Ῥωμαικωτέρα πως, καὶ τῶν νόμων τούτων εἶναι πιστευθεῖσα παιδευτήριον

[44] Some veterans were established there at an earlier date, after Actium and before 27: *CIL* III 14165.6. For Berytus, J. Lauffray, 'Beyrouth : Archéologie et histoire, époques gréco-romaines. I Période hellénique et Haut Empire romain', *ANRW* 2.8.135–63; Millar, 'The Roman Coloniae', 10–18.

[45] P. Collinet, *Histoire de l'école de droit de Beyrouth* (Paris, 1925), is merely the last of a venerable series of works published since the seventeenth century, listed by Collinet, 6–9; Millar, 'The Roman Coloniae', 16–17; Rochette, *Le Latin dans le monde grec*, 167–74. Other centres were Alexandria and Antioch: Rochette, *Le Latin dans le monde grec*, 174–7. For the substitution of Greek for Latin as the language of legal instruction, see Collinet, *Histoire*, 211–18. The school functioned till the mid-sixth century. Most of the literary sources which shed light on the institution are later than the period considered in the present chapter. There are a few from the third century (Collinet, *Histoire*, 26–30) and more from the fourth (at 30–42). For a recent treatment: L. J. Hall, *Roman Berytus: Beirut in Late Antiquity* (London, 2004).

[46] *CIL* III 6687; *ILS* 2683; L. Boffo (ed.), *Iscrizioni greche e latine per lo studio della bibbia* (Brescia, 1994), 182–203, no. 23; Cf. Isaac, *Limits of Empire*, 60–2.

[47] Bowersock, 'Roman Senators from the Near East', nos. 11 and 12: M. and S. Sentius Proculus, possibly brothers. Cf. J.-P. Rey-Coquais, 'Un légat d'Afrique', in A. Mastino (ed.), *L'Africa romana: Atti*

five) equestrian officers are attested as originating from Berytus.[48] Two (or possibly three) of these refer to the only attested first-century equestrian officers from Syria. The number of attested equestrian officers of this town was surpassed only by Palmyra in the second century.[49]

I am aware of twenty-three inscriptions representing private individuals, setting up dedications to gods in Latin on their own behalf.[50] We find only purely Latin personal names on thirteen of these, but on eight the names are a combination of Latin and Greek or Semitic. The former reflect a tradition of Roman nomenclature which goes back to the settlement of veterans in the city while the latter could either mean that local families received the citizenship or that descendants of the group of citizens intermarried with local families. Both must have happened regularly, but it is interesting to see it reflected in the personal names. Next there are nine epitaphs or statue dedications with inscriptions in Latin.[51] Four of these represent private persons with fully Latin names, one of them recording those of freedmen and one a soldier. One inscription has a mixture of Latin and Greek names.

There are a few relevant inscriptions from other parts of the Empire: the worshippers of Jupiter Heliopolitanus from Berytus who lived in Puteoli (*CIL* III 6680; *ILS* 300) and a dedication from Nîmes to this god and to the god Nemausus by a *primipilaris* from Berytus (*ILS* 4288).

For Berytus the limited epigraphic material confirms the impression derived from the literary sources that this was a substantial Roman veteran colony where the Latin tradition was maintained for centuries after the foundation. The city produced some members of the higher classes and

del IX Convegno di Studio su 'L'Africa Romana' Nuoro, 13–15 dicembre 1991 (Sassari, 1992), 345–52 = AÉ 1992. 1689.

[48] H. Devijver, 'Equestrian Officers from the East', in P. Freeman and D. Kennedy (eds.), *The Defence of the Roman and Byzantine East: Proceedings of a Colloquium held at the University of Sheffield in April 1986* (Oxford, 1986), 109–225, at 183.

[49] Devijver, 'Equestrian Officers', 183. For military inscriptions see further *CIL* III 14165/6; AÉ 1998. 1435: career inscription of a centurion, probably a local man (*tribus Fabia*), mentioned also in *IGLS* VI, no. 2955; 2956, first half of the second century.

[50] H. Seyrig, *Antiquités Syriennes*, 1st ser. (Paris, 1934), 5; *Antiquités Syriennes*, 3rd ser. (Paris, 1946), 46–7, no. 18; 48, no. 19; *CIL* III 14165/5; 9; AÉ 1900.191; 1903.361, for which see also 1905, p. 7: the dedicator, Q. Antonius Eutyches, appears also on another dedication: 1924.138; 1905.29; 1906.188 and p. 41; 1906.189 and 190; 1922.60; 1924.137; 1926.56; 1939.69; 1950.231; 1950.233: a dedication to 'Fortunae Geni coloniae' by M(arcus) Iulius Avidius Minervinus from Emesa; 1955.85: one slave made a vow and another placed the dedication; 1957.118; 1958.164; 1998.1436: a private dedication in Latin to I.O.M.H. by Q. Longinus, a freedman. 1437: another freedman.

[51] AÉ 1898.20; 1906.189; 1907.191; 1926.61; 1939.68; 1947.143; 1950.230; 1958.162. 1928.62 = 1954, p. 77 s.n. 258; 1947, p. 49 s.n. 135 is the famous text: *Regina Berenice regis magni A[grippae f(ilia)] et rex Agrippa templum?] / [qu]od rex Herodes proavos(!) eorum fecerat ve[tustate conlapsum a solo restituerunt] / marmoribusque et columnis [se]x [exornaverunt].*

some of its citizens expressed themselves in Latin on public monuments and had proper Roman names.

Ptolemais (Acco)

The next veteran colony established in the region was Ptolemais.[52] Veterans of the four Syrian legions were settled in a new colony at Ptolemais between 51/2 and 54, and a new road was constructed from Antioch in Syria to the colony.[53] Ulpian describes Ptolemais as lying between Palaestina and Syria.[54] The foundation of the colony involved the usual thorough reorganization of the territory and land grants to veterans. The land, whether bought or confiscated, was taken from its original possessors and the infusion of veterans entailed the imposition of a new local leadership. The site of the ancient town has been occupied continuously since antiquity. As in Jerusalem, there are therefore very few inscriptions, but the few that have been discovered do not contradict the pattern one might expect to see if there had been more evidence.[55] As noted above, the imposition of

[52] See L. Kadman, *The Coins of Akko-Ptolemais* (Tel Aviv, 1961); N. Makhouly and C. N. Johns, *Guide to Acre*, rev. edn (Jerusalem, 1946); H. Seyrig, 'Le monnayage de Ptolemaïs en Phénicie', *RN* 4 (1962): 25–50; 'Divinités de Ptolemaïs', *Syria* 39 (1962): 192–207; E. Schürer, *The History of the Jewish People in the Age of Jesus Christ (175 BC–AD 138)*, 3 vols., ed. G. Vermes, F. Millar, and M. Goodman (Edinburgh, 1973–9), 121–5; see also E. Stern (ed.), *The New Encyclopedia of Archaeological Excavations in the Holy Land*, I (Jerusalem, 1993), 16–31; V (2008), 1554–61; Tsafrir *et al.*, *Tabula Imperii Romani-Iudaea-Palaestina* (Jerusalem, 1994), 204–5; B. Isaac, 'Roman Colonies in Judaea: The Foundation of Aelia Capitolina', *Talanta* 12–13 (1980–1): 31–53, at 37–9 = Isaac, *Near East under Roman Rule*, 92–4; Millar, 'The Roman *Coloniae*', 23–6.

[53] The last pre-colonial coin-issue of Ptolemais dates from AD 51/2: Kadman, *Coins of Akko-Ptolemais*, 108, nos. 86–90; Seyrig, 'Le monnayage de Ptolemaïs en Phénicie', 39. For further bibliography see A. Kindler and A. Stein, *A Bibliography of the City Coinage of Palestine* (Oxford, 1987), 5–18. The foundation by Claudius (died 54) is mentioned by Pliny, *NH* 5.17.75: *Colonia Claudi Caesaris Ptolemais, quae quondam Acce* ... Milestones of 56 record the construction of a road *ab Antiochea ad novam coloniam Ptolemaida*. See R. G. Goodchild, 'The Coast Road of Phoenicia and its Roman Milestones', *Berytus* 9 (1948–9), 91–127, esp. 120. For the legions, see the founder's coins with *vexilla*, AD 66, see Kadman, *Coins of Akko-Ptolemais*, no. 92.

[54] Ulpian, *Dig.* L 15, 1, 3: *Ptolemaeensium enim colonia, quae inter Phoenicen et Palaestinam sita est, nihil praeter nomen coloniae habet.* That is, the colony had no additional financial privileges, such as the *ius Italicum*, or the exemptions from taxation enjoyed by Caesarea and Aelia Capitolina. Perhaps it received *ius Italicum* in the reign of Elagabalus, for city coins of his reign show Marsyas (Kadman, *Coins of Akko-Ptolemais*, no. 163).

[55] See M. Avi-Yonah, 'Newly Discovered Greek and Latin Inscriptions', *QDAP* 12 (1946): 84–102, at 85, n. 2: *Imp. Ner. Caesari Col. Ptol. Veter. Vici Nea Com. et Gedru*; 86, n. 3: *Pago Vicinal(i)*, which shows that the territory, like that of Heliopolis, was organized in *pagi*. See also Y. Soreq, 'Rabbinical Evidences about the Pagi Vicinales in Israel', *JQR* 65 (1975): 221–4. A centurial *cippus* was found a kilometre and a half south of the first inscription, see J. Meyer, 'A Centurial Stone from Shavei Tziyyon', *SCI* 7 (1983–4): 119–25, with S. Applebaum, 'A Centurial Stone from Shavei Tziyyon: Appendix', *SCI* 7 (1983–4): 125–8. A fragment of another Latin inscription was found not far from this spot, see Meyer, 'A Centurial Stone', 117.

the veteran colony was a measure that had a drastic impact on the existing community and cannot have been welcome. There is one hint that families of distinction may have lived in the city. It produced at least one distinguished person: the consular Flavius Boethus, governor of Palestine, AD 162–6, known from the works of Galen as a scholar and philosopher with an interest in medicine.[56]

Caesaraea on the Sea

The case of Caesarea is difficult as the nature of and reason for the grant of colonial status to the city are not clearly established. It became a colony in the reign of Vespasian but it is a matter of debate whether this change in status was accompanied by the settlement of legionary veterans.[57] There is good evidence for the existence of several honorary or titular colonies from the reign of Claudius at the latest, so Caesarea would definitely not have been the first case of a grant of colonial status without settlement of veterans and the literary and archaeological evidence, though capable of a different interpretation, cumulatively points to Caesarea not receiving a veteran settlement.[58] Most explicitly, *Digest.* L 15 8 states that *Divus*

---

[56] See references in E. M. Smallwood, *The Jews under Roman Rule*, 2nd edn (Leiden, 1981), 552.

[57] I have argued that Caesarea received colonial status without receiving a contingent of veteran settlers in my article 'Roman Colonies in Judaea'; reprinted in *The Near East under Roman Rule*, 87–111. A different scenario has been proposed by H. M. Cotton and W. Eck, 'A New Inscription from Caesarea Maritima and the Local Elite of Caesarea Maritima', in L. V. Rutgers (ed.), *What Athens has to Do with Jerusalem: Essays on Classical, Jewish and Early Christian Art and Archaeology in Honor of Gideon Foerster* (Leuven, 2002), 375–91, who argue that the epigraphic evidence indicates the presence of a group of veteran settlers in the city, planted there at the time of the change in status. See also Eck, 'Language of Power', and my own forthcoming paper: 'Caesarea-on-the-Sea and Aelia Capitolina: Two Ambiguous Roman Colonies', in C. Brélaz (ed.), *L'héritage grec des colonies romaines d'Orient*: Proceedings of a Conference, 8–9 November 2013, in Strasbourg. This paper evaluates the evidence from the inscriptions collected in the *Corpus Inscriptionum Iudaeae/Palaestinae*, I, part I, Jerusalem (2010), and II, Caesarea and the Middle Coast (2011), nos. 1128–2107, historical introduction on pp. 17–38.

[58] F. Vittinghoff, 'Die "Titularkolonie"', in W. Eck (ed.), *Civitas Romana: Stadt und politisch-soziale Integration im Imperium Romanum der Kaiserzeit* (Stuttgart, 1994), 34–40, notes that 'die "Titularkolonie"' is rare before the end of the first century, but perhaps was granted already under Caesar to especially meritorious peregrine communities. Dio 43.39.5, referring to Spain, in 45 BC states: 'to those who had displayed any good-will toward him he granted lands and exemption from taxation, to some also citizenship, and to others the status of Roman colonists' (ἔδωκε … πολιτείαν τέ τισι, καὶ ἄλλοις ἀποίκοις τῶν Ῥωμαίων νομίζεσθαι). This could refer, according to Vittinghoff, 35, n. 44, to Nova Carthago, Ucubi, and Tarraco, unless Dio is anachronistic here. Caesarea in Mauretania was possibly also a Claudian titular colony; cf. Pliny, *NH* 5.20: *oppidum … Caesarea Iubae regia a divo Claudio coloniae iure donate – eiusdem iussu deductis veteranis Oppidum Novum*. There can be no doubt regarding the case of Vienna in Gaul (Vittinghoff, 36 with n. 48). Vienna was promoted from a colony with the *ius Latii* to a titular *Colonia Civium Romanorum*. The date is uncertain, but the Latin status was probably granted by Caesar, following Vittinghoff, and the status

Vespasianus Caesarienses colonos fecit (the divine Vespasian made the people of Caesarea *coloni*), suggesting that the existing Caesareans became citizens of the new Roman colony. Given that this is a legal source, the phrasing may be significant, though it is possible that the source is confused, conflating generally later practice in creating 'honorary' colonies with generally earlier practice in establishing veteran settlements. Yet the best informed contemporary source, Josephus, explicitly denies that Vespasian founded any city of his own in Judaea: 'For he founded there no city of his own while keeping their territory [i.e. the land of the Jews], but only to eight hundred veterans did he assign a place for settlement called Emmaus.'[59] This would seem clearly to exclude the establishment of a veteran settlement at Caesarea.

The absence of clear archaeological or iconographic evidence of a military settlement is also persuasive. Founder's coins with legionary *vexilla* and symbols are invariably found on coins of the Eastern veteran colonies. Accordingly, they are frequent on the coins of Berytus, Acco, and Aelia Capitolina, but are absent on those of Caesarea.[60] There is also no evidence in the vicinity of Caesarea of centuriation, such as is found at Acco (see below). The absence of centuriation suggests that there was no reorganization or redistribution of land in the territory of the city consonant with the arrival of new settlers.

The grant of colonial status could result from two vastly different historical scenarios. Briefly, the granting of 'honorary' colonial status can be seen as a reward for political loyalty while the implanting of veterans on a community, with the economic and political disruption this entailed, should be seen as a punishment. The introduction of a foreign elite over and above

---

of a full citizen colony was no later than AD 41. This is clear from Claudius' speech in Lyon: *CIL* XIII 1668; *ILS* 212; *FIRA* I 43: *Ante in domum consulatum intulit quam colonia sua solidum civitatis Romanae beneficium consecuta est.* Vienna is known as *Colonia Romana* to Pliny, *NH* 3.36, but not to Strabo 4.186. Puteoli received colonial status from Nero: Tac. *Ann.* 14.27: *vetus oppidum Puteoli ius coloniae et cognomentum a Nerone apiscuntur*; cf. Vittinghoff, 'Die "Titularkolonie"', 35, n. 44. See also A. N. Sherwin-White, *The Roman Citizenship*, 2nd edn (Oxford, 1973), 244.

[59] Jos. *BJ* 7.6.6 (216): οὐ γὰρ κατῴκισεν ἐκεῖ πόλιν ἰδίαν αὐτῷ τὴν χώραν φυλάττων, ὀκτακοσίοις δὲ μόνοις ἀπὸ τῆς στρατιᾶς διαφειμένοις χωρίον ἔδωκεν εἰς κατοίκησιν, ὃ καλεῖται μὲν Ἀμμαοῦς, Cf. B. Isaac, 'Judaea after A.D. 70', in Isaac, *Near East under Roman Rule*, 112–21, at 114. Pliny, *NH* 5.13.69: *Stratonis turris, eadem Caesarea ab Herode rege condita, nunc colonia prima Flavia a Vespasiano imperatore deducta* might (but need not) be construed as implying veteran settlement, but his passage should clearly be regarded as less significant than the two sources cited above.

[60] Werner Eck regards the absence of such coinage in the case of Caesarea as insignificant, arguing that they are to be expected only from the mints of colonies established during the period of large-scale discharges following the civil wars: Eck, 'Language of Power', 34. However, both Claudian Acco and Hadrianic Aelia Capitolina produced such coins, and I therefore conclude that the failure to do so by the mint of Caesarea after AD 70 is indeed indicative.

the existing non-Jewish population definitely would have been punishment, even if landed property from Jews had become available for distribution after the suppression of the Jewish revolt. There was indeed every reason not to punish the citizens of Caesarea, but to reward them. They had supported the Roman army, killed many Jews, and it was the place where Vespasian had been proclaimed emperor (hence the name *prima Flavia*). Such a reward would parallel the lesser honours granted to smaller towns in the aftermath of 70. Ma'abartha at the foot of Mt. Gerizim was founded as the city of Flavia Neapolis (Nablus).[61] Jaffa received the name of Flavia Joppa.[62] Both towns had been ravaged during the war. It is worth observing that, elsewhere in the wider region, Samosata, the old royal capital of Commagene, annexed by Vespasian, became 'Flavia Samosata', but did not receive colonial status.[63] Additionally, it is difficult to find advantages for Vespasian in establishing a veteran colony at Caesarea. Such colonies had no useful military function; on the contrary, in wartime they had to be protected by the regular troops.[64] A group of elderly veterans had nothing to contribute to the security of the province of Judaea. In fact, the presence of veteran colonists would have had an adverse effect: forming an irritant among people who had formed a bulwark of support for Rome among the Jewish insurgents. Furthermore, Caesarea was a prosperous urban centre that did not need reinforcement, unlike Jerusalem, sacked and not rebuilt, and seen by Hadrian, sixty years afterwards, as ripe for development.

Even the presence in fair numbers of veterans and soldiers at Caesarea cannot be taken as conclusive evidence for the planting of a veteran colony. As is stated by Josephus, Caesarea (and Sebaste) supplied numerous recruits for special units of the provincial army before AD 70 – another reason to reward the city. There is every reason to assume that the same population continued to do so after 70, when they could do so as Roman citizens. In fact, they could serve in the provincial legions and would have increasingly done so as local recruitment became the norm, at least in the

[61] Jos. *BJ* 3.8.32 (307–15); for the (re)foundation, see G. F. Hill, *British Museum Catalogue of the Greek Coins of Palestine* (London, 1914), 45–7, nos. 1–19, and pp. xxvi–xxvii. The civic area began in 72/3. Cf. Schürer, *History of the Jewish People*, I, 520–1.

[62] Jos. *BJ* 2.18.10 (507–9); 3.9.2–4 (414–31); Hill, *British Museum Catalogue*, 44, nos. 1–2, cf. pp. xxiv–xxv. For the city in general, see now *CIIP* III, 19–146.

[63] W. Wroth, *British Museum Catalogue of the Greek Coins of Galatia, Cappadocia and Syria* (London, 1899), 117–23.

[64] Isaac, *Limits of Empire*, ch. 7, and see now the discussion for Asia Minor by C. Brélaz, 'Les colonies romaines et la sécurité publique en Asie Mineure', in G. Salmeri, A. Raggi, and A. Baroni (eds.), *Colonie romane nel mondo greco, Minima epigraphica et papyrologica Supplementa*, III (Rome, 2004), 187–209.

second century. These recruits would have tended to use Latin like other members of the military and this can serve as sufficient explanation for any use of Latin by private persons on inscriptions in Caesarea. How little we know of linguistic usage in first-century Judaea will be clear also from the fact that we do not know what would have been the first language of such military men: did they speak Greek at home? Or Aramaic? Did they speak Greek or Latin in daily life in the army?

The literary sources, few as they are, the coins, and the historical circumstances all strongly suggest that Caesarea received colonial status as a reward and was spared the establishment of a contingent of veteran legionaries in the city. The argument in support of the claim that it was a genuine veteran colony could only be based on the Latin inscriptions discovered in the city.[65] The systematic excavations carried out in Caesarea have uncovered a large number of those, brought together in vol. II of the *CIIP*.[66] The inscriptions of Caesarea are numbers 1128–2079 on pp. 37–798 of *CIIP*, vol. II, with inscriptions from the vicinity, nos. 2080–2107, on pp. 799–820. Even with all the inscriptions published, there still is a problem of method. Caesarea was not only a Roman colony; it was also the provincial capital, the seat of both the governor and the financial procurator. Moreover, it was not far from the legionary base of the *VI Ferrata* at Legio. We must therefore assume that a substantial number of Latin inscriptions was to be expected there anyway from those circles, as in Bostra and Gerasa (see below), where no planting of veteran settlers occurred.

For the purposes of analysis, the inscriptions must therefore be divided into the following categories:

(1) Inscriptions related to the imperial or provincial authorities and their officials. These normally have nothing to do with the city or local society as such.

(2) Military monuments, related to the provincial garrison and military personnel attached to the governor's office. Again, such inscriptions are frequently unconnected with the city and its permanent inhabitants.

(3) Public inscriptions, related to or set up by the city authorities. These, like the city coinage, ought to be in Latin because of the colonial status

---

[65] Gregorius Thaumaturgus travelled to Caesarea to study Roman law there, rather than in Berytus as he had wanted originally: *Panegyr. ad Origenem* 5. *PG* 10. 1067–8. The fact that one could study Roman law in Caesarea in the third century is certainly significant, but it is no indication that there was a presence of Roman veterans in the first century.

[66] An attempt at evaluation of the material now available will come out in the already cited forthcoming work in C. Brélaz, *L'héritage grec des colonies romaines d'Orient*. This evaluation has not led to different conclusions on my part.

of the city. Such a use of Latin does not prove that the language had roots in the local population.

(4) Public building inscriptions.

(5) Inscriptions set up by and for private individuals.

Only texts belonging to category 5 might be taken as unambiguously reflecting Latinity among the citizens of Caesarea. From an analysis of all the available material I conclude that the discussion about the nature of the colony of Caesarea cannot be decided on the basis of the epigraphic material. What we do recognize, however, in a vivid manner, is its colonial status as such and the fact that it was the capital of a province with a substantial military presence. Even so Greek dominates at least in numbers of texts. This in itself need not surprise us, for over time the legions and *auxilia* in the Near East were recruited in the region among people whose mother tongue was not Latin. Caesarea was and remained a major Hellenized city in the Near East. My point is that the inscriptions known so far do not provide evidence to contradict the conclusion, based on other indications, that Vespasian gave Caesarea the rank of a colony as a reward for good behaviour without imposing a group of veteran settlers on the city.

Aelia Capitolina

The refoundation of Jerusalem as Aelia Capitolina[67] represented the last establishment of a genuine veteran colony in the region, as opposed to the grant of colonial status to an existing community.[68] It was an exceptional foundation, first, because it replaced the city of Jerusalem and, second, in Roman terms, because it was situated side by side with a functioning legionary base. As in the case of Caesarea, but for different reasons, this means that it is not easy to interpret the epigraphic evidence, since it must be determined whether Latin inscriptions derive from the legionary base or from the colony. Unlike Caesarea, however, Jerusalem has produced very few Latin texts for the period under consideration.[69] Aelia Capitolina, at the time of its foundation as a Roman colony, was a small and rather isolated settlement. It became a major city only in the fourth century. The

---

[67] For the inscriptions from Aelia Capitolina, see now *CIIP*, I/ii, historical introduction in I/i. For an evaluation, see again my forthcoming paper.

[68] Isaac, 'Roman Colonies in Judaea', esp. 101–6 = Isaac, *Near East under Roman Rule*, 99–107; Millar, 'The Roman *Coloniae*', 28–30.

[69] As already noted, the inscriptions from Jerusalem and vicinity are now available in *CIIP* I/i and ii. For a related topic, see now P. Arnould, *Les arcs romains de Jérusalem: Architecture, décor et urbanisme* (Göttingen, 1997).

epigraphical evidence for this period is correspondingly meagre. It mostly reflects the presence of a legion, soldiers, and a city administration. Just to give an impression: funerary inscriptions of serving military people are small in number (three, excluding one from Abu Ghosh).[70] Of particular interest is no. 732, perhaps for an *optio* of the legion *X Fretensis*, set up by a relative. If indeed this was the case we may possibly face a case of local recruitment, one example of what must have been very common at the time. Other funerary inscriptions of the period under consideration are again not large in number. Five are in Greek,[71] eight in Latin, two of them military, and one of those antedating the foundation of Aelia Capitolina. One (no. 740) is interesting: the Latin funerary inscription for Glaucus son of Artemidorus from Zeugma. It gives no clue how the man came to Aelia.

The evidence from the two Near Eastern cities considered provides a lively impression of the significant impact of Roman administrative presence and army there. Yet this influence remains limited. Greek dominates, at least in the numbers of texts. This completes our little survey of evidence from the Roman colonies in the region. For comparison, it will now be useful briefly to discuss the Latin inscriptions from several towns in the Near East that were not veteran colonies.

Palmyra

A recent inventory of the Latin inscriptions of Palmyra[72] divides them into two main groups:

(1) Six trilingual grave inscriptions (Latin, Greek, and Palmyrene), most of which concern people occupying prominent positions in the city, dated to the first and second centuries (from AD 52 to 176). The Latin is always brief, the Greek longer, and the Palmyrene longest. The presence of Latin here is no indication that the language was spoken locally, but must be seen as a gesture or a declaration of loyalty towards the Roman Empire. Interestingly, Latin is not used locally after Palmyra received colonial rank, probably under Severus.[73]

(2) Military inscriptions which are divided into three sub-groups: inscriptions linked with the imperial family, inscriptions concerning officers,

[70] No. 732; 733 may have been part of 732; 734 (perhaps pre-colonial); 735 (from Abu Ghosh); 736.
[71] Nos. 737, 738, 746, 749, 750. Note the Hebrew/Aramaic and Greek graffito, no. 752.
[72] K. As'ad and C. Delplace, 'Inscriptions latines de Palmyre', *REA* 104 (2002): 363–400.
[73] Millar, *Roman Near East*, 326–7.

and funerary inscriptions. These reflect the presence of a military garrison at Palmyra.

Bostra

The town of Bostra in Arabia served as a legionary base and seat of the provincial governor.[74] It received colonial status in the third century, a grant that had no impact on the social composition of the city. The inscriptions have been published very well in one accessible volume. Numerous inscriptions were set up by serving military men,[75] by governors,[76] or members of the governor's entourage.[77] These need not detain us here.[78]

Generally speaking, there is a separation between city and army in the sense that there are no careers of men who served both as officers in the army and as city magistrates, such as we have encountered in Heliopolis[79] and Berytus,[80] but not, so far, at Caesarea. The city made dedications in Latin to such officials but private inscriptions in Latin are rarer.[81] Nevertheless, we have some epitaphs set up by civilians for their military relatives or by military for civilians.[82] Of particular interest are inscriptions by civilians for civilians in Latin.[83] These presumably represent the relatives of military people who settled in Bostra. These cases provide evidence of some local use of Latin even though there is no question that there ever was a veteran settlement. The Latin must be ascribed to families somehow related to the

---

[74] For the inscriptions from Bostra: *IGLS* XIII/1 (ed. M. Sartre). For the city, see M. Sartre, *Bostra, des origines à l'Islam* (Paris, 1985). For the coinage see A. Spijkerman, *The Coins of the Decapolis and Arabia* (Jerusalem, 1978) and A. Kindler, *The Coinage of Bostra* (Warminster, 1983).

[75] *IGLS* XIII/1, e.g. nos. 9050, 9051, 9064, 9065(?), 9067, 9069, 9070, 9072, 9078, 9079, 9081, 9082, 9085, 9086, 9087, 9098; note also 9169.

[76] *IGLS* XIII, nos. 9060, 9062.

[77] *IGLS* XIII, nos. 9071, 9077.

[78] Note also the more recently published inscriptions: *AÉ* 2000. 1527a–b: emperors; 1528: military; 1529–32; 1536: governors; 1540: military building inscriptions.

[79] *IGLS* VI, nos. 2786–7, 2793–4, 2796.

[80] *CIL* III 6687 = *ILS* 2683, discussed above.

[81] *IGLS* XIII/1, no. 9029. One inscription in honour of Iulia Domna represents a dedication by an individual who came from Parthicopolis in Thrace (9053). He may have been the relative of a soldier or government official. Iulia Domna, born in Emesa, appears frequently on inscriptions in the region: on milestones (*CIL* III 13689), on honorary inscriptions in the Galilee (*IGR* III 1106) and in Berytus (*AÉ* 1950. 0230).

[82] 9170: by a freedman and heir named Ianuarinius Florinus for a centurion. 9172: Mercurius, freedman of a *beneficiarius tribuni*. See also 9179 (234–5): the mother and sister of an *optio hastati* of the VI *Ferr.* from Philadelphia; 9181: a centurion for his adopted son.

[83] 9171: Antonius Eutices for his spouse; 9177 (232); 9184 (240); 9189 (245); 9190 (246); 9195: the father was perhaps a former soldier, the son, 9 years old, an *eques* (250); 9197 (251).

provincial government or the army who preferred to use this language for public consumption.

Gerasa

This city was apparently the seat of the provincial procurator of Roman Arabia,[84] and there was a local garrison. It received colonial status in the third century. We rule out of our discussion Latin inscriptions set up by people or military units temporarily present in the city, such as the *equites singulares* of Hadrian who made a dedication when the emperor was in the region,[85] anonymous dedications to emperors, or inscriptions set up in the city by high provincial officials, legates, and procurators (105, 160), their subordinates, notably the procurator's staff (165, 208) and their relatives (207), and serving soldiers and officers (171, 178).

Of the remaining, the most remarkable is no. 175, a Latin inscription in honour of Maecius Laetus, procurator, set up by the heirs of Allius Vestinus, *advocatus fisci, ex testamento eius*. This strongly suggests that the heirs were local people. The funerary inscriptions of serving soldiers are in Latin, as expected, and mark the presence of a garrison in town, but give no indication of Latinity among the permanent population (200, 201, 211), nor does the tombstone of a procurator set up by his widow and son (207). Some, however, may possibly indicate that there was at least *some* local Latin culture. For instance, no. 199, the epitaph of an *optio* of the *Ala I Thracum*, perhaps locally based, was set up in both languages by his brother, who is not listed as a soldier himself. Other epitaphs, in Latin only, were set up for imperial freedmen who fulfilled various functions in the procurator's office by their spouses, children, and relatives (202, 203, 204, 210; also 215, 216). The procurator's staff would seem to have formed a milieu in the city which preferred at least to have their tombs marked in Latin, but little can be said about the origins of those staff members.[86]

Furthermore, there are a number of interesting but ambivalent cases. No. 177 is engraved upon a cylindrical stele, in honour of Marcus Aurelius Faustus, an imperial freedman, and lists various equestrian functions, all in Latin. One might suggest that the dedicants were citizens of Gerasa

[84] R. Haensch, *Capita provinciarum: Statthaltersitze und Provinzialverwaltung in der römischen Kaiserzeit* (Mainz, 1997), 244.

[85] C. Kraeling, *Gerasa: City of the Decapolis* (New Haven, 1938), no. 30.

[86] No. 204 gives the origin of one *tabularius*, an imperial freedman, as Puteoli. His mother and sister have Greek names.

who wrote Latin because of their social basis in the army. No. 179 refers to Gerasa as a Roman colony and is thus of the third century. The dedicants, an Aurelius Longinianus ... and his son, may have written Latin because of a military career, but this cannot be simply assumed.

The least that can be said for Gerasa is that there are sufficient inscriptions in Latin to demonstrate that there was a habit of using that language in formal texts. Mostly, these texts can be connected to people and their relatives who were associated with the army and provincial government. Yet many of the inscriptions are epitaphs and therefore should be regarded as belonging to the personal sphere, independent of a formal or administrative framework where the use of Latin was obligatory.

Petra

Whatever the status of the old Nabataean capital after the annexation of the Province of Arabia,[87] it is certain that the governors regularly visited it.[88] It received colonial status under Elagabalus, probably in 221–2.[89] The Latin inscriptions reflect the presence of the governor and of military personnel.[90]

Caesarea Philippi

The excavations at the Pan sanctuary of Caesarea Philippi (Banias) have uncovered a substantial number of inscriptions (twenty-nine texts).[91] There is an obvious preponderance of Roman personal names (fifteen Roman, five Greek, five Semitic). A special case is inscription no. 5 of AD 222, which mentions eight members of a family, five of them with names that are connected with 'Agrippa'. This presumably reflects a local tradition of more than a century of loyalty to the Herodian house. There are few regular

---

[87] M. Sartre, *IGLS* XXI: *Inscriptions de la Jordanie*, 4 (Paris, 1993).

[88] G. W. Bowersock, *Roman Arabia* (Cambridge, 1983), 86; M. Sartre, *Bostra*, 68–70; *IGLS* XXI, 11, 30.

[89] S. Ben-Dor, 'Petra colonia', *Berytus* 9 (1948): 41–3; Millar, 'The Roman *Coloniae*', 51.

[90] *IGLS* XXI, nos. 1–8: dedications by the governor Q. Aiacius Modestus, AD 205–7; nos. 40–1: to Diocletian (fragment); 44: soldiers of a legionary cohort, unnamed emperor; 45: for Claudius Severus, governor, AD 107–15; 47: in honour of a governor, *opt(iones) l[egio]nis*; 51: tomb of T. Annius Sextius Florentinus, governor, AD 127; 52: C. Antonius Valens, *eques* of the *legio III Cyr.*, epitaph; 53: fragmentary epitaph.

[91] The excavations were carried out by Dr Zvi Maoz, formerly of the Antiquities Authority, and I have prepared the inscriptions for publication in the periodical *'Atiqot*. I mention them here to provide preliminary information and hope that the full publication will appear in print before long, after a quite considerable delay.

Greek names, and only four Semitic ones, including two patronymics. Seven inscriptions are in Latin, not including boundary markers and mile-stones. This is remarkable for material from an essentially rural sanctuary in this region, demanding a particular explanation. There is no information about any settlement of Roman veterans in the locale and there is no reason to assume that there was one. It is very likely that the first- and second-century inscriptions in Latin should be assigned to men from the region who also served in the Roman army and had undergone a measure of Latinization.[92] It is quite likely that these were men serving in the units of Ituraeans, recruited in part from the territory of Caesarea Philippi.[93]

Arados

This was the most important northern Phoenician city, located on an island off the coast. A few Latin inscriptions have been found here.[94] The city and council dedicated a statue to an equestrian officer, who may have been either commander of a local garrison or a native Aradian serving in the army.[95] The latter situation is almost certainly the case attested in the bilingual inscription of L. Septimius Marcellus for his brother M. Septimius Magnus, centurion in various legions.[96] There is some further evidence of men from Arados serving in the army.[97]

Military Presence

To end this limited survey, it may be useful to note that a number of cities have produced Latin texts that are limited strictly to the military sphere

---

[92] Two inscriptions are directly related to the military, but do not prove this hypothesis. A Greek inscription mentions 'Taia the son of Silas, *signifer*'. Another is set up by a centurion in honour of a commander of the *Cohors Milliaria Thracum* in the reign of Trajan, which shows that this unit must have been in the region in this period.

[93] J. C., Mann, *Legionary Recruitment and Veteran Settlement during the Principate* (London, 1983).

[94] J.-P., Rey-Coquais, *Arados et sa Pérée aux époques grecque, romaine et byzantine* (Paris, 1974); Rey-Coquais, *IGLS* VII, *Arados et régions voisines* (1970). For Dio Chrysostom's disparaging remarks about the city, see above, pp. 159–60.

[95] *IGLS* VII, no. 4009 (= *CIL* III 14165/10): *Civitas et Bule Aradia / L Domitio Cf Fab Catullo [p]raef* ... There is no explicit evidence of a garrison in the city, but note coins of the city countermarked 'L XV': Hill, *British Museum Catalogue of the Greek Coins of Phoenicia*, p. xxxvii.

[96] No. 4016. Compare 4015: The boule and demos set up a statue with dedication in Greek for M. Septimius Magnus.

[97] *IGLS* VII, 90, no. 40; *CIL* VIII 18084, l. 1: *–ius Severus Arado*; 24: *[Cl]emens Gabal(a)*. Note, finally, *IGLS* 4028 from Hosn Soleiman in the Alawite Mountains, the great sanctuary of Arados at Baetocece. It is bilingual and records five documents affirming the privileges bestowed upon the sanctuary by various Seleucid rulers and reconfirmed in an imperial rescript of the mid-third century (Gallienus *et al.* AD 253–60).

and reflect the presence of a military garrison at some stage. The most remarkable case is that of Apamea in Syria.[98] Other towns to be mentioned are Neapolis (Nablus),[99] Samaria-Sebaste,[100] Emmaus-Nicopolis,[101] Tiberias,[102] and, finally, Dura Europos.[103]

Conclusions

All empires are necessarily multilingual. The Roman Empire in the East had two languages of government of unequal status, Latin and Greek. Greek could be used for some official functions in the Roman army, but, as formulated by Adams, Latin 'had super-high status which made it suitable for various symbolic purposes, whether in legalistic documents, or to highlight the Roman identity of a soldier, or to mark or acknowledge overriding authority'.[104]

---

[98] J. Balty and W. van Rengen, *Apamea in Syria: The Winter Quarters of Legio II Parthica* (Brussels, 1993); cf. *AÉ* 1993. 1571–97.

[99] (a) A fragmentary inscription mentions a *tribunus* and a *primus pilus* or *praepositus*: Ch. Clermont-Ganneau, *Archaeological Researches in Palestine* (London, 1896), II, 318–19. (b) Countermarks of the legion *XII Fulminata* on coins struck up to AD 86/7: C. J. Howgego, 'The XII Fulminata: Countermarks, Emblems and Movements under Trajan or Hadrian', in S. Mitchell (ed.), *Armies and Frontiers in Roman and Byzantine Anatolia* (Oxford, 1983), 41–6. The coins were countermarked after AD 86/7 and probably before 156/7. This almost certainly shows that the legion (or part of it) was based at Neapolis in 115–17 or 132–5. (c) The tombstone of M. Ulpius Magnus, centurion of the legion *V Macedonica*, presumably from the years of the revolt of Bar Kokhba: F.-M. Abel, 'Nouvelle inscription de la Ve légion Macedonique', *RBi* 35 (1926): 421–4: figs. 1 and 2. (d) A city coin: *obv.* Tribonianus Gallus (251–3); *rev. COL NE[A]POLI* and emblems of the legion *X Fretensis*: S. Ben Dor, 'Quelques rémarques à propos d'une monnaie de Néapolis', *Revue Biblique* 59 (1952): pl. 9,1. (e) City coin: *obv.* Volusianus Augustus (251–3); *rev. COL NEAPOLIS* and emblems of the legion *III Cyrenaica*: A. Kindler, 'Was there a Detachment of the Third Legion Cyrenaica at Neapolis in A.D. 251–253', *Israel Numismatic Journal* 4 (1980): 56–8.

[100] G. Reisner, C. S. Fisher, and D. Gordon Lyon, *Harvard Excavations at Samaria,* I (Cambridge, 1924), 251, no. 1, recording a *vexillatio* of the *legio VI Ferrata*. *AÉ* 1938.13: *mil(ites) v(e)xi(lationis) coh(ortium) Pa(nnoniae) Sup(erioris), cives Sisci(ani) (et) Varcian(i) et Latobici*. *AÉ* 1948. 150, 151.

[101] Josephus says that the legion *V Macedonica* stayed there in the Jewish War before the siege of Jerusalem: Jos. *BJ* 4.8.1 (445); see also: 5.1.6 (42); 2.3 (67). Five inscriptions referring to this legion have been found there: *CIL* III 6647; 14155.11; 14155.12; J. H. Landau, 'Two Inscribed Tombstones', *'Atiqot* 2 (1976): 98–102. At least two of these are epitaphs of serving soldiers who died at Emmaus some time in the later first century AD: cf. M. Fischer, B. Isaac, and I. Roll, *Roman Roads in Judaea*, II, *The Jaffa–Jerusalem Roads* (Oxford, 1996), 14–15, 152, 174. This shows that they stayed there long enough for a stone-mason's workshop to be set up. Another inscription mentions the *coh(ors) VI Ulpi(a) Petr(aeorum)*: *AÉ* 1924. 132. A fragmentary inscription mentions an unknown cohort: *CIL* III 13588. It is therefore quite possible, although not certain, that army units were permanently based here.

[102] *AÉ* 1948. 146: the epitaph of a centurion of the legion *VI Ferrata*. Cf. 1988. 1053: a stamped brick of the same legion, found on Har Hazon, NW of Tiberias.

[103] Millar, *Roman Near East*, 467–71; N. Pollard, *Soldiers, Cities, and Civilians in Roman Syria* (Ann Arbor, 2000).

[104] Adams, *Bilingualism* (2003), ch. 5, part IV: 'Latin as a Language of Power'. Certain types of legalistic documents concerning Roman citizens had to be in Latin, even if the citizens did not know

The question asked in this chapter is what we can deduce from the surviving texts, invariably inscriptions on stone, about the use of Latin in cities of the Roman East. Such use of Latin may, but need not, have been a very deliberate expression of some form of identity (political, cultural, or ideological) rather than reflecting intensive and 'everyday' use and knowledge of Latin among the authors of the texts. We have no way of knowing whether Latin was a first, second, or third language for most of the individuals involved in the Latin dedications, but whether Latin was imposed or preferred by these users, it represents an ideological expression. The Latinity of those who used Latin on epitaphs may have been superficial, but its use implies a declaration of social and political loyalty. Latin was a minority language in the epigraphic culture of the East, and certainly in the oral culture of the cities. Its use, therefore, is necessarily a conscious attempt to differentiate its users from the surrounding Greek or Semitic populations. We can compare this to the use of Hebrew in funerary inscriptions. Traditionally, the tombstones of Jews in the diaspora are in Hebrew or in both Hebrew and the local language. This does not mean that the deceased or their relatives have any serious knowledge of Hebrew. Another example of the investment of significance in language-choice is a famous graffito, scratched in the rocks of the Wadi Mukatteb in Sinai: *Cessent Syri ante Latinos Romanos* (The Syrians will cease before [? yield to] the Latin Romans). The words of the traveller are not exactly Ciceronian Latin, but his meaning is more or less clear.[105]

Inscriptions represent, first of all, a public declaration of political and social identity. Nevertheless, a switch of language clearly did not have the same meaning in every context. The significance ascribed to the choice of language probably depended on the particular epigraphic culture of the city. These cultures appear not to have been straightforwardly related to accepted or plausible claims of Greek origin. Thus, Dio Chrysostom in his thirty-third discourse, where he harangues the citizens of Tarsus: 'And would any one call you colonists from Argos, as you claim to be, or more likely colonists rather of those abominable Aradians? Would he call you Greeks, or the most licentious of Phoenicians?'[106] Yet the self-perception of the citizens may have been very different. Dio himself was well aware that the Hellenic credentials of Tarsus were more impressive than those of his

---

Latin. Birth certificates and wills of Roman citizens had to be in Latin and so were building inscriptions.

[105] *CIL* III 86.

[106] D. Chr. 33.41; cf. 42 and on this B. Isaac, *The Invention of Racism in Classical Antiquity* (Princeton, 2004), 345–6, 395. Cf. p. 159, above. For Latin in Arados, see above.

native Prusa. We do not know what the citizens of Tarsus thought of Dio's harangue, but we can be quite certain that the Hellenized inhabitants of Aradus would not have been pleased if they had heard him speaking. An inscription from Trachonitis is dedicated by 'The Hellenes in Danaba'.[107] Even the Hellenized Syrian and Palestinian cities might claim to be genuinely Hellenic, as shown by an inscription from Scythopolis-Beth Shean, which refers to the city of Nysa-Scythopolis as 'one of the Hellenic cities in Coele-Syria'.[108] The continued Latin tradition in Roman colonies such as Berytus and Aelia Capitolina may be due in part to active involvement on the part of the inhabitants of the Eastern colonies in the Roman army. In Greek-speaking Roman colonies in the West, epitaphs of the early imperial period are found written in Greek, but influenced by Latin formulae, probably reflecting the particular cultural status of the two languages in those cities.[109]

The least problematic cases we have surveyed are those of Berytus and Heliopolis, known to have been populated by veteran settlers. Heliopolis in particular has produced a good quantity of inscriptions which show that private citizens used Latin on their public monuments, as did distinguished citizens who served in senior imperial positions and as city magistrates. These types of inscriptions show that Latin was to some extent integrated into civilian life. There is some evidence that the same was the case in Aelia Capitolina where veterans certainly took root in a depopulated city. There is no such published evidence from Caesarea, which, I have argued, was a titular colony. Bostra, legionary base and seat of the governor of Arabia, has also provided copious epigraphic evidence. Significantly, there is no evidence of senior military men or imperial magistrates serving also as city magistrates, an indication of social separation. It is not surprising that we encounter epitaphs set up by civilians for their military relatives or by military for civilians in Bostra. Noteworthy, however, are a limited number

---

[107] M. Sartre, 'Communautés villageoises et structures sociales d'après l'épigraphie de la Syrie du sud', in A. Calbi, A. Donati, and G. Poma (eds.), *L'epigrafia del villaggio, Actes du VIIe colloque international Borghesi à l'occasion du cinquantenaire d'Epigraphica (Forli, 27–30 septembre 1990)* (Faenza, 1993), 117–35; *AÉ* 1993. 1636 from Dhunaybeh (Danaba) οἱ ἐν Δαναβοις Ἕλληνες Μηνοφίλῳ εὐνοίας ἕνεκεν. It is suggested that this might be connected with the Herodian settlers in Trachonitis. See also above, p. 132 and p. 153.

[108] G. Foerster and Y. Tsafrir, 'Nysa-Scythopolis: A New Inscription and the Titles of the City on its Coins', *Israel Numismatic Journal* 9 (1986–7): 53–8: τῶν κατὰ Κοίλην Συρίαν Ἑλληνίδων πόλεων. See the comments by P.-L. Gatier, *Syria* 67 (1990): 204–6, and A. Stein, 'Studies in Greek and Latin Inscriptions on the Palestinian Coinage under the Principate' (PhD thesis, Tel Aviv University, 1991). See also above, pp. 120, 131, and 153.

[109] K. Korhonen, 'Three Cases of Greek/Latin Imbalance in Roman Syracuse', in E. N. Ostenfeld (ed.), *Greek Romans and Roman Greeks* (Aarhus, 2002), 70–8, at 73.

of inscriptions by civilians for civilians which presumably represent the relatives of military people who settled in Bostra and, as such, are evidence of some local use of Latin even though there is no question that there ever was a planned veteran settlement at Bostra. A similar pattern is found at Gerasa, where the financial procurator had his headquarters and various units appear to have been based. Finally, we must note rare and surprising pockets of Latin culture attested in minor provincial centres such as Caesarea Philippi.

The use of Latin on inscriptions in a few, but not many, cities of the Roman East represents a variety of social situations, which, given the scarcity of sources, are not always easy to determine. It may not tell us much about the language actually spoken in daily life. It is, however, a clear indication of a direct Roman impact on the life of a city: settlement of Roman army veterans is but one such phenomenon, the presence of a garrison or provincial offices is another constituting factor, but there are more possibilities such as the settlement of retired soldiers and officers from a local or regional garrison. These might be either retired locals who had served in the army or immigrants who had served and then retired locally. Although the use of Latin on, for instance, epitaphs does not necessarily mean that Latin was the first language spoken by the dead or the dedicants, the choice of Latin was a significant decision. It broke with the linguistic practices of the surrounding communities and thus set apart those who used the language. The association with the Roman rulers means that the most obvious understanding of the choice of language is as a reflection of political loyalty and of association with the imperial power. Latin does not simply represent one of the languages spoken locally, but had a particular social and political resonance, and the study of the epigraphic material opens up these resonances to historical analysis.

CHAPTER 13

Ancient Antisemitism

Terminology

In considering enmity towards the Jews, it is generally acknowledged that there is a problem of terminology: 'Antisemitism' is a modern term with, in itself, clearly racist connotations. Those who take the book of Genesis seriously may believe all Semites are descendants of Sem. However, according to current usage, 'Semitic' indicates a language group. Yet antisemitism usually entails hostility only towards Jews, not towards speakers of Arabic or Amharic. Antisemitism is therefore a term which denotes hostility to an imaginary race. The *OED* defines it as: 'Theory, action, or practice directed against the Jews. Hence *anti-Semite*, one who is hostile or opposed to the Jews.'

It has often been observed that fear is an inseparable part of modern antisemitism. Hence *Judenhass*, 'hatred of Jews', the term used by Zvi Yavetz, or *Judeophobia*, the title of Peter Schäfer's book on the subject.[1] The disadvantage of the latter term is that it emphasizes the element of fear and ignores that of hostility and does not adequately describe the delusional nature of antisemitism, whether or not this quality is applicable in antiquity. The term 'xenophobia' has the same disadvantage. There 'misoxenia' might have been preferable to indicate hatred of foreigners, but there is little point in trying to invent a new term, since people will just go on using the old one.

I would say there is nothing very wrong with the definition of antisemitism found in the *OED,* cited above. It is, however, necessary to go at least one step further. Antisemitism is defined properly only if it is recognized as a form of either racism or collective prejudice. We can speak of racist antisemitism if it attributes to the Jews' collective traits, physical,

---

[1] Z. Yavetz, *Judenfeindschaft in der Antike* (Munich, 1971); P. Schäfer, *Judeophobia: Attitudes toward the Jews in the Ancient World* (Cambridge, 1997).

mental, and moral, which are unalterable by human will, because they are
caused by hereditary factors or external influences, such as climate and
geography. Antisemitism is not racist, but a form of ethnic or religious
prejudice, if it does not deny in principle the possibility of change or variation at an individual or even collective level. The presumed group characteristics are not then held to be stable, unalterable, or imposed from
the outside through physical factors: biology, climate, or geography. This
is not an academic difference. If Jews are accepted as converts, then this
is non-racist hostility: the Jews can, if they choose, cease to be Jews and
are then accepted, in theory and up to a point. This is social and religious
prejudice and intolerance. However, if Jews are regarded with hostility
whatever they do, simply because they are what they are, namely Jews,
and have no choice, then this is racist hostility. History has seen both
varieties and the conceptual difference is significant and so is that in the
practice of daily life.

Hellenistic Egypt

Classical Greece is not relevant to us here, for, as far as we know, the
Greeks lived in their classical age unaware of the existence of Jews.[2] The
Greeks became familiar with the Jews and their land only after the death
of Alexander, in the Hellenistic period. At first there is no obvious hostility
to be found in the texts, all of them collected and easily accessible in the
major collection of Menahem Stern.[3] Hostility towards Jews developed in
the Hellenistic period and for a proper understanding we need to consider
separately, as far as possible, (a) Alexandrian authors, (b) Hellenistic, non-
Egyptian authors, (c) Roman literature.

The particular features in the works of Alexandrian authors on Jews
and Judaism stem from two factors: (i) the circumstance that Jews formed
a significant part of the population of the city and were from the earliest
period of its existence involved in fierce conflict with the other population
groups there. In other words, this was urban hostility, caused by proximity
and ensuing social friction, (ii) the fact that Egypt, unlike other parts of
the Mediterranean world, plays a large and negative role in Jewish traditions concerning their origins and early history as a people.

---

[2] As noted above, p. 134, Herodotus may possibly be referring to the Jews in 2.104.3, where he mentions 'The Phoenicians and Syrians of Palestine' who acknowledged having learnt the custom of
circumcision from the Egyptians.
[3] M. Stern, *Greek and Latin Authors on Jews and Judaism*, 3 vols. (Jerusalem, 1974–94).

In response the surviving Alexandrian texts give their own, alternative versions of the exodus story, aiming at denigrating the Jews who allegedly have inferior origins. These sources have in common the assertion that the Jews are descendants of a group of polluted derelicts, suffering from leprosy and other impure diseases, who were expelled from Egypt and marched to Judaea under Moses who was then responsible for building a society that was both misanthropic or xenophobic and atheist or godless. The surviving references range from the third century BC (Manetho) to the first century AD (Apion and Chaeremon; Lysimachus is not dated, but falls within this range).[4] This version is found also in Diodorus, whose source is unknown.[5] Speculation is not profitable. The only Latin author to repeat these assertions in their hostile form is Tacitus.[6] Strabo gives a related, but entirely positive version.[7] Clearly, this was a subject of concern to Egyptians far more than to Greeks and Romans. Tacitus, a scholar who disliked Jews, used the subject for his own purposes, but no other Greek or Latin author did so in this form.

Moses, the first legislator of this people, after the traditional Greek model, is then depicted as a sort of Lycurgus who prescribed religious customs and a lifestyle, the opposite of those of the Egyptians, including a rule that they were permitted to have intercourse only among themselves.[8] Interestingly, this is the sort of general accusation levelled precisely at Egyptians by Greek and Latin authors, from Hecataeus of Miletus onwards (ca. 500 BC).[9]

In the Alexandrian texts Jews were also accused of practising both human sacrifice and cannibalism. In antiquity and in later periods human sacrifice and, even more, cannibalism are among the most serious accusations levelled at foreign peoples. Such an assertion, without substantiation, was enough to reduce foreigners to a level felt to be close to that of animals. It takes away their humanity.[10] Two Alexandrian authors maintained that the Jews practised ritual slaughter of foreigners. One is Damocritus,[11] of

---

[4] Manetho: Stern, no. 19; Lysimachus; Apion: Stern, no. 165, pp. 395–7; Chaeremon: Stern, no. 178, pp. 417–21. Cf. Schäfer, *Judeophobia*, 15–31.

[5] Diodorus 34/35.1.1–5; Stern, no. 63, I, 181–5.

[6] Tacitus, *Hist.* 5. Cf. R. S. Bloch, *Antike Vorstellungen vom Judentum: Der Judenexkurs des Tacitus im Rahmen der griechisch-römischen Ethnographie* (Stuttgart, 2002), esp. 87–90, 170–6.

[7] Schäfer, *Judeophobia*, 24–6.

[8] Manetho (Stern, no. 19), echoed by Tacitus, *Hist.* 5.4.1. Also: Diodorus 34/35.1.1–5; Stern, n. 63, 'misanthropic and lawless customs'.

[9] Parmenides, fr. 8.57; cf. B. Isaac, *The Invention of Racism in Classical Antiquity* (Princeton, 2004), ch. 7.

[10] Isaac, *Invention of Racism*, 207–11.

[11] Damocritus, *De Iudaeis*, apud Suda s.v. Damocritus; Stern, no. 247, I, 530–1.

uncertain date, probably first century AD. The second is Apion, cited by
Josephus (first half of the first century AD):[12] 'The practice was repeated
annually at a fixed season. They would kidnap a Greek foreigner, fatten
him up for a year, and then convey him to a wood, where they would
slaughter him, sacrificing his body with their customary ritual, partake
of his flesh, and, while immolating the Greek, swear an oath of hostility
to the Greeks. The remains of their victim were then thrown into a pit.'
Cassius Dio reports Jewish cannibalism during the revolt in Cyrene and
Egypt under Trajan.[13] This is almost certainly based on an Alexandrian
source, for Dio relates no such stories in his (abbreviated) passage on the
Bar Kokhba revolt.[14]

Here then we have two of the most hostile traditions from antiquity that
are clearly attributable to Alexandrian circles. Apart from echoes in the work
of Tacitus they do not recur in the literature of the Roman Empire. There is
another feature found once in Hellenistic sources which does not recur in
Roman literature, namely a call for the total eradication of the Jewish people.
Diodorus Siculus reports that the advisers of the Seleucid king Antiochus
Sidetes urged him 'to make an end of the people completely, or, failing that,
to abolish their laws and force them to change their ways'.[15] The reason given
is the fact the Jews are xenophobic and have perverse laws imposed by Moses.
It is to be noted that Diodorus observes with approval that the king rejected
the advice. Concerning Jewish religion a clearly Alexandrian theme is furthermore the claim that the Jews worshipped an ass.[16]

Hellenistic, Non-Egyptian

A hostile claim which appears in several authors is worth noting. According
to Josephus it is found first in the work of Apollonius Molon, a highly
influential orator from Asia Minor (first century BC). He 'adds that we are
the most witless of all barbarians, and are consequently the only people
who have contributed no useful invention to civilization'.[17] It is repeated

---

[12] Josephus, *Contra Apionem* 2.89.91–6; Stern, no. 171, I, 410–12. Stern, I, 141–4, 148–9, argues that
Josephus is unconvincing when he claims that Apion based his claims on Posidonius and Apollonius
Molon; for a similar conclusion, based on different arguments: Schäfer, *Judeophobia*, 55–62.

[13] Dio 68.32.1.

[14] Dio 68.12.1–14.3. Cf. Stern, no. 437, II, 385–9.

[15] Diodorus Siculus 34/35.1.5; Stern, no. 63, I, 181–5. A roughly similar account is found in Josephus,
Ant. 13.8.3 (245).

[16] Mnaseas of Patara in Lycia (200 BC), a student of Eratosthenes (representing the Alexandrian tradition), cited by Apion, cited by Josephus: see Stern, no. 28, I, 100; Apion: Stern, no. 170, I, 412–13.

[17] Josephus, *Contra Apionem* 2.148 (Stern, no. 49).

by Apion who, again according to Josephus, claims that the Jews 'have not produced any remarkable men, for instance inventors in the arts and crafts or men remarkable for their wisdom'.[18] This assertion occurs also in a quotation from Celsus[19] and, with a different emphasis, in the writings of the Emperor Julian,[20] who says that the Hebrews did not originate any science or any philosophical study, nor did they have a single commander like Alexander or Caesar. Even anyone inferior to those two great men deserves more admiration than all the commanders of the Jews put together. It should be noted that this particular idea is not found in the central works of Roman literature. It originated in Hellenistic circles, was taken over by Alexandrian authors, and recurs in the writings of a second-century Middle Platonic philosopher and in those of a fourth-century emperor with a mostly Greek education. As it occurs four times over a lengthy period it is worth mentioning, since the accusation that the Jews do not contribute to civilization is familiar from recent antisemitism. Thus the idea was there, although not found very frequently, in antiquity. If we may trust Josephus, it did not originate in Alexandria, but was taken over there as well.

In the social sphere the Jews are accused of cutting themselves off from the rest of humanity. This idea is expressed by Diodorus, citing Hecataeus of Abdera,[21] which would make it a relatively early tradition (around 300 BC). In the text transmitted by Diodorus, the means by which the Jews keep themselves apart are bizarre customs: not sharing meals and hating all other peoples.[22] It recurs in two parallel passages in Diodorus and Josephus, cited above, where this served as an argument for the extermination of the Jews. A variant appears in Philo's work (first century AD), who defends the Jews against claims that their laws command misanthropic and unsociable practices.[23] Apollonius Molon, according to Josephus, called the Jews atheists and misanthropes. Apollonius, mentioned before, was from Alabanda in Caria, and later established himself at Rhodes. He does represent the Hellenistic, but not the Alexandrian tradition, although, of course, he may have been familiar with earlier Alexandrian sources such as Manethon, where, as we saw, these accusations are already represented.

---

[18] *Contra Apionem* 2.135 (Stern, no. 175).

[19] Celsus, ap. Origenes, *Contra Celsum* 1.16, 4.31 (Stern, no. 375).

[20] Julian, *Contra Galilaeos* 176, 178, 218B–C (Stern, no. 481a).

[21] Diodorus 40.3.4 (Stern, no. 11); for discussion of Hecataeus on the Jews: Bloch, *Antike Vorstellungen*, 29–41. Cf. Jos., *Contra Apionem* 2.258 (Stern, no. 258), which represents the Alexandrian tradition.

[22] Diodorus 34/35.1.1–5; Stern, no. 63, I, 181–5, source unknown. Cf. Schäfer, *Judeophobia*, 170–7.

[23] Philo, *De virtutibus* 141.

Apollonius adds that the Jews are also cowards and characterized by temerity and reckless madness.[24]

It is important to note that classical Greek and Latin authors considered sociability an indispensable feature of a civilized people. Thus Aristotle states: 'The man who is isolated – who is unable to share (κοινωνεῖν) in the benefits of political association, or has no need to share because he is already self-sufficient – is no part of the polis, and must therefore be either a beast or a god.'[25] Strabo and Diodorus consider it a characteristic of remote barbaric people that they are cut off from other peoples. These, however, are regarded as wild and distant people, which the Jews are not.

As regards the charge of atheism, this obviously did not mean the Jews denied the existence of any god at all, in the modern sense. It meant that they rejected the legitimate and commonly recognized gods of civilized (Hellenic) society.

One of the most peculiar Jewish customs in Greek and Roman opinion was the keeping of the Sabbath. The first known author to comment on this was Agatharchides (second century BC) who commented on the conquest of Palestine and the capture of Jerusalem by Ptolemy I Soter in 302 which succeeded because the Jews foolishly refused to fight on the seventh day.[26]

To sum up: an especially fierce Alexandrian form of hostility may clearly be distinguished in the sources. Some of this appears to have influenced non-Alexandrian, Hellenistic and Roman authors, but essential elements were not taken over elsewhere. These are the hostile rewriting of the origins of the Jewish people as rendered in the Exodus story and the accusations of human sacrifice and cannibalism. The Hellenistic, non-Alexandrian tradition seems to have included at least one distinct claim which was that the Jews contributed no useful invention to civilization. The assertions that the Jews cut themselves off from humanity and were misanthropic and that they were atheist are represented in both traditions. It may be unwise to press the sources for clear evidence where these arguments originated, whether in Alexandria or in Seleucid Syria. It will be useful, in concluding this section, to point out once again that the confrontation between Jews and Egyptians was one between large groups in an urban setting, while the main conflict between Seleucids and Jews was located in the Jewish homeland where Jews formed a majority in a province of the Seleucid kingdom.

[24] Stern, no. 49, I, 154–5; Schäfer, *Judeophobia*, 21–2.
[25] Aristotle, *Pol.* 1253a (trans. Ernest Barker).
[26] Josephus, *Contra Apionem* 1.205–11; Stern, no. 30a, I, 104–8; Schäfer, *Judeophobia*, 82–4.

The former was marked by constant tension and occasional large-scale violence; the latter was a clash between Palestinian Jewish inhabitants and Seleucid rulers.

Roman

Roman feelings about Jews are often hostile, as is clear from the language used: *sceleratissima gens* ('a most villainous people', Seneca); *taeterrima gens* ('a most disgusting people', Tacitus); *perniciosa gens* ('a pernicious people', Quintilian); 'much lower than reptiles' (Cleomedes); 'a graceless people' (γένος ἔκσπονδον) (Synesius).[27] The works of Juvenal and Martial speak for themselves. Most of these belong to the mainstream of Latin literature and are representative of a broad section of Roman upper-class opinion. In trying to understand these attitudes it is essential to keep in mind that there was a substantial presence of Jews inside the city of Rome. Then, when the Empire became Christian, an even stronger hostility towards Jews became the norm. Constantine refers to the Jews as 'bloodstained men (who) are, as one might expect, mentally blind' and 'a detestable mob', a 'deadly' or a 'nefarious sect'.[28]

This discussion of Roman attitudes towards the Jews, which is more extensive than the discussion of Hellenistic attitudes, will be divided into several sections: social criticism, criticism of the Jewish religion (monotheism), and a number of specific topics – dietary restrictions, Sabbath and circumcision.

Social Criticism

The Hellenistic insistence on the lack of sociability of the Jews was, like other themes of that period, taken up by Tacitus. 'To establish his influence over this people for all time, Moses introduced new religious practices, quite opposed to those of all other religions. The Jews regard as profane all that we hold sacred; on the other hand, they permit all that we abhor.'[29] The Jews are thought to have cut themselves off from the remainder of

---

[27] Synesius, *Ep.* 5 (Stern, no. 569). The full description is: 'a graceless people and fully convinced of the piety of sending to Hades as many Greeks as possible'.

[28] Constantine's letter about the date of Easter, Eusebius, *Life of Constantine* 18.2 (trans. A. Cameron and S. G. Hall, Oxford, 1999), 3.18.2–3. Cf. *CTh* 16.8.1; *CJ* 1.9.3: *feralem sectam*; *nefariam sectam*. See the comments by G. Stemberger, *Juden und Christen im Heiligen Land: Palästina unter Konstantin und Theodosius* (Munich, 1987), 45–6.

[29] Tacitus, *Hist.* 5.4.1.

humanity by adopting religious customs and morals distinct from, or even opposed to those of all other peoples. It was an ancient tradition among the Romans to claim that those whose religion they did not respect had morals which were not worthy of respect either. Thus similarly, in the next chapter of his *Histories*, Tacitus repeats that the Jews, while maintaining strict loyalty towards one another, feel hostility and hatred towards all others ... They instituted circumcision to distinguish themselves thereby from other peoples. Those who are converted to their way of life accept the same practice, and the earliest habit they adopt is to despise the gods, to renounce their country, and to regard their parents, children and brothers as of little consequence.[30]

There are several themes here, but the essence of the passage is, again, that it is the Jews who erect a barrier between themselves and others. Tacitus refers to dietary laws[31] and circumcision, but also introduces sexual customs. Concerning the latter he combines the ideas of unsociability and moral corruption: they keep themselves apart, even in their sexuality, but have no morals among themselves, this in contrast with the incorrupt Germans who maintain the sanctity of marriage and of the relationship between husband and wife.[32] In this connection it is certainly interesting that Tacitus, whatever he thought of the Jews, never calls them barbarians.[33]

The idea of unsociability was repeated in rather similar terms by Celsus (second century AD), as cited by Origen: 'they are proud and refuse the society of others'.[34] It is expressed in a particularly fierce form by Philostratus in the third century in a speech which he attributes to the Stoic Euphrates:

> For the Jews have long been in revolt not only against the Romans but against humanity; and a people that has made its own a life apart and irreconcilable, that cannot share with the rest of mankind in the pleasures of the table nor join in their libations or prayers or sacrifices, are separated from ourselves by a greater gulf than divides us from Susa or Bactra or the more distant Indies. What sense then or reason was there in chastising them for revolting from us, whom we had better never annexed?[35]

It is interesting to see the specific reasons: the refusal to eat and worship together. Noteworthy is furthermore the assertion that the Jews are more remote than the farthest peoples of the world. The assertion that it would

[30] *Hist.* 5.5.1: *contemnere deos, exuere patriam, parentes liberos fratres vilia habere.*
[31] Herodotus already uses diet as a criterion of ethnicity: 3.23.1; 9.82.
[32] Tacitus, *Germ.* 17, 18, discussed also in Isaac, *Invention of Racism* (2004), 432.
[33] Bloch, *Antike Vorstellungen*, 154.
[34] Celsus, ap. Origenes, *Contra Celsum* 5.2.41 (Stern, no. 375, p. 256).
[35] Philostratus, *Vita Apollonii* 5.33 (trans. F. C. Conybeare, Loeb).

have been better not to annex the Jews is new and relatively rare. It is found also in a much later statement by Rutilius Namatianus (fifth century).[36]

Tacitus twice says that proselytes to Judaism are the worst (*pessimus quisque*), for they are traitors to their religion, country, and family. In accepting the foreign cult they abandon their own and, with it, all the social obligations that every decent man respects. Conversion, it is important to note, is a subject that plays no role in the earlier, Hellenistic sources. The idea that Jews are exclusively loyal towards each other occurs first in Cicero's work (*Pro Flacco*).[37] Cicero explicitly asserts that there were large numbers of Jews in Rome who were hostile to the *optimates* and could influence public meetings. This is judicial rhetoric, but it must have been at least credible to those present or, to say the least, have corresponded with their prejudices. The issue of conversion clearly is a new one that disturbed Roman authors. Jews were regarded as disloyal elements in society. Non-Jews who converted to Judaism were therefore traitors.

In the reign of Augustus, Horace wrote his much-discussed lines: 'This is one of those lesser frailties I spoke of, and if you should make no allowance for it, then would a big band of poets come to my aid – for we are the big majority – and we, like Jews, will compel you to become one of our throng.'[38] It has often been claimed that this refers to Jewish proselytizing practices. Other scholars argue that it portrays Jews as prone to use pressure to achieve their political ends and that it implies nothing about gentiles being compelled to become Jewish.[39] Since the subjects of these lines are poets, and Jews are merely an object for comparison, it is hardly likely that Horace is speaking of forced conversion. It is more probable that, like Cicero, he is referring here to the political pressure which Jews could exert thanks to their mutual loyalty.

We find the issue of loyalty and conversion again in the work of Juvenal who attacks proselytes along similar lines as Cicero: 'Having been wont to deride Roman laws, they learn and follow and revere Jewish law, and all that Moses passed on in his secret volume, prohibiting to point the way to anyone not following the same rites, and leading none but the circumcised

---

[36] Rutilius Namatianus, *De reditu suo* 1.395–8: Stern, no. 542, II, 664; Schäfer, *Judeophobia*, 87–9.

[37] Cicero, *Pro Flacco* 66–7.

[38] *Sermones* I, 4.139–3 (Stern, no. 127, I, 321; 323 with references to earlier literature). Cf. the trans. of N. Rudd, *Satires of Horace and Persius* (Penguin, 1973): 'and, like the Jews, we make you fall in with our happy band'.

[39] J. Nolland, 'Proselytism or Politics in Horace, *Satires* I, 4, 138–143?' *Vigiliae Christianae* 33 (1979), 347–55, emphasizing the parallel with Cicero, *Pro Flacco* 6.6; E. Will and C. Orrieux, '*Prosélytisme Juif*? *Histoire d'une erreur* (Paris, 1992), 103–5; M. Goodman, *Mission and Conversion: Proselytizing in the Religious History of the Roman Empire* (Oxford, 1994), 74; Schäfer, *Judeophobia*, 107–8.

to the desired fountain.'[40] This part of his satire is aimed against Jewish proselytes, but there are several characteristics Juvenal sees these proselytes as sharing with born Jews, the most important of which is that they deride Roman law while honouring Jewish law. The two sets of laws are thus considered mutually exclusive. In becoming Jewish, Juvenal is saying, Romans cut themselves off from civilized Roman society. This is further illustrated by the claims that proselytes refuse to point the way to gentiles and that Moses had produced a secret book.[41] There is a background to this statement: the fear of foreign secret cults was already prevalent in Republican Rome.[42]

In any case, from Cicero to Tacitus we notice a strand of thinking in Latin authors which holds that the Jews are loyal to one another, form an effective pressure group, and are hostile to non-Jews. The same would hold true for converts, who thereby become traitors to their country and family. It is important to keep in mind that all these texts reflect reactions to the presence of Jews in the city of Rome. They are not vague feelings about a distant people or a minority in various provinces, but direct responses to a significant element in the city population. The presence of Jews living according to their own customs in Rome on the other side of the Tiber was tolerated by Augustus and Tiberius, according to Philo.[43] From time to time efforts were made to halt the spread of Judaism among Romans in Rome.[44] We recognize here themes that are clearly different from those that reached Rome through the Hellenistic literature. There the Jews are accused of being misanthropic and unsociable, but the matter of conflicting loyalty did not come up because the Hellenistic kingdoms did not represent integrated empires. The Jews formed a substantial group in Alexandria and were the focus of frequent friction, but their position never took the form represented in Rome, where their collective loyalty became the focus of attention. In this respect the opinions on the role of Jews in Rome resemble the arguments of later centuries far more than they did in the Hellenistic world.

---

[40] Juvenal, 14.100–4 (Stern, no. 301, comments on II, 107): This is a passage from a satire whose main theme is the bad influence that the vices of parents have on their children; cf. Courtney's comments *ad loc.*, 571–2; J. P. Stein, *CP* 65 (1970), 34ff.; Will and Orrieux, '*Prosélytisme Juif?*, 111–12. Possibly in response to accusations like these, Josephus, *Contra Apionem* 2.211, asserts that Jews must, among other services rendered to foreigners, point out the road. Cf. *Ant.* 4.8.31 (276).

[41] The meaning of this sentence is not quite certain, see Stern's comments.

[42] Livy describes the Bacchanalia, against which action was taken in 186 BC, as 'dark and nocturnal rites' (39.8.4).

[43] Philo, *Leg.* 23 (156–7). For the status of the Jews in Rome: Isaac, *Invention of Racism*, 447–50.

[44] Isaac, *Invention of Racism*, 236–7, 408, 456–8.

The suspicion of dual loyalty could develop into something worse: the fear of being taken over by the subject people.

Seneca hated Jews, a *sceleratissima gens*, 'a most villainous people'. He considered their influence pernicious, as expressed in a statement transmitted by Augustine. In this text Augustine says Seneca expressed criticism of Jewish customs, especially the Sabbath, and he adds a direct quotation: 'Meanwhile the customs of this accursed people have gained such influence that they are now received throughout all the world. The vanquished have given laws to their victors.'[45] It is important here to consider the clear sense conveyed that the vanquished are conquering the victors.[46] This shows how threatening Romans found some of their subjects as soon as they sensed a certain influence in the religious, social, or cultural sphere. In the present case it concerns religious influence. Juvenal's attack on proselytes, cited above, in combination with his well-known assertion that the Syrian Orontes is now flowing into the Tiber, shows that he harboured similar sentiments.[47] Foreign cults penetrated the households of Roman magistrates, says Cassius Longinus in AD 61, in a speech attributed to him by Tacitus.[48]

Domitian, in a famous description by Suetonius, is reported to have gone to great lengths to identify Jews for the sake of the special tax on them.[49] Domitian, in his campaign, sought two categories in particular: non-Jews who lived as Jews without publicly acknowledging this, and born Jews who concealed their origin. Domitian is also on record as having put to death his relative Flavius Clemens and his wife Flavia Domitilla on the charge of atheism. This, according to Cassius Dio, was a charge on which many who inclined to Jewish customs were condemned.[50] Above we saw that this was one of the traditional accusations aimed at Jews, first attributed to Apollonius Molon.

Elsewhere Cassius Dio, who is unusual in his fairly tolerant description of the Jewish God, refers to both Jews by birth and proselytes as *Ioudaioi*: 'I do not know how they obtained this appellation, but it applies also to other people, even if they are of alien descent, who adopt their customs. This

---

[45] Augustine, *De civitate dei* 6.11 (Stern, no. 186, I, 431–2); discussion: Stern, I, 429–32; Schäfer, *Judeophobia*, 111–13.

[46] For the concept: Isaac, *Invention of Racism*, 225–35.

[47] Juvenal, *Sat.* 3.60–72. Cf. below, p. 316.

[48] Tacitus, *Ann.* 14.44.3.

[49] Suetonius, *Domitianus* 12.2 (Stern, no. 320). Dio 68.1.2, notes that, after Nerva succeeded Domitian, he would not permit anyone to accuse anybody of *maiestas* (an offence against the authority of the Emperor) or of adopting the Jewish mode of life.

[50] Dio 67.14.1–3, for which see Stern, I, 435, with comments, 380–4. Above, p. 289.

group also exists among the Romans, and although it has been repressed often, it has increased very much and has succeeded in obtaining the right of freedom in its way of life.'[51] The passage is important because it states explicitly that there was an increase in the number of proselytes by the early third century, which Dio mentions without disapproval in spite of the fact that 'they are different from other people in virtually their entire way of life'.

Dio has this idea of separateness in common with earlier, hostile authors, but he is unusual in that he considers Jewish proselytes to be just like Jews by birth. However, a different view of this aspect is expressed in the address which Dio assigns to Maecenas. The latter advises Augustus 'to hate and punish those who are involved in foreign cults, not only for the sake of the gods – for if they do not respect them they will not honour any other being – but also because such people preferring new gods persuade many to adopt strange cults and this leads to conspiracies, factions and political societies which do not profit the monarchy in the least'.[52] Dio is here explicit in his rejection of foreign cults: not only are they a threat to religion and religious values, but they are also a focus of political danger. The Jews were exceptional in being allowed to assemble for religious services while other foreign religions were forbidden to do so in Rome in the reigns of Caesar and Augustus. It seems then that Dio did not regard the Jews as practitioners of one of those foreign cults that he wanted suppressed. It may be relevant that Dio was not a native of the city of Rome, but of Nicaea in Bithynia.

The condemnation of Jewish proselytism and the idea that the vanquished dominate the victors recurs in particularly hostile form in the work of the fifth-century author Rutilius Namatianus, already referred to above.[53]

The feelings described above, we see, were expressed by Roman authors over a period of some 500 years and therefore may be regarded as a truly representative feature of the trends in Roman attitudes towards the Jews. The background is clear: a superbly successful empire should be superior in every respect, not just through arms and politics, and it should not be influenced at all by its subjects in cultural and, even more important, in religious matters. It is hard not to conclude that this sensitivity was to some extent irrational. I firmly disagree with scholars who tend to interpret

---

[51] Dio 37.17.1. Cf. above, p. 296.
[52] Dio 52.36.2.
[53] Rutilius Namatianus, *De reditu suo* 1.395–8 (Stern, II, no. 542).

such Roman attitudes towards the Jews and the policies that followed from these attitudes as generally rational and justified by reality.[54]

In any case, there are enough texts to conclude that there was a marked sensitivity to a perceived presence of Jewish proselytes in Rome which expressed itself in hostile reactions. It is quite clear that this happened in response to the novel forms of religious and social choice exhibited by some Roman citizens. They abandoned the traditional religion and the community of loyal citizens, committing themselves to a different conception of religion and a separate community.

Other Topics: Religion, Dietary Restrictions, Sabbath, Circumcision

The importance of religion in Roman evaluations of other peoples and their influence on Roman religion and society should not be underestimated. 'Nothing is more deceptive in appearance than a false religion.'[55] 'For men wisest in all divine and human law used to judge that nothing was so potent in destroying religion as the replacement of native sacrifices by foreign ritual.'[56] Foreign cults were usually regarded as a potential threat to the stability of the state. Roman citizens practising foreign rites was punishable as a criminal act in principle, even if the law was not always upheld in practice.[57] The term *superstitio* has been discussed frequently. It is important to realize that the Roman state religion (replaced in the Later Roman Empire by Christianity) is always called *religio* and never *superstitio*, while other religions are sometimes called *religio* and sometimes *superstitio*. The latter term was originally almost devoid of negative judgement – like the Greek *barbaros* – but became over time increasingly hostile. For the Jewish religion Cicero uses both terms and he is the first to call it a *barbara superstitio*.[58] He makes it clear that the practice of Jewish religion (*istorum religio sacrorum*) is incompatible with Roman institutions,[59] for the organization of rites 'is not only of concern to religion, but also to the well-being of the state'.[60]

---

[54] See, for instance, H. Solin, 'Juden und Syrer im westlichen Teil der römischen Welt: Eine ethnisch-demographische Studie', *ANRW* 2.29.2 (1983): 607ff. esp. 686: the Jews in Rome were 'a continuous source of agitation and unrest'.

[55] Livy 39.16.6: a speech which Livy attributes to a consul in 186 BC.

[56] Livy 39.16.9.

[57] Tac., *Ann.* 13.32.2.

[58] Cicero, *Pro Flacco* 67.

[59] *Pro Flacco,* 29.69.

[60] Cic., *De legibus* 2.12.30.

A distinction should be made between attitudes towards religions
and cults represented in Rome and Italy, and those which were actively
practised only in the provinces. The local religions in the annexed provinces were left alone, provided there was no practice of human sacrifice and the religion did not call into question Roman authority. The
antiquity of their cult practices in particular made them respectable.
This is the reason why Josephus devotes a considerable part of his work
against Apion to the citation of records demonstrating the antiquity of
Judaism.[61] Foreign cults, such as those from Egypt and Judaism, which
attracted attention in Roman society because they were a presence
clearly felt inside Rome, however, were regarded in a different light from
those which were known only through indirect sources as a provincial
phenomenon.

Many Roman authors had a low opinion of the Jews and their religion. Their criticism extended to particulars of Jewish religious custom,
as far as they knew it, and to characteristics that were attributed to the
Jews. There is no need here to discuss in detail how Roman authors
viewed Jewish religion, since that has been done in modern works that
are easily accessible.[62] It will suffice to review briefly a number of important subjects.

More than anything else it was the exclusive monotheism of the Jews,
with the concomitant absence of a cult-statue in the Temple in Jerusalem
before its destruction, that struck Roman authors.[63] Several authors
approve,[64] but many others disapprove: they regard the Jewish concept of
one God as an aberration.[65] It was even suggested that monotheism fitted
their anti-social attitudes described above: their God refuses to associate
with other gods, as asserted by Numenius of Apamea (second half of the
second century AD), who says that the Jewish God is ἀκοινώνητος, 'not
sociable, exclusive'.[66] This is precisely the expression used by Diodorus and
others to describe the Jews themselves, as cited above. In peoples this was a
quality which Greeks and Romans rejected and the same was true for their

[61] Josephus, *Contra Apionem* 13.69–23.218.
[62] All the sources are available in Stern's major work. J. G. Gager, *The Origins of Anti-Semitism*
(New York and Oxford, 1983), 55–66, contains a succinct discussion. Schäfer, *Judeophobia*, part I,
has a full treatment of the subject.
[63] Varro (116–27 BC); Schäfer, *Judeophobia*, 34–65. Also: Tacitus, *Hist.* 5.5.4; Plutarch, *Quaestiones convivales* 4.6, 'Who the god of the Jews is' (Stern no. 25); Cassius Dio 37.17.2.
[64] Stern, no. 72, I, 207–12.
[65] Julian, *Ep.* 20.454a, *Ad Theodorum*, no. 89a (Stern, no. 483), respects the Jewish God for the qualities
ascribed to him, but rejects the idea that he should be the only god.
[66] Numenius of Apamea, ap. Lydus, *De mensibus* 4.53, pp. 109–10 (Stern no. 367).

divinity. The particularly hostile tradition that the Jews really worshipped an ass, whose statue stood in the Temple, has been mentioned already.[67] It is found in Roman sources in derivative form, but does not play a significant role in Roman ideas about Jewish religion.

The second subject which appears frequently in the sources is dietary restrictions, notably the abstinence from pork.[68] It was not in itself remarkable for peoples to have their own specific diet. In the case of the Jews their special diet is not in itself a subject of criticism. What was criticized fiercely was the idea that the Jews would not share meals with non-Jews, as has already been discussed under the heading of 'sociability'.

The third topic familiar from the sources is the Sabbath.[69] As seen above, it was ridiculed by Agatharchides (second century BC). It is mentioned as a well-known institution without negative emphasis by several poets in the reign of Augustus,[70] another indication that there were enough Jews in the city of Rome in this period for their customs to be familiar in broad circles. Some later authors, hostile on other subjects as well, consider the Sabbath wasteful and a proof of the idleness of Jews.[71] Several authors want to demonstrate the absurdity of the Sabbath by claiming that Jerusalem was conquered because the Jews would not defend themselves on that day.[72] Plutarch lists keeping of the Sabbath as one of the bad barbarian customs which are taken up by Romans, yet another critical remark about foreign customs penetrating contemporary society.[73] Several authors in the reign of Augustus and afterwards refer erroneously – and sometimes ironically – to the Sabbath as a fast day.[74] A curious late attack may be found in a letter from Synesius (ca. 365–413/414) to his brother, where he describes

---

[67] See in particular E. J. Bickerman, 'Ritualmord und Eselskult: Ein Beitrag zur Geschichte antiker Publizistik', in Bickerman, *Studies in Jewish and Christian History* (Leiden, 1980), II, 225–55, at 245–55; Stern, I, 97–8, bibliography on p. 98, 184, 530, 563; II, 18, 36; Schäfer, *Judeophobia*, 55–62.

[68] Schäfer, *Judeophobia*, 66–81.

[69] Schäfer, *Judeophobia*, 82–92.

[70] Tibullus, 1.3.15–18 (Stern no. 126); Horace, *Serm.* 1.9.67–72 (Stern, no. 129); Ovid, *Ars amatoria* 1.413–16 (Stern no. 142).

[71] Seneca, *De superstitione*, ap. Augustine, *De civitate dei* 6.11 (Stern, no. 186); Tacitus, *Hist.* 5.4.3 (Stern, no. 281, comments in II, 37–8).

[72] Dio 37.16.2 (Stern, no. 406) on Pompey's capture of the city; Frontinus, *Stratagemata* 2.1.17 (Stern, no. 229 with comments on I, 510–11) on Titus' capture of Jerusalem (the passage is erroneous in several respects); Plutarch, *De superstitione* 8 (Stern, no. 256); cf. Stern, comments on II, 549. The earliest is Agatharchides already cited.

[73] Plutarch, *De superstitione* 3 (Stern, no. 255), see also the previous note. Note also Seneca's hostile remark: *Ep. Mor.* 95.47 (Stern, no. 188).

[74] Pompeius Trogus, ap. Iustinus, *Ep.* 36.2.14 (Stern no. 137) and other authors, cited by Stern in the commentary, I, 341 and 277; Petronius, *Carmen* 50, fr. 37 (Stern, no. 195); Martial, *Ep.* 4.4 (Stern, no. 239).

how a Jewish skipper and his Jewish sailors stopped functioning at sunset on Sabbath eve and almost let the vessel go down.[75] It cannot be said that such mockery of Sabbath practices amounts to hostility. It is one of the numerous customs and habits which were seen to single out the Jews and raised little sympathy, if not criticism.

An unusual accusation found in the fifth-century author Rutilius Namatianus is that the Jewish God is soft or effeminate, because he rested on the seventh day.[76] Here criticism of the Jewish nation and their Sabbath is extended or transferred to their God. Yet the Jews, together with the Parthians, were the two Eastern nations that were not normally regarded as soft or effeminate by Greek and Roman authors, unlike the Syrians and various peoples in Anatolia.[77]

Finally, there is the particularly sensitive topic of circumcision.[78] This was the essential mark of the Jewishness of the men and the final step taken by a convert.[79] It is usually mentioned with great disapproval. Strabo mentions it as one of the bad customs of the Jews which were typical of their decline, adopted when, after Moses and his first successors, 'superstitious men were appointed to the priesthood and then tyrannical people'.[80] Tacitus, as already mentioned, says that the Jews 'adopted circumcision to distinguish themselves from other peoples by this difference'. The idea of the social separateness of the Jews has been described above. Circumcision was the one physical feature emphasizing this separateness. In spite of the circumstance that there were other peoples who also had this custom, it became the obvious distinguishing mark of a Jewish male, for the other peoples were not present in such numbers in Italy.[81] Jews could be referred to as simply 'the circumcised'.[82] Petronius lists it among other remarkable or even ludicrous physical characteristics of foreign peoples.[83] Martial repeatedly mentions

---

[75] Synesius, *Ep.* 5 (Stern, no. 569).

[76] Rutilius Namatianus, *De reditu suo* 1.391–2 (Stern, no. 542). Cf. Celsus, ap. Origenes, *Contra Celsum* 6.61 (Stern, no. 375).

[77] Isaac, *Invention of Racism*, 63, 65, 209, 307–8.

[78] Schäfer, *Judeophobia*, 93–105; cf. P. Cordier, 'Les Romains et la circoncision', *Revue des Études juives* 160 (2001): 337–55.

[79] Goodman, *Mission and Conversion*, 67, 77, 81–2. Schäfer, *Judeophobia*, 96–7. See, for instance, Petronius, *Carmen* 50, fr. 37 (Stern, no. 195), cited already in connection with the Sabbath; Juvenal 14.99 (Stern, no. 301).

[80] Strabo 16.2.37 (761) (Stern, no. 115).

[81] As appears from the well-known story told by Suetonius, *Domitianus* 12.2 (Stern, no. 320).

[82] Horace, *Serm.* 1.9.70 (Stern, no. 129): *curti Iudaei*; Persius, *Sat.* 5.184 (Stern, no. 190): *recutita sabbata*.

[83] Petronius, *Satyricon* 102.14.

circumcised Jews, each time from the perspective of his persistent pre-occupation with their sexuality.[84]

A later, satirical reference to circumcision appears in the Historia Augusta: 'At this time the Jews started a war because they were forbidden to mutilate their genitals'.[85] This statement is famous because it is the only source which appears to state explicitly that the cause of the Bar Kokhba war in the reign of Hadrian was a prohibition of circumcision.[86] Whatever the merit of this theory, it is worth noting that the SHA does not use the word circumcision, but mutilation. The implication is that this was a ludicrous rebellion, for who in his right senses would go to war because he was forbidden to mutilate himself? The statement about the origins of the Bar Kokhba war puts the war as a whole in a ridiculous light and it is therefore worth considering whether this does not call into question the trustworthiness of this statement in a source which is anyway of dubious reliability. The equation of circumcision with mutilation, on the other hand, is found also in the work of a contemporary Christian author, John Chrysostom: 'Watch out for the dogs, watch out for the evil-workers, watch out for those who mutilate the flesh. For we are the true circumcision, who worship God in spirit ...'[87]

Yet, in spite of all this hostility, Judaism was permitted in Judaea, in Rome, and in the provinces. It was permitted, in spite of the fact that the religion as such was regarded by many with highly negative feelings, but yet the Jews had the status of a recognized people and a people had a right to its religion, whatever it was. It did not have a right to accept foreigners into its midst and when this happened, as was seen to happen among the Jews, counter-measures were taken from time to time. Religion was an inseparable part of ethnic and social identity, and the Romans therefore seriously restricted freedom of religion. Children had the right and duty

---

[84] Martial, *Ep.* 7.30.5; 7.35; 7.82.6 (Stern, no. 243); 11.94 (Stern, no. 245).

[85] SHA, *Hadrian* 14, 2: *moverunt ea tempestate et Iudaei bellum, quod vetabantur mutilare genitalia.* See: B. Isaac, *The Near East under Roman Rule* (Leiden, 1998), 277–8.

[86] See below, Chapter 14. The subject has been much debated. Cf. E. Schürer, *The History of the Jewish People in the Age of Jesus Christ (175 BC–AD 138)*, 3 vols. (Edinburgh, 1973–9), I, 536–40; E. M. Smallwood, *The Jews under Roman Rule* (Leiden, 1981), 429–31; Stern, II, comments on pp. 619–21, all with extensive bibliography. Note also J. Geiger, 'The Ban on Circumcision and the Bar-Kokhba Revolt', *Zion* 41 (1976), 139–47 (Hebrew); Schäfer, *Der Bar Kokhba-Aufstand* (Tübingen, 1981); B. Isaac and A. Oppenheimer, 'The Revolt of Bar Kokhba: Ideology and Modern Scholarship' = B. Isaac, *The Near East Under Roman Rule*, 220–52, at 233–4; additional bibliography on pp. 254–6; Schäfer, *Judeophobia*, 103–5.

[87] J. Chrysostom, *Homilia adversus Judaeos*, PG 48. 845. Chrysostom is here quoting Paul: Philippians 3:2. On Chrysostom and the Jews: R. L. Wilken, *John Chrysostom and the Jews: Rhetoric and Reality in the Late Fourth Century* (Berkeley, CA, 1983).

to practise the religion of their parents, but nobody had an automatic right to practise the religion of another people. That was considered a politically significant act. In the case of Roman citizens it was also regarded as a breach of the required loyalty, for religion was an inseparable part of the state.

Under the Empire, the imperial cult became part of this complex. Rome accepted that the Jews had a peculiar fanaticism which made it impossible to demand of them what was demanded of everybody else, but they were suffered as an exception. On the part of the Romans, this was a realistic policy, rather than an expression of tolerance, for they were aware that Jews would rather let themselves be killed than revere a mortal ruler as if he were a god. For the same reason Jews were exempted from army service and other duties which impinged on their customs. The Romans succeeded in building an empire because they were realists and they did not usually attempt to enforce the unenforceable.

As already observed, the Jews are not described as soft or effeminate in Roman sources, unlike other peoples from the same area. Cicero is the only one who ever calls them 'born slaves', so apparently this was not a theme which caught the imagination either. The stereotypes of Jews did not correspond with those applied to most Eastern peoples and Jews were not classified with the weak and spineless peoples.

Conclusion

The evaluation of these matters will always depend on the attitude of the evaluator. Those who cherish their antipathies towards other nations, groups, or minorities always claim that their dislike is based on objective realities. There are similar patterns in the analysis of antiquity. Those who dislike Jews in the present will conclude that there were objective reasons for the Greeks and Romans to dislike them.[88] One difficulty in

---

[88] Ruth Benedict wrote her monograph *Race and Racism* (London, 1942) with the clear intention of clarifying the concept of race and attacking racism in a time which saw extravagant abuse of the concept. She strongly insists that racism is a creation of our own time. However, on p. 103, she states: 'The Hebrew law and the prophets also contributed to the foundations of Jesus's teaching. The ancient Mosaic Law lays down gracious rules: ... After the Assyrian (*sic*) captivity, however, an opposition party arose which advocated separatism ... Fanatical racism therefore occurred in Israel long before the days of modern racism, but no trace of it is to be found in the words of Christ. His teachings of a great community of peoples without regard to race agreed with the older Hebraic law, and were given a solid basis, also, by the achievements of the Roman Empire.' It is curious that we should find such a traditional form of Christian antisemitism and bigotry in an American anthropologist and thinker, writing in 1939 and publishing in 1942 precisely to combat racism.

understanding the relationships in antiquity properly is that we have no numerical information. There is no way of knowing how many Jews there were in the various provinces and in Rome, and how many proselytes. However this may be, it is clear that people of every period are guided more by emotions than by numbers and facts when thinking about social groups, and it should not be difficult to accept that most of the ancient authors discussed in this chapter were not guided by rational considerations in their judgements and fears.

We have now reached the point where a number of essential questions can be answered.

(1) Was Greek and Roman hatred of the Jews essentially different from hatred of other non-Greek and non-Roman groups?
(2) Was it different from the Hellenized Egyptian hatred of the Jews?
(3) Were Roman attitudes different from those encountered in the Hellenistic and Alexandrian tradition?
(4) Can a clear impact be felt of the various wars and revolts on the attitudes towards Jews?
(5) Which common anti-Semitic stereotypes of later periods are absent in Graeco-Roman antiquity?

1. The answer to the first question will be unambiguous.[89] The attitudes toward Jews are indeed quite different from those towards other foreigners. Although some points of resemblance are found in criticism of Egypt, this must not be taken too far. As mentioned, there is an old tradition, first attributed to Hecataeus of Miletus (ca. 500), that Egypt was different in every respect from the rest of the world. Greek and Roman critical attitudes focused on the peculiarities of the Egyptian religion. Still, the total of the hostile attitudes towards the Jews is different: the insistence on their social attitudes and religious practices has no parallel in the criticism of, for instance, Syrians, Phoenicians, and Parthians.

2. Alexandrian hostility towards the Jews contained various significant elements that are not echoed elsewhere: the efforts to prove the inferior origin of the Jewish people – inspired by a distortion of the Exodus story – are repeated only by Tacitus. The story seems not to have become a major feature of attitudes towards Jews in the Roman world. The accusations concerning human sacrifice and cannibalism, so prominent in Alexandrian sources, play no role in non-Egyptian Hellenistic and Roman literature.

---

[89] Attitudes towards other peoples: Isaac, *Invention of Racism*, chs. 4–12.

A specific point: the claim that the Jews worshipped an ass was not taken over either. It may or may not be significant also that only Seleucid circles are reported as having contemplated the total elimination of the Jewish people.

3.   I would say that the Hellenistic period clearly saw the development of particular forms of hostility towards the Jews, but the differences between the Alexandrian and non-Egyptian traditions are significant. Roman authors took over some of the themes that appealed to them and adapted those to their peculiar social, moral, and ideological framework. There are, in other words, elements of continuity, but there is no linear development to be found. Dislike of the Jews was not invented at any particular stage or in any given place. The dislike developed in specific social settings – what were transmitted were specific ideas.

4.   While it seems obvious in principle that there was a connection between specific periods of violence and warfare and the attitudes of Greeks and Romans towards Jews, it is less easy to be concrete. When the advisers of the Seleucid king Antiochus Sidetes urged him 'to make an end of the [Jewish] people completely, or, failing that to abolish their laws and force them to change their ways', as already cited, this was obviously connected with the Hasmonaean war. It is reasonable to assume that the particular hostility of the Alexandrian authors Apion and Chaeremon in the first half of the first century AD was connected with the serious tension and violent clashes between Jews and non-Jews in Alexandria in that period.[90] It is less easy to point at a direct connection between the statements of specific authors and the major Jewish revolts against Rome. An exception here would seem to be Cassius Dio's extraordinary description of bloody violence during the revolt in the Diaspora, inspired perhaps by Egyptian sources. As for the authors in the city of Rome, these must have been more influenced by the urban social relationships in the city than by events in the provinces.

5.   It will be instructive to see which common antisemitic stereotypes of later periods are absent in Graeco-Roman antiquity. The first absence to be mentioned is the blood libel. This clearly belongs to a later period, although we saw that accusations of cannibalism are found in the Alexandrian tradition. Another feature absent in this period is the idea of the wandering Jew (Ahasverus), the eternal, cosmopolitan foreigner or, perhaps more relevant for antiquity, the idea that the Jews were and always remained a nomadic

---

[90] Gager, *Origins of Anti-Semitism*, 43–51.

people. There are various reasons why one might expect such assertions not to have come up in antiquity. There is another idea, however, that one could have looked for in Roman literature, namely that of the Jew as a typical oriental or Asiatic. Indeed no less a scholar than Theodor Mommsen assumed as a matter of course that it was there, even though in fact it nowhere occurs in any of the sources.[91]

No stereotype has been encountered more frequently during the past centuries concerning the Jews than that of the grabby, materialistic trader. This is nowhere to be found in Greek and Latin literature. The typical unreliable trader in Graeco-Roman tradition is the Phoenician.[92] The latter people, incidentally, are also among those described as stereotypically oriental. An obvious reason for the fact that Jews were not seen as treacherous traders is that very few of them were in fact engaged in trade before the Middle Ages. On the contrary, in Rome there was a familiar stereotype of impoverished Jews hanging around synagogues.[93]

Finally, there is no suggestion that the Jews were rootless conspirators who aimed to gain world domination through secret plotting. While it is true that there was a fear in Rome that the provincial subjects, including the Jews, were in fact taking over the Empire, that is clearly a different proposition from the notion that there was a Jewish plot to take over the world, developed in the nineteenth century.[94]

---

[91] Mommsen, *Römische Geschichte*, III, 549: 'Also in this period we encounter the characteristic hostility of the Westerner to this so thoroughly Oriental race and its strange opinions and customs.'

[92] Isaac, *Invention of Racism*, 324–35.

[93] Martial, *Ep.* 12.57.13; Juvenal, *Sat.* 3.10–18. For the Jews in the city of Rome: Schürer, *History of the Jewish People*, III, 73–81; D. Noy, *Jewish Inscriptions of Western Europe*, II, *The City of Rome* (Cambridge, 1995); M. Williams, 'The Structure of the Jewish Community in Rome', in M. Goodman (ed.), *Jews in a Graeco-Roman World* (Oxford, 1998), 215–28.

[94] The Elders of Zion; Hermann Goedsche (aka Sir John Redcliffe), *Biarritz* (1868).

CHAPTER 14

Roman Religious Policy and the Bar Kokhba War

The cause or causes of the Bar Kokhba revolt are still reported in only two sources, for the documents discovered in recent years do not add any direct references to its origins. We have to choose between the information given by the Historia Augusta and Cassius Dio, or combine these two.[1] If Jerusalem was refounded as *Colonia Aelia Capitolina* before the outbreak of the revolt, this reinforces the statement of Dio that this was the cause of the revolt. However, this in itself does not contradict or invalidate the explicit statement in the Historia Augusta that a general ban on circumcision was the cause. Generations of scholars have firmly expressed their preference for one cause or the other and – as is often the case in our field – most of them have assumed that their arguments annihilated the opposite view, which their captious critics then refused to acknowledge.[2]

One point is now clear. Excavations of the Eastern Cardo of Aelia Capitolina have produced convincing evidence that the Eastern Cardo was constructed in the 120s. The conclusion of the excavator is that the Roman city was planned and its main thoroughfares paved in the early years of Hadrian's reign, about a decade before his visit to the East of AD 129–30. The least that can be said is that building activity is attested well before the outbreak of the Bar Kokhba revolt.[3] Since the city was, in fact, the location of legionary headquarters it is also possible that construction was initiated ahead of a formal decision regarding the status of the city. In this connection it is worth keeping in mind that two Flavian milestones

---

[1] SHA, *Hadrian* 14.2; Dio 69.12.

[2] For my own share in this discussion: B. Isaac, *The Near East under Roman Rule: Selected Papers* (Leiden, 1998), nos. 8, 11–16, 18. See now R. Baker, 'Epiphanius, on Weights and Measures §14: Hadrian's Journey to the East and the Rebuilding of Jerusalem', *ZPE* 182 (2012): 157–67. This paper shows conclusively that Epiphanius does not state that Hadrian visited the area in 117 and the passage cannot therefore serve as evidence for actions of Hadrian in the area at that time.

[3] S. Weksler-Bdolah, 'The Foundation of Aelia Capitolina in Light of New Excavations along the Eastern Cardo', *IEJ* (2014): 38–62. These publications report on excavations that firmly date the first construction of the 'Eastern Cardo', which runs past the Temple Mount, to the 120s.

were found in excavations in the same part of the city. This means that fifty years before the construction of the Eastern Cardo and sixty years before the Second Jewish Revolt there was activity here, clearly carried out by the legion stationed in Jerusalem.

Whatever our views are, it still is the case that the two opposing views have one feature in common: they both regard the Bar Kokhba revolt as a religious war. This does not exclude other factors as a possibility and it has, for instance, been suggested that problems of land and tenure were among the chief factors that preoccupied the Jews who took part in the second revolt and were among its chief causes.[4] The advantage of such an explanation is that it focuses the mind on local problems, which may be appropriate in considering a local rebellion. Given the inadequacy of the available information, however, such explanations are inevitably speculative. The aim of this chapter then will be to consider the two alleged causes of the revolt in the light of what we know about Roman religious policy[5] and Roman attitudes towards the Jews in general.[6] I will attempt to reinforce the arguments of those who conclude that there never was a general ban on circumcision for Jews. Since it did not exist it was no cause of the Revolt. I will argue furthermore that the ban on circumcision for converts, which did exist, was part of a long-term policy against conversion. This chapter has therefore two aims, one negative, the other positive: the first, to show that a general ban on circumcision makes no sense in the light of what we know about Roman religious policy. Consequently it is easily understood that there is no evidence that there ever was such a ban. The second aim is to show that the ban on the circumcision of converts to Judaism, which we know to have existed, was part of the long-standing policy against proselytism.

The Jews were among several peoples whose religion was disapproved of by various Roman authors.[7] The importance of religion in Roman evaluations of other peoples and their influence on Roman religion and society should not be underestimated. It is clearly expressed, for instance, in the speech which Livy attributes to the consul who took action against the

---

[4] S. Applebaum, *Prolegomena to the Study of the Second Jewish Revolt (ad 132–135)* (Oxford, 1976), 9–15.

[5] For general accounts of Roman religion: M. Beard, J. North, and S. Price (eds.), *Religions of Rome*, 2 vols. (Cambridge, 1998); R. MacMullen, *Paganism in the Roman Empire* (New Haven, 1981).

[6] The texts are well known and easily accessible, M. Stern, *Greek and Latin Authors on Jews and Judaism*, 3 vols. (Jerusalem, 1974–84). For evaluation, see now P. Schäfer, *Judeophobia: Attitudes toward the Jews in the Ancient World* (Cambridge, 1997).

[7] Tac., *Hist.* 1.11.1: *provinciam aditu difficilem, annonae fecundam, superstitione ac lascivia discordem et mobilem, insciam legum, ignaram magistratuum* … Also: *Hist.* 4.81.

Bacchanalia in 186 BC. Of course this speech does not reflect anything like the actual words of the consul at the time, but it is instructive because it shows what Livy himself, in the reign of Augustus, felt the magistrate might have said at the time. 'Nothing is more deceptive in appearance than a false religion.'[8] 'For men wisest in all divine and human law used to judge that nothing was so potent in destroying religion as the replacement of native sacrifices by foreign ritual.'[9] Foreign cults were definitely regarded as a potential threat to the stability of the state. The citizens were warned that it would be *superstitio* to fear action taken against the Bacchanalia.[10] For Romans to indulge in foreign superstition was punished as a criminal act in principle, even if foreign cults were not always prosecuted in practice.[11] However, people were allowed to practise their own traditional religion, if it was well established.

The antiquity of some cult practices made them respectable. This is the reason why Josephus devotes a considerable part of his work against Apion to the citation of records demonstrating the antiquity of Judaism.[12] Conversely, it was the novelty of Christianity which made it despicable in Roman eyes. However, whatever their antiquity, all foreign cults which attracted followers in the city of Rome and in Italy were resisted. The issue is emphasized in the address which Dio assigns to Maecenas. The latter is represented as advising Augustus 'to hate and punish those who are involved in foreign cults, not only for the sake of the gods – for if he does not respect them he will not honour any other being – but also because such people preferring new gods persuade many to adopt strange cults and these originate in conspiracies, factions and political societies which do not profit the monarchy in the least'.[13] Dio's speech is explicit in his rejection of

---

[8] Livy 39.16.6: *Nihil enim in speciem fallacius est quam praua religio.* The Bacchanalia were the subject of a decree of the Senate, the substance of which is transmitted in an inscription (*CIL* I 196; *ILS* 18; *ILLRP* 511). For critical discussion: M. Gelzer, 'Die Unterdrückung der Bacchanalien bei Livius', *Hermes* 71 (1936): 275–87, esp. 285–6, who compares accusations of horrible deeds aimed at the Bacchanalia with similar ones targeted later at the Christians; Gelzer argues for an early and later phase in the sources, whereby the later one is responsible for the reports of horrors; J. A. North, 'Religious Toleration in Republican Rome', *PCPS* 25 (1979): 85–103; J.-M. Pailler, *Bacchanalia: La répression de 186 av. J.-C. à Rome et en Italie: Vestiges, images, tradition* (Rome, 1988); E. S. Gruen, *Studies in Greek Culture and Roman Policy* (Leiden, 1990), 34–78.

[9] 39.16.9: *iudicabant enim prudentissimi uiri omnis diuini que iuris nihil aeque dissoluendae religionis esse quam ubi non patrio sed externo ritu sacrificaretur.*

[10] 39.16.10: *haec uobis praedicenda ratus sum, ne qua superstitio agitaret animos uestros, cum demolientes nos Bacchanalia discutientes que nefarios coetus cerneretis.*

[11] Tac., *Ann.* 13.32.2.

[12] *Contra Apionem* 13.69–23.218.

[13] Dio 52.36.2: τοὺς δὲ δὴ ξενίζοντάς τι περὶ αὐτὸ καὶ μίσει καὶ κόλαζε, μὴ μόνον τῶν θεῶν ἕνεκα, ὧν ὁ καταφρονήσας οὐδ' ἄλλου ἄν τινος προτιμήσειεν, ἀλλ' ὅτι καὶ καινά τινα δαιμόνια οἱ

foreign cults: not only are they a threat to religion and religious values, but they are also a focus of political danger. We shall see that this is precisely the argument which Trajan uses for his prohibition of Christianity. The Jews were exceptional in being allowed to assemble for religious services while other foreign religions were forbidden to do so in Rome in the reigns of Caesar and Augustus.

Some of the religions which the Romans despised were influential in Rome and others were marginal. Of the former some were found threatening because of their appeal to Romans, such as some Egyptian and Asiatic cults, Judaism, and Christianity. Others, although marginal, were considered immoral, excessive, or primitive, such as the Gallic, British, or Germanic cults. These were not influential in Rome, but they were important to the local population. A distinction should be made therefore between attitudes towards religions and cults represented in Rome and Italy, and those which were actively practised only in the provinces. Foreign cults, such as those from Egypt[14] and Judaism, which attracted attention in Roman society and thus were a presence clearly felt in Rome, were regarded in a different light from those which were known only through indirect sources as a provincial phenomenon.

An example of a foreign religion which attracted many followers in Rome and hence evoked great antagonism is that of the Egyptians. These were best known in antiquity for their unusual religion: the cult of animals and the practice of mummification made a strong impression on the Greeks and Romans, particularly on the latter.[15] The animal cult attracted a good deal of attention, mostly negative. Cicero is particularly vehement.

τοιοῦτοι ἀντεσφέροντες πολλοὺς ἀναπείθουσιν ἀλλοτριονομεῖν, κἀκ τούτου καὶ συνωμοσίαι καὶ συστάσεις ἑταιρεῖαί τε γίγνονται, ἅπερ ἥκιστα μοναρχίᾳ συμφέρει.

[14] The bibliography on ancient attitudes towards Egypt is quite substantial: G. Nenci (ed.), *Hérodote et les peuples non grecs* (Geneva, 1990), esp. A. B. Lloyd, 'Herodotus on Egyptians and Libyans', 215–44; Loyd, *Herodotus Book II*, 3 vols. (Leiden, 1975); C. Préaux, 'La singularité de l'Égypte dans le monde gréco-romain', *Chronique d'Égypte* 49 (1950): 110–23; 'Les raisons de l'originalité de l'Égypte', *Museum Helveticum* 10 (1953): 203–21; M. Reinhold, 'Roman Attitudes toward Egyptians', *Ancient World* 3 (1980): 97–103; K. A. D. Smelik and E. A. Hemelrijk, 'Opinions on Egyptian Animal Worship in Antiquity', *ANRW* 2.17.4 (1984): 1852–2000; H. Sonnabend, *Fremdenbild und Politik: Vorstellungen der Römer von Ägypten und dem Partherreich in der späten Republik und frühen Kaiserzeit* (Frankfurt, 1986); Isaac, *The Invention of Racism in Classical Antiquity* (2004), ch. 7. See also: M. Swetnam-Burland, '"Egyptian" Priests in Roman Italy', in E. Gruen (ed.), *Cultural Identity in the Ancient Mediterranean* (Los Angeles, 2011), 336–53; P. J. E. Davies, '*Aegyptiaca* in Rome: Adventus and Romanitas', in Gruen, Cultural Identity, 354–70.

[15] See the detailed treatment by Smelik and Hemelrijk, 'Opinions'; Sonnabend, *Fremdenbild und Politik*, 118–42. The Egyptians are described as very pious by Isocrates, *Busiris* 24–9.

He speaks of 'degraded superstitions'.[16] Egyptian ideas represent not merely erroneous ideas, but *pravitas,* depravity, a term which Cicero uses frequently when he calls something not just mistaken, but utterly wrong. Elsewhere he describes Egyptian religion as a form of *dementia,* insanity. These pronouncements by Cicero have the advantage of not appearing in juridical speeches. It is therefore clear that they represent Cicero's true opinion rather than special pleading for the law courts.

There can be no doubt that this hostile response was caused by the fact that Egyptian cults exerted some influence in Rome and attracted followers, for Cicero did not really care what happened in far-away countries. He was sensitive to the mood in Rome. Confirmation of this is found in the decree of 53 BC to tear down the temples of Serapis and Isis, which private individuals had built in Rome, although outside the *pomerium.*[17] Augustus was ambivalent. Among measures taken in 28 BC for the benefit or the pleasure of the urban population, Dio relates that Augustus 'did not allow the Egyptian rites to be celebrated inside the *pomerium,* but made provision for the temples; those which had been built by private individuals he ordered their sons and descendants, if any survived, to repair, and the rest he restored himself'.[18] Although Dio does not say so, this clearly means that Augustus rescinded the decree issued twenty-five years earlier.[19] In the city of Rome the result of this policy was apparently a rapid flourishing of Egyptian cults, for in 21 BC Agrippa took measures restricting their performance in the city.[20] When in Egypt, Augustus claimed to have a high regard for the god Serapis, while he himself refused to worship Apis and the remains of the Ptolemies.[21]

Like many such regulatory measures, they had either little effect, or their effect did not last long, This is clear, for instance, from Tacitus' comments

---

[16] Cic., *Tusc.* 5.78: *Aegyptiorum morem quis ignorat? quorum inbutae mentes pravitatis erroribus quamvis carnificinam prius subierint quam ibim aut aspidem aut faelem aut canem aut crocodillum violent, quorum etiamsi inprudentes quippiam fecerint, poenam nullam recusent.*

[17] Dio 40.47.

[18] Dio 53.2.4.

[19] It is thus an error to list this as an instance of Octavian's aversion to Egyptian gods and rites, as stated by M. Reinhold, 'Roman Attitudes toward Egyptians', 98. For the Isis temple *antiquo quae proxima surgit ovili*: Juvenal 6.529.

[20] Dio 54.6.6.

[21] 51.16.3. Cf. Julian, *Ep.* III: "ανδρες εἶπεν Ἀλεξανδρεῖς ἀφίημι τὴν πόλιν αἰτίας πάσης αἰδοῖ τοῦ μεγάλου θεοῦ Σαράπιδος.., Sarapis is not mentioned in the parallel passage Plutarch, *Antonius* 80.3. Reinhold, 'Roman Attitudes', 98 (and others cited n. 20), believes that Augustus' expression of veneration for Serapis was only a political expedient of the moment, for in fact, they say, Augustus harboured a deep antipathy toward Egyptian cults. Whether true or not, it does not matter. What matters is not what Augustus thought but what he said.

on the 4,000 descendants of enfranchised slaves of Jewish origin, together with Isis worshippers, who were to be shipped to Sardinia and employed there in suppressing brigandage in AD 19: 'if they succumbed to the pestilential climate, it was a cheap loss (*vile damnum*)'.[22] We shall return to these events. Other sources report sharp repression of the cult of Isis at this time. A temple was destroyed again, having been destroyed earlier in 53 BC and subsequently restored by order of Octavian, and the cult-statue was thrown in the Tiber.[23] The Egyptian cults in the city of Rome, then, were a subject of ever recurring tension between those who fiercely disapproved and adherents among the city populace.

Some other religions in the provinces exerted little influence in Rome, but were considered immoral. Tacitus writes that the Britons practised human sacrifice and were given to inhuman superstitions.[24] Gallic superstition under the spiritual guidance of the Druids is well known and so was that of many Germans.[25] Druidism was banned by the Romans in the reigns of Tiberius[26] and of Claudius.[27] The prohibition was apparently not fully effective, for Druids were involved in the revolt of Boudicca (Tac. *Ann.* 14.30.3) and in that of AD 69.[28] It is not clear, therefore, how active the Romans were in suppressing Druidism and with how much success, or even why they thought it desirable to do so.[29] It may not be very wrong to accept the Elder Pliny's explicit statements about the reason. In chapters discussing *magicae vanitates* and *ars portentosa* – which he dislikes – he

---

[22] Tac., *Ann.* 2.85. Cf. R. Syme, *Tacitus* (Oxford, 1958), I, 468. See below, p. 318, n. 69.

[23] Suetonius, *Tiberius* 36.1; Josephus, *Ant.* 18.3.4 (79); not mentioned by Tacitus. As observed by Syme, *Tacitus*, this is a paradoxical omission.

[24] Tac., *Ann.* 14.30.3: *praesidium posthac impositum victis excisi que luci saevis superstitionibus sacri: nam cruore captivo adolere aras et hominum fibris consulere deos fas habebant.* Also: *Agricola* 11.3; cf. Syme, *Tacitus*, I, 457–8.

[25] Tac., *Germ.* 39.2; also *Hist.* 4.61.

[26] See below, reference to Pliny.

[27] Suetonius, *Claudius* 25.5, where it is noted that under Augustus this religion had been prohibited to Roman citizens. Cf. Caesar, *BG* 6.13–14, 16, 18; Tacitus, *Hist.* 4.54; Pliny, *NH* 29.54.30; Pomponius Mela 3.2.19; Aurelius Victor, *Liber de Caesaribus* 4.2. H. Last, 'Rome and the Druids: A Note', *JRS* 39 (1949), 1–5, argues that the Roman explanation has to be accepted. The Druids were truly savage and disgusting. Syme, *Tacitus*, 2.457–8; S. Piggott, *The Druids* (London, 1968); A. Ross, 'Ritual and the Druids', in M. J. Green (ed.), *The Celtic World* (London and New York, 1995), 423–44 and, in general, B. Cunliffe, *The Ancient Celts* (Oxford, 1997). On religion in Roman Gaul: G. Woolf, *Becoming Roman* (Cambridge, 1998), ch. 8 and the works by P. M. Duval, *Les dieux de la Gaule* (Paris, 1976); J.-J. Hatt, *Mythes et dieux de la Gaule* (Paris, 1989). The Cimbri are typically the sort of people associated with human sacrifice: Strabo 7.2.3 (294).

[28] The figure of Veleda: Tacitus, *Hist.* 4.65; 5.24.5; *Germ.* 8.3.2; Statius, *Silvae* 1.4.90.

[29] M. Goodman has suggested that it was not druidic practices but the druids' authority with the Celtic population which shocked Romans: *The Ruling Class of Judaea: The Origins of the Jewish Revolt Against Rome AD 66–70* (Cambridge, 1987), 240–7.

includes human sacrifice as a particularly despicable rite, abolished even in
Rome not until 97 BC, 'so that down to that date it is manifest that such
abominable rites were practised'.[30] It recurs in a digression on Gaul by
Ammianus.[31] Usually, we may conclude, foreign cults were left alone in the
provinces, especially if they could claim to be ancient, as long as no human
sacrifices were practised.

It emerges therefore that Roman attitudes towards foreign religions and
cults depended to a large extent on two factors: foreigners were permitted to practise their ancestral cults as long as they were regarded as morally acceptable. However, it was considered dangerous if they appealed to
Romans in the city and Italy. John North has put it in simple terms: 'You
might, of course choose to make your vow to one deity rather than another,
but you could not make an act of commitment to a new cult, which would
cut you off from the old ones; there are no alternative religious systems
available.'[32] Or as formulated by J. Scheid: 'Public religion may be defined
as a social religion and a religion of cultic acts. Social religion is practised
by a person as member of a community and not as a subjective individual,
as a person ...'[33]

So far Roman attitudes towards foreign religions in the Empire. In considering Roman comments on the Jews it will be useful again to distinguish between Rome and the provinces. We should separate comments
on Jews in Rome and on those in Judaea or in general. While it is always
possible to cherish hatred of far-away peoples, it is clearly the case that
social friction, caused by day-to-day contact, is a different phenomenon
from more abstract forms of hostility.

First, however, it will be useful briefly to review the formal status of the
Jews in Rome and the provinces in the early Empire.[34] Julius Caesar and

[30] Pliny, *NH* 30.3 (trans. W. H. S. Jones, Loeb): *palamque in tempus illut sacra prodigiosa celebrata.* It
was a source of embarrassment that Rome itself used to follow instructions by the Sibylline books
to bury alive two Greeks and two Gauls, not only at the time of the war with the Insubres after
the First Punic War (Plutarch, *Marcellus* 3.7.1), but even in the late second century (*Quaestiones
Romanae* 83/283F). Plutarch is puzzled: 'It definitely seems illogical that they themselves do this
and yet reproach barbarians that they practice sacrilege.' Cf. A. Fraschetti, 'Le sepolture rituali de
Foro Boario', in *Le délit religieux dans la cité antique*, Table ronde (Rome, 1978, 1981), 51–115, esp. 83;
North, 'Religious Toleration', 99, n. 5.
[31] Ammianus 15.9–12.
[32] North, 'Religious Toleration', 85–103, esp. 85.
[33] J. Scheid, 'Religion et superstition à l'époque de Tacite: Quelques reflexions', in *Religion, supersticion
y magia en el mundo romano* (Cadiz, 1985), 19.
[34] E. Schürer, *The History of the Jewish People in the Age of Jesus Christ (175 BC–AD 135)*, rev. edn by
G. Vermes, F. Millar, and M. Goodman (Edinburgh, 1973), I, 275; III, ch. 2, 107–25; W. Horbury,
W. D. Davies, and J. Sturdy (eds.), *The Cambridge History of Judaism*, III, *The Early Roman Period*
(Cambridge, 1999), ch. 6 (by E. M. Smallwood), esp. 172–7.

Augustus in particular took various measures to confirm the formal recognition of the Jews in the Roman Empire. A considerable number of official documents have been preserved by Josephus.[35] All of them are intended to ensure the Jews had the right to practise their own religion and to retain their privileges.[36] Caesar stipulates that the Jews are an *ethnos* ruled in Judaea by a recognized *ethnarch*/high priest, with the status of friend and ally.[37] These rulers are allowed to decide on all questions concerning the Jews' way of life.[38] Through Caesar's favour, Jews living outside Palestine may also have been granted important privileges, notably the right of free association, a topic much discussed and not entirely clear, like so much else in ancient Jewish history.[39]

One document cited by Josephus seems to indicate that the general ban on associations did not apply to the Jews. They are said to have been excluded because of the antiquity of their institutions and previous precedent.[40] Recently, however, it has been argued that the document is not reliable evidence of such an exemption.[41] Philo too testifies to the toleration

---

[35] Josephus, *Ant.* 14.10 (185–267) and 16.6 (160–79); Suetonius, *Augustus* 93. Cf. J. Juster, *Les Juifs dans l'empire romain* (1914), I, 213–42, 391–408; II, 1–27; A. M. Rabello, 'The Legal Conditions of the Jews in the Roman Empire', *ANRW* 2.13 (1980): 662–762; T. Rajak, 'Was there a Roman Charter for the Jews?', *JRS* 74 (1984): 107–23 = *The Jewish Dialogue with Greece and Rome: Studies in Cultural and Social Interaction* (Leiden, 2001), 301–33; J.-E. Bernard, 'Transferts historiographiques: Josèphe, César et les privilèges juifs', *Bull. du Centre de la Recherche français de Jérusalem* 2 (1998): 13–24; see now M. Pucci Ben-Zeev, *Jewish Rights in the Roman World* (Tübingen, 1998).

[36] Rajak, 'Roman Charter for the Jews?', 112, asks whether any of this material had, in the Roman perception, a general application or any validity as precedent, beyond the specific context. In spite of Josephus' suggestion to this effect, her conclusion is that this was not the case.

[37] *Ant.* 14.10.2 (194–5): Ὑρκανὸν Ἀλεξάνδρου καὶ τὰ τέκνα αὐτοῦ ἐθνάρχας Ἰουδαίων εἶναι ἀρχιερωσύνην τε Ἰουδαίων διὰ παντὸς ἔχειν κατὰ τὰ πάτρια ἔθη εἶναί τε αὐτὸν καὶ τοὺς παῖδας αὐτοῦ συμμάχους ἡμῖν ἔτι τε καὶ ἐν τοῖς κατ᾽ ἄνδρα φίλοις ἀριθμεῖσθαι ὅσα τε κατὰ τοὺς ἰδίους αὐτῶν νόμους ἐστὶν ἀρχιερατικὰ φιλάνθρωπα ταῦτα κελεύω κατέχειν αὐτὸν καὶ τὰ τέκνα αὐτοῦ· Also: 14.10.4 (199).

[38] ἄν τε μεταξὺ γένηταί τις ζήτησις περὶ τῆς Ἰουδαίων ἀγωγῆς ἀρέσκει μοι κρίσιν γίνεσθαι [παρ᾽ αὐτοῖς].

[39] Caesar's ban on *collegia*: Suetonius, *Div. Iul.* 42.3; *Div. Aug.* 32. For associations, permitted, and political clubs, forbidden, in the first centuries BC and AD: W. Cotter, 'The Collegia and Roman Law: State Restrictions on Voluntary Associations 64 BCE–200 CE', in J. S. Kloppenborg and S. G. Wilson, *Voluntary Associations in the Graeco-Roman World* (London, 1996), 74–89, esp. 74–6. As noted on p. 76, the first prohibition occurred in 64 BC, when the Senate dissolved all suspect *collegia*, when synagogues were also exempt. Possible reasons for this exemption are discussed on p. 77.

[40] See *Ant.* 14.10.8 (213–16): The Jews alone were permitted to assemble, 'or to collect contributions of money or to hold common meals. Similarly do I forbid other religious societies but permit these people alone to assemble and feast in accordance with their native customs and ordinances.'

[41] M. Williams, 'The Jewish Community in Rome', in M. Goodman (ed.), *Jews in a Graeco-Roman World* (Oxford, 1998), 215–28, esp. 217–21, where the reliability of Josephus' document is questioned. Williams goes on to argue that the Romans did not formally classify the synagogues of the city of Rome as *collegia*. There was, she suggests, some form of supra-synagogal structure, a common

of the Jews in Rome in the reign of Augustus.[42] After Caesar's death, his decisions regarding the Jews in the provinces were also confirmed.[43] This included the right to send money to the Temple in Jerusalem which Cicero and Tacitus found objectionable.[44] The usual expression is that the Jews are permitted to follow 'the laws of their fathers'. The emphasis here all the time is on the *ethnarch* and the *ethnos,* and on children and their fathers. The Jews have these privileges because they were an *ethnos,* a people. A much discussed episode in the reign of Claudius may have led to temporary restrictions of the freedom of assembly, if we follow Cassius Dio.[45]

Turning now to concepts and stereotypes about Jews, as distinct from their formal status in the Empire, it is clear that they are accused of being anti-social, cutting themselves off from the rest of humanity. This idea originates in the Hellenistic literature.[46] The essential phrase here appears to be that the Jews are unsociable (μόνους γὰρ ἀπάντων ἐθνῶν ἀκοινωνήτους). This must be understood in the light of contemporary ideas about foreign peoples. It was regarded as typical of remote and primitive peoples and of nomads that they lived in isolation and were unsociable.[47] This was not at all a familiar pattern among civilized peoples who lived in cities. According to Diodorus, the Jews are regarded as unique, because they cut themselves off from other peoples by their own choice. In the text transmitted by Diodorus, the instruments by which the Jews keep themselves apart are bizarre customs: not sharing meals and hating all other peoples.[48] Tacitus,

---

council. The problem is discussed also by E. S. Gruen, *Diaspora: Jews amidst the Greeks and Romans* (Cambridge, 2002), 24–6.

[42] Philo, *Leg.* 23 (155–7); cf. Cotter, 'Collegia', 78–9.

[43] *Ant.* 14.10.10 (219–22); 14.10.11–12 (223); 14.10.20 (241).

[44] 16.6.1 (16).

[45] Dio 60.6.6: Τούς τε Ἰουδαίους πλεονάσαντας αὖθις ὥστε χαλεπῶς ἂν ἄνευ ταραχῆς ὑπὸ τοῦ ὄχλου σφῶν τῆς πόλεως εἰρχθῆναι οὐκ ἐξήλασε μέν, τῷ δὲ δὴ πατρίῳ βίῳ. Suetonius, *Claudius* 25.4, states that the Jews were in fact expelled, 'because they all the time made disturbances at the instigation of Chrestus'. There has been much discussion whether this refers to Jesus or not, but this is apparently an untenable assumption. See also Acts 18:2; Orosius 7.6.16. For extensive discussion of the statement by Dio, with full references to secondary literature, H. Botermann, *Das Judenedikt des Kaisers Claudius: Römischer Staat und Christiani im 1. Jahrhundert* (Stuttgart, 1996), 103–40; H. D. Slingerland, *Claudian Policymaking and the Early Imperial Repression of Judaism at Rome* (Atlanta, GA, 1997); Gruen, *Diaspora,* 36–41.

[46] Diodorus 40.3.4 (Stern, *Greek and Latin Authors,* no. 11), citing Hecataeus of Abdera: ἀπάνθρωπόν τινα καὶ μισόξενον βίον εἰσηγήσατο. Cf. Jos., *Contra Apionem* 2.258 (Stern, no. 258). This, however, represents the Alexandrian tradition which is not discussed here in detail. Stern, II, 39, also refers to the formulation of Paul in 1 Thess 2:14–15: Ἰουδαίων ... πᾶσιν ἀνθρώποις ἐναντίων. Two parallel passages in Diodorus and Josephus may or may not be based on Posidonius: Diodorus, *Bibliotheca Historica* 34/35.1.1–2 (Stern, no. 63, with comments on pp. 183–4). It recurs in the second century: Celsus ap. Origenes, *Contra Celsum* 5.2.41 (Stern, no. 375, p. 256).

[47] See for instance Diodorus 3.18.5–6; Strabo 2.1.2 (137); 3.3.8 (156). See above, Chapter 10.

[48] The themes of misanthropy and xenophobia are analysed by Schäfer, *Judeophobia,* 170–7.

however, also gives another explanation for the Jewish social themes: 'To establish his influence over this people for all time, Moses introduced new religious practices, quite opposed to those of all other religions. The Jews regard as profane all that we hold sacred; on the other hand, they permit all that we abhor.'[49] Tacitus essentially follows the same line as the source of Josephus and Diodorus, but reinterprets the origin of their customs in characteristic fashion. The historian of the Principate sees Moses as a sort of Augustus who fashioned the constitution so as to leave his mark forever on the state he created.[50] Similarly, in the next chapter of his *Histories*, Tacitus touches on many themes, but the essence of the passage is, again, that it is the Jews who erect a barrier between themselves and others. Above all, it is circumcision which distinguishes Jewish men from others.[51]

It is important to keep in mind that all these texts reflect reactions to the presence of Jews in the city of Rome. They are not vague feelings about a distant people or a minority in various provinces, but direct responses to a significant element in the city population. In several texts the matter of conversion is significant. Something therefore has to be said about proselytes. This is certainly not a suitable topic for discussion on the present occasion. The issue of proselytism is a hotly debated one and has been discussed in important studies.[52] It should not concern us here whether Judaism was a missionary religion or not; nor is the number of actual converts of pressing concern. It is relevant, however, to observe that it was rather significant, and hence threatening, in the perception of Romans. Roman politics in this matter were not determined by statistics or Jewish literature, but by the perception of members of the Roman upper class.

---

[49] Tacitus, *Hist.* 5.4.1: *Moyses quo sibi in posterum gentem firmaret, novos ritus contrariosque ceteris mortalibus indidit. Profana illic omnia quae apud nos sacra, rursum concessa apud illos quae nobis incesta.*

[50] Livy 39.13.11: *nihil nefas ducere, hanc summam inter eos religionem esse.*

[51] *Hist.* 5.5.1–2: *et quia apud ipsos fides obstinata misericordia in promptu, sed adversus omnes alios hostile odium. Separati epulis, discreti cubilibus, proiectissima ad libidinem gens, alienarum concubitu abstinent; inter se nihil inlicitum. Circumcidere genitalia instituerunt, ut diversitate noscantur. Transgressi in morem eorum idem usurpant, nec quidquam prius imbuuntur quam contemnere deos, exuere patriam, parentes liberos fratres vilia habere.*

[52] For major statements of the opposing views: L. H. Feldman, *Jew and Gentile in the Ancient World: Attitudes and Interactions from Alexander to Justinian* (Princeton, 1993), advocates vigorous and successful Jewish proselytism; Scot McKnight, *A Light among the Gentiles: Jewish Missionary Activity in the Second Temple Period* (Minneapolis, 1991), challenges this view, arguing that 'Judaism never developed a clear mission to the Gentiles that had as its goal the conversion of the world'. It was not truly a 'missionary religion', although there is evidence of conversion to Judaism through a variety of means. Other important studies: M. Goodman, *Mission and Conversion: Proselytizing in the Religious History of the Roman Empire* (Oxford, 1994); E. Will and C. Orrieux, *'Prosélytisme Juif'? Histoire d'une erreur* (Paris, 1992); and discussion in Schäfer, *Judeophobia*, 106–18.

Juvenal attacks proselytes as follows: 'Having been wont to deride Roman laws, they learn and follow and revere Jewish law, and all that Moses passed on in his secret volume, prohibiting to point the way to anyone not following the same rites, and leading none but the circumcised to the desired fountain.'[53] This part of his satire is aimed against Jewish proselytes, but there are several characteristics Juvenal sees these proselytes as sharing with born Jews, the most important of which is that they deride Roman law while honouring Jewish law. The two are thus considered mutually exclusive. In becoming Jewish, Juvenal is saying, Romans cut themselves off from civilized Roman society.

If indeed the Jews and Egyptians took no active steps in winning converts, this did in fact not make much difference to the views of many Romans, who blamed them all the same. Seneca considered Jewish influence pernicious:[54] 'Meanwhile the customs of this accursed race have gained such influence that they are now received throughout the entire world. The vanquished have given laws to their victors.'[55] This looks like a paraphrase of Horace's famous dictum about Rome and Greek culture.[56] The formulation leaves no doubt as to the author's emotions on the subject. There is no need here to determine whether he refers to sympathizers or full converts or what we can learn from this passage about the spread of conversion to Judaism at the time.[57]

Juvenal's attack on proselytes cited above, in combination with his well-known claim that the Syrian Orontes is now flowing into the Tiber, shows that he harboured similar sentiments.[58] Tacitus, writing in roughly the

---

[53] Juvenal, 14.100–4 (Stern, no. 301, comments on II, 107): *Romanas autem soliti contemnere leges | Iudaicum ediscunt et servant ac metuunt ius, | tradidit arcano quodcumque volumine Moyses: | non monstrare vias eadem nisi sacra colenti, | quaesitum ad fontem solos deducere verpos.* This is a passage from a satire whose main theme is the bad influence that the vices of parents have on their children; cf. Courtney's comments *ad loc.*, 571–2; J. P. Stein, 'The Unity and Scope of Juvenal's Fourteenth Satire', *CP* 65 (1970): 34–6; Will and Orrieux, 'Prosélytisme Juif'?, 111–12. For the passages cited here, see also above, pp. 293–4.

[54] Cf. Schäfer, *Judeophobia*, 111–13.

[55] Augustine, *De civitate dei* 6.11 (Stern, no. 186): *Cum interim usque eo sceleratissimae gentis consuetudo convaluit, ut per omnes iam terras recepta sit; victi victoribus leges dederunt.* See above, pp. 291 and 295.

[56] Horace, *Ep.* 2.1.156: *Graecia capta ferum victorem cepit et artis intulit agresti Latio.* Cf. Pliny, *NH* 24.5.5: *ita est profecto, magnitudine popul<us> R. perdidit ritus, vincendoque victi sumus*; Florus, *Epitoma* 1.47.7.

[57] Stern, I, 429–32, assumes this statement, derived from a work composed in the 60s of the first century, reflects Seneca's feelings 'at the height of the Jewish proselytizing movement and the diffusion of Jewish customs throughout the Mediterranean world'. Schäfer, *Judeophobia*, 111–13, does not accept this and maintains that we cannot learn from this or other passages that there was proselytizing activity. Goodman does not discuss the present passage.

[58] *Sat.* 3.60–72: 'I cannot stand, Quirites, a Greek city of Rome; and yet what part of the dregs comes from Greece? The Syrian Orontes has long since flowed into the Tiber, bringing with it its language and its habits, its flutes and its loud harps; bringing too the tambourines, and the prostitutes who

same period, also despised proselytes: 'The worst elements (among other peoples) disregarded their ancestral religions and used to send tribute and contributed it to Jerusalem, thus increasing Jewish wealth.'[59] Foreign cults penetrated the households of Roman magistrates, says Cassius Longinus in AD 61, in a speech attributed to him by Tacitus.[60] This referred to slaves, but senatorial families themselves were also affected. Under Nero a Roman matron, Pomponia Graecina, was accused of foreign superstition.[61] Her husband, A. Plautius, was ordered to investigate the matter (and found her innocent). Domitian is on record as having put to death his relative Flavius Clemens and his wife Flavia Domitilla on the charge of atheism (ἔγκλημα ἀθεότητος). This, according to Cassius Dio, was a charge on which many who inclined to Jewish customs were condemned.[62]

Relevant, in this connection, is the particularly sensitive topic of circumcision.[63] This marked the Jewish male and it was the final step taken by a convert.[64] It is usually mentioned with great disapproval. Strabo mentions it as one of the bad customs of the Jews which were typical of their decline and adopted when, after Moses and his first successors, 'superstitious men were appointed to the priesthood and then tyrannical people'.[65] Tacitus, as already mentioned, says that the Jews 'adopted circumcision to distinguish themselves from other peoples by this difference'. Male circumcision

are ordered to do their job at the Circus ... One comes from lofty Sicyon, another from Amydon or Andros, others from Samos, Tralles or Alabanda; all are making for the Esquiline, or for the hill that takes its name from osier-beds; all are ready to worm their way into the houses of the great and become their masters.' Cf. above, p. 295.

[59] Tacitus, *Hist.* 5.5.1: *Nam pessimus quisque spretis religionibus patriis tributa et stipes illuc <con>gerebant, unde auctae Iudaeorum res.*

[60] Tacitus, *Ann.* 14.44.3: *postquam vero nationes in familiis habemus quibus diversi ritus, externa sacra aut nulla sunt* ... This is the speech in which Cassius Longinus argues for the execution of 400 slaves because one of them had murdered their owner, the city-prefect. As observed by Syme, *Tacitus*, 533, Tacitus furnishes through the oration of Cassius Longinus the arguments for severity, but none for mercy.

[61] Tacitus, *Ann.* 13.32.2: *et Pomponia Graecina insignis femina, A. Plautio, quem ovasse de Britannis rettuli, nupta ac superstitionis externae rea, mariti iudicio permissa.* She could have been accused of being involved in an Egyptian cult, in Judaism or Christianity.

[62] Dio 67.14.1–3 (Stern, 435) with comments on pp. 380–4 on the question whether the two inclined to Judaism, as Dio himself asserts, or to Christianity. Cf. E. M. Smallwood, 'Domitian's Attitude toward the Jews and Judaism', *CP* 51 (1956): 3–4; adherents of Judaism and atheism: 6–7. As observed by Smallwood (9), there is no evidence that born Jews were attacked in the reign of Domitian. See also T. Rajak, *JRS* 69 (1979): 192–4; Williams, 'Jewish Community in Rome', 206–7. Williams (208–9) does not accept that proselytism in itself cannot have been a decisive factor in the action taken against Flavius Clemens, his wife Flavia Domitilla, and M. Acilius Glabrio. She argues that political motives and Domitian's dislike of the Jews were the reasons.

[63] Schäfer, *Judeophobia*, 93–105.

[64] Goodman, *Mission and Conversion*, 67, 77, 81–2; Schäfer, *Judeophobia*, 96–7 (see, for instance, Petronius, cited already in connection with the Sabbath); Juvenal, 14.99 (Stern, no. 301).

[65] Strabo 16.2.37 (761) (Stern, no. 115), adding excision of the females, cf. Stern, comments on p. 306.

was the one physical feature emphasizing the separateness of the Jews. In spite of the circumstance that there were other peoples who also had this custom, it became the obvious distinguishing mark of a Jewish male, for other peoples who practised circumcision were not present in such numbers in Italy.[66] Jews could be referred to as simply 'the circumcised'.[67] The Historia Augusta refers to circumcision as a form of mutilation, in the satirical statement on the cause of the revolt.[68]

From time to time efforts were made to halt the spread of Judaism among Romans in Rome, possibly in 139 BC and, better attested, in AD 19, when 4,000 descendants of enfranchised slaves 'infected by this religion' were expelled together with Isis worshippers.[69] Others had to leave Italy or 'renounce the impious rites'. As formulated by Tacitus, this concerns proselytes, for they were 'infected' with foreign cults and required to renounce them.[70] A fragment which derives from Dio states explicitly that Jews were

---

[66] As appears from Suetonius, *Domitianus* 12.2 (Stern, no. 320), already cited.

[67] There is no need here to prove the point: it can be seen by anyone reading through Stern's collection of texts and has been commented upon frequently. See Horace, *Serm.* 1.9.70 (Stern, no. 129): *curti Iudaei*; Persius, *Sat.* 5.184 (Stern, no.190): *recutita sabbata*. Cf. Will and Orrieux, 'Prosélytisme Juif', 105.

[68] SHA, *Hadrian* 14.2: *moverunt ea tempestate et Iudaei bellum, quod vetabantur mutilare genitalia*. The passage is much discussed. See now A. Oppenheimer, 'The Ban on Circumcision as a Cause of the Revolt: A Reconsideration', in P. Schäfer (ed.), *The Bar-Kokhba War Reconsidered: New Perspectives on the Second Jewish Revolt Against Rome* (Tübingen, 2003), 55–69. For my own views on this passage: B. Isaac, *The Near East under Roman Rule*, 277–8. In the light of what I have just said, I regard as a red herring the view of Mary Smallwood that the ban was not peculiar to the Jews, because it also extended to Arabs, Samaritans, and Egyptians: E. M. Smallwood, 'The Legislation of Hadrian and Antoninus Pius against Circumcision', *Latomus* 18 (1959): 334–47; 'The Legislation of Hadrian and Antoninus Pius against Circumcision: Addendum', *Latomus* 20 (1961): 93–6; accepted in the revised edition of E. Schürer, *The History of the Jewish People in the Age of Jesus Christ* (Edinburgh, 1973), I, 537–8; rejected by P. Schäfer, *Der Bar Kokhba-Aufstand* (Tübingen, 1981), 40–2. Both the Historia Augusta and the decree of Antoninus Pius mention only the Jews and that is what concerns us here.

[69] Tacitus, *Ann.* 2.85 (Stern, no. 284 with comments on pp. 69–73); Suetonius, *Tiberius* 36; Josephus, *Ant.* 18.3.5. (81ff.); Dio 57.18.5a. Cf. E. M. Smallwood, 'Some Notes on the Jews under Tiberius', *Latomus* 15 (1956): 314–29, where it is argued that the affair was caused by Roman anger about proselytism. E. Abel, 'Were the Jews Banished from Rome in AD 19?', *REJ* 127 (1968): 383–6, argues that the 4,000 expelled were not born Jews but proselytes. A different view: M. H. Williams, 'The Expulsion of the Jews from Rome in AD 19', *Latomus* 48 (1989): 765–84, with further references to earlier literature on p. 765, n. 2; Williams suggests that the Jews were expelled in an attempt to suppress unrest caused by problems with the corn supply; L. V. Rutgers, 'Roman Policy towards the Jews: Expulsions from the City of Rome during the First Century C.E.', *Classical Antiquity* 13 (1994): 56–74, repr. in Rutgers, *The Hidden Heritage of Diaspora Judaism* (Leuven, 1998) and also in K. P. Donfried and P. Richardson (eds.), *Judaism and Christianity in First-Century Rome* (Grand Rapids, 1998). Rutgers, 'Roman Policy', 60–5, finds Williams' suggestion attractive, but insists that important questions remain unanswered. The whole issue of the expulsions of the Jews from Rome is discussed extensively by Gruen, *Diaspora*. Cf. above, p. 311, n. 22.

[70] Suetonius suggests that both proselytes and born Jews were concerned. This follows from the phrases 'qui superstitione ea tenebantur' and 'reliquos gentis eiusdem vel similia sectantes'.

actively engaged in converting non-Jews.[71] As a result, Tiberius ordered the entire Jewish community in Rome to leave the city.

Thus, in spite of the variations, there is a consensus in the sources that the cause of friction was the conversion of Romans to Judaism and to Egyptian cults, even if we accept the argument that the former was not the result of proselytizing activities initiated and pursued by Jews.[72] If we accept the argument of Williams that not proselytism, but social and economic unrest was the reason for the expulsion, it is still the case that proselytism is portrayed as a significant factor in the affair by several authors. There may not in fact have been very many proselytes in Rome in this period,[73] but for our attempt to trace the Roman views of Judaism it is no less significant when ancient sources say there were a large number. It is popular perspective of reality which counts, not actual reality. Similarly, in modern wealthy countries, what determines policies towards foreign workers is not whether they really affect the employment of citizens of those countries, but whether this is thought to be the case. In such cases politicians respond to popular pressure more than to economic reality.[74]

Turning now briefly to the Roman legal sources for their actual measures regarding the Jews, we see once more that the subject of conversion occupied the authorities both before and after the Empire became Christian. First there is the rescript of Antoninus Pius which permits Jews to circumcise only their own sons, and states that the circumcision of non-Jews is punishable.[75] The rescript determines in fact that Jewish religion may be acquired exclusively by birth, as Jews are only permitted to circumcise their own sons. It should be noted, however, that it deals only with circumcision and not with other forms of Jewish activity.[76] The reason

---

[71] Dio 57.18.5a.

[72] As argued by Goodman, *Mission and Conversion*, 68, against Stern and others. Cf. Will and Orrieux, 'Prosélytisme Juif', 105–9; Schäfer, *Judeophobia*, 109–11.

[73] Williams, 'Expulsion of the Jews', 769–72.

[74] Gruen, *Diaspora*, suggests a connection with the tensions engendered by the death of Germanicus in 19. He also points out that, three years earlier, astrologers and magicians were expelled from Italy, following the accusation of Libo Drusus of treasonable ambitions in which practitioners of obscure arts were involved (Tac. *Ann.* 2.27–32; Suetonius, *Tiberius* 36; Dio 57.15.8). All this may reflect a climate of increased suspicion of foreign cults and foreigners in general in those years.

[75] *Dig.* 48.8.11 (Modestinus): *Circumcidere Iudaeis filios suos tantum rescripto divi Pii permittitur: in non eiusdem religionis qui hoc fecerit, castrantis poena irrogatur.* Cf. A. Linder, *The Jews in Roman Imperial Legislation* (Detroit and Jerusalem, 1987), 99–102.

[76] We may ignore for the present the question whether Antoninus' rescript modifies a hypothetical Hadrianic law banning circumcision. I accept the argument that it does not; cf. J. Geiger, 'The Ban on Circumcision and the Bar-Kokhba Revolt', *Zion* 41 (1976): 139–47 (Hebrew). Geiger's argument has not been accepted by all scholars, cf. A. M. Rabello, 'The Ban on Circumcision as a Cause of Bar

for this prohibition is clear enough. Jews are not allowed to circumcise non-Jews because it represents a formal act of conversion. Jews are allowed to circumcise Jews because they are Jews anyway. Towards the end of the third century, the jurist Paul states that only Jews by origin are allowed to practise circumcision. Gentiles who allow themselves or their slaves to be circumcised voluntarily as well as the doctors who are involved are to be punished. Jews who circumcise non-Jewish slaves are liable to deportation or capital punishment.[77] The least this shows is that there was felt to be a need for such legislation. Whether these laws actually prevented such acts as they were intended to is another matter. What is clear, however, is that the Jews, as a recognized people – but only they themselves and their descendants – were allowed to practise their religion without hindrance, both in Judaea and elsewhere, and even in Rome. This did not change when Judaea was incorporated as a province, nor was the essence of this status affected by the Jewish revolts against Rome.[78]

According to the Historia Augusta, Septimius Severus again forbade conversion to Judaism and Christianity[79] – to little purpose, if we may believe Dio.[80] Both the contents and the style of legislation changed immediately in the reign of Constantine. A law of 329 prohibited proselytism and it imposed the death penalty on Jews persecuting Jewish converts to Christianity, while indicating that such persecutions did indeed take place.[81] Legislation during the following centuries clearly shows that the matter of conversion to and from Judaism remained a subject which preoccupied the authorities.

It has been seen that the Jews were allowed to practise their religion because it was the religion of their ancestors and Jewish identity was inherited, not acquired, for conversion was prohibited. By contrast, Christianity was never an inherited and always an acquired religion, for the Christians were not a people, even if there existed a tendency, among

Kokhbah's Rebellion', repr. in Rabello, *The Jews in the Roman Empire: Legal Problems from Herod to Justinian* (Aldershot, 2000), ch. 5; 'A Tribute to Jean Juster', repr. Rabello, ch. 15, esp. 222–4.

[77] Paulus, *Sententiae* 5.22.3–4: *Cives Romani, qui se Iudaico ritu vel servos suos circumcidi patiuntur, bonis ademptis in insulam perpetuo relegantur: medici capite puniuntur. Iudaei si alienae nationis comparatos servos circumciderint, aut deportantur aut capite puniuntur.* Cf. Linder, *The Jews in Roman Imperial Legislation*, 117–20.

[78] After the destruction of the Temple the money sent by Jews to Jerusalem was converted into the *fiscus Iudaicus*. This was a punitive measure, but not one which restricted individual Jews in practising their religion.

[79] SHA, *Severus* 17.1: *Iudaeos fieri sub gravi poena vetuit. Idem etiam de Ch<h>ristianis sanxit.* Cf. Stern, II, 625, for comments. It is possible that we can trust this source on this point.

[80] Dio 37.17.1.

[81] *CTh.* 16.8.1; *CJ* 1.9.3, cf. Linder, *The Jews in Roman Imperial Legislation*, 125–32.

some Christian authors, to describe themselves as a people. Thus, while the Christians were, at best, 'a sort of men' (*genus hominum*), the Jews were always called 'a people' (*gens*), even by those who disliked them. The status of the Christians in the Empire is thus immediately connected with problems of ethnicity or group status. Naturally, the secondary literature is extensive.[82]

For this we may turn to Pliny the Younger's famous exchange of letters with Trajan, written ca. 110.[83] Consulting Trajan about the Christians in his province, Pliny asks the emperor two questions relevant here: (1) is it possible to repent, retract, and be pardoned? (2) Is being a Christian criminal in itself, or only when carrying out misdeeds in association with this group of people? Trajan answers that being a Christian itself is a crime.[84] If the people accused insisted that they were Christian they were executed. If they were Roman citizens Pliny sent them to Rome. When they denied they were, or ever had been Christians, they had to prove this by repeating after the governor 'a formula of invocation to the gods and making offerings of wine and incense to an imperial statue brought there for this purpose and furthermore by reviling the name of Christ'.[85] If they recanted they were pardoned, like the Jews and practitioners of the Isis cult expelled from Rome in AD 19. Only if they kept insisting that they were Christians,

---

[82] A lucid treatment: G. E. M. de Ste. Croix, 'Why were the Early Christians Persecuted?', *Past and Present* 26 (1963): 6–38; also: A. N. Sherwin-White, 'Why were the Early Christians Persecuted? An Amendment', *Past and Present* 27 (1964): 23–7; and de Ste. Croix's, 'Why were the Early Christians Persecuted? A Rejoinder', *Past and Present* 27 (1964): 28–33; W. H. C. Frend, *Martyrdom and Persecution in the Early Church: A Study of Conflict from the Maccabees to Donatus* (Oxford, 1965), chs. 4, 6, 7, and 8; R. Freudenberger, *Das Verhalten der römischen Behörden gegen die Christen im 2. Jahrhundert dargestellt am Brief des Plinius und Trajan und den Reskripten Trajans und Hadrians* (Munich, 1967; repr. 1969). This is essentially an extensive commentary on the two letters in Pliny; for 'die drei Rechtsfragen', see 73–6; T. D. Barnes, 'Legislation Against the Christians', *JRS* 58 (1968): 32–50.

[83] Pliny, *Ep.* 10.96, and Trajan's reply. Cf. A. N. Sherwin-White, *The Letters of Pliny: A Historical and Social Commentary* (Oxford, 1966; reissued 1985), 691–710, appendix 5, 772–8; Barnes, 'Legislation Against the Christians', 36–7.

[84] Pliny, *Ep.* 10.97: *si deferantur et arguantur, puniendi sunt.* Barnes, 'Legislation Against the Christians', 48, observes: 'whereas all other criminals, once convicted, were punished for what they had done in the past, the Christian was punished for what he was in the present, and up to the last moment could gain pardon by apostasy'. This is perhaps unnecessarily paradoxical. As Trajan states unequivocally: those who repent are pardoned (*veniam ex paenitentia impetret*). They are no different from other pardoned criminals. This was a policy designed to prevent Christianity from spreading.

[85] Pliny, *Ep.* 10.96.5–6: *Qui negabant esse se Christianos aut fuisse, cum praeeunte me deos adpellarent et imagini tuae, quam propter hoc iusseram cum simulacris numinum adferri, ture ac uino supplicarent, praeterea male dicerent Christo, quorum nihil cogi posse dicuntur qui sunt re uera Christiani, dimittendos putaui.* The demand that those who were suspected of Christianity should bring offerings to pagan gods was also made *ceteris paribus* of the Jews in Antioch in 66/7 (Jos. *BJ* 7.2.3 (41–53), esp. (50–1)); cf. Freudenberger, *Das Verhalten der römischen Behörden*, 141–54.

having been asked three times, were they executed.[86] It is thus clear that the crime was inherent in being a Christian, not in any specific act associated with this status. Such a crime could be pardoned by giving clear proof of a return to traditional religion.[87]

Judaism, disliked by many Romans, was yet permitted because it was the religion of a people with a recognized status, while Christianity was not – hence Christian services were forbidden under the edict which banned all political associations. In the words of Gibbon: 'The Jews were a people which followed, the Christians a sect which deserted the religion of their fathers.'[88]

It is curious that the reason for the ban on Christianity should have been a matter of dispute among scholars, since the Roman attitude towards religion ever since the Republican period is well known, as already described. The inhabitants of the Empire were not permitted to make an act of commitment to a new cult which would cut them off from their old ones.[89] The Jews were allowed to practise their religion, but they were forbidden to accept converts; the Christians were forbidden to do either. As argued by some scholars, it is possible that the Jews were not very active in attracting proselytes, but there is no doubt that the early church held that all humans must convert.[90]

Conclusions

There was a long-standing policy of recognition of ancestral cults and religions. Any people in the Empire had a right to practise its ancestral religion as long as due recognition was given to the emperor and the Roman state. This included the Jews, both those in Judaea and those who lived in

---

[86] Pliny adds that their *pertinacia* and *obstinatio* ought to be punished. Some authors have argued improbably that the essence of their crime was thus stubborness and obstinacy: see most recently A. N. Sherwin-White, 'Why were the Early Christians Persecuted? An Amendment'; refuted by de Ste. Croix, 'Why were the Early Christians Persecuted?', 18–19; 'Why were the Early Christians Persecuted? A Rejoinder'; similarly, at length: Freudenberger, *Das Verhalten der römischen Behörden*, 99–110. Christian obstinacy is criticized also by Marcus Aurelius 11.3; cf. comments by A. S. L. Farquharson, *The Meditations of the Emperor Marcus Aurelius* (Oxford, 1951), II, 859-10.

[87] De Ste. Croix, 'Why were the Early Christians Persecuted?', 19; Barnes, 'Legislation Against the Christians', 37.

[88] E. Gibbon, *The Decline and Fall of the Roman Empire*, ch. 20. Cf. T. Barnes, *Tertullian: A Historical and Literary Study* (Oxford, 1971), 90; A. Momigliano, 'The Social Structure of the Ancient City: Religious Dissent and Heresy', in S. C. Humphreys, *Anthropology and the Greeks* (London, 1978), 190–1.

[89] J. A. North, 'Religious Toleration', 85.

[90] Goodman, *Mission and Conversion*, 106–8, argues that proselytizing by Christians may have been less predominant in the second half of the second century.

dispersion. An exception was made if cults were regarded as particularly barbaric – human sacrifice was regarded as especially unacceptable.

In the city of Rome and in Italy there was a constant interaction between the local population and groups of foreigners and immigrants who practised their own cults. This resulted in mutual influence, notably in religion and cult practice. The Romans were highly sensitive to this and strongly disapproved of what was perceived as the undue appeal of some foreign cults. This created tension and was resisted through occasional countermeasures aimed at suppressing the influence exerted by such cults, notably expulsions from the city and the banning of formal conversion. In this connection it is easily understood that Jews were forbidden to circumcise non-Jews. This was a tangible, physical expression of conversion, easier to define than informal cult acts, widely regarded, moreover, as a bad custom anyway. It is therefore not hard to understand any legislation against circumcision of those not born as Jews without assuming a connection with anything that happened before or after the Bar Kokhba war.

This was the combination of restricted freedoms and well-defined restrictions which existed for centuries and continued to exist till the conversion of Constantine and the fourth century. It is, of course, possible to argue that Hadrian was an eccentric ruler who took a frivolous decision to ban circumcision of all men throughout the Empire. Yet it must be acknowledged that the general pattern of Roman religious policy through the ages does not easily account for such a measure, merely because the emperor found the custom distasteful. Furthermore, there is nothing in the Roman pattern of behaviour which would exclude the foundation of a Roman colony on the site of Jerusalem, which we know to have existed. A ban on conversion, including the circumcision of non-Jews, also corresponds with what we know of Roman religious policy.

CHAPTER 15

Jews, Christians, and Others in Palestine
The Evidence from Eusebius

Demography is one of those topics which are as important as they are frustrating to those interested in numbers in the ancient world. The absence of information is such that some specialists consider any effort at serious study an idle undertaking. Palestine is known to have been populated by pagans, Jews, and Christians in the Roman and Byzantine periods. I shall not be dealing here with problems of social identity, nor will I attempt to reach any conclusions about numbers, which would seem an unprofitable enterprise in the absence of hard facts. My aim is to raise a related question that should at least be asked, even if no clear-cut answer can be given at this stage. What was the distribution of the various population groups in Palestine: pagans, Jews, and Christians? The situation in the cities has been discussed in several works and there are various sources. Avi-Yonah is, indeed, remarkably confident in giving concrete numbers.[1] Even so we do not know much about the physical aspects concerned. It is generally admitted that the larger cities such as Caesarea had mixed populations, but this is information which derives from literary sources and we have no clear idea of what this meant in

---

[1] M. Avi-Yonah, *Geschichte der Juden im Zeitalter des Talmud* (Berlin, 1962), 16–20. He asserts that, after the Bar Kokhba war, there were fifty-six Jewish communities (i.e. non-mixed villages) in Galilee; see also 133, 224, 241–2. Avi-Yonah, *The Holy Land: From the Persian to the Arab Conquest. A Historical Geography* (Grand Rapids, 1977), ch. 3: 'Population', 212–21, esp. 219–21: 'Numbers'. G. Alon, *The Jews in their Land in the Talmudic Age* (Jerusalem, 1980-04), 750–7, tends less to cite specific numbers, but he is fairly confident that he can make valid statements about the relative strength of the various communities. F.-M. Abel, *Géographie de la Palestine* (Paris, 1967), II, does not discuss these questions at all. For Roman Palestine we should mention M. Broshi, 'The Population of Western Palestine in the Roman-Byzantine Period', *BASOR* 236 (1979): 1–10. For an attempt to assess the situation in southern Palestine: J. Schwartz, *Jewish Settlement in Judaea After the Bar-Kochba War until the Arab Conquest* (Jerusalem, 1986; Hebrew). Schwartz seems to allow for the existence of mixed communities, for instance in the area of Beth Guvrin (97, 107). There is now an extensive recent bibliography on the demography of the Roman Empire. For up-to-date introductory entries on ancient demography, see W. Scheidel, 'Demography', in W. Scheidel, I. Morris, and R. Saller (eds.), *The Cambridge Economic History of the Greco-Roman World* (Cambridge, 2007) with bibliography in n. 1.

practice over time.[2] The excavations at Sepphoris give us a glimpse of a surprisingly mixed city centre in a town which the sources might have led us to believe was overwhelmingly Jewish.[3] Other important towns, such as Lydda and Beth Guvrin, have been explored less, and we cannot know whether systematic excavations, where possible, would add new information or raise new questions. There is, in any case, a clear aware- ness among scholars that most Roman and Byzantine cities had mixed populations to some extent at least.[4] It should be added that this is well known and not in dispute for the cities and villages of Asia Minor, unlike those of Palestine.[5]

Even less is known about the situation in the countryside. Did the vari- ous groups live together in the same villages, or did each have their own villages?[6] To what extent were there regional patterns that can be traced? How did these develop over time? These questions are essential to any effort at understanding social relationships. It is usually assumed that, while most cities had mixed populations, the villages were monocultures inhabited by representatives of a single ethnic and religious group.[7] Yet it must be admitted that little thought has been given to the nature of the

---

[2] For Caesarea, see R. L. Vann (ed.), *Caesarea Papers* (Ann Arbor, 1992) and several contributions in J. Humphrey (ed.), *The Roman and Byzantine Near East: Some Recent Archaeological Research* (Ann Arbor, 1995). See now *CIIP* II, *Caesarea and the Middle Coast*, with the Introduction, 17–35 and, on the Jewish presence: 28–30.

[3] Alon, *Jews in their Land*, 751: 'Jews *were* the overwhelming majority in those towns'. Avi-Yonah, *The Holy Land*, 218: 'Sepphoris-Diocaesarea in the fifth century was still purely Jewish.' A historical monograph, S. S. Miller, *Studies in the History and Traditions of Sepphoris* (Leiden, 1984), does not discuss the presence of gentiles in the city. He seems to assume that there were no Christian inhabit- ants there before they are actually attested in the fifth century (p. 4 with n. 19). For the recent excava- tions: E. M. Meyers, E. Netzer, and C. L. Meyers, 'Sepphoris: "Ornament of All Galilee"', *Biblical Archaeologist* 49 (1986): 4–19; E. Netzer and Z. Weiss, *Zippori* (Jerusalem, 1994).

[4] Alon, *Jews in their Land*. For Lydda, A. Oppenheimer, 'Jewish Lydda in the Roman Era', *Hebrew Union College Annual* 59 (1988): 115–36; J. Schwartz, *Lod (Lydda), Israel*, BAR International Series (Oxford, 1991).

[5] For Asia Minor and Sardis in particular: T. Rajak, 'Jews Pagans and Christians in Late Antique Sardis: Models of Interaction', in *The Jewish Dialogue with Greece and Rome* (Leiden, 2002), 447–62.

[6] M. Sartre, *L'Orient romain* (Paris, 1991), 389–90, and F. Millar, *The Roman Near East* (Cambridge, 1993), 348–51, 374–7, are cautious and do not express an opinion on the distribution of social groups in rural Palestine.

[7] Avi-Yonah does not say so explicitly in his *Geschichte der Juden*, but the assumption is implicit throughout, for instance, on pp. 132–4; in *The Holy Land*, 215–19, he refers frequently to 'Jewish settlements', 'Jewish villages'. He assumes without argument that the Roman government made specific, regional decisions about the ethnic composition of the population (215, 219). There is no evidence that the Roman authorities tried to do this, or that they could have if they had wanted. Incidentally, on p. 217 Avi-Yonah assumes that the units mentioned in the *Notitia Dignitatum* were still ethnic in character. This is erroneous, for the old ethnic names may still be used for units manned with locally recruited troops. Alon, *Jews in their Land*, discusses the distribution of the population exclusively in regional terms.

evidence for this assumption and its implications. It is, in principle, quite possible that many villages had a mixed population. The distribution of pagans and Christians, for example, must have depended on the manner in which Christianity spread in the rural parts of Palestine during the Late Roman and Byzantine periods. If conversion took place more often on an individual rather than a group basis, many villages must inevitably have been inhabited by both unconverted pagans and converted Christians. It is usually asserted – and there is good evidence to support this – that the Jewish population of Palestine was considerably reduced by the time of the Moslem conquest. Since the population as a whole saw a huge increase during the Byzantine period[8] we have to consider the possibility that the Jewish population decreased less in absolute numbers than in proportion to the vastly increased gentile population. Again, we must ask how Christianization worked in Palestine: were entire villages taken over? Was there a gradual, individual process at work? One point to note briefly at this stage is the significance of synagogues and churches in rural settlements: villages which boasted such buildings were not necessarily inhabited by representatives of one group only.

It is not the aim of this chapter to discuss these problems in general, but rather to focus on a unique source which, I claim, is not sufficiently understood, and is well worth closer scrutiny, namely the *Onomasticon* of biblical place-names by Eusebius. This is a mine of information about Palestine in the Roman and Byzantine periods of a kind which does not exist for any other part of the Empire. It is unique because it is the only text which is concerned solely and consistently with regional matters. It contains more than 900 lemmas, which refer to twenty-nine cities and hundreds of villages. Eusebius mentions the location of settlements along twenty roads and knows of the presence of military garrisons at eleven sites. His aim in the work is to focus not primarily on the cities, but on biblical sites, most of which were villages and small places. Thus while cities regularly serve as a point of reference, the setting of the work is essentially rural, a rare feature in classical texts. Of course the work has been studied intensively by scholars interested in the Holy Land,[9] but it is not a book which has drawn much attention from historical geographers of the Roman Empire. Yet it

---

[8] This may be seen in any of the publications of the 'Archaeological Survey of Israel', published by the Israel Antiquities Authority. The increase in settlement in the area between Lydda and Jerusalem is discussed by M. Fischer, B. Isaac, and I. Roll, *Roman Roads in Judaea*, II, *The Jaffa–Jerusalem Roads*, BAR International Series (Oxford, 1996), part V, 301–7.

[9] The work is used extensively in all the works about the historical geography of the Holy Land, cited above. Specific studies: E. Klostermann (ed.), *Eusebius, Das Onomastikon der biblischen*

is a rare source, giving us an insight into the level of detailed geographical knowledge available locally, in a provincial capital rather than at the centre of the Roman Empire. It has been cited most frequently for its information about administrative matters and specific sites, but there is little genuine discussion about the nature of the document as such, the sources which Eusebius used, and his geographical methods. In the following pages I shall attempt to show that the *Onomasticon* if properly interpreted has more to tell us about the distribution of population groups in Palestine in the third century than it has been given credit for by most scholars.[10]

Among the large number of villages that Eusebius mentions there is a fairly small group which he qualifies in some manner. Thus he describes thirty-three as 'very big villages' (μεγίστη κώμη) and three as 'big villages' (κώμη μεγάλη). He refers to eleven 'villages of Jews' of which seven are 'very big'. Three villages are inhabited 'entirely by Christians' (ὅλη Χριστιανῶν). Two of these are also 'very big' villages. Eusebius further mentions four 'villages of Samaritans' (κώμη Σαμαρέων) or villages 'founded by the Samaritans from Babylonia'.[11] In the entire work he does not mention any specifically 'pagan' villages. The term (τὰ ἔθνα) only occurs when he refers to three rural sanctuaries as being 'still venerated by the pagans'.[12] Galilee is also described as 'belonging to the gentiles', but that derives from Matthew and thus indirectly from Isaiah.[13]

The first question to be asked is why so few villages are assigned to specific groups, eighteen out of hundreds of villages which Eusebius mentions

---

Ortsnamen (Leipzig, 1904; repr. Hildesheim, 1966), introduction, pp. vii–xxxiv; W. Kubitschek, 'Ein Strassennetz in Eusebius' Onomasticon', *JÖAI* 8 (1905): 119–27; M. Noth, 'Die topographischen Angaben im Onomasticon des Eusebius', *ZDPV* 66 (1943): 32–63; T. Barnes, 'The Composition of Eusebius' Onomasticon', *JTS* NS 26 (1975): 412–15. Matters of method: Avi-Yonah, *The Holy Land*, 127–9; criticized by B. Isaac and I. Roll, *Roman Roads in Judaea*, I, *The Scythopolis–Legio Road*, BAR International Series (Oxford, 1982), 11–13. Note the recent publications: G. S. P. Freeman-Grenville, R. L. Chapman III, and J. E. Taylor, *The Onomasticon by Eusebius of Caesarea* (Jerusalem, 2003); R. S. Notley and Z. Safrai, *Eusebius, Onomasticon* (Leiden, 2005), a problematic publication; S. Timm, *Das Onomastikon der biblischen Ortsnamen: Edition der syrischen Fassung mit griechischem Text, englischer und deutscher Übersetzung* (Berlin, 2005).

[10] I have discussed the administrative information contained in Eusebius' *Onomasticon* in a paper: 'Eusebius and the Geography of Roman Provinces', in D. Kennedy (ed.), *The Roman Army in the East* (Ann Arbor, 1996), 153–68; repr. in B. Isaac, *The Near East under Roman Rule* (Leiden, 1998), 284–309.

[11] The expression ταύτην ἔκτισαν οἱ ἀπὸ Βαβυλῶνος Σαμαρεῖται is almost certainly just a reference to 2 Kings 17:30. An interesting misunderstanding is the village of Nerigel (138.16), which Eusebius derives from the mention of the god Nergal in the text of Kings. However, Socho (see below) was a genuine Samaritan village. For Bainith (58.3) he also seems to have a specific village called Baithanne, in mind. Eusebius is critical of the Samaritan tradition regarding Mt. Gerizim and Ebal (Gaibal) (64.12).

[12] The oak of Mamre: 6.8; Mt. Hermon: 20.11; Galgala: 64.24.

[13] Γαλιλαία τῶν ἐθνῶν (116.7; 120.3); Matt 14:5.3; Isa 8:23.5.

in his work. There are several possible explanations. It could be assumed that he provides random information, correct in itself, but not significant in its relationship to other villages which he also mentions in his work. If this were the case nothing could be deduced from negative information, from the fact that he does *not* assign a village to a specific group. In other words, he describes a few villages as Christian while there were many others, also mentioned in the work, which he could and should have included among the Christian villages. His failure to do so could have been due to inconsistency or ignorance. If we are to accept the proposition that Eusebius' information about Jewish and Christian villages was the result of an entirely random selection nothing further could be deduced from the material, except that it might be true for the relevant settlements. However, this is not a likely hypothesis, for it does not agree with other aspects of Eusebius' *Onomasticon*. As I have argued elsewhere, there is a clear and demonstrable pattern in the references to garrisons, roads, and city-territories, all of which represent valid and consistent contemporary information.[14] While this is an obvious fact in the case of the garrisons and roads, the conclusion regarding city-territories is based on a rather complex argument which cannot be used in support of considerations about other aspects of the work. Nevertheless it can safely be said that Eusebius, where he provides contemporary information, does so in a consistent manner.

A second claim could be that Eusebius does not provide a representative sample, since he only refers to villages identified with biblical places. This too is an unsatisfactory explanation, for the number of places which he mentions is very large in absolute terms. Even if he gives the names of only one-fifth of the villages existing in Palestine in his time, the ratio would not change drastically. Among thousands of settlements only fifteen would have been Christian. A third possibility is to assume that the information is representative in some way and requires an explanation in its own right.

Before we pursue this further we ought to consider whether there is any correlation between the evidence from Eusebius and other material. Apart from the evidence in Eusebius, what else can we know about villages? We should consider:

- Other written sources, notably Talmudic literature.
- The presence of an early church or synagogue and the question of what we can infer from this as regards the composition of the population.

---

[14] Isaac, *The Near East under Roman Rule*, 284–309.

The first question is whether places which Eusebius knows as Jewish are mentioned as such in Talmudic sources. In any comparison between information in Talmudic material and Eusebius it is important to note that the latter almost certainly represents a narrow time-span. Since his information about cities and army-units derives exclusively from the late third or the early fourth century, the same may be assumed for his statements about villages. Talmudic literature, on the other hand, developed over centuries.

The first thing we must note here, then, is that there is little correlation between Jewish villages recorded by Eusebius and those occurring in the Talmud. Of ten villages described as Jewish by Eusebius, only four are mentioned in Talmudic literature: Kefar Dagon[15], Naaran[16], En Geddi, and Naveh in Arabia[17]. There are also villages which occur in Talmudic sources, which Eusebius mentions without describing them as Jewish: Mikhmas[18], Zoar[19], Haifa,[20] and many sites in the north. We may add that Jericho is mentioned in the Talmudic literature as a place typically inhabited by gentiles, as opposed to nearby Naaran.[21] This approach clearly does not get us any further, for there are good explanations as to why there might be little correlation between the two sources. Talmudic literature does not single out places inhabited exclusively by Jews, but refers to them for other reasons, apart from the exceptional passage reflecting the reality of the fourth to fifth century which mentions a number of pairs of neighbouring gentile

---

[15] Tos. Ahilot 3:9.

[16] Leviticus Rabbah xxiii 5 (ed. Margulies, 533); Lamentations Rabbah (Buber) i 17, p. 91; Canticles Rabbah ii 2 (5). Naaran is mentioned also in later sources, discussed by P. Mayerson, 'Antiochus Monachus' Homily on Dreams: an Historical Note', *JJS* 35 (1984): 51–6 = *Monks, Martyrs, Soldiers and Saracens* (New York and Jerusalem, 1994), 216–21; the synagogue found there dates to the sixth century: *NEAEHL* III, 1075–6.

[17] See the Talmudic sources cited in the previous note. For the remains of a synagogue at Naveh, see below.

[18] *On.* 132.3: Large village. m. Menahot 8:1, indicating that it produced fine flour. Note also a Hebrew inscription on a coffin from the village: *ZDPV* (1914): 135–6 (*CII* 1191).

[19] Tos. Shevi'it 15:7 (ed. Lieberman, 198). Near the site a Jewish cemetery has been found, cf. *TIR* 263, s.v. Zoora; Schwartz, *Jewish Settlement*, 111–12; M. Sartre (ed.), *IGLS* XXI: *Inscriptions de la Jordanie*, 4 (Paris, 1993), 133–7, nos. 105, 106. Near Zoar was Mahoza which is mentioned frequently in the Babatha archive: N. Lewis (ed.), *The Documents from the Bar Kokhba Period in the Cave of Letters, Greek Papyri* (Jerusalem, 1989); Y. Yadin and J. C. Greenfield, *Aramaic and Nabatean Signatures and Subscriptions* (Jerusalem, 1989). At that time, the early second century, it was inhabited by both Jews and Nabataeans.

[20] Haifa: Eusebius, *On.* 108.31; for Talmudic sources, see Tsafrir *et al.*, *Tabula Imperii Romani: Iudaea/Palaestina* (1994), 141.

[21] See n. 20. Note the presence of a group of important sages recorded in Tos. Berakhot iv 16 (ed. Lieberman, 21). This shows that Jericho was either not entirely gentile, or not at all times, yet another indication that we should not blindly rely on sources which seem to suggest that specific places were inhabited exclusively by one group.

and Jewish places: Halamish and Naveh, Sussita (Hippos) and Tiberias, Castra and Haifa, Jericho and Naaran, Lod and Ono. Although of quite unequal importance, these places were apparently all remarkable for the fact that they were predominantly Jewish or gentile. There is also an interesting reference to Kefar Nahum, described as a place where there was a presence of 'minim' in the period of the Bar Kokhba revolt.[22] Apparently it was inhabited by Jews, interspersed with sectarian elements. The village is known for its synagogue, the date of which is disputed.[23] New Testament Capernaum is also mentioned in a well-known, and particularly relevant statement made by Epiphanius in his story about the *comes* Joseph. According to Epiphanius, writing in the last quarter of the fourth century, Joseph obtained permission from Constantine to build churches 'in the cities and villages of the Jews, where nobody has been able to build churches, because there are no Hellenes, Samaritans or Christians among them. This remains the case particularly in Tiberias, in Diocaesarea, which is now called Sepphoris, in Nazareth and in Capernaum, that there are no gentiles among them.'[24] It must be stressed that this is a dubious source, but, taken at face value, it would confirm that the absence of gentiles in settlements inhabited by Jews is the exception rather than the rule. Epiphanius here mentions the two main cities of Galilee and two villages in which the presence of Christians would have been particularly desirable, from his point of view, because of their prominence in the Gospels. In any case, the two contemporary explicit statements, cited above, about the ethnic and religious separation or mix in Palestinian towns and villages support rather than contradict the assumption that the different elements of the population usually lived together in the same settlements.

When we consider the presence of synagogues in rural settlements we should, of course, refer only to those firmly dated to the period under

---

[22] Ecclesiastes Rabbah i 8 (4). Eusebius, *On.* 120.2, merely mentions that it is an extant village in 'Galilee of the Gentiles'.

[23] F. Hüttenmeister and G. Reeg, *Die antiken Synagogen in Israel* (Wiesbaden, 1977), I, 260–9; J. E. Taylor, *Christians and the Holy Places: The Myth of Jewish-Christian Origins* (Oxford, 1994), 'The Question of the Synagogue', 290–1, with up-to-date bibliography and discussion. If the synagogue dates to the fourth–fifth century, this may not be relevant for the period to which Eusebius refers.

[24] Epiphanius, *Panarion* 30.4–12 (*GCS* 25.1.347): κόμητα γὰρ αὐτὸν κατέστησε, φήσας αὐτῷ αἰτεῖν πάλιν ὃ βούλεται· ὁ δὲ οὐδὲν ᾐτήσατο πλὴν τοῦτο μέγιστον χάρισμα τυχεῖν παρὰ τοῦ βασιλέως τὸ ἐπιτραπῆναι [καὶ] διὰ προστάγματος βασιλικοῦ οἰκοδομῆσαι Χριστοῦ ἐκκλησίας ἐν ταῖς πόλεσι καὶ κώμαις τῶν Ιουδαίων, ἔνθα τις οὐδέποτε ἴσχυσεν προστήσασθαι ἐκκλησίας διὰ τὸ μήτέ Ἕλληνα μήτε Σαμαρείτην μήτε Χριστιανὸν μέσον αὐτῶν εἶναι. τοῦτο δὲ μάλιστα ἐν Τιβεριάδι καὶ ἐν Διοκαισαρείᾳ τῇ καὶ Σεπφουρὶν καὶ ἐν Ναζαρὲτ καὶ ἐν Καπερναοὺμ φυλάσσεται ⟨τὸ⟩ παρ᾽ αὐτοῖς [τοῦ] μὴ εἶναι ἀλλόεθνον.

consideration. This excludes many, for the majority of synagogues are dated to a much later period. Again, this approach is not very productive.

- Synagogues have been found in villages which Eusebius mentions, but does not describe as Jewish, for instance: Apheka/Fiq[25], Maon in Judaea[26], Gabatha (Gevat)[27]. Kana[28] may also belong to this category.[29] Did Eusebius not know these were Jewish settlements? Or does he not describe them as Jewish because they had a mixed population?

- There are quite a few villages which Eusebius describes as Jewish for which we do have contemporary corroborating evidence: Anim (Anaia)[30], Carmel (?)[31], En Rimmon (Eremmon)[32], Eshtemo(a)[33], En Geddi[34], Nineve/Nave[35]. In the case of the Samaritan villages this may be true for the village of Socho (modern Shuweika)[36].

- There are villages which Eusbius describes as Jewish for which we have no other evidence, literary or archaeological, of their Jewishness in this

---

[25] Hüttenmeister and Reeg, *Die antiken Synagogen*, 2–4 (second–third centuries).

[26] *On.* 130.12; the synagogue: *NEAEHL* III, 942–5 (fourth–seventh centuries).

[27] *On.* 78.3: village in the territory of Diocaesarea. Hüttenmeister and Reeg, I, 137–8, mentions the discovery there of a pillar with a menorah and a stone with Jewish symbols. Hüttenmeister notes that this does not prove there was a synagogue, which is true, but it does demonstrate a Jewish presence in the area.

[28] In the case of Kana it is impossible to say whether a synagogue was indeed discovered at the site which Eusebius had in mind since there are various places with related names and problems in identification: G. Schmitt, *Siedlungen Palästinas in griechisch-römischer Zeit* (Wiesbaden, 1995), 115–16.

[29] For Kapharnaoum (Kefar Nahum), see below. Khorazin may also be a special case. Eusebius, *On.* 174.23, describes it as 'now deserted'. The excavations are said to have confirmed that the settlement with its synagogue were partially destroyed in the early fourth century: *NEAEHL* I, 301–4. The Babylonian Talmud refers to it, but in a context related to the period of the Second Temple: b. Menahot 85a.

[30] Eusebius, *On.* 26.9–13. *NEAEHL* I, 62, s.v. Horvat 'Anim (fourth–seventh centuries). Note that there are two neighbouring villages of this name. The other, a smaller village, mentioned also below, is described as Christian by Eusebius, *On.* 26.9–13. *Mart. Pal.* 10.2 (*GCS* 9, 931) thus notes the two villages of Anaia as one Jewish and one Christian. As pointed out to me by Susan Weingarten, it might be relevant that he does *not* say this about the two villages of Socho (156.18), where an underground hideaway has been found (upper site) as well as a church (lower site); see references in *TIR* 234, s.v. Socho I.

[31] *On.* 92.20: Jewish; 118.5: garrison. Remains of a synagogue at Kh. Kirmil, possibly brought from there to Yatta: Hüttenmeister and Reeg, I, 253. Cf. below, pp. 336; 339.

[32] *NEAEHL* IV, 1284 (third–fourth centuries).

[33] *NEAEHL* II, 423–6; Hüttenmeister and Reeg, I, 117–21 (fourth–fifth centuries).

[34] *NEAEHL* II, 399–409 (late second/early third century until Islamic conquest); Hüttenmeister and Reeg, I, 108–14. For Naveh in Talmudic sources, see above.

[35] Hüttenmeister amd Reeg, 336–9. Full references in G. Reeg, *Die Ortsnamen Israels nach der rabbinischen Literatur* (Wiesbaden, 1989), 433–5; Schmitt, *Siedlungen*, 266. See also above, n. 20.

[36] It is mentioned in the Samaritan Chronicle, *REJ* 44 (1902): 225–7. Abel, *Géographie*, II, 467, s.v. Socho (3); Hüttenmeister and Reeg, II, 668. Note that this is a different site from the two villages of the same name, mentioned above, n. 30.

period: Akkaron /Eqron[37], Ietta[38], Thala[39], Dabeira[40]. The same is true for the Samaritan village of Tharsila in Batanea[41].

It is clear therefore, that we cannot solve these problems by simply combining or mixing the archaeological evidence with that from Eusebius, even when the two refer to the same period. Other literary sources are sometimes helpful, but the Talmudic material can be no more a basis for systematic comparison with the evidence in Eusebius than the archaeological remains. What we can do is to keep an open mind in considering the material and watch out for indications of the existence of mixed communities, e.g. in Talmudic and patristic sources, through the distribution of dated inscriptions.

My suggestion is that the overwhelming majority of villages had a mixed population: pagan, Jewish, Christian, and Samaritan. Eusebius would have considered that the norm and found it worth mentioning only if a settlement was purely Jewish, Christian, or Samaritan (purely pagan settlements would have been of no interest to him). This is important if it is true. Jews and gentiles would have lived side by side both in the cities and in the countryside. The parallel midrashic sources which mention well-known pairs of neighbouring settlements inhabited by gentiles and Jews respectively have been cited above.[42] It could be argued that the point is emphasized because this was not the usual pattern. When did this pattern develop? After one of the two revolts? In any case, around AD 300 very few villages could be described as homogeneous. It will be clear that Eusebius – whatever the precise date of the *Onomasticon* – wrote before the Christianization of Palestine took a decisive momentum. This is not to deny the impact of the Jewish presence in Galilee in this period or afterwards. If this situation continued into the following centuries it has consequences for our understanding of the presence of synagogues in rural settlements. These are clearly evidence of a prosperous Jewish

---

[37] *On.* 22.9. This is an ancient site where extensive excavations of the biblical period have been undertaken (*NEAEHL* III, 1051–9, s.v. Miqne, Tel). These have not produced information on the Late Roman/Byzantine village; cf. *TIR*, 56, s.v. Accaron.

[38] Ietta (*On.* 108.8) or Iutta, modern Yatta, was a bishopric by 450 (ACO 2.1.2 (p. 103)): Μαρκιανὸς ὁ εὐλαβέστατος ἐπίσκοπος Ἰωτάνης; 2.2.2 (p. 70)), cf. Abel, *Géographie*, II, 366–7, s.v. Jouttah; *TIR*, 155. A church has been noted there, but no synagogue.

[39] Thala almost certainly should be identified with the excavated site of Tel Halif, a flourishing settlement in the Late Roman and Byzantine periods: *NEAEHL* II, 558–9.

[40] *On.* 78, 5–7 (Dabaritta). A church, but no synagogue, is reported to have been found there, cf. *TIR* 106.

[41] *On.* 102.4. M. Avi-Yonah, *Gazetteer of Roman Palestine* (Jerusalem, 1976), 100: modern Tsil?

[42] Above, n. 30. Two of the five Jewish settlements are also mentioned by Eusebius as Jewish.

presence in their villages, but they do not prove the absence of gentiles in such communities.

μεγίστη κώμη
Total 33 villages, 7 Jewish
Machmas
Adolam (Odollam)
Aendor
Akkaron (Jewish)
Akkrabein
Anaia (Jewish)
Aser/Asor
Beelmeon (Arabia)
Bersabee (garrison)
Carmel (Jewish)
Chasalon
Douma
Eleale
Engeddi (Jewish)
Ephraim
Eremmon (En Rimmon, En Remmon Jewish)
Esthemo (Jewish.)
Gaulon
Gedrous
Gethremmon
Giththam
Hebron (see also Mamre)
Ietheira
Ietta (Iutta, Jewish)
Kaparadagon
Karnaia (Carnaea, Transjordan)
Mabsara (in Gebalene, ὑπακούουσα τῇ Πέτρᾳ)
Namara (in Batanea)
Thaanach
Thala (Jewish)
κώμη μεγάλη
Apheka (Fiq)
Thamna
Magdiel
Jewish, not μεγίστη

Dabeira
Nineve (Nave, Arabia)
Noorath (Na'aran)
Total Jewish: 11
Christian
Anaia (not μεγίστη)
Ietheira (also μεγίστη)
Karaiatha (10 miles west of Madaba)

CHAPTER 16

Roman Organization in the Arabah in the Fourth Century AD

Following the survey work carried out by Fritz von Frank in the Negev, Albrecht Alt made an extensive attempt to trace a string of Diocletianic *castella* in the Wadi Arabah.[1] The assumption here was that there must have been a *limes* system in the Negev such as allegedly existed in Germany.

The existence of such a system was firmly denied by Beno Rothenberg, based on his survey of the Arabah in the 1960s:

> The Diocletianic reform brought no essential military changes to the 'Arabah. Only three small fortlets were erected there, all sited at the extreme ends of the 'Arabah, and protecting essential water-sources on major west-east roads. There was never a line of fourth century *castella* in the 'Arabah, and no traces of any north-south road running all the way from the Dead Sea to the Red Sea have ever been found. A quantity of Byzantine sherds in the remains of an Iron Age watch-tower or a Nabataean khan do not make it a Roman fortress.[2]

This chapter reconsiders the available sources in an attempt to assess the merits of these two contradictory opinions and any possible alternatives. I will argue that Rothenberg was right in challenging the view that there was a line of fourth-century *castella* in the Arabah, but wrong in denying the existence of a fourth-century north–south road through it. Furthermore, I will argue that the archaeological evidence attesting the existence of this road corresponds with the evidence from the literary sources, as long as the dates of these sources are carefully interpreted.

---

[1] A. Alt, 'Aus der Araba II: Römische Kastelle und Strassen', *ZDPV* 58 (1935): 1–59. Numerous publications by M. Gichon argued that there was a '*limes* system' in the Negev from the Flavian period onwards. For my own discussion of these theories see B. Isaac, *The Limits of Empire: The Roman Army in the East* (Oxford, 1992).

[2] B. Rothenberg, 'The Arabah in Roman and Byzantine Times in the Light of New Research', in S. Applebaum (ed.), *Roman Frontier Studies* (Tel Aviv, 1967), 211–23, at 220. For the road to Elath see Y. Aharoni, 'The Roman Road to Aila (Elath)', *IEJ* 4 (1954): 9–16; 'Tamar and the Roads to Elath', *IEJ* 130 (1963): 30–42.

First of all, Eusebius' *Onomasticon*³ will be brought to bear on this issue. Additional sources are the *Notitia Dignitatum*, *P. Colt* 39, the Beer Sheva Edict(s),⁴ and the Madaba Map. The confusing evidence from the *Tabula Peutingeriana* will also be discussed.

The evidence of Eusebius' *Onomasticon* for the state of the road-system in the late third century is of crucial importance.⁵ This source contains more than thirty references to twenty roads in Palestine, Arabia, and Syria. Usually this takes the form of a statement that a site 'is x miles from A as one goes to B'. As argued elsewhere, Eusebius used up-to-date information regarding the Roman public roads which he found in the governor's office in Caesarea. The *Onomasticon* thus contains fairly full evidence for the public roads in the province in the late third century AD. Moreover, it often states explicitly which locations the roads were seen as linking, thus providing evidence regarding the nodal points of the system. The sources listed at the end of this chapter therefore give us the following decisive information. There was a public road from Aelia Capitolina to Hebron through Bethlehem (Sources 1 and 2). This road continued from Hebron to Aila (Elath/Aqaba) past Mampsis (Source 5). A look at the map shows that this road can only have run through the Arabah. As regards garrisons, it is clear from Sources 3 and 4 that the village of Carmel, situated on the road between Hebron and Mampsis was garrisoned in this period.⁶ Other garrisoned sites on this road are Malatha,⁷ Mampsis,⁸ and Thamara which has

---

³ Klostermann (ed.), 1904. See now: G. S. P. Freeman-Grenville, R. L. Chapman III, and J. E. Taylor, *The Onomasticon by Eusebius of Caesarea* (Jerusalem, 2003); S. Timm, *Das Onomastikon der biblischen Ortsnamen: Edition der syrischen Fassung mit griechischem Text, englischer und deutscher Übersetzung* (Berlin, 2005).

⁴ *P. Colt* refers to the papyri discovered at Nessana, see C. Kraemer (ed.), *Excavations at Nessana*, III, *Non-Literary Papyri* (Princeton, 1958); cf. L. Casson, 'The Administration of Byzantine and Early Arab Palestine', *Aegyptus* 32 (1952): 54–60. For the Beer Sheva edict(s) see also L. Di Segni, 'The Beersheba Tax Edict Reconsidered in the Light of a Newly Discovered Fragment', *Scripta Classica Israelica* 23 (2004): 131–58.

⁵ For the date of this work and the nature of the underlying sources, see above, Chapter 15.

⁶ Other sources relevant for the site of Carmel are *Notitia Dignitatum Orientis* 34.20 which gives the *Equites Scutarii Illyriciani* as the local garrison. It is also mentioned in *P. Colt* 39, which suggest it was a military site. It lies on the road from Hebron to Malatha. Cf. above, Chapter 15, p. 331 and below, pp. 339; 343.

⁷ For this site see Josephus, *Ant.* 18.6.2 (147), describing it as a tower which served as a refuge to Agrippa I. It is mentioned by Ptolemy, *Geogr.* 5.17.4: Μαλιάτθα; and by Eusebius, *On.* 14.3; 88.4; 108.3; as a reference point, but not as a garrison. It was garrisoned by a *Cohors Prima Flavia* according to *Not. Dig. Or.* 34.45. For the excavations, see E. Stern (ed.), *The New Encyclopedia of Archaeological Excavations in the Holy Land* (Jerusalem, 1993), III, 934–7 s.v. Tel Malhata.

⁸ Eusebius mentions it as a site on the road from Hebron to Aela, but does not include it among the military sites (Source 5). However, it is mentioned in *P. Colt* 39 and the Beer Sheva Edict(s), which suggests there was a garrison at a later stage, i.e. in the fifth–sixth century. See also: Stern et al., *New Encyclopedia*, III, 882–93 s.v. Kurnub.

not been identified with certainty (Source 5).[9] Finally, the last military site identified in the literary sources is the legionary base at Aela on the Gulf of Aqaba/Elath (Source 6), where the old Trajanic road through Transjordan and the road here discussed came together.[10] Eusebius' *Onomasticon* is the earliest source which locates the *legio X Fretensis* there rather than in Jerusalem. As is well known, in this period the legion would have been smaller in size than at the time it was first based in Jerusalem in the first century.[11] It is almost certain, therefore, that the base at Aela was smaller in size than the average second-century legionary base as known in the West.

This evidence from literary sources must be interpreted in combination with newly discovered epigraphic material from the Arabah.[12]

Milestones in the Arabah

Three Tetrarchic and Constantinian mile stations[13] have been found, each of them numbering eight to ten pieces, all of them north of Yotvata. One of those, found at Yahel, 12 miles north of the fort, gives the distance *ABOSIA* 12 m, i.e. 'ab Osia' or 'a Bosia' 12 miles. They are dated to the Tetrarchic and Constantinian reigns (AD 284–324). The existence of mile stations along a road from Aela which continues northwards beyond

---

[9] Thamara is also mentioned by Ptolemy, *Geogr.* 5.16.8, which shows that it existed under that name before the mid-second century AD. I am not convinced by the tentative identification of the site now called Mezad Thamar with ancient 'Thamara'. The excavations by Gichon have produced evidence of occupation from the end of the third century to the late sixth or early seventh century (Isaac, *Limits of Empire*, 193–5).

[10] The excavations at Aqaba by S. T. Parker have not uncovered remains of the legionary base. See now S. T. Parker and A. M. Smith II, *The Roman Aqaba Project Final Report*, I, *The Regional Environment and the Regional Survey*, ASOR archaeological reports 19 (Boston, 2013). Note the fragments of a building inscription found at Aila (Aqaba) dated AD 324–6: *IGLS* XXI/4, no. 150; cf. H. I. MacAdam, 'Epigraphy and the *Notitia Dignitatum* (*Oriens* 37)', in D. French and C. S. Lightfoot (eds.), *The Eastern Frontier of the Roman Empire* (Oxford, 1989), 295–309.

[11] As has been pointed out, however, it is quite possible that the base in Jerusalem contained the headquarters and only part of the legion, even in the first century, as there is evidence of vexillations (detachments) based elsewhere (see Isaac, *Limits of Empire*, 427–8, 431, 433).

[12] U. Avner, 'The Southern Arava – Roman Milestones', *Hadashot Arkheologiyot* 104 (1995): 120–1 (Hebrew); S. R. Wolff, 'Archaeology in Israel', *AJA* 100 (1996): 725–68

[13] Esp. photographs in Wolff, 'Archaeology in Israel', 762–4: three Tetrarchic and Constantinian milestations, 16056.93645; 16230.93868; 16145.93765 (see also D. L. Kennedy, *The Roman Army in Jordan* (London, 2000), 193–4). Along the eastern slope of the Arabah, further evidence of ancient roads has been found: (a) a stretch of surfaced road running towards the south of Gharandal, (b) a quarry with five discarded milestones 10 km north of Gharandal at Qa'a es-Sa'idiyeen, (c) a possible anepigraphic milestone at Bir Madkhur, and (d) stretches of what is said to be an old road further north (see A. M. Smith *et al.*, 'The Southeast Araba Archaeological Survey: A Preliminary Report on the 1994 Season', *BASOR* 305 (1997): 45–71, at 59–621 and figs. 12, 14; M. Perry and A. M. Smith, 'Bir Madkur', *AJA* 102 (1998): 592–595, at 594).

Yotvata proves that there was a public road all along the Arabah in the Tetrarchic period.

Inscription from Yotvata (AD 296–306)

From the excavations carried out by Z. Meshel it appears that the Roman fort south of Yotvata[14] was not occupied later than the fourth century. Yotvata, approximately 34 km or one day's march in military terms north of Elath, is the most important of all sites in the western section of the southern Arabah because it has the best water supply in this otherwise extremely arid region. All over the area underground water is accessible.[15] The remains are visible of an ancient water collecting system called in English 'chains of wells' (*qanat, foggara*) and with it were associated shards of the Persian and Roman periods.[16] The reason for the existence of a fort on this site, even though it lasted less than a century, is obvious. It served as a road-station in an oasis on an important road, perhaps a junction or crossroads. It policed the oasis and, conversely, it could exist where it did thanks to the water supply. It lies one kilometre south of the earlier remains of the Chalcolithic period and Iron Age I.

In combination these sources and finds show that we may regard the following road as attested in the ancient literary and epigraphic sources listed above: Jerusalem (Aelia)–Bethlehem–Hebron–Mampsis–Thamara–Aela. The Tetrarchic date of the southern part of this road is attested by the milestones. The descents from the Hebron Mountains and into the Arabah, now called 'Ma'aleh Deragot' and 'Ma'aleh 'Aqrabim', are elaborately

---

[14] I. Roll (ed.), 'A Latin Imperial Inscription from the Time of Diocletian Found at Yotvata', *IEJ* 39 (1989): 239–60 (*ed. princeps*), interprets this as architectural terminology. I prefer to read this as a reference to a unit of horsemen and the name of the unit (*Constantianam?*), see Isaac, *Limits of Empire*, 188; similarly *Année Epigraphique* 1990, no. 1015. Eck sees *Costia* as a place-name in the ablative: W. Eck, '*Alam costia constituerunt*: Zum Verständnis einer Militärinschrift aus dem südlichen Negev', *Klio* 74 (1992): 395–400. That leaves us with the question what 'Bosia' or 'Osia' of the milestones just mentioned refers to. The inscription mentions a governor of Palaestina, Aufidius Priscus, who now occurs also on inscriptions from Caesarea: *CIIP* II, nos. 1268, 1271, 1272. Cf. Kennedy, *Roman Army in Jordan*, 209. See also: Z. Meshel, 'A Fort at Yotvata from the Time of Diocletian', *IEJ* 39 (1989): 228–38; A. Kindler, 'The Numismatic Finds from the Roman Fort at Yotvata', *IEJ* 39 (1989): 261–6. See below, source 7.

[15] The first description known to me is by A. Musil, *Arabia Petraea* (Vienna, 1907), II, 254 with figs. 139–40. See also: F. von Frank, 'Aus der Araba', *ZDPV* 57 (1934): 240–50; N. Glueck, 'Explorations in Eastern Palestine', *AASOR* 15 (1935): 40; Aharoni, 'The Roman Road to Aila (Elath)'; Rothenberg, 'The Arabah in Roman and Byzantine Times', in S. Applebaum (ed.), *Roman Frontier Studies 1967* (Tel Aviv, 1971), 211–23.

[16] M. Evenari et al., *The Negev: The Challenge of a Desert*, 2nd edn (Cambridge, 1982).

constructed with carefully made steps and watchtowers, possibly in the Tetrarchic period.[17]

Along this road a number of military posts is attested in literary sources and epigraphy: Carmel, Malatha, Mampsis, (B)Osia (Yotvata), Aela. The dates of these are as follows.

Carmel is mentioned by Eusebius, in the *Notitia* and in *P. Colt* 39: i.e. it was occupied from the Tetrarchic period–sixth century. Malatha is mentioned as a reference point by Eusebius and as military site in the *Notitia Dignitatum*, i.e. it was garrisoned before the end of the fourth century. Mampsis is listed in *P. Colt* and the Beer Sheva Edict(s),[18] i.e. it almost certainly was a military site in the fifth and sixth centuries, but the town was certainly inhabited already in the fourth century, as attested by the excavations. It may be significant that Eusebius does not mention it as a garrisoned town. (B)osia is Tetrachic–mid-fourth century as attested by an inscription and excavations. Aela was a legionary base from the Tetrarchic period onwards.[19]

Note also the following two sites: Mo'ah (Moyet 'Awad, ancient Calgouia?),[20] usually described as a road-station in the Arabah on the Petra–Gaza road. It could equally well have serviced travellers along the north–south road through the Arabah if it existed before the Tetrarchic period. Second, and perhaps more relevant for the present chapter: En Hazeva (= Eusebius' Thamara?) on the crossroads Mampsis–Phaenon and the north–south road through the Arabah.[21] En Hazeva certainly was occupied in the fourth century AD and would naturally have served as a station on the road from Mampsis to the southern Arabah, here discussed.

The Tabula Peutingeriana

The Peutinger map has important information, which, however, is hard to correlate with the facts on the ground. It shows three routes coming together at a site called Ad Dianam.[22]

---

[17] M. Harel, 'The Roman Road at Ma'aleh Aqrabim', *IEJ* 9 (1959): 175–9.

[18] Above, Chapter 15.

[19] The *legio X Fretensis* must have been transferred in the second half of the third century or the beginning of the fourth: cf. *CIIP* I/i, 25–6 with references.

[20] R. Cohen, 'Excavations at Moa 1981–85', *Qadmoniot* 20 (1987): 26–31; Isaac, *Limits of Empire*; Y. Tsafrir *et al.*, *Tabula Imperii Romani: Iudaea-Palaestina* (Jerusalem, 1994). Calgouia is listed by Ptolemy 5.16.8.

[21] Y. Tsafrir *et al.*, *Tabula Imperii Romani*. For Thamara/Thamaro see above and n. 9.

[22] To judge from the vignette on the map, Ad Dianam was a more significant site than Aela.

(1) The Clysma–Phara–Haila road in Sinai.[23]

(2) The *via nova Traiana* through Transjordan.[24] The Peutinger Table lists beyond Petra: Zadagatta (= Sadaqa), Hauarra,[25] and Praesidio (Khirbat al-Halde?). Between Humayma and Aqaba there are three known ancient sites: Quweira, Khalde, and Kithara, for one (or two) sites named on the Peutinger map.

(3) The road from Jerusalem to Elusa and from there to Oboda–Lysa–Gypsaria–Rasa–Ad Dianam, indicated on the Peutinger Table. This corresponds with the known route from Avdat past the Ramon Crater and thence southeast past Mezad Shaharut to Yotvata.[26]

This requires brief comment:

(1) Mayerson reconstructs the route and observes that the distance from Phara to Haila is given as 50 miles while it is in fact some 250 km So, it is clear that at least this distance given on the map is incorrect.

(2) The customary identification of Ad Dianam with Yotvata is a hypothesis, based on the traditionally recorded Arabic place-name Ghadian and on the fact that it is the only significant site in the Arabah north of Aqaba/Elath. It must now be considered uncertain whether Ghadian/Yotvata is to be identified with Ad Dianam of the Peutinger Table, for it certainly was named 'Osia' or 'Bosia' in the Tetrarchic period.[27] Furthermore I do not regard it as likely that the same place would have been called 'Costia' on the official Roman inscription of the same date cited above, as suggested by Werner Eck.[28] It will not do simply to claim that official, local Roman inscriptions of a single period have garbled the name of a military site to such an extent. As part of a solution it has been suggested that Ad Dianam was in fact one of

---

[23] P. Mayerson, 'The Clysma – Phara – Haila Road on the Peutinger Table', repr. in Mayerson (ed.), *Monks, Martyrs, Soldiers and Saracen* (Jerusalem, 1994), 173–82; 'The Pilgrim Routes to Mount Sinai and the Armenians', repr. in Mayerson (ed.), *Monks, Martyrs, Soldiers and Saracen*, 183–196; Tsafrir *et al.*, *Tabula Imperii Romani*; Kennedy, *Roman Army in Jordan*.

[24] D. F. Graf, 'The *Via Nova Traiana* in Arabia Petraea', in J. Humphrey (ed.), *The Roman and Byzantine Near East: Recent Archaeological Research* (Ann Arbor, 1995), 141–67, repr. in Graf, *Rome and the Arabian Frontier: From the Nabataeans to the Saracens* (Aldershot, 1997); Kennedy, *Roman Army in Jordan*.

[25] Auara: Ptolemy, *Geogr.* 5.16; Haura of the *Notitia Dignitatum* = modern Humayma.

[26] Lysa and Gypsaria are not identified with certainty, see Tsafrir *et al.*, *Tabula Imperii Romani*, map and p. 172, s.v. Lysa; 137, s.v. Gypsaria. Both are listed by Ptolemy, *Geogr.* 5.16. Rasa has not been identified. See F. M. Abel, *Géographie de la Palestine* (Paris, 1967), I, 214 for a suggestion.

[27] It is also quite unclear how the *via nova Traiana* would have reached Aela past the site of Yotvata.

[28] Above, n. 14.

the unidentified ancient sites along the *via nova Traiana*. That solves a problem along this road, but creates another problem, no less serious.

(3) Ad Dianam is a meeting point of three roads on the map, all three well identified. If we move Ad Dianam away from the Arabah it is hard to see how it could have been connected with road three here described and, besides, we would have another site (Yotvata) not listed. We must conclude that the Peutinger Table here has been corrupted and all efforts at engineering create new problems instead of the ones they are meant to solve. It may be better not to try to force a decision on the ancient name(s) of the fort at Yotvata in the presence of so much uncertain or conflicting evidence.

One far more important point is certain. The Peutinger Table fails to indicate a Roman road that is attested by Eusebius and has now been confirmed beyond doubt by Tetrarchic milestones, namely the north–south road through the Arabah discussed in this chapter. This is all the more remarkable, since the Peutinger Table lists Thamaro. Eusebius specifically mentions this as a village along the road from Hebron and Mampsis to Aela, but the Peutinger Table places it on an east–west road running from Rabba on to Elusa.[29] The obvious explanation for the absence of this road from the map is that this road really belongs to the Tetrarchic period and was not organized as a Roman road before the late third century. This reinforces – if reinforcement were needed – the view that the basic material of the Peutinger Table for this particular area reflects the second-century state of affairs and is based on a source of that period.[30]

It is clear now that Rothenberg was partly right and partly wrong in his conclusions. He was right in claiming that there was never a line of fourth-century *castella* in the Arabah, but there definitely was a north–south road running through it and almost certainly it was first constructed and organized in the Tetrarchic period. The existence of Roman milestones confirms that there was a public road, organized in the late third century, and the literary evidence clearly shows what were regarded as the main destinations for those travelling along the road. To the same period belong a number of military positions along the road – at least four, possibly five. There can be no doubt that construction and organization of the road, laid out in

---

[29] For Thamaro, spelled Θαμαρώ, see also Ptolemy, *Geogr.* 5.16.8. It is mentioned also by the *Notitia Dignitatum* 34.46, is listed in the Beer Sheva Edict(s) and appears on the Madaba Map.

[30] G. W. Bowersock, *Roman Arabia* (Cambridge, 1983), 169–71. Of course this is not meant to suggest that all of the map reflects material of this period. It is perfectly obvious that the map as we have it contains information from many stages.

the Tetrarchic period, was connected with the transfer of *legio X Fretensis* from Aelia (Jerusalem) to Aela (Aqaba). We should see this then as a part of the measures which accompanied the transfer of the legion to the Red Sea shore. Since the early second century there had been, of course, a road linking Aela with Transjordan, the *via nova Traiana*, as it is described on milestones. This road linked the southern part of the province of Arabia with the northern part, more specifically with the legionary headquarters and provincial centre at Bostra. Now, in the Tetrarchic period, the legion in Jerusalem was transferred to Aela on the Red Sea, and a public highway was organized through the Arabah, linking the new legionary base with the region of the abandoned legionary headquarters in Jerusalem. Aela was now linked with western Palestine as previously it had been connected with Transjordan, a conception that was expressed administratively by the transfer of the Negev to the province of Palaestina.

The Sources

Source 1

Eusebius, *Onomasticon* 6.8–16, Ἀρβώ (Gen 23:2)

"αὕτη ἐστὶ Χεβρών", κώμη νῦν μεγίστη, μητρόπολις οὖσα τὸ παλαιὸν τῶν ἀλλοφύλων, καὶ γιγάντων οἰκητήριον, καὶ βασίλειον μετὰ ταῦτα Δαυίδ.

Hieronymus 7.11–18

Arboc ... haec est autem eadem Chebron, olim metropolis Filistinorum ... distat ad meridianam plagam ab Aelia milibus circiter viginti duobus.

Arbo ... this is Hebron, now a very large village, once the capital of the Philistines... it is about twenty-two miles south of Aelia.

Source 2

Eusebius 42.10–13, Βηθλεέμ (Gen 35:19)

φυλῆς Ἰούδα, Αἰλίας ἄποθεν σημείοις ἐπὶ τὰ νότια περὶ τὴν φέρουσαν εἰς Χεβρὼν ὁδόν,

Hieronymus 43.19–21

Bethleem ... in sexto ab Aelia miliario contra meridianam plagam iuxta viam quae ducit Chebron.

Bethlehem ... six miles south of Aelia on the Hebron road.

Source 3

Eusebius 118.5–10, Κάρμηλος (1 Sam 25:2)

ἔνθα ἦν Νάβαλ. κώμη ἐστὶν εἰς ἔτι νῦν Χερμαλὰ ὀνομαζομένη, ἥτις ἑρμηνεύεται Κάρμηλος, ἀπὸ δεκάτου σημείου Χεβρὼν πρὸς ἀνατολάς, ἔνθα φρούριον ἐγκάθηται.

Hieronymus 119.4

Carmelus, ubi Nabal quondam Carmelius fuit, et nunc villa est Chermela nomine, in decimo lapide oppidi Chebron, vergens ad orientalem plagam, ubi et Romanum praesidium positum est.

Carmel ... is now a village named Chermela, ten miles east of Hebron, where a Roman garrison is located.

Source 4

Eusebius 172.20–24, Χερμέλ (Jos 15:55)

φυλῆς Ἰούδα, κώμη μεγίστη Χερμέλ ἐν τῷ Δαρωμᾷ, ὅθεν ἦν Ναβάλ, πλησίον Χεβρὼν πρὸς νότον. ἔνθα φρούρια κάθηται στρατιωτῶν.[31]

Chermel ... of the tribe of Juda, a very large village in the Daroma, whence Nabal, near Hebron and south of it, where a Roman garrison is based.

Source 5

Eusebius 8.7–9

λέγεται δέ τις Θαμαρὰ κώμη διεστῶσα Μάψις ἡμέρας ὁδόν, ἀπιόντων ἀπὸ Χεβρὼν εἰς Ἀϊλάμ, ἥτις νῦν φρούριόν ἐστι τῶν στρατιωτῶν.

Hieronymus 9.6

est ed aliud castellum Thamara, unius diei itinere a Mampsis oppido separatum, pergentibus Ailam de Chebron, ubi nunc praesidium positum est.

There also is a village Thamara, one day from the town of Mampsis on the road from Hebron to Aela, where now a garrison is located.

[31] Cf. *On.* 92.20.

Source 6

Eusebius 6.17–8.5, Αἰλάμ (Gen 14:1)

ἐν ἐσχάτοις ἐστὶ <Παλαιστίνης> παρακειμένη τῇ πρὸς μεσημβρίαν ἐρήμῳ
καὶ τῇ πρὸς αὐτὴν ἐρυθρᾷ θαλάσσῃ, πλωτῇ οὔσῃ τοῖς τε ἀπ᾽ Αἰγύπτου
περῶσι καὶ τοῖς ἀπὸ τῆς Ἰνδικῆς. ἐγκάθηται δὲ αὐτόθι τάγμα Ῥωμαίων
τὸ δέκατον. καλεῖται δὲ νῦν Ἄϊλά.

Hieronymus 7.25

Ailat in extremis finibus Palaestinae iuncta meridianae solitudini et mari
rubro, unde ex Aegypto Indiam et inde ad Aegyptum navigatur. sedet
autem ibi legio Romana cognomento decima. et olim quidem Ailath a vet-
eribus dicebatur.[32]

Aela is on the border of Palaestina, near the southern desert and the Red
Sea, from where they sail from Egypt to India and from India to Egypt.
There is based the so-called tenth Roman legion. Once it was called Ailath
by the ancients.

Source 7

AÉ 1986. 699; 1987. 961; 1990. 1015; 1992. 1714.

Perpetuae Paci / Diocletianus Augus(tus) et / [[Maximianus Aug(ustus) et]]
/ Constantius et Maximianus / nobilissimi Caesares / alam costia constit-
uerunt / per providentia(m) Prisci pr(a)esidis [[[provinciae —]]] / [[[——
]]] // Mul(tis) XX // Mul(tis) XL

---

[32] Hieronymus, *Comm. in Ez.* 47.18ff.: *lingua maris rubri, in cuius littore Ahila posita est, ubi nunc
moratur legio et praesidium Romanorum.* Cf. Ptolemy, *Geogr.* 5.17.1: ἡ δὲ Ἐλάνα κώμη κατὰ τὸν
μυχὸν κειμένη τοῦ ὁμωνύμου κόλπου ἐπέχει μοίρας

CHAPTER 17

Hatra Against Rome and Persia
From Success to Destruction

In the literary sources available to us Hatra is prominent during four episodes. According to Cassius Dio Hatra revolted against Trajan.[1] From this we may deduce that it had been part of the region under Roman control immediately after Trajan's campaign of conquest, but without having been besieged previously. This immediately shows our ignorance of the history of Hatra before Trajan besieged it and, more in general, of the course of Trajan's Parthian War.[2] We do not know what was the degree or form of dependence of Hatra on Parthia until 114 and we do not know what the state of affairs preceding the revolt was. We may assume there was no previous siege. It is possible that Hatra came to an agreement with Trajan and accepted some form of integration into the Roman Empire. It is also possible that Hatra's 'revolt' (ἀφειστήκεσαν) merely represents a phrase indicating that foreigners refused to accept Roman sovereignty and resisted it.[3] In any case, it clearly was part of the region Trajan wanted to annex into the provincial system of the Empire. Another element to be noticed in Dio's passage on Trajan's siege is the fact that the sun-god is believed to have taken an active part in the war. He was the origin of thunder, lightning, etc. that played a role during the siege to the advantage of the besieged.[4]

This is a revised version of a paper read at a conference in December 2009 in Amsterdam, organized by Lucinda Dirven, on 'Hatra: Politics, Religion and Culture Between Parthia and Rome (Amsterdam)'. It was published in L. Dirven (ed.), *Hatra: Politics, Culture and Religion between Parthia and Rome* (Stuttgart, 2013), 23–32.

[1] Dio 68, 31.

[2] As acknowledged by F. Lepper, *Trajan's Parthian War* (Oxford, 1948), ch. 1.

[3] Frontinus, describing Domitian's campaigns in Germany, says that by crushing the ferocity of these savage tribes 'he acted for the benefit of the provinces' (*Stratagems* 1.1.8). Plautius Silvanus Aelianus is on record as having 'brought over to the river bank under his protection kings hitherto unknown or hostile to the Roman people to pay homage to the Roman standards' (*ignotos ante aut infensos p. R. reges signa Romana adoraturos in ripam, quam tuebatur, perduxit*): ILS 986.

[4] See J. Tubach, 'The Triad of Hatra', in Dirven, *Hatra*, 201–11.

Turning to the second reported siege – or pair of sieges – of the city, in AD 197/8,[5] the fact that Septimius Severus spent time and effort to take the city during his march back shows and illustrates the importance of the location. In Dio's description it is worth noting that Severus marched south along the Euphrates, but withdrew northwards along the Tigris because the Roman army had exhausted supplies of every kind while advancing into Mesopotamia. We should keep this in mind when considering the effect of the army's progress, withdrawing northwards along the Tigris, and the reasons why Hatra would have resisted Rome at the time. The passing of an army with its demands for provisions could reduce a community to poverty.

The main reason for Severus' persistence, however, was according to Dio the matter of disgrace. This element may even be more important if the report by Herodian is right, that Barsemius, ruler of Hatra, sent Severus' enemy Niger a troop of archers.[6] Septimius Severus is on record as having punished other cities that supported Niger in the civil war. Antioch on the Orontes was deprived of many of its privileges and Neapolis (Shekhem) in Palestine – the traditional centre of the Samaritans – lost its city status, while neighbouring Samaria-Sebaste was awarded colonial rank in the same years.[7] After siding with Pescennius Niger against the victorious Septimius Severus, the city of Byzantium was besieged by Roman forces and suffered extensive damage and the loss of city-status in AD 196.[8] However, it was rebuilt toward the end of Severus' reign and afterwards by Caracalla.[9]

---

[5] D. B. Campbell, 'What Happened at Hatra? The Problem of the Severan Siege Operations', in P. Freeman and D. Kennedy (eds.), *The Defence of the Roman and Byzantine East* (Oxford, 1986), 51–8.

[6] Herodian 3.1.3.

[7] For Antiochia and Neapolis, see SHA, *Septimius Severus* 9.4–5: *Ant[h]ioc<h>ensibus iratior fuit, quod et administrantem se in oriente <in>riserant et Nigrum etiam victum iuverant. denique multa his ademit. Neapolitanis etiam Pal<a>estinensibus ius civitatis tulit, quod pro Nigro diu in armis fuerunt.* For the colonial status awarded Sebaste: Paulus, *Dig.* L 15, 8, 7: *Divus quoque Severus in Sebastenam civitatem coloniam deduxit.* Colonial coinage: G. F. Hill, *British Museum Catalogue, Palestine*, pp. xxxix, 80, nos. 12–13. The latest pre-colonial coinage dates to 201/2: A. Kindler and A. Stein, *A Bibliography of the City Coinage of Palestine: From the 2nd Century* BC *to the 3rd Century* AD (Oxford, 1987), 226–9. How long Neapolis' punishment was maintained is not clear. The city later received colonial status as well, as appears from coins of 251–3: S. Ben Dor, 'Quelques remarques à propos d'une monnaie de Néapolis', *Revue Biblique* 59 (1952): 251–2, pl. 9.1; K. Harl, 'The Coinage of Neapolis in Samaria, A.D. 244–52', *American Numismatic Society, Museum Notes* 29 (1984), nos. 151 and 154 with comments on p. 68; A. Kindler, 'Was there a Detachment of the Third Legion Cyrenaica at Neapolis in AD 251–253?', *Israel Numismatic Journal* 4 (1980): 56–8. From both Neapolis and Samaria there is evidence of a military presence at some stage in the first and second centuries: B. Isaac, *The Limits of Empire: the Roman Army in the East*, 2nd edn (Oxford, 1992), 430–1.

[8] Dio 74.6–14; Herodian 2.14–3.6; Hesychius 36, ed. Praeger 1, p. 15.

[9] Hesychius 38.

Herodian's remark about archers from Hatra is yet another testimony of the prominence of the Hatreni in this capacity. Also: if Herodian is right this shows that in Dio's information some matters of importance are missing, to say the least.[10] Finally, it raises the possibility that Hatra regularly provided Rome with troops like other dependent or client states during the period of Roman ascendancy in Northern Mesopotamia – following the campaign of Lucius Verus in the 160s.[11] They would have been in a similar relationship as, for instance, the Batavi in the first century. It almost certainly is significant that this also appears to be the period in which Hatra became a kingdom, whatever the relationship of those kings with respectively Parthia and Rome. It is possible, although there is no direct proof, that this was the result of Roman interference, following the war in the 160s. After all, it is well known that Rome determined the rank and titles of the rulers of friendly, dependent states. In other words: Hatra may have become a client kingdom in this phase of its existence.[12] It remains a hypothesis, but is a possibility. This too was the period in which extensive fortifications and numerous major public buildings in the city were constructed.[13]

In connection with the subject of honour, image, and status, we may note the remarkable statement that Severus watched the storming of the

---

[10] Cf. C. R. Whittaker, *Herodian* (London and Cambridge, 1969), II, 317, n. 4: 'Herodian's chronology differs seriously from the order of events in Xiphilinus' epitome of Dio, which records two attacks on Hatra, both after the capture of Ctesiphon (AD 197/8); see Dio 75.9ff. But the words of Dio give no real chronology.' In any case, we cannot be certain whether Severus tried and failed once or twice to capture the city.

[11] M. Sommer, 'In the Twilight: Hatra between Rome and Iran', in Dirven, *Hatra*, 33–44, considers it more likely that Hatra, during this period, was dependent on Parthia than on Rome. Cf. S. R. Hauser, 'Hatra und das Königreich der Araber', in J. Wiesehöfer (ed.), *Das Partherreich und seine Zeugnisse* (Stuttgart, 1998), 493–528, opting also for the theory that it belonged to Parthia.

[12] M. R. Cimma, *Reges socii et amici populi romani* (Milan, 1976); D. Braund, *Rome and the Friendly King* (London and New York, 1984). I do not claim more than I state here explicitly. It is therefore incorrect to assert that in my view 'Hatra and its region were very much part of the Roman Empire in the second and third centuries CE': Dirven, in Dirven, *Hatra*, 12–13. The presence of a Roman garrison in the period 238–40 has indeed been proved. Below I argue that Hatra resisted any attempt on the part of major empires to take full control.

[13] D. Kennedy and D. Riley, *Rome's Desert Frontier from the Air* (London, 1990), 105–7; M. Gawlikowski, 'A Fortress in Mesopotamia: Hatra', in E. Dabrowa (ed.), *The Roman and Byzantine Army in the East: Proceedings of a Colloquium held at the Jagiellonian University, Krakow in September 1992* (Krakow, 1994), 47–56, at 49: recent excavations of ramparts; M. Sommer, *Hatra* (Mainz, 2003), 47–79; more recently: M. Sommer, *Roms Orientalische Steppengrenze: Palmyra – Edessa – Dura-Europos – Hatra. Eine Kulturgeschichte von Pompeius bis Diocletian*, Oriens et Occidens 9 (Stuttgart, 2005). Note also W. al-Salihi, 'Military Considerations in the Defence of Hatra', *Mesopotamia* 26 (1991): 187–94, at 188: outer earth wall, ca. 500 m from main wall. diam. ca. 3 km (excavation report awaits publication); 188 for the main wall, description, discussion.Hikmat Basher al-Aswad, 'Water Sources at Hatra', *Mesopotamia* 26 (1991): 195–211.

city seated on a lofty tribunal, an image which evokes the more famous one of Xerxes witnessing the defeat of his fleet at Salamis in 480, as described by Herodotus and Aeschylus.[14] This shows a clear difference in the execution of the role of the two commanders. Trajan was almost wounded himself at Hatra over eighty years before and therefore clearly involved in the battle himself. Severus, at least on this occasion, was very distant.[15]

Noteworthy is the importance of the cavalry and archers, said to be Arabians, which in Semitic languages in antiquity is a term for nomads rather than an ethnic or linguistic designation.[16] However, Dio here refers to Arabs in an ethnic sense as is clear, for instance, from the statement that he expected 'the Arabians to come to terms'. This refers to the Hatrene ruler and his people. The name of the province of Arabia, *Arabia Provincia*, established in Trajan's reign also indicates that the Romans understood this to be an ethnic designation, for they were well aware that the Nabataeans in Petra and Bostra were no nomads.[17] It is not unlikely that the name 'Arabia' had broader associations than 'Nabataea'. The Province of Arabia had a grandiose name, like the two provinces of Germania which somehow conveyed the message that Rome controlled all of Germania. To return to Hatra: its rulers are described as sovereigns of Hatra and Arabs in local inscriptions.[18] Arabs were therefore understood to be the non-urban Hatreni.

Here, as in the passage about Trajan's siege there is an emphasis on divine interference (by the sun-god), reflecting a widely held belief in antiquity in the active role played by gods on the battle field. Dio was obviously aware of the importance of the cult to the city and its inhabitants. One further point to make here is the usual stereotype encountered also in Tacitus that Syrian troops are inferior to those recruited from Europe.[19] In this

---

[14] Hdt. 8.90; Aeschylus, *Persae* 465–70.

[15] For the place of the commander on the battle field in this period: A. K. Goldsworthy, *The Roman Army at War: 100 BC–AD 200* (Oxford, 1996), 152–63.

[16] For the meaning of the term 'Arab' indicating 'nomadic' or 'nomadic origin' in the sense of a way of life, see R. Zadok, *On West Semites in Babylonia during the Chaldaean and Acheaemenian Periods: n Onomastic Study* (Jerusalem, 1977), 192; I. Eph'al, '"Ishmael" and "Arabs": A Transformation of Ethnological Terms', *Journal of Near Eastern Studies* 35 (1976): 225–35; *The Ancient Arabs. Nomads on the Borders of the Fertile Crescent 9th-5th Centuries bc* (Leiden, 1982). B. Aggoula, *Inventaire des inscriptions Hatréennes* (Paris, 1991), translates 'ARABY' as Bédouins, e.g. nos. 336, 343. This seems anachronistic. For the relationship between Hatra and the nomads in the region, see K. Dijkstra, 'State and Steppe: The Socio-Political Implications of Hatra Inscription 79', *Journal of Semitic Studies* 35 (1990): 81–98 with references to earlier discussion on pp. 90–3, nn. 26–31. See Chapter 6, pp. 144–7.

[17] There is no obvious reason why they refrained from calling the new province 'Nabataea'.

[18] The king, Sanatruq, and his son are called mlk' d'arab, king of Arabia, e.g. in inscriptions nos. 79, 195–9, 373, 378.

[19] D. L. Kennedy, '"European" Soldiers and the Severan Siege of Hatra', in Freeman and Kennedy, *Defence of the Roman and Byzantine East*, 397–429. Kennedy has shown that Severus' failure at Hatra

connection: it ought to be superfluous to point this out again, but appears not to be so, that the troops meant are indeed units from Europe, the continent, not from Dura Europos on the Orontes.[20] This is obvious: Cassius Dio was a Roman senator, writing in Greek for an empire-wide public, not for our contemporary specialists on the Roman Near East or the army there. For Dio and his readers Europeans were inhabitants of a continent, not of a small town on the Euphrates. When Dio refers elsewhere to 'Europeans' he does so also in clear contrast to Asians or Africans.[21] If he had meant to refer to soldiers from Dura Europos he would have explained what was meant, just as, in our times, someone would add an explanation if he mentions Amsterdam, meaning the village of Amsterdam, Ohio, rather than the city of Amsterdam in the Netherlands.

The third episode, the first of the two sieges of the city by Ardashir, the newly victorious Sasanian ruler, clearly implies that Hatra had gone over to the Roman side without a siege by 229.[22] There was a detachment of Roman troops there by 238–40, as indicated by three famous Latin inscriptions.[23] However, the city was attacked by Ardashir already in 229, shortly after he had defeated the Parthians (226) and gained power. Hatra now resisted the Sasanian Ardashir when he marched against Rome, so it appears that the policy of Hatra was to resist any foreign power that attempted to interfere

may have been less damaging, at least diplomatically, than Dio represents it. For the stereotype, see E. L. Wheeler, 'The Laxity of the Syrian Legions', in D. L. Kennedy, *The Roman Army in the East* (Ann Arbor, 1996), 229–76; B. Isaac, *The Invention of Racism in Classical Antiquity* (Princeton, 2004), ch. 5. Whittaker, *Herodian*, II, 320, n. 1, comments on Herodian: Herodian does not mention the mutiny of the European legions reported by Dio. He argues that this probably stemmed from the executions of a praetorian tribune, Julius Crispus, and Severus' commander, Laetus. It is also possible that the entire episode is tendentious. In any case, as noted, it represents a stereotypical difference between eastern and European troops.

[20] Kennedy's publication cited in the previous note should have sufficed, but it appears that there are still proponents of the theory that Dio referred to troops from Dura.

[21] *Zonaras Gallorum in Italiam incursionem enarrans 7.23 sua hausit e Plutarcho et Dione. Dionea haec sunt:* 1) οἱ δ' Εὐρωπαῖοι Γαλάται, ὧν οἱ Ἀσιᾶται νομίζονται ἄποικοι ... 13.54.10: τάς τε Ἄλπεις πρῶτος ἀνθρώπων τῶν οὐκ Εὐρωπαίων, ὅσα γε ἡμεῖς ἴσμεν, σὺν στρατῷ διέβη. 290.18-21: Ὁ δέ γε Μάλλιος τότε Πισιδίαν Λυκαονίαν τε καὶ Παμφυλίαν τῆς τε Γαλατίας τῆς Ἀσιανῆς πολλὰ προσηγάγετο. ἔστι γάρ τι κἀνταῦθα γένος αὐτῶν, ἐκ τοῦ Εὐρωπαίου ἀποδάσμιον. Βρέννον γάρ ποτε βασιλέα σφῶν προστησάμενοι τήν τε Ἑλλάδα καὶ τὴν Θρᾴκην ἐπέδραμον ... 251.20–252: Δίων δὲ ὁ Κοκκηιανὸς ταύτας πλησίον φησὶ Ἴβηρος εἶναι ποταμοῦ, πλησίον τῶν Εὐρωπαίων Ἡρακλείων στηλῶν, ἃς νήσους Ἕλληνες μὲν καὶ Ῥωμαῖοι κοινῶς Γυμνησίας φασίν, Ἴβηρες δὲ Βαλερίας ἤτοι ὑγιεινάς. Tzetz. *Ad Lycophr.* 633.

[22] See S. R. Hauser, 'On the Significance of the Final Siege of Hatra', in Dirven, *Hatra*, 119–39.

[23] (1) *AE* 1983. 935. F. Vattioni, *Le iscrizioni di Hatra* (Naples, 1981), 109–10, no. 3 (B) – *AE* 1983. *AE* 1958.240. D. Oates, 'A Note on Three Latin Inscriptions from Hatra', *Sumer* 11 (1955): 40–3, no. 81; fig. 2. (B) – *AE* 1958. A. Maricq, 'Les dernières années de Hatra: L'alliance romaine', *Syria* 34 (1957): 288–96 (B) – *AE* 1958. (2) *AE* 1958. 238. *PIR* (2. Aufl.) C 1025. *PIR* (2. Aufl.) C 992. (3) *AE* 1958. 239.

directly or impose direct control. The Sassanians wanted to re-occupy all
of Mesopotamia (at least), occupied Carrhae and Nisibis in 238 and Nisibis
again in 260. As part of these operations they wanted to occupy Hatra,
just like the Roman emperors who campaigned in Mesopotamia. Dio says
Ardashir wanted to use it as a base for attacking the Romans.[24] Whatever
he had in mind, once Ardashir captured the city in 240,[25] it was destroyed
and never refounded. Ammianus saw the site in 363 and describes it as an
'old settlement, long abandoned in absolute solitude'.[26]

If we want to understand the significance of Hatra against the background of the relationship of the two empires in general, we are immediately faced with the reality that this relationship itself has been a matter of
debate on the part of modern scholars.[27] This is not the occasion to review
all of this in its complexity – and even if I decided to make such an attempt,
this still would not resolve matters to the satisfaction of everybody. It will
have to suffice here briefly to give my own views on the role Hatra played
in the conflict between Rome and Persia. Among present company there
is no need to insist on the limitations of the literary documentation found
in the Roman literature, while the Persian sources are almost non-existent.
Obviously we must be very cautious in accepting any statement made in
Roman sources about Persian aims, motivation, and ambitions, except as
an expression of what the Romans thought about Persia or wanted others
to think. This is not to say that opinions among the Romans were uniform
or remained the same over time. Strabo describes the Parthians as powerful but virtually part of the Roman Empire.[28] Tacitus states that Artabanus
III, in AD 35, a few decades after Strabo wrote, made extreme demands,
requiring restoration of the old border between Persia and Macedonia as it
was before Alexander's campaign.[29] In the third century Dio reports similar
far-reaching claims on the part of Ardashir.[30] A modified and slightly more

---

[24] D. Potter, *Prophecy and History* (Oxford, 1990), 372–5, suggests that the wars between the first
Sassanid kings and Rome were caused by the desire of Ardashir to establish control over the frontier
client kingdoms like Hatra and Armenia which Rome considered part of her empire. It may not
be wise to limit Sasanian ambition to such an extent. For the siege: Campbell, 'What Happened at
Hatra?'

[25] *Codex Manichaicus Coloniensis* 18.1-16, Koenen and Römer (eds.), pp. 10–12 (Dodgeon and Lieu,
p. 33): 'When I was twenty[-four] years old, in the year in which Dariadaxir (i.e. Ardashir), the king
of Persia, subjugated the city of Hatra.'

[26] Ammianus 25.8.5.

[27] E. Kettenhofen, *Die römisch-persischen Kriege des 3. Jahrhunderts n. Chr. nach der Inschrift Šāhpuhrs
I* (Wiesbaden, 1982). For my views on these matters, see Isaac, *Limits of Empire*, ch. 1.

[28] Strabo 6.4.2 (288).

[29] Tacitus, *Ann.* 6.31.

[30] Dio 80.3; cf. Herodian 6.2.2.

moderate demand is ascribed to Shapur II in the fourth century.[31] These then are Roman reports concerning enemy demands over the centuries that are a subject of debate. I will not return to this discussion on this occasion.

It will suffice to say that my view still is that there is little basis for the argument that Sasanian demands were consistently more militant than those of the Parthians. Diplomacy has to be seen and checked against the background of reality, of deeds and military action. Let us briefly note some salient points. In the first century BC the first extended period of warfare between Rome and Parthia saw Crassus' invasion and defeat in Parthia (54 BC) and, during the civil wars, an extended Parthian invasion of Roman territory (41–38 BC). In the first century AD a Roman Eastern campaign turned a diplomatic conflict regarding Armenia into a military one (AD 57–8, 61–2). The second century saw Trajan's failed attempt to annex all of Mesopotamia, down to the Persian Gulf (114–17). It ended in failure, but Armenia remained under Roman control, a situation unacceptable to Parthia. The result was a Parthian invasion in 155, followed by a Roman counter-attack, involving raids deep into Mesopotamia, including the plundering of Seleucia and Ctesiphon. The Roman army withdrew from Babylonia, but the long-term effect was a continued Roman presence in parts of Northern Mesopotamia from the 160s onwards. In the 190s Septimius Severus attacked again, plundered Seleucia and Ctesiphon again, and annexed Northern Mesopotamia as a province. Further attacks, attempting to expand Roman control under Caracalla, failed and were followed by a negotiated peace. When the Sasanian Ardashir took over from the Parthian Artabanus he inherited a seriously reduced empire as a result of these sixty years of Roman attacks. There is no need to assume a radical change in imperial ideology following the succession of ruling dynasties to explain the Persian counter-attacks in the third century. Persia lost an important and affluent region and the Sasanian military offensive against Rome was as predictable a response to this encroachment as were the Parthian raids in the years 41–38 BC to Crassus' major invasion in 54. The two powers continued their struggle for another four centuries, but the sequel no longer concerns us on this occasion, since Hatra ceased to exist.

The location of Hatra clearly was a position felt to be essential for those who wanted to gain control of Northern Mesopotamia – if they were based in Babylonia, or for those who wanted to act militarily in the South, if they controlled the North. Hence the efforts made by Trajan, Septimius Severus, and Ardashir. Yet it was not a place that needed to function as a city, at least

---

[31] Ammianus 17.5.4–5; also 17.14.1.

in the eyes of Ardashir, for he destroyed it. Its location remained essential, as is clear from the fact that Julian's army passed the site during their withdrawal in 363.[32] It was hostile to Rome at stages, resisting Trajan and Severus, but had a modest garrison under Gordian, presumably because it was opposed to the Sassanian efforts to assert themselves, using their city as a base. Like Palmyra, Hatra profited from a key position in times of peace, but even more than Palmyra it paid for its profitable location when this invited intervention in times of war. It succeeded at least three times in defending itself against besiegers and when, on a fourth (or fifth) occasion, it failed, that was the end, joining a long list of minor players who succeeded for a while in maintaining themselves in the Near East, between the major powers in the West and East, but that eventually were crushed.

The evidence concerning Hatra in peacetime is far less extensive and vivid than that from Palmyra. It is not mentioned in Talmudic sources, unlike Palmyra.[33] The rich epigraphical material from Palmyra splendidly shows its role policing the caravan trade, even if essential information can be gained only by systematic interpretation.[34] Such material is missing at Hatra, which, none the less, had quite an epigraphic habit, but a different one from that maintained by the Palmyrenes.[35]

Another clear instance of the economic significance that being a trade centre on a main road in the desert could have is Batnae/Batnai (Suruc). It lies in the Syrian desert on the road from Antioch–Beroia (Aleppo)–Hierapolis/Bambyke (Mambij)–Euphrates.[36] The distance from Batnai to the Euphrates along the road is about 60 km, which is only a little more than that from Hatra to the Tigris.

Key is the description by Ammianus:

> The town of Batne, founded in Anthemusia in early times by a band of Macedonians, is separated by a short space from the river Euphrates; it is filled with wealthy traders, when, at the yearly festival, near the beginning of the month of September, a great crowd of every condition gathers for the

[32] Above, n. 26.

[33] A. Oppenheimer et al., *Babylonia Judaica in the Talmudic Period* (Wiesbaden, 1983), 477–8: Hutra and Hatar in Talmudic sources are not to be identified with Hatra. Unlike Palmyra (Tadmor) therefore Hatra is not mentioned in any Talmudic source.

[34] L. Dirven, 'The Nature of the Caravan Trade between Palmyra and Dura Europos', *ARAM* 8 (1996), 39–54, has shown that a direct link between Palmyra and Dura on the Euphrates complements the long familiar route to Sura, cf. M. Sommer, *Hatra*, 44–6, for Hatra as a trade centre.

[35] Aggoula, *Inventaire* (991). Most of the relevant texts are statue bases. If I am not mistaken only one inscription, no. 65, mentions merchants.

[36] F. V. M. Cumont, *Etudes syriennes* (Paris, 1917), 19–23; E. Honigmann, *Evêques et évêchés monophysites d'Asie antérieure au VIe siècle* (Louvain, 1951), I, 102.

fair, to traffic in the wares sent from India and China, and in other articles that are regularly brought there in great abundance by land and sea. This district the above-mentioned leader [sc. Nohodares, a Persian commander who had received instructions to invade Mesopotamia in 354] made ready to invade, on the days set for this celebration, through the wilderness and the grass-covered banks of the Abora; but he was betrayed by information given by some of his own soldiers ...[37]

Here we have an explicit and unambiguous statement concerning the essential commercial importance of a town along a desert route which served as an annual market for the long-distance trade. Ammianus emphasizes that the Persian commander, if he had been successful, would 'have devastated the whole region like thunderbolt'.[38] The passage shows (a) how important Batnae was as a commercial centre, (b) it played this role only during an annual market, not continuously, (c) the crucial military importance a place like this could have.

The importance the Romans attached to this kind of centre is shown by the legislation limiting markets for the exchange of goods between Rome and Persia to specific locations agreed upon by treaty between Rome and Persia.[39] The locations are Nisibis, Callinicum, and Artaxata. The reason is stated: in order to prevent the secrets of either kingdom from being disclosed. It should be noted that Nisibis at that time was under Persian control, while Artaxata was the capital of Armenia.

A comparable regulation is found in a treaty of 562.[40] This contains a clause stipulating that merchants must import their wares through the traditionally appointed toll-stations. Another relevant clause, in this connection, stipulates that 'Saracen and other barbarian merchants are not allowed to use unknown and little used routes, but must pass through Nisibis and Dara and with formal permission only'.

To return to the evidence concerning Hatra, one interesting exception is an inscription found 20 km from the site: it commemorates the

---

[37] Ammianus 14.3.3–4: *Batnae municipium in Anthemusia conditum Macedonum manu priscorum ab Euphrate flumine breui spatio disparatur refertum mercatoribus opulentis, ubi annua sollemnitate prope Septembris initium mensis ad nundinas magna promiscae fortunae conuenit multitudo ad commercanda, quae Indi mittunt et Seres, alia plurima uehi terra mari que consueta. Hanc regionem praestitutis celebritati diebus, invadere parans dux ante dictus, per solitudines Aborae amnis herbidas ripas, suorum indicio proditus ...*

[38] *Quod si impetrasset, fulminis modo cuncta vastarat.*

[39] *Cod. Iust.* 4.63.4 (Krueger), dated 408–9. Cf. Oppenheimer *et al.*, *Babylonia Judaica*, 327. The text refers to an agreement that probably goes back to Jovian, AD 363.

[40] Menander Protector, fr. 11 (Müller, *FHG* IV, 208ff.); cf. E. Winter, 'Handel und Wirtschaft in sasanidisch-(ost)römischen Verträgen und Abkommen', *Münstersche Beiträge zur antiken Handelsgeschichte* 6 (1987): 46–74.

construction of a caravan station at a watering hole along the road, set up by the commander of the guards.[41] This is an exception, but there can be little doubt that Hatra played a role somewhat similar to that of Palmyra, Batnae, and other centres of commercial transit.[42] It was situated on a main road along the Tigris, parallel to the route along the Euphrates – which explains its importance in war as well. Whatever the sources of its obvious wealth, it dominated an important route,[43] namely the one linking Singara (only roughly 100 km away) with the Tigris and Seleucia-Ctesiphon with Nisibis. This was the route Zeugma–Edessa, Rhesaina, Nisibis, Singara, Hatra, Tigris. We should note that it appears as such on the *Tabula Peutingeriana*, the Peutinger Map which here apparently reflects the second and third centuries and locates it on a main route: it lists the locations Singara–Hatra–Naharra–Seleucia/Ctesiphon. Singara is shown to be connected with Rhesaina and Nisibis. The extent of our ignorance concerning essential matters is shown by the fact that we have not the slightest idea whether any other centre replaced Hatra in the role it must have played during the period of its prosperity, or how else its destruction affected trade along the Tigris route. The oldest firmly dated monument in Hatra appears to be a shrine build in 98. The building of the great iwans started in the second century.[44] We may therefore assume that the city played its successful role during roughly a century-and-a-half.

---

[41] Aggoula, Appendice, no. 5 from Sa'rdiyya. Note also H.65, l. 5: lgr tgry', 'en l'honneur des commerçants' (Aggoula), but the reading is not quite certain.

[42] The question whether it was a 'caravan city' and whether this is an appropriate description of other cities has been discussed again in L. Gregoratti, 'Hatra: On the West of the East', in Dirven, *Hatra*, 45–54, basically positive although the term 'caravan city' is not used; T. Kaizer, 'Questions and Problems Concerning the Sudden Appearance of Material Culture of Hatra in the First Centuries CE', in Dirven, *Hatra*, 57–72, at 62–6, reaching a negative conclusion.

[43] G. Widengren, 'The Establishment of the Sasanian Dynasty in the Light of New Evidence', in *Atti del convegno internazionale sul tema: La Persia nel Medioevo* (Rome, 1971), 711–82, at 757; H. J. W. Drijvers, 'Hatra, Palmyra und Edessa', *ANRW* 2.8 (1977), 803–7 and bibl. on 877–9. For other tentative explanations regarding the source of Hatrene wealth, there are the papers by Sommer, 'In the Twilight', and by Gregoratti, 'Hatra: On the West of the East'. The latter in particular analyses the relationship of the site of Hatra to the road-system.

[44] M. Gawlikowski, 'A Fortress in Mesopotamia: Hatra', 52; 'The Development of the City of Hatra', in Dirven, *Hatra*, 73–80, at 77–9; R. V. Ricciardi and A. Peruzzetto, 'The Ancient Phases of the Great Sanctuary at Hatra', in Dirven, *Hatra*, 81–90; H. B. al-Aswad, 'New Discoveries in Temple XIV in Hatra', in Dirven, *Hatra*, 107–14.

Bibliography

Abel, F.-M., *Géographie de la Palestine* (Paris, 1967).

Adams, J. N., 'Language Use in the Army in Egypt', in Adams, J. N., Janse, M. and Swain, S. (eds.), *Bilingualism in Ancient Society: Language Contact and the Written Text* (Oxford, 2002), 599–623.

Bilingualism and the Latin Language (Cambridge, 2003).

Aggoula, B., *Inventaire des inscriptions Hatréennes* (Paris, 1991).

Aharoni, Y., 'The Roman Road to Aila (Elath)', *IEJ* 4 (1954): 9–16.

Alon, G., *The Jews in their Land in the Talmudic Age* (Jerusalem, 1980–4).

Alston, R., *Soldier and Civilian in Roman Egypt: A Social History* (London, 1995).

Amato, E. (ed.) and Julien, Y. (trans.), *Favorinos d'Arles, Oeuvres*, I. *Introduction général – Témoignages – Discours aux Corinthiens – Sur la Fortune* (Paris, 2005).

Andrade, N. J., *Syrian Identity in the Greco-Roman World* (Cambridge, 2013).

Applebaum, S. (ed.), *Roman Frontier Studies* (Tel Aviv, 1967), 211–23.

Prolegomena to the Study of the Second Jewish Revolt (AD 132–135) (Oxford, 1976)

Asheri, D., Lloyd, A. and Corcella, A., *A Commentary on Herodotus Books I–IV* (Oxford, 2007).

Attridge, H. W. and Oden, R. A., *Philo of Byblos: The Phoenician History, Introduction, Critical Text, Translation, Notes*, CBQMS 9 (Washington, DC, 1981).

Avi-Yonah, M., *Geschichte der Juden im Zeitalter des Talmud* (Berlin, 1962).

The Holy Land: From the Persian to the Arab Conquest, A Historical Geography (Grand Rapids, MI, 1977).

Barnes, T. D., 'The Family and Career of Septimius Severus', *Historia* 16 (1967): 87–107.

'Legislation Against the Christians', *JRS* 58 (1968): 32–50.

Baumgarten, A. I., *The Phoenician History of Philo of Byblos: A Commentary* (Leiden, 1981).

Beard, M., North, J. and Price, S. (eds.), *Religions of Rome*, 2 vols. (Cambridge, 1998).

Beaujeu, J., *La religion romaine à l'apogée de l'empire* (Paris, 1955).

Bekker-Nielsen, T., 'Academic Science and Warfare in the Classical World', in Bekker-Nielsen, T. and Hannestad, L. (eds.), *War as a Cultural and Social Force: Essays on Warfare in Antiquity* (Copenhagen, 2001), 120–9.

Bell, H. I., *et al.*, *The Abinnaeus Archive* (Oxford, 1962).

Bikerman, E., 'La Coelé-Syrie: Notes de Géographie Historique', *Revue Biblique* 54 (1947): 256–68.

Boffo, L., *Iscrizioni greche e latine per lo studio della bibbia* (Brescia, 1994).

Botermann, H., *Das Judenedikt des Kaisers Claudius: Römischer Staat und Christiani im 1. Jahrhundert* (Stuttgart, 1996).

Bowersock, G. W., *Greek Sophists and the Roman Empire* (Oxford, 1969).

'Roman Senators from the Near East: Syria, Judaea, Arabia, Mesopotamia', in *Atti del colloquio internazionale AIEQL su epigrafia e ordine senatorio, Roma 1981* (Rome, 1982), II, 651–68.

'The Three Arabias in Ptolemy's Geography', in Gatier, P.-L., Helly, B., and Rey-Coquais, J.-P. (eds.), *Géographie historique au Proche Orient: Syrie, Phénicie, Arabie, grecques, romaines, byzantines* (Paris, 1988), 47–53.

Bréguet, E., 'Urbi et Orbi', in Bibauw, J. (ed.), *Hommages à Marcel Renard*, Collection Latomus 101 (Brussels, 1969), 140–52.

Brodersen, K., *Studien zur römischen Raumerfassung* (Hildesheim, 1995).

Brunt, P. A., 'Laus Imperii', in Garnsey, P. D. A. and Whittaker, C. R. (eds.), *Imperialism in the Ancient World* (Cambridge, 1978), 162–78.

Calame, C., *Alcman: Introduction, texte critique, témoignages, traduction et commentaire* (Rome, 1983).

Campbell, D. A., *Greek Lyric* (Cambridge, 1938).

Campbell, D. B., 'What Happened at Hatra? The Problem of the Severan Siege Operations', in Freeman, P. and Kennedy, D. (eds.), *The Defence of the Roman and Byzantine East* (Oxford, 1986), 51–8.

Campbell, J. B., *The Emperor and the Roman Army* (Oxford, 1984).

The Roman Army, 31 BC–AD 337: A Sourcebook (London, 1994).

Chaniotis, A. and Ducrey, P. (eds.), *Army and Power in the Ancient World* (Stuttgart, 2002)

Champion, T. C. (ed.), *Centre and Periphery: Comparative Studies in Archaeology* (London, 1989).

Champlin, E., *Fronto and Antonine Rome* (Cambridge, 1980).

Charlesworth, M., '*Providentia* and *Aeternitas*', *HTR* 29 (1936): 107–32.

Christof, E., *Das Glück der Stadt: die Tyche von Antiocheia und andere Stadttychen* (Frankfurt am Main, 2001).

Cohen, S. J. D., *The Beginnings of Jewishness* (Berkeley, CA, 1999).

Collinet, P., *Histoire de l'école de droit de Beyrouth* (Paris, 1925).

Conché, M., *Héraclite, Fragments* (Paris, 1986).

Corcella, A., *Libro IV: La Scizia e la Libia/Erodoto* (Rome, 1993).

Cotter, W., 'The Collegia and Roman Law: State Restrictions on Voluntary Associations 64 BCE–200 CE', in Kloppenborg, J. S. and Wilson, S. G., *Voluntary Associations in the Graeco-Roman World* (London, 1996), 74–89.

Cotton, H. M. and Eck, W., 'A New Inscription from Caesarea Maritima and the Local Elite of Caesarea Maritima', in Rutgers, L. V. (ed.), *What Athens has to Do with Jerusalem: Essays on Classical, Jewish and Early Christian Art and Archaeology in Honor of Gideon Foerster* (Leuven, 2002), 375–91.

Cotton, H. M., Hoyland, R. G., Price, J. J., and Wasserstein, D. J. (eds.), *From Hellenism to Islam: Cultural and Linguistic Change in the Roman Near East* (Cambridge, 2009),

Courtney, E., *A Commentary on the Satires of Juvenal* (London, 1980).

Crawford, M. H., *Roman Republican Coinage*, 2 vols. (London, 1974).

Cumont, F., 'L'éternité des empereurs romains', *Revue d'histoire et de literature religieuses* 1 (1896): 435–52.

de Jonge, P., *Philological and Historical Commentary on Ammianus Marcellinus, XVI* (Groningen, 1972).

Philological and Historical Commentary on Ammianus Marcellinus, XVII (Groningen, 1976).

de Ste. Croix, G. E. M., 'Why were the Early Christians Persecuted?', *Past and Present* 26 (1963): 6–38.

'Why were the Early Christians Persecuted? A Rejoinder', *Past and Present* 27 (1964): 28–33.

Deonna, W., 'L'ex-voto de Cypsélos à Delphes: Le symbolisme du palmieret des grenouilles', *RHR* 139 (1951): 162–207; 140 (1951), 5–58.

Derow, P. and Parker, R. (eds.), *Herodotus and his World* (Oxford, 2003).

Devijver, H., 'Equestrian Officers from the East', in Freeman, P. and Kennedy, D. (eds.), *The Defence of the Roman and Byzantine East* (Oxford, 1986), 109–225.

Diels, H. A. and Schramm, E., *Herons Belopoiika, Philons Belopoiika: Griechisch und Deutsch* (Berlin, 1918–19; repr. Leipzig, 1970).

Dirven, L. (ed.), *Hatra: Politics, Culture and Religion between Parthia and Rome* (Stuttgart, 2013).

Dodds, E. R., *The Ancient Concept of Progress* (Oxford, 1973).

Dubuisson, M., 'Y a-t-il une politique linguistique romaine?', *Ktema* 7 (1982): 187–210.

Ducrey, P., 'Armée et pouvoir dans la Grèce antique, d'Agamemnon à Alexandre' in Chaniotis, A. and Ducrey, P. (eds.), *Army and Power in the Ancient World* (Stuttgart 2002), 51–60.

Ebach, J., *Weltentstehung und Kulturentwicklung bei Philo von Byblos: Ein Beitrag zur Überlieferung der biblischen Urgeschichte im Rahmen des altorientalischen und antiken Schöpfungsglaubens* (Stuttgart, 1979).

Eck, W., 'The Language of Power: Latin in the Roman Near East', in Cotton, H. M. *et al.* (eds.), *From Hellenism to Islam: Cultural and Linguistic Change in the Roman Near East* (Cambridge, 2009), 15–42.

Edwards, C., *Writing Rome: Textual Approaches to the City* (Cambridge, 1996).

Eliav-Feldon, M., Isaac, B. and Ziegler, J. (eds.), *The Origins of Racism in the West* (Cambridge, 2009).

Elsner, J., *Imperial Rome and Christian Triumph* (Oxford, 1998)

Feldman, L. H., *Jew and Gentile in the Ancient World: Attitudes and Interactions from Alexander to Justinian* (Princeton, 1993).

Finkelberg, M., *Greeks and Pre-Greeks* (Cambridge, 2005).

The Homer Encyclopedia (Oxford, 2011).

Fischer, M., Isaac, B. and Roll, I., *Roman Roads in Judaea, II. The Jaffa–Jerusalem Roads*, BAR International Series (Oxford, 1996).

Florescu, F. B., *Monumentul de la Adamklissi: Tropaeum Traiani* (Bucharest, 1960).

Foerster, G. and Tsafrir, Y., 'Nysa-Scythopolis: A New Inscription and the Titles of the City on its Coins', *Israel Numismatic Journal* 9 (1986–7), 53–8.

Formigé, J., *Le trophée des Alpes (La Turbie)*, Gallia Suppl. 2 (Paris, 1949).

Fraenkel, E., *Agamemnon: Edited with a Commentary*, 3 vols. (Oxford, 1950).

Frank, F. von, 'Aus der Araba', *ZDPV* 57 (1934), 240–50.

Freeman-Grenville, G. S. P., Chapman, R. L. III and Taylor, J. E., *The Onomasticon by Eusebius of Caesarea* (Jerusalem 2003).

Freudenberger, R., *Das Verhalten der römischen Behörden gegen die Christen im 2. Jahrhundert dargestellt am Brief des Plinius und Trajan und den Reskripten Trajans und Hadrians* (Munich, 1967; repr. 1969).

Gager, J. G., *The Origins of Anti-Semitism* (New York and Oxford, 1983).

Garnsey, P. D. A. and Whittaker, C. R. (eds.), *Imperialism in the Ancient World* (Cambridge, 1978).

Garnsey, P. D. A., *Ideas of Slavery from Aristotle to Augustine* (Cambridge, 1996).

Gatier, P.-L., 'Philadelphie et Gerasa du Royaume Nabatéen à la Province d'Arabie', *Géographie historique au Proche Orient* (Paris, 1988), 159–70.

'Décapole et Coelé-Syrie: Deux inscriptions nouvelles', *Syria* 67 (1990): 204–6.

Gawlikowski, M., 'A Fortress in Mesopotamia: Hatra', in Dabrowa, E. (ed.), *The Roman and Byzantine Army in the East: Proceedings of a Colloquium held at the Jagiellonian University, Krakow in September 1992* (Krakow, 1994), 47–56.

Geiger, J., 'Notes on the Second Sophistic in Palestine', *Illinois Classical Studies* 9 (1994): 221–30.

Hellenism in the East: Studies on Greek Intellectuals in Palestine (Stuttgart, 2014).

Gersht, R., 'Representations of Deities and the Cults of Caesarea', in Raban, A. and Holum, K. G. (eds.), *Caesarea Maritima: A Retrospective After Two Millennia* (Leiden, 1996).

'The Tyche of Caesarea Maritima', *PEQ* 116 (1984): 110–14.

Glucker, J., *Antiochus and the Late Academy* (Göttingen, 1978).

Gomme, A. W. *et al.*, *A Historical Commentary on Thucydides*. 5 vols. (Oxford, 1956–81).

Goodchild, R. G., 'The Coast Road of Phoenicia and its Roman Milestones', *Berytus* 9 (1948–49), 91–127.

Goodman, M., *The Ruling Class of Judaea: The Origins of the Jewish Revolt Against Rome AD 66–70* (Cambridge, 1987).

Mission and Conversion: Proselytizing in the Religious History of the Roman Empire (Oxford, 1994).

Gow, A. S. F. and Page, D. L. (eds.), *The Greek Anthology: Hellenistic Epigrams*, 2 vols. (Cambridge, 1965).

Gregoratti, L., 'Hatra: On the West of the East', in Dirven, L. (ed.), *Hatra: Politics, Culture and Religion between Parthia and Rome* (Stuttgart, 2013), 45–54.

Gruen, E. S., *Studies in Greek Culture and Roman Policy* (Leiden, 1990).

Diaspora: Jews amidst the Greeks and Romans (Cambridge, 2002).

Rethinking the Other in Antiquity (Princeton, 2011).

(ed.), *Cultural Identity in the Ancient Mediterranean* (Los Angeles, 2011).

Hall, E., *Inventing the Barbarian: Greek Self-Definition through Tragedy* (Oxford, 1989).

Hall, J., *Ethnic Identity in Greek Antiquity* (Cambridge, 1997).

Hellenicity: Between Ethnicity and Culture (Chicago, 2002).

Hamdorf, F. W., *Griechische Kulturpersonifikationen der vorhellenistischen Zeit* (Mainz am Rhein, 1964).

Hanson, V. D. and Heath, J., *Who Killed Homer: The Demise of Classical Education and the Recovery of Greek Wisdom* (New York, 1998).

Harl, K. W., *Civic Coins and Civic Politics in the Roman East AD 180–275* (Berkeley, CA, 1987).

Harley, J. B. and Woodward, D. (eds.), *History of Cartography*, I (Chicago, 1987).

Harrison, S. J., *Apuleius: A Latin Sophist* (Oxford, 2000).

Hauser, S. R. 'Hatra und das Königreich der Araber', in Wiesehöfer, J. (ed.), *Das Partherreich und seine Zeugnisse* (Stuttgart, 1998), 493–528.

'On the Significance of the Final Siege of Hatra', in Dirven, L. (ed.), *Hatra,: Politics, Culture and Religion between Parthia and Rome* (Stuttgart, 2013), 119–39.

Heubner, H., *P. Cornelius Tacitus: Die Historien*, I (Heidelberg, 1963).

Hill, G. F., *British Museum Catalogue of the Greek Coins of Palestine* (London, 1914).

Hinks, R., *Myth and Allegory in Ancient Art* (London, 1939; repr. 1968).

Holdsworth, C. and Wiseman, T. P. (eds.), *The Inheritance of Historiography 350–900* (Exeter, 1986).

Hölscher, T., 'Beobachtungen zu römischen historischen Denkmälern III', *AA* (1988): 523–41.

Horden, P. and Purcell, N., *The Corrupting Sea: A Study of Mediterranean History* (Oxford, 2000).

Hüttenmeister, F. and Reeg, G., *Die antiken Synagogen in Israel* (Wiesbaden, 1977).

Instinsky, H. V., 'Kaiser und Ewigkeit', *Hermes* 77 (1942): 313–55.

Isaac, B. and Roll, I., *Roman Roads in Judaea*, I. *The Scythopolis – Legio Road*, BAR International Series (Oxford, 1982),

Isaac, B., 'Roman Colonies in Judaea: The Foundation of Aelia Capitolina', *Talanta* 12–13 (1980–1): 31–53.

The Limits of Empire: The Roman Army in the East, 2nd edn (Oxford, 1992).

'Jews, Christians and Others in Palestine: the Evidence from Eusebius', in Goodman, M. (ed.), *Jews in a Graeco-Roman World* (Oxford, 1998), 65–74.

The Near East under Roman Rule: Selected Papers (Leiden, 1998).

The Invention of Racism in Classical Antiquity (Princeton, 2004).

Isaac-Edersheim, E., 'Messias, Golem, Ahasver. Drei mythische Gestalten des Judentums' (The Messiah, Golem and Ahasuerus. Three Mythical Figures of the Jews), *Internationale Zeitschrift für Psychoanalyse und Imago* 26.1 (1941): 50–80, 26.2: 177–213 and 26.3/4:, 287–315.

Jones, C. P., *The Roman World of Dio Chrysostom* (Cambridge, 1978).

Kadman, L., *The Coins of Akko-Ptolemais* (Tel Aviv, 1961).

Kennedy, D. L., ' "European" Soldiers and the Severan Siege of Hatra', in Freeman, P. and Kennedy, D. L. (eds.), *The Defence of the Roman and Byzantine East: Proceedings of a Colloquium held at the University of Sheffield in April 1986* (Oxford, 1986), 397–429.

The Roman Army in Jordan (London, 2000).

Kennedy, G., *A New History of Classical Rhetoric* (Princeton, 1994).

Kindler, A. and Stein, A., *A Bibliography of the City Coinage of Palestine: From the 2nd Century* BC *to the 3rd Century* AD (Oxford, 1987).

Konstan, D., 'Defining Ancient Greek Ethnicity', *Diaspora* 6 (1997), 97–110.

Kuttner, A. L., *Dynasty and Empire in the Age of Augustus: The Case of the Boscoreale Cups* (Berkeley, CA, 1995).

Lehmann, C. M. and Holum, K. G., *The Greek and Latin Inscriptions of Caesarea Maritima* (Boston, 2000).

Lehmann, K., Review of P. G. Hamberg, *Studies in Roman Imperial Art*, *Art Bulletin* 29 (1947): 136–9.

Lepper, F., *Trajan's Parthian War* (Oxford, 1948).

Levi, A. C., *Barbarians on Roman Imperial Coins and Sculpture* (New York, 1952).

Levick, B., *The Government of the Roman Empire: A Sourcebook* (Beckenham, 1985).

Lightfoot, J. L., *Lucian on the Syrian Goddess* (Oxford, 2003).

Linder, A., *The Jews in Roman Imperial Legislation* (Detroit and Jerusalem, 1987).

Lloyd, G. E. R., *Disciplines in the Making: Cross-Cultural Perspectives on Elites, Learning, and Innovation* (Oxford, 2009).

Loring Brace, C., *'Race' is a Four-Letter Word: the Genesis of the Concept* (Oxford, 2005).

MacMullen, R., *Soldier and Civilian in the Later Roman Empire* (Cambridge, 1963). *Paganism in the Roman Empire* (New Haven, 1981)

Maenchen-Helfen, J. O., *The World of the Huns: Studies in their History and Culture*, ed. Knight, M. (Berkeley, CA, 1973).

Makhouly, N. and Johns, C. N., *Guide to Acre*, rev. edn (Jerusalem, 1946).

Marcovich, M., *Heraclitus: Greek Text with a Short Commentary*, Editio Maior (Merida, 1967).

Mason, S., 'Jews, Judaeans, Judaizing, Judaism: Problems of Categorization in Ancient History', *Journal for the Study of Judaism* 38 (2007): 457–512.

Mattern, S. P., *Rome and the Enemy: Imperial Strategy in the Principate* (Berkeley, CA, 1999).

Matthew, W. D., *Climate and Evolution*, 2nd edn with additions (New York, 1939; repr. 1974).

Matthews, J., *The Roman Empire of Ammianus* (Baltimore and London, 1989).

Mellor, R., 'The Goddess Rome', *ANRW* 2.17.2 (1991): 950–1030.

Messerschmidt, W., *Prosopopoiia: Personifikationen politischen Charakters in spät-klassischer und hellenistischer Kunst* (Cologne, 2003).

Meyer, J., 'A Centurial Stone from Shavei Tziyyon', *SCI* 7 (1983–4): 119–25.

Millar, F., *A Study of Cassius Dio* (Oxford, 1964).

The Emperor in the Roman World: 31 BC – AD 337 (London, 1976).

'The Roman Coloniae of the Near East: A Study of Cultural Relations', in Solin, H. and Kajave, F. M. (eds.), *Roman Policy in the East and Other Studies in Roman History: Proceedings of a Colloquium at Tvärmine, 1987* (Helsinki, 1990), 7–57.

The Roman Near East: 31 BC–AD *337* (Cambridge, 1993).

Moore, F. G., 'On *Urbs Aeterna* and *Urbs Sacra*', *TAPA* 25 (1894): 34–60.

Neils, J., *The Parthenon Frieze* (Cambridge, 2001).

Nicolet, C., *Space, Geography, and Politics in the Early Roman Empire* (Ann Arbor, 1991).

North, J. A., 'Religious Toleration in Republican Rome', *PCPS* 25 (1979): 85–103.

Oppenheimer, A. *et al.*, *Babylonia Judaica in the Talmudic Period* (Wiesbaden, 1983).

'The Ban on Circumcision as a Cause of the Revolt: A Reconsideration', in P. Schäfer (ed.), *The Bar-Kokhba War Reconsidered: New Perspectives on the Second Jewish Revolt Against Rome* (Tübingen 2003), 55–69.

Page, D. L., *Poetae Melici Graeci* (Oxford, 1962).

Paschoud, F., *Roma Aeterna* (Rome, 1967).

Pfanner, M., *Der Titusbogen* (Mainz am Rhein, 1983).

Picard, G. C., *Les trophées romains, contribution à l'histoire de la Religion et de l'Art triomphal de Rome* (Paris, 1957).

Pratt, K. J., 'Rome as Eternal', *Journal of the History of Ideas* 26 (1965): 25–44.

Pucci Ben-Zeev, M., *Jewish Rights in the Roman World* (Tübingen, 1998).

Raeburn, D. and Thomas, O., *The Agamemnon of Aeschylus* (Oxford, 2011).

Rajak, T. 'Ethnic Identities in Josephus', in *The Jewish Dialogue with Greece and Rome* (Leiden, 2002), 137–46.

'Jews Pagans and Christians in Late Antique Sardis: Models of Interaction' (1999), reprinted in *The Jewish Dialogue with Greece and Rome* (Leiden, 2002), 447–62.

'Was There a Roman Charter for the Jews?' *JRS* 74 (1984), 107–23, reprinted in *The Jewish Dialogue with Greece and Rome* (Leiden, 2002), 301–33.

The Jewish Dialogue with Greece and Rome: Studies in Cultural and Social Interaction (Leiden, 2002)

Reinhold, M., 'Roman Attitudes toward Egyptians', *Ancient World* 3 (1980): 97–103.

Rey-Coquais, J.-P., 'Philadelphie de Coelesyrie', *ADAJ* 25 (1981), 25–31.

Inscriptions Grecques et Latines de la Syrie (IGLS), VII. *Arados et régions voisines* (Paris, 1970).

'Des montagnes au désert: Baetocécé, le *Pagus Augustus* de Niha, la Ghouta à l'Est de Damas', in Frézouls, E. (ed.), *Sociétés urbaines, sociétés rurales dans l'Asie Mineure et la Syrie hellénistiques et romaines. Actes du colloque organisé à Strasbourg (novembre 1985)* (Strasbourg, 1987), 191–216.

'Syrie romaine de Pompée à Dioclétien', *JRS* 68 (1978), 44–73

Inscriptions Grecques et Latines de la Syrie (IGLS), VI. *Baalbek et Beqa* (Paris, 1967).

Rochette, B., *Le Latin dans le monde grec: Recherches sur la diffusion de la langue et des lettres latines dans les provinces hellénophones de l'Empire romain* (Brussels, 1997).

Romeo, I., 'The Panhellenion and Ethnic Identity in Hadrianic Greece', *Classical Philology* 97 (2002): 21–40.

Romm, J. S., *The Edges of the Earth in Ancient Thought: Geography, Exploration and Fiction* (Princeton, 1992).

Rothenberg, B., 'The Arabah in Roman and Byzantine Times in the Light of New Research', in Applebaum, S. (ed.), *Roman Frontier Studies* (Tel Aviv, 1967), 211–23.

Rotman, Y., *Byzantine Slavery and the Mediterranean World* (Cambridge, MA, 2009).

Rowlands M., Larsen, M., and Kristiansen, K. (eds.), *Centre and Periphery in the Ancient World* (Cambridge, 1987).

Rutgers, L. V., 'Roman Policy towards the Jews: Expulsions from the City of Rome during the First Century C.E.', *Classical Antiquity* 13 (1994): 56–74.

Sartre, M., 'La Syrie Creuse n'existe pas', in Gatier, P.-L., Helly, B. and Rey-Coquais, J.-P. (eds.), *Géographie historique au Proche Orient: Syrie, Phénicie, Arabie, grecques, romaines, byzantines* (Paris, 1988), 15–40.

Bostra, des origines à l'Islam (Paris, 1985).

Inscriptions Grecques et Latines de la Syrie (IGLS), XXI. Inscriptions de la Jordanie, 4 (Paris, 1993).

Schäfer, P., *Judeophobia: Attitudes toward the Jews in the Ancient World* (Cambridge, 1997).

The Bar-Kokhba War Reconsidered: New Perspectives on the Second Jewish Revolt Against Rome (Tübingen, 2003).

Schmitt, G., *Siedlungen Palästinas in griechisch-römischer Zeit* (Wiesbaden, 1995).

Schneider, R. M., *Bunte Barbaren: Orientalenstatuen aus farbigem Marmor in der römischen Repräsentationskunst* (Worms, 1986).

Schürer, E., *The History of the Jewish People in the Age of Jesus Christ (175 BC–AD 138)*, ed. Vermes, G., Millar, F. and Goodman, M., 3 vols. (Edinburgh, 1973–9).

Schwartz, J., *Jewish Settlement in Judaea after the Bar-Kochba War until the Arab Conquest* (Jerusalem, 1986).

Semple, E. C., *Influences of Geographic Environment* (New York, 1911).

Seyrig, H., 'Le monnayage de Ptolemaïs en Phénicie', *RN* 4 (1962): 25–50.

Shapiro, H. A., *Personifications in Greek Art: The Representation of Abstract Concepts, 600–400 BC* (Zürich, 1993).

'The Invention of Persia in Classical Athens', in M. Eliav-Feldon *et al.* (eds.), *The Origins of Racism in the West* (Cambridge, 2009), 57–87.

Shaw, B. D., '"Eaters of Flesh, Drinkers of Milk": The Ancient Mediterranean Ideology of the Pastoral Nomad', *Ancient Society* 13/14 (1982–3), 3–52; reprinted in Shaw, *Environment and Society in Roman North Africa: Studies in History and Archaeology* (Aldershot, 1995).

'Fear and Loathing: The Nomad Menace and Roman Africa', in Wells, C. M. (ed.), *Roman Africa/L'Afrique romaine: The 1980 Governor-General Vaniers Lectures*. Revue de l'Université d'Ottawa 52 (Ottawa, 1982), 25–46, reprinted in Shaw, *Rulers, Nomads, and Christians in Roman North Africa* (Aldershot, 1995).

Environment and Society in Roman North Africa: Studies in History and Archaeology (Aldershot, 1995).

Sherwin-White, A. N., 'Why were the Early Christians Persecuted? An Amendment', *Past and Present* 27 (1964): 23–7.

Shipley, G., *Pseudo-Scylax's Periplous: The Circumnavigation of the Inhabited World, Text, Translation and Commentary* (Exeter, 2011).

Silberman, A. (ed.), *Pomponius Mela, Chorographie* (Paris, 1988).

Smallwood, E. M., 'The Legislation of Hadrian and Antoninus Pius Against Circumcision', *Latomus* 18 (1959): 334–47.

'The Legislation of Hadrian and Antoninus Pius against Circumcision: Addendum', *Latomus* 20 (1961): 93–6.

The Jews under Roman Rule: From Pompey to Diocletian. A Study in Political Relations (Leiden, 1981)

Smelik, K. A. D. and Hemelrijk, E. A., 'Opinions on Egyptian Animal Worship in Antiquity', *ANRW* 2.17.4 (1984): 1852–2000.

Smith, R. R. R., 'The Imperial Reliefs from the Sebasteion at Aphrodisias', *JRS* 77 (1987), 88–138.

Snowden, F. M. Jr., *Blacks in Antiquity* (Cambridge, 1970).

'Iconographical Evidence on the Black Populations in Greco-Roman Antiquity', in Vercoutter, J. *et al.* (eds.), *L'image du Noir dans L'art occidental*, I (Fribourg, 1976), 133–245.

Before Color Prejudice (Cambridge, 1983).

Sommer, M., *Hatra* (Mainz, 2003).

'In the Twilight: Hatra between Rome and Iran', in Dirven, L. (ed.), *Hatra: Politics, Culture and Religion between Parthia and Rome* (Stuttgart, 2013), 33–44.

Sonnabend, H., *Fremdenbild und Politik: Vorstellungen der Römer von Ägypten und dem Partherreich in der späten Republik und frühen Kaiserzeit* (Frankfurt, 1986).

Stern, E. *et al.* (eds.), *The New Encyclopedia of Archaeological Excavations in the Holy Land* (Jerusalem, 1993).

Stern, M., *Greek and Latin Authors on Jews and Judaism*, 3 vols. (Jerusalem, 1974–84).

Swain, S., *Hellenism and Empire: Language, Classicism and Power in the Greek World* AD *50–250* (Oxford, 1996).

Syme, R., *Tacitus* (Oxford, 1958).

The Augustan Aristocracy (Oxford, 1986).

The Provincial at Rome and Rome and the Balkans 80 BC–AD *14*, ed. Birley, A. (Exeter, 1999).

Taylor, T. G., *Environment, Race and Migration*, 2nd enlarged edn (Chicago, 1945).

Thomsen, P., *Die lateinischen und griechischen Inschriften der Stadt Jerusalem und ihrer nächsten Umgebung* (Leipzig, 1922).

Timm, S., *Das Onomastikon der biblischen Ortsnamen: Edition der syrischen Fassung mit griechischem Text, englischer und deutscher Übersetzung;* (Berlin, 2005).

Touati, A. M. L., *The Great Trajanic Frieze: The Study of a Monument and of the Mechanisms of Message Transmission in Roman Art* (Stockholm, 1987).

Toynbee, J. C. M., *The Hadrianic School: A Chapter in the History of Greek Art* (Cambridge, 1934).

Trousset, P., 'Signification d'une frontière: Nomades et sedentaires dans la zone du limes d'Afrique', in Hanson, W. S. and Keppie, L. J. F. (eds.), *Roman Frontier Studies 1979: Papers Presented to the 12th International Congress of Roman Frontier Studies* (Oxford, 1980), III, 931–43.

Tsafrir, Y., Di Segni, L. and Green, J., *Tabula Imperii Romani: Iudaea-Palaestina* (Jerusalem, 1994).

Vittinghoff, F., 'Die "Titularkolonie"', in Eck, W. (ed.), *Civitas Romana: Stadt und politisch-soziale Integration im Imperium Romanum der Kaiserzeit* (Stuttgart, 1994), 34–40.

Vlassopoulos, K., *Greeks and Barbarians* (Cambridge, 2013).

Vyverberg, H., *Historical Pessimism in the French Enlightenment* (Cambridge, 1958).

Wallerstein, I., *The Modern World-System: Capitalist Agriculture and the Origins of the European World-Economy in the Sixteenth Century* (New York and London, 1974).

The Capitalist World-Economy (Cambridge and Paris, 1979).

Unthinking Social Science: The Limits of Nineteenth-Century Paradigms (Cambridge, 1991).

Weksler-Bdolah, S., 'The Foundation of Aelia Capitolina in Light of New Excavations along the Eastern Cardo', *IEJ* 64 (2014), 38–62.

Wenning, R., 'Die Stadtgöttin von Caesarea Maritima', *Boreas* 9 (1986), 113–29.

Whitmarsh, T., *Local Knowledge and Microidentities in the Imperial Greek World* (Cambridge, 2010).

Whittaker, C. R., *Herodian* (London and Cambridge, 1969).

Will, E. and Orrieux, C., *'Prosélytisme Juif'? Histoire d'une erreur* (Paris, 1992).

Williams, M. H., 'The Expulsion of the Jews from Rome in AD 19', *Latomus* 48 (1989): 765–84.

'The Jewish Community in Rome', in Goodman, M. (ed.), *Jews in a Graeco-Roman World* (Oxford, 1998), 215–28.

Wolff, S. R., 'Archaeology in Israel', *AJA* 100 (1996): 725–68.

Woolf, G., 'World-Systems Analysis and the Roman Empire', *JRA* 3 (1990): 44–58.

Becoming Roman (Cambridge, 1998).

Yang, H., 'Invention of Barbarian and Emergence of Orientalism: Classical Greece', *Journal of Chinese Philosophy* 37 (2010): 556–66.

'Perceiving the Nomadic Other: A Note on Herodotus' Scythians and Sima Qian's Xiongnu', in Heil, A., Sauer, M. and J. (eds.), *Noctes Sinenses: Festschrift für Fritz-Heiner Mutschler zum 65. Geburtstag* (Heidelberg, 2011), 196–200.

'Perceptions of the Barbarian in Ancient Greece and China', *Research Bulletin* (Center for Hellenic Studies) 2 (2013).

Zanker, P., *The Power of Images in the Age of Augustus* (Ann Arbor, 1988).

'Die Frauen und Kinder der Barbaren auf der Markussäule', in Scheid, J. and Huet, V. (eds.), *La colonne Aurélienne: Geste et image sur la colonne de Marc Aurèle à Rome* (Turnhout, 2000).

Zirkle, C. 'The Early History of the Idea of the Inheritance of Acquired Characters and of Pangenesis', *Transactions of the American Philosophical Society*, NS 35 (1946): 91–151.

Index

Printed in Great Britain
by Amazon

21373692R10220